Work Psychology

Work Psychology

Understanding Human Behaviour in the Workplace

JOHN ARNOLD

CARY L COOPER

IVAN T ROBERTSON

Third Edition

 Prentice Hall

FINANCIAL TIMES

An imprint of **Pearson Education**

Harlow, England • London • New York • Boston • San Francisco • Toronto • Sydney • Singapore • Hong Kong
Tokyo • Seoul • Taipei • New Delhi • Cape Town • Madrid • Mexico City • Amsterdam • Munich • Paris • Milan

Pearson Education Limited
Edinburgh Gate
Harlow
Essex CM20 2JE
England

and Associated Companies throughout the world

Visit us on the World Wide Web at:
http://www.pearsoneduc.com

First published in Great Britain in 1991
Third edition 1998

ISBN 0 273 62868 2

British Library Cataloguing in Publication Data
A CIP catalogue record for this book can be obtained from the British Library

10 9 8
06 05 04 03

Printed and bound in Great Britain by
Ashford Colour Press Ltd, Gosport, Hants

CONTENTS

LIST OF FIGURES

LIST OF TABLES

LIST OF CASE STUDIES

Case studies are provided for those chapters which focus on a single topic in work psychology. The last case listed for each chapter is suitable for a session of up to 1 hour. The other cases are usually short vignettes which take 10–20 minutes to work on.

PREFACE

Work psychology is about people's behaviour, thoughts and emotions related to their work. It can be used to improve our understanding and management of people (including ourselves) at work.

All too often, work organisations have sophisticated systems for assessing the costs and benefits of everything except their management of people. Lip service is paid to the value of staff, but it is hard to avoid the conclusion that in some organisations employees are seen as necessary evils to be tolerated as good-humouredly as possible. Consequently, the thinking behind how they are managed can be rather careless or simplistic. Work psychologists seek to counter that tendency by carefully studying how people can best be assessed, motivated, led, trained and developed at work. They are also concerned about the ethical use of psychological theory and techniques, and the impact such techniques may have on power relationships at work.

This book is intended for undergraduate students in business and management, and psychology, as well as those studying for professional qualifications with bodies such as the United Kingdom's Institute of Personnel and Development (IPD). We have tried to make it suitable both for people encountering the subject for the first time and for those who already have some familiarity with it. We aim to give a clear and straightforward – but not simplistic – account of many key areas of contemporary work psychology. More specifically, we try to achieve several objectives in order to make this book as useful as possible to its readers.

First, we seek to blend theory and practice. Both are important. Without good theory, practice is blind. Without good practice, theory is not being properly used. We therefore describe key theories and evaluate them where appropriate. We also discuss how the concepts described can find practical application. We provide short *case studies* to which material in the book can readily be applied. These can be used as classroom exercises, or as assignments for individual students. An *Instructor's Manual* provides additional notes on the *case studies* and describes how they can be used. A pack of overhead projector master sheets is available to lecturers adopting the book. For these and for the *Instructor's Manual* please contact the publishers.

Second, we try to present material at a level which the reader should find intellectually stimulating, but not *too* difficult. It is all too easy to use a slick, glossy presentation at the expense of good content. There is always the temptation to descend to oversimple 'recipes for success' which insult the reader's intelligence. On the other hand, it is equally easy to lose the reader in unnecessarily complex debates. We hope that we avoid both these fates.

Third, we try to help the reader to gain maximum benefit from the book by providing several aids to learning. Each chapter begins with clearly stated learning objectives, and concludes with some short and long self-test questions which reflect these objectives. At the end of each chapter we provide a small number of suggestions for further reading, and a glossary of important terms used in the chapter. Throughout the text we specify key learning points which express succinctly the main message of the preceding two or three pages of text. We include a number of diagrams as well as text, in recognition that pictures can often express complex ideas in an economical and memorable way.

Fourth, we have chosen topics that we judge to be the most useful to potential readers of this book. Some usually appear in organisational behaviour texts, whereas others are generally found in books of a more specifically psychological orientation. Thus, we include chapters on: the nature of work organisations and cultures; human intellectual and personality characteristics; employee selection and appraisal; learning and behaviour modification; work motivation; decision making by individuals, groups and organisations; leadership; training; career choice and development; stress in employment and unemployment; and job redesign and new technology: in this edition we have added a new chapter on organisational change, courtesy of our friend and colleague Bernard Burnes, who is a renowned expert in this area.

We also include some material which we think deserves greater emphasis than it usually receives in other books. Thus, in Chapter 2, we provide a brief overview of basic traditions in psychology and how they have contributed to understanding people at work. This should be especially useful for students of business and management, who, we have found in our experience as teachers, need a base from which to understand work psychology. In Chapter 3 we examine how work psychologists obtain their data, and we devote Chapter 4 to a simple introduction to statistical techniques for dealing with those data. Explanation is provided in English as well as algebra! Again, we feel that students are too often left ignorant of data-analytic techniques. This makes it hard for them to evaluate what they read, as well as depriving them of useful techniques for evaluating data of their own.

In Chapter 5, we provide some context of a quite different kind: the problems facing minority groups at work and how they might be overcome. Then, in several other chapters, we use advances in social psychology and apply them to the world of work. This is particularly true of Chapter 9 on attitudes (including job satisfaction and organisational commitment), Chapter 12 on perceiving people and Chapter 13 on decision making.

Fifth, we provide up-to-date coverage of our material. There are currently exciting advances in many areas of work psychology, and we try to reflect these. At the same time, where the old stuff is best, we include it. There is nothing to be gained by discussing recent work *purely* because it is recent.

Sixth, we attempt to avoid being *entirely* reliant on material from North America. Many North American texts virtually ignore work conducted in other parts of the world. No doubt we have our own blinkers, but we try to include perspectives from places other than North America, especially the UK and other European countries. Nevertheless, the USA and Canada provide much valuable material. We therefore also make use of research and theory originating in those countries.

DEVELOPMENTS FROM THE SECOND EDITION

Readers familiar with the second edition of this text, published in 1995, may find it helpful if we describe the changes we have made. First, though, we should say that the changes represent incremental development of the second edition, rather than a fundamental reorientation. Feedback from readers of the second and first editions clearly indicated that they appreciated the clarity of style and the combination of theoretical and practical considerations. They also very much valued the substantial list of references, many quite recent, at the end of each chapter. Naturally, we have tried to preserve these features in this third edition. The style remains the same and the reference lists have been revised and updated. We are grateful for the feedback we have received from readers of the first and second editions, and wherever possible we have reflected it in this third edition. As well as learning objectives, glossary of terms and self-test questions, each chapter now has a short list of suggested reading, and key learning points designed to summarise important themes. We have increased the extent to which cross-cultural issues are discussed, in recognition that, to a large extent, there is now a global economy.

All chapters have been updated. Regarding specific changes to some chapters, the following comments may be helpful:

- we have expanded Chapter 1 to include an analysis of the changes occurring in work organisations and labour markets in the 1980s and 1990s;
- Chapter 3 now includes more coverage of competing philosophies of research and the history of work psychology;
- Chapters 7 and 8, on personnel selection, have been restructured in order to present an easier-to-follow account;
- Chapter 9 has been revised so that there is less emphasis on older social-psychological attitude research, and more on the significance of attitudes specific to the workplace;
- Chapter 13 has been reorientated and renamed in order to give greater coverage to groups and teams at work;
- Chapter 15, on training and learning, now has more on management development;
- Chapter 16, on careers, has been altered so that (like Chapter 1) it takes much more account of how the workplace is changing. It also discusses the topical concept of the psychological contract;
- there is now a new chapter on organisational change. The subject of change crops up in one form or another throughout the book. However, the topic of organisational change has its own theories and practices, and is clearly highly relevant to the current changing workplace. We are very grateful to Bernard Burnes for contributing this chapter.

The best judges of whether we meet our objectives in this book will be those who read it. Comments and suggestions are most welcome, and should be directed to Dr John Arnold, The Business School, Loughborough University, Ashby Road, Loughborough, Leicestershire LE11 3TU, UK; e-mail: j.m.arnold@lboro.ac.uk.

Finally, we wish to acknowledge with gratitude the help of our colleagues in preparing this book. Ann Shaw did an efficient and skilful job in tackling complex revisions to many of the chapters, and in deciphering the words and diagrams generated by the first author. In Manchester, Olga Hladyk played a similar role. Penelope Woolf and then Beth Barber at our publishers yet again kept us going with a well-judged mixture of encouragement and pressure. Last, but not least, our academic colleagues at the Manchester School of Management and the Business School, Loughborough University are stimulating and knowledgeable sparring partners whose perspectives contribute much to our work.

Loughborough and Manchester　　　　　　　　　　　　　　　　　*John Arnold*
February 1998　　　　　　　　　　　　　　　　　　　　　　　*Cary L. Cooper*
　　　　　　　　　　　　　　　　　　　　　　　　　　　　　　Ivan T. Robertson

Perspectives on work organisations and cultures

After studying this chapter, you should be able to:

1 specify the characteristics of the 'formal' organisation;

2 describe the interplay between structure, the technology and the environment;

3 describe the organisation as a complex open system;

4 describe the organisation as a socio-technical system;

5 describe the organisation as a series of metaphors;

6 describe the organisation as a culture;

7 understand the changing nature of organisations in the new millennium.

INTRODUCTION

In modern society, most people spend their working lives in an organisation of some sort and, therefore, have first-hand experience of organisational life. This chapter considers some of the research findings and theoretical work that help to provide a better understanding of the nature of organisations. An examination of the structural aspects of organisations revealed by organisation charts and other formal documents leads to a consideration of some of the complex interrelationships that exist between factors such as organisation structure, technology and environment. The second half of the chapter discusses the use of system concepts, as a means for describing and gaining insights into organisational behaviour. In addition, contemporary, open systems approaches to organisation theory are outlined. And finally, organisations as metaphors are explored to help us in construing and understanding them.

CHARACTERISTICS OF ORGANISATIONS

An organisation is 'a collection of interacting and interdependent individuals who work toward common goals and whose relationships are determined according to a certain structure' (Duncan, 1981, p. 5). This definition provides a useful starting point for an examination of organisations, although as this chapter and many other chapters throughout the book demonstrate, the nature of organisations and the behaviour of the people who create them and work in them are so complex that any brief definition is bound to be imperfect. The above definition does, however, make some important points, which can be elaborated upon:

1. organisations are human creations and, fundamentally, they consist of people, rather than buildings, equipment, machinery etc.;

2. the term 'organisation' is general and not restricted to industrial or commercial firms. Educational and medical institutions, social clubs and a wide range of other organised human activities fall within the definition;

3. people within organisations must, to some extent, be working to common goals and co-ordinate their activities to this end. This does not, however, mean that everyone in the organisation has the same set of goals and priorities, nor that all the goals are explicit and clear to everyone;

4. although relationships between people are determined according to a certain structure, informal or unofficial groups and structures can be at least as important as the formal organisation structure.

FORMAL ORGANISATION STRUCTURE

The structure of an organisation is often depicted with the aid of an organisation chart; a typical chart (*see* Fig. 1.1) provides an indication of the formal relationships between the management, supervisory and other staff in the organisation. Such charts indicate the overall shape of the organisation, and provide an outline of the formal decision-making structure. Usually, for instance, positions higher up the chart have more power and authority than those lower down. The lines linking the positions in the chart show

Fig. 1.1 The organisational chart for Savor Products Unit, a subunit of Ashborne Pure Foods Ltd

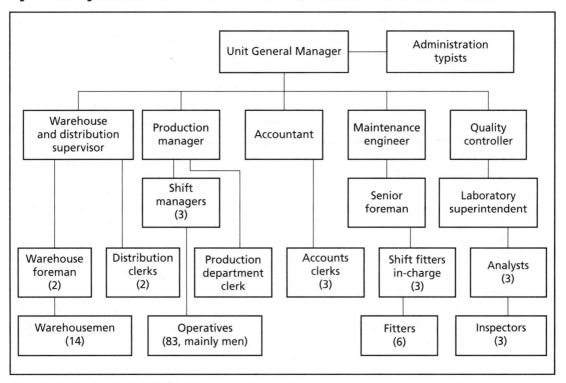

Source: Reproduced courtesy of J.R.K. Berridge

the formal channels of communication used to exercise this authority, and the overall shape of the chart also shows the number of levels of authority that exist within the organisation. A wide, flat chart, for example, depicts an organisation with few levels of authority, where the vertical distance between the most junior and most senior position is relatively small. A narrow, tall chart shows the opposite case of an organisation with many levels of authority.

Roles not people

Organisation charts show the relationship between specific jobs or roles within the organisation. In some cases, named individuals are shown to be the holders of specific positions, but the basic function of the chart is to represent the organisation structure, regardless of the particular people who fill the positions shown. This distinction between roles and people is supported in an extreme form by structural sociologists such as Perrow, who argue that in the design and analysis of organisations, it makes sense to focus on 'the roles people play rather than the personalities in the roles' (Perrow, 1970, p. 2). Others (e.g. Makin *et al.*, 1996) argue that individual personalities are important considerations. The widespread use of organisation charts suggests that there is at least some value in making a distinction between organisational roles and the individuals who fill them. The interrelationships between factors such as organisation structure and the people who work within the organisation is a theme that will be explored at various stages in this chapter.

Specialisation (division of labour)

In many organisations, it is impossible for one person to carry out all of the tasks involved, and some degree of specialisation or division of labour usually takes place. Division of labour involves dividing up the activities of the organisation and distributing tasks among people, so that different people do not find themselves doing the same collection of tasks. The basic division of labour used by most organisations is shown by the horizontal divisions in the organisation chart (*see* Fig. 1.1). Often the required specialisation is achieved not only by allocating different tasks to individuals, but by dividing the organisation into separate departments or subunits either on a functional basis (e.g. sales, marketing, personnel) or a product basis, or perhaps into geographical regions.

Organisation charts reflect not only the horizontal division of labour that is a feature of modern organisations, but also show that organisations are subdivided on a vertical basis. The organisation chart reveals the chain(s) of command in the organisation, and it is usually possible to trace a chain of command through from the most junior to the most senior member of the organisation. In some organisations, authority and decision making may be centralised and be allocated to a relatively small number of people, while in others authority is decentralised.

A further characteristic of organisation structure is span of control. At its simplest, the span of control of a manager or supervisor is indicated by the number of subordinates reporting directly to that person, and it is usually revealed on a comprehensive organisation chart.

Bureaucracy and classical organisation theory

Many of the aspects of organisation structure considered above were first examined in work carried out by early organisation theorists and management scientists, such as Taylor (1911), Fayol (1930) and Weber (1947), who developed their ideas about organisations during the early part of the twentieth century. Weber, for example, produced a series of publications concerned with the structure of organisations, and the exercise of power and authority within them. He proposed the 'bureaucratic' model of organisations, where work is organised and conducted on an entirely rational basis. Some of the essential features of a bureaucracy are:

- specialisation or division of labour
- a hierarchy of authority
- written rules and regulations
- rational application of rules and procedures.

Since Weber's time, bureaucracy has become a derogatory term associated with the excessive and often completely irrational use of rules and regulations. In many ways, however, Weber's work represents the beginning of modern theories of organisations, and many of the issues addressed by Weber and other 'classical' theorists are of lasting importance.

Dimensions of organisation structure

Much of the work of the early organisation theorists such as Weber was concerned with the ways in which organisations should be structured to ensure maximum efficiency, and structural aspects are still important when an attempt is made to build up a comprehensive picture of an organisation.

A long-term series of studies, begun at the University of Aston in Birmingham, examined various aspects of organisation structure and, by extensive studies of real organisations, attempted to identify some of the major dimensions of structure. The structural variables examined by the Aston team were:

- *specialisation*: the extent to which specialised tasks and roles are allocated to members of the organisation
- *standardisation*: the extent to which an organisation has standard procedures
- *formalisation*: the degree to which rules, procedures, instructions etc. are written down
- *centralisation*: the degree to which certain aspects of authority and decision making are located at the top of the organisational hierarchy
- *configuration*: the shape of the organisation's role structure (e.g. whether the chain of command is long or short).

After considerable data collection and analysis, the researchers were able to show that three underlying factors seemed to underpin the variations in organisation structure that they observed. These underlying factors were summarised by Payne and Pugh (1976). They are:

- *structuring of activities*: the extent to which employee behaviour is defined by specialised jobs, routines, procedures etc. (Factor I)
- *concentration of authority*: the degree to which the authority to take decisions is concentrated at the higher levels in the organisation's hierarchy (Factor II)
- *line control of work-flow*: the degree to which control is exercised through line personnel or through impersonal procedures (Factor III).

Some examples of organisations with differing structural characteristics are given in Fig. 1.2. Others (e.g. James and Jones, 1976) have proposed slightly different sets of organisation structure variables.

Whichever structural factors are considered, it must be emphasised that factors such as specialisation or standardisation are concerned with the structure of the organisation only, and do not provide direct evidence of how members of the organisation behave in practice. As Pugh and Hickson (1976, p. 185) noted:

> none of the variables of structure are directly related with individual behaviour in the organization. Specialization is concerned with the existence of separate functions and roles, not whether the individuals in them trespass outside their territories or not; standardization is concerned with the existence of procedures, not whether they are conformed to.

Fig. 1.2 Underlying dimensions of structure in five organisations

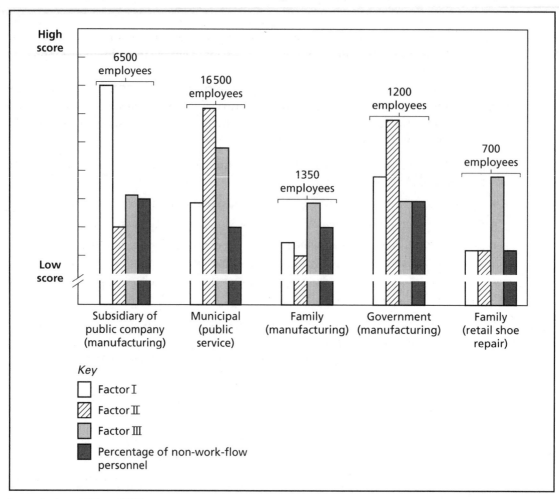

Source: Pugh and Hickson (1976)

■ **KEY LEARNING POINT**

Organisation structure depends on specialisation, standardisation, formalisation and centralisation.

STRUCTURE, TECHNOLOGY AND ENVIRONMENT

The fact that organisations can be described by using certain basic concepts of structural form raises the possibility that some structures will be more efficient than others. Woodward (1958) carried out research designed to examine the links between organisation success, size and structural form. The research examined 1000 British organisations ranging in size from 250 to over 1000 employees. The commercial success of each firm was assessed and relationships between commercial success and structural form were examined. The analysis, in the first instance, established no correlations between the structural factors and successful performance. Subsequently the researchers grouped the organisations into categories on the basis of the production methods (or technology) that they were using. Organisations were categorised into three groups:

1 small batch and unit production, where products are designed and manufactured on a 'custom-made' basis, involving the production of single units or small batches, often to customer specifications, e.g. prototype electronic equipment;

2 large batch and mass production, where standard products are manufactured in large quantities, e.g. motor cars, production of liquids or gases in the chemical industry;

3 process production, such as the continuous flow production of liquids or gases in the chemical industry.

When the organisations were regrouped on the basis of technology, various links with the structural factors became apparent (*see* Fig. 1.3). As Fig. 1.3 reveals, organisations in the different categories showed marked differences in span of control. The research also established links between technology and the number of levels in the management hierarchy, and the ratio of managers and supervisory staff to other personnel.

The most important point is that the successful organisations in each category had different structures. For example, the spans of control of successful organisations in the unit-production category were lower than those in the mass-production category. For the present purposes, the main issues of interest are the demonstrations that in the sample of organisations studied:

Fig. 1.3 Illustrative results from Woodward's study

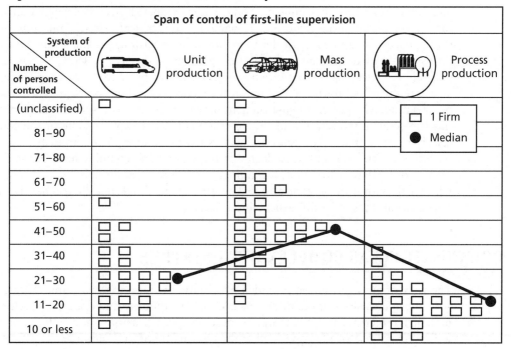

Source: Woodward (1958). Crown copyright. Reproduced with the permission of the Controller of Her Majesty's Stationery Office.

- there was no general link between organisational success and structural form;
- successful organisations had different structural forms, depending on the technology that they were using.

Woodward herself recognised many imperfections in the study carried out (Woodward, 1965). The specific findings and methodology of the study have also been criticised by others (e.g. Davis and Taylor, 1976). Nevertheless, the study represented a landmark in research in organisations.

A substantial amount of further research has been done to examine technology–structure relationships (*see*, for example, Pugh and Hickson, 1976). An examination of the available work reveals that although structure and technology seem to be related, it is not clear whether structure influences technology, technology influences structure, or how much other factors affect both (*see* Bedeian, 1980, for a review). Regardless of the detailed relationship between technology and structure, it is clear that there is no single ideal structural form for all organisations.

Other researchers have shown how factors other than structure can be linked with aspects of organisational design and management. Burns and Stalker (1961), for example, have shown that organisations tend to use different management practices depending on the environmental conditions (e.g. rate of technological change in the industry concerned), and Lawrence and Lorsch (1967) have examined the links between environmental factors and effective organisation design.

The findings of both Lawrence and Lorsch (1967) and Burns and Stalker (1961) suggest that different types of organisations are likely to be successful in different environments, and few people would dispute that organisational success is dependent, to some extent, on the existence of a good match between the organisation's characteristics and the surrounding environment. Some evidence does, however, suggest that the need for a good organisation–environment match is not a critical determinant of an organisation's success. Taken as a whole, the evidence concerning organisation–environment interaction provides some rather conflicting results (Filley *et al.*, 1976). It has been suggested (e.g. Weick, 1977) that organisations do not respond to the external environment as it actually is, but to the perception of the environment built up by the members of the organisation. The perceived environment may or may not correspond with 'reality', and this subjective interpretation of the environment could explain some of the conflicting research results that have been obtained. Notwithstanding the complexities of many of the issues for the moment, it is clear that there are many complex links between factors such as organisation structure, technology, environment and the individuals and groups who work within the organisation. Any attempt to develop a comprehensive view of organisations must take this aspect into account.

ORGANISATIONS AS COMPLEX OPEN SYSTEMS

The view of an organisation provided by a static organisation chart and reflected in the structural dimensions of organisations is clearly incomplete and does not provide a comprehensive picture. In an attempt to describe organisations more adequately, many writers make use of ideas derived from systems theory (Cummings, 1980). An open system in its simplest form involves an input, a transformation process and an output. A 'closed' system, by contrast, does not involve inputs and outputs, and is independent of

Fig. 1.4 An open system view of an organisation

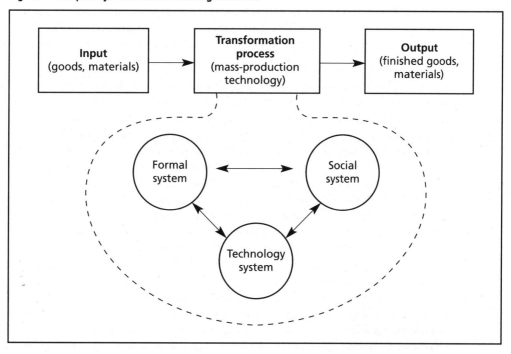

external forces. Organisations that are part of the social and economic fabric of the environment in which they exist should clearly be represented as open systems. Thus, a system view of an organisation manufacturing motor cars (*see* Fig 1.4) would involve an input of goods and materials, and the use of mass-production technology to transform the inputs into motor cars, the outputs. Other organisations have different inputs, transformation processes and outputs.

One important feature of the systems approach is that a particular system may be subdivided into smaller subsystems. Many organisations (including car factories) could, for instance, be subdivided into a formal system, involving the formal or structural aspects of organisations discussed earlier, a technology or production system, and a social system, concerned with the individuals and groups of employees within the organisation (*see* Fig. 1.5). Each subsystem interacts with every other subsystem, and the organisation also interacts with the external environment. In turn, the subsystems in Fig. 1.5 could be further subdivided, and, of course, the organisation itself is merely a subsystem of other supersystems – the economic system of the country, for example.

Describing organisations with the aid of systems concepts highlights two important issues:

1 *interaction and interrelatedness*: Ackoff and Emery (1972) defined a system as a 'set of interrelated elements, each of which is related directly or indirectly to every other element, and no subset of which is unrelated to any other subset'. Using 'systems' concepts to understand organisations helps to emphasise the point that any aspect of the organisation, e.g. structure, technology, individuals, work groups, departments etc., cannot be considered as separate, self-contained elements or units of analysis. The elements or subsystems in the organisation system are part of a complex interconnected network;

2 *levels of analysis*: any system is part of a wider supersystem and can be subdivided into subsystems. For example, the social system of an organisation could be considered as a whole, subdivided into systems based on groups of workers, or broken down into individual (single person) systems. Which level of analysis is most useful?

Although some writers have proposed a specific answer to this question (e.g. Katz and Kahn, 1978), it seems that the important contribution of the systems approach is that it draws attention to the existence of different levels of analysis, rather than specifying a 'correct' one. In most circumstances the level of analysis that is most useful depends on the problem being addressed and, just as there is no single ideal organisation structure to adopt, there is no ideal level of analysis for all purposes. This view is confirmed to some extent by the fact that organisational psychologists and sociologists have made use of 'systems' concepts to study organisations at various levels of analysis. Katz and Kahn (1978) have provided a thorough discussion of the use of systems theory to gain insights into some important psychological aspects of organisations. They also covered most of the more technical aspects of systems theory that have been omitted from the above discussion.

Systems theory in its strongest and most technical form takes detailed proposals about the properties of systems and the processes involved in system survival, growth and decay. Buckley (1967) and Silverman (1970) have provided some strong criticism of the use of systems theories in the study of organisations. They are critical, for instance, of the fact that some systems theorists appear to consider organisations as 'natural' systems, which are capable of initiating action and, for example, attempt to ensure their own survival. In other words, some theorists treat organisations as if they were living organisms capable of an independent life of their own. As Silverman pointed out, when discussing the influences of the environment, 'organisations do not react to their environment, their members do' (p. 37).

Silverman was also concerned that the models developed by systems theorists may represent the important features of organisations from the theorists' point of view, but fail to capture adequately the way in which the organisational factors involved are seen by members of the organisation: 'People act in terms of their own and not the observer's definition of the situation'.

Many work psychologists use systems ideas in a fairly dilute form, often merely to indicate the interaction and interrelatedness of organisational factors, and to identify different variables and possible levels of analysis. They do not necessarily employ many of the more technical and often more controversial aspects of systems theory. Payne and Pugh (1971), for instance, made some use of systems ideas to present 'a framework for behaviour in organisations' (p. 375). Their framework incorporated a series of interlocking systems divided into four different levels of analysis:

1 organisation
2 department or segment within organisation
3 work team or group
4 individual.

They suggested that the main purpose of the framework is to provide an indication of the main features in organisational life, the levels of analysis and interrelationships involved. This somewhat non-technical way of using systems concepts (which is also apparent in the model proposed by Kotter (1978) and described later in this chapter) does seem to provide a helpful way of conceptualising organisational variables.

> ■ KEY LEARNING POINT
> *It is important to think of organisations as organic systems.*

Socio-technical systems

A good demonstration of the interacting nature of social and technological systems is provided in some work carried out by the Tavistock Institute of Human Relations (Trist and Bamforth, 1951). The research examined the consequences of changes in methods of production in British coal-mines. The traditional method of mining, known as the short-wall method, involved small groups of eight to ten men working together as a team. The teams worked fairly independently of each other and each one concentrated on removing coal from a small section of the coal-face. The teams were very tightly-knit systems, and close relationships often formed between team members; competition between teams, however, was often fierce. The bonds of friendship and enmity were reflected both at work and in the wider community.

Improvements in mining technology led to the installation of new mechanical coal-cutting and removing systems. To operate the new equipment the small teams of miners were reorganised into much larger groups of forty to fifty, divided into specialised task groups and reporting to a single supervisor. These much larger social groups created as a consequence of the new technology were associated with many unsatisfactory changes. The new working procedures (the long-wall method) caused miners to be spread out over much larger distances, making supervision difficult. The social and psychological experiences associated with the earlier small teams were never adequately replaced under the new system.

Also, under the long-wall method, more extensive division of labour (specialisation) was introduced, and miners became responsible for a more limited range of tasks than under the short-wall method. By and large the miners found this reduction in the scope of their jobs distasteful. With the long-wall method, low productivity predominated. The Tavistock researchers suggested that a 'composite' long-wall method would be a better means of organising production. Under the composite method, the new technology was used, but aspects of the earlier short-wall method were also incorporated. For example, groups were allowed in order to introduce more variety into the work. The composite method, which paid attention to the interacting nature of the social and technical system, produced higher output, less absenteeism and was estimated to be working at 95 per cent of its potential. The conventional long-wall method had lower output, higher absenteeism and worked to only 78 per cent of its potential.

Some more recent socio-technical systems research (Trist *et al.*, 1977; Cummings, 1980) has examined the changes in quality of working life that can result from attempts to make the best possible match between social and technical systems (*see also* Chapter 1).

Major elements of organisational dynamics

So far four different and interrelated elements of organisational dynamics have been mentioned: formal (structural) organisational characteristics, technology, environment and social system. Kotter (1978) has integrated these and other aspects into an overall framework for examining organisations (*see* Fig. 1.5).

Fig. 1.5 Kotter's model of organisational dynamics

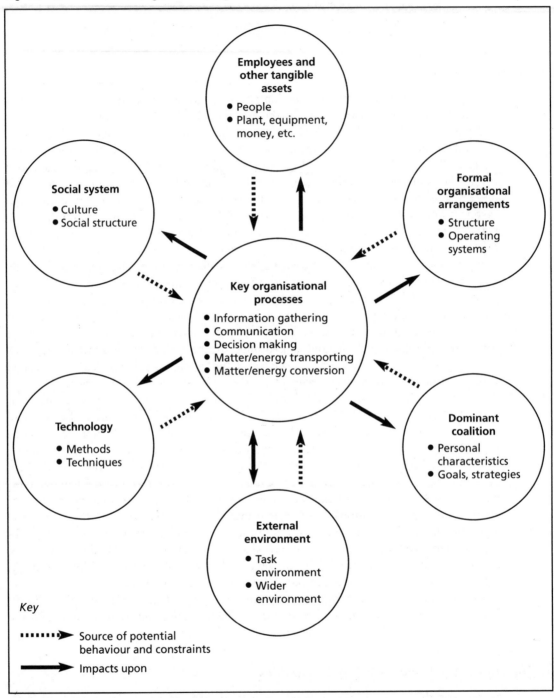

Source: J.P. Kotter (1978) *Organizational Dynamics* © 1978 Addison-Wesley Publishing Company Inc. Reprinted by permission of Addison Wesley Longman Inc.

The following notes apply to Fig. 1.5:

- *key organisational processes*: the major information-gathering, communication, decision-making, matter/energy transporting and matter/energy converting actions of the organisation's employees and machines;
- *external environment*: an organisation's task environment includes suppliers (of labour, information, materials and so on), markets, competitors and other factors related to the organisation's current products and services. The wider environment includes factors such as public attitudes, the economic and political systems, laws etc.;
- *employees and other tangible assets*: employees, plant and offices, equipment, tools etc.;
- *formal organisational arrangements*: formal systems explicitly designed to regulate the actions of employees (and machines);
- *the social system*: culture (i.e. values and norms shared by employees) and structure (i.e. relationships between employees in terms of such variables as power, affiliation and trust);
- *technology*: the major techniques that are used by employees while engaging in organisational processes and that are programmed into an organisation's machines;
- *the dominant coalition*: the objectives and strategies, the personal characteristics and the internal relationships of that minimum group of co-operating employees who oversee the organisation as a whole and control its basic policy making.

Schein (1980, pp. 277–8) has commented as follows on Kotter's work.

> In summary, Kotter's model provides a systematic check list of elements to analyze ... types of interactions among elements to consider ... This type of model takes the open systems point of view to its logical conclusion in identifying the wide variety of interactions that must be analyzed if adaptability is to be maximized.

In this respect, Kotter's model is in keeping with most contemporary attempts to deal with organisations, in that it does not attempt to provide a total picture of every possible element involved, nor does it seek to understand or explain all of the possible interconnections and interrelationships, a task that is well beyond our current state of knowledge and perhaps always will be.

■ **KEY LEARNING POINT**

The most significant contribution to British social sciences is to understand organisational behaviour as socio-technical systems.

ORGANISATIONS AS METAPHORS

In more recent times, organisational theorists have been building on the use of metaphors to understand the nature of organisational behaviour and life. The most influential proponent of this approach has been Morgan (1986) in his book *Images of*

Organization. In his framework, he sees organisations as complex entities, sometimes machine-like and other times organic. He has identified eight different ways of construing organisations: as machines, as organisms, as brains, as cultures, as political systems, as psychic prisons, as flux and transformation, and as instruments of domination.

Organisations as machines

'Organisations as machines' simply means that they can be designed and operated as if they are machines, with highly visible structures, levels and routines: in other words, bureaucracies. Although these types of organisations provide continuity, form and security, they tend, according to Morgan (1986), to 'limit rather than mobilize the development of human capacities, molding human beings to fit the requirements of mechanical organization rather than building the organization around their strengths and potentials'. These organisations seem to function better in protected and stable industries or fields.

Organisations as organisms

When an industry is more turbulent, competitive and fast moving, it usually requires a different type of organisation, an adaptable or organismic type. When we refer to an organisation as being 'an organism', we mean it behaves in similar ways to our own biological mechanisms. When the environment around and within us changes, our bodies adapt. Organisations that are dynamic tend to have more organismic structures and response modes. Kanter (1983), in her book *The Change Masters*, found that highly successful companies demonstrated many of the characteristics of an organismic organisation.

Organisations as brains

Some organisations in some industries need to be not only resilient and flexible, but also inventive and rational. Seeing the organisation as brain is in effect thinking about the system as not only being capable of change, but also of rational or intelligent change, about 'improving capacities for organisational intelligence'. As Morgan has suggested, 'innovative organizations must be designed as learning systems that place primary emphasis on being open to inquiry and self criticism ... The challenge to design organizations that can innovate is thus really a challenge to design organizations that can self-organize'.

Organisations as cultures

When we speak of 'organisations as cultures', we are basically referring to the fact that complex systems are made up of values, principles, attitudes and ways of viewing and relating to the world that are unique to it, and different from other organisations. To quote Morgan (1986): 'shared meaning, shared understanding, and shared sense making are all different ways of describing culture.' It is those aspects of the organisation that help us make sense of the world around us, and guide us in our interactions and relationships.

The concept of 'organisational culture' has grown enormously over recent years. This has occurred because of the increasing concerns about *matching* the right cultures in 'mergers and acquisitions' (Cartwright and Cooper, 1992), creating the culture through 'total quality management' (Dale, Cooper and Wilkinson, 1998), and in *privatising* former public sector organisations and encouraging *entrepreneurial* cultures (Nelson *et al.*, 1994).

Schein (1980) defines organisational culture as:

> (a) a pattern of basic assumptions, (b) invented, discovered, or developed by a given group, (c) as it learns to cope with its problems of external adaptation and internal integration, (d) that has worked well enough to be considered valid and, therefore (e) is to be taught to new members as the (f) correct way to perceive, think and feel in relation to those problems.

Not only can we now define organisational culture, but a great deal of research has gone into it (Cartwright and Cooper, 1992), although there have been many critiques of the methods and measures, with new measures emerging all the time (Sharfman and Dean, 1991; Dess and Rasheed, 1991).

Organisations as political systems

Organisations are not only about hierarchies and structures, or about shared cultures, but also about politics. They are about power, authority, responsibility, political activity, patronage and a host of activities and issues one might term political with a small 'p'. Organisational life is about wheeling and dealing, negotiating, compromising, politicking, and influencing behaviour and decisions. Each organisation, in other words, has its own political system. It has its own political order, such as autocratic management style or representative democracy or some hybrid of systems. It has its own system for control of information, alliances and communications networks – this is basically the concept of an organisation as a political system. Understanding this metaphor, and assessing an organisation in these terms, is important in appreciating its current activities, as well as predicting its behaviour and future ability to survive or grow.

Organisations as psychic prisons

Perhaps the most interesting of Morgan's concepts is 'organisations as psychic prisons'. He draws on Plato's *Republic*, and the famous allegory of shadows in a cave, and their reality and meaning:

> The allegory pictures an underground cave with its mouth open toward the light of a blazing fire. Within the cave are people chained so that they cannot move. They can see only the cave directly in front of them. This is illuminated by the light of the fire, which throws shadows of people and objects onto the wall. The cave dwellers equate the shadows with reality, naming them, talking about them, and even linking sounds from outside the cave with the movements on the wall. Truth and reality for the prisoners rest in this shadowy word, because they have no knowledge of any other.

Many organisations are constrained by their shadows or 'psychic prisons'. They are confined by their own representation of themselves to the outside world, by the mythical pasts they have inherited or created, by the distortions of their own culture. By using the metaphor of the psychic prison, we can go below the surface of organisational behaviour, and look at the collective unconscious in the system, and understand what is reality and what is fantasy. In other words, we can delineate more clearly the true shape of the shadows in our organisational world.

Organisations as flux and transformation

But the shadows or 'psychic prisons' are also changing all the time, so organisations can be seen to be in 'flux and transformation'. To truly understand an organisation, therefore, we have to appreciate fully the generative processes of the system, that is, how it develops, grows and regenerates. To appreciate and understand organisations, it is necessary, as Morgan contends, to 'attempt to fathom the nature and source of change, so that we can understand its logic', particularly if we are to manage these complex systems.

Organisations as vehicles for domination

Finally, organisations are also 'instruments of domination', that is, they impose their will on others. We have to attempt to highlight what Morgan terms the 'dysfunctional or unintended consequence of an otherwise rational system of activity'. If we do not fully understand what organisations can do to their inhabitants, how they can dominate and control their constituents, their long-term future is potentially in jeopardy.

Overview of metaphors of organisation

Morgan's metaphors for organisational life are not fixed categorical systems, that is, you are either one or another; or you change from one to another. In fact, an organisation can be a mix of each of the metaphors, predominately two or three of them, and these combinations can change over time (almost by definition), as Morgan suggests:

> A machine-like organization designed to achieve specific goals can simultaneously be: a species of organization that is able to survive in certain environments but not others; an information-processing system that is skilled in certain kinds of learning but not in others; a cultural milieu characterized by distinctive values, beliefs, and social practices; a political system where people jostle to further their own ends; an arena where various subconscious or ideological struggles take place; an artifact or manifestation of a deeper process of social change; an instrument used by one group of people to exploit and dominate others; and so on.

This typology is enormously helpful in understanding, diagnosing and changing organisations. This is particularly the case for organisational change, where it is vital to understand the dynamics and nature of organisation, as Machiavelli in *The Prince* suggested:

> It should be borne in mind that there is nothing more difficult to arrange, more doubtful of success, and more dangerous to carry through than initiating changes … The innovator makes enemies of all those who prospered under the old order, and only lukewarm support is forthcoming from those who would prosper under the new.

> ■ **KEY LEARNING POINT**
> *Organisations can be viewed as metaphors: as machines, organisms, brains, cultures, political systems and the like.*

CHANGING NATURE OF ORGANISATIONS

Organisations of the 1980s reflected the 'enterprise culture' of the times, with people working longer and harder in an effort to achieve individual success, personal achievement and material rewards. During this period, we had privatisations, process re-engineering, mergers and acquisitions, strategic alliances, joint ventures and the like, transforming the culture of organisations into hothouse, free-market environments. In the short term, this approach to the 'work ethic' and entrepreneurial business culture certainly did have an impact on the UK's economic competitiveness in international markets, but the strains were already beginning to show. For UK industry in the 1980s, 'stress' had found as firm a place in modern business vocabularies as 'junk bonds', 'software packages' and 'downsizing'. The costs of stress in the workplace that were highlighted during that period were legend (Cartwright and Cooper, 1997):

> Mental illness is responsible for 80 million lost working days each year at an estimated cost to UK industry alone of £3.7 billion;

> 35 million working days are lost annually through coronary heart disease and strokes at an estimated annual cost to the average UK organisation of 10 000 employees of £2.5 million;

> 8 million working days each year are lost through alcohol and drink related disease at an estimated cost of over £1.3 billion.

So what have the 1990s brought, and where are organisations of the future going? The following describes the recent history of organisations and the move towards what Cooper (1996) describes as the 'short-term contract' culture of the next millennium organisations. It is certainly true that the end of the 1980s and the early 1990s have been dominated by the effects of the recession and efforts to get out of it. Organisations have 'downsized', 'delayered', 'flattened', 'right-sized' or whatever euphemism you care to use to massage the hard reality of job loss, which has meant that there are fewer people at work, doing more work and feeling extremely job insecure. This has had the effect of forcing people to work longer hours to deal with increased workloads, with new technology rather than being our saviour (as predicted in the 1960s) creating the added burden of information overload as well as accelerating the pace and flow of work, as a greater immediacy of response (e.g. faxes, e-mail) becomes the standard business expectation. In addition, job insecurity is creating a climate of *presenteeism*, as individuals vie to demonstrate 'organisational commitment' in an effort to avoid the second or third tranche of redundancies. Whether it is out of fear or an intrinsic organisational norm, many work organisations are creating 'workaholic cultures', where hours of work equate in their minds to productivity – 'the longer the better' – and in some curious but unproven way, 'the longer the more efficient'.

In a recent national UK survey carried out by Austin Knight of a sample of employees from 22 large UK organisations representing over one million white-collar workers, it was found that (1) although three-quarters of employees sampled had contracted hours of between 35 and 37 hours per week, two-thirds regularly worked more than 40 hours and 25 per cent more than 50 hours per week; (2) 76 per cent said that continually working long hours had adversely affected their physical health; (3) 47 per cent admitted that their families suffered from their absence, but fewer than one-third would 'stand up to their boss in order to improve their family time'; (4) 57 per cent acknowledged that their 'personal life suffered because of long hours'; and finally, but ironically, (5) 90 per cent of *employers* surveyed saw long hours as a corporate problem in terms of reduced performance and lowered morale.

In addition, the Institute of Management (IM), in its recent national survey (*Survival of the Fittest*) of over 1300 middle to senior managers throughout the UK, found that 81 per cent of managers 'often or always' are working in excess of their official hours (with 55 per cent 'always' working extra hours); 54 per cent 'often or always' work in the evenings; and 36 per cent 'often or always' work at weekends. The IM concludes that 'longer working hours do not necessarily result in enhanced productivity. Excessive hours may reduce individuals' efficiency and effectiveness and consequently have a negative impact on the organisation'. This was also supported by the independent think-tank DEMOS, whose report *Time Squeeze* in 1995 found that 25 per cent of all British male employees work more than 48 hours a week; a fifth of all manual workers work more than 50 hours a week; one in eight managers work more than 60-hour weeks; and that seven out of ten British workers want to work a 40-hour week, but only three out of ten do.

But do the long working hours and job insecurity cultures that many people now work in explain fully the 'feel bad' factor in UK plc, at a time when the UK has, in contrast to many of its European competitors, comparatively positive economic indicators, or is there something more insidious going on in the organisations that people work and increasingly *live* in? The recent IM report referred to earlier may provide some clues to the answers to this question. Although a large majority of UK managers found their work stressful, the hours long, and the demands of their jobs on their personal relationships intrusive (with over 50 per cent expressing grave concern), the real crunch of their concerns were their attitudes toward the future nature of work. Although 72 per cent of managers perceive themselves to be 'core employees', a large minority (28 per cent) consider themselves to be on a short-term contract, a part-timer or selling their services to organisations. In addition, more than 40 per cent of them 'do not feel in control of their future career development' (the figure is even higher for middle managers – the next generation of senior executives – 58 per cent), and only 25 per cent 'expect their next move to be a promotion within their existing organisation', while nearly 30 per cent see their future outside the organisation. Indeed, one in four UK managers 'thought it highly likely that they would be responsible for a dispersed workforce supported by IT by the year 2000' – a future move toward the 'virtual organisation'.

The nature of our work environments, therefore, seems to be dramatically changing, as more and more employees, from top floor to shop floor, take on part-time work, or short-term contracts or a portfolio of jobs/careers. More and more organisations are implementing the dreaded words of 'outsourcing', 'market-testing', 'interim management' and the like, which effectively means that many more people will be selling their services to organisations on a freelance or short-term contract basis – blue collar, white collar, managerial, and professional temps. And this trend is growing faster in the UK than in any other industrialised country, partially, I suspect, because the natural extension of privatising the public sector is privatising the private sector! Currently in the UK more than one in eight British workers are self-employed, and part-time working is growing at a much faster rate than full-time work (e.g. the last quarter of 1994 showed an increase of over 173 000 new part-time jobs and the disappearance of over 74 000 full-time ones). In addition, the number of men in part-time employment nearly doubled between the mid-1980s and mid-1990s, while fewer women (under 4.5 per cent) and more men (nearly 10.5 per cent) are unemployed. In addition, not only are we moving out of manufacturing industries (with just over a quarter of workers in that sector), but also the number of people employed by firms of over 500 employees has declined dramatically to just over a third of the employed population.

The trend toward a short-term contract or freelance culture in work organisations is likely to have a number of significant consequences. First, more and more people will be working from home, as more sophisticated IT helps to create and support the 'virtual organisation'. This will affect, and in some cases, has already affected, family life. With two out of every three families 'two-earner' or 'dual-career' families, the problems of who plays what role in the family, and the conflicts surrounding work and domestic space, will exacerbate an already delicate work–home balance. Second, if employers increasingly look for and recruit 'flexible workers', the likelihood is that more women as opposed to men will be employed, displacing men as the main breadwinner and in the short term making them increasingly vulnerable in the labour market. Women have throughout their careers worked part-time or on short-term contracts, whereas men, by and large, have not. For example, in 1984 there were over four million women in part-time work, whereas during that same year there were only 570 000 men in part-time employment. By 1994, the figures were over five million women and 990 000 men in part-time work – a narrowing but still significant gap. Indeed, in order for women to pursue families as well as careers/jobs, substantially more women than men have had discontinuous careers. If you were an employer and looking for individuals who would be prepared to take short-term contract or part-time or project management work, who would you tend to choose, a man or woman? Third, the individuals who are likely to survive the 'new millennium' or 'virtual organisation' of the future will have to possess or be prepared to develop some of the following skills: be able to accurately diagnose their abilities and skills, will know where and how to get appropriate training in deficient skills, will be able to market themselves professionally to organisations, will be capable of and know how to network, will have well-developed interpersonal skills, will be able to tolerate ambiguity and a certain level of insecurity, and will be able to manage their time efficiently and be prepared to prioritise work and family issues. T.S. Eliot hinted at the frame of mind of the people who may be able to cope with this fluid and changing nature of the world of work in his *Four Quartets*:

> We shall not cease from exploration
>   And the end of all our exploring
> Will be to arrive where we started
>   And know the place for the first time.

Will this trend toward stable insecurity, freelance working and virtual organisational life continue? Individuals may question their need to commit to organisations that do not commit to them. We do know one thing, that to convert the current climate of 'feel bad' to 'feel good' is not simply a matter of higher salaries or greater personal rewards or a reduction in income tax, but about quality of life issues, like workloads, hours of work, family time, control over one's career and some sense of security in employment. It is important for the future of an effective and less stressful work environment that organisations begin to think about their structures, policies and working practices with regard to their human resources, and not just tediously mouth the platitude 'the most valuable resource is our human resource'. As Alastair Mant suggested in his book *The Rise and Fall of the British Manager*:

> A great deal of what wants doing in this naughty world seems to be reasonably obvious to men and women of goodwill and common sense everywhere. But we have not, it seems, mastered the trick of creating the intervening institutions that help us to get things done ... We rush headlong from analysis to action, without stopping en route to build sound constitutional structures to support our endeavours.

We must view employees as individuals who have needs, personalities and commitments outside the confines of organisational life, and begin to realise (and put into practice) our intuitive or gut feeling that the performance, efficiency and satisfaction of an employee is linked to his or her total life experience. As John Ruskin said in 1871, 'in order that people may be happy in their work, these three things are needed: they must be fit for it; they must not do too much of it; and they must have a sense of success in it'.

■ **KEY LEARNING POINT**

Work organisations are in transition, from secure, hierarchy-based to more temporary cultures.

SUMMARY

The organisations that we live and work in are fundamental to our well-being and productivity. The structure, technology and environment of the organisation influence human activity, and are interrelated in complex ways. We can best understand organisations by seeing them anthropomorphically. They are in a sense living organisms with cultures, brains and complex systems, which create their own political systems, change, barriers and roles. It is essential that we understand the dynamics of organisations, as well as their structures, if we are to have accurate communications within them. As Saul Gellerman, the American management guru, suggested:

> Nothing is more central to an organization's effectiveness than its ability to transmit accurate, relevant understandable information among its members. All the advantages of organizations – economy of scale, financial and technical sources, diverse talents, and contracts – are of no practical value if the organization's members are unaware of what other members require of them and why. Nevertheless, despite its overwhelming and acknowledged importance, the process of communication is frequently misunderstood and mismanaged.

TEST YOUR LEARNING

Short-answer questions

1 What were the structural variables examined by the Aston research team?

2 What is meant by 'socio-technical' systems in organisations?

3 What are the characteristics of 'organisational culture'?

4 What does 'organisations as machines' mean?

5 List the likely trends in the organisations of the future.

Essay questions

1 Describe the essential features of Weber's (1947) 'bureaucratic' model of organisations.

2 What are Morgan's (1986) organisational metaphors?

3 If the current trend in work continues, why might women become the main bread-winners?

GLOSSARY OF TERMS

Centralisation The degree to which certain aspects of authority and decision making are located at the top of an organisation.

Closed system Involves no inputs or outputs and is independent of external forces.

Open system Involves inputs, a transformation process and an output (e.g. manufacturing costs).

Organismic culture An adaptable organisation, like a biological organism.

Organisation chart A chart depicting the formal report on relationships in an organisation.

Organisational culture Norms, values and attitudes shared by all in an organisation.

Process production Continuous flow of production, such as liquids/gases in the chemical industry.

Role The expected and perceived boundaries that define a particular job.

Small-batch productions Products designed and manufactured on a 'custom-made' basis, small units of production.

Socio-technical system Interacting nature of social (e.g. people and groups) and technological (e.g. plant, machinery) systems of work.

Span of control The number of subordinates reporting directly to a manager.

System theory All aspects of an organisation are interrelated (e.g. structure, technology, people, work groups etc.) and cannot be treated as self-contained units or elements.

SUGGESTED FURTHER READING

1   *Organizations and the Psychological Contract* by Peter Makin, Cary Cooper and Charles Cox (BPS Books, 1996) is an attempt to highlight the changing psychological contract between employees and employers, from the perspective of both managers and workers.

2   *International Review of Industrial and Organizational Psychology* by Cary Cooper and Ivan Robertson (John Wiley & Sons, 1997) is an annual review volume which explores a range of issues in depth relating to work organisations, cultures and human resource management.

3   *Trends in Organizational Behavior* by Cary Cooper and Denise Rousseau (John Wiley & Sons, 1997) is a collection of ideas, concepts and issues to do with macro organisational issues, from the psychological contract to corporate culture measurement to cross-cultural issues.

REFERENCES

Ackoff, R.L. and Emery, F.E. (1972) *On Purposeful Systems*. London: Tavistock.

Bedeian, A.G. (1980) *Organizations: Theory and Analysis*. Hinsdale, IL.: Dryden Press.

Buckley, W. (1967) *Sociology and Modern Systems Theory*. Englewood Cliffs, NJ: Prentice Hall.

Burns, T. and Stalker, G.M. (1961) *The Management of Innovation*. London: Tavistock.

Cartwright, S. and Cooper, C.L. (1992) *Mergers and Acquisition: The Human Factor*. Oxford: Butterworth Heinemann.

Cartwright, S. and Cooper, C.L. (1997) *Managing Workplace Stress*. London: Sage Publications.

Cooper, C.L. (1996) 'Hot under the collar', *Times Higher Education Supplement*, 21 June 1996, p. 15.

Cummings, T. (1980) *Systems Theory for Organizational Development*. Chichester: John Wiley.

Dale, B., Cooper, C.L. and Wilkinson, A. (1998) *Managing Quality and Human Resources: A Guide to Continuous Improvement*. Oxford: Blackwell.

Davis, L.E. and Taylor, J.C. (1976) 'Technology, organization and job structure' in Dubin, R. (ed.) *Handbook of Work, Organization and Society*. Chicago, IL.: Rand McNally.

Dess, G.G. and Rasheed, A.M.A. (1991) 'Conceptualizing and measuring organizational environments: a critique and suggestions', *Journal of Management*, vol. 17, no. 4, pp. 701–10.

Duncan, W.J. (1981) *Organizational Behavior*. 2nd edn. Boston, MA: Houghton Mifflin.

Fayol, H. (1930) *Industrial and General Administration*, trans. J.A. Coubrough. Geneva: International Management Institute (originally published 1916).

Filley, A.C., House, R.J. and Kerr, S. (1976) *Managerial Process and Organizational Behavior*. 2nd edn. Glenview, IL: Scott, Foresman.

James, L.R. and Jones, A.P. (1976) 'Organizational structure: a review of structural dimensions and their conceptual relationships with individual attitudes and behaviour', *Organizational Behavior and Human Performance*, vol. 16, pp. 74–113.

Kanter, R.M. (1983) *The Change Masters*. London: Unwin Hyman.

Katz, D. and Kahn, R.L. (1978) *The Social Psychology of Organizations*. 2nd edn. New York: John Wiley.

Kotter, J.P. (1978) *Organizational Dynamics: Diagnosis and intervention*. Reading, MA: Addison-Wesley.

Lawrence, P.R. and Lorsch, J.W. (1967) 'Differentiation and integration in complex organizations', *Administrative Science Quarterly*, vol. 12, pp. 1–47.

Makin, P.J., Cooper, C.L. and Cox, C. (1996) *Organizations and the Psychological Contract*. Leicester: BPS Books.

Mant, A. (1977) *The Rise and Fall of the British Manager*. London: Pan Publications.

Morgan, G. (1986) *Images of Organization*. London: Sage.

Nelson, A., Cooper, C.L. and Jackson, P. (1995) 'Privatisation and employee satisfaction and well being: the effects of uncertainty', *Journal of Occupational and Organizational Psychology*, vol. 68, no. 1, pp. 57–72.

Payne, R.L. and Pugh, D.S. (1971) 'Organizations as psychological environments' in Warr, P.B. (ed.) *Psychology at Work*. Harmondsworth: Penguin.

Payne, R.L. and Pugh, D.S. (1976) 'Organizational structure and climate' in Dunnette, M.D. (ed.) *Handbook of Industrial and Organizational Psychology*. Chicago, IL.: Rand McNally.

Perrow, C. (1970) *Organizational Analysis*. Belmont, CA: Wadsworth.

Pugh, D.S. and Hickson, D.J. (1976) *Organization Structure in its Context*. Farnborough: Saxon House, D.C. Heath.

Schein, E.H. (1980) *Organizational Psychology*. 3rd edn. Englewood Cliffs, NJ: Prentice Hall.

Sharfman, M.P. and Dean, J.W. Jr. (1991) 'Conceptualizing and measuring the organizational environment: a multidimensional approach', *Journal of Management*, vol. 17, no. 4, pp. 681–700.

Silverman, D. (1970) *The Theory of Organizations*. London: Heinemann.

Taylor, F.W. (1911) *The Principles of Scientific Management*. New York: Harper.

Trist, E.L. and Bamforth, K.W. (1951) 'Some social and psychological consequences of the long-wall method of coal getting', *Human Relations*, vol. 4, pp. 3–38.

Trist, E.L., Susman, G.I. and Brown, G.R. (1977) 'An experiment in autonomous working in an American underground coal mine', *Human Relations*, vol. 30, pp. 201–36.

Weber, M. (1947) *The Theory of Social and Economic Organization*, ed. and trans. A.M. Henderson and T. Parsons. Oxford: Oxford University Press (originally published 1922).

Weick, K.E. (1977) 'Enactment processes in organizations' in Staw, B.M. and Salancik, G.R. (eds) *New Directions in Organizational Behavior*. Chicago, IL.: St. Clair Press.

Woodward, J. (1958) *Management and Technology*. London: HMSO.

Woodward, J. (1965) *Industrial Organization: Theory and practice*. Oxford: Oxford University Press.

2

Concepts of the person in work psychology

LEARNING OBJECTIVES

After studying this chapter, you should be able to:

1 describe five areas of basic psychology;

2 examine the relationship between basic psychology and work psychology;

3 describe the key features of each of the following traditions in psychology:

  a psychoanalytic

  b trait

  c behaviourist

  d phenomenological

  e social cognitive.

4 identify the main similarities and differences between the traditions;

5 specify how each tradition contributes to work psychology.

INTRODUCTION

This chapter outlines the basic areas of psychology and briefly describes how each addresses some issues relevant to work psychology. Then five fundamental theoretical traditions in psychology are described. Each tradition has made a contribution to work psychology, even though the traditions contradict each other in some respects. The nature of their contributions is briefly outlined and the portions of this book which examine those contributions in more detail are identified. The aim of this chapter is to place work psychology in the context of psychology as a whole. It is intended to act as a useful refresher for the psychology student, and as an orientation to some fundamental ideas in psychology for the non-specialist reader.

BASIC PSYCHOLOGY AND WORK PSYCHOLOGY

Psychology has been defined in various ways. Perhaps the simplest yet most informative definition is that provided by Miller (1966): 'the science of mental life'. Mental life refers to three phenomena: behaviours, thoughts and emotions. Most psychologists these days would agree that psychology involves all three.

The notion that psychology is a science is perhaps rather controversial. Science involves the systematic collection of data under controlled conditions, so that theory and practice can be based on verifiable evidence rather than on the psychologist's intuition. The aims are to describe and predict behaviours, thoughts and emotions (*see* Chapter 3 for more on psychological theory). Not everyone agrees that it is appropriate to study behaviours, thoughts and emotions in a scientific manner. Some argue that human behaviour is too complex for that, and anyway people's behaviour changes in important ways when they are being observed or experimented upon (*see also* Chapter 3). Nevertheless, most psychologists do favour a scientific approach. As a result, most courses and training in psychology place considerable emphasis on practical classes and statistical analysis of data – somewhat to the surprise of some students.

The discipline of psychology can be divided into several subdisciplines, each with its own distinctive focus. Collectively they can be termed *basic psychology*. There are several ways of splitting psychology. Perhaps the most helpful is as follows:

- *physiological psychology* concerns the relationship between mind and body. For example, physiological psychologists might investigate the electrical activity in the brain associated with particular behaviours, thoughts and emotions, or they might be interested in the bodily changes associated with feeling stressed at work;

- *cognitive psychology* focuses on our cognitive functioning; that is, our thought processes. This includes topics like how well we remember information under various conditions, and how we weigh up information when making decisions;

- *developmental psychology* concerns the ways in which people grow and change psychologically. This includes issues like how and when children become able to understand particular concepts, and how they learn language. Also, developmental psychology is beginning to pay more attention to change and growth throughout adult life;

- *social psychology* concerns how our behaviours, thoughts and emotions affect, and are affected by, other people. Topics include how groups of people make decisions, and the extent to which a person's attitudes towards particular groups of people influence his or her behaviour towards them;

- *personality psychology* focuses on people's characteristic tendency to behave, think and feel in certain ways. It is concerned with issues like how people differ from each other psychologically, and how those differences can be measured. It also increasingly recognises that situations as well as personality influence a person's behaviour, thoughts and emotions. Hence some attention is also paid to defining how *situations* differ from each other.

Work psychology is defined in terms of its context of application (*see* Fig. 2.1), and is not in itself one of the subdisciplines of psychology defined above. It is an area of applied psychology. Work psychologists use concepts, theories and techniques derived from all areas of basic psychology. The same is true of psychologists working in other applied contexts such as education and health. (Clinical psychology involves the investigation and treatment of psychological difficulties and handicaps.)

■ KEY LEARNING POINT

The five areas of basic psychology all contribute ideas and techniques to work psychology.

Fig. 2.1 The relationship between areas of psychology

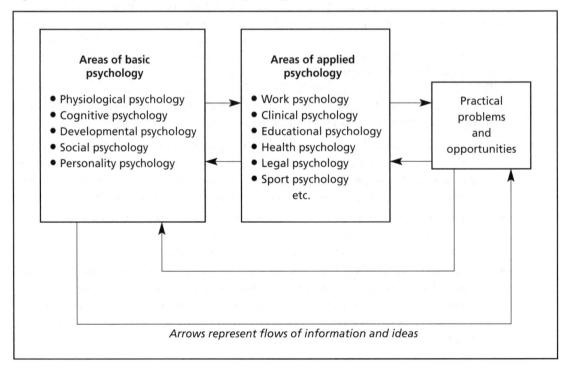

Arrows represent flows of information and ideas

As shown in Fig. 2.1, areas of applied psychology use ideas and information from basic psychology. Conversely, they can also contribute ideas and information to the development of basic psychology. Sometimes theory from basic psychology can directly contribute to the solution of problems, and problems can stimulate developments in basic psychology. But more often, applied psychology rather than basic psychology offers theories and techniques directly applicable to practical problems in real-life situations. In fact, it might be argued that some applied psychologists are more interested in solving practical problems than in theory and ideas from basic psychology. Thus there may be a danger that the areas of applied psychology will fail to reflect advances in basic psychology. It might also be the case that some more theoretically-inclined psychologists fail to take sufficient account of work in applied psychology, or of current real-world issues. The development of psychology as a profession that can be put to good use depends upon the information flows shown in Fig. 2.1.

The relationship between basic and applied psychology was the subject of several articles published in the journal *Applied Psychology: An International Review* in January 1993. In the main article, Schönpflug argued that applied psychology has not benefited much from basic psychology. Applied psychologists are interested in solving problems, while basic psychologists are driven by a love of knowledge for its own sake. Schönpflug believes that applied psychology now has a high academic and professional status. Several other psychologists contributed short papers commenting on Schönpflug's. Some of the points made are as follows. First, applied psychology could progress faster if there was more communication between applied psychologists working in different settings. Second, the development of applied psychology, and indeed psychology as a whole, might be influenced as much by university politics and individual psychologists' career aspirations as by philosophical considerations. Third, applied psychology contributes much more to advances in basic psychology than vice versa. Fourth, basic psychology and applied psychology are more closely linked than Schönpflug believes, but time lags of up to twenty years between the emergence of ideas in basic psychology and their use in applied psychology tend to hide the link. Fifth, and in contrast to the previous point, basic psychology and applied psychology are almost entirely separate. The latter could be renamed practical psychology in order to indicate its separateness.

Whatever the strength of these diverse and sometimes contradictory viewpoints, it can be said that work psychology, as one branch of applied psychology, does have its own theories and techniques. The following chapters will demonstrate this. Some draw upon basic psychology a lot, others less so.

■ **KEY LEARNING POINT**

Psychology is a discipline that includes many different views of what a person is. Some of the views contradict each other.

It would be dishonest to pretend that psychology is a well-integrated discipline with generally accepted principles. Underlying it are several competing and quite different concepts of the person. These are most apparent in personality psychology – not surprisingly since personality psychology is the subdiscipline most concerned with the essence of human individuality. These competing conceptions of humanity will now be briefly examined. The interested reader can find much fuller coverage of each in texts such as Mischel (1993) and Pervin (1993).

THE PSYCHOANALYTIC APPROACH

This approach, also sometimes known as *psychodynamic*, was developed by Sigmund Freud (1856–1939). Freud is probably the best-known psychologist who ever lived. He developed a completely new approach to human nature which has had a great influence on many areas of pure and applied social science, literature and the arts. Perhaps in reaction to the stilted Viennese society in which he spent much of his life, Freud proposed that our psychological functioning is governed by instinctive forces, many of which exert their effect outside our consciousness. He developed his ideas in a series of famous published works (e.g. Freud, 1960).

Freud identified three facets of the psyche:

1 the *id*: the source of instinctual energy. Prominent among those instincts are sex and aggression. The id operates on the *pleasure principle*: it wants gratification and it wants it now. It has no inhibitions, and cannot distinguish between reality and fantasy;

2 the *ego*: this seeks to channel the id impulses so that they are expressed in socially acceptable ways at socially acceptable times. It operates on the *reality principle*. It can tolerate delay, and it can distinguish between reality and fantasy. But it cannot eliminate or block the id impulses, only steer them in certain directions;

3 the *superego*: the conscience – the source of morality. It develops during childhood and represents the internalised standards of the child's parents. It defines ideal standards and operates on the principle of *perfection*.

According to Freud, these parts of the psyche are in inevitable and perpetual conflict. Much of the conflict is unconscious. Indeed, Freud's concept of the psyche has often been likened to an iceberg, of which two-thirds is under water (unconscious) and one third above water (conscious). When conflicts get out of hand we experience anxiety, though often we cannot say *why* we feel anxious. Anxiety can arise from:

- fear that id impulses will be uncontrollable

- feelings of guilt about behaviour or desires

- realistic fear about what is going to happen.

Because anxiety is unpleasant, people try to avoid it. One way to do this is to distort reality and push unwelcome facts out of consciousness. Freud proposed a number of *defence mechanisms* which accomplish this. They include:

- *projection*: we see in other people what we do not like in ourselves. It is easier to cope with righteous indignation about somebody else's faults than to come to terms with our own;

- *denial*: we pretend things are not as they really are;

- *reaction formation*: we deal with an unacceptable impulse by expressing its opposite. Thus, for example, anti-pornography campaigners may be expressing indirectly their own sexual impulses.

Defence mechanisms consume energy, and therefore detract from a person's capacity to live a full life. When asked what a psychologically healthy person should be able to do, Freud replied 'love and work' (not necessarily at the same time, presumably!). Even many people who have little time for his general approach regard this as a valid point.

For Freud, the key to understanding a person is to uncover unconscious conflicts. Most of these have their origins in childhood and are very difficult to change. They are revealed most clearly when the person's guard is down – for example, in dreams or in apparently accidental slips of the tongue ('Freudian slips') where the person expresses what he or she *really* feels. Freud believed that virtually no behaviour is truly accidental, but that people can rarely account for it accurately. Some psychologists working from other perspectives in psychology would agree that people cannot report accurately the causes of their own behaviour (Nisbet and Wilson, 1977). If correct, this would make a mockery of current work psychology, much of which is based on self-reports (e.g. using questionnaires, *see* Chapter 3) which are taken more or less at face value.

■ **KEY LEARNING POINT**

The psychoanalytic approach places a high emphasis on unconscious psychological conflicts which can reduce personal effectiveness at work.

Some psychologists who initially followed Freud subsequently broke away from him, though they remained within the psychoanalytic school of thought. The work of one, Erik Erikson, is covered briefly in Chapter 16. Their biggest quarrels with Freud were that the drives he proposed were too few and too simple, and that the ego was more powerful than he gave it credit for. They tended to place greater emphasis than Freud on social behaviour, and believed that strivings for ideals reflect something more noble than rationalisation of instincts. Perhaps the best known of these post-Freudian psychoanalytic psychologists is Carl Jung. He extended the concept of the unconscious to include the *collective unconscious* as well as the personal unconscious. Jung saw the collective unconscious as an inherited foundation of personality. It contains images which have never been in consciousness such as God, the wise old person and the young hero. Jung (1933) also examined the ways in which different people relate to the world. He distinguished between *introversion* (a tendency to reflect on one's own experiences) and *extroversion* (a preference for social contact). He identified *sensing, intuition, feeling* and *thinking* as other alternative ways of experiencing the world. Some of these concepts have been taken up in trait-based approaches to personality (*see* next section).

Within psychology as a whole, the psychoanalytic school of thought lost its earlier domination around the 1950s, and has never regained it. Critics complain that it is highly interpretative, incapable of being proved or disproved, and therefore unscientific. They argue that Freud was a product of his time (but aren't we all?), and was over-influenced by its hang-ups about sex. Many also claim that he does not account for women's psychological functioning nearly as well as men's.

Nevertheless, the psychoanalytic approach is far from dead. Freudian terms and concepts (e.g. defence mechanisms) have found their way into common parlance. Kline (1988) has argued that some Freudian concepts can be demonstrated satisfactorily and ought to be used more in investigating people's everyday functioning. Although most people in work organisations do not have the time (or the inclination) for the detailed, somewhat mystical and time-consuming procedures required by the psychoanalytic approach, some psychologists have nevertheless used psychoanalytic concepts in the world of work. For example, in their book *The Neurotic Organization*, Kets de Vries and Miller (1984) argued that 'sick' organisations needed to resolve these neuroses, which are usually reflected by their most senior managers. They identified five neurotic styles:

1 *paranoid*: suspicion of others and hypervigilance for hidden threats;

2 *compulsive*: perfectionism and concern for the 'proper' way of doing things;

3 *dramatic*: frequent drawing of attention to self, and a desire for activity and excitement;

4 *depressive*: feelings of guilt, inadequacy and hopelessness;

5 *schizoid*: withdrawal, lack of involvement and lack of excitement or enthusiasm.

Schneider and Dunbar (1992) have analysed media coverage of hostile takeover bids, where one business makes an unwelcome attempt to take over another one. They identify several different themes in media accounts of these events (e.g. growth, control, dominance and synergy) and relate these to developmental themes identified by psychoanalytic psychologists, including dependency, control, mastery and intimacy.

Work of the kind done by Kets de Vries and Miller (1984) and Schneider and Dunbar (1992) seeks to demonstrate that individual and collective behaviour in business is not driven by straightforward pursuit of profit but by the personal concerns of the people involved. Further, they argue that these personal concerns are best analysed using psychoanalytic concepts.

> ■ **KEY LEARNING POINT**
> *The psychoanalytic approach tries to explain why behaviour at work can often seem irrational, hostile or self-defeating.*

THE TRAIT APPROACH

This approach is essentially concerned with measuring a person's psychological characteristics. These characteristics, which include intellectual functioning, are generally assumed to be quite stable. That is, a person's personality is unlikely to change much, especially during adulthood (McCrae and Costa, 1990). Some theorists have developed personality types, or 'pigeon-holes' in which any individual can be placed. One good example dates back to ancient Greek times when Hippocrates wrote of four types: phlegmatic (calm); choleric (quick-tempered); sanguine (cheerful, optimistic); and melancholic (sad, depressed).

These days psychologists more often think in terms of traits than types. A trait (usually pronounced 'tray') is an underlying dimension along which people differ one from another. Hence rather than putting people into a pigeon-hole, trait theorists place them on a continuum, or rather a number of continua. Trait psychologists such as Eysenck (1967) and Cattell (1965) have identified specific traits through much careful experimental and statistical investigation. Some of this work is covered in more detail in Chapter 6. Favoured assessment devices of trait psychology are personality questionnaires, which consist of a number of questions about people's behaviour, thoughts and emotions. The better questionnaires are painstakingly developed to ensure that the questions are clear and responses to them are stable over short time periods (*see also* Chapter 6). Of course, ideally one would collect information about a person's actual behaviour rather than their *reports* of their behaviour. Indeed, Cattell among others has done this. However, normally that would be too time consuming. Personality questionnaires are the best alternative.

Most trait psychologists argue that the same traits are relevant to everyone, though for any individual some traits (usually those on which they have extreme scores) will be more evident than others in his or her behaviour. However, some trait psychologists have taken a rather more flexible approach. Allport (1937) argued that for any given person, certain traits may be *cardinal* (that is, pervasive across all situations), *primary* (evident in many situations), or *secondary* (evident only in certain quite restricted situations). So if we wanted to predict a person's behaviour, it would be important to identify his or her cardinal traits. These traits would be different for different people. For one person, sociability might be a cardinal trait. Another person may also be sociable, but his or her sociability might be less important than another trait (for example, conscientiousness) in dictating behaviour. Hence if each of these two sociable people had a choice one evening between going out with friends or completing a coursework assignment, the first one would be the more likely to go out.

In recent years there has been a growing consensus among trait theorists that there are five fundamental dimensions of personality – the so-called 'Big Five' (Digman, 1990; *see also* Chapter 6). Interestingly, there is perhaps more agreement on the *number* of traits than in *what* the traits are, but probably the following is about right:

1 extroversion, e.g. sociability, assertiveness

2 emotionality, e.g. anxiety, insecurity

3 agreeableness, e.g. conforming, helpful to others

4 conscientiousness, e.g. persistent, organised

5 intellect, e.g. curiosity, openness to experience.

The last of these is not the same as intelligence as measured by intelligence tests, but is related to it.

Most advocates of the trait approach argue that traits are at least partly genetically determined, which is one reason why they are stable. Research comparing the personalities of identical and non-identical twins tends to support this conclusion, though it is very difficult to separate the effects of environment from those of genes. About one-quarter of the variation in personality seems to be due to genetic factors (Bouchard and McGue, 1990). This of course means that three-quarters of the variation is due to other factors.

Trait theory carries the danger of circularity. How do we know somebody scores high on a particular personality trait? Because they behave in a certain way. Why does the person behave in that way? Because they score high on that personality trait. Behaviour is therefore taken as a sign of certain traits, which is all very well so long as the underlying traits not only exist but also determine behaviour. There has been considerable debate in psychology on this latter point. Increasing attention is now being paid to identifying how traits and situations interact to determine behaviour (Mischel, 1984). For example, in situations where social rules are strict and widely understood (e.g. funerals), personality will influence behaviour less than in unstructured situations which lack clearly defined codes of behaviour. One problem with selection interviews is that they have fairly clear social rules. For example, the candidate must answer questions fully, and avoid interrupting the interviewer. Thus the demands of this situation dictate the candidate's behaviour to a considerable extent. This makes it difficult for the interviewer to make inferences about the candidate's personality.

In spite of such caveats, the trait approach has had a great influence in work psychology. This is particularly evident in selection (*see* Chapter 8) and vocational guidance (*see* Chapter 16), where the aim is to establish whether one or more persons will be good at, and/or enjoy, certain kinds of work. The idea that people have stable characteristics which strongly influence their behaviour is central to those endeavours, since it offers the prospect of matching individuals to work environments which suit them. The possibility that experience changes personality is less often considered, even though there is some evidence for it. Also, it is probably fair to say that managers find trait psychology quite attractive. After all, it brings an aura of stability and predictability to the behaviour of their staff, which all too often seems changeable and confusing. Underlying this is perhaps our tendency to see people, not situations, as the cause of behaviour (*see* Chapter 12).

> ■ **KEY LEARNING POINT**
>
> *Trait approaches emphasise the importance of stable and measurable differences between people's psychological functioning which are frequently reflected in their work behaviour.*

Large sums of money are spent on the development and use of personality tests such as the 16PF (published by ASE, 1994; see also Institute for Personality and Ability Testing, 1986) and the Occupational Personality Questionnaires (SHL, 1984). The latter was developed by the British consultancy firm Saville and Holdsworth with the backing of many large organisations. Such ventures testify to the continuing prominence of the trait approach in work psychology.

THE BEHAVIOURIST APPROACH

In its more extreme forms, behaviourism makes no inferences whatever about what is going on inside the organism. It is concerned only with observable behaviour and the conditions (situations) which elicit particular behaviours. A person, and his or her personality, is a set of behaviours; nothing more and nothing less. There is no need to invoke invisible concepts such as traits or defence mechanisms when what we are really interested in – behaviour – can be observed directly. A leading advocate of this position was B. F. Skinner (*see*, for example, Skinner, 1971). He and other learning theorists argued that our behaviour is environmentally controlled. He used the concept of *reinforcer* to refer to any favourable outcome of behaviour. Such an outcome reinforces that behaviour, i.e. makes it more likely to occur again in a similar situation. *Punishment* is where a behaviour is followed by an unpleasant outcome. A more detailed description of this and other related concepts can be found in Chapter 10.

Behaviourists therefore argue that the behaviour a person performs (which is his or her personality) is behaviour which has been reinforced in the past. If a child is consistently reinforced for being polite, he or she will behave in a polite manner. Abnormal behaviour is the result of abnormal reinforcement. If a child's parents only pay attention to him or her when he or she misbehaves, the child may learn to misbehave because parental attention is a reinforcer. Behaviour problems can also rise from *conflicts*. One is an *approach-avoidance conflict*. This occurs when a particular behaviour is associated with both reinforcement and punishment. For example, a person may find that volunteering to take on extra tasks at work is reinforced by a pay rise, but also punished by the disapproval of work-mates.

The behaviourist approach to personality implies that behaviour (and therefore personality) can be changed if reinforcement changes. The introduction of a reward for arriving at work on time is likely to lead to greater frequency of staff arriving on time. This change in behaviour would *not* mean that staff had changed their position on a personality trait of punctuality or conscientiousness. Behaviourists do not believe in traits. The change would simply be the result of reinforcement.

Of course, when we ask *why* a particular outcome reinforces a particular behaviour, it becomes difficult to avoid reference to a person's internal states. We might say a person liked or wanted that outcome, and then we would probably enter a debate about *why* they liked or wanted it. Some behavioural psychologists have acknowledged the necessity of taking internal states into account, and have suggested that biologically-based drives or needs are the bases for reinforcement (Hull, 1952). Skinner's reliance solely on observable behaviour may perhaps have been viable for the rats and pigeons with which he performed many of his experiments, but most psychologists these days agree that it is insufficient for human beings.

> ■ **KEY LEARNING POINT**
> *Behaviourism focuses on what people do, and how rewards and punishments influence that.*

A more recent offshoot of behaviourist theory is *social learning* (e.g. Bandura, 1977). This differs from traditional learning theory in a number of ways, and is examined in more detail in Chapter 10. Briefly, advocates of social learning theory stress our capacity to learn from the reinforcements and punishments experienced by other people as well as ourselves. They also point out that we do not necessarily *immediately* do something that will obtain reinforcement. We may choose to delay that behaviour if we would prefer to be reinforced some other time. Also, reinforcement can be self-administered. For example, we might allow ourselves to eat a chocolate biscuit as a reward for reading and taking notes on a difficult section of a text book. In short, social learning ideas portray people as much more self-controlled and thinking than traditional behaviourist theory.

Concepts from learning and social learning have been used quite a lot in work psychology. In training (*see* Chapter 15), rewards can be used to reinforce the desired behaviours when trainees perform them. Trainees can also learn appropriate behaviours if they are performed (modelled) for them by a competent performer. More generally, in *organisational behaviour modification*, rewards are used to reinforce behaviours such as arriving for work on time or taking appropriate safety precautions (*see* Chapter 10). Some organisations make extensive use of *mentoring* in their career development (*see* Chapter 16), based partly on the assumption that the experienced mentor will model desirable behaviours that the less experienced young employee will learn. Social learning has in recent years developed further into what is now termed social cognition (*see* below). Social cognition emphasises the ways in which we regulate our own behaviour by analysing it and measuring its success. Some of the more recent motivation theories described in Chapter 11 rely quite heavily on these ideas.

PHENOMENOLOGICAL APPROACHES

Phenomenology concentrates on how people experience the world around them. It emphasises our capacity to construct our own meaning from our experiences (Spinelli, 1989). With roots in philosophy as well as psychology, phenomenologists assert that our experience of the world is made up of an interaction between its 'raw matter' (i.e. objects) and our mental faculties. Thus, for example, a piece of music exists in the sense that it consists of a series of sounds, but only has meaning when we place our own interpretation on it.

Phenomenologists argue that what appears to be objectively-defined reality is in fact merely a widely-agreed *interpretation* of an event. They also assert that many interpretations of events are highly individual and not widely agreed. Thus phenomenology places a high value on the integrity and sense-making of individuals. That general sentiment underlies many somewhat different perspectives that can loosely be called phenomenological – hence the title of this section refers to 'approaches', not 'approach'. Several of these perspectives also portray the person as striving for personal growth or *self-actualisation*; that is, fulfilment of his or her potential. This optimistic variant of phenomenological theory is often called *humanism*.

A good example of humanism is provided by Carl Rogers (e.g. Rogers, 1970). He has argued that if we are to fulfil our potential, we must be *open to our experience*. That is, we must recognise our true thoughts and feelings, even if they are unpalatable. Unfortunately we are often not sufficiently open to our experience. We may suppress experiences that are inconsistent with our self-concept, or that we feel are in some sense morally wrong. Rogers has argued that often we readily experience only those aspects of self which our parents approved of when we were children. Parents define *conditions of worth* – in effect, they signal to children that they will be valued and loved only if they are a certain sort of person.

For Rogers, the antidote to conditions of worth is *unconditional positive regard* (UPR). In order to become a fully functioning person, we need others to accept us as we are, 'warts and all'. This does not mean that anything goes. Rogers argues for a separation of person and behaviour, so that it is all right (indeed desirable) to say to somebody 'that was not a sensible thing to do', and if necessary punish him or her for it. But it is not all right to say 'you are not a sensible person', because that signals disapproval of the person, not just his or her behaviour. Only when people realise that their inherent worth will be accepted whatever their actions can they feel psychologically safe enough to become open to their experience. Further, since Rogers believes that people are fundamentally trustworthy, he has argued that they will not take advantage of UPR to get away with murder. Instead, UPR encourages more responsible behaviour.

■ KEY LEARNING POINT

Phenomenological approaches put high emphasis on personal experience and the inherent potential of people to develop and act responsibly.

Humanism has been criticised for being naive. Certainly in the authors' experience some business/management students do not find it convincing. Social workers and others in the caring professions are, however, much more sympathetic, as are psychology students. As far as work psychology is concerned, the basic point that people's *interpretations* of events are crucial has been heeded to some extent. Many questionnaire-based measures of people's experiences at work (for example, their supervision) have been developed (*see* Cook *et al.*, 1981). On the other hand, people's responses on such questionnaires are often taken as approximations of an objective reality rather than as a product of the individual's interpretative faculties, which rather contradicts the humanist position.

Phenomenological approaches find expression in some theories of work motivation (*see* Chapter 11). The idea that people strive to express and develop themselves at work is quite a popular one, though by no means universally held. Trends in management towards empowerment of employees and total quality management (TQM) are based on the assumption that people can and will use their skills to help their organisation, not sabotage it. Phenomenology has also contributed to career development (Chapter 16) and to the design of jobs (Chapter 19). Many counsellors make extensive use of Rogers' ideas when working with clients on career decisions and other work-related issues. They work on the assumption that showing a client unconditional positive regard will allow him or her to bring true career interests and ambitions into consciousness. By and large, though, phenomenological approaches are not currently dominant in work psychology.

THE SOCIAL COGNITIVE APPROACH

From around the mid-1970s, psychology has become increasingly influenced by a fusion of ideas chiefly from social psychology and cognitive psychology but also from behaviourism and phenomenology. *Social cognition* focuses on how our thought processes are used to interpret social interaction and other social–psychological phenomena such as the self. There is also a recognition that our thought processes reflect the social world in which we live, as well as formal logic. There is little role here for emotions, in spite of some arguments that feelings take precedence over thoughts (Zajonc, 1980).

Advocates of social cognition see the person as motivated to understand both self and the social world in order to establish a sense of order and predictability. The existence of other people (whether or not they are actually physically present) affects the nature of thought processes. Also, conceptions of self act as a filter through which information is processed. For example, we tend to process information about ourselves which is consistent with our self-concept more readily than inconsistent information. We also remember it better.

To some extent, social learning (*see* 'The behaviourist approach' above; *see also* Chapter 10) has fused with social cognition. After all, learning from the experiences of others requires thought, including the relatively complex cognitive operation of imagining oneself in the position of somebody else.

Advocates of the social cognitive approach also pay a great deal of attention to *information processing* (Schneider, 1991). High emphasis is placed on memory, and it is assumed that the ways in which people process information are general – that is, the same across different kinds of situation. It is assumed that how we store new information depends partly upon how our existing knowledge is structured, and that we are biased towards preserving existing cognitive structures. In other words, although we can assimilate new information, we are normally unwilling to let it change our general outlook.

The *self* is seen by some social cognitive psychologists as playing a very important regulatory role in behaviour. Our ideas about the type of person we are, and about our goals and interests (i.e. our self-concept), influence the type of situations we seek and the behaviours we choose to perform. One especially important concept here is *self-efficacy* (Bandura, 1982; *see also* Chapter 10), which concerns the extent to which a person believes he or she can perform the behaviour required in any given situation. Self-efficacy is frequently a good predictor of behaviour.

The *schema* is another key concept in social cognition. It is a knowledge structure that a person uses to make sense of situations. For example, a stereotype is a schema (*see* Chapter 12). Schemas are in effect ready-made frameworks into which one's experiences can be fitted. Schemas which involve sequences of actions are termed *scripts* (Abelson, 1981). For example, we might have a script of the sequence of events we expect to happen when we enter a restaurant. Scripts guide our own behaviour and also enable us to develop expectations about the behaviour of other people in any given type of situation. Events which cannot be accommodated within our schemas and scripts are experienced as puzzling, and may lead us to revise them. This is analogous to scientists changing their theories in the light of new evidence (Kelly, 1951).

> ■ **KEY LEARNING POINT**
> *Social cognition examines the ways in which people think about and regulate themselves and their behaviour.*

The impact of social cognition on work psychology has not yet been very great, though it is growing. As a general rule, work psychology is slow to incorporate new theoretical perspectives (Webster and Starbuck, 1988). This is partly because it usually takes some time to identify how new theories can be applied. In the case of social cognition, however, there is also the 'problem' that its relative complexity limits its capacity to generate straightforward 'off the shelf' techniques that can be applied across a range of situations.

Nevertheless, ideas from social cognition are certainly highly relevant to the world of work. In Chapter 12, this can be seen in the context of person perception. In Chapter 10, the importance of self-efficacy in work settings is examined. Other work has shown how social cognitive phenomena can enhance our understanding of work behaviour. For example, Gioia and Manz (1985) argued that scripts play a key part in learning behaviour from others (vicarious learning) at work. Social cognition is becoming more prominent in work psychology, especially when coupled with social learning.

SUMMARY

Modern psychology can be divided into several subdisciplines which reflect different facets of human psychological functioning. Cutting across these divisions are competing theoretical traditions in psychology. These are the psychoanalytic, trait, behavioural, phenomenological and social cognitive traditions. None of them can be described as correct, though the social cognitive tradition is the most recent, and makes most use of other traditions. They make some contradictory assumptions about the fundamental nature of the person. Their differences and similarities are summarised in Table 2.1. Each tradition finds some expression in work psychology. The differences between them emphasise that any apparent coherence of work psychology is due to the fact that it always takes place in the work setting. It does not possess a generally agreed view of human nature.

Table 2.1 Key characteristics of five theoretical traditions in psychology

	Thinking/ reasoning	Self-actualisation	The unconscious	Biologically based needs/drives	Personal change	Self-determination
Psychoanalytic (Freud)	✗	✗	✓	✓	✗	✗
Trait	✓	✗	✗	✓	✗	0
Behaviourist (Skinner)	✗	✗	✗	✗	✓	✗
Phenomenological (Rogers)	0	✓	0	0	✓	✓
Social cognitive	✓	0	0	✗	0	✓

✓ = Emphasised **0** = Acknowledged but not emphasised ✗ = De-emphasised or considered rare

Short-answer questions

1 What are the areas of basic psychology, and what kind of issues does each area address?

2 Examine the relationship between basic psychology and work psychology.

3 In psychoanalytic psychology, what are (i) the id, (ii) the ego, (iii) the superego and (iv) defence mechanisms?

4 What is a trait? Briefly describe two key features of the trait approach to personality.

5 In behaviourism, what is reinforcement? Why do behaviourist psychologists think that personality can be changed?

6 In phenomenological psychology, what are (i) conditions of worth, (ii) unconditional positive regard and (iii) self-actualisation?

7 Why is the self an important concept in the social cognitive approach?

Essay questions

1 Compare and contrast any two approaches to personality.

2 Select any two approaches to personality. Imagine two managers. One believes one approach is correct; the other supports the other approach. Examine the probable impact of their beliefs on the way they deal with other people at work.

GLOSSARY OF TERMS

Behaviourist approach to personality The approach which focuses on behaviour, rather than thoughts and emotions.

Cognitive psychology The branch of basic psychology that concerns the study of human perception, memory and information processing.

Conditions of worth In phenomenological approaches to personality, conditions of worth are the conditions under which other people are prepared to value us as a person.

Defence mechanisms In the psychoanalytic approach to personality, these are the methods we use to deal with intrapsychic conflicts that provoke anxiety.

Developmental psychology The branch of basic psychology that concerns how people develop and change throughout their life.

Ego In the psychoanalytic approach to personality, the ego is the part of the psyche which seeks to channel id impulses in socially acceptable ways.

Freudian slip When a person accidentally says something that reflects his or her unconscious desires.

Humanism *See* Phenomenological approach to personality.

Id In the psychoanalytic approach to personality, the id is the part of the psyche which consists of basic instincts and drives.

Personality psychology The branch of basic psychology that concerns how and why people differ from each other psychologically.

Phenomenological approach to personality An approach to personality which emphasises how personality is shaped by a person's individual interpretations, experiences and choices.

Physiological psychology The branch of basic psychology that concerns the relationship between brain and body.

Psychoanalytic approach to personality The approach which focuses on unconscious drives and conflicts as determinants of behaviour.

Psychology Sometimes defined as the science of mental life, psychology concerns the systematic study of behaviour, thoughts and emotions.

Punishment In the behaviourist approach to personality, punishment is the occurrence of an unpleasant stimulus or the removal of a pleasant stimulus following a specific behaviour.

Reinforcement In the behaviourist approach to personality, reinforcement is the occurrence of a pleasant stimulus (positive reinforcement) or the removal of an unpleasant stimulus (negative reinforcement) following a specific behaviour.

Schema In the social cognitive approach to personality, a schema is an organised set of beliefs and expectations held by a person.

Science A branch of knowledge based upon systematically-collected data under controlled conditions.

Script In the social cognitive approach to personality, a script is an expected sequence of events that a person associates with a particular type of situation.

Self-concept The total set of beliefs a person holds about himself or herself.

Social cognitive approach to personality The approach to personality which emphasises how we process information in a social context.

Social psychology The branch of basic psychology which concerns how the social world affects the behaviour, thoughts and emotions of individuals and groups.

Superego In the psychoanalytic approach to personality, the superego is the part of the psyche which concerns moral values, or conscience.

Trait A dimension upon which people differ psychologically.

Trait approach to personality The approach to personality which concerns the number and nature of traits, and how to assess people's position on them.

Unconditional positive regard In the phenomenological approach to personality, unconditional positive regard is the acceptance of one person by another, irrespective of his or her behaviour.

SUGGESTED FURTHER READING

1 The article by Schiönpflug (full reference below) gives a helpful, though quite technical, account of the relationships between different areas of psychology.

2 Most fairly up-to-date general psychology texts provide an overview of different approaches to personality, though not always divided up exactly as they have been here. A good example is Henry Gleitman's book *Psychology* (4th edn published by Norton, 1995), chapters 11, 16 and 17.

REFERENCES

Abelson, R.P. (1981) 'Psychological status of the script concept', *American Psychologist*, vol. 36, pp. 715–29.

Allport, G.W. (1937) *Personality: A psychological interpretation*. New York: Holt, Rinehart and Winston.

ASE (1994) 16PF, 5th edn. Available to qualified users from ASE, Windsor, Berkshire SL4 1BU, UK.

Bandura, A. (1977) *Social Learning Theory*. Englewood Cliffs, NJ: Prentice Hall.

Bandura, A. (1982) 'The self-efficiancy mechanism in human agency', *American Psychologist*, vol. 37, pp. 122–47.

Bouchard, T.J. and McGrue, M. (1990) 'Genetic and rearing environmental influences on adult personality: an analysis of adopted twins reared apart', *Journal of Personality*, vol. 58, pp. 263–92.

Cattell, R.B. (1965) *The Scientific Analysis of Personality*. Harmondsworth: Penguin.

Cook, J.D., Hepworth, S.J., Wall, T.D. and Warr, P.B. (1981) *The Experience of Work*. London: Academic Press.

Digman, J.M. (1990) 'Personality structure: emergence of the five-factor model', *Annual Review of Psychology*, vol. 41, pp. 417–40.

Eysenck, H.J. (1967) *The Biological Basis of Personality*. Springfield, IL: Charles C. Thomas.

Freud, S. (1960) *The Psychopathology of Everyday Life*. London: Hogarth (first published 1901).

Gioia, D.A. and Manz, C.C. (1985) 'Linking cognition and behavior: a script processing interpretation of vicarious learning', *Academy of Management Review*, vol. 10, pp. 527–39.

Hull, C.L. (1952) *A Behavior System*. New Haven, CT: Yale University Press.

Institute for Personality and Ability Testing (1986) *Administrator's Manual for the Sixteen Personality Factor Questionnaire*. Champaign, IL.

Jung, C.G. (1933) *Psychological Types*. New York: Harcourt, Brace and World.

Kelly, G.A. (1951) *The Psychology of Personal Constructs*, vols 1 and 2. New York: Norton.

Kets de Vries, M.F.R. and Miller, D. (1984) *The Neurotic Organization*. London: Jossey-Bass.

Kline, P. (1988) *Psychology Exposed*. London: Routledge.

McCrae, R.R. and Costa, P.T. (1990) *Personality in Adulthood*. New York: Guilford Press.

Miller, G.A. (1966) *Psychology: The science of mental life*. Harmondsworth: Penguin.

Mischel, W. (1984) 'Convergences and challenges in the search for consistency', *American Psychologist*, vol. 39, pp. 351–64.

Mischel, W. (1993) *Introduction to Personality*. 5th edn. New York: CBS College Publishing.

Nisbett, R. and Wilson, T. (1977) 'Telling more than we know: verbal reports on mental processes', *Psychological Review*, vol. 84, pp. 231–59.

Pervin, L.A. (1993) *Personality*. 6th edn. Chichester: John Wiley.

Rogers, C.R. (1970) *On Becoming a Person*. Boston, MA: Houghton Mifflin.

Schiönpflug, W. (1993) 'Applied psychology: newcomer with a long tradition', *Applied Psychology: An International Review*, vol. 42, pp. 5–30.

Schneider, D.J. (1991) 'Social cognition', *Annual Review of Psychology*, vol. 42, pp. 527–61.

Schneider, S.C. and Dunbar, R.L.M. (1992) 'A psychoanalytic reading of hostile takeover events', *Academy of Management Review*, vol. 17, pp. 537–67.

SHL (1984) *The Occupational Personality Questionnaires*. Available to qualified users from Saville and Holdsworth Ltd, Thames Ditton, Surrey, UK.

Skinner, B.F. (1971) *Beyond Freedom and Dignity*. New York: Knopf.

Spinelli, E. (1989) *The Interpreted World*. London: Sage.

Webster, J. and Starbuck, W.H. (1988) 'Theory building in industrial and organisational psychology' in Cooper, C.L. and Robertson, I.T. (eds) *International Review of Industrial and Organizational Psychology*, vol. 3. Chichester: John Wiley.

Zajonc, R.B. (1980) 'Feeling and thinking: preferences need no inferences', *American Psychologist*, vol. 35, pp. 151–75.

3

Work psychology: its origins, subject matter and research techniques

After studying this chapter, you should be able to:

1 describe important landmarks in the history of work psychology;

2 specify the topics covered by work psychologists;

3 describe the employers and roles adopted by work psychologists;

4 describe the main elements of a psychological theory, and explain the links between those elements;

5 discuss the relationship between work psychology and common sense;

6 list four ethical principles governing the activities of work psychologists;

7 distinguish between two opposing philosophies in the conduct of psychological research;

8 describe five methods of data collection used in research by work psychologists;

9 describe the key features, advantages and disadvantages of four research designs used by work psychologists.

INTRODUCTION

This chapter begins with a brief look at the roots and history of work psychology, including the Hawthorne studies and other key milestones. Attention then turns to present-day work psychology: the topics it covers, the relationship between theory and practice, and professional affairs. The issue of whether work psychology is more useful than so-called common sense is examined. If it is to be useful, work psychology must be based on sound information and appropriate techniques. This chapter therefore concludes with an analysis of how work psychologists obtain information using research methods. The strengths and weaknesses of each method are illustrated with examples. By the end of the chapter the reader should know the topics that work psychology covers, and be able to describe and evaluate the research methods used by work psychologists.

THE ORIGINS OF WORK PSYCHOLOGY

Work psychology has at least two distinct roots. One resides in a pair of traditions that have often been termed 'fitting the man [sic] to the job' (FMJ) and 'fitting the job to the man [sic]' (FJM). The FMJ tradition manifests itself in employee selection, training and vocational guidance. These endeavours have in common an attempt to achieve an effective match between job and person by concentrating on the latter. The FJM tradition focuses instead on the job, and in particular the design of tasks, equipment and working conditions that suit a person's physical and psychological characteristics.

Much early work in these traditions was undertaken in response to the demands of two world wars. In the UK, for example, there was concern about the adverse consequences of the very long hours worked in munitions factories during the First World War and again in the Second World War (Vernon, 1948). The extensive use of aircraft in the Second World War led to attempts to design cockpits that optimally fitted pilots' capacities. In both the UK and the USA, the First World War highlighted the need to develop methods of screening people so that only those suitable for a post were selected for it. This need was met through the development of tests of ability and personality. One major source of such work in the UK was the National Institute of Industrial Psychology (NIIP), which was established in 1921 by the influential psychologist C. S. Myers and a business colleague named H. J. Welch, and survived in various forms until 1977. The brief of the NIIP was 'to promote and encourage the practical application of the sciences of psychology and physiology to commerce and industry by any means that may be found practicable'. The UK Civil Service began to employ a considerable number of psychologists after the Second World War. Their brief was, and largely still is, to improve Civil Service procedures, particularly in selection and training. Especially in the 1960s and 1970s, some other large organisations also employed psychologists. Organisational and labour market trends since the 1980s have reduced the proportion of work psychologists employed in large organisations, and increased the proportion who are self-employed or employed by small consultancy firms.

> ■ **KEY LEARNING POINT**
> *Two important traditions in work psychology concern how jobs can be fitted to people and how people can be fitted to jobs.*

The FMJ and FJM traditions essentially concern the relationship between individuals and their work. The other root of work psychology can be loosely labelled *human relations*. It is concerned with the complex interplay between individuals, groups, organisations and work. It therefore emphasises social factors at work much more than FMJ and FJM. The importance of human relations was highlighted in some famous research now known as the *Hawthorne studies*. These were conducted in the 1920s at a large factory of the Western Electric Company at Hawthorne, near Chicago, USA. The studies were reported most fully in Roethlisberger and Dickson (1939). Originally, they were designed to assess the effect of level of illumination on productivity. One group of workers (the experimental group) was subjected to changes in illumination while another (the control group) was not. The productivity of both groups increased slowly during this investigation; only when illumination was at a small fraction of its original level did the productivity of the experimental group begin to decline. These strange results suggested that other factors apart from illumination were determining productivity.

This work was followed up with what became known as the *relay assembly test room study*. A small group of female assembly workers was taken from the large department, and stationed in a separate room so that working conditions could be controlled effectively. Over a period of more than a year, changes were made in the length of the working day and working week, the length and timing of rest pauses, and other aspects of the work context. Productivity increased after every change, and the gains were maintained even after all conditions returned to their original levels.

Why did these results occur? Clearly, factors other than those deliberately manipulated by the researchers were responsible. For example, the researchers had allowed the workers certain privileges at work, and had taken a close interest in the group. Hence some factor probably to do with feeling special, or guessing what the researchers were investigating, seemed to be influencing the workers' behaviour. The problem of people's behaviour being affected by the knowledge that they are being researched has come to be called the *Hawthorne effect*. The more general lessons here are: (i) it is difficult to experiment with people without altering some conditions other than those intended, and (ii) people's behaviour is substantially affected by *their interpretation* of what is happening around them (Adair, 1984).

These conclusions were extended by a study of a group of male workers who wired up equipment in the bank wiring room. A researcher sat in the corner and observed the group's activities. At first this generated considerable suspicion, but apparently after a time the men more or less forgot about the researcher's presence. Once this happened, certain phenomena became apparent. First, there were social *norms*; that is, shared ideas about how things should be. Most importantly, there was a norm about what constituted an appropriate level of production. This was high enough to keep management off the men's backs, but less than they were capable of. Workers who either consistently exceeded the productivity norm or fell short of it were subjected to social pressure to conform. Another norm concerned supervisors' behaviour. Supervisors were expected to be friendly and informal with the men: one who was more formal and officious was strongly disapproved of. Finally, there were two informal groups in the room, with some rivalry between them.

The bank wiring room showed clearly how social relationships between workers were important determinants of work behaviour. These relationships were often more influential than either official company policy or monetary rewards.

> ■ KEY LEARNING POINT
>
> *The human relations tradition in work psychology emphasises individuals' experiences and interpretations in work.*

There has been much criticism of the experimental methods used by the Hawthorne researchers and considerable debate about the exact reasons for their findings. However, subsequent research by other social scientists confirmed and extended the general message that human relations matter. For example, Trist and Bamforth (1951), working in British coal-mines, showed that if technology is introduced which disrupts existing social groups and relationships, then there are serious consequences for productivity, industrial relations and employee psychological well-being. Their work gave birth to the *socio-technical systems* approach to work design (*see also* Chapter 19).

WORK PSYCHOLOGY TODAY

What is work psychology?

One source of confusion is that work psychology has a lot of different names. In the UK and the USA, the old-established term (still sometimes used) is *industrial psychology*. The newer label in the USA is *industrial/organisational psychology* (or I/O psychology for short). In the UK, it is often called *occupational psychology*, but this term is uncommon in most other countries. Throughout Europe, increasing use is made of *the psychology of work and organisation* and *work and organisational psychology* to describe the area. Just to confuse things further, some specific parts of the field are given labels like *vocational psychology*, *managerial psychology* and *personnel psychology*. Meanwhile, there are also some bigger areas of study to which psychology contributes greatly. These include *organisational behaviour* and *human resources management*.

Our advice for the confused reader is: don't panic! The differences between these labels do mean something to some people who work in the field, but should not unduly worry most of us. The main distinction mirrors that made in the earlier section between individually-orientated versus group- or organisation-orientated topics. In the UK, the label 'occupational psychology' is most commonly applied to the first, and 'organisational psychology' to the second (Blackler, 1982). But many psychologists in the workplace regularly cross this rather artificial boundary. We use the term *work psychology* because of its simplicity, and because to us it encompasses both the individual and organisational levels of analysis.

A reading of the previous two chapters and this one so far should have given the reader a reasonable idea of what work psychology is. In order to be more specific, we now list twelve areas in which work psychologists operate as teachers, researchers and consultants. This list is adapted from the British Psychological Society (1986) register of the Division of Occupational Psychology members. To simplify things a bit, we have divided the twelve areas into five groups, as shown in Fig. 3.1. Inevitably, some of the twelve in reality relate to more than one group – for example, performance appraisal is often partly about development as well as assessment.

Fig. 3.1 The domains of work psychology

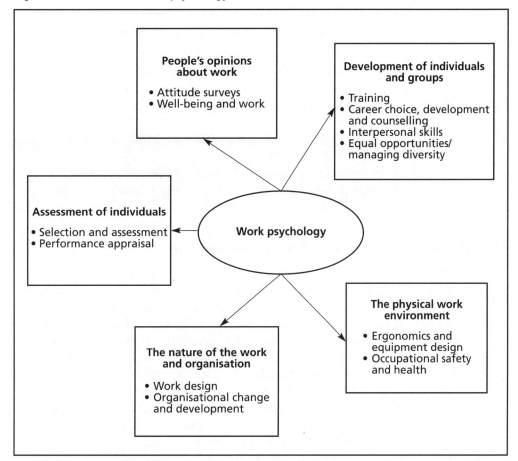

1   *selection and assessment*: for all types of job by a variety of methods, including tests and interviews;

2   *training*: identification of training needs; the design, delivery and evaluation of training;

3   *performance appraisal*: identification of key aspects of job performance; design of systems for accurate performance assessment; training in appraisal techniques;

4   *organisational change and development*: analysis of systems and relationships with a view to possible change; implementation of any such change (e.g. new technology);

5   *ergonomics and equipment design*: analysis and design of work equipment and environments to fit human physical and cognitive capabilities;

6   *career choice, development and counselling*: analysis of a person's abilities, interests and values, and their translation into occupational terms;

7   *interpersonal skills*: identification and development of skills such as leadership, assertiveness, negotiation, group working and relationships with other individuals;

8   *equal opportunities*: monitoring and enhancing opportunities for minority groups at work. In recent years this has broadened into *managing diversity*, where the aim is to harness the skills and perspectives of many different cultural and other groups;

9 *occupational safety and health*: examination of causes of accidents and introduction of measures to reduce their frequency of occurrence;

10 *work design*: allocation of tasks so that jobs are as satisfying and motivating as possible;

11 *attitude surveys*: design, conduct and analysis of surveys (e.g. by questionnaire or interview) of employee opinions and experiences at work;

12 *well-being and work*: investigation of factors which lead to stress in work and unemployment, and identification of ways to prevent and manage stress.

> ■ **KEY LEARNING POINT**
> *Work psychology concerns all aspects of human behaviour, thoughts, feelings and experiences concerning work.*

The qualifications and roles of work psychologists

How can one tell whether somebody who claims to be a work psychologist is in fact appropriately qualified? In the UK, the British Psychological Society (BPS) oversees the professional practice of psychologists. To become a Chartered Psychologist (C. Psychol.) a person must possess not only an approved degree in psychology (or the equivalent), but also several years of appropriate specialist postgraduate training and/or work experience. It is also possible to be a Chartered *Occupational* Psychologist, though some people who could become one prefer to stick with the generic C. Psychol. To be a Chartered Occupational Psychologist, a person must be eligible for membership of the Division of Occupational Psychology of the BPS. In turn, this requires demonstrable *practical expertise* and experience in several of the areas listed above – *knowledge* is not enough. Certain tests of ability and personality (*see* Chapter 8) can only be administered by Chartered Psychologists or (in some cases) by people who have been awarded a Certificate of Competence in Occupational Testing after training from a Chartered Psychologist.

Chartered Psychologists and Chartered Occupational Psychologists in the UK are bound by BPS ethical guidelines and disciplinary procedures. Information on all of these matters, including lists of Chartered Psychologists, can be obtained from the British Psychological Society. The Directory of Chartered Psychologists is also available for consultation in many UK public libraries. The names and addresses of psychological associations in the UK and other countries are listed in an appendix to this chapter.

The ethical code of conduct produced by the BPS (British Psychological Society, 1991) covers a range of topics. They include the ways in which work psychologists are allowed to advertise their services, guidelines for the use of non-sexist language, and guidelines on conduct in professional practice and in psychological research. Regarding the last of these, psychologists are required to consider the following issues:

● *consent*: those who participate in the research should normally be made aware beforehand of all aspects of it that might reasonably be expected to influence their willingness to participate;

- *deception*: deception of those who participate in the research should be avoided wherever possible. If deception is necessary for the effective conduct of the research, it should not be the cause of significant distress when participants are debriefed afterwards;

- *debriefing*: after participation, the participants should be given any information and other support necessary to complete their understanding of the research, and to avoid any sense of unease their participation might have engendered;

- *withdrawal from the investigation*: the psychologist should tell participants of their right to withdraw from the research at any time;

- *confidentiality*: subject to the requirements of legislation, including (in the UK) the Data Protection Act, information obtained about a participant is confidential unless agreed otherwise in advance. This is in some ways especially important in work psychology where, for example, a senior member of an organisation may put pressure on the researcher to reveal what a junior member has said;

- *protection of participants*: the investigator must protect participants from physical and mental harm during the investigation. The risk of harm should normally be no greater than the participant's normal lifestyle.

> ■ **KEY LEARNING POINT**
> *Work psychologists' activities are governed by ethical principles, many of which concern the rights and well-being of people who pay for their services and/or participate in their research.*

Whatever country they live in, work psychologists can be teachers, researchers and consultants. Many are found in institutions of higher education, where they tend to engage in all three activities, especially of course the first two. Shimmin and Wallis (1994), among others, have noted that work psychologists in higher education are now much more often employed in departments of business and management than in departments of psychology. This reflects both a tendency for work psychology to be used primarily to achieve management goals, and a mixing of psychology with other disciplines in a subject that has come to be called organisational behaviour (OB). (Indeed, this book is recommended reading on many OB courses.) Other work psychologists operate as independent consultants, advising organisations and individuals who seek their services on a fee-paying basis. There are also some specialist firms of psychologists and/or management consultants. Some psychologists are employed full-time by such firms. Others work for them on an occasional basis as independent associates. Still other psychologists are employed by larger organisations to give specialist advice, in effect acting as internal consultants. In the UK, the Civil Service, the armed forces, the Post Office and British Telecom have been prominent in this regard. As noted earlier, however, large organisations now employ fewer psychologists than was once the case.

Theory and research in work psychology

A theory in psychology can be defined as an organised collection of ideas which serves to predict what a person will do, think or feel. To be successful, it needs to specify the following five elements (*see also* Fig. 3.2):

Fig. 3.2 A simplified structure of psychological theory

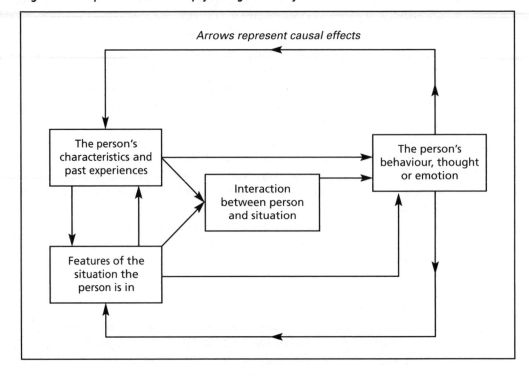

1 the particular behaviours, thoughts or emotions in question. These should have significance for human affairs;

2 any differences between people in the degree to which they characteristically exhibit the behaviours, thoughts or emotions in question;

3 any situational factors that might influence whether the behaviours, thoughts or emotions in question occur;

4 any consequences of the interaction between 2 and 3 for the behaviours, thoughts or emotions;

5 any ways in which the occurrence of particular behaviours, thoughts or emotions might feed back to produce change in 2 and 3.

To take an example, let us suppose that a psychologist wishes to develop a theory to explain and predict the occurrence of arriving late for work. Relevant individual characteristics might include a person's job satisfaction and the extent to which he or she tends to be well organised. Relevant past experiences might include punishments for being late. Situational features might include the distance of home from work, the simplicity or complexity of travel between home and work, and the expectations of the person's work-mates. They may also include factors which change day by day such as the weather. These might all directly affect the person's actual incidence of arriving late for work. But so might the *interaction* between person and situation. For example, a well-organised person may have no difficulty making complex travel arrangements between home and work. For such a person, complexity of travel arrangements would *not* have much effect on time of arrival at work. A poorly organised person may be able to cope with straightforward travel arrangements but not complex ones. For that person, the complexity of travel to work could make a big difference to punctuality.

Just to make things more complicated, it is likely that person and situation influence each other. This can occur in at least three ways. Two of these will have happened before the specific events of interest to the psychologist. First, people's characteristics can affect the types of situation they expose themselves to. Second, they may be able to change features of their situation, or features of their situation may change them. Third, a person's behaviour right now may lead him or her to change ('I'm late again; I must become a better organised person') or may cause a change in his or her situation (in an extreme case, being dismissed for being late once too often).

Naturally, it is possible to suggest many other personal characteristics and situational features which might influence lateness for work. The choice of which to investigate might itself be guided by theory. Testing and application of a theory of lateness for work would also require appropriate methods for assessing personal characteristics, situational features and lateness for work.

It is important to note that theories, or at least good ones, are not conjured out of thin air. The concepts and proposed relationships between them are based on past research and theory, and the psychologist's reflections upon them. The choice of what to study in the first place can also be influenced by current events and public opinion. Weick (1989) has urged social scientists to be more careful and imaginative in how they formulate theory, and has suggested some ways to achieve this.

> ■ KEY LEARNING POINT
> *The conventional view of good theory in work psychology is that the theory should be precise in specifying the behaviour, thoughts or feelings it is designed to predict, and the individual and situational characteristics which influence them.*

Some might argue that theory has little to offer practice. There are various reasons for advancing that argument. Theories in a particular area may not be very good, in the sense that they do not adequately or accurately specify the phenomena portrayed in Fig. 3.2. A psychologist may find that a particular technique seems to work well, and not be concerned about theoretical reasons why it works. But the present authors firmly believe that a good theory is essential to *good* practice. It is incorrect to say, as people sometimes do, that an idea is good in theory but not in practice. A good theory does a good job of describing, explaining and predicting behaviour, thoughts or emotions which have important outcomes. Basing practice on it *is* better than basing it on nothing, or on an inferior theory. As the distinguished social psychologist Kurt Lewin (1945) long ago argued, there is nothing so practical as a good theory.

The point was made in Chapter 2 that psychology is not a united or unified discipline. The multiplicity of views certainly extends to what research and theory are about and how research should be conducted. The most fundamental polarity has been described nicely by, among others, Easterby-Smith *et al.* (1991, chapter 3) as positivism versus phenomenology. Each of these positions has distinct and very different philosophical roots, though in practice nowadays much research includes a bit of both.

Positivism assumes that the social world exists objectively and should therefore be measured using objective methods rather than subjective ones such as intuition. This usually implies quantitative (i.e. numerical) data. Science is seen as advancing through making hypotheses about laws and causes of human behaviour and then testing those hypotheses, preferably by simplifying the problem of interest as much as possible. It is also assumed that the researcher can investigate without influencing what is being investigated: that is, his or her conduct and presence are assumed to have no impact on the social world.

The other extreme is labelled phenomenology by Easterby-Smith *et al.* (1991; *see also* Chapter 2). This viewpoint suggests that reality is not objective. Instead, the meaning of events, concepts and objectives is constructed and interpreted by people, through their thought processes and social interactions. Research conducted on the basis of this philosophy will aim 'to understand and explain why people have different experiences, rather than search for external causes and fundamental laws to explain their behaviour' (Easterby-Smith *et al.*, 1991, p. 24). So instead of measuring how often certain behaviours occur, the aim of research is to examine the different ways in which people interpret and explain their experience. The data produced by such research tend to be harder to obtain and to summarise than those produced by positivist research, but also richer in meaning, detail and explanation.

Many topics in work psychology can be investigated from both perspectives and all points in between. To continue the example of arriving late for work, a positivist research project (which was the sort implied in the example given earlier) would assess the frequency of this behaviour and try to link it with objective factors such as distance from work as well as perhaps more subjective ones such as job satisfaction. The assumption would be that such factors may *cause* lateness for work, irrespective of the sense individuals might make of their situation. On the other hand, phenomenologically-orientated research on lateness at work would focus much more on how individuals thought and felt about being late for work, and how they explained their own behaviour in this area. The general theoretical framework outlined in Fig. 3.2 would still have some relevance, but aspects of the person and situation to be examined would be treated as part of people's ways of understanding their own behaviour rather than as objectively verifiable forces causing it.

> ### ■ KEY LEARNING POINT
> *There is an important philosophical disagreement in psychology between positivism and phenomenology. The former emphasises objectively verifiable causes of behaviour, thoughts and emotions; the latter focuses more on people's subjective explanations and accounts.*

Work psychology is predominantly problem centred. There is no single dominant theoretical perspective, and work psychology has sometimes been somewhat isolated from theoretical developments in mainstream psychology (*see* Chapter 2). Herriot (1984) for example criticised work psychologists for ignoring developments in social psychology in their study of employee selection. Another issue concerns the influence of work psychologists on organisations which purchase their services. Many tend to see themselves as technical experts (Blackler and Brown, 1986), able to advise on the detail of specific procedures – for example, psychometric tests, assertiveness training, ergonomics and so on. On the other hand, human resource managers are attempting to play an increasingly central and strategic role in their organisations. If work psychologists are to influence organisational functioning, they need to move away from a technical specialist role toward that of a general business consultant (Anderson and Prutton, 1993). They must understand the organisational impact of their techniques, be able to work on 'macro' issues like organisational change and human resource planning, and be able to demonstrate the likely financial impact of their recommendations. They must be able to speak the language of business, and to communicate with a wide range of people. They need to be open to new ideas and techniques, including those originating outside psychology (Offerrmann and Gowing, 1990). They need to recognise the politics of doing work psychology – that is, the power relationships between individuals and organisations involved in it. Regarding research, this means being able to 'sell' a research proposal so that practical benefits for the potential sponsoring organisation are apparent (and exceed the costs), to be prepared to negotiate and renegotiate on how the research will be conducted, and to develop and maintain contacts within the organisation. All of this must be done without contravening the ethical guidelines described earlier.

Some would, however, argue that ethical and practical issues go deeper than this. Who, exactly, is the psychologist working for? Because most research in organisations is paid for by senior managers, it is likely that the research agenda will be driven by their perspectives and priorities. Obtaining the informed consent of people at lower levels of the organisation does not really get round that reality. An alternative is to work only on behalf of individuals or groups and communities with low power and resources. Decisions like this have obvious links with the psychologist's own values and political stance, and equally obvious consequences for the level of financial rewards he or she enjoys. Most work psychologists take the view that usually organisations are sufficiently unitarist (that is, united in objectives and values) to permit all constituencies within them to gain from the psychologist's interventions, or at least not *lose*. Some might argue that this is a convenient assumption, as opposed to a carefully considered and justified position, and that ensuring that a person or group is not harmed by the work psychologist's activities is not the same as actively working for their interests.

In an excellent article, Gary Johns (Johns, 1993) has analysed why techniques advocated by work psychologists (e.g. in personnel selection or job design) are not always adopted in organisations, even if they seem to be based on good research and have potential to save (or make) money. He argues that work psychologists often neglect the political and social contexts of organisations. Yet these considerations loom larger in managers' minds than the finer points of a psychologist's arguments concerning the technical merit of, for example, a particular personality test. Managers are likely to respond to factors like how rival companies do things, what legislation requires, and what their bosses are likely to find readily acceptable. Evidence for the effectiveness of a psychological technique is often derived from quite complex, abstract research, where the social and political context in which the research was carried out is either not adequately reported or non-existent. Johns argues that work psychologists should place more emphasis on influencing legislation. For example, the American Psychological Association supported a bill to ban the use of the polygraph (lie detector) in pre-employment screening. They should also be prepared to publicly name organisations that adopt good practice, since permission to do so is usually granted, and managers are more impressed by information about named organisations than unnamed ones. Work psychologists should also actively seek to publish their work in managers' journals as well as academic ones.

Given Johns' analysis, it is perhaps not surprising that Miner (1984) found that organisational science theories which had been generally supported by research were no more likely than other theories to have spawned practical techniques. Perhaps more optimistically, he found that most of the theories which had both high validity and high usefulness of application had been produced by people whose initial training had been in psychology (as opposed to, for example, political science, organisational behaviour or sociology). Most of those theories concerned motivation (*see* Chapter 11). Miner's analysis is dependent on his own judgements of scientific validity and usefulness of application. It must therefore be treated cautiously. On the other hand, he claimed that he had no wish to see psychology do so well, so undue favouritism can probably be ruled out.

■ **KEY LEARNING POINT**

If work psychology is to have a substantial influence on organisational and public policy, work psychologists must address the political acceptability as well as the technical merit of their recommendations.

Staw (1991) notes that psychologists tend to concentrate on 'micro' organisational behaviour, which includes attitudes, motivation, absenteeism and work stress. Sociologists focus more on 'macro' phenomena like organisational structure, strategy and environment. Staw argues that psychological theories may help explain 'macro' phenomena, partly because the actions of organisations are often really those of individuals or small groups of people. A good example of this can be seen in the Schneider and Dunbar (1992) article mentioned in Chapter 2. If Staw is correct, the potential of psychology in the workplace is great, but has not yet been achieved. Sociological theories may have a role to play in explaining 'micro' organisational behaviour, as Pfeffer (1991) pointed out in an article published in the same issue of the *Journal of Management* as Staw's article. This lends further weight to the need noted by Offerrmann and Gowing (1990) for work psychologists to be more aware of what other academic disciplines can offer.

■ **KEY LEARNING POINT**

A schematic summary of some key points of this section is shown in Fig. 3.3. The formulation, conduct, output and utilisation of research in work psychology are all part of a complex process.

Where can one find out about advances in work psychology? Some can be found in books. General texts like this give a necessarily brief account of major developments. Other specialist books are devoted to particular topics and sometimes even to particular theories. For example, Warr (1987) brought together much evidence from diverse sources to explain psychological well-being in employment and unemployment. He also developed an analogy with the impact of vitamins on *physical* health in order to improve our understanding of environmental influences on *mental* health.

Fig. 3.3 The research process in work psychology

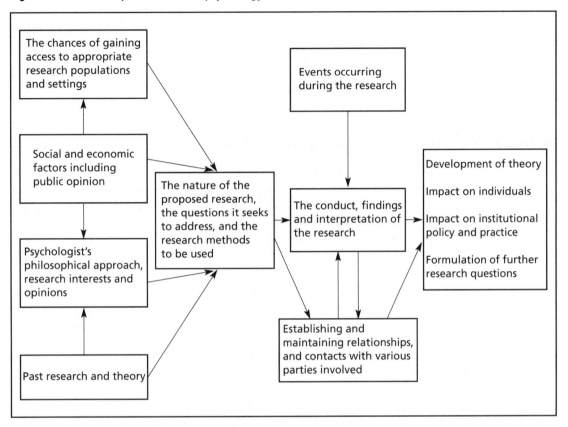

Many new theoretical developments, and also tests of established theories, can be found in certain academic journals. Leading journals of work psychology include *Journal of Occupational and Organizational Psychology* (published in the UK), *Journal of Applied Psychology* (USA), *Journal of Organizational Behavior* (USA/UK), *Applied Psychology: An International Review* (The International Association of Applied Psychology – mainly European), *Organizational Behavior and Human Decision Processes* (USA), *Personnel Psychology* (USA), *Human Relations* (UK/USA) and *Journal of Vocational Behavior* (USA). There are also other prestigious journals which include work psychology along with other disciplines applied to work behaviour. These include *Academy of Management Journal* (USA), *Academy of Management Review* (USA), *Administrative Science Quarterly* (USA), and *Human Resource Management Journal* (UK). Some other journals concentrate more on the concerns of practitioners; that is, people who earn their living by supplying work psychology to organisations. These include *The European Work and Organizational Psychologist* (various European countries) and *Selection and Development Review* (UK).

This is of course a long list of journals, and plenty more could be added to it. But there are subtle differences between journals in content and approach which soon become evident to the observant reader. This makes information search easier if one has carefully defined the topic one wishes to explore. Also, computerised literature searches can be accomplished by most academic libraries. Many journals and academic or professional bodies have World Wide Web sites which are useful sources of information about current research and other activities. Electronic searches help to make the quest for knowledge much quicker and less tedious. Most of the journals listed above concentrate on carefully designed evaluations of theories or psychological techniques. They also publish review articles summarising the current position and perhaps proposing new directions. Some of the material in the remainder of this chapter and the next should help the reader to evaluate journal articles.

WORK PSYCHOLOGY AND COMMON SENSE

One of the better jokes about psychologists is that they tell you what you already know in words that you do not understand. Like most good jokes, it has a grain of truth – but only a grain. To see why, let us look more closely first at the notion of common sense, and then at its relationship with work psychology.

Common sense is sometimes expressed in proverbs such as 'look before you leap'. Yes, one says, that's common sense – after all, it would be stupid to proceed with something without checking first to see if it was wise. But the reader may already have called to mind another proverb: 'He who hesitates is lost'. Well, yes, that's common sense too. After all, in this life we must take our chances when they come, otherwise they will pass us by. This example illustrates an important characteristic of common sense: it can be contradictory. Interestingly, one research study found that students sometimes endorsed pairs of contradictory proverbs of this kind as both having high 'truth value' (Halvor Teigen, 1986). And so they should. Both *are* true – sometimes, and in some circumstances. Psychologists are in the business of working out when, and in what circumstances.

Another feature of common sense is that people often disagree about what it is (Schweiso, 1984). Quite often, in debates, both (or all) parties claim that common sense is on their side. Usually they do not get to grips with the assumptions they are making about what common sense is. But perhaps the most pervasive feature of common sense is that often it comes *after the event*. We observe what happens, reflect upon what we have seen, and construct an explanation for it. We forget that we could equally well have explained the event differently, and that we could have explained it just as readily if it had happened to turn out quite differently. Indeed, this capacity to generate explanations is an important part of being human. We have a variety of 'theories' in our heads for explaining what goes on around us (*see also* Chapter 12). But we too readily assume that the one we choose is the one everyone else would choose, and call it common sense.

One good example of so-called common sense in the work setting concerns the maxim 'a happy worker is a productive worker'. This is often taken to mean that if we increase a person's job satisfaction (though note that this is only one aspect of happiness), he or she will then work better. Note that there is a conceptual leap here from happiness *being associated with* productivity, to happiness *causing* productivity. This is a small change in wording but a major change in meaning (*see also* Chapter 4).

Most people, including those who might agree with the notion that job satisfaction leads to improved work performance, can soon see possible reasons why this might not in fact be so. Some of us might derive our job satisfaction from social relationships at work and invest energy in those rather than work performance. Limitations of people's ability or the machines they work with may be the key determinants of performance.

Even if satisfaction and performance are linked, doing a good job may cause satisfaction rather than satisfaction leading to doing a good job. In fact, according to Iaffaldano and Muchinsky (1985) the correlation (*see* Chapter 4) between job satisfaction and work performance is 0.17. This means, in effect, that 'a happy worker is a productive worker about 3% more than we would expect just by chance'. Somehow this statement does not carry the comforting certainty of the original!

All this is not to claim that only psychologists can see beyond the end of their nose. As is made clear above, people readily abandon simplistic versions of common sense. We can argue that even without psychologists, our understanding of how the world works generally seems to be good enough to live a reasonably successful life (Furnham, 1983). In fact, psychologists are increasingly interested in how we make sense of our day-to-day lives (*see* Chapter 12), and how we use language to construct a coherent account of our reality (Potter and Wetherell, 1987).

> ■ KEY LEARNING POINT
> *Work psychology seeks to go beyond 'common-sense' views of work behaviour, thoughts and feelings.*

It is now time to ask how work psychologists collect their information and what they do with it. After all, if psychologists want people to believe them, they need to show that their conclusions are based on sound data and analysis. The remainder of this chapter, and the next, examine these issues.

RESEARCH TECHNIQUES IN WORK PSYCHOLOGY

Methods and designs

Work psychologists use a variety of techniques in their research on human behaviour, thoughts and emotions in the workplace. In considering these techniques, it is helpful to distinguish between research *designs* and research *methods*. The former concerns the overall research strategy employed. This strategy depends on the researcher's beliefs about scientific investigation as well as the nature of the phenomena being researched. Research methods are the specific ways in which information is gathered within the overall research strategy. Drawing on Bryman (1989, p. 29), a number of designs and methods can be identified. There is more than one way of carrying out each design and each method. The designs are discussed later in this chapter. First, it is necessary to make a few points about each of the methods.

> ■ KEY LEARNING POINT
> *Research design refers to the overall strategy in conducting research, whereas research methods are the procedures by which information is collected.*

Research methods

Questionnaires/psychometric tests

Many research projects in work psychology, especially surveys, use one or both of these. Questionnaires are often used to assess a person's attitudes, values, opinions, beliefs or experiences (*see also* Chapter 9). Psychometric tests are normally employed to measure ability or personality (*see also* Chapter 8). Questionnaires and tests normally require a person to answer a series of written questions presented on paper or sometimes on a computer screen. Answers are often multiple-choice; that is, the person has to select the most appropriate response from a choice of several. Responses are usually expressed as a number representing, for example, a person's intelligence, extroversion or job satisfaction. Some questionnaires and tests need to be administered by the researcher in person. Others are designed to be self-explanatory and can be filled in by the respondent without supervision.

Interviews

A work psychologist may conduct one or more interviews, normally with an individual, but sometimes with a group of people. The work psychologist asks questions and records responses, either by making notes or using a tape recorder. The questions may be specified in advance, in which case it is a *structured interview*. On the other hand, the interviewer may define only the general topic he or she wishes to investigate and permit respondents to talk about whatever they wish within that topic. This is an *unstructured interview*.

Psychophysiological assessment

This involves measurement of a people's neurological, biological or physiological state, as it relates to their psychological functioning. So, for example, in a study of work stress, blood samples may be taken to gauge the concentration of fatty acids in a person's bloodstream. This method of data collection is less common in work psychology than in some other areas of psychology.

Observation

A work psychologist may observe people's behaviour by stationing himself or herself as unobtrusively as possible, and recording the frequency, source and timing of behaviour. This can be termed *structured observation*. Alternatively, the work psychologist may participate in the events he or she is studying. For example, King (1992) investigated innovations on a hospital ward while also working as a nursing assistant. This is *participant observation*. Where people are being observed in their workplace, they are normally informed, or asked about it in advance. Their awareness may itself affect their behaviour, but that is usually preferable to the alternatives of secrecy or even deception. Observation may also include observing the consequences of behaviour; for example, a person's work productivity.

Diaries

People may be asked to keep a diary of key events and/or their behaviour, thoughts and feelings. It is normally necessary to give people a fair amount of structure to help them to focus their written comments, and to stay in contact with them as an encouragement to keep up the diary-filling.

Archival sources

As Bryman (1989, p. 31) pointed out, this is strictly speaking a source of data rather than a method of collecting it. Achival information already exists before the work psychologist's investigation. Examples include absenteeism data, company accounts, productivity records, human resource policy documents, accident statistics and many others. Data from archival sources are most often used either to provide a context for a particular research project, or to investigate the impact of an event on the functioning of an organisation.

> ■ KEY LEARNING POINT
>
> *A work psychologist's research data can be obtained using questionnaires, psychometric tests, interviews, observation of behaviour, measurement of bodily activity, and existing data banks.*

The survey design

The key distinguishing feature of a survey is that it does not intervene in naturally occurring events, nor does it control them. It simply takes a snapshot of what is happening, usually by asking people about it. The aim is usually to gather quantitative information about certain phenomena (for example, events, attitudes) from a large number of people. On occasions this will be done simply to ascertain the frequency of occurrence of a certain event, such as feeling anxious at work. But more commonly, a survey will attempt to discover the relationships of variables with each other – for example, whether anxiety at work tends to be accompanied by low job satisfaction.

The survey design could involve use of any of the methods described above. However, it most commonly involves questionnaires. Questionnaires cannot be just thrown together (as they are in some popular magazines) if they are to do a proper job. They must be carefully devised so that they unambiguously measure what they are supposed to measure – i.e. so that they are *valid* (*see* Chapter 6). It is important to ask the right people to participate in the survey. Ideally, the respondents should be a *random sample* of all those people to whom the survey is relevant. That means that everyone to whom the survey was relevant would have an equal chance of participating in it. In practice, of course, this is rarely the case.

But to whom is a survey relevant? Let us suppose that a psychologist wanted to examine whether doing work where the pace of work is not under one's own control (e.g. on an assembly line) makes people feel negative about their work (*see* Cox, 1978, chapter 7). If a work psychologist sent questionnaires only to people doing work of con-trolled pace, there would be no basis for comparison with anybody else. One way round this might be to include some questions asking people what effect they think the paced nature of their work has on them. For some psychologists, how people make sense of such things is important in its own right. But for most, this would not be sufficient. They would insist that comparison was necessary with people whose work was *not* paced. The trouble is, these people may be different in a number of ways from those whose work *is* paced. Any one (or more) of these differences could explain differences between the groups in work attitudes.

This leads to another point: exactly what information should be collected in the survey? Continuing our example, the work psychologist might ask about any number of things. Age, sex, work experience, educational attainment, abilities required by work, job status, supervision, friendships at work, wage levels and working conditions are just a few. If the paced and non-paced groups differed on one or more of these, it would be difficult to tell what was responsible for any difference between the groups in job satisfaction. Also we could not be certain whether paced work led to (low) job satisfaction, or low job satisfaction led to paced work. The latter might occur if managers allocated the jobs with controlled pace to those employees who expressed dissatisfaction. Another possible interpretation would be that some third factor, for example prior work experience, determined *both* a person's job satisfaction *and* the kind of work he or she did. Unless we knew about his or her prior experience, we could not tell.

Thus the survey has both advantages and disadvantages (*see* Fowler, 1984). It can be used with people directly involved in the issues to be investigated. It can investigate their experiences in their day-to-day setting. It is normally fairly easy to conduct, and makes relatively low demands on people's time. These are advantages. On the other hand, the survey does not involve any manipulation of the variables being investigated. This makes it very difficult to establish cause and effect. The survey takes the world as it is. The world is complicated, and unless the survey takes all relevant factors into account, it may lead the psychologist to draw incorrect conclusions. Various sophisticated statistical techniques can reduce this danger, but not eliminate it.

■ **KEY LEARNING POINT**

Surveys are relatively easy to conduct and they investigate the real world in which people work. However, it is often difficult to be sure about causes and effects.

Longitudinal surveys can help to clarify what causes what. In a longitudinal survey, data are gathered on more than one occasion. This contrasts with *cross-sectional* surveys, where data are collected on one occasion only. Longitudinal data can help to tease out possible causal connections. Conditions pertaining at time 1 may cause those at time 2 but not, presumably, vice versa! Again, though, there remains the danger of key information not being collected. Also, even if event A happens before event B, that does not necessarily mean that A *causes* B.

Sometimes survey research involves collection of information from sources other than the people concerned (for example, from the personnel records of a company). But often *all* the data consist of people's *self-reports* of their behaviour, thoughts and/or emotions. These may not be accurate or complete. It can also lead to a problem called *common method variance*, which is where the relationship between variables is artificially high simply because all of the data are obtained by the same method.

Finally, survey information can be collected using interviews (*see* Brenner, 1981). Market researchers and social researchers often conduct them. The interview is in effect often used as a talking questionnaire. However, it can also be employed to explore issues with respondents in more depth than a questionnaire allows. Conducting research interviews is a skilled business. Care must be taken to gain the trust of the respondent, to explore issues to the extent required, and to avoid accidentally influencing the respondent's answers. Some would say that this last goal cannot be achieved.

The experimental design

The claim of psychology to be a science rests partly on its extensive use of experiments. One key advantage of an experiment is that it allows the psychologist *control* over what happens. This in turn permits inference about causes and effects. On the other hand, there are some disadvantages too. These are discussed below, but first let us examine a concrete example.

The most controlled environment is the psychologist's laboratory. To return to our earlier example concerning paced work, the psychologist might set up a conveyor belt in the laboratory. He or she would probably choose a task typical of conveyor belt work – perhaps checking that boxes of chocolates have been properly packed. The boxes travel along the conveyor belt at a set speed, and the worker has to remove any faultily packed ones. People might be asked to work on this task for a period of several weeks, and to indicate their job satisfaction at various points during that period.

All of this would, of course, cost a lot of money. A large research grant would be required. The psychologist would probably also take the opportunity to record other things apart from job satisfaction, such as work performance (proportion of incorrectly packed boxes identified) and perhaps some physiological measures of stress (e.g. heart rate, blood cholesterol levels).

But this would not be enough on its own. It would also be necessary to include a *control* group as well as the *experimental group* already described. People in the control group should as far as possible do the same job as the experimental group, except that their task would not be machine-paced. Hence, the control group would perhaps be given piles of boxes of chocolates, and instructed to check them. Data on job satisfaction etc. would be collected from members of the control group in the same way and at the same times as from the experimental group.

The work psychologist would try to ensure that the conditions experienced by the experimental and control groups differed *only* in whether or not their task was machine-paced. The two groups have the same task. They perform it in the same laboratory (though the groups may not see each other or even be aware of each other's existence). They can be paid the same amount with the same pay rules, and be supervised in the same way, though the difference between paced and non-paced work may make these last two similarities difficult to achieve in practice. The groups can be given the same opportunities (or lack of them) for interaction with other workers. It would not be easy to ensure that the two groups did the same *amount* of work. The control group could be told that they had to check the same number of boxes per day or week as the experimental group. This would introduce some degree of pacing, though not nearly as much as a conveyor belt running at a constant speed.

Two key terms in experimental jargon are as follows. The *independent variable* is what the psychologist manipulates in order to examine its effect on the *dependent variable*. In this example, therefore, the independent variable is whether or not the work is machine-paced, and the dependent variable is job satisfaction. More complex experiments often have more than one independent variable, and more than one dependent variable.

Another important point concerns the people who undertake the work for the sake of the experiment (often called the *subjects*). Ideally, they would be typical of people who do that kind of work. If so, this would increase the confidence with which experimental results could be applied to the 'real world'. An attempt to recruit such people to the experiment could be made by advertising in local newspapers. This might not be successful, however. Since most researchers work in higher education, they would be tempted to recruit students because they are easy to find – and they usually need the money that is often paid for participation in experiments! But because students are unlikely to work at conveyor belts for much of their career, their reactions in the experiment might not be typical of those who do. Whoever participates in the experiment, individuals would normally be *assigned at random* to either the experimental group or the control group. This random assignment helps to ensure that the people in the two groups do not differ in systematic ways.

It should now be clear that the laboratory experiment allows the psychologist to make unambiguous inferences about the effects on job satisfaction of machine-paced work. Or does it? The psychologist's control necessarily makes it an artificial situation because the real world is rarely so neat and tidy. Unless the psychologist indulges in a huge (and unethical) deception, the experimental subjects will know that they are not in a real job, and that the experiment will only last a few weeks. This could crucially affect their reactions to the work. So could the guesses they make about what the psychologist is investigating. These guesses will be influenced by unintentional cues from the experimenter via (for example) tone of voice and body posture. Such cues are termed *demand characteristics*. Every experiment has them.

> ■ **KEY LEARNING POINT**
>
> *Laboratory experiments allow the work psychologist to control and manipulate the situation in order to establish whether there are causal relationships between variables. But it is not clear whether the same relationships would hold in real-life situations.*

The artificiality of the laboratory experiment is seen by some as a fatal flaw. Sometimes it is possible to conduct a *field experiment* instead. For a work psychologist this would take place in a real work setting, probably with the people who worked there. It would gain over the laboratory experiment in realism, but almost certainly lose in control. Even if managers and union officials at a factory were prepared to allow the psychologist to create an experimental and control group on the factory floor, they would probably not allow random assignment of subjects to groups. Also, they probably could not arrange things like identical supervision and identical opportunities to interact with co-workers even if they wanted to.

Occasionally, it is possible for psychologists to conduct a field experiment using events that are occurring anyway. This is sometimes called a *natural experiment*. For example, a chocolate factory may be changing some, but not all, of its chocolate inspection from self-paced work to conveyor belts (*see* Kemp *et al.*, 1983, for a rather similar situation). The psychologist could use this profitably, especially if he or she was able to obtain data on job satisfaction etc. both before and after the change was made. Here again, though, the gain in realism is balanced by a loss of control and the consequent presence of confounding factors. For example, the people working at the factory might have some choice of which form of work they undertook. This immediately violates the principle of random allocation to groups. On the other hand, one might argue that if this is the way the world works, there is nothing to be gained by trying to arrange conditions which do not reflect it.

> ■ **KEY LEARNING POINT**
>
> *It is occasionally possible to conduct experiments in real-world settings, though usually the work psychologist has less control over the situation than in laboratory experiments.*

Qualitative design

Both surveys and experiments normally express data using numbers (i.e. quantitatively). They allow the people participating in the research little chance to express their opinions in their own words, since the work psychologist investigates a limited number of variables of his or her own choice, selected in advance. Hence surveys and experiments do not obtain a detailed picture of any individual's world. They both involve the psychologist in a fairly detached, quasi-scientific role, and tend to reflect the positivist research philosophy described earlier.

Qualitative research involves a much greater emphasis on seeing the world from the point of view of the subjects who participate in it (Bryman, 1989). That is, it tends to reflect the phenomenological research philosophy described earlier. This normally means collecting detailed information over weeks, months or years using observation and/or unstructured interviews from a fairly small number of individuals or organisations – perhaps only one. This information is intended to paint a picture rather than measure a limited number of specific phenomena. It is therefore normally in the form of words, not numbers.

Rather than testing a pre-specified theory, the work psychologist may well begin the research with some loose theoretical ideas and develop theory in the light of the data obtained during the course of the research. Data collection should also be influenced by developing theoretical ideas as the research proceeds. This process has been termed *grounded theory* by Glaser and Strauss (1967).

Returning to our earlier example, a work psychologist engaging in qualitative research would most likely be interested in how people working on paced and/or unpaced inspection of boxes of chocolates made sense of their situation, and how they coped with it. The psychologist might work on the task as a participant observer, and might also interview individuals or groups about it.

> ■ **KEY LEARNING POINT**
>
> *Qualitative research usually involves an attempt to describe how individuals make sense of the situations they are in.*

Qualitative research usually produces a large amount of data, which requires some editing and interpretation by the researcher. It is time consuming and difficult to carry out. Even obtaining the necessary access to people in their workplace can prove impossible. It leaves researchers vulnerable to the accusation that they have simply discovered in the data what they expected to find. Because this research is usually conducted with relatively small numbers of people, it is often not clear whether the findings would be repeated with a bigger, different sample. For all of these reasons, there are relatively few articles reporting qualitative research in leading work psychology journals. On the other hand, qualitative work has the advantages outlined in the second paragraph of this section. It is becoming more popular as dissatisfaction with the shortcomings of surveys and experiments slowly grows. Some journals (for example the *Journal of Occupational and Organizational Psychology*) explicitly state an editorial policy encouraging qualitative research.

Action research design

Lewin (1946) coined the term *action research* to describe research where the researcher and the people being researched participate jointly in it. Action research is intended both to solve immediate problems for the people collaborating with the researcher, and to add to general knowledge about the topic being researched. It involves not only diagnosing and investigating a particular problem, but also making changes in a work organisation on the basis of research findings, and evaluating the impact of those changes. Increasingly, it also involves the development of an organisation's capacity to solve problems without external help in the future (Eden and Chisholm, 1993).

Action research can involve any of the research methods described earlier but, like qualitative research, is most likely to use interviews and participant observation (*see* Symon and Clegg, 1991, for a good example of an action research project). Much more than other research designs, it is driven by a specific problem in an organisation and what to do about it. It completely abandons the detachment of survey and experimental designs. Like qualitative research, it seeks to examine how people participating in the research see things, and it usually covers fairly long periods of time. Unlike most qualitative research, it involves attempting to solve a problem, and monitoring the success of that attempt.

From the point of view of the researcher, action research can be exciting, difficult and unpredictable. Because of its problem orientation, it requires close involvement with an organisation. This in turn requires careful negotiation and renegotiation of the researcher's role in the organisation, particularly concerning who in the organisation (if anyone) the researcher is 'working for'. Also, people in the organisation may reject the researcher's recommendations for dealing with a problem. This creates obvious difficulties for the evaluation of attempts to deal with the problem, though the researcher may be permitted to evaluate the success of any alternative strategy produced by organisation members. In action research, therefore, the process of conducting the research can become as much a focus of interest as the problem it was originally designed to address.

> ■ **KEY LEARNING POINT**
> *Action research involves the psychologist and people involved in the situation being researched working together to define the aims of the research and solve practical problems.*

SUMMARY

Work psychology concerns both the interaction between an individual and his or her work, and the relationships between people in the work setting. This includes staff selection, training, vocational guidance, management development, ergonomics, organisational development, equal opportunities and job redesign, among other things. Work psychologists act as researchers, teachers and consultants in these areas. In the UK, the British Psychological Society oversees professional qualifications of work psychologists. Psychology can sometimes seem like common sense, but the latter is a slippery concept. It is often contradictory, and people do not always agree about what it is. Common sense is invoked *after* the event, whereas theory aims to *predict* what will happen given a certain set of circumstances. Research designs used by work psychologists include surveys, experiments, qualitative research and action research. These designs vary in the amount of control exerted by the work psychologist, the degree of difficulty in carrying out the research, the role of theory, and the nature of the data obtained. Research designs can be distinguished from methods of data collection. Methods include questionnaires, tests, interviews, observation, psychophysiological measures and archival sources. The characteristics of research published in leading journals of work psychology have been summarised by Schaubroeck and Kuehn (1992, p. 107):

> a majority of published studies were conducted in the field, although laboratory work comprises nearly one-third of the research. Half of the published research was experimental ... most studies minimized common method factors by using diverse data sources. On the down side, a majority of field studies were cross-sectional in nature, there was very little cross-validation of findings, 'hard' data such as physiological measures and archival records were used infrequently ... Researchers appeared to invest in particular design strengths and compromise on others.

TEST YOUR LEARNING

Short-answer questions

1 What were the key lessons learned by work psychologists from the Hawthorne studies?

2 Name and briefly describe eight areas of work undertaken by work psychologists.

3 If you were a manager considering buying the services of a work psychologist, what would you want to know about the psychologist's (i) qualifications and experiences; and (ii) method of working?

4 How would you evaluate whether the research undertaken by a work psychologist was ethical?

5 Imagine that you are trying to develop a theory to explain successful performance in telephone sales work. For each box in Fig. 3.2, suggest at least two possible factors.

6 List three important differences between positivist research and phenomenological research.

7 List five methods by which work psychologists obtain research information.

8 Write a short paragraph on the fundamental differences between experimental and survey research in work psychology.

9 What is action research?

Essay questions

1 Describe any issue in work psychology which interests you. Examine how different research designs might be used to tackle that issue. Is any one design better than the others?

2 'It is not worth distinguishing between research designs and research methods in work psychology because the choice of design dictates the choice of method.' Discuss.

GLOSSARY OF TERMS

Action research A form of research which concentrates on solving practical problems in collaboration with the people and organisations experiencing them.

Archival data Research information obtained from written, computerised or audiovisual sources that exist independent of the research.

BPS British Psychological Society – the governing body for psychologists in the UK.

Chartered Psychologist (C. Psychol.) Title conferred by the BPS recognising the qualifications and experience of psychologists in the UK. Appropriately qualified work psychologists may also use the title Chartered Occupational Psychologist.

Common method variance The extent to which people's scores on two or more psychological variables are related solely because the variables were assessed using the same research method.

Control group In an experiment investigating the impact of one or more interventions, the control group of research subjects does *not* experience an intervention. This group provides a comparison with groups which do experience an intervention.

Cross-sectional research Research where data is collected at only one point in time.

Cross-validation A research technique where a piece of research is repeated on a second sample to see if the same results as first time are obtained.

Demand characteristics Features of experiments which convey clues to subjects about the hypotheses being investigated.

Dependent variable The variable on which the impact of one or more independent variables is investigated in an experiment.

Ethics Rules based on moral principles (such as protecting people from harm and maintaining confidentiality), which govern the research and practice of work psychologists.

Experiment A research design in which the researcher controls or manipulates one or more independent variables in order to investigate their effect on one or more dependent variables.

Experimental group The group of subjects in an experiment which experiences one or more interventions in an investigation of the impact of those interventions.

Grounded theory Theory which develops during the process of data collection in a research project, and which influences data collection later in the same project.

Hawthorne studies A series of investigations of work behaviour conducted at the Hawthorne factory of the Western Electric Company near Chicago, USA in the 1920s.

Independent variable A variable that is manipulated or controlled in an experiment in order to examine its effects on one or more dependent variables.

Interview method Research method where the researcher asks questions face to face or on the telephone with one or more subjects.

Longitudinal research Research where data are collected at two or more points in time, usually months or years apart.

Participant observation Research method where the researcher observes events, and perhaps asks the people involved about them, while also participating in the events.

Phenomenological research Research based on the assumption that there are few objective facts about the social world, and that it is therefore necessary to focus on people's subjective interpretations rather than objectively verifiable causal laws.

Positivist research In contrast to phenomenological research, positivist research takes the view that human behaviour, thoughts and feelings are substantially influenced by objectively measurable factors which exist independent of the researchers and people being researched.

Psychometric test A test, usually using written questions, of one or more aspects of a person's cognitive ability or personality.

Psychophysiological assessment Research method where information is obtained about some aspect of a person's neurological, physiological or medical condition.

Qualitative research Research design where the researcher aims to obtain a detailed picture of the way in which a limited number of people interpret one or more aspects of their world, normally using words rather than numbers.

Questionnaire A written list of questions designed to obtain information about a person's life history, beliefs, attitudes, interests, values or self-concept.

Random sample A set of people who act as subjects in a research project, chosen at random from the population to which the research applies.

Structured observation A research method where the researcher remains uninvolved in events, but records what occurs using a predetermined system.

Subjects People who contribute data in a research project (in non-experimental methods, they are sometimes called respondents).

Survey Research design where a sample of respondents/subjects provides data in a standard form on one or more variables.

SUGGESTED FURTHER READING

Note: full references for all three pieces of suggested reading are given in the reference list below.

1 The book by Sylvia Shimmin and Don Wallis, *Fifty Years of Occupational Psychology in Britain*, provides a well-written description of how work psychology has evolved in the UK and the topics it focuses on. Although the historical details are of course specific to the UK context, much of the content of this book can be generalised to other countries.

2 Although about management rather than work psychology, the book by Mark Easterby-Smith, Richard Thorpe and Andy Lowe, *Management Research: An Introduction*, gives a clear and practical guide to key issues in formulating and doing research.

3 Alan Bryman's book, *Research Methods and Organisation Studies,* is in many respects a rather more advanced and detailed version of Easterby-Smith *et al.*, with slightly greater emphasis on conceptual as well as practical issues.

REFERENCES

Adair, J.G. (1984) 'The Hawthorne effect: a reconsideration of the methodological artifact', *Journal of Applied Psychology*, vol. 69, pp. 334–45.

Anderson, N. and Prutton, K. (1993) 'Occupational psychology in business: strategic resource or purveyor of tests?', *The Occupational Psychologist*, no. 20, 3–10.

Blackler, F. (1982) 'Organizational psychology' in Canter, S. and Canter, D. (eds) *Psychology in Practice*. Chichester: John Wiley.

Blackler, F. and Brown, C. (1986) 'Alternative models to guide the design and introduction of the new information technologies into work organizations', *Journal of Occupational Psychology*, vol. 59, pp. 287–314.

Brenner, M. (1981) 'Skills in the research interview' in Argyle, M. (ed.) *Social Skills and Work*. London: Methuen.

Bryman, A. (1989) *Research Methods and Organization Studies*. London: Unwin Hyman.

British Psychological Society (1986) *Register of Members of the Division of Occupational Psychology*. Leicester: BPS.

British Psychological Society (1991) *Code of Conduct, Ethical Principles and Guidelines*. Leicester: BPS.

Cox, T. (1978) *Stress*. London: Macmillan.

Easterby-Smith, M., Thorpe, R. and Lowe, A. (1991) *Management Research: An introduction*. London: Sage.

Eden, M. and Chisholm, R.F. (1993) 'Emerging varieties of action research', *Human Relations*, vol. 46, pp. 121–42.

Fowler, F.J. (1984) *Survey Research Methods*. London: Sage.

Furnham, A. (1983) 'Social psychology as common sense', *Bulletin of the British Psychological Society*, vol. 36, pp. 105–9.

Glaser, B.G. and Strauss, A.L. (1967) *The Discovery of Grounded Theory*. Chicago, IL: Aldine.

Halvor Teigen, K. (1986) 'Old truths or fresh insights? A study of students' evaluations of proverbs', *British Journal of Social Psychology*, vol. 25, pp. 43–9.

Herriot, P. (1984) *Down from the Ivory Tower: Graduates and their jobs*. Chichester: John Wiley.

Iaffaldano, M.T. and Muchinsky, P.M. (1985) 'Job satisfaction and job performance: a meta-analysis', *Psychological Bulletin*, vol. 97, pp. 251–73.

Johns, G. (1993) 'Constraints on the adoption of psychology-based personnel practices: lessons from organizational innovation', *Personnel Psychology*, vol. 46, pp. 596–602.

Kemp, N.J., Wall, T.D., Clegg, C.W. and Cordery, J.L. (1983) 'Autonomous work groups in a greenfield site: a comparative study', *Journal of Occupational Psychology*, vol. 56, pp. 271–88.

King, N. (1992) 'Modelling the innovation process: an empirical comparison of approaches', *Journal of Occupational and Organizational Psychology*, vol. 65, pp. 89–100.

Lewin, K. (1945) 'The Research Center for Group Dynamics at Massachusetts Institute of Technology', *Sociometry*, vol. 8, pp. 126–36.

Lewin, K. (1946) 'Action research and minority problems', *Journal of Social Issues*, vol. 2, pp. 34–6.

Miner, J.B. (1984) 'The validity and usefulness of theories in an emerging organizational science', *Academy of Management Review*, vol. 9, pp. 296–306.

Offerrmann, L.R. and Gowing, M.K. (1990) 'Organizations of the future', *American Psychologist*, vol. 45, pp. 95–108.

Pfeffer, J. (1991) 'Organization theory and structural perspectives on management', *Journal of Management*, vol. 17, pp. 789–803.

Potter, J. and Wetherell, M. (1987) *Discourse and Social Psychology – Beyond attitudes and behaviour*. London: Sage.

Roethlisberger, F.J. and Dickson, W.J. (1939) *Management and the Worker*. New York: John Wiley.

Schaubroeck, J. and Kuehn, K. (1992) 'Research design in industrial and organizational psychology' in Cooper, C.L. and Robertson, I.T. (eds) *International Review of Industrial and Organizational Psychology*, vol. 7. Chichester: John Wiley.

Schneider, S.C. and Dunbar, R.L.M. (1992) 'A psychoanalytic reading of hostile takeover events', *Academy of Management Review*, vol. 17, pp. 537–67.

Schweiso, J. (1984) 'What is common to common sense?', *Bulletin of the British Psychology Society*, vol. 37, pp. 43–5.

Shimmin, S. and Wallis, D. (1994) *Fifty Years of Occupational Psychology in Britain*. Leicester: British Psychological Society.

Staw, B.M. (1991) 'Dressing up like an organization: when psychological theories can explain organizational action', *Journal of Management*, vol. 17, pp. 805–19.

Symon, G. and Clegg, C.W. (1991) 'Technology-led change: a study of the implementation of CADCAM', *Journal of Occupational Psychology*, vol. 64, pp. 273–90.

Trist, E.L. and Bamforth, K.W. (1951) 'Some social and psychological consequences of the long-wall method of coal getting', *Human Relations*, vol. 4, pp. 3–38.

Vernon, H.M. (1948) 'An autobiography', *Occupational Psychology*, vol. 23, pp. 73–82.

Warr, P. (1987) *Work, Unemployment and Mental Health*. Oxford: Clarendon Press.

Weick, K.E. (1989) 'Theory construction as disciplined imagination', *Academy of Management Review*, vol. 14, pp. 516–31.

APPENDIX: PSYCHOLOGICAL ASSOCIATIONS IN VARIOUS COUNTRIES

Albania	**Association of Albanian Psychologists** Faculty of Social Sciences, Tirana University, Tirana, Albania
Argentina	**Association Argentina de Ciencias del Comportamiento** Tte. Gral. Peron 2158, 1040 Buenos Aires, Argentina
Armenia	**Union of Psychologists of Armenia** Yerevan Abovyan Pedagogical Institute, Yerevan, Republic of Armenia
Australia	**The Australian Psychological Society Ltd** PO Box 126, Carlton South, Victoria 3053, Australia
Austria	**Berufsverband Österreichischer Psychologinnen und Psychologen** Garnisongasse 1, A-1090 Vienna, Austria
Bangladesh	**Bangladesh Psychological Association** c/o Bangladesh National Insurance Company, 21 Rajuk Avenue, Motijheel C/A, Dhaka-1000, Bangladesh
Barbados	**Psychological Association of Barbados** PO Box 931, National House, Roebank Street, Bridgetown, Barbados
Belgium	**Belgian Psychological Society** Laboratoire de Psychologie Experimentale, Université Libre de Bruxelles, 117 Avenue A. Buyl, 1050 Bruxelles, Belgium
Brazil	**Sociedade Brasileira de Psicologia** R. Florencio de Abreu, 681, sala 1105, 14015-060 Ribeirao Preto SP, Brazil

Bulgaria	**Bulgarian Psychological Society** Druzhestvo na Psycholosite v Balgaria, 14 Lulin Planina Street, Bulgaria
Canada	**Canadian Psychological Association** 151 rue Slater St, Suite 205, Ottawa, Ontario, Canada K1P 5H3
Chile	**Colegio Psicologos de Chile A.G.** Av. Gral. Bustamante No. 250 Depto. H. 3oPiso, Providencia, Santiago, Chile
China	**Chinese Psychological Society** c/o Institute of Psychology, Academia Sinica, PO Box 1603, Beijing 100 012, People's Republic of China
Colombia	**Colombian National Committee of Psychology** Apartado 88754, Bogota, Colombia
Croatia	**Croatian Psychological Association** Ivana Lucica 3, HR-41000 Zagreb, Croatia
Cuba	**Psychologists Union of Cuba** School of Psychology, University of Habana, San Rafael y Mazon, Habana, Cuba
Czech Republic	**Czech–Moravian Psychological Society** Kladenska 48, 16000 Praha 6, Czech Republic
Denmark	**Dansk Psykolog Forening** Stockholmsgade 27, DK-2100 Kobenhavn 0, Denmark
Egypt	**Egyptian Association for Psychological Studies** 1 Osiris Street, Tager Building, Egyptian Scientific Union, Garden City, Cairo, Egypt
Estonia	**Union of Estonian Psychologists** PO Box 572, EE-0010, Tallinn, Estonia
Finland	**Finnish Psychological Society** Mariankatu 7 B, SF-00170, Helsinki, Finland
France	**Société Française de Psychologie** 28-32 rue Serpente F-75006, Paris, France
Georgia	**Georgian Psychological Association** D. Uznadze Institute of Psychology, 22 Iashvili St, Tbilisi 380007, Republic of Georgia
Germany	**Federation of German Psychological Associations** Geschäftsstelle des BDP, Heilsbachstr. 22-24, D-53123 Bonn, Germany
Greece	**Hellenic Psychological Society** Department of Psychology, School of Philosophy, University of Athens, Panepistemiopolis, Athens 15784, Greece
Hong Kong	**Hong Kong Psychological Society** Department of Psychology, Chinese University of Hong Kong, Shatin, Hong Kong

Hungary	**Hungarian Psychological Association** Budapest, Tcrezkrt 13, H-1536 Budapest, PO Box 220, Hungary
Iceland	**Icelandic Psychological Society** Lágmúli 7, IS-108 Reykjavik, Iceland
India	**Indian Psychological Association** 27-A, Masjid Moth (Village), New Delhi 110049, India
Indonesia	**Indonesian Psychologists Association** Brawijaya IV/no.20, Kebayoran Baru, Jakarta Selatan, Indonesia
Iran	**Iranian Association of Psychology** Faculty of Education, Teheran University, Martyr Chamran Highway, Al-Ahmad Ave, Opposite Nasr. St, Teheran, Iran
Iraq	**Iraqi Educational and Psychological Association** c/o Al-Mistansiriyah University, PO Box 46017, Codeno 12506, Baghdad, Iraq
Ireland	**Psychological Society of Ireland** 13 Adelaide Road, Dublin 2, Ireland
Israel	**Israel Psychological Association** 74a Frishman Street, Tel-Aviv 64375, Israel
Italy	**Società Italiana di Psicologia** via Reggio Emilia 29, 00198, Rome, Italy
Japan	**Japanese Psychological Association** 2-40-14-902, Hongo, Bunkyo-ku, Tokyo 113, Japan
Jordan	**Jordanian Psychological Association** PO Box 1336, Jubeiha 11941, Amman, Jordan
Korea	**Korean Psychological Association** Department of Psychology, Seoul National University, Shillim-Dong, Kwanak-Gu, Seoul 151-742, Korea
Liechtenstein	**Berufsverein der Psychologen Innen** Liechtenstein, FL 9485 Nendeln, Furetentum, Liechtenstein
Luxembourg	**Association Luxembourgeoise des Psychologues** Service Medico-Psycho-Pedagogique, 3 Place Norbert Metz, L-4239 Esch-sur-Alzette, Luxembourg
Malta	**Malta Union of Professional Psychologists** PO Box 341, Valletta, Malta
Mexico	**Sociedad Mexicana de Psicologia A.C.** Apartado Postal 22-2II, 14001 Tlalpan, Mexico D.F
Morocco	**Association Marocaine des Etudes Psychologiques** B.P. 6414 Rabat-Instituts, Rabat, Morocco
Namibia	**Psychological Association of Namibia** PO Box 9500, Windhoek 9000, Namibia
Nepal	**Nepalese Psychological Association** Post Box 3213 GPO, Kathmandu, Nepal

The Netherlands	**Nederlands Instituut van Psychologen** Postbus 9921, NL-1006 AP Amsterdam, The Netherlands
New Zealand	**New Zealand Psychological Society** PO Box 4092, Wellington, New Zealand
Nicaragua	**Association Nicaraguense de Psicologos** PO Box C-142, Managua, Nicaragua
Nigeria	**Nigerian Psychological Association** Department of General and Applied Psychology, University of Jos, PMB 2084 Jos, Nigeria
Norway	**Norsk Psykologforening** Storgata 10A, 0155 Oslo, Norway
Pakistan	**Pakistan Psychological Association** Department of Psychology, Government College, Lahore, Pakistan
Panama	**Panamanian Association of Psychologists** Apartado 6-1835, El Dorado, Panama
The Philippines	**Psychological Association of the Philippines** Philippines Social Science Centre, Don Mariano Marcos Avenue, Diliman 1101, Quezon City, U.P. Box 205, The Philippines
Poland	**Polish Psychological Association** ul. Stawki 5/7, PL-00-183 Warszwawa, Poland
Portugal	**Associacao dos Psicologos Portugueses, APPORT** Beco do Fanado, No. 3-4o, Apartado 469-3000 Coimbra, Portugal
Puerto Rico	**Association de Psicologos de Puerto Rico** PO Box 363435, San Juan 00936-3435, Puerto Rico
Romania	**Romanian Psychologists Association** Calea 13 Septembrie, no. 13, Sector 5, Bucharest, Romania
Russia	**Russian Psychological Society** Institute of Psychology, Russian Academy of Sciences, Yaroslavskaya St. 13, Moscow 129366, Russia
Serbia	**Psychological Association of Serbia** Djustina 7/111 YU-11000 Beograd, Serbia
Singapore	**Singapore Psychological Society** Institute of Mental Health, 10 Buangkok Green 539747, Singapore
Slovenia	**Slovenian Psychological Association** Prushnikova 74, SI-1210 Ljubljana-Sentvid, Slovenia
South Africa	**Psychological Association of South Africa** PO Box 74119, Lynnwood Ridge, 0040, South Africa
Spain	**Federacion Espanola de Asociaciones de Psicologia** Facultad de Filosofia, Edificio A, Despacho 41, Departamento de Psicologia, Univsidad Complutense, Ciudad Universitaria, Madrid 28040, Spain

Sweden	**Swedish Psychological Association**	
	Box 3287, 10365 Stockholm, Sweden	

Sweden | **Swedish Psychological Association**
Box 3287, 10365 Stockholm, Sweden

Switzerland | **Swiss Psychological Society**
Psychologisches Institut, Universitat Zurich,
Schmelzbergstrasse 44, CH-8044 Zurich, Switzerland

Thailand | **The Thai Psychological Association**
Building 3, 8th Floor, Education, Phyathai Road,
Pratumwan, Bankok 10330, Thailand

Turkey | **Turkish Psychologists Association**
P.K. 117 Kucukesat, 0662, Ankara, Turkey

Uganda | **Uganda National Psychological Association**
PO Box 7062, Kampala, Uganda

Ukraine | **Ukrainian Psychological Society**
Pankovskaya str. 2, 252003 Kiev, Ukraine

United Kingdom | **The British Psychological Society**
St Andrews House, 48 Princess Road East, Leicester LE1 7DR, UK

USA | **American Psychological Association**
750 First St, NE Washington, DC 20002-4242, USA

Uruguay | **Sociedad de Psicologia del Uruguay**
Colonia 1342, Esc. 19 y 20, C.P. 11100 Montevideo, Uruguay

Venezuela | **Venezuelan Federation of Psychologists**
Av La Guaira con, Av Naiguata, Macaracuay, Caracas, Venezuela

Vietnam | **Vietnam Psycholopedagogical Association**
101 Tran Hung Dao Street, Hanoi, Vietnam

Zimbabwe | **Zimbabwe Psychological Association**
PO Box 8346, Causeway, Harare, Zimbabwe

4

Basic statistics and data analysis in work psychology

After studying this chapter, you should be able to:

1 define the null and alternative hypotheses in psychological research;

2 explain the concept of statistical significance;

3 explain the concepts of power and effect size in statistical testing;

4 define in words the circumstances in which the following statistical tests would be used: *t*-test; analysis of variance; chi-square; correlation; and multiple regression;

5 with this chapter available for reference, calculate a *t*-test, chi-square and correlation on simple data sets (see the 'Test your learning' section at the end of this chapter for the data to do this).

INTRODUCTION

In this chapter we examine a topic which is given too little coverage in most texts of this kind, but highly detailed and daunting treatment in specialist books on behavioural science statistics. We attempt to explain key concepts concerning how data can be examined and how conclusions can (or cannot) be drawn from them. We do this in words as well as equations. This should enable the reader unfamiliar with statistics and/or uncertain of his or her ability in that area to grasp the basics without feeling much pain. We also provide some worked examples which put the principles into practice. The concepts and techniques described here are important. They are applicable to data of many kinds. Inevitably, we can cover only the basic ideas and techniques. Many complex issues are involved in the appropriate use and interpretation of statistical tests, and psychologists often ignore them (Judd *et al.*, 1995). The interested reader will find more detailed information in texts such as Rosenthal and Rosnow (1984) and Ferguson and Takane (1989).

KEY PRINCIPLES IN HYPOTHESIS TESTING

Much research in work psychology examines one or both of the following questions:

1 Do two or more groups of people *differ* from each other?
2 Do two or more variables *covary* (that is, go together) within a particular group of people?

Work psychologists ask these questions because the answers to them enhance our understanding of human behaviour in the workplace. For example, the first question is central to the issue described in the previous chapter concerning the effect of machine-paced work on job satisfaction. If a psychologist conducted an experiment something like that described in Chapter 3, he or she would obtain job satisfaction data from each individual within the experimental group (which experienced machine-paced work) and the control group (which experienced self-paced work). Clearly, to establish the effect of machine-pacing on job satisfaction, it is necessary to compare the job satisfaction scores of the two groups. This could be done using a statistical technique called a *t*-test, which is described later in this chapter.

To move on to the second question, a psychologist might conduct a survey (*see* Chapter 3) in order to establish whether or not people's age is associated with the amount of job satisfaction they experience. It would be possible to divide people into age-groups (e.g. 20–29; 30–39 etc.) and compare pairs of groups using a *t*-test. But this would lose information about people's ages – for example, 29-year-olds would be lumped together with 20-year-olds. Also, the age-grouping would be arbitrarily chosen. It would be better to see whether age and job satisfaction go together by means of a *correlation*. This essentially plots each person's age against their job satisfaction on a graph, and assesses the extent to which as age increases, job satisfaction either increases or decreases. Correlation is discussed further below.

Psychologists often test *hypotheses* in their research. An important concept here is the *null hypothesis* (H_0). Essentially, this is the hypothesis that there is 'nothing going on'. Thus, if a psychologist is investigating whether two or more groups differ in their job satisfaction, the null hypothesis would be that they do not. If the psychologist is investigating whether age and job satisfaction are associated, the null hypothesis would be that they are not. That is, knowing someone's age would tell you nothing about their level of job satisfaction, and vice versa.

In each case, we can also make an *alternative* or *experimental hypothesis* (H_1). This can either be directional or non-directional. For example, directional alternative hypotheses would specify whether people doing machine-paced work would experience higher or lower job satisfaction than those doing self-paced work, or whether job satisfaction increases or decreases as age increases. Non-directional hypotheses would be less specific. They would simply state that there was a difference between groups in levels of job satisfaction (but not which group was higher) or that age and job satisfaction do go together (but not whether older people are more satisfied or less satisfied).

Hypotheses refer to the *population(s)* from which the sample(s) of people who participate in research are drawn. They do *not* refer to those samples alone. In essence, then, when doing research, a psychologist is asking: 'given the data I have obtained from my research sample, is the null hypothesis or the alternative hypothesis more likely to be true for the population as a whole?' Note that 'population' does not mean everyone in the whole world, or even in a particular country. It should refer to those people to whom the psychologist wishes to generalise the results. This might be 'production line workers in Denmark' or 'people currently employed in the Netherlands'.

Interestingly, researchers are sometimes not very specific concerning what population they wish to draw conclusions about. Also, they sometimes use *samples of convenience* – that is, people they can get hold of easily. Ideally, those who participate in the research should be a *random sample* of the population of interest (*see also* Chapter 3, 'The survey design'). That is, everyone in the population should stand an equal chance of participating in the research. This is rarely, if ever, achieved. Surveys often involve questionnaires being sent to a *random sample* of people from a given population but of course not everybody replies. One inevitably wonders whether responders differ in important ways from non-responders. Responders may, for example, be more conscientious/conforming, or simply have more time on their hands.

Therefore, rather than attempting to obtain a random sample, it is more common for researchers to try to show that their inevitably non-random sample is reasonably *representative* (for example in age, sex, type of employment, location) of the population as a whole. Put another way, the proportions of people of each age, sex, and so on, among those participating in the research should not differ much from those in the wider population. But it is still possible that participants differ from non-participants in other respects, including those of interest in the research. So, for example, it may be that people high on the conscientiousness dimension of personality are more likely to respond than others. This obviously matters if, for example, the research concerns overall levels of conscientiousness in the population.

Statistical analysis of data in work psychology most often involves assessment of *the probability of accepting the alternative hypothesis when the null hypothesis is in fact true for the population*. The lower this probability, the more confident the psychologist can be that the alternative hypothesis can be accepted, and the null hypothesis can be rejected. This probability is also called *statistical significance* – a crucial concept in psychology. Typically, psychologists are not prepared to accept the alternative hypothesis (thus rejecting the null hypothesis) unless there is only a probability of 0.05 or less that the null hypothesis is true given the data the psychologist has collected. Erroneously rejecting the null hypothesis is sometimes called *type I error*.

> ■ **KEY LEARNING POINT**
> *The concept of statistical significance refers to the probability of the null hypothesis being true, given the data obtained.*

The psychologist is therefore saying 'I must be at least 95 per cent sure that I can reject the null hypothesis before I am prepared actually to do so'. This might be considered pretty conservative – perhaps *too* conservative. After all, how many of us wait until we are 95 per cent certain of something before we act on the basis of it in our day-to-day lives? There is also the other side of the coin, less often considered by psychologists: the probability of accepting the null hypothesis when the alternative hypothesis is in fact true. Erroneously accepting the null hypothesis is sometimes called *type II error*.

If the psychologist finds that, on the basis of his or her data, there is less than a 0.05 (i.e. one in twenty) chance of mistakenly rejecting the null hypothesis, he or she will usually declare that the result is *statistically significant at the 0.05 level*. If the probability is less than 0.01 (i.e. one in a hundred), the result is *statistically significant at the 0.01 level*. A similar rule applies for a probability of 0.001 (one in a thousand). These are of course arbitrary cut-off points. Basically, the lower the probability, the more confident the psychologist is in rejecting the null hypothesis. Notice also that the lower the probability, the more 'highly statistically significant' the result is said to be.

But how do psychologists calculate statistical significance given their research data? They use one or more techniques referred to collectively as *statistical tests* of the data. We now examine these in general terms. There are some worked examples later in the chapter, each of which demonstrates a particular statistical test procedure.

SOME COMMON STATISTICAL TESTS

The *t*-test

Suppose for a moment that a psychologist is interested in seeing whether production managers are more or less numerate than accountants. He or she administers a test of numeracy to (say) 20 of each and obtains a mean score of 25 for the production managers and 30 for the accountants. Clearly, the accountants score higher on average, but what other information is required before deciding whether to accept or reject the null hypothesis that the populations of production managers and accountants do not differ in their numeracy?

First, we need to consider whether the difference between sample means is large relative to the overall range of scores. After all, if scores in the sample ranged from 10 to 50, a difference of 5 between the two means might not mean very much. But, if scores ranged only from (say) 20 to 35 that difference of 5 might seem quite large in comparison.

The most commonly used measure of the spread of scores is the *standard deviation*. The formula for calculating it appears later in this chapter. Here, we can note that the standard deviation is a function of the differences between each individual score and the overall mean score, and of the sample size. Hence if all scores were exactly the mean, the standard deviation would be zero because there would be no differences between individual scores and the mean. Apart from this exceptional case, we can normally expect about 68 per cent of all individual scores to be within one standard deviation either side of the mean. About 96 per cent of scores are within two standard deviations of the mean.

Sample size is also important in evaluating the significance of a difference between two means. Suppose for a moment that the null hypothesis was in fact true. If a psychologist repeatedly took samples of 20 production managers and 20 accountants, he or she would *on average* expect their mean scores to be equal. But of course in small samples, it only takes one or two exceptional scores to make quite a big difference between the two group means. Thus, although on average the mean scores for the samples should be equal, in some samples there would be quite big differences. If the psychologist repeatedly took bigger samples (say 100 production managers and accountants), then the influence of a few extreme scores would be more diluted. If the null hypothesis was in fact true, we would again expect the difference between the two group means to be zero, but this time there would be less variation from that figure between samples.

So, to evaluate the statistical significance of a difference between two mean scores in a research study, we need to consider not only the magnitude of difference between means, but also the *standard deviation* and the *sample size*. For any given difference between means, the smaller the standard deviation, and the larger the sample size, the more likely it is that the psychologist could reject the null hypothesis.

Typically, in order to assess whether two mean scores show a statistically significant difference, psychologists use a *t*-test. This statistical procedure takes into account the factors noted above. A worked example appears later in this chapter. A *t* score of more than about 2 or less than about −2 generally indicates a statistically significant difference between means but the exact value required for significance depends on sample size. Most statistics text books include tables which show the minimum values (sometimes called *critical values*) of *t* required to achieve statistical significance at the 0.05, 0.01 and 0.001 levels for any given sample size.

■ **KEY LEARNING POINT**

The t-*test assesses the significance of a difference between two group mean scores, taking into account the sample sizes and the amount of variation in scores within groups.*

The *t*-test requires that the data are *quantitative*. That is, the data should reflect scores on a dimension along which people vary, not different types, or pigeon-holes, into which they fall. Strictly, the data should also be such that a difference of a given number of units between two scores should reflect the same amount of difference no matter what the absolute level of the scores. So, a score of 100 should be the same amount more than 90 as 20 is more than 10. This may seem straightforward, but with many self-report measures (e.g. job satisfaction) we cannot strictly be sure whether it is the case. Further, scores should approximate to a *normal distribution* (*see* Fig. 4.1). This is a technical term for a bell-shaped distribution of scores, which peaks at the mean, and drops off at equal rates on either side of it, with that rate being linked to the standard deviation. Fortunately, the *t*-test is not usually invalidated if the data do not approximate a normal distribution (Sawilowsky and Blair, 1992). In the jargon, it is a *robust* test. This is just as well, because the research data obtained by psychologists are often very unlike the normal distribution (Micceri, 1989).

A somewhat different version of the *t*-test can be employed if we wish to see whether the means of two sets of scores from the *same* people differ significantly. So, for example, we might be interested in assessing people's performance at a task before and after training. The formula is somewhat different (a worked example appears later in this chapter), but most of the principles for this *t*-test for non-independent samples are the same as those for the independent samples *t*-test described above.

Analysis of variance

What happens when the scores of more than two groups are to be compared? In this situation, another very common statistical test is performed – it is called *analysis of variance*. Essentially, it is an extension of the *t*-test procedure. The resulting statistic is called *F*, and the principles concerning statistical significance are applied to *F* in the same way as to *t* (see above). The same limitations to the use of *t* also apply to *F*. *F* can also be used instead of *t* to compare just two means. Indeed, $F = t^2$ in this instance.

Fig. 4.1 The normal distribution

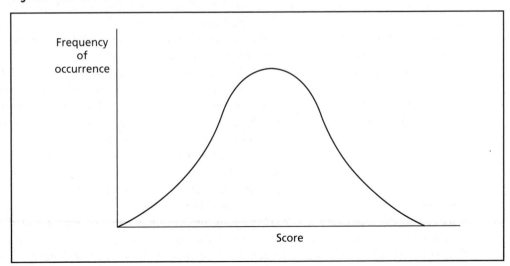

F reflects the ratio of variation in scores between groups to variation in scores within groups. The greater the former relative to the latter, the higher the F value, and the more likely it is that the population means differ (i.e. there is a low probability of obtaining our results if the null hypothesis is in fact true for the population). If a statistically significant F value is obtained, we can reject the null hypothesis that the population means are identical. If we wish, we can then use a modified form of the t-test to identify which particular pair or pairs of groups differ significantly from each other.

> ■ **KEY LEARNING POINT**
> *The statistical technique called analysis of variance extends the principles of the t-test to more than two groups.*

Data from more complex research designs can be analysed using analysis of variance. Suppose, for example, the psychologist was interested in the effects of both machine-paced work *and* style of supervision on job satisfaction. He or she runs an experiment with four groups of people. One group does machine-paced work under close supervision. Another does the same work under distant supervision. The third does self-paced work under close supervision, and the fourth performs self-paced work under distant supervision. Analysis of variance can be used to examine the statistical significance of the separate effects of each factor (pacing of work and style of supervision) on job satisfaction. It can also identify *interaction effects*. For example, the impact of close versus distant supervision might be greater (or even opposite) when work is self-paced than when it is machine-paced.

Chi-square

As indicated earlier, data are sometimes qualitative rather than quantitative. Suppose, for example, that a psychologist wishes to examine whether production managers and marketing managers differ in their views of 'human nature' at work. The psychologist devises a way of assessing whether each of 50 production managers and 50 marketing managers believes in 'theory X' (people have to be controlled and forced to work), 'theory Y' (people are essentially responsible and trustworthy) or 'social' (people are most concerned with social relationships at work) (*see* Chapter 11). Each manager is classed as believing in one of these three views of human nature.

The psychologist cannot use t or F because the data are *categorical*, not quantitative. Believing in one view of human nature is not 'more' or 'less' than believing in another – it is simply different. Hence although the psychologist might arbitrarily give managers a score of 1 if they believe in theory X, 2 for theory Y and 3 for social, the numbers are not a scale. Believing in theory Y is not 'more' or 'less' than believing in theory X. The psychologist is therefore interested in determining whether there is a statistically significant difference in the frequency with which members of the two groups of managers endorse each view of human nature. The statistical test employed in this instance is known as chi-square. The more the groups differ, the higher the chi-square figure for the data, and the less likely it is that the null hypothesis is true. As with t and F, critical values of chi-square at various levels of statistical significance can be checked in tables in most statistics texts. Unlike t and F, these critical values do not depend directly on sample size. Instead, they depend on the number of rows and columns in the data when tabulated. In the above example, the table would contain six cells altogether: 2 (types of manager) × 3 (views of human nature). The figure in each cell would be the number of managers falling into that category. The chi-square procedure compares the observed numbers with those that would be expected if the proportion subscribing to each view of human nature was the same for each type of manager. A worked example of chi-square appears later in this chapter.

> ■ KEY LEARNING POINT
> *The statistical technique called chi-square is used to test differences between groups in the frequency with which group members fall into defined categories.*

Correlation

The second question posed at the start of this chapter concerned whether two or more variables tend to go together. Correlation is most commonly used in survey research (*see* Chapter 3, 'Methods and designs'). Thus, for example, a psychologist might wish to find out whether job satisfaction and intention to leave one's job are connected. Alternatively, he or she might be interested in seeing whether self-esteem and salary are connected. In these cases, the variables are on continuous scales, as for *t*-tests, but unlike *t*-tests the psychologist is not looking to compare mean scores. Instead, he or she wishes to find out whether the two variables correlate (co-relate).

There are several different but similar statistical tests of correlation, each of which produces a *correlation coefficient*. The most common of these is Pearson's product–moment correlation coefficient, or *r* for short. Correlation coefficients cannot exceed a value of one, and cannot be lower than minus one. A Pearson's *r* of one would mean that when scores on the two variables of interest were plotted on a graph, a straight line could be drawn which would go through all of the plotted points (*see* Fig. 4.2a). This line would rise from left to right, indicating that as variable *A* increased, so did variable *B*. This line would not need to be at any particular angle, nor would it necessarily go through the origin. An *r* of minus one would also mean that a straight line could be drawn through all of the plotted points, but this time it would slope the other way, so that as *A* increased, *B* decreased (*see* Fig. 4.2b). An *r* of zero would mean not only that it was impossible to draw a straight line through all of the data points, but also that there was no tendency whatever for scores on either of the two variables to rise or fall with scores on the other one (*see* Fig. 4.2c).

The reader may already have grasped that an *r* of zero is a statistical representation of the null hypothesis, that there is no linear relationship between the variables. The psychologist therefore typically asks 'Does the correlation coefficient I have obtained with my sample differ sufficiently from zero for me to reject the null hypothesis?' Just as with other statistics, for any given sample size we can look up the critical value of *r* required to achieve particular levels of statistical significance. Thus, for example, with a sample size of 20, the critical value of *r* for significance at the 0.05 level is ± 0.444. Corresponding values at the 0.01 and 0.001 levels are 0.590 and 0.708.

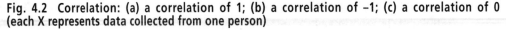

Fig. 4.2 Correlation: (a) a correlation of 1; (b) a correlation of −1; (c) a correlation of 0 (each X represents data collected from one person)

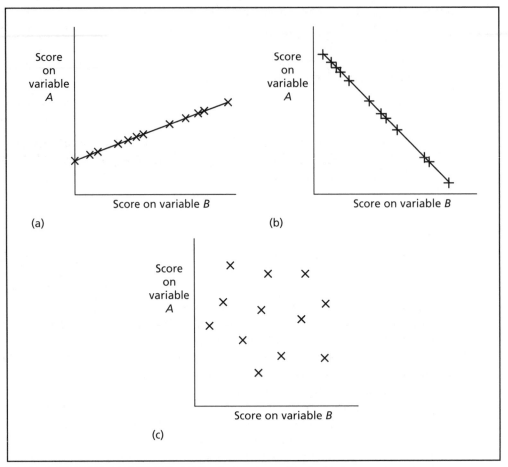

A worked example of Pearson's *r* appears later in this chapter. At this point, however, it is worth saying a little about how it can be calculated. One method (*see* later in this chapter for another) is as follows. First, each score on each variable is converted to a *z-score*. That is, it is transformed to reflect the number of standard deviations it is above or below the sample mean: *z*-scores greater than zero (i.e. positive) are above the mean and those less than zero (i.e. negative) are below it. Then for each person in the sample, the *z*-score on variable *A* is multiplied by that on variable *B*. These *cross-products* for each person are added together and divided by the total sample size. With a little imagination, the reader can perhaps see how an *r* of zero is obtained when variables *A* and *B* are unrelated. In this situation, the following four occurrences are about equally frequent (*see* Fig. 4.3a):

1 positive *z*-scores on both variables

2 positive *z*-score on variable *A*, and a negative one on *B*

3 negative *z*-score on variable *A*, and a positive one on *B*

4 negative *z*-scores on both variables.

Fig. 4.3 Cross-products in correlation: (a) a correlation of 0; (b) a positive correlation (each X represents data collected from one person)

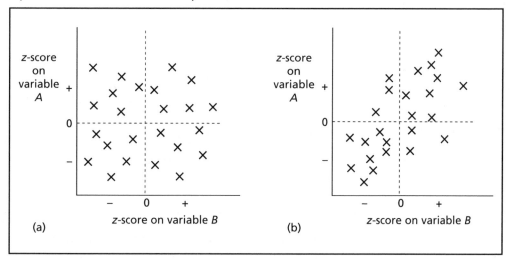

(a)   z-score on variable B

(b)   z-score on variable B

In the first and last cases above, the cross-product will be a positive number (i.e. greater than zero), while in the second and third it will be negative. When the cross-products for each person are added, the positive and negative ones will cancel each other out, thus giving an *r* of zero. But when there is a positive correlation between the variables (*see* Fig. 4.3b) most of the cross-products are positive (remember, a negative number multiplied by another negative number produces a positive number).

> ■ **KEY LEARNING POINT**
>
> *The statistical technique called correlation tests the extent to which scores on two variables tend to go together (i.e. covary).*

A special case of *r* occurs when one of the variables has only two values. This is analogous to a non-independent samples *t*-test, since in effect the two levels of one variable are being examined to see if they are associated with significantly different mean scores on the other variable. The values of *r* and *t* are not identical, but their associated levels of statistical significance are.

Another form of correlation is the *Spearman rank correlation (rho)*. This is used when the data do not reflect absolute scores, but only a rank order. This would mean that we know, for example, that score *x* is greater than score *y*, but not by how much. The formula for calculating *rho* looks different from that for *r*, but in fact boils down to the same thing. *Rho* can also be useful when the data are highly *skewed* (*see* Fig. 4.4) and when there are a few scores hugely different from the others. In both cases, *r* can be distorted, but because the highest score gets a rank of one whether it is two units or a hundred greater than the next highest score, *rho* get rid of such difficulties.

Whatever the exact correlation technique, it is important to remember the old maxim *correlation does not imply causality*. Often, a psychologist would like to infer that the

Fig. 4.4 Skewed distributions: (a) a positively skewed distribution; (b) a negatively skewed distribution

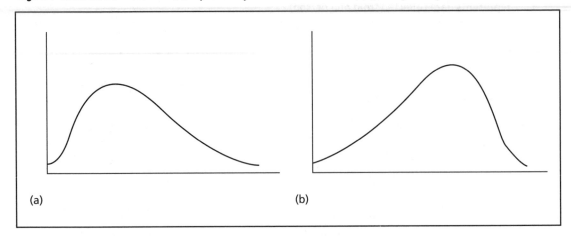

(a)   (b)

reason why two variables are correlated is that one causes the other. This may seem plausible, but it is hard to be sure. Suppose that a psychologist finds a highly significant positive correlation between self-esteem and salary. If both are measured at the same time, there is no basis on which to decide whether self-esteem causes salary or salary causes self-esteem. It is fairly easy to think of possible explanations for either causal direction. It is also possible that some other variable(s) (e.g. social status, educational attainment) cause both self-esteem and salary, but unless we have measured them, we can only speculate.

Obtaining data over time (a *longitudinal study*) can help, in so far as it may help uncover whether scores on one variable at time 1 predict scores on the other at time 2. But even then, the fact that phenomenon A happens before B does not necessarily mean that A *causes* B (*see* Chapter 3). We could also enter an interesting philosophical debate about the notion of causality – but now is not the time!

Multiple regression

Just as analysis of variance is an extension of the *t*-test for more than two groups, so multiple regression is an extension of correlation for more than two variables. Suppose a psychologist wishes to assess the correlation with self-esteem of each of salary, educational attainment and social status. He or she might well find that the latter three variables are all correlated with each other, and also with self-esteem. In this case, the psychologist might wonder which one(s) really matter in predicting self-esteem.

Multiple regression is a statistical technique that allows the social scientist to assess the *relative* importance of each of salary, educational attainment and social status as predictors of self-esteem. It involves estimation of the correlation of each of the three with self-esteem *independent of the other two* (the technique can of course be extended to larger numbers of variables). In this way the researcher can end up with an equation that specifies the weighting to be given to each predictor variable in predicting self-esteem, as well as an overall indication of just how predictable self-esteem is using all of the predictor variables. But note: just because variables are designated 'predictors' in multiple regression analyses, it does not mean that they are necessarily 'causes' of the variable to be predicted.

Multiple regression is a much-used technique in work psychology. It is quite complex. Its intricacies are beyond the scope of this book, but the interested reader can find out more by consulting Berry and Feldman (1985) or Cohen and Cohen (1983).

OTHER PHENOMENA IN STATISTICAL TESTING

Effect size

The reader may have wondered whether statistical significance is necessarily the same as significance for practical purposes. At least one behavioural science statistics text (Rosenthal and Rosnow, 1984) repeatedly reminds its readers that statistical significance depends on the size of the effect (e.g. the difference in means between two groups relative to the standard deviation; or the value of r for two variables) *multiplied by* the size of the study. Thus, when research uses large samples, quite small effect sizes can lead us to reject the null hypothesis – probably correctly, of course, *but* if the effect is so small, albeit detectable, are we going to worry about it? For example, a psychologist might find that, in a large sample, marketing managers score on average two points higher on a numeracy test than production managers, and that this difference is highly statistically significant. So what? Should anybody be concerned? One way of addressing this issue is to assess the relationship between numeracy and work performance, focusing particularly on the extra work performance one could expect given a specified increase in numeracy, and then translating this into practical benefits (*see* Chapter 8 concerning utility analysis).

However, it is also useful to consider effect size in more abstract terms. We can think of it as *the degree to which the null hypothesis is false*. For t, we can consider the difference between group means as a proportion of the standard deviation of scores (d) to be a measure of effect size. For r, we can use the proportion of variance in scores common to both variables. This is r^2. Thus, a correlation of 0.60 indicates that $0.60 \times 0.60 = 0.36$, or 36 per cent of the variance in one variable is 'accounted for' by scores in the other. With large samples, it is often possible for a correlation of only 0.2 or less to be statistically significant. In this case, the variables share just 4 per cent of variance. This sounds small, but Rosenthal and Rosnow (1984, pp. 207–11) have demonstrated that it can nevertheless reflect practical outcomes of real importance.

> ■ **KEY LEARNING POINT**
> *Effect size goes beyond statistical significance by assessing the magnitude of the relationship obtained, rather than how confident one can be that the relationship is not zero.*

For F, one often-used indicator of effect size is called *eta*. It reflects the proportion of total score variation that is accounted for by group membership. Like r^2, eta^2 can be considered an indicator of the proportion of total variance accounted for.

There is nothing mysterious about indices of effect size. They are often quite simply derived, and are sometimes even routinely calculated on the way to a test of statistical significance. Examples are given later in this chapter.

Statistical power

Statistical power refers to the probability of rejecting the null hypothesis when it is indeed false and therefore should be rejected. It is, in other words, the probability of avoiding making a type II error (*see* above, 'Key principles in probability testing'). Like all probability estimates, it can vary from zero to one.

The level of power operating in any particular research study depends on the level of statistical significance the psychologist wishes to work at, the size of the sample, and the size of the effect under examination. The chief practical lesson to be learned is that small sample sizes have very low power – that is, a high probability of missing a relationship that does exist in the population from which the sample is drawn.

Cohen (1977) has produced tables which specify the sample sizes required to achieve certain levels of power for particular statistical tests at specified significance levels and effect sizes. One example will illustrate the point about sample size. Suppose that there *is* a difference in numeracy between production managers and marketing managers, such that the difference in means is half a standard deviation (i.e. $d = 0.5$). If a psychologist had a sample of 20 of each type of manager, the chance of detecting the difference in means at the 0.05 significance level would be only 0.3, or 30 per cent. So there would be a 70 per cent chance of obtaining a non-significant result, even though there is a difference between population means. It would require 85 in each group to achieve a power level of 0.90, which would mean that there was only a 10 per cent chance of failing to find a difference significant at the 0.05 level when the difference between population means was half a standard deviation. To some extent, then, the outcome of a test of statistical significance reflects the statistical power of the research study rather than the validity of the research hypothesis (Tukey, 1991).

These observations about statistical power are very important. Often in research, one investigator reports a statistically significant finding with a moderate to large sample size. Then another researcher attempts to replicate the result with a smaller sample, fails to find a statistically significant effect, and declares that the original finding must have been a fluke. But close examination shows that the *effect size* in the second study is as large as the first – only the smaller sample prevents statistical significance being achieved.

> ■ **KEY LEARNING POINT**
> *There is a high probability that small-scale studies will fail to find effects which exist in the population of interest.*

Garbage in, garbage out

One final point should be noted before we turn to some worked examples. No statistical wizardry can rescue poor sampling, or poor measures. If the psychologist's measure of numeracy is a poor one (for example, it only assesses one aspect of numeracy, or people's scores are unreliable – *see* Chapter 7), then it is unlikely that he or she will draw any useful conclusions.

STATISTICAL EXAMPLES

This section provides examples of the main statistical techniques discussed earlier. In keeping with our objective of imparting statistical knowledge in the most straightforward way possible, we have provided only the necessary minimum when it comes to formulae and the examples are as direct and uncluttered as possible. The whole section is preceded by the introduction of statistical terms and formulae that are of use in most of the examples. Terms and formulae peculiar to each example are introduced in the preamble to the relevant example. Readers are advised to familiarise themselves with the general terms and formulae before tackling the examples. In the interests of clarity, we have used a simplified version of statistical notation (e.g. subscripts have been omitted where possible). We hope that this will benefit the reader and not offend the statistical purist.

Relevant statistical terms and formulae of general use

$\sum$ = the sum of

Example: for four scores $x_1 = 2, x_2 = 3, x_3 = 2, x_4 = 5,$

$\sum x = 2 + 3 + 2 + 5 = 12$

Mean = sum of scores divided by the number of scores = $\bar{x}$

Example: for five scores $(x_1 \ldots x_5) = $ 4, 3, 6, 3, 4

$$\bar{x} = \frac{x_1 + x_2 + x_3 + x_4 + x_5}{5}$$

$$= \frac{4 + 3 + 6 + 3 + 4}{5} + \frac{20}{5} = 4$$

$$\bar{x} = \frac{\sum x}{n}$$

Deviation = distance from the mean = $x_i - \bar{x}$

(where x_i = any of i different scores)

Example: for five scores

x_i (Score)	$-$	$\bar{x}$ (Mean)	$=$	$x_i - \bar{x}$ (Deviation)
x_1 (= 4)	$-$	$\bar{x}(=4)$	=	0
x_2 (= 3)	$-$	$\bar{x}(=4)$	=	-1
x_3 (= 6)	$-$	$\bar{x}(=4)$	=	2
x_4 (= 3)	$-$	$\bar{x}(=4)$	=	-1
x_5 (= 4)	$-$	$\bar{x}(=4)$	=	0

Sum of squares = sum of squared deviation scores = SS

Example: for five scores

$$SS = (x_1 - \bar{x})^2 + (x_2 - \bar{x})^2 + (x_3 - \bar{x})^2 + (x_4 - \bar{x})^2 + (x_5 - \bar{x})^2$$

$$= 0^2 + (-1)^2 + 2^2 + (-1)^2 + 0^2$$

$$= 0 + 1 + 4 + 1 + 0 = 6$$

Computational formula for *SS*

$$\sum x^2 - \frac{(\sum x)^2}{n}$$

i.e. 1 square each score and add them;

2 add up all of the scores, square the total and divide by the number of scores;

3 Subtract the value obtained in step 2 from that obtained in step 1.

Variance = average squared deviation = sum of squared deviations divided by number of scores

$$= \frac{SS}{n} = \delta^2$$

Sample variance = sum of squared deviations divided by one less than the number of scores in sample

$$= \frac{SS}{n-1} = S^2$$

Note that because we are using a specific sample to estimate – rather than the whole available population – the variance $n - 1$, rather than n, should be used.

Sample standard deviation = square root of average squared deviation

$$= \text{square root of variance} \sqrt{S^2} = S$$

Level of statistical significance = probability of committing a type I error = α

Degrees of freedom = the number of scores that are free to vary = d.f.

Example: in a sample of five scores with a mean of 4; once four scores (4, 3, 6, 4) are known, the fifth score *must* be 3; hence d.f. = 5 – 1 = 4

Standard score = scores expressed in 'deviation from the mean' units

$$= \frac{x_i - \bar{x}}{S} = Z$$

Example:

	Score	Mean	S	z
x_1	4	4	1.23	0.0
x_2	3	4	1.23	−0.81
x_3	6	4	1.23	1.63
x_4	4	4	1.23	0.0
x_5	3	4	1.23	−0.81

Statistical test: Student's *t*-test

'Student' was a pseudonym of the statistician who invented the test. In this example the investigator is interested in assessing whether there is a statistically significant difference in mean scores on a particular variable (V_1) for two specific groups of people (A and B). This may be, for example, because the groups have been exposed to different treatments (e.g. different training procedures) or because the groups differ in some way (e.g. male versus female; employed versus unemployed; over 35 years versus under 35 years old) which is expected to be associated with differences on the dependent variable. The formula used in the example below is appropriate if the variances in the two groups are similar (homogeneous). (Note that a pooled variance estimate is calculated and used.) If the variances in the groups are not homogeneous a different formula is needed. Another different formula is needed if the two groups involved are not independent samples, for example, if the study had involved the same group on two occasions.

Relevant formulae

(i) $\quad t = \dfrac{\bar{x}_A - \bar{x}_B}{S_{\bar{x}_A} - S_{\bar{x}_B}}$

S^2 = pooled variance for both groups

$$S^2 = \frac{(n_A - 1)S_A^2 + (n_B - 1)S_B^2}{(n_A - 1) + (n_B - 1)}$$

$$S_{\bar{x}_A} - S_{\bar{x}_B} = \sqrt{\frac{S^2}{n_A} + \frac{S^2}{n_B}}$$

Substituting $\sqrt{\dfrac{S^2}{n_A} + \dfrac{S^2}{n_B}}$ for $S_{\bar{x}_A} - S_{\bar{x}_B}$ in formula (i)

(ii) $\quad t = \qquad \dfrac{\bar{x}_A - \bar{x}_B}{S} \times 2 \quad \dfrac{1}{\sqrt{1/n_A + 1/n_B}}$

$\qquad$ Significance test $\quad$ Effect size $\qquad$ Size of study

Data

Group A	Group B
12.5	19
14.5	21
8	14.5
10	17
13	20
$\bar{x}_A = 11.6$	$\bar{x}_B = 18.3$
$S_A^2 = 6.68$	$S_B^2 = 6.70$

$$S^2 = \frac{4 \times 6.68 + 4 \times 6.70}{8}$$

$$= \frac{26.72 + 26.80}{8} = 6.69$$

Using formula (ii) for t:

$$t = \frac{\bar{x}_A - \bar{x}_B}{S} \times \frac{1}{\sqrt{1/n_A + 1/n_B}}$$

$$t = \frac{11.6 - 18.3}{\sqrt{6.69}} \times \frac{1}{\sqrt{0.2 + 0.2}}$$

$$= \frac{-6.7}{2.59} \times \frac{1}{0.63}$$

$$= -2.59 \times 1.58$$

$$= \underline{-4.10}$$

Interpretation

At the 95 per cent level (i.e. $\alpha = 0.05$; minimising the possibility of type I error to 5 per cent) the critical value of t [for $(n_A - 1) + (n_B - 1) = 8$ degrees of freedom] = 2.31. The observed value of 4.10 exceeds this value, therefore there is a statistically significant difference between the means of the two groups and the null hypothesis of no difference between the groups is rejected. Note that the sign (+ or −) of t is merely a function of which mean is used as the first term in the calculation of t. It has no effect on the interpretation of significance, when a two-tailed test is being used. The test is said to be two-tailed when the investigator is interested in whether one (either) group is different from another. If he or she is investigating a more specific hypothesis: that one (specific) group has the larger mean, then a one-tailed test is needed. Put simply, a two-tailed test allows either of the two means to be larger; in a *one*-tailed test *one* (specific) mean must be larger if statistical significance is to be attained. The value of t needed to show statistical significance in a one-tailed test is smaller than that needed for a two-tailed test.

Statistical test: analysis of variance

This example is similar to the previous one in that the investigator is interested in differences between groups. In this case, however, a third group (C) has been utilised in addition to groups A and B. Of course it would be possible to do several different *t*-tests to check for statistically significant differences (i.e. A versus B, A versus C, B versus C). With only three groups this would probably be acceptable. The problem with multiple *t*-tests, or the multiple use of any test on the same samples, is that as more tests are done, the overall probability of committing a type I error is increased.

$1 - \alpha$ = the probability of committing no error; i.e. for each test at the 95 per cent (a = 0.05) level = $1 - 0.05 = 0.95$

The probability of no error on a second test = $(1 - \alpha)(1 - \alpha) = 0.95 \times 0.95 = 0.90$

The general formula is $(1 - \alpha)^T$, where T equals the number of tests done: hence, with $\alpha = 0.05$, when there are three groups and three *t*-tests the experiment-wise probability of no error is reduced to $0.95^3 = 0.86$ (i.e. an 86 per cent chance of avoiding an error). With five separate tests the chance of avoiding error falls to 77 per cent. The procedures involved in the analysis of variance ensure that the selected alpha level applies to the total risk of type I error for the study. In effect the analysis procedures perform all of the relevant comparisons simultaneously.

The analysis of variance procedure literally divides up the variance in a set of data into different components. Initially the total variance is divided up into variance within the groups and variance between the groups. By comparing these variances it is possible to assess differences between the groups. If all groups were similar the mean value for each group would be similar and so would the variance about this mean. The variation between groups would be much the same as the variation within groups, and in this case the F ratio, obtained by dividing between-group variance by within-group variance would be close to one. If the F ratio is large, implying more variation between groups than within them, this would indicate that the groups' scores differ from each other.

Relevant formulae

$$SS_{total} = \sum x^2 - \frac{(\sum x)^2}{nk}$$

where k = number of groups

        N = total sample = nk

$SS_{within} = \sum SS$ within each group

$SS_{between}$ = the number of observations in each group multiplied by the SS of the group means

Note that $SS_{total} = SS_{between} + SS_{within}$

Variance (usually called mean square in analysis of variance) = $\dfrac{SS}{\text{degrees of freedom}} = MS$

$$F = \frac{MS_{between}}{MS_{within}}$$

Data

Group A	Group B	Group C
12	14	16
14	11	15
11	12	14
13	14	17
10	11	14
$\bar{x}_A = 12$	$\bar{x}_B = 12.4$	$\bar{x}_C = 15.2$
$\sum x_A = 60$	$\sum x_B = 62$	$\sum x_C = 76$
$\sum x_A^2 = 730$	$\sum x_B^2 = 778$	$\sum x_C^2 = 1162$

$N = 15$ $\sum x = 198$ $\sum x^2 = 2670$ $(\sum x)^2 = 39\,204$ $k = $ number of groups $= 3$

$$SS_{total} = \sum x^2 - \frac{(\sum x)^2}{N}$$

$$= 2670 - \frac{39204}{15} = 56.4$$

$$SS_{within} = SS_A + SS_B + SS_C$$

$$= 10 + 9.2 + 6.8$$

$$= 26$$

$$SS_{between} = 5[(12 - 13.2)^2 + (12.4 - 13.2)^2 + (15.2 - 13.2)^2]$$

Analysis of variance (ANOVA) table

Source of variance	d.f.	SS	MS	F
Between groups	$(k - 1) = 3 - 1 = 2$	30.4	$\dfrac{SS}{d.f.} = 15.2$	$F = 7.00$
Within groups	$(N - k) = 15 - 3 = 12$	26	$\dfrac{SS}{d.f.} = 2.17$	
Total	$(N - 1) = 15 - 1 = 14$	56.4		

Interpretation

At $\alpha = 0.05$ the critical value for F with d.f. (2, 12) is 3.59.

The observed value of 7.00 exceeds this and we conclude that there are statistically significant differences between groups and the null hypothesis of no differences between the groups is rejected.

Statistical test: chi-square (χ^2)

As noted in the earlier part of this chapter, researchers may sometimes have access to important data that are in categorical form, rather than continuous scores. For example a researcher might be interested in organisational roles (e.g. x, y) and preferred management style (style A, B or C). In such a situation a t-test or analysis of variance cannot be used since the variables in the study are not measured on a continuous scale and the calculation of various statistics needed to compute t or F (e.g. means) for the groups would be meaningless.

Chi-square provides a useful procedure for examining statistical significance in categorical data. The basis of the chi-square test involves casting the data into a contingency table. In the case of this example this will be a two (x, y) by three (A, B, C) table. If there was an even distribution of styles across the organisational roles then the number of cases in each cell of the table would reflect this. In other words the null hypothesis of no relationship between organisational role and management style would lead us to *expect* a certain number of cases in each cell.

Relevant formulae

Expected frequency in a cell, $E = \dfrac{TR \times TC}{N}$

where: TR = total number of cases in the row in which the cell belongs
TC = total number of cases in the column in which the cell belongs
N = total number of cases

Chi-square = $\chi^2 = \Sigma \dfrac{(0 - E)^2}{E}$

where: O = observed number of cases in each cell
E = expected number in each cell

Data

Person	Organisational role	Preferred management style	Person	Organisational role	Preferred management style
1	x	A	17	y	C
2	x	B	18	y	C
3	x	A	19	y	C
4	x	B	20	y	B
5	x	C	21	y	C
6	x	A	22	y	C
7	x	B	23	y	A
8	x	A	24	y	C
9	x	B	25	y	B
10	x	A	26	y	C
11	x	B	27	y	C
12	x	A	28	y	B
13	x	A	29	y	C
14	x	B	30	y	A
15	x	A	31	y	C
16	y	B	32	y	C

Organisational role	Preferred management style			Row totals
	A	B	C	
x	8	6	1	15
y	2	4	11	17
Column totals	10	10	12	32

Calculation of χ^2

Example of calculation of expected frequencies (for top left-hand cell)

$$E = \frac{15 \times 10}{32} = 4.6875$$

$$\chi^2 = \frac{(8 - 4.6875)^2}{4.6875} + \frac{(6 - 4.6875)^2}{4.6875} + \frac{(11 - 5.625)^2}{5.625}$$

$$+ \frac{(2 - 5.3125)^2}{5.3125} + \frac{(4 - 5.3125)^2}{5.3125} + \frac{(11 = 6.375)^2}{6.375}$$

$$\chi^2 = 2.3408 + 0.3675 + 3.8028 + 2.0654 + 0.3243 + 3.3553$$
$$= 12.26$$

d.f. $= (3 - 1)(2 - 1) = 2$

Interpretation

Critical value of χ^2 for $\alpha = 0.05$ is 5.99. Therefore, since the observed χ^2 is larger than this value, we conclude that the null hypothesis of no relationship is rejected.

Statistical test: Pearson product–moment correlation coefficient

The Pearson product–moment correlation coefficient is one of the most widely used procedures in work psychology. In many studies investigators wish to know whether two variables are associated with each other. Variables are said to be associated if they vary together (i.e. large or small values on one variable are consistently associated with large or small values on the other).

The Pearson product–moment correlation coefficient provides a single statistic (usually referred to as r) which indicates the precise magnitude of the linear association between two variables. The values of r vary from +1 through 0 to –1 (*see* earlier in this chapter). The square of the correlation coefficient r^2 represents the proportion of variability in one variable that is associated with the other.

If two sets of scores are positively correlated (i.e. values on one variable increase as values on the other increase) the standard (z-) scores (*see* earlier in this chapter) will also vary together. This is obvious if you recognise that *for a correlation to be large and positive*, an extreme high score on one variable (and hence a high z-score) must be coupled with a similarly high score on the other variable.

The formula

$$r = \frac{\Sigma z_x z_y}{n}$$

makes sense when considered in this light. For example, if high scores on one variable (i.e. positive z values) are consistently linked with low scores (i.e. negative z values) on the other the product of the two scores $z_x z_y$ will be negative (since a negative multiplied by a positive is a negative) and the value for r will be between zero and minus one. If there is no consistent link between the variables the size and direction of the product term $z_x z_y$ will vary, and when the values for each pair of scores are added together (summed) they will cancel each other out, giving an r of zero. Notice that in the formula the sum of the product terms $z_x z_y$ is divided by N, which will be the same as the number of product terms added together (*see* Fig. 4.5). In other words r is the mean of the sum of the products of the z-scores. Remembering that z-scores represent distances from the mean (sometimes referred to as *moments*) makes the use of the term 'product–moment correlation' obvious.

The formula for the correlation coefficient provides a basis for estimating values on one variable from values on the other. For example, if the correlation between two variables is known (i.e. the value of r is known) then if we know someone's z-score on one variable (x) the best estimate of their score on the other (y) is given by:

$$z_y = r z_x$$

Fig. 4.5 Correlation and standard scores

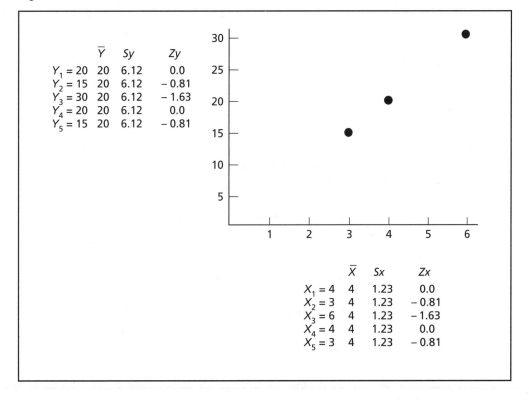

Of course unless the correlation is perfect (i.e. $r = 1$) our estimate will not be entirely accurate.

It is possible to translate the estimated z-score, in this case z_y, to an estimated raw score $\hat{y}$. As noted above, however, this score will not necessarily correspond to the observed score y_i (unless $r = 1$). Notice that if $r = 0$ the best estimate of z_y will be $z_y = 0$). In other words when there is no correlation and hence no basis for predicting any specific value of y, the best guess is the mean score. Indeed (until $r = 1$), the estimated scores tend to be closer to the mean than the real scores. The deviation scores for these estimated values and the sum of squares for the deviation scores (*see above*, 'Statistical test: Student's t-test') are:

Deviation scores for estimates = $\hat{y}_i - \bar{y}$
Sum of squares for estimates = $\Sigma(\hat{y}_i - \bar{y})^2$

Similarly the deviation scores and sum of squares for the actual values (which will always be larger than those for the estimated values) can be calculated:

Deviation scores for actuals = $y_i - \bar{y}$
Sum of squares for actuals = $\Sigma(y_i - \bar{y})^2$

$\Sigma(\hat{y}_i - \bar{y})^2$ represents the part of the total variation in Y that is associated with X. This is made clear by considering what would happen to this value if none of the variation in Y was associated with X. In this case r would be zero, all estimates of $\hat{y}$ would be $\bar{y}$ (i.e. the mean) and the value in question, $\Sigma(_i - \bar{y})^2$ would also be zero. As the degree of association between X and Y increases, r will increase and the value of $\Sigma(_i - \bar{y})^2$ will increase relative to the actual sum of squares, $\Sigma(y_i - \bar{y})^2$.

The ratio of these terms:

$$\frac{\Sigma(\hat{y}_i - \bar{y})^2}{\Sigma(y_i - \bar{y})^2}$$

represents the proportion of variability in Y that is associated with X

As noted earlier in this chapter (*see above*, 'Correlation'), the square of the correlation coefficient (r^2) can also be interpreted to represent the proportion of variability in Y that is associated with X. Indeed:

$$r^2 = \frac{\Sigma(\hat{y}_i - \bar{y})^2}{\Sigma(y_i - \bar{y})^2} = \text{proportion of variability in Y associated with X}$$

Computation of r

As is often the case, the definition formulae for a statistic – in this case r – are not convenient for computation. The following formula, which produces identical results to those given earlier, is much more convenient for calculation:

$$r_{xy} = \frac{n\Sigma x_i y_i - (\Sigma x_i)(\Sigma y_i)}{\sqrt{[n\Sigma x_i^2 - (\Sigma x_i)^2][n\Sigma y_i^2 - (\Sigma y_i)^2]}}$$

where each value for xy is obtained by multiplying the value obtained for x by the value obtained for y on the same person.

Data

Person	x	y	xy
1	5	3.0	15
2	9	2.1	18.9
3	15	1.7	25.5
4	13	1.5	19.5
5	7	2.9	20.3
6	10	3.4	34.0
7	11	4.2	46.2
8	4	1.0	4.0
9	16	3.2	51.2
10	8	1.5	12.0
	$\sum x = 98$	$\sum y = 24.5$	$\sum xy = 246.6$
	$(\sum x)^2 = 9604$	$(\sum y)^2 = 600.25$	
	$\sum x^2 = 1106$	$\sum y^2 = 69.65$	

$(n = 10)$

$$r_{xy} = \frac{n\sum x_i y_i - (\sum x_i)(\sum y_i)}{\sqrt{[n\sum x_i^2 - (\sum x_i)^2][n\sum y_i^2 - (\sum y_i)^2]}}$$

$$r_{xy} = \frac{2466 - (98)(24.5)}{\sqrt{[11060 - 9604][696.5 - 600.25]}}$$

$$r_{xy} = \frac{2466 - 2401}{\sqrt{[1456][96.25]}}$$

$$r_{xy} = 0.17$$

For $\alpha = 0.05$ with $(n - 2)$ 8 degrees of freedom the critical value for $r = 0.63$. Therefore (since the observed value for r is less than this), we accept the null hypothesis that there is no correlation between variables X and Y.

TEST YOUR LEARNING

Note: worked answers to questions 3, 4 and 5 appear in the *Instructor's Manual*.

1 Briefly describe a psychological study of your own invention and specify a null hypothesis and an alternative hypothesis suitable for that study.

2 Explain in words the concepts of statistical significance, statistical power and effect size.

3 Use the appropriate statistical test to calculate the association between cash value of sales over the last month and years of sales experience in the following data obtained from fifteen sales staff from a single company.

Sales person number	1	2	3	4	5	6	7	8	9	10	11	12	13	14	15
Cash value of sales (£K)	8	6	5	9	11	7	13	8	9	4	5	5	9	10	14
Years of sales experience	6	5	5	8	10	12	12	9	6	3	7	8	10	10	13

4 A research study was conducted in a company to examine whether women and men were equally likely to leave the company. Examination of company personnel records revealed that during the last year 30 women left the company while 270 did not. The figures for men were 30 and 350. Use the appropriate statistical test to answer the research question.

5 On one university course, there are some students from the same country as the university and some from abroad. The scores out of 10 in a work psychology examination of 12 students of each group were as follows:

'Home' students	6	7	9	9	6	4	2	9	6	3	3	5
'Abroad' students	3	10	10	6	9	10	9	9	8	7	4	6

Using the appropriate statistical test, discover whether one group scored statistically significantly higher than the other.

Note: you will need to work out for yourself which statistical test to use for which example. For the data given here, the values of statistics that must be exceeded to achieve statistical significance at the $P < 0.05$ level (two-tailed) are:

Chi-square: 3.84
t 2.23
Correlation: 0.50

GLOSSARY OF TERMS

Alternative hypothesis (also called the **experimental hypothesis**) The hypothesis that is the alternative to the null hypothesis. The alternative hypothesis essentially proposes that 'something is going on' in the data. That is, that two or more groups of people do differ on a psychological variable, or that two or more variables are correlated with each other.

Analysis of variance A statistical technique used to test whether two or more samples have significantly different mean scores on one or more variables.

Chi-square A statistical technique used to test whether two or more groups of people differ in the frequency with which their members fall into different categories.

Correlation A statistical technique used to test whether scores obtained from one sample on two variables are associated with each other, such that as scores on one variable increase, scores on the other either increase (positive correlation) or decrease (negative correlation).

Cross-sectional research Research where data are collected from each respondent on only one occasion.

Effect size The magnitude of an association between scores on one or more variables, or of the differences in mean scores between two or more samples.

Experimental hypothesis *See* **Alternative hypothesis.**

Longitudinal research Research where data are collected from each person on two or more occasions.

Multiple regression A statistical technique used to identify which of two or more variables are most strongly correlated with another variable (usually called the criterion variable).

Normal distribution The term given to a particular distribution of scores on a variable where the distribution curve is symmetrical about the mean, with unit area and unit standard deviation.

Null hypothesis The null hypothesis essentially proposes that 'nothing is happening' in the data. That is, that the variables measured are not correlated, or that there are no differences in mean scores between groups of people.

Random sample A number of people selected from a population in such a way that everyone in that population had an equal chance of being selected.

Respondent A term often given to a person who provides data in psychological research, particularly a survey research sample.

Sample A number of people drawn from a defined population (e.g. all people; all females; all sales managers).

Standard deviation A measure of how much variability around the mean there is in a set of data.

Statistical power A measure of the probability that a statistically significant effect will be observed in a sample of given size if such an effect does actually exist in the population from which the sample is drawn.

Statistical significance The probability of rejecting the null hypothesis on the basis of data obtained from a sample when it is in fact true for the population from which the sample is drawn. Psychologists are normally only willing to reject the null hypothesis if there is, at most, a one in twenty chance of it being true.

Subject A term often given to people who provide data in psychological research, particularly experimental research.

***t*-test** A statistical technique used to test whether two samples have significantly different mean scores on a variable.

Type I error This occurs when the null hypothesis is erroneously rejected on the basis of research data.

Type II error This occurs when the alternative hypothesis is erroneously rejected on the basis of research data.

***z*-score** An individual's score on a variable expressed as the number of standard deviations above or below the mean.

SUGGESTED FURTHER READING

1 The book by Adamantios Diamantopoulos and Bodo Schlegelmilch, *Taking the Fear out of Data Analysis* (published by Dryden Press, 1997), is a gentle and entertaining introduction for those who feel they are not particularly numerate but want to understand how to apply basic statistics appropriately. The examples used are not confined to psychology.

2 A more advanced and detailed but still very readable guide to the appropriate use of statistics is provided by Cohen and Cohen (full reference in the list below). Watch out for the authors' dry humour!

REFERENCES

Berry, W.D. and Feldman, S. (1985) *Multiple Regression in Practice*. London: Sage.

Cohen, J. (1977) *Statistical Power Analysis for the Behavioral Sciences*. London: Academic Press.

Cohen, J. and Cohen, P. (1983) *Applied Multiple Regression/Correlation Analysis for the Behavioral Sciences*. 2nd edn. Hillsdale, NJ: Lawrence Erlbaum.

Ferguson, G.A. and Takane, S.(1989) *Statistical Analysis in Psychology and Education*. 6th edn. London: McGraw-Hill.

Judd, C.M., McClelland, G.H and Culhane, S.E. (1995) 'Data analysis: continuing issues in the everyday analysis of psychological data', *Annual Review of Psychology*, vol. 46, pp. 433–65.

Micceri, T. (1989) 'The unicorn, the normal curve, and other improbable creatures', *Psychological Bulletin*, vol. 105, pp. 156–66.

Rosenthal, R. and Rosnow, R.L. (1984) *Essentials of Behavioral Research, Methods and Data Analysis*. New York: McGraw-Hill.

Sawilowsky, S.S. and Blair, R.C. (1992) 'A more realistic look at the robustness and type II error properties of the *t*-test to departures from population normality', *Psychological Bulletin*, vol. 111, pp. 352–60.

Tukey, J.W. (1991) 'The philosophy of multiple comparisons', *Statistical Science*, vol. 6, pp. 100–16.

5 | Minority groups at work

LEARNING OBJECTIVES

After studying this chapter, you should be able to:

1 identify the problems experienced by women in the workplace;

2 explore the policies and procedures that organisations can develop to create equal opportunity environments for women;

3 identify the ways in which racial discrimination manifests itself at work;

4 explore what can be done to help ethnic minorities at work;

5 identify and explore the issues associated with disabled workers in the workplace.

INTRODUCTION

Increasingly, women, ethnic minorities, the disabled and other minority groups are entering the workforce in ever burgeoning numbers. If we are to overcome the obvious entry obstacles, work-related and career blockages problems of these minority groups, we must know something about the extent and nature of their difficulties at work. This chapter explores three minority groups in the workplace – women, ethnic minorities and the disabled – and helps to identify the sources of their stress, as well as suggesting ways of remedying them.

WOMEN AT WORK

The role of women in society is radically changing in most Western countries (Lewis and Cooper, 1989). Vast numbers of women are beginning to work full-time and to aspire to climb the same 'organisational ladders' as their male counterparts (Davidson and Cooper, 1984).

In the UK, for instance, the male labour force has increased at a much slower rate than the female one. In addition, in the early 1950s there were 2.7 million married women in jobs, but by the early 1980s that figure had risen by 143 per cent to over 6.7 million. And, most interesting of all, at the start of the 1950s only a quarter of working women were married, whereas today over two-thirds of all women who are working are married.

But what does this trend mean for the health and well-being of women? Will they join the growing number of men who suffer from stress-related illnesses as a result of work? Cooper *et al.* (1988) reviewed the literature in the field to answer these types of questions: what follows in this section is a summary of their work.

More and more research work is being conducted to answer the question above, and although there are medics who feel that working women are less at risk than men (Lancet, 1979), the early studies in this field have been disturbing. One of the most interesting and comprehensive investigations was carried out by Haynes and Feinleib (1980). Their sample was drawn from the Framingham Heart Study, which is the most comprehensive investigation of heart disease yet conducted. Many of the inhabitants of Framingham, Massachusetts, USA, had been undergoing regular medical screening for the past twenty years. The main purpose of the study was to identify the precursors to heart disease in that population. Interested to identify the impact of employment on working women, Haynes and Feinleib collected data on the employment status and behaviour of 350 housewives, 387 working women (employed outside the home for over one-half of their adult years) and 580 men (between the ages of 45 and 64) in the Framingham study. All 1317 subjects in the investigation were followed for the development of coronary heart disease over an eight-year period.

The main finding was that working women did not have a significantly higher incidence of coronary heart disease than housewives, and their rates were lower than for working men. Haynes and Feinleib then analysed the data in terms of married (including divorced, widowed and separated) versus single working women, and found a substantial increase in incidence of heart disease in married working women. But the most revealing of all their results appeared when they compared married working women with children, and those without children. In this case they found that 'among working women, the incidence of coronary heart disease rose as the number of children increased'. This was not the case, however, for women who were housewives; indeed, that group showed a slight decrease with an increasing number of children.

In addition to these results, Haynes and Feinleib found that working women as a whole 'experienced more daily stress, marital dissatisfaction, and aging worries and were less likely to show overt anger than either housewives or men'. Indeed, in a review of the research literature on marital adjustment in dual-career marriages, Staines *et al.* (1978) found that of the thirteen major studies in this area, using either an American national or regional sample, at least eleven showed that marital adjustment was worse for dual-career wives than for non-working wives. This has more recently been confirmed by a study of 350 dual-career couples (Cooper and Lewis, 1993) in the UK, which is particularly the case for women in two-earner families without the active participation of the husband/partner in carrying out the domestic or family responsibilities.

On the other hand, Newberry *et al.* (1979) examined the psychiatric status and social adjustment of a matched group of working married women and housewives drawn from a community sample. They used the Social Adjustment Scale, Gurin's Symptom Check List and the Schedule for Affective Disorders and Schizophrenia. They found that although there was no difference between the two groups on overall psychiatric symptoms, depressive symptoms, diagnosable psychiatric disorders or treatment for an emotional problem in the past year, married working women did differ from housewives in their attitudes towards work and the home. Indeed, they found that housewives suffered from greater 'work impairment', feelings of inadequacy, disinterest and overall work maladjustment than working wives. On the other hand, working wives were found to be more impaired, disinterested and inadequate in respect of their housework as compared to their work.

Although there is some scattered evidence, as above, that working women may not be 'at risk' of stress-related illness or other negative social consequences, the data are beginning to mount to the contrary, particularly for working women who are married with a family. In a study of psychiatric disorders among professional women, Welner *et al.* (1979) found, for example, that women GPs had a significantly higher rate of psychiatric depression than a control, and that women with children had significantly more career disruption than those without children. In addition, Davidson and Cooper (1980a) found that married female executives with children were under greater stress than single or divorced working women. Indeed, Hall and Hall (1980) suggest that the main source of stress among two-career couples stems from the fact that the number of demands on the partners exceeds the time and energy to deal with them. Families, in this context, add a further series of potential problem areas, particularly when work organisations are doing very little, if anything, to help the dual-career family, and specifically the wife who is expected to be both mother and worker.

Aside from these findings, some startling results have emerged from the total Framingham sample in regard to Type A coronary-prone behaviour and women. Two distinguished cardiologists, Friedman and Rosenman (1974), found a significant relationship between behavioural patterns of people and their prevalence to stress-related illness, particularly coronary heart disease. Type A behaviour is characterised by 'extremes of competitiveness, striving for achievement, aggressiveness, haste, impatience, restlessness, hyperalertness, explosiveness of speech, tenseness of facial muscles, feelings of being under pressure of time and under the challenge of responsibility'. Type B behaviour, on the other hand, is characterised by the relative absence of the behaviour associated with Type A individuals. On the basis of large-scale prospective research work, Rosenman *et al.* (1966) found that this Type A behaviour pattern in all groups of people is a significant precursor to coronary heart disease and other stress-related illnesses: Type A men between the ages of 39 and 49, and 50 and 59, had respectively 6.5 and 1.9 times the incidence of coronary heart disease of Type B men.

In this context, one interesting finding of the Framingham study is that working women who score high on Type A are twice as likely to develop coronary heart disease as male Type As. Indeed, in a study in the UK carried out by one of the authors (Davidson and Cooper, 1980b), it was found that senior female executives had significantly higher Type A behaviour scores than male executives, which in terms of these Framingham results may mean that female professional women may be at greater risk of actual coronaries than the mythical 'high-flying' male executive.

> ■ KEY LEARNING POINT
> *The pressures on women at work are growing as they confront the glass ceiling.*

Sources of stress for women at work

As we can see, woman at work can suffer, but what are some of the determinants of this stress? A number of causes of stress can arise from 'within the woman' herself (Davidson and Cooper, 1992). Many women, those taking on management positions in particular, may discover conflicts within themselves. It is obvious that a great deal of learning about sex roles takes place among women during the early phases of their lives, and this can translate into an attitude that creates difficulties later in work life or life generally. Larwood and Wood (1979), in their book *Women in Management*, described internal blocks that women experience which derive from early sex stereotyping and socialisation. First, many women are caught in a 'low expectation trap', particularly when performing a job usually done by men. Women can feel that their performance is unequal to the task. This feeling is often a self-fulfilling prophecy. Second, some theorists believe that certain women fear success, and may avoid success in order to 'behave in a socially approved manner' (Horner, 1970). This feeling can inhibit further effort and achievement. Third, most women are not socialised to be assertive or aggressive or to seek power and control. As McClelland (1975) has pointed out, the most successful male managers are the most assertive and have considerable desire for power. Women would, therefore, seem disadvantaged from their 'pink' cradle of birth. It can be countered, however, that there is a different management style that is compatible with the more traditional, less aggressive female role. Fourth, many women have been expected and encouraged to be dependent upon men, a fact that some researchers believe makes women less self-reliant and more amenable to influence.

This 'culture trap' creates difficulties for working women because most organisations are dominated by male values and behaviours, while women are still encouraged to pay a less achievement-orientated, less aggressive and more dependent role. Perhaps, as women gain hold of more significant and powerful positions in industry, the more aggressive values of contemporary business will change, to be replaced by an amalgam of female and male values. In the meantime, however, women are at a disadvantage and are forced to use the behavioural armoury of their male associates to succeed. Some common stress factors faced by female managers and the resulting symptoms of strain are pointed out in Fig. 5.1

Role expectations

A major source of stress for career women derives from the concept of the professional women held by themselves and others. While a man can suffer from lack of role clarity and role conflict, he does so because of his individual situation, not because he is a man. The same cannot be said of a women attempting to fill a role previously held only by men. Self-doubt and concern about meeting other people's expectations must continually hover over the thoughts and actions of women at work.

It has been suggested by many writers and researchers in the women in management field that there is a strong tendency for women to be externalisers (that is, feeling that events affecting them are the result of luck or chance rather than the result of their own actions), whereas men are more likely to be internalisers (that is, feeling that events are the result of their own actions) (Harlan and Weiss, 1980). Thus, men are more likely to attribute success to their own actions but attribute failure to external events, whereas

Fig. 5.1 Stress and women at work

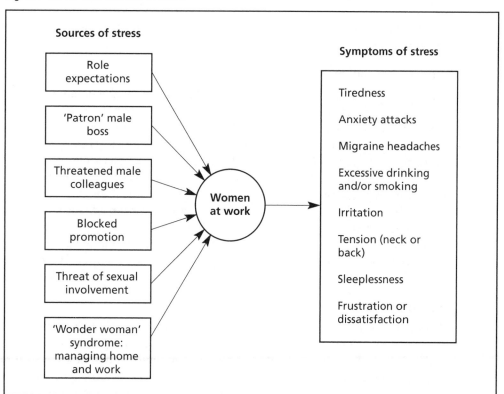

the opposite is the case for women. Indeed, Blackstone and Weinreich-Haste (1980) found that young girls do indeed attribute their success to luck or extra effort, and their failure to lack of ability – with young boys the reverse applied. It appears that an internalised locus of control is an important asset in management, and that successful female managers have been found to attribute their success no more to external factors than their male counterparts (Place, 1979). Moreover, in at least one study, the development of an internalised locus of control was reported as being an important factor contributing towards female managerial success, and was found to develop in a girl who perceived herself as controlling and mastering her adolescent environment (Place, 1979).

'Patron' male boss

While some male bosses may feel threatened by a young career woman who works doubly hard to prove herself, most research indicates that most men are supportive of their female subordinates. This especially holds true for a highly competent female subordinate who does not threaten her boss's relationship with male colleagues. The supportive male boss plays a 'patron' role, which holds potential strains of its own for the woman. The patron protects and advances his protégée, but at the same time uses her competence for his own advancement. Although this shielding and advancement has definite advantages, it also holds built-in pressures. First, the woman may feel she must always perform at her best to meet her patron's expectations. Second, she can identify with him and suffer the professional 'trials and tribulations' that he experiences. Third, significant people within the organisation may not recognise her talents, which are always seen as fused with his. Fourth, the career woman in this case is still playing a dependent role by not 'making a mark' based on her own resources. All of these factors intertwine to create layers of expectations, which can place significant stress on the career woman.

Threat of sexual involvement

Sexuality at work is a double-edged sword for the working woman. On the one hand, she may experience the pressures of sexual harassment from men who hold the keys to her future success. On the other hand, a woman may utilise her sexual role to achieve career objectives, often resulting in unforeseen complications. Although there is little evidence that this manipulative sexual role is often played by career women, it is certain that both males and females can potentially use sexuality at work. More often than not, the main stress factor a woman experiences as a result of an explicit sexual advance from a colleague involves the many issues surrounding the advance. Is he attracted to her physical attributes or her intellect and work capabilities? If he is interested in her as a woman, what does this mean to her about her skill, and about his professional attitude towards her? This conflict can present an enormous source of stress for women, especially perhaps at the beginning of their careers, when they may lack self-confidence.

Threatened male colleagues

Although many woman claim they are helped by their male bosses, they often report that male colleagues of similar rank are excessively competitive, create stress for them and seem to feel threatened by them. Some men at junior and middle levels, for example, feel particularly threatened because they see their organisations promoting women as 'tokens' of equality. Male colleagues who are threatened by their female counterparts, for whatever reason, can and do create strains for women. This reaction can be as subtle as failing to provide complete information needed to make an important decision or by maintaining a distant and cool working relationship. It can be argued that this is common enough for men working together; why should women be shielded?

Blocked promotion

Women struggling up the career ladder face obstacles at all levels, some of which involve the conflict between work and home. Many companies expect an employee to be willing to move for a job promotion or to take on short-term assignments away from home. Female managers with a family, for example, are unlikely to be able to do either, often appearing less of a 'company man' than their male counterparts.

The 'wonder woman' syndrome

Most working women also have the responsibility for a home and family as well. Juggling a job and a family is often done at the expense of a woman's physical and psychological health. The dual-career family is becoming the norm, a fact that involves considerable strain for the women and men involved. Evidence that women are paying a price for the 'wonder woman' role appears in coronary heart disease figures, as mentioned previously.

> ■ KEY LEARNING POINT
> *Women at work face problems with role expectations, threatened male colleagues, blocked promotion and expectations to be 'wonder women'.*

What organisations can do

Cooper *et al.* (1988), Lewis and Cooper (1989) and Cooper and Lewis (1993) have all highlighted the kinds of strategies that might help to minimise the problems of working woman and dual-career couples in general. Such strategies should provide a firm foundation by means of which the alleviation of home–work interface stresses and strains can be accomplished.

Flexible working arrangements

There is a wide range of flexible working arrangements that organisations can provide for their male and female employees which can help them to accommodate to changing family patterns (Cooper and Lewis, 1998). Flexitime is obviously one good example. In order that a dual wife or husband can meet the psychological responsibilities associated with their children's education or, indeed, free themselves of guilt, many parents feel that they must take their children to school and/or pick them up. This is very difficult to accomplish under the current 9 to 5 (or later) arrangements, and would be made much easier under flexitime conditions – as long as it was applicable for both husband and wife. Flexitime is useful not only during the work week, so why should it not be extended to school vacation times?

Many dual-career parents are concerned about arrangements for their children during the summer months when they are at home. There are several ways of coping with this problem: allowing the dual wife or husband to have a lighter load during these months; allowing them to build up a backlog of working time during other months to relieve them during these ones; providing facilities on site during the summer months for young children (perhaps by the use of students training in the field of primary education); or some combination of all of these.

Another more flexible working arrangement could be achieved by introducing more part-time work in a variety of different forms: limiting the number of days a week by allowing individuals to work three- or four-day, 40-hour weeks. This last suggestion is growing in popularity, and if dual husband and wife were able to work on this basis they could, by careful planning, easily manage their domestic work arrangements between them. In 1972 an American Management Association survey estimated that between 700 and 1000 firms of over 100 000 employees in toto were on a four-day, 40-hour week in the United States. By the 1980s, the number of firms grew to 3000 covering over one million workers. Indeed, many firms are moving to a three-day, 38-hour week without decline in productivity and job satisfaction (Foster *et al.*, 1979).

Allied to many of these suggestions is the notion that organisations provide crèche or nursery facilities in the workplace. There is an increasing growth of these in many of the 'advanced thinking' organisations. Many educationalists and psychologists consider this to be a good idea, since it provides the mother or father with the opportunity of seeing the children some time during working hours. A less satisfactory solution would be community-based nurseries, but these may be necessary for those who work for small companies, or who are self-employed. The benefits that organisations could derive from the introduction of the industrial kibbutzim seem so obvious that it is surprising that more companies have not followed suit.

Working at home

With the advent of the microprocessor revolution, it should become easier for dual husbands and wives in certain types of jobs to work at home. The need for a central workplace should decrease quite dramatically over the next decade or two. Already, employees can take home a computer terminal or indeed a minicomputer itself to carry out many of the tasks that they were once able to do only in a centralised work environment. In order to allow such practice, work organisations will have to rid themselves of their deep-rooted, nefarious suspicion of their fellow workers, namely, that the latter will always take every opportunity to exploit their employers and work as little as possible, and that only by overseeing them will the work get done! Indeed, it is this very control that has made the process of work unsatisfying and has encouraged the compartmentalisation of work and home life, to the detriment of the former. As C. Wright Mills (1959) suggested: 'Each day men sell little pieces of themselves in order to try and buy them back each night and weekend with little pieces of fun'.

Some organisations may one day realise that they may not need a centralised workplace at all. For the time being, however, work organisations ought to explore the variety of jobs that could easily be done at home and provide their employees with the necessary degree of flexibility to enable them to work there. At the very least, it is worth an experiment.

Smoothing the way for women

Many women who have played the traditional family 'caring' role need particular help if they are to change the pattern of their marriage and fulfil a more dual role. One problem these women may face, after many years away from work, is lack of confidence and the feeling that they are out of date (or, in fact, actually are out of date). It is in the interest of employers and the wider community to provide opportunities for these women to be brought up to date with current developments. This might best be done by professional associations or, indeed, by work organisations providing updating courses for ex-employees who have temporarily left employment to raise a family. As Fogarty *et al.* (1971) have suggested, 'The important thing in the interests of both employers and of young mothers themselves is to minimize the interruption to a highly qualified woman's career and to keep her as closely in touch as possible with her particular world of work'. Any help the industrial organisation can give its former employees in maintaining their skills may pay off greatly in the future, not only in terms of 'goodwill' but in reducing costs of retraining or initial training of replacement staff. As far as the question of confidence is concerned, this can be achieved during the updating activity or by specialised courses prior to retraining or updating, depending on the time gap between the termination of full employment and the return to work.

Maternity and paternity leave

It is obvious that what many women at work need, if they are preparing to have a family, is some sense of security about their job. In this respect it seems only sensible to have some reasonable maternity leave with a guaranteed right to return to work after it, and with some financial security during the leave period. Most countries in the European Union have guarantees against dismissal during pregnancy, a guarantee of paid maternity leave (usually between eight and twelve weeks and up to six months in many Eastern European countries), and guarantees of the right to return to work either immediately following the paid maternity leave period or unpaid leave after some prearranged return period (in some cases up to two or three years later). Different countries have different arrangements in this respect (Davidson and Cooper, 1994).

Paternity leave is also particularly important in the changing circumstances of the family. Few organisations provide this contemporary innovation, but many will have to consider it in the near future if they want to deal more systematically with what may end up, if ignored, as an uncontrolled absenteeism problem in the years ahead. Dual-career families will increasingly need the flexibility of short leave periods, and provision of leave for both men and women should help to ease the problem.

Changing corporate policy towards equal opportunities

In 1980, a report by the Industrial Society recommended the following action:

1 stimulate industry into encouraging able women to take up careers in management and improve, therefore, attitudes among parents, teachers and women generally;

2 ensure that girls are given guidance and opportunities at schools and in higher education;

3 reduce sex bias in education and particularly in subject choice.

The issue, however, was how do we achieve these lofty goals? Perhaps one way to start the process moving is to encourage organisations to provide formal equal opportunity guidelines. Certainly, during the 1980s, a large number of organisations introduced formal equal opportunities, although the majority tended to have limited content and structure, and consequently no power to initiate real change. In her review of UK local authorities, for example, Coyle (1989) reported that of the 200-plus who had adopted formal equal opportunities policies between 1982 and 1987, less than a quarter had introduced any formal structures for women's equality. A survey of a representative sample of 20 companies from *The Times* Top 1000 Index (for 1987) was carried out by Aitkenhead and Liff (1991), in order to ascertain how equal opportunities were understood. Respondents constituted the person in the organisation who had responsibility for equal opportunities. Results from this study, according to the authors, 'were depressing', and indicated that the majority had a view of equal opportunities such that:

1 they already prevailed;

2 they were not conceived of in terms of organisational structures requiring adaptation to suit individual needs;

3 distributional changes were regarded as unnecessary;

4 criteria for evaluating them, if they existed, were only vaguely conceived of.

Aitkenhead and Liff (1991) concluded that their results painted a gloomy picture of the present or future development of equal opportunities. In their words (p. 39), 'Since most respondents felt little needed to be done within their organizations, it is not surprising that little was being done'.

The report of the Hansard Society Commission, *Women at the Top* (1990), provides a summary of both the barriers that hamper women from progressing up the organisational hierarchy and the strategies adopted by employers.

One overriding barrier which undoubtedly restricts the application of equal opportunity policy is the discriminatory attitudes of managers and employers, linked often to assumptions that individuals (because of their sex and marital status) possess characteristics that would make them unsuitable for employment/promotion. Beck and Steel (1989) give the following examples of possible assumptions:

• lack of commitment to work

• have outside commitments which would interfere with work

• possess poor mental/physical ability

• produce an anticipated unfavourable reaction in other staff and members of the public

• be unsuitable for the job because of the feeling that certain types of work are only suitable for a member of the opposite sex of single status

• be unable to supervise

• possess limited career intentions

• be unwilling to undertake training.

Organisations that have initiated systematic and structured equal opportunity policies usually carry out equal opportunity audits and monitoring (Davidson, 1989). According to the Hansard Society Commission (1990, p. 78):

Equal opportunity audits are designed to provide an organization with a comprehensive picture of the patterns of employment of women; the effect of the organization's working arrangements upon the potential for career development among women; the relationship between current recruitment, training, promotion and general employment policies and practices, and the development of equal opportunities; and the attitudes of employers and their supervisors/managers towards the present position and any potential changes.

Audits such as these should include both in-depth statistical analysis and in-depth interviews with a cross-section of both males and females throughout the organisation. Based on the results of equal opportunity audits, recommendation for a continued programme of action to overcome actual and potential barriers can be proposed, and periodic monitoring of progress can commence.

Some companies, such as ICI, BP and the Bank of England, have surveyed their pattern of female employment and issued a code of practice to improve job appraisal and training for women, which, it is anticipated, may increase the number of female managers at middle and senior levels over the next few years. The Bank of England, for example, as a result of a policy review and systematic equal opportunities audit, is introducing additional measures, including an improved career break scheme and equal opportunities training for all staff (Hansard Society Commission, 1990).

> ■ KEY LEARNING POINT
> *What is needed to help women at work are flexible working arrangements, changing corporate personnel policies and family friendly audits.*

ETHNIC MINORITIES AT WORK

The United Kingdom is a multi-racial and multi-cultural society. As in many multi-cultural societies, we find experiences of discrimination, inequality and certain injustices (Alderfer and Thomas, 1988). The workplace is no exception to this rule, with many ethnic minorities suffering at all stages of the employment process, in recruitment, selection, career development, type of job etc. We focus in this section on the problems of the ethnic minorities, which in the UK context refers to people of Asian, African and Caribbean descent. In this regard, we will be drawing on the excellent work of Iles and Auluck (1991) for this review of the experience of ethnic workers in Britain.

Ethnic minorities in the workforce

Much of the information we can glean on ethnic minority workers comes from the Labour Force Survey, published by the Department of Employment (1988), which was based on a 60 000 household survey between 1985 and 1987. In this survey, it was discovered that nearly 5 per cent of the working population is from the ethnic minorities (African, Afro-Caribbean or Asian origin). It was also found that significantly more individuals from these groups, as opposed to the indigenous white population, are unemployed and less economically active. If we take male employment, for example, 61 per cent of ethnic minority males are economically active, while the figure for white males is 84 per cent. In addition, for nearly all age groups, nearly twice as many of these minorities are unemployed than their white counterparts. However, more recent figures suggest that the unemployment rates are declining at a faster rate than for whites. This increase in employment, however, is in the secondary labour market, casual employment and lower paid jobs.

Although the unemployment and activity rates of ethnic minority women are comparable to those of their male counterparts, in contrast to their white female equivalents they tend to be more economically active later in life, particularly Afro-Caribbean women (Department of Employment, 1988). Nevertheless, ethnic minority women have been found to earn significantly less than white women, and ethnic women graduates earn only 71 per cent of their white counterparts (Breugel, 1989). Also, minority group women at work are more likely to be found in manual jobs, in full-time employment, and in jobs below their qualification level (Breugel, 1989).

Discrimination against ethnic minorities at work

There seems to be substantial evidence of racial discrimination in the workplace for ethnic minorities in the UK (Smith, 1976). In a study by the Commission for Racial Equality (1985) in Leicester, it was found that significantly more white applicants for jobs in a shopping centre were successful than ethnic minority applicants, even when their qualifications and experience were similar. Another study by Brown and Gay (1985) found that ethnic minority applicants matched to whites in terms of gender, experience and qualifications were less successful in being called for interview in three major UK cities. Much of these studies suggest that it is the acceptability of the applicants in terms of white standards, such as attitudes, appearance etc., that decide their fate (Jenkins, 1986). This particularly adversely affects applicants from the ethnic minorities during the recruitment and selection process.

This not only applies to blue-collar workers, but also to graduates. In a study of non-university graduates (Brennan and McGeevor, 1988), it was found that below 50 per cent of ethnic graduates were employed 12 months after graduation, while over 70 per cent of whites were in full-time employment. In addition, it has been found that ethnic minority university graduates (Johnes and Taylor, 1989) were significantly less likely to find employment after graduation, and a significant number were still unemployed six months after obtaining their qualifications.

It will not be surprising to many that the major professions contain few people from ethnic minorities. It was found, for instance, by the Commission for Racial Equality (1987) that in the accounting profession white applicants were significantly more successful than equally qualified ethnic minorities, that all partners in these firms were white and that 95 per cent of the professional staff were white. This also applies to some extent in education, the police service, nursing (in terms of senior nursing jobs) etc. (Commission for Racial Equality, 1988a, b; Oakley, 1987). In the USA, it has also been found that progress toward middle and senior management positions for ethnic minorities is slow or in some industries non-existent (Fernandez, 1975). This is also the case in the UK, with very few attending appropriate management courses in higher education and few employed in the larger organisations.

Problems faced by ethnic minorities at work

There are a range of problems faced by minorities in the workplace (Davidson, 1997). First, the selection and recruitment process is biased against them in one form or another. Second, they have very few role models in the work environment, who could mentor them and socialise them toward organisational life. Third, they do not get the feedback they need in terms of performance appraisal to guide them through the turbulent waters of career ladders. Fourth, employing organisations do not know how to deal with subtle discrimination at work from bosses and colleagues alike. This is not helped by differentiation in pay, conditions and training and development for ethnic minorities found in some companies in some industries, and at all levels.

What can be done to help ethnic minorities at work?

Iles and Auluck (1991) make a number of very useful suggestions about what can be done to help the ethnic minorities at work. First, there should be recruitment initiatives by organisations to employ more ethnic minorities. This is a likely scenario in any case given the demographic downturn of the 1990s in the UK. Second, they suggest that more systematic or formalised selection procedures should be introduced to minimise selection bias and match the skills, qualifications and personal characteristics of the applicants to the job itself. In this regard, it is particularly important to train selection interviewers to be aware of their implicit biases and possible discriminatory practices (Toplis, 1983). Assessment centres must also prove useful to minimise the impact of the interview, using multiple activities and approaches to selection.

This kind of initiative could also be extended to 'equality training' for work groups, where work teams could explore the ways in which they subtly utilise discriminatory practices and behaviours in the course of their productive activity. Third, it is also vital to encourage more accurate and less biased performance appraisal at work. It has been found time and time again (Schmitt and Lappin, 1980) that assessors are biased or have more confidence in appraising people similar to themselves. Unfortunately, white and ethnic minority workers are frequently assessed against different performance criteria, which will ultimately affect their development and advance. And finally, one ought to consider the issue of 'positive action' in recruiting ethnic minorities in the workplace. This is a controversial area, which has been the policy of the USA for decades, but has only recently been discussed in the UK. Positive action at least can provide the first steps in equality of opportunities for minority groups in society, and should be given a fair hearing, examining in detail the American experience.

> ■ **KEY LEARNING POINT**
> *As more and more ethnic minorities are confronted by barriers at work, organisations should develop more recruitment incentives, formalise selection procedures, and encourage training at work.*

THE DISABLED WORKER

There has always been a confusion in people's minds about the differences between disability and handicap. Haggard (1985) has provided a useful differentiation: 'disability refers to a reduced repertoire of generally valuable biological, physical and social skills … handicap refers to the reduced personal, social, educational, economic and cultural opportunities available as a consequence'. With the introduction of new technology, which now makes a disability less of a handicap, more and more is being done to encourage and develop the disabled in the workplace.

McHugh (1991) provides a very thorough and useful summary of problems and opportunities for the disabled, including those suffering from epilepsy, deafness, blindness, heart disease, motor deficits, severe learning difficulties and neurological disorders. He outlines how the disabled are stigmatised in society and in the workplace, but how efforts are being made to 'normalise' them by providing vocational training, career opportunities etc. However, we still have the problem in people's minds about the cost and benefits associated with providing these opportunities, particularly among senior managers, to whom the costs loom large. Nevertheless, the demographic changes about to take place early in the next millennium will mean that we will increasingly need to recruit from many sources not considered in the past. In addition, as Hurley (1989) has suggested, the movement toward computer aided design, office technology, computer aided learning and the wide range of computer assisted production systems will mean 'a shift from manual bodily-dependent work, towards more mental ideas-dependent work'. As McHugh (1991) highlights, this will mean 'more and more work will be done from home through a link to a central computer, and there will be considerable flexibility of working hours and days'. This may mean that the 'homebound' disabled will have more contact with people outside their previously bounded world, although not as much as they would if they were able to operate in a centralised work environment (Flack, 1981).

The future will also hold more opportunities for the disabled in terms of learning networks through computers, or equipment that will enable otherwise severely handicapped people to use equipment or, from a work point of view, be more mobile, by the touch of a computer key. But to provide the opportunities, equipment, facilities and infrastructure, we will need the willing participation and involvement of senior management to invest in the future of the disabled. Up until now, this process has been very slow and difficult to progress, because of management's concern about the 'bottom line', the investment in equipment in terms of its payoff. The changes in demography and society's attitude towards the disabled are rapidly developing, together with the improved cost–benefit ratio, which should mean that the start of the next millennium should create a role in the workplace for the disabled – and not a marginal role, in 'disabled type' jobs, but in all walks of work life. As Lord Snowdon once remarked, 'just because someone is disabled doesn't mean he or she doesn't have a range of other talents. If you mention the names of Milton, Beethoven and Nelson, probably the last thing you would think they had in common was that they were disabled' (McHugh, 1991).

MANAGING DIVERSITY AT WORK

To ensure that women, ethnic minorities and the disabled are encouraged and supported in the work environment, it is essential that organisations manage their diverse workforce in a structured way. Iles and Hayers (1996) suggest, in their working in managing diversity in transnational project teams, that there are five key diversity competences that organisations ought to build on:

1 cultural awareness, in essence understanding cultural differences
2 communicative competence, or communicating across the differences
3 cognitive competence, or acknowledging stereotypes
4 valuing differences
5 gaining synergy from the differences.

These are competences that need to be learned and developed, and approaches within organisations should be targeted for this purpose.

This is reinforced by Thornberg (1994), who suggests that a three-phase approach is needed by organisations to manage diversity:

1 bring in more women and minorities;
2 emphasise working on understanding how people are different and why, by concentrating on problems of individual and group behaviour associated with race and gender;
3 focus on company culture which involves evaluating all of the organisation's procedures and policies.

As Davidson (1997) suggests in her book *The Black and Ethnic Minority Woman Manager*, 'the barriers that prevent all women (regardless of ethnic origins) from progressing up the organisational hierarchy and the strategies adopted by employers in order to try to create more equal opportunities for women are well documented ... such policies as selection and promotion procedures, flexible working, mobility issues, age limits'. In the end, it is a matter of principle and determination, a real desire on the part of organisations to change and encompass all.

SUMMARY

There are a number of groups of workers who are obviously less advantaged than others. These include women, the ethnic minorities and the disabled. By any measures we can see that members of these groups do not have the same access, opportunities and career prospects. We need to ensure that these groups are provided with the opportunities, facilities and resources necessary for them to enter and develop in the workforce. This might be helped by the so-called 'demographic timebomb' of the next decade. This will be greatly helped by more systematic and valid personnel selection techniques, which minimise inherent bias (*see* Chapter 7), by flexible working arrangements to accommodate the disabled and working mothers, by 'flexiplace' as well as flexitime, and by new technology which meets the needs of people working from home or is more 'user friendly'. The UK workforce will, in the short and medium term, need to utilise all its human resources if it is to survive into the future as a competitive economy. In the longer term, it must begin to truly grapple with the problems of discrimination of minorities at work, if we are to survive as a society.

TEST YOUR LEARNING

Short-answer questions

1 What is meant by the 'culture trap' in respect of women at work?

2 Is it important for women to have some kind of mentor at work, and why?

3 What are the advantages and disadvantages of parental leave as opposed to maternity leave?

4 Is affirmative action a good way to deal with discrimination against minorities at work?

5 How should an organisation avoid labelling certain jobs as 'disabled jobs'?

Essay questions

1 Is a flexitime policy enough to help women cope with the dual demands of work and family?

2 What evidence is there that there is discrimination against ethnic minorities at work?

CASE
STUDY
5.1

Female manager's relationship with boss

'The trouble that I have with my male boss is that he finds it hard having to work with a woman. Some situations like travelling together are so uncomfortable that I have had to talk to him about them, especially when we sign in at a hotel. He cannot readily accept inviting me to lunch even though I tease him about it sometimes and try to make light of it. He likes to always keep control, even with his male colleagues, and I somehow threaten that control. I cope by trying not to joke too much about it as I think that puts me down. I tend to walk away from the situation, hoping in time we will develop a closer relationship.

It causes me a great deal of anxiety as I sometimes need to consult him – we once didn't speak for two months! One of the people who does respect and listen to me is the Chief Executive, and the fact that I am a woman is helpful there. However, he is my boss's boss and that can cause problems as it may seem I am going above my immediate boss's head.'

Suggested exercise

If you had this dilemma, how would you deal with it? Either discuss in small groups, or role-play your approach.

GLOSSARY OF TERMS

Affirmative action A form of positive discrimination for members of a minority group to help them obtain a position or achieve promotion in an organisation with few members of this minority, whether women, disabled or ethnic minorities.

Culture trap Women trying to cope with organisational cultures created by male values of achievement orientation, competition and success at all costs.

Disability According to Haggard (1985), 'disability refers to a reduced repertoire of generally valuable biological, physical and social skills'.

Dual-career couple When both members of a family unit work.

Handicap According to Haggard (1985), 'handicap refers to the reduced personal, social, educational, economic and cultural opportunities available as a consequence' (of disability).

Parental leave When both members of a working couple share the childcare of their new offspring, by taking time off work alternately.

Patron male boss A male senior colleague who acts as mentor to a woman subordinate in terms of her career development.

Type A behaviour Hard-driving, ambitious, time-conscious, aggressive and impatient behaviour associated with heart disease and other stress-related illnesses.

'Wonder woman' syndrome When a woman takes it upon herself or feels forced to take on not only work commitments but also all of the domestic responsibilities without asking for help from her spouse/partner (or not getting the support).

SUGGESTED FURTHER READING

1 *Shattering the Glass Ceiling: The Woman Manager* by Marilyn Davidson and Cary Cooper, published by Paul Chapman Ltd in 1994, highlights the problems, obstacles and approaches to overcome the glass ceiling women are currently experiencing in the workplace.

2 *Vulnerable Workers: Psychosocial and Legal Issues* by Marilyn Davidson and Jill Earnshaw, published by John Wiley & Sons in 1991, explores problems with all minority workers; women, disabled, ethnic and the like, discussing both the psychosocial and legal issues surrounding them in the workplace.

3 *How to Manage Your Career, Family and Life* by Cary Cooper and Suzan Lewis, published by Kogan Page in 1998, explores the career and family issues for men and women at work, what can be done both at home and in the workplace to help lessen the burdens.

REFERENCES

Aitkenhead, M. and Liff, S. (1991) 'The effectiveness of equal opportunity policy' in Firth-Cozens, J. and West, M.A. (eds) *Women at Work*. Bristol: Open University Press.

Alderfer, C. and Thomas, D.A. (1988) 'The significance of race and ethnicity for understanding organisation behaviour' in Cooper, C.L. and Robertson, I.T. (eds) *International Review of Industrial and Organizational Psychology*. Chichester: John Wiley, pp. 1–41.

Beck, J. and Steel, M. (1989) *Beyond the Great Divide*. London: Pitman Publishing.

Blackstone, T. and Weinreich-Haste, H. (1980) 'Why are there so few women scientists and engineers?', *New Society*, vol. 51, pp. 383–5.

Brennan, J. and McGeevor, P. (1988) *Graduates at Work: Degree Courses and the Labour Market*. London: Jessica Kingsley.

Breugel, I. (1989) 'Sex and race in the labour market', *Feminist Review*, vol. 32, Summer, pp. 49–68.

Brown, C. and Gay, P. (1985) *Racial Discrimination 17 Years after the Act*, working paper no. 646. London: Policy Studies Institute.

Commission for Racial Equality (1985) *Positive Action and Equal Opportunity in Employment*. London: Commission for Racial Equality.

Commission for Racial Equality (1987) *Chartered Accountancy Training Contracts: Report of a Formal Investigation*. London: Commission for Racial Equality.

Commission for Racial Equality (1988a) *Medical School Admissions: Report of a Formal Investigation*. London: Commission for Racial Equality.

Commission for Racial Equality (1988b) *Ethnic Minority School Teachers: A Survey in Eight Local Education Authorities*. London: Commission for Racial Equality.

Cooper, C.L. and Lewis, S. (1993) *The Workplace Revolution: Managing Today's Dual Career Families*. London: Kogan Page.

Cooper, C.L. and Lewis, S. (1998) *How to Manage your Career, Family and Life*. London: Kogan Page.

Cooper, C.L., Cooper, R.D. and Eaker, L.H. (1988) *Living with Stress*. Harmondsworth: Penguin.

Coyle, A. (1989) 'The limits of change: local government and equal opportunities for women', *Public Administration*, vol. 67, pp. 39–50.

Davidson, M.J. (1989) 'Restructuring women's employment in British Petroleum' in Pearson, R. and Ellias, D. (eds) *Women's Employment and Multinationals in Europe*. London: Macmillan.

Davidson, M.J. (1997) *The Black and Ethnic Minority Woman Manager: Cracking the Concrete Ceiling*. London: Paul Chapman.

Davidson, M.J. and Cooper, C.L. (1980a) 'The extra pressure of women executives', *Personnel Management*, June, pp. 48–51.

Davidson, M.J. and Cooper, C.L. (1980b) 'Type A coronary prone behaviour and stress in senior female managers and administrators', *Journal of Occupational Medicine*, vol. 22, pp. 801–6.

Davidson, M.J. and Cooper, C.L. (1984) *Working Women: An International Survey*. Chichester: John Wiley.

Davidson, M.J. and Cooper, C.L. (1992) *Shattering the Glass Ceiling: The Woman Manager*. London: Paul Chapman Publishing.

Davidson, M.J. and Cooper, C.L. (1994) *European Women in Business and Management*. London: Paul Chapman Publishing.

Department of Employment (1988) *Labour Force Survey*. London: HMSO.

Fernandez, J.P. (1975) *Black Managers in White Corporations*. New York: John Wiley.

Flack, J. (1981) 'Minicomputers and the disabled user', *Bulletin of the British Psychological Society*, vol. 34, p. 209.

Fogarty, M.P., Rapoport, R. and Rapoport, R.N. (1971) *Sex, Career and Family*. Beverly Hills, CA: Sage.

Foster, L.W., Latack, J.C. and Riendl, L.J. (1979) 'The effects and promises of the shortened work week', in *Proceedings of the Academy of Management Annual Conference*, August.

Friedman, M. and Rosenman, R.H. (1974) *Type A Behaviour and Your Heart*. London: Wildwood House.

Haggard, M.P. (1985) 'Concepts of impairment, disability and handicap', *Bulletin of the British Psychological Society*, vol. 38, p. 83.

Hall, D.T. and Hall, F. (1980) 'Stress and the two career couple' in Cooper, C.L. and Payne, R.L. (eds) *Current Concerns in Occupational Stress*. Chichester: John Wiley.

Hansard Society Commission (1990) *Women at the Top*. London: Hansard Society.

Harlan, A. and Weiss, C. (1980) *Moving Up: Women in Managerial Careers; Third Progress Report*. Wellesley, MA: Wellesley Centre for Research on Women.

Haynes, S.G. and Feinleib, M. (1980) 'Women, work and coronary heart disease: prospective findings from the Framingham Heart Study', *American Journal of Public Health*, vol. 70, pp. 133–41.

Horner, K. (1970) *Femininity and Successful Achievement: A basic inconsistency. Feminine Personality and Conflict.* Pacific Grove, CA: Brooks/Cole.

Hurley, J. (1989) 'The new technologies and the changing nature and organization of work', *Irish Journal of Psychology*, vol. 10, no. 3, pp. 368–80.

Iles, P. and Auluck, R. (1991) 'The experience of black workers' in Davidson, M.J. and Earnshaw, J. (eds) *Vulnerable Workers.* Chichester: John Wiley.

Iles, P. and Hayers, P.K. (1996) 'Managing diversity in transnational project teams: a tentative model and case study', *Journal of Managerial Psychology*, vol. 12, no. 2, pp. 95–117.

Industrial Society (1980) *Women in Management – Onwards and Upwards?* London: Industrial Society.

Jenkins, R. (1986) *Racism and Recruitment: Managers, Organisations and Equal Opportunities in the Labour Market.* Cambridge: Cambridge University Press.

Johnes, G. and Taylor, J. (1989) 'Ethnic minorities in the graduate labour market', *New Community*, vol. 15, no. 4, pp. 527–36.

Lancet (1979) 'Women, work and coronary heart disease' (editorial), 12 July 1979, pp. 76–7.

Larwood, L. and Wood, M. (1979) *Women in Management.* London: Lexington Books.

Lewis, S. and Cooper, C.L. (1989) *Career Couples.* London: Unwin Hyman.

McClelland, D.C. (1975) *The Inner Experience.* New York: Irvington.

McHugh, M.F. (1991) 'Disabled workers – psychosocial issues', in Davidson, M.J. and Earnshaw, J. (eds) *Vulnerable Workers.* Chichester: John Wiley.

Mills, C. Wright (1959) *The Power Elite.* New York: Oxford University Press.

Newberry, P., Weissman, M. and Myers, J. (1979) 'Working wives and housewives: do they differ in mental status and social adjustment?', *American Journal of Orthopsychiatry*, vol. 49, pp. 282–91.

Oakley, R. (1987) *Employment in Police Forces: A Survey of Equal Opportunities.* London: Commission for Racial Equality.

Place, H. (1979) 'A biographical profile of women in management', *Journal of Occupational Psychology*, vol. 52, pp. 267–76.

Rosenman, R.H., Friedman, M. and Strauss, R. (1966) 'CHD in the Western Collaborative Group Study', *Journal of the American Medical Association*, vol. 195, pp. 86–92.

Schmitt, N. and Lappin, I. (1980) 'Race and sex as determinants of the mean and variance of performance ratings', *Journal of Applied Psychology*, vol. 65, pp. 428–35.

Smith, D. (1976) *The Facts of Racial Disadvantage.* London: Political and Economic Planning.

Staines, G.L., Pleck, J.H., Shepard, L. and O'Connor, P. (1978) 'Wives' employment status and marital adjustment', working paper, University of Michigan, Institute of Social Research.

Thornberg, I. (1994) 'Journey toward a more inclusive culture', *HR Magazine*, February, pp. 79–96.

Toplis, J.W.C. (1983) 'Training interviewers to avoid unfair discrimination', paper to British Psychological Society, London, December.

Welner, A., Marten, S., Wochnick, E., Davis, M., Fishman, R. and Clayton, J. (1979) 'Psychiatric disorders among professional women', *Archives of General Psychiatry*, vol. 36, pp. 169–73.

6

Individual differences

After studying this chapter, you should be able to:

1 describe the approach to the testing of human intelligence adopted by Binet and Simon;

2 describe the technique of factor analysis;

3 explain the difference between Spearman's 'g' factor and Thurstone's 'primary mental abilities' approach to intelligence testing.

4 outline Vernon's Hierarchical Theory of Human Intelligence.

5 state some criticisms of intelligence tests and contrast the conventional approach with practical intelligence;

6 compare and contrast the personality theories of Eysenck and Cattell;

7 define the 'big five' personality constructs;

8 name three personality questionnaires available in the UK;

9 distinguish between cognitive ability, personality and work competencies.

INTRODUCTION

Although there are many approaches to conceptualising and understanding human individual differences, only one kind of approach (which represents individual differences as measurable, structural concepts) has been widely influential in work psychology research and practice. This approach, which has been applied to both cognitive abilities and personality, is the trait-factor analytic approach. The basis of trait theory is that there are cross-situational generalities in behaviour. In other words, personality traits explain why people behave in similar ways in different circumstances. This emphasis on the person as the source of individual differences contrasts most sharply with the emphasis in behaviour theory on the situation as the source of individual differences in behaviour (*see* Chapter 2).

In their attempts to explain personality, psychologists have tended to emphasise the role of either internal (person) factors or external (situational) factors. It is important to understand that debate about the relative importance of people and situations in determining behaviour is a long-standing issue within psychology. To most of us it is clear, from everyday experience, that our behaviour is not completely at the mercy of situational influences. There is some cross-situational consistency in how we behave from one setting to another, particularly in terms of key features of our psychological make-up, such as extroversion, agreeableness and anxiety. On the other hand most people will behave quite differently at a lively party and at a very important business event.

The relative influence of person and situation variables has been a topic of some controversy. Some people have argued very strongly for the predominance of situational influences, suggesting that stable individual differences in psychological make-up have a relatively small role to play (e.g. Mischel, 1968). Despite these historical differences of opinion, it is clear that modern psychology allows for the influence of both person and situation variables (*see* Pervin, 1989). The approaches described below focus on the structure and measurement of individual differences; they do not emphasise the role of situational factors in determining behaviour. It would be a mistake, however, to conclude that the approaches described do not recognise the potential for situations to influence how people behave. Eysenck, whose theory of personality is dealt with below, has captured the essential futility of trying to identify a single cause by writing, 'Altogether I feel that the debate is an unreal one. You cannot contrast persons and situations in any meaningful sense ... No physicist would put such a silly question as: which is more important in melting a substance – the situation (heat of the flame) or the nature of the substance?' (quoted by Pervin, 1980, p. 271).

Recent theoretical and research work has developed an important, more sophisticated concept than the idea that both people and situations are important. This is the idea that people and situations interact with each other to determine behaviour. An influential current theory which adopts an interactionist perspective is the social cognitive (previously referred to as social learning) theory of Bandura (1977, 1986). The impact of this theory can be seen in various fields of work psychology, including behaviour analysis and modification (Chapter 10) and training and learning (Chapter 15).

■ **KEY LEARNING POINT**
Personal and situational factors interact to determine behaviour.

COGNITIVE ABILITY

Some people are better at processing information than others. We are constantly exposed to evidence that, when it comes to cognitive (thinking) ability, there are wide variations between people. It is equally clear that some of these differences are the result of differences in opportunities to learn (i.e. they are situationally or environmentally determined). Psychologists have expended a great deal of time and effort trying to understand and measure differences in cognitive ability. One approach to the issues involved has a long history and is particularly relevant to personnel selection and assessment. The core of this approach involves the use of carefully designed tests to assess people's levels of cognitive ability. Such tests need to be administered under standardised conditions and require people to attempt to answer written questions, all of which have been evolved through a highly technical process of trialling and analysis (*see* Table 6.2 for illustrative questions). Because of the need for standardisation in administration and test content, this approach cannot assess people on their capacity to conduct everyday, real-life tasks. This is seen by some psychologists as a serious weakness.

An alternative view of the cognitive abilities that people possess involves seeking to examine what has been termed 'practical intelligence' (*see* Sternberg and Wagner, 1986). Practical intelligence refers to the intelligence that underlies the performance of real-life tasks. Scribner (1986) suggested that practical thinking has a number of defining features which help to distinguish it from the kind of thinking required to complete traditional tests of intelligence. Practical thinking involves: problem formulation as well as problem solution; flexibility in devising solutions to the 'same problem'; incorporating the environment into the problem-solving system; conscious use of 'least-effort strategies' and the acquisition and use of specific knowledge that is important to the context in which the problem is embedded. As Table 6.1 shows, these features of practical thinking mark it out as different from the thinking involved in completing traditional tests of intelligence. In organisational settings practical thinking underlies the development and use of work-related competencies (*see* Boyatzis, 1982; Boam and Sparrow, 1992). This point is taken further in a later section of this chapter.

■ **KEY LEARNING POINT**

The thinking needed for practical intelligence seems to be different from the thinking required in traditional intelligence tests.

In the early years of the twentieth century, two French psychologists, Alfred Binet and Theodore Simon, developed what is generally accepted as the first satisfactory test of human intelligence. At the turn of the nineteenth century, France, in common with other industrialised nations, had introduced compulsory education. Most of the children entering the schools seemed well able to benefit from the regular schools. Some were perhaps in need of special help, but could be dealt with by the regular system. A third group, however, was retarded to the point of being unable to benefit from the regular system. It was not always easy to identify the children in need of special treatment, and the test developed by Binet and Simon was intended to help in identifying these children by assessing their intellectual capabilities.

Table 6.1 Practical thought and intelligence testing

Practical thought	Intelligence tests
Problem formulation	Usually the problem is stated in a clear unambiguous fashion and there is no call to reconstruct or explore its nature or relevance
Flexibility in devising solutions, i.e. the 'sample' problem is solved in different ways, each suited to the occasion. For example, a waiter uses many strategies to remember a round of drinks	Familiar and generally inflexible algorithms used to tackle all problems of a certain type
Incorporation of the environment into the problem. Expert problem solvers take account of the environment in work settings or items in the environment to help with the problem	The environment is standardised and irrelevant to problem solving
Least effort strategies are used	Probably similar
Use of setting-specific knowledge	The construction of tests tries to ensure that general intellectual processes, rather than setting-specific knowledge, determines success

The approach adopted by Binet and Simon is still the basis for contemporary intelligence tests. In essence, Binet and Simon considered that intelligence could be measured by assessing a person's ability to answer a carefully selected collection of questions. Although the questions in modern tests (*see* Table 6.2) sometimes differ from those used by Binet and Simon, the principle of sampling behaviour on a carefully selected set of tasks is still at the basis of most tests. Clearly, by sampling behaviour one runs the risk of drawing false conclusions about a person – perhaps because of the particular questions asked, the circumstances in which the test is taken, or various other reasons. Binet and Simon certainly recognised that test scores alone were not enough and they proposed that, before any decision about a child was taken, other types of assessment should also be made.

Since the pioneering work of Binet and Simon, psychologists have carried out a considerable amount of work in their attempts to measure intelligence and to understand its structure. Much of this work makes use of statistical methods, developed to aid research into human intelligence. These statistical methods (the principal ones are correlation and factor analysis) are now used in many disciplines. Some elementary grasp of these methods is essential to an understanding of the psychology of human mental abilities. Correlation is dealt with in Chapter 4 and the reader who is unfamiliar with correlation and the calculation and interpretation of correlation coefficients should consult that chapter before going further. Factor analysis, because of its important influence on theoretical work in intelligence, is outlined at the appropriate point in this chapter.

Table 6.2 Some items from an intelligence test

Q7	Mountain is to molehill as valley is to ...

1	2	3	4	5
hollow	chasm	hill	plain	mound

Q8	The third member of this series is omitted. What is it?

0.1, 0.7, ..., 34.3, 240.1

Q9	Which one of the five words on the right bears a similar relation to each of the two words on the left?

	1	2	3	4	5
Class; shape	Rank	Grade	Analyse	Size	Form

Q10	Here are five classes. Write down the number of the class which contains two, and two only, of the other four classes:

1	2	3	4	5
Terriers	Mammals	'Scotties'	Dogs	Canines

Q11	Sniff is to handkerchief as shiver is to ...

1	2	3	4	5
blow	fire	catarrh	burn	sneeze

Q12	How many members of the following series are missing?

1, 2, 5, 6, 7, 11, 12, ..., 20, 21 22, 23

Q13	Which one of the five words on the right bears a similar relation to each of the two words on the left?

	1	2	3	4	5
Stream; tolerate	Brook	Contribute	Bear	Support	Pour

Q14	Working from the left, divide the fourth whole number by the fifth fraction:

8, 6, 5/7, 3, 9, 2/9, 3/8, 1, 17/31, 4/9

Source: The AH5 Test. Reprinted by permission of the National Foundation for Educational Research Publishing Company Limited.

Structure of intelligence

Human beings are capable of showing considerable ability in a wide range of pursuits. For some (e.g. a bookmaker's clerk), considerable numerical skill is required; for others (e.g. a journalist), the ability to use words correctly and fluently is important; while yet others (e.g. an architect) need the ability to visualise objects in three dimensions. It would be possible to suggest many further occupational areas and associated abilities. The important point, however, is that it may be superficial to consider intelligence as a single or unitary attribute that can be represented by an overall measure.

Table 6.3 shows a typical correlation matrix derived by intercorrelating the results of a group of people in a collection of tests. Notice that although some of the correlations are smaller than others, none of them is negative. In other words people who do well in

Table 6.3 Correlations between some intellectual tests

	Maths	English	Geography	IQ
Maths test				
English test	+0.51			
Geography test	+0.52	+0.34		
IQ test	+0.55	+0.50	+0.48	

Source: adapted from Satterly (1979).

one test, do well (or at least not very badly) in the others. The results in Table 6.3 are typical of those obtained when people are tested on a wide range of intellectual tasks. Results such as this led Spearman (1927) to propose the so-called two-factor theory of the structure of intelligence. This suggested that an underlying factor of general intelligence ('g') was helpful in performance in all areas of human ability. The existence of such a factor would explain why there is a persistent positive correlation between such a wide range of tests of human intellectual ability. Spearman explained the fact that performance in different types of test varied by proposing that, as well as 'g', there was a series of test-specific factors ('s').

Other researchers, notably Thurstone (1938), opposed Spearman's view. The view of Thurstone was that intelligence is made up of a loosely related set of 'primary abilities' and that the relationships between the various aspects of human performance could be explained more effectively by these underlying primary abilities than by a general factor or 'g'. Thurstone proposed twelve or so 'primary mental abilities', including:

1 *verbal comprehension* (v): important in reading, comprehension and verbal reasoning;
2 *space or visualisation* (s): concerned with the perception and visualisation of objects in space;
3 *number* (n): the speed and accuracy of straightforward arithmetic calculation.

Factor analysis

Investigations of the structure of human abilities usually involved the use of a statistical technique known as factor analysis. Factor analysis is a mathematical technique that can be used to analyse a correlation matrix. It shows how each of the tests used to produce the original correlation matrix can be divided up and allocated to a smaller collection of underlying factors. Table 6.4 shows a correlation matrix. To simplify things the actual correlation coefficients have not been given, but merely an indication of where the correlations have high values.

> ■ **KEY LEARNING POINT**
> *Statistical methods such as correlation and factor analysis have been useful in exploring the structure of human intelligence.*

Table 6.4 Sizes of correlations in a correlation matrix

	A			B		
	1	2	3	4	5	6
1 Verbal reasoning	✗					
2 Vocabulary		✗				
3 Spelling	High		✗			
4 Spatial reasoning				✗		
5 Drawing accuracy					✗	
6 Geometry				High		✗

The correlations between the tests in group A (1–3) are high, as are the correlations between the tests in group B (4–6). The correlations of tests from group A with tests from group B are only moderate. What this pattern of correlations suggests is:

1 the tests in group A all have something in common (probably a 'verbal' factor);

2 the tests in group B also have something in common (probably a 'spatial' factor).

Notice also that all of the tests are correlated positively with each other (the correlations in the shaded areas, although lower, are still positive). These positive correlations between all of the tests suggest:

3 the existence of some factor common to all tests (presumably 'g').

Table 6.5 shows how a factor analysis for this matrix might appear. The factor analysis provides a numerical statement of the factors underlying the correlation matrix, and the loading of each test on each factor indicates the extent to which the test involves this factor. The first test (verbal reasoning), for example, loads heavily on factor I ('g'), less heavily on factor II (verbal) and not at all on factor III (spatial).

A hierarchy of abilities

The factor analysis in Table 6.5 produces both a general intelligence factor (which would offer support for Spearman) and some specific factors (supporting Thurstone).

Table 6.5 The results of a factor analysis

	Factors		
	I (g)	II (verbal)	III (spatial)
Verbal reasoning	0.6	0.5	
Vocabulary	0.7	0.4	
Spelling	0.8	0.3	
Spatial reasoning	0.4		0.6
Drawing accuracy	0.5		0.5
Geometry	0.5		0.7

Some of the differences between the theories of Spearman and his followers and Thurstone and his were due to the use of different techniques of factor analysis, the use of different samples for investigation and so on. In fact, a reconciliation of the two theories is not as difficult as it might at first seem.

The 'compromise' theory was proposed by Burt (1940) and elaborated by Vernon (1969). The hierarchical organisation of mental abilities that they proposed (*see* Fig. 6.1) incorporates both general and specific factors. At the top of the hierarchy is 'g', the broad general ability factor that is involved in all intellectual performance. But intellectual performance is not explained by 'g' alone. Differences of intermediate generality are also important, between verbal–numerical–education (v : ed), for example, and practical–mechanical–spatial–physical (k : m) factors. In turn, the major group factors may be subdivided into increasingly less general minor and specific factors. In general, psychologists in the UK have adopted this hierarchical view of mental abilities. American psychologists have been inclined to adopt a view more in line with Thurstone's original ideas and have continued to search for related specific abilities. Guilford (1967), for instance, developed a 'structure of the intellect' model that classifies abilities by operation, product and content (*see* Fig. 6.2). Guilford argued and attempted to demonstrate that it should be possible to produce tests that are independent (i.e. not intercorrelated) for each cell in the cube shown in Fig. 6.2 (i.e. 120 separate abilities in all). Despite the general acceptance of Vernon's theory the distinction between 's' and 'g' has been retained in many theories of human mental ability. Cattell (1987) put forward the view that an initial general ability, referred to as fluid 'g' or 'g_f' is utilised in specific experience and 'crystallises' into more specific skills. Cattell refers to this as crystallised intelligence (g_c) (*see* Jensen, 1992).

Fig. 6.1 The hierarchical structure of human abilities

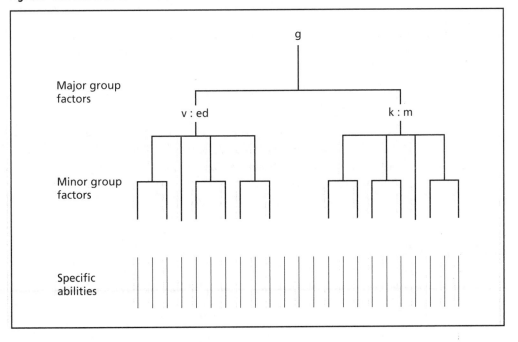

Fig. 6.2 Guilford's structure of the intellect model

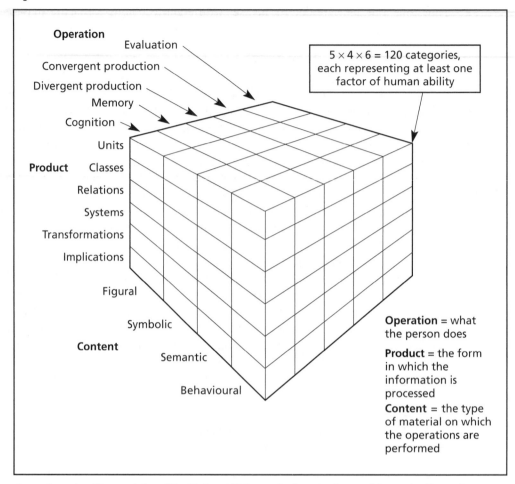

Source: Reproduced by permission of The McGraw Hill Companies from the *Nature of Human Intelligence* by J.P. Guilford (1967).

■ **KEY LEARNING POINT**

Various different models for the structure of intelligence have been proposed. Vernon's hierarchical model has been widely accepted as a solution which combines the key features of the major competing models.

INTELLIGENCE TESTS

So far we have managed to discuss the underlying structure of intelligence without directly confronting the problem of what intelligence actually is! The defining of intelligence presents problems for psychologists, and to this day there is no universally accepted definition. Many psychologists will settle for the definition first proposed by Boring (1923, p. 35): 'Intelligence is what intelligence tests measure'. In fact, this definition is not as meaningless as it seems at first sight. Tests of general intelligence are designed to examine the ability of people to carry out certain mental operations. The various tests of general intelligence ('g') are all interrelated and people obtain similar scores in different tests. Thus, 'g' is a quality that can be measured reliably and with some precision; but as Eysenck and Kamin (1981, p. 25) have pointed out, 'we cannot at this stage say that "g" is the same as the term as understood by the man in the street'. Eysenck, however, clearly considers that what intelligence tests measure is pretty close to what most people think of as intelligence. Others, such as Kamin (Eysenck and Kamin, 1981), hold a different view and argue that IQ tests do not provide a good measure of what most people regard as intelligence. Both of these authors are eminent psychologists but hold quite different views about our current ability to measure intelligence. They do not disagree that the available tests measure something with reasonable accuracy – they disagree fundamentally about *what* such tests do measure.

Regardless of whether the available tests measure what we think of as intelligence or some other qualities, tests of intelligence and specific abilities have been used with some success in personnel selection (*see* Chapter 8). Many tests of specific abilities (mechanical, verbal, numerical etc.) and of 'g' can be used to provide quite good predictions of people's competence in certain jobs. Tests have been criticised on various grounds. One criticism is based on the argument that intelligence tests do not measure pure underlying intelligence, but a mixture of it and of taught or acquired knowledge. Vernon (1956, p. 157) distinguished between intelligence and attainments in the following way:

> the former refers to the more general qualities of thinking – comprehension, level of concept developing, reasoning and grasping relations – qualities which seem to be acquired largely in the course of normal development without specific tuition; whereas the latter refers more to knowledge and skills which are directly trained.

Unfortunately, it is one thing to make such a distinction in writing but quite another to put it into practice by developing tests that are 'pure' tests of one or other factor. Proponents of intelligence tests believe that this can be done; others consider that it has not been done properly and is probably impossible.

In the personnel selection context, tests are also criticised because they are biased in favour of certain ethnic or cultural groups. Consider Vernon's description of intelligence given above – as qualities which seem to be acquired largely in the course of normal development. What is the 'normal environment' in which this 'normal development' takes place? White middle-class family groups, some critics would say! The argument of cultural bias asserts that the intellectual development that takes place naturally is dependent on the specific environmental and cultural background in which a person develops, so that perfectly bright and intelligent people from certain socio-economic or ethnic backgrounds will fail to develop the normal qualities assessed in the tests. The consequence will be that, despite their underlying intelligence, the tests will label them as unintelligent.

A rational and unbiased examination of the advantages and disadvantages of psychological tests in the light of criticisms such as the ones raised above is of value to both the science of psychology and to society. The criticism that intelligence tests are biased against certain ethnic groups is, at least in part, based on the frequently replicated finding that ethnic minority groups (mostly black Americans) produce lower scores on cognitive tests than whites (*see* Schmitt and Noe, 1986, for a review of evidence).

Despite these subgroup differences, the prevailing view of the scientific community is that it is not unfair to use such tests for selection decision making. In essence this conclusion is based on the finding that although there are consistent differences between subgroups in mean scores, the accuracy of prediction of the tests (i.e. the prediction of future levels of work performance) is the same for different ethnic groups. Most of the evidence on the fairness or otherwise of cognitive testing in selection is from studies in the USA and such data may need to be interpreted differently in the European context.

There is a wide range of different tests available to measure general intelligence (i.e. Spearman's 'g' factor) and various specific abilities (mechanical, spatial, numerical etc.) and several publishers of psychological tests are operating in the UK. Evidence concerning the value of cognitive tests and the fairness of such tests is discussed in Chapter 8. A widely used test of g which requires minimal special experience or training is Raven's progressive matrices – which measures g through a series of abstract diagrammatic problems (Raven *et al.*, 1996).

> ■ **KEY LEARNING POINT**
> *There are consistent differences in the general mental ability test scores obtained by different subgroups.*

TRAIT VIEWS OF PERSONALITY

Psychoanalytic theories of human personality such as Freud's are often criticised by other psychologists for their lack of scientific rigour, lack of satisfactory definition of key concepts and the fact that the theories either do not generate testable predictions about human behaviour or, when predictions are made, that they do not work out in practice (*see* Chapter 2 for an introduction to alternative views of personality. One of the strongest critics of these theories is Eysenck (e.g. Eysenck and Wilson, 1973), who has developed an alternative approach to personality based on the rigorous application of scientific methods and statistical analysis. Eysenck, working in Britain, and the British- born psychologist Cattell, working in the United States, pursue an approach that attempts to uncover the underlying personality traits which they believe can be used to explain human behaviour in a variety of different situations.

Trait theories perhaps come closest to describing the structure of personality in a way that matches our everyday use of the term. Trait theories use words such as shy, outgoing, tense and extroverted to describe the basic factors of human personality. These basic elements – traits – represent predispositions to behave in certain ways, in a variety of different situations. In the UK the main exponent of the approach is Hans Eysenck (1970, 1981; Eysenck and Eysenck, 1985).

'Trait theorists such as Eysenck (1970) and Cattell *et al.* (1970) use the technique of factor analysis in attempts to identify the underlying structure of human personality. Eysenck argues that personality is best understood in terms of a hierarchical organisation (*see* Fig. 6.3). The underlying building blocks for personality can be represented by a small number of basic dimensions (types) that have been identified from the factor

Fig. 6.3 The hierarchical organisation of personality

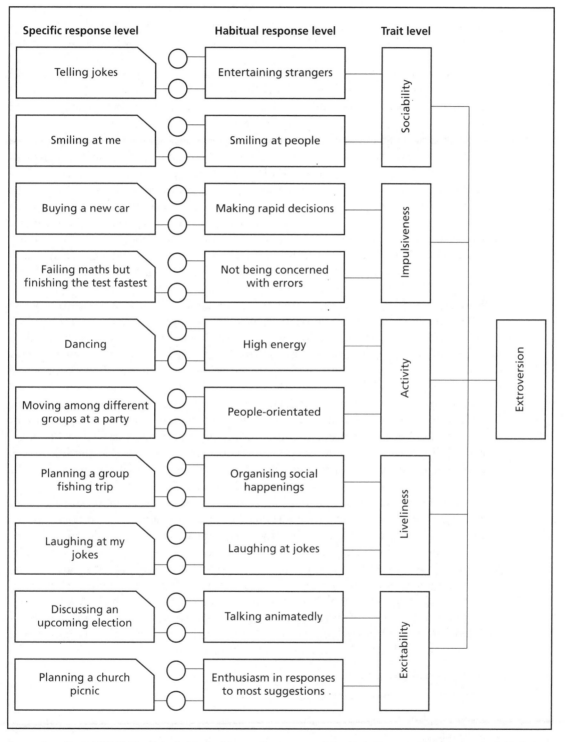

Source: From Eysenck (1967) *The Biological Basis of Personality*, courtesy of Charles C. Thomas Publisher Ltd, Springfield, Illinois, USA.

analysis of large numbers of personality questionnaires asking people how they behave and feel in various situations. Two major dimensions emerging consistently from factor analytic studies conducted by Eysenck and others are *extroversion* and *neuroticism*. Extroverts are lively, sociable, excitable people and neurotics are characterised by high levels of anxiety and tension. Two important points should be borne in mind in relation to these dimensions. The first is that they are continuous dimensions and most people are not extreme in either extroversion or neuroticism. The second point is that the dimensions are independent; in other words, someone's position on one dimension bears no relationship to his or her position on the other.

As well as providing empirical evidence concerning basic human personality factors, Eysenck's work provides a theory concerning the origins and development of personality. This involves the impact of both inherited, neurological differences and environmental influences due to the processes of conditioning and socialisation. The main measuring instruments associated with Eysenck's theory are the Eysenck Personality Inventory (EPI) (Eysenck and Eysenck, 1964), a self-report questionnaire that measures the factors extroversion and neuroticism, and the Eysenck Personality Questionnaire (EPQ) (Eysenck and Eysenck, 1975) which measures extroversion and introversion, together with a third factor – psychoticism. The EPQ is now incorporated into the Eysenck Personality Scales (Eysenck and Eysenck, 1991).

Working in the United States, Cattell, using similar statistical techniques to those of Eysenck, also pursues a trait approach to personality. One notable difference between the two theorists is the number of stable factors that they feel need to be used to describe and measure personality structure. Although neither Cattell nor Eysenck bases theories entirely on data from self-report questionnaires, some of the differences between them become apparent when the questionnaires used by each of them are compared. The EPI uses two dimensions (extroversion – introversion and neuroticism), and Eysenck recognises the existence of a third important factor – psychoticism. Cattell's main personality questionnaire (the 16PF) includes sixteen personality factors. To some extent the differences are due to the different statistical procedures that the researchers employ. The latest version of the 16PF available for use in the UK is the 16PF5. UK norms for this version are available (Russell and Karol, 1994; Smith, 1994).

Research exploring the similarities and differences between the models of Eysenck, Cattell and other trait-orientated theorists has produced some fairly consistent evidence of the existence of five (the so-called big five) major personality factors. A series of studies has administered the leading personality questionnaires to large groups of people. With the aid of factor-analytic techniques, the investigators have sought to identify the minimum number of underlying personality dimensions that will account for the range of responses produced in people's answers to the questionnaires. A high degree of consensus has emerged and investigators have agreed that a five-factor structure represents an adequate way of describing the basic dimensions of personality (Digman and Takemoto-Chock, 1981; McCrae and Costa, 1990). This fivefold structure involves:

1 extroversion–introversion
2 neuroticism (i.e. emotional instability, anxiety)
3 conscientiousness
4 agreeableness
5 openness to experience.

Extroversion and neuroticism have already been described. Conscientiousness, as the label suggests, concerns an individual's predisposition to be well organised and to focus on targets, goals and deadlines. Agreeableness concerns the extent to which someone is good natured, eager to co-operate with others and concerned to avoid conflict. Openness to experience is related to a person's tendency to be influenced by new experiences.

> ■ KEY LEARNING POINT
> *The 'big five' provides a very useful organising framework for understanding the structure of human personality.*

Substantial evidence exists that the 'big five' structure is consistent across various national groups. For example, McCrae and Costa (1997) reported results comparing six diverse samples (German, Portuguese, Hebrew, Chinese, Korean and Japanese) showing substantial similarity in a 'big five' structure with a large American sample. This and other evidence suggests very strongly that the big five structure is a useful general framework although, as McCrae and Costa acknowledge, this may be limited to modern, literate, industrialised cultures like those mentioned above.

At first glance, the emergence of the big five may seem to suggest that perhaps the Eysenck scales focus on a more limited set of factors than is useful whereas Cattell's 16PF uses too many. It is certainly true that several attempts to replicate Cattell's 16 factors have not been very successful (*see*, for example, Kline and Barrett, 1983) and have generally suggested that a smaller number of factors fits the data more efficiently.

The identification of the big five personality factors is a marked development in the trait-factor analytic approach. It is important to realise, though, that the establishment of the big five does not mean that other conceptualisations of personality become redundant. The big five provide a useful view of the minimum factors that must be included in any description of human personality. In many circumstances it may make sense to use a more detailed set of dimensions. Hough (1992), for example, makes an important distinction between the use of personality variables for description and their use for predicting job performance. In other words, while the big five may be a useful framework for describing the minimum dimensions of personality, they may not be as valuable for other purposes, such as predicting job performance. Evidence that Hough (1992) presents shows different patterns of criterion-related validity (*see* the glossary for Chapter 8) for at least nine different personality constructs. The role of personality in personnel selection decision making is discussed further in the next chapter. For the moment it is sufficient to recognise that the big five provide a level of description for personality that is not always the most relevant.

PERSONALITY TESTS

Although several studies have shown that the factors measured by many personality tests can be related to the big five, the tests themselves provide scores on a variety of personality dimensions. For example, as already mentioned, the EPQ assesses three personality factors (extroversion, neuroticism and psychoticism). Table 6.6 gives some information on the better-known personality questionnaires available in the UK.

Table 6.6 Personality questionnaires

Instrument	Personality characteristics measured
Eysenck Personality Questionnaire (EPQ; Eysenck and Eysenck, 1964)	Extroversion, neuroticism (or emotional stability), psychoticism
The Sixteen PF (16PF; Cattell *et al.*, 1970). Several versions of short/long forms are available and measure second-order personality factors etc., in addition to the 16 factors mentioned here	Sixteen personality factors, e.g. submissiveness (mild, humble, easily led, docile, accommodating); self-assurance (placid, serene, secure, complacent); tender-mindedness (sensitive, clinging, over-protected)
The Occupational Personality Questionnaire (OPQ; SHL, 1990)	Thirty personality dimensions are measured in the most detailed version of the OPQ (the concept model). Other versions/models of the questionnaires are available. Illustrative personality dimensions are: • caring (considerate to others, helps those in need, sympathetic, tolerant) • emotional control (restrained in showing emotions, keeps feelings back, avoids outbursts) • forward planning (prepares well in advance, enjoys target-setting, forecasts trends, plans projects)
The revised NEO Personality Inventory (NEO PI-R, Costa and McCrae, 1992)	The big five personality factors, plus facet scores for six subscales within each of the big five domains

As with all kinds of psychological measures, personality tests need to satisfy various well-established psychometric criteria before they can be considered to be acceptable measuring instruments. These criteria are concerned with assessing the extent to which the test measures what it is intended to measure (the issue of validity) and the precision or consistency of measurement that the test achieves (reliability). The British Psychological Society has produced a detailed review of all of the most widely used personality tests in the UK (Bartram, 1995). This review gives a thorough technical evaluation of each test. These concepts are discussed in relation to personnel selection and psychometric testing in Chapter 7.

Work competencies

One helpful and increasingly widely used way of describing the qualities needed by candidates is the identification of the *work competencies* required by effective performers. In this approach, rather than describing the attributes required by candidates with the aid of established psychological frameworks, such as personality dimensions or subcomponents of cognitive ability, a direct description of the competencies needed for the job is attempted.

This approach represents a fusion of the common-sense approach adopted by human resource practitioners in organisations, who have long described candidate requirements in terms of skills, and the work of psychologists (*see* earlier in this chapter), attempting to capture the essence of 'practical intelligence'. Sternberg and Wagner (1986) provide a useful exploration of the distinction between conventional psychological thinking about intelligence and this approach. They argue that 'tacit knowledge' – that is, knowledge that is usually not openly expressed or stated – is of crucial importance in the skilful performance of work tasks. In some interesting studies they show that measures of tacit knowledge provide good predictions of people's performance on real-work tasks. They also show that scores on their tests of tacit knowledge are not strongly correlated with scores on traditional tests of mental ability, suggesting that tacit knowledge is distinct from intelligence, as defined in earlier sections of this chapter. A final important feature of their work is the finding that individual differences in tacit knowledge are general, rather than specific, in nature. In much the same way that Spearman found high intercorrelations between different tests of mental ability and hypothesised a general intelligence, 'g' factor, Sternberg and Wagner, for similar reasons, suggest that tacit knowledge may also be a general, rather than specific, psychological construct.

With these findings and ideas in mind, it is interesting to look at the work that has been conducted by various investigators, studying the competencies required by people in particular jobs, or families of jobs. For example, investigators looking at managerial work have repeatedly found the need for job holders to display similar sorts of competencies, even though the specific jobs were different. Indeed, several researchers have suggested generic sets of competencies applicable to managerial work as a whole. Table 6.7 gives examples of two such competency frameworks, proposed by Dulewicz (1989) and Klemp and McClelland (1986). The similarities between the frameworks

Table 6.7 Competency frameworks

Klemp and McClelland	Dulewicz
The intellectual competencies • Planning/causal thinking • Diagnostic information seeking • Conceptualisation/synthetic thinking	*Intellectual* • Strategic perspective • Analysis and judgement • Planning and organising
The influence competencies • Concern for influence (the need for power) • Directive influence (personalised power) • Collaborative influence (socialised power) • Symbolic influence	*Interpersonal* • Managing staff • Persuasiveness • Assertiveness and decisiveness • Interpersonal sensitivity • Oral communication
Additional competency • Self-confidence	*Adaptability* • Adaptability and resilience *Results orientation* • Energy and initiative • Achievement motivation • Business sense

Source: Klemp and McClelland (1986) and Dulewicz (1989).

themselves are obvious. Looking at this work, it is tempting to propose that such competencies may well be predicted very accurately by scores on traditional cognitive ability tests plus scores on measures of tacit knowledge.

> ■ KEY LEARNING POINT
> *The knowledge, skills and abilities required for jobs may be described in terms of key competencies.*

SUMMARY

Individual differences in personality and cognitive ability have been the subject of much psychological research. Although there are many different theoretical frameworks (*see* Chapter 2), the trait-factor analytic approach is most important in work psychology. Factor-analytic research has uncovered stable, underlying structures for both cognitive ability (a general factor and specific abilities) and personality (five major factors). Measures have been developed for cognitive ability and personality. To be of value in work psychology, such measures need to be both reliable and valid (*see* Chapter 7).

TEST YOUR LEARNING

Short-answer questions

1 Explain the hierarchical organisation of mental abilities favoured by British psychologists.

2 Will a person's scores on tests of different cognitive abilities be likely to be similar? Explain your answer.

3 Outline the role that factor analysis has played in identifying the structure of intelligence.

4 What two major personality factors were identified by Eysenck?

5 What are the 'big five' personality factors?

6 Give an example of a set of work competencies.

Essay questions

1 Critically evaluate the trait-factor analytic approach to cognitive ability.

2 Discuss the extent to which the 'big five' provide a comprehensive picture of human personality.

GLOSSARY OF TERMS

Agreeableness A positive orientation towards others, sympathetic, eager to help – preferring collaboration to conflict.

Anxiety *See* **Neuroticism**.

Cognitive ability Also referred to as intelligence or general mental ability. Refers to the capacity of individuals to process information and use the information to behave effectively (including the capacity to learn from experience).

Competence A term that has become popular recently and is used to describe attributes of individuals (skills, knowledge etc.) that are responsible for effective work performance.

Conscientiousness A predisposition to prefer active control and organisation. A conscientious person will like to be purposeful and well organised and see life in terms of tasks to be accomplished.

Correlation Usually expressed as a correlation coefficient, which can vary from –1 to +1. Positive correlations indicate that as one variable increases, so does the other. A correlation of zero indicates that there is no relationship between the variables.

Emotional instability *See* **Neuroticism**.

Extroversion A personality factor characterised by lively, sociable, excitable and impulsive behaviour.

Factor analysis A statistical technique used to identify key factors that underlie relationships between variables.

General mental ability *See* **Cognitive ability**.

Introversion A personality factor characterised by a lack of enthusiasm for the company of others and a low-key, risk-averse and unexcitable approach to life.

Intelligence *See* **Cognitive ability**.

Neuroticism A predisposition to be tense and anxious. Sometimes referred to as emotional instability, or anxiety.

Openness to experience A tendency to be curious about inner (psychological) and outer worlds with a willingness to entertain novel ideas and unconventional values.

Practical intelligence A view of intelligent behaviour that focuses on real-world activity, rather than controlled behaviour assessed by conventional intelligence testing.

Social cognitive theory A theory which developed from behaviourist origins and sees the behaviourist view as incomplete, rather than wrong. In social cognitive theory internal cognitive processes (e.g. expectancies about what might happen) and external (social/situational) factors play a key role in determining behaviour.

Trait-factor analytic theory An approach to individual differences that uses factor analysis to identify the major structural dimensions (traits) of personality.

SUGGESTED FURTHER READING

1 Paul Kline's book (Routledge, 1993) *Personality: The psychometric view* gives a very clear and succinct view of the trait factor-analytic approach.

2 In their book, *Modern Psychometrics: The science of psychological measurement* (Routledge, 1989), John Rust and Susan Golombok give in-depth coverage of all of the issues raised in this chapter concerned with intelligence and intelligence testing – including a very readable account of factor analysis.

REFERENCES

Bandura, A. (1977) *Social Learning Theory*. Englewood Cliffs, NJ: Prentice Hall.

Bandura, A. (1986) *Social Foundations of Thought and Action: A social cognitive theory*. Englewood Cliffs, NJ: Prentice Hall.

Bartram, D. (ed.) (1995) *Review of Personality Assessment Instruments (Level B) for use in Occupational Settings*. The British Psychological Society: Leicester.

Boring, E.C. (1923) 'Intelligence as the tests test it', New Republic, vol. 35, pp. 35–7.

Boam, R. and Sparrow, P. (1992) *Designing and Achieving Competency*. London: McGraw-Hill.

Boyatzis, R.E. (1982) *The Competent Manager: A model for effective performance*. New York: John Wiley.

Burt, C. (1940) *The Factors of Mind*. London: University of London Press.

Cattell, R.B. (1987) *Intelligence: Its structure, growth and action*. New York: Elsevier Science.

Cattell, R.B., Eber, H.W. and Taksuoka, M.M. (1970) *Handbook for the Sixteen Personality Factor Questionnaire*. Windsor: National Foundation for Educational Research.

Costa, P.T. and McCrae, R.R. (1992) *The NEO PI-R Professional Manual*. Odessa, FL: Psychological Assessment Resources Inc.

Digman, J.M. and Takemoto-Chock, N.K. (1981) 'Factors in the natural language of personality: re-analysis and comparison of six major studies', *Multivariate Behavioral Research*, vol. 16, pp. 149–70.

Dulewicz, V. (1989) 'Assessment centres as the route to competence', *Personnel Management*, November, pp. 56–9.

Eysenck, H.J. (1970) *The Structure of Human Personality*. London: Methuen.

Eysenck, H.J. (1967) *The Biological Basis of Personality*. Springfield, IL.: Charles C. Thomas.

Eysenck, H.J. (1981) 'General features of the model' in Eysenck, H.J. (ed.) *A Model for Personality*. New York: Springer-Verlag.

Eysenck, H.J. and Eysenck, M.J. (1985) *Personality and Individual Differences: A natural science approach*. New York: Plenum Press.

Eysenck, H.J. and Eysenck, S.B.G. (1964) *Manual of the Eysenck Personality Inventory*. London: University of London Press.

Eysenck, H.J. and Eysenck, S.B.G. (1975) *Manual of the Eysenck Personality Questionnaire*. Sevenoaks: Hodder and Stoughton.

Eysenck, H.J. and Eysenck, S.B.G. (1991) *Manual of the Eysenck Personality Scales*. London: Hodder and Stoughton.

Eysenck, H.J. and Kamin, L. (1981) *Intelligence: The battle for the mind*. London: Pan.

Eysenck, H.J. and Wilson, G.D. (1973) *The Experimental Study of Freudian Theories*. London: Methuen.

François, G. Le (1980) *Psychology*. Belmont, CA: Wadsworth.

Guilford, J.P. (1967) *The Nature of Human Intelligence*. New York: McGraw-Hill.

Hough, L.M. (1992) 'The "Big Five" personality variables-construct, confusion: description versus prediction', *Human Performance*, vol. 5, pp. 139–55.

Jensen, A.R. (1992) 'Commentary: Vehicles of g', *Psychological Science*, vol. 3, pp. 275–8.

Klemp, G.O. and McClelland, D.C. (1986) 'What characterizes intelligent functioning among senior managers' in Sternberg, R.J. and Wagner, R.K. (eds) *Practical Intelligence*. Cambridge: Cambridge University Press.

Kline, P. and Barrett, P. (1983) 'The factors in personality questionnaires among normal subjects', *Advances in Behavioral Research and Therapy*, vol. 5, pp. 141–202.

McCrae, R.R. and Costa, P.T. (1990) *Personality in Adulthood*. New York: Guildford.

McCrae, R.R. and Costa, P.T. (1997) 'Personality trait structure as a human universal', *American Psychologist*, vol. 52, pp. 509–16.

Mischel, W. (1968) *Personality Assessment*. New York: John Wiley.

Pervin, L.A. (1980) *Personality: Theory, Assessment and Research*. 3rd edn. New York: John Wiley.

Pervin, L.A. (1989) 'Persons, situations, interactions: the history of a controversy and a discussion of situational models', *Academy of Management Review*, vol. 14, pp. 350–60.

Raven, J., Raven, J.C. and Court, J.H. (1996) *Raven's Progressive Matrices, Professional Manual*. Oxford: Oxford Psychologists Press.

Russell, M.T. and Karol, D.L. (1994) *The UK Edition of the 16PF5: Administrator's Manual*. Windsor: National Foundation for Educational Research.

Satterly, D.J. (1979) 'Covariation of cognitive styles, intelligence and achievement', *British Journal of Educational Psychology*, vol. 49, pp. 179–81.

Schmitt, N. and Noe, R.A. (1986) 'Personnel selection and equal employment opportunity' in Cooper, C.L. and Robertson, I.T. (eds) *Internatonal Review of Industrial and Organizational Psychology*. Chichester: John Wiley.

Scribner, S. (1986) 'Thinking in action: some characteristics of practical thought' in Sternberg, R.J. and Wagner, R.K. (eds) *Practical Intelligence*. Cambridge: Cambridge University Press.

SHL (1990) *Occupational Personality Questionnaire Manual*. Saville and Holdsworth Ltd, Thames Ditton, Surrey, UK.

Smith, P. (1994) *The UK Standardization of the 16PF5: A supplement of norms and technical data*. Windsor: National Foundation for Educational Research.

Spearman, C. (1927) *The Abilities of Man*. London: Macmillan.

Sternberg, R.J. and Wagner, R.K. (eds) (1986) *Practical Intelligence*. Cambridge: Cambridge University Press.

Thurstone, L.L. (1938) *Primary Mental Abilities*, Psychometric Monographs no. 1. Chicago, IL: University of Chicago Press.

Vernon, P.E. (1956) *The Measurement of Abilities*. London: University of London Press.

Vernon, P.E. (1969) *Intelligence and Cultural Environment*. 2nd edn. London: Methuen.

7

Personnel selection: design and validation

After studying this chapter, you should be able to:

1 name and outline four different job analysis procedures;

2 outline the personnel selection design and validation process;

3 define four different types of validity in the context of personnel selection: face validity; content validity; construct validity; and criterion-related validity;

4 distinguish between predictive and concurrent designs for establishing criterion-related validity;

5 state the major sources of error that arise when graphical rating scales are used;

6 give examples of different types of rating scales for job performance;

7 state advantages and disadvantages of different types of rating scales.

INTRODUCTION

As the contents pages of this book show, work psychology has an important contribution to make in many areas of organisational life. Personnel selection and assessment is probably the area where the biggest and most consistent contribution has been made. Personnel selection and assessment is an aspect of work psychology that overlaps with the interests of others, such as human resource professionals (*see* Torrington and Hall, 1991). In fact, the contribution of psychology to this area of activity is distinctive and complements the work of other professional groups. Whereas others may have interests in administrative or managerial issues, such as the collection and storage of information about the competencies of employees, the focus of attention for psychologists has always been the assessment process itself. Research and development work has concentrated on the production and evaluation of technically sound assessment procedures. Given the centrality of psychological measurement to psychological science in general, this is right and proper.

Two main principles underlie the roles that personnel selection and assessment procedures play in organisational settings. The first principle is that there are individual differences between people (e.g. differences in aptitudes, skills and other personal qualities). This simple principle leads to the very important conclusion that people are not equally suited to all jobs, and suggests that procedures for matching people and jobs could have important organisational benefits. The second principle is that future behaviour is, at least partly, predictable. The goal of selection and assessment activities is to match people to jobs and ensure the best possible levels of future job performance; the belief that *future job performance* can be estimated is an important facet of the second principle mentioned above. The essential function of personnel selection and assessment procedures (e.g. interviews, psychometric tests) is to provide means of estimating the likely future job performance of candidates.

Since the early part of this century a great deal of research within work psychology has concentrated on the development and evaluation of personnel selection procedures. Much of this work will be considered in the next chapter. This chapter is not concerned with personnel selection methods as such, but focuses on those aspects of psychological theory and practice that underlie the successful application of personnel selection procedures. The main topics covered in this chapter are related to the two principles given above. First, since personnel selection involves the matching of people to the requirements of jobs, job analysis is covered (individual differences between people were covered in Chapter 6). The second part of the chapter concentrates on topics concerned with the development of procedures for predicting future job performance; specifically, validation processes and the measurement of job performance.

Figure 7.1 provides an outline of the main elements involved in designing a personnel selection procedure. The process begins with a job analysis, followed by the choice of selection instruments. Information on the work performance of job holders is then used to examine the validity of the selection instruments (i.e. whether high and low scores on the selection instruments are associated with good and poor work performance).

A thorough job analysis provides a basis for suggesting that candidates who display particular characteristics are likely to be suitable for the job in question. The analysis may suggest, for example, that certain personality and dispositional characteristics are desirable together with specific previous experience, technical qualifications and levels of intelligence and specific abilities. The next stage in the process is to identify selection

Fig. 7.1 The personnel selection, design and validation process

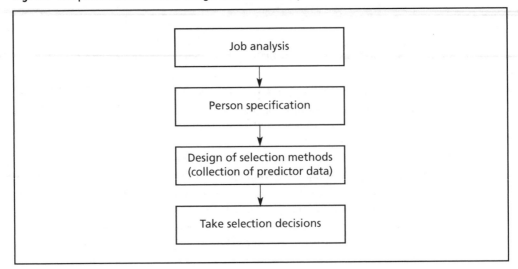

instruments (e.g. intelligence tests, group discussion exercises, interviews, application forms) that can be used to examine whether candidates display the required characteristics or not. These instruments are then used to assess candidates and selection decisions are taken.

> ■ **KEY LEARNING POINT**
> *Personnel selection is one of the most important topic areas in work and organisational psychology.*

JOB ANALYSIS

Job analysis procedures are designed to produce systematic information about jobs, including the nature of the work performed, equipment used, the working conditions and the position of the job within the organisation. It is worth noting that satisfactory job analyses are prerequisites for many decisions and activities that have a crucial influence on the lives of personnel within the organisation, including the design and validation of personnel selection procedures, training and career development schemes, job design or redesign, job evaluation and safety. There is a wide range of techniques and procedures available; Algera and Greuter (1989), Greuter and Algera (1989) and Spector *et al.* (1989) provide overviews and critical examinations of the principal techniques.

Although not always clearcut, there is an important distinction between job-orientated and worker-orientated job analysis procedures. As the term suggests, job-orientated procedures focus on the work itself, producing a description in terms of the equipment used, the end results or purposes of the job, resources and materials utilised, and so on. By contrast, worker-orientated analyses concentrate on describing the psychological or behavioural requirements of the job, such as communicating, decision making, reasoning.

> ■ KEY LEARNING POINT
> *Job analysis procedures are generally either worker-orientated or job-orientated.*

Sources of job analysis data may be divided into four categories: written material, job holders' reports, colleagues' reports and direct observation.

Written material

In many organisations written job descriptions are available (except for newly created jobs) and can provide the analyst with useful information. It is worth checking by observation and other methods that available descriptions are up to date and provide comprehensive information about the job. If so, a great deal of time and effort may be saved. Unfortunately, in many organisations existing job descriptions are rarely up to date, comprehensive or detailed enough. Published analyses of jobs may provide useful leads but are of limited value, since jobs analysed elsewhere are likely to be similar but not identical to the one under consideration. An accountant's, secretary's or production manager's job will vary considerably from one organisation to another, perhaps in ways that are crucial. Other written material such as production data, organisation charts, training manuals, job aids and so on may also provide useful additional information.

Job holders' reports

Interviews in which job holders are asked, through careful questioning, to give a description of their main tasks and how they carry them out provide extremely useful information, and such interviews are usually an essential element in any job analysis. On the other hand, it is difficult to be sure that all of the important aspects of the job have been covered by the interview and that the information provided by the job holder is not too subjective, biased (owing to faulty memory, perhaps) or even deliberately untrue.

Workers' reports may also be obtained by asking them to complete a diary or activity record. Since this is done on a regular basis as the job is being carried out, it avoids problems associated with faulty memory and so forth. It is, however, a difficult and time-consuming procedure. Stewart (1967) has provided an example of the use of this method to analyse the jobs of British managers.

Flanagan (1954) developed a procedure known as the critical incident technique. In brief, using this technique involves asking the interviewee to recall specific incidents of job behaviour that are characteristic of either very good or very poor performance on the job. This can provide the analyst with a clear grasp of the job behaviour(s) that are important and enable him or her to differentiate between good and poor job holders – extremely useful information in the context of personnel selection!

McCormick *et al.* (1972) have produced the *position analysis questionnaire* (PAQ), which is an example of a structured questionnaire approach to job analysis. The elements in the questionnaire are worker-orientated in that they focus on generalised aspects of human behaviour and are less tied to the technology of specific jobs. The PAQ consists of nearly two hundred items organised into six basic divisions:

1 information input

2 mediation processes (i.e. the mental processes of reasoning, decision making etc.)

3 work output

4 interpersonal activities (i.e. relationships with others)

5 work situation and job context

6 miscellaneous aspects.

One problem with the PAQ is that it requires a fairly high level of reading ability on the part of respondents. Nevertheless, the PAQ is an extremely well-researched and valuable means of analysing jobs.

> ■ **KEY LEARNING POINT**
> *The PAQ is a generic job analysis questionnaire which is well researched and can be used to analyse a wide variety of jobs.*

The development work for the PAQ was carried out in the United States by McCormick and others, and the development of British job analysis questionnaires has been a particularly welcome development. Banks and colleagues (Banks *et al.*, 1983; Banks, 1988) have developed the *job components inventory* (JCI). This inventory focuses on both job and worker facets, and the outputs from the analysis include quantified profiles of the absolute and relative skills required for the job under investigation. The JCI was developed within an education and training context and as yet it has not been used extensively with personnel selection.

Another British questionnaire is the Work Profiling System (WPS), developed by Saville and Holdsworth (SHL, 1988) and updated in 1995 for use with a PC. The WPS makes use of a set of some eight hundred items. Depending on the level of job being analysed, a subset of about two hundred items is usually used.

A self-contained technique for analysis, which is job rather than worker orientated, has been described by Fine and Wiley (1974). Known as *functional job analysis* (FJA), this approach makes use of a standardised language to describe what job holders do and provides a means of examining the complexity and the orientation of the job. Orientation here is described as the extent to which the job is directed towards 'data', 'people' or 'things', and, as a result of analysis, can be expressed in percentage terms. The basic unit of analysis in FJA is the task – that is, an action or action sequence organised over time and designed to contribute to a specific end result or objective. Using a very similar definition of the task, Annett and others (Annett *et al.*, 1971; Shepherd, 1976) have developed a means of analysis known as *hierarchical task analysis* (HTA). Since HTA is particularly useful in the development of training, this procedure is discussed in more detail in Chapter 15.

A popular procedure for collecting job analysis information in the UK involves the use of Kelly's (1955) repertory grid technique (e.g. Smith, 1980). This approach provides systematic worker-orientated data. It has an advantage over other means of obtaining worker-orientated data such as PAQ, in that it does not limit the responses of the job holder by providing a prestructured set of categories.

Colleagues' reports

In addition to gleaning information directly from job holders, it can be useful to obtain data from subordinates, peers and superiors. For example, when collecting critical incident data the views of a job holder, a subordinate and a superior on the nature of such critical incidents might provide for interesting comparisons.

For structured job analysis questionnaires, a comparison of the responses of job holders and their supervisors provides a basis for assessing the (convergent) validity of the questionnaire. Although some studies have looked at other instruments (e.g. Banks and Miller, 1984, and the JCI) most of this work has used the PAQ. These studies have revealed reasonably good agreement between job incumbents and supervisors. A more puzzling and troublesome finding, however, has been the reasonably high correlations found between the PAQ results of job experts and naive raters, often students working from job titles or written descriptions of the job (*see*, for example, Freidman and Harvey, 1986). The concern raised by these findings is that even trained analysts' responses on the PAQ are influenced at least partly by commonly held stereotypes (hence the correlation with untrained raters working only from a job title), rather than entirely by valid and substantive job factors.

Direct observation

In any job analysis exercise some direct observation of the job being carried out is invariably helpful. It is, of course, possible that the presence of the analyst may alter the job holder's behaviour, and as with the approaches described earlier the data obtained cannot be perfect. Yet data derived from observation, perhaps even from participant observation, where the analyst does all or some of the job, can provide insights that no other method can.

It is often useful to conduct a job analysis using a variety of methods rather than just one. On this basis, as well as being useful for personnel selection, the resulting information may be helpful in other areas of the organisation, such as training and development or job evaluation. One procedure that explicitly uses more than one method is Levine's (1983) *combination job analysis method* (C-JAM).

> ■ **KEY LEARNING POINT**
> *Job analyses are usually best developed by using as many different approaches and means of data collection as possible and pooling the results.*

USING JOB ANALYSIS INFORMATION

The job analysis is used in a number of ways. A job description can be prepared from the job analysis data. It can be useful in the selection procedure to give candidates some understanding of the job, and can also be used within the organisation to provide information for training, job evaluation and other purposes. The job analysis also provides information that might be used when recruitment advertisements and so forth are prepared to attract candidates for the job.

A personnel specification represents the demands of the job translated into human terms. It involves listing the essential criteria that candidates must satisfy and also those criteria that would exclude candidates from consideration. Moving from a job analysis to a clear specification of the psychological qualities thought to be required by a successful job holder is a difficult process. Various procedures have been suggested and used to make this step but it is important to remember that none of them is entirely objective and that some inferences are required. It is also worth noticing that the inferential steps needed and the nature of these inferences are different, depending on whether one is designing a sign- or sample-based selection procedure. Wernimont and Campbell (1968) made an important distinction between what they described as *signs* and *samples* of behaviour; the distinction is relatively straightforward, though rather important. Consider, for example, how a candidate for a sales position may react to being asked to complete a personality questionnaire, containing questions like 'Do you often wish that your life was more exciting?' Consider also how the same candidate may react to being required to conduct a role-play exercise and expected to persuade a client to make a purchase. The relevance of the role-play exercise and its obvious potential to provide the selection decision makers with a realistic *sample* of the candidate's behaviour is obvious. Although it may not be so obvious to the candidate, the results of the personality test may also provide important *signs* relating to certain job-relevant psychological characteristics. For example, success in sales jobs may be more likely when someone is extroverted, emotionally stable and agreeable (*see* Chapter 6). Job analysis data may be used in two broadly different ways in the design of selection procedures depending on whether the selection procedure will be used to assess samples or signs of behaviour.

Figure 7.2 illustrates these two approaches. The more traditional use of job analysis involves moving from the analysis to make inferences about the kind of psychological

Fig. 7.2 Using job analysis information

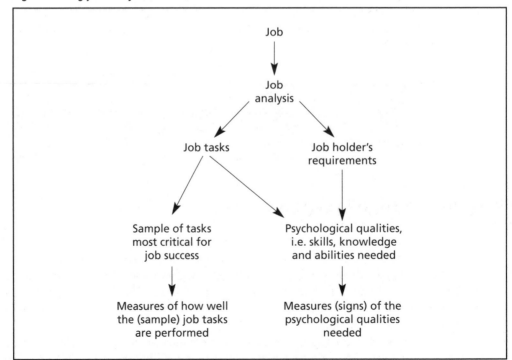

characteristics (signs) needed for successful job performance. By contrast, the sample approach involves focusing on the job tasks and designing selection procedures that provide representative samples of the actual behaviour needed for successful jobs. Alternative approaches are described later in this chapter.

■ **KEY LEARNING POINT**

Job analysis information may be used to design sign- or sample-based personnel selection procedures.

CASE STUDY 7.1

Using job analysis procedures

Royal Tobacco Industries (RTI) had been diversifying for several years to minimise their dependence on tobacco products. One of their most recent acquisitions was The Bridge Engineering Company. Bridge Engineering was a specialist engineering company in the West Midlands of England which specialised in precision engineering for the motor car, light goods vehicle and aeroplane industries. RTI felt that Bridge Engineering had a strong customer base and a highly skilled and experienced workforce. This provided the potential for Bridge to become the market leader in the supply of certain precision parts on a European and eventually worldwide basis. Karl-Heinz Tissen was installed by RTI as managing director. Although the potential of Bridge Engineering was substantial, its current performance was based mainly on a small number of experienced personnel in various key roles throughout the company. Their skill and expertise was crucial to the company's success, but it was also important to recruit highly competent people into the company to fill the roles that would emerge if RTI's plan was successful. Karl-Heinz Tissen's first project on the personnel front was to arrange for a systematic job analysis of the key functions in the existing company structure.

Suggested exercises

Explain why it was so important for Tissen to conduct the job analysis project and consider how he might have used the resulting information.

VALIDATION PROCESSES

The key stage in the personnel selection process occurs when the selection decision is taken and a candidate is either offered a position within the organisation, or turned away. At this point various pieces of evidence concerning the current or past performance of candidates (e.g. behaviour at an interview, psychological test scores or references), usually referred to as predictors, are used to decide whether or not a candidate is suitable for the job in question. Although job analysis may suggest that certain candidate characteristics might be desirable, alone it cannot *prove* that candidates with these characteristics will do better than others on the job. This evaluation of the accuracy of the selection methods is obtained by assessing the criterion-related validity of the predictors.

Criterion-related validity

Criterion-related validity refers to the strength of the relationship between the predictor (e.g. psychological test scores or interview ratings) and the criterion (e.g. subsequent work behaviour indicated by measures such as output figures or supervisor's ratings). Criterion-related validity is high if candidates who obtain high predictor scores obtain high criterion scores *and* candidates who obtain low scores on a predictor also obtain low criterion scores. Figure 7.3 shows a scatterplot of some hypothetical data obtained by using two predictors:

1 a job knowledge test score; and

2 an intelligence test score;

and one criterion:

3 average number of units produced per day.

Inspection of the scatterplot in Fig. 7.3b shows that the criterion-related validity of the intelligence test appears to be quite good. Participants' scores in this test correspond closely with the number of units produced. Although the predictor and criterion scores are obviously closely related it is worth noting that the correspondence is not perfect. For perfect correspondence all of the points would lie exactly on the diagonal line drawn in on Fig. 7.3b. For the job knowledge test there is no correspondence at all and, as Fig. 7.3a clearly shows, the points are distributed more or less in a circle and high scores on one variable can be associated with either high or low scores on the other variable.

The strength of the relationship between predictor scores and criterion scores is usually expressed as a correlation coefficient (referred to as a validity coefficient). Perfect correlation between two variables will produce a correlation of one. No correlation at all, as in Fig. 7.3a, will produce a coefficient of zero (*see also* Chapter 4).

Fig. 7.3 Some hypothetical predictor and criterion scores: (a) job knowledge test; (b) intelligence test

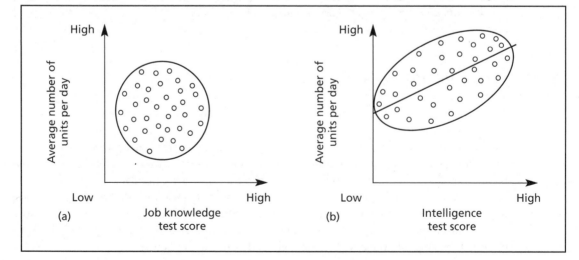

CORRELATION AND PREDICTION

When the correlation between two variables is high it is possible to predict the score of one when supplied with the score on the other. Consider, for example, Fig. 7.4, where the predictor–criterion relationship is perfect (i.e. a validity (correlation) coefficient of +1.0). In the case of a new candidate, it would be possible to obtain his or her score on predictor A and thus predict a score on the criterion. For example, if the organisation wished to select staff who would produce an average of at least 75 units per day, what should be done?

As Fig. 7.4 shows, if only people who obtained a score of above 80 on predictor A were offered jobs by the organisation, all future employees would be likely to produce 75 units (or more) per day. Unfortunately, in practice selection can rarely be conducted in such an idealised and clear-cut fashion and there are several practical problems that must be considered.

Less than perfect predictor–criterion relationships

Research (e.g. Muchinsky, 1986; Smith and George, 1992) has shown that it is most unusual in practical situations to obtain validity coefficients much in excess of +0.5 much less the coefficient of +1.0 that will allow perfect prediction. Nevertheless, validity coefficients of considerably less than +1.0 can provide a basis for improved personnel selection.

Fig. 7.4 Prediction of criterion scores from selection test scores

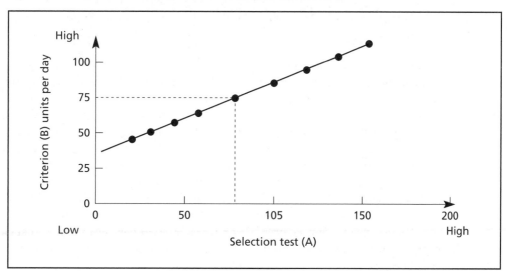

Theoretically the ideal way to collect criterion-related validity data is to use a predictive (or follow-up) design. This design involves collecting predictor information (e.g. interview ratings, test scores) for candidates and then following up the candidates (e.g. during their first year of employment) to gather criterion data on their work performance. One important feature emerging from data collected in this way is that the work performance of people with both high and low predictor scores may be examined. An accurate picture of the true relationship between predictor and criterion scores can be established by allowing candidates with the full range of predictor scores to be given an opportunity to conduct the job.

What this means in practice is that the predictor scores should not be used to take selection decisions until after a validity study has been conducted. In other words, until the relationship between predictor and criterion is firmly established, candidates should be offered employment regardless of their performance on the predictors. Often this is a difficult step for an organisation to take. If job analysis and other information (in the absence of validity data) suggest that the use of certain predictors should improve their selection decisions, many organisations would not be happy to allow candidates with low scores on these predictors to enter employment. Sometimes it is possible to convince an organisation not to use the results of potential predictors and to continue to use their existing methods while a validation study is carried out. Often, however, organisations cannot accept the constraints of a complete predictive validity (follow-up) design and some compromise is needed.

Another practical problem with the predictive validity design is that of ensuring that the predictor results obtained by new employees are not revealed to other members of the organisation before a validity study has been conducted. Obviously a supervisor who is given a new employee with either a high or low predictor score could be affected by these results. The supervisor's behaviour towards the new employee might be influenced and/or estimates of the new employee's work performance could be biased.

> ■ **KEY LEARNING POINT**
> *Predictive validity designs are the most rigorous but their implementation usually presents a number of practical problems.*

An alternative design for conducting criterion-related validity studies is the concurrent design. In the concurrent design, predictor data are obtained from existing employees on whom criterion data are already available. One advantage of the concurrent design is that the organisation is not required to collect predictor data from candidates (for employment) without making use of the data for selection decisions. Predictor data are collected from existing employees only. A second advantage of the concurrent design is that there is no time delay between the collection of predictor and criterion data. Existing employees' predictor scores are correlated with their criterion performance. The criterion data are likely to be available already, or at least can be collected quickly. There is certainly no need to wait for the lengthy follow-up period involved with the predictive design. Figure 7.5 compares the two designs in a hypothetical situation and indicates the considerable differences in time scales and data collection effort that can occur.

Fig. 7.5 A comparison of predictive and concurrent designs

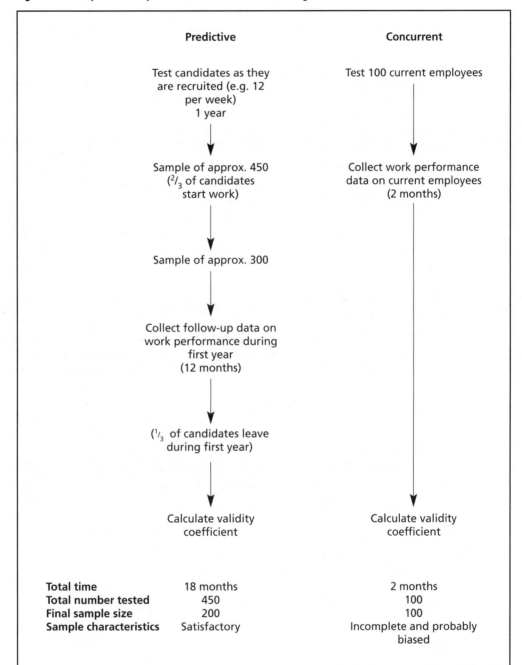

Because of these advantages the concurrent design is attractive to many organisations. However, there are disadvantages. The workers presently employed by an organisation provide a population that may be very different from the population of job applicants. Current job holders have already survived existing company selection procedures and represent a preselected group of people who have been with the organisation for some time. No data are available on people who were not hired by the company, nor on those who were hired but have subsequently left it. Thus the concurrent sample is incomplete and not representative of the potential workforce. If, as a result of a concurrent validity study, a link between, say, scores in an arithmetic test and job performance is established, it is difficult to be sure if the people tested come to the job with such skills or whether arithmetic skills are acquired as a result of training and job experience. Such problems make it hard to be certain about the actual predictive value of results derived from a concurrent validity study.

One important point to make about any validity study, regardless of whether predictive or concurrent procedures are used, concerns the fact that the initial validity study should always be followed by a 'cross-validation' study on a second sample of people to cross-check the results obtained. For studies that involve relatively few predictors this requirement is perhaps not essential and represents a 'counsel of perfection'. However, when a study has investigated many possible predictors and those with the strongest predictor–criterion relationship are to be used for selection purposes, cross-validation is more important. The more potential predictors are used, the more likely it becomes that random or chance variations will produce apparent relationships between some of these predictors and the criterion measure(s). Relationships due to chance would be unlikely to occur again in the cross-validation sample – only 'real' relationships would produce the same results in both samples.

> ■ KEY LEARNING POINT
> *Cross-validation is necessary to be confident of the results from a validation study, unless the sample is very large.*

OTHER TYPES OF VALIDITY

Criterion-related validity is the most important type of validity as far as selection is concerned, but there are other important types of validity as well.

Face validity

A selection test or procedure displays face validity if it 'looks right'. For example, requiring an applicant for a carpenter's job to make a 'T-joint' from two pieces of wood would show face validity. On the other hand asking the applicant to carry out a test of general intelligence would probably have much less face validity for the candidate, since the link between that test and job performance would probably be less obvious to the candidate.

Content validity

Like face validity, content validity is established on a logical basis rather than by calculating validity coefficients or following other technical statistical procedures. A predictor shows content validity when it covers a representative sample of the behaviour domain being measured. For example, a content valid test of car-driving ability would be expected to cover all of the essential activities that a competent driver should be able to carry out. A test that did not include an emergency stop and a reversing exercise would be lacking in content validity.

Construct validity

This involves identifying the psychological characteristics (or constructs) such as intelligence, emotional stability or manual dexterity which underlie successful performance on the task (such as a test or performance on the job) in question. Since construct validity involves relationships between predictors and characteristics that are not directly observable, it can be assessed only by indirect means. Often this is done by correlating a well-established measure of a construct with a new measure. A poor relationship would suggest that the new measure may lack construct validity. Exploring the construct validity of any psychological instrument is an important facet of understanding what the instrument actually measures. As material in Chapter 8 shows, the construct validity of several frequently used personnel selection methods is not well understood.

TASK *Think about some of the jobs that you have done and how you were selected. Did the selection procedure seem to display face validity and content validity? What were the main competencies needed in the job?*

RELIABILITY

Validity, in its various forms, deals with the extent to which a test or other measuring techniques measures what it sets out to measure. Another extremely important characteristic of any measurement technique is reliability. Reliability refers to the consistency with which a test (or other technique) provides results. In essence a predictor (or criterion) is reliable if it produces consistent conclusions. Equally, if the same candidate produces very different scores when he or she takes a test on two different occasions, the reliability of the test must be questioned. Any measuring instrument (whether predictor or criterion) used in a selection procedure must be both valid and reliable. In technical (psychometric) terms reliability refers to the extent to which a measuring instrument is free from random variation. Various well-established procedures and formulae are available for assessing the reliability of a measure and further details may be found in a more advanced text (e.g. Anastasi, 1988; Smith and Robertson, 1993).

> ■ KEY LEARNING POINT
> *To be effective personnel selection methods must be both valid and reliable.*

Personality and job performance

Paul Wessenberg had been managing director of Linguafrank, a company producing language training material, since he began the company ten years ago. Browsing through a trade magazine Karl noticed and was impressed by an advert for JIC Associates. JIC Associates was a small but dynamic human resources company which specialised in the assessment of senior personnel in organisations. At this time Karl had a difficult decision to make concerning the selection of a new editor for Linguafrank's highly successful but now rather out-of-date series of *Travellers Aid* audio-cassette tapes. The previous editor was about to move on to a job with a TV company.

The JIC consultant who visited Karl in his office showed him some very attractively produced psychological testing material. After a brief discussion of the kind of person needed to fill the editor's role and an extremely impressive demonstration of the computer-produced reports by the JIC testing system, Karl was very enthusiastic about enlisting JIC's help to solve his selection problem. In due course JIC prepared advertisements, tested a small group of the large number of applicants and made a recommendation to Karl on the two best candidates. Karl chose Charles Smith as his new editor.

Charles was a disaster almost from the first day. Although he was clearly highly intelligent, his personality and attitudes were completely unsuited to Linguafrank. Charles Smith's outgoing, rather laid-back, style was seen as much too casual by the Linguafrank personnel. He found that the job was not what he expected in a variety of ways and was desperately unhappy in the job.

Suggested exercises

1 *Consider what went wrong and why.*

2 *Prepare some briefing notes explaining what Paul Wessenberg should have done and the kinds of questions he should have asked in his initial contacts with JIC.*

MEASURING WORK PERFORMANCE

The discussion of the processes of personnel selection has shown how satisfactory selection decisions are based on strong relationships between predictors and criteria. The only specific criterion measure mentioned has been 'average output per day'. The average output per day produced by an employee is clearly an important measure of success, but what about other factors such as absenteeism? An average output figure that did not take absences into account would all too easily give a false impression of an employee's value to the organisation. What about less clear-cut factors such as his or her attitude to co-workers, willingness to do overtime, and potential for promotion to a supervisory position? The point being made is that the identification of employees who will produce high daily outputs (or other single factor) may not be the sole requirement of an organisation's selection system.

Thus, in any organisation, there is a wide range of criteria that could be used to assess an employee's value to the company. Some possible measures are:

- production records (including quality and quantity of output, wastage, attainment of targets)

- absenteeism, lateness, disciplinary record
- ratings made by managers, supervisors, co-workers, subordinates.

The use of ratings and other methods to provide information on an employee's job performance is an established procedure within most organisations. Performance appraisal information is used for a variety of purposes, including promotion, salary, career development, counselling and training, as well as in the validation of personnel selection procedures. Of the available methods of obtaining appraisal data, rating scales are by far the most widely used (*see* Landy and Rastegary, 1989). More recently the use of 360° appraisal systems has been increasing (Edwards and Ewen, 1996). In a 360° appraisal system each person is appraised by several others, usually including peers, boss and subordinates. The appraisal is intended to discover the full range of different points of view on the appraisee – hence the term '360°'.

Rating scales

As Fig. 7.6 shows, a variety of different graphical rating scales can be used to elicit performance appraisal data. Such scales vary in the extent to which they provide a satisfactory basis for performance appraisal. Like many forms of psychological measurement, the key issues revolve around the problems of reliability and validity. Such scales should provide a clear indication of the meaning that can be assigned to each point on the scale (validity) so that both the rater and anyone else who needs to interpret the rating on the scale can make a valid inference. Clearly with a scale such as Fig. 7.6a clear and unambiguous interpretation is impossible, since the scale provides so little information. It is also important that the scale can be used consistently, either by different raters or by the same rater on different occasions. Again a scale such as Fig. 7.6a presents problems, since so much subjective judgement is needed that the judgements may well change from rater to rater or from trial to trial. Although a scale such as Fig. 7.6c probably provides a better basis for validity and reliability, such graphical rating scales still contain many possible sources of error.

Leniency

This relates to a characteristic of the person doing the rating. Some people appear to be 'easy' raters and tend to provide a greater proportion of high scores (positive leniency). At the other extreme are the harsh or severe raters (negative leniency). Leniency can often be observed when the results of two or more judges are compared.

Halo

The halo error involves a tendency to let our assessment of an individual on one trait influence our evaluation of that person on other specific traits. In other words, if we believe that someone is outstandingly good in one important area of performance, we might rate them high in all areas, regardless of their true performance.

Central tendency error

Many raters are very reluctant to provide ratings at the extremes of the scale that they are using and may tend to produce ratings that group around the mid-point of the scale. This may not necessarily be because the 'true' distribution of ratings should be like this, but because the rater is inhibited about assigning very high or low ratings.

Fig. 7.6 Graphical performance rating scales of various kinds

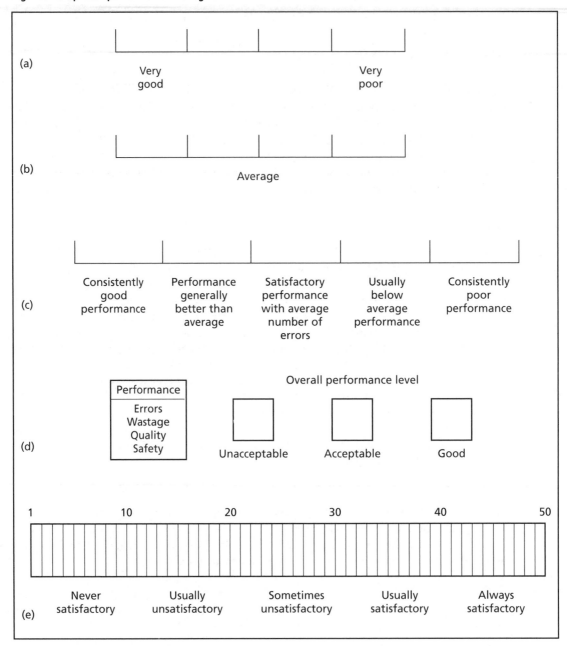

One straightforward way of helping to minimise the error in any type of rating scale is to use multiple questions (items) for each of the qualities being rated. Any individual item is open to some degree of misinterpretation by the rater. A set of items, all of which are relevant to the construct being rated, will help to reduce overall error. This is because the misinterpretations and errors related to each item will probably be random in their effect and will therefore balance each other out. A score based on the average of all items will almost certainly be more reliable than a score derived from a single item (*see* Fig. 7.7).

■ KEY LEARNING POINT

Multiple items help to improve the reliability of rating scales.

Fig. 7.7 Multiple item, BARS and BOS rating scales

Multiple item

		Strongly agree					Strongly disagree	
1	The lecturer speaks clearly	1	2	3	4	5	6	7
2	Overhead projector slides are visible and contain a small number of relevant points	1	2	3	4	5	6	7
3	etc.							

Single item

		Strongly agree					Strongly disagree	
1	The lecturer presents material well.	1	2	3	4	5	6	7

Behaviourally anchored rating scale (BARS)

Presentation

```
                          9
                          8   ←   Could be expected to speak audibly, without
                          7       hesitation and respond to student reaction
                          6
                          5   ←   Could be expected to use overheads in correct
                          4       order and give summary at end of lecture
Could fail to define some →  3
(non-central) concepts       2   ←   Could fail to be audible on several occasions
                          1
```

Behaviour observation scale (BOS)

Prepares overhead projector slides
and key points in advance of lecture

1	2	3	4	5
Never	Seldom	Sometimes	Generally	Always

Another very useful method of increasing the accuracy of ratings is to use more than one rater. In many ways the same principles as in the use of multiple items are relevant here. Errors and bias will be likely to balance out and the resulting average ratings will be more accurate. It is also important that the raters are sufficiently expert and well trained to give accurate ratings. Several studies have shown that combined expert ratings give very accurate scores (e.g. Smither *et al.*, 1989).

Behaviourally anchored scales

One problem with many unsatisfactory rating scales is that the 'anchors' which define the points on the scale are such broad, generalised descriptions – such as 'average', 'good' or 'excellent' – that it is impossible to be sure that the terms are interpreted in the same way by everyone who uses the scales. One promising means of providing unambiguous anchor points on a scale is to use *behaviourally anchored rating scales* (BARS). BARS use anchors that describe specific behaviour which is critical in determining levels of job performance (Smith and Kendall, 1963). BARS are developed using a four-step procedure:

1 with the aid of a group of 'experts' (employees/supervisors/managers) define the factors needed for successful job performance;

2 use a second group of 'experts' to provide examples of specific behaviour associated with high, average or low performance on the factors;

3 a third group takes the examples from step 2 and independently matches them with the factors from step 1. This 'retranslation' acts as a cross-check on the two previous steps. Examples that are not assigned correctly to the aspect for which they were written do not provide unambiguous behavioural anchors for that aspect of job performance and should not be used;

4 the final step involves using more 'experts' to assign scale values to the surviving items, which then serve as the behavioural anchors for the scale.

The research evidence concerning BARS suggests that they produce results which are slightly better than well-constructed graphic rating scales. These results lead some people to question whether the effort involved is worth the trouble. Two points are worth bearing in mind here. First, a well-constructed graphic scale may require an amount of effort equal to that involved in constructing a BARS. Second, if the correct procedure is followed, a BARS is highly likely to be worth while and have good psychometric properties. Other more recent scale development procedures include *behaviour observation scales* (BOS) (e.g. Weirsma and Latham, 1986). BOS development procedures will also ensure the development of reasonably sound scales. In essence BOS, like BARS, are based on critical examples of behaviour. With BOS the rater assesses the ratee in terms of the frequency of occurrence of the relevant behaviour (*see* Fig. 7.7).

> ■ **KEY LEARNING POINT**
> *When designed according to the correct procedure, BARS and BOS are likely to produce psychometrically sound results.*

Some research has shown that, when used for appraisal (which is rather different from using a rating scale to provide criterion data in a validation study), there is a preference among users for BOS. BOS are seen as better for providing feedback, determining training needs, setting goals and overall ease of use (*see* Latham *et al.*, 1993).

Somewhat disappointingly, however, no procedures have been able to produce scales immune to rating errors. Research concerning the appropriateness and benefits of different procedures has been reviewed by Latham and Fry (1986).

Other criteria

Although rating scales have always been the dominant criteria within personnel selection validity studies, a variety of other criteria can and should be used. The relevance and quality of criteria that can be predicted by any personnel selection method are of overriding importance. Logical evaluation of any method makes it obvious that it is only as useful as the criteria that it can predict. For example, a method that predicts supervisors' ratings of job performance quite well may not predict job tenure at all. Thus an organisation wishing to select future employees who will stay with them for a long time (e.g. because training is long and costly) would get little benefit from such a selection procedure. Alternative criteria, used in personnel selection research include: absenteeism, turnover/tenure, accidents/safe working behaviour, promotion, salary/grade progression, job performance tests. As Chapter 8 will explain, selection procedures need to be designed with specific work criteria in mind. In essence, any selection method is only as good as the criteria it can predict. A selection method which was designed to identify high performers may not predict candidates' absenteeism rates very accurately.

MULTIPLE VERSUS SINGLE CRITERIA

When utilising data on someone's performance within an organisation one important issue to consider is whether to use a single overall measure or multiple criteria (i.e. many measures of job success). In a much-quoted and important article, Dunnette (1963, pp. 251–2) made the following points:

> Over the years our concept of the criterion has suggested the evidence of some single all encompassing measure of job success against which other measures (predictors) might be compared ... Much selection and validation research has gone astray because of an overzealous worshipping of the criterion ... Thus, I say: junk the criterion! Let us cease searching for single or composite measures of job success and proceed to undertake research which accepts the world of success dimensionality as it really exists.

This issue still arouses controversy and not all personnel psychologists share Dunnette's desire always to use multiple criteria.

It is important to point out that the use of a single criterion does not necessarily mean utilising only one measure of success; normally it involves combining the data from several measures to form a composite single criterion. By and large, in the specific context of personnel selection, most psychologists would agree with Dunnette that it is more efficient to use multiple criteria rather than a single composite. One predictor, for instance, may predict the ability of a manager to influence colleagues and subordinates, while another might predict his or her technical problem-solving skills. The use of a single composite criterion would not allow such detailed (and surely useful) validity data to be obtained. Despite the desirability of multiple criteria, practical considerations, including the difficulties involved in communicating with non-specialists, usually mean that only a small number of criteria are used in any validation study. For other purposes, such as job evaluation or the development of incentive payment systems, composite criteria may be more or less essential.

SUMMARY

The basis of personnel selection is that there are job-relevant, individual differences between people, which can be assessed. Assessment in organisational settings is a common activity which can have a useful impact on individual and organisational success and well-being. Job analysis provides the basis for many human resource activities in organisations and it is particularly important in personnel selection. A range of structured approaches to job analysis is available, though the most thorough and reliable information may be obtained using structured questionnaires. Job analysis information may be used to develop (sign- or sample-based) selection procedures. Since the reliability and validity of such procedures determines the quality of personnel entering the organisation it is crucial that selection procedures provide valid assessments of future work behaviour. Several different (e.g. predictive or concurrent) validation processes are available for assessing validity. When properly designed, rating scales can provide good, though not perfect, indications of people's performance at work.

TEST YOUR LEARNING

Short-answer questions

1 Name the six main divisions in the position analysis questionnaire (PAQ) produced by McCormick *et al.* (1972).

2 For what purposes can a job analysis be used?

3 Draw a diagram of the personnel selection design and validation system.

4 What is a 'predictive (or follow-up) design' when used to collect criterion-related validity data?

5 What is the difference between content and construct validity?

6 Explain how 'sign' and 'sample' approaches to personnel selection differ.

7 Outline the procedure for the construction of behaviourally anchored rating scales (BARS).

8 What are the advantages of using multiple criteria for assessing employees' performance?

Essay questions

1 Discuss the importance of job analysis in personnel selection.

2 Evaluate the role of validity and reliability in the measurement of individual differences.

GLOSSARY OF TERMS

Behaviourally anchored rating scales (BARS) Rating scales that use anchors that describe specific behaviour. The behaviours provide anchors for a spread (good–poor) of performance standards and are derived from a systematic development procedure.

Concurrent validity A form of criterion-related validity in which data on the predictor and criterion are obtained at the same time.

Construct validity An indication of the extent to which the test or procedure measures the psychological construct that it is intended to measure.

Content validity A form of validity based on a logical analysis of the extent to which a test or procedure embodies a representative sample of the behaviour from the domain being measured.

Correlation Usually expressed as a correlation coefficient which can vary from –1 to +1. Positive correlations indicate that as one variable increases, so does the other. A correlation of zero indicates that there is no relationship between the variables.

Criterion-related validity The extent to which a predictor (e.g. a selection test score) is related to a criterion (e.g. work performance). In personnel selection, high criterion-related validity indicates that a selection measure gives an accurate indication of candidates' performance on the criterion.

Critical incident technique A technique developed by Flanagan (1954), still widely used, to obtain information about jobs by concentrating on specific examples (incidents) of outstandingly good or poor performance.

Face validity A very weak form of validity based on the extent to which a test or procedure appears to measure a particular construct.

Functional job analysis An approach to job analysis which uses a standardised language and concentrates on the tasks (rather than skills) required for the job.

Job analysis Procedures (there is more than one way to do a job analysis) for producing systematic information about jobs, including the nature of the work performed, position in the organisation, relationships of the job holder with other people.

Job components inventory (JCI) A job analysis technique developed in the UK (Banks *et al.*, 1983) which can provide profiles of the skills required for the job in question.

Personnel specification A representation of the demands of a job translated into human terms (i.e. a statement of the attributes needed for successful job performance).

Position analysis questionnaire (PAQ) A questionnaire-based procedure for job analysis which produces information about the major job elements involved, broken down into six divisions.

Predictive validity A form of criterion-related validity in which data on the criterion are obtained after data on the predictor.

Reliability An indicator of the consistency which a test or procedure provides. It is possible to quantify reliability to indicate the extent to which a measure is free from error.

Validity A general term indicating the extent to which a test or procedure measures what it is intended to measure.

SUGGESTED FURTHER READING

1 For more depth on the issues raised in this chapter, consult a comprehensive text on personnel selection, such as *Systematic Personnel Selection* by Mike Smith and Ivan Robertson (full reference in the list below).

2 A very detailed treatment of validity and reliability is given in Anastasi's book, *Psychological Testing* (full reference in the list overleaf).

REFERENCES

Algera, J. and Greuter, M. (1989) 'Job analysis for personnel selection' in Smith, M and Robertson, I.T. (eds) *Advances in Selection and Assessment*. Chichester: John Wiley.

Anastasi, A. (1988) *Psychological Testing*. New York: Macmillan.

Annett, J., Duncan, K.D., Stammers, R.B. and Gray, M.J. (1971) 'Task analysis', Training Information Paper no. 6. London: HMSO.

Banks, M.H. (1988) 'Job components inventory' in Gael, S. (ed.) *Job Analysis Handbook*. New York: John Wiley.

Banks, M.H. and Miller, R.L. (1984) 'Reliability and convergent validity of the job components inventory', *Journal of Occupational Psychology*, vol. 57, pp. 181–4.

Banks, M.H., Jackson, P.R., Stafford, E.M. and Warr, P.B. (1983) 'The job components inventory and the analysis of jobs requiring limited skill', *Personnel Psychology*, vol. 36, pp. 57–66.

Dunnette, M.D. (1963) 'A note on the criterion', *Journal of Applied Psychology*, vol. 47, pp. 251–4.

Edwards, M.R. and Ewen, A.J. (1996) *360° feedback*. AMACOM: New York.

Fine, S.A. and Wiley, W.W. (1974) 'An introduction to functional job analysis' in Fleishman, E.A. and Bass, A.R. (eds) *Studies in Personal and Industrial Psychology*. Homewood, IL: Dorsey Press.

Flanagan, J.C. (1954) 'The critical incident technique', *Psychological Bulletin*, vol. 51, pp. 327–58.

Freidman, L. and Harvey, R.J. (1986) 'Can raters with reduced job descriptive information provide accurate position analysis questionnaire (PAQ) ratings?', *Personnel Psychology*, vol. 39, pp. 779–89.

Greuter, M. and Algera, J. (1989) 'Criterion development and job analysis' in Herriot, P. (ed.) *Assessment and Selection in Organizations*. Chichester: John Wiley.

Kelly, G.A. (1955) *The Psychology of Personal Constructs*. New York: Norton.

Landy, F.J. and Rastegary, H. (1989) 'Criteria for selection' in Smith, M. and Robertson, I.T. (eds) *Advances in Selection and Assessment*. Chichester: John Wiley.

Latham, G.P. and Fry, L.W. (1986) 'Measuring and appraising employee performance' in Gael, S. (ed.) *Analysis Handbook*. New York: John Wiley.

Latham, G.P., Skarlicki, D., Irvine, D. and Siegal, J.P. (1993) 'The increasing importance of performance appraisals to employee effectiveness in organizational settings in North America' in Cooper, C.L. and Robertson, I.T. (eds) *International Review of Industrial and Organizational Psychology*, vol. 8. Chichester: John Wiley.

Levine, E.L. (1983) *Everything you Always Wanted to Know about Job Analysis*. Tampa, FL: Mariner Publishing.

McCormick, E.J., Jeanneret, P. and Meacham, R.C. (1972) 'A study of job characteristics and job dimensions as based on the position analysis questionnaires', *Journal of Applied Psychology*, vol. 36, pp. 347–68.

Muchinsky, P.M. (1986) 'Personnel selection methods' in Cooper, C.L. and Robertson, I.T. (eds) *International Review of Industrial and Organizational Psychology*. Chichester: John Wiley.

SHL (1988) *The Work Profiling System*. Saville and Holdsworth Ltd, Thames Ditton, UK.

Shepherd, A. (1976) 'An improved tabular format for task analysis', *Journal of Occupational Psychology*, vol. 47, pp. 93–104.

Smith, M. (1980) 'An analysis of three managerial jobs using repertory grids', *Journal of Management Studies*, vol. 17, pp. 205–13.

Smith, M. and George, D. (1992) 'Selection methods' in Cooper, C.L. and Robertson, I.T. (eds) *International Review of Industrial and Organizational Psychology*, vol. 7. Chichester: John Wiley.

Smith, M. and Robertson, I.T. (1993) *Systematic Personnel Selection*. London: Macmillan.

Smith, P.C. and Kendall, L.M. (1963) 'Retranslation of expectations: an approach to the construction of unambiguous anchors for rating scales', *Journal of Applied Psychology*, vol. 47, pp. 149–55.

Smither, J.W., Barry, S.R. and Reilly, R.R. (1989) 'An investigation of the validity of expert true score estimates in appraisal research', *Journal of Applied Psychology*, vol. 74, pp. 143–51.

Spector, P.E., Brannick, M.T. and Coovert, M.D. (1989) 'Job analysis' in Cooper, C.L. and Robertson, I.T. (eds) *International Review of Industrial and Organizational Psychology*. Chichester: John Wiley.

Stewart, R. (1967). *Managers and their Jobs*. London: Macmillan.

Torrington, D.P. and Hall, L.A. (1991) *Personnel Management: A new approach*. London: Simon & Schuster.

Wernimont, P.F. and Campbell, J.P. (1968) 'Signs, samples and criteria', *Journal of Applied Psychology*, vol. 52, pp. 372–6.

Wiersma, U. and Latham, G.P. (1986) 'The practicality of behavioural expectation scales and trait scales', *Personnel Psychology*, vol. 39, pp. 619–28.

Personnel selection and assessment processes: validity and utility

LEARNING OBJECTIVES

After studying this chapter, you should be able to:

1 list seven personnel selection methods and describe three in more detail;

2 state five major evaluative standards for personnel selection procedures;

3 name the chief sources of distortion in validation studies;

4 describe the technique of meta-analysis and explain its contribution to personnel selection research;

5 specify advantages and disadvantages of several selection methods, including: interviews; psychometric tests; work-sample tests and assessment centres;

6 explain how some selection techniques could lead to bias and unfairness to some subgroups;

7 describe the role that validity, selection ratio and other factors play in determining financial utility;

8 explain the terms used in the financial utility equation.

INTRODUCTION

Although a large variety of personnel selection procedures have been developed and used in organisational settings, the relevant research shows rather clearly that not all of the methods are equally useful. This chapter examines the main personnel selection procedures that are available for use. As well as understanding the methods available for personnel selection and assessment procedures it is also useful to have a clear grasp of the research evidence concerning each method. After examining the evidence concerning the validity of each of the main methods, this chapter also explores the extent to which the various methods are used and shows how the costs and benefits derived from selection procedures may be expressed in financial terms.

Table 8.1 Personnel selection methods

1 Interviews
Many involve more than one interviewer. When several interviewers are involved, the term *panel interview* is used. The most important features of an interview are the extent to which a preplanned structure is followed and the proportion of questions that are directly related to the job.

2 Psychometric tests
This category includes tests of cognitive ability (such as general intelligence, verbal ability, numerical ability) and self-report measures of personality.

3 References
Usually obtained from current or previous employers, often in the final stages of the selection process. The information requested may be specific or general and open-ended.

4 Biodata
Specifications of biographical information about a candidate's life history. Some biodata inventories may contain many (e.g. 150+) questions and ask objective questions, such as professional qualifications held, and more subjective ones, such as preferences for different job features.

5 Work-sample tests
Such tests literally use samples of the job in question (e.g. the contents of an in-tray for an executive position or specific kinds of typing for a secretarial post). The applicant is given instructions and then a specific amount of time to complete the tasks.

6 Handwriting analysis
Inferences are made about candidates' characteristics by examining specific features of their handwriting (e.g. slant, letter shapes). Obviously, a reasonably lengthy sample of the candidate's normal writing is required.

7 Assessment centres
This procedure involves a combination of several of the previously mentioned techniques (e.g. psychometric tests, interviews, work samples). Candidates are usually dealt with in groups and some of the techniques used require the candidates to interact (e.g. simulated group decision-making exercises).

PERSONNEL SELECTION METHODS

Table 8.1 shows the major personnel selection methods that are available for use and also gives a brief explanation of what the methods involve. Most of the methods are well known; many readers will have first-hand experience of some of them and detailed explanations of what is involved are superfluous. One or two methods do, however, require a little explanation. Brief explanations are therefore given below for work-sample tests, biodata and assessment centres.

Work-sample tests, as their name suggests, require candidates to conduct a sample of the kind of work that is involved in the job for which they are being considered. The most widely used work-sample test is the typing test; that is, a test given to applicants for jobs that require typing skills. A well-known work-sample test used for executive positions is the in-tray or in-basket test. This requires candidates to work through the contents of a typical in-tray (containing memos, notes, letters, production data, sales information etc.) and decide what action they will take.

When using predictors such as interviews, psychological tests or work-sample tests, the specific areas to be investigated in the interview or the particular tests to be used are normally derived from job analysis data (*see* Chapter 7). The information from the job analysis provides a basis for deciding which factors (e.g. numerical ability, good personal relationships) might be important for job success. Biographical data are often developed in a different way. When candidates apply for a job with an organisation it is likely that they will complete an application form and other documents in which they are expected to provide certain biographical information concerning factors such as age, previous employment, personal history and education. The basic procedure for using biographical data is to collect information on a number of candidates and correlate it with subsequent performance. Items of information that predict subsequent performance can then be identified. Items of information chosen on this basis do not necessarily have any obvious link with the job; it has merely been demonstrated, on a statistical basis, that they predict future performance.

In most practical situations it is not sensible to base selection decisions on the use of one predictor only (such as the results of one test) or even on one type of predictor. When several different predictors are used together the basic aim should be to ensure that the various predictors complement rather than duplicate each other. One successful method of selection that makes use of many different predictors is the 'assessment centre' approach. Assessment centres make use of many different predictors, including interviews, psychological tests, in-basket exercises and group discussions. They extend for a period of, say, two to three days, although they may be as short as a day or as long as a week. Candidates are usually assessed by trained assessors, who are often senior managers in the organisation. A typical assessment centre would involve groups of six candidates being assessed by three to six assessors. Assessment centres are used frequently to evaluate people who already work within an organisation. The information gained from the assessment centre is then used to help take decisions concerning promotion and career development in general.

■ **KEY LEARNING POINT**

In most situations it is best to use a combination of several personnel selection techniques.

HOW WELL DO SELECTION METHODS WORK?

Before it is feasible to consider how well selection methods work it is necessary to be clear about what it means for a selection method to work. The previous chapter introduced the concept of criterion-related validity and demonstrated how this could be evaluated by means of validation procedures. Obviously, criterion-related validity is an essential requirement for a selection method but other features are also important. Table 8.2 lists a number of other features of personnel selection methods that are also important. A comprehensive evaluation of any selection method would require a thorough examination of the method in relation to each of the features given in Table 8.2. In the interests of clarity and simplicity, the evaluation of selection methods that follows is concentrated almost exclusively on criterion-related validity.

Table 8.2 Major evaluative standards for personnel selection procedures

1 Discrimination The measurement procedures involved should provide for clear discrimination between candidates. If candidates all obtain similar assessments (i.e. scores, if a numerical system is used), selection decisions cannot be made.
2 Validity and reliability The technical qualities of the measurement procedures must be adequate.
3 Fairness/adverse impact The measures must not discriminate unfairly against members of any specific subgroup of the population (e.g. ethnic minorities).
4 Administrative convenience The procedures should be acceptable within the organisation and capable of being implemented effectively within the organisation's administrative structure.
5 Cost and development time Given the selection decisions (e.g. number of jobs, number of candidates, type of jobs) involved, the costs involved and the time taken to develop adequate procedures need to be balanced with the potential benefits. This is essentially a question of utility.

> ■ **KEY LEARNING POINT**
>
> *One of the key evaluative standards for personnel selection methods is criterion-related validity.*

Estimating the validity of personnel selection procedures

As the previous chapter explained, predictive or concurrent validation processes may be used to estimate the criterion-related validity of a selection procedure. Most of the selection procedures mentioned so far in this chapter have been examined in this way and investigators have conducted validation studies on many selection procedures in many industries. Any single validation study is unlikely to provide a definitive answer on the validity of a selection method. This is because any particular study can be conducted on only a *sample* of relevant people and, of course, has to be conducted in a specific organisation, at a particular time, using particular measures. There may be specific factors, to do with the sample of people used, the measures, the timing of the study and so on, which influence the study and bias the results in some way. It is obvious, then, that to estimate the validity of a particular selection procedure, more than one study is needed, so that any bias due to specific features of any particular study will not have an unduly large influence. But how many studies are required and how can we summarise and aggregate the results of several studies in order to draw conclusions? This problem of cumulating the results of many studies is not unique to personnel selection research and has exercised the minds of psychologists in many fields in recent years. Various statistical techniques have been developed to resolve the problem and an outline is given below. The techniques described below are discussed within the context of personnel selection but have applications in many areas of work psychology (*see* Hunter and Hirsh, 1987, for a review).

An example will help to illustrate the way in which the results of validation studies may be cumulated and summarised. A researcher may, for example, be interested in the extent to which a particular individual difference characteristic, such as intelligence, achievement motivation or verbal ability (call this factor X) is predictive of managerial performance.

As already noted, any individual study, using a particular sample of managers, will not give a definitive result for the validity of factor X. Consider for a moment why this is so. In other words consider what things might cause the results of any specific study to be less than perfectly accurate. Table 8.3 provides a list of these features with a brief explanation of how they may influence the accuracy of the result obtained from any study. As Table 8.3 makes clear, some of the problems are caused by sampling error

Table 8.3 Major sources of distortion in validation studies

1 Sampling error

The small samples (e.g. 50–150) used in many validation studies mean that the results obtained may be unduly influenced by the effects of small numbers of people within the sample whose results are unusual. As sample size increases, these irregularities usually balance each other out and a more reliable result is obtained.

2 Poor measurement precision

The measurement of psychological qualities at both the predictor (i.e. selection method) and criterion (i.e. job performance) stage of the validation process is subject to unsystematic error. This error (unreliability) in the scores obtained will reduce the ceiling for the observed correlation between predictor and criterion: the error is unsystematic and random, thus this element of the predictor or criterion score will not correlate systematically with anything. This means that as reliability decreases, the maximum possible correlation between predictor and criterion will decrease.

3 Restricted range of scores

The sample of people used in a validation study may not provide the full theoretically possible range of scores on the predictor and/or criterion measures. A restricted range of scores has a straightforward statistical effect on limiting the size of the linear correlation between two variables. So, like unreliability, range restriction in a sample serves to reduce the magnitude of the observed correlation coefficient.

(item 1) and imperfect reliability in the selection method, imperfect reliability in the criterion measure (item 2) and range restriction in the selection method scores (item 3). Consider these sources of error in relation to our example of the predictive validity of factor X. The sources of error are usually referred to as artefacts since they are not part of the natural relationship under investigation, but are a consequence of the particular investigative procedures used in the study. If the researcher in our example was able to identify ten studies of the predictive validity of factor X each study would be inaccurate due to the artefacts. Sampling error would be present because in each study the sample involved would not be perfectly representative of the population. Studies with larger samples would of course be less prone to sampling error.

TASK *To get a clearer idea of the importance of sampling error think about how confident you would be that a random sample of six people from your family gave a good estimate of the average height of human beings. Then consider what you would need to do – and how large the sample would need to be – to get a good estimate.*

As far as unreliability and range restriction are concerned, these artefacts will adversely affect observed validity coefficients. Test reliability (*see* Chapter 6) may be calculated and expressed in a numerical form, with zero indicating total unreliability (i.e. in a totally unreliable test someone's score on a second administration could not be predicted from his or her score on the first). To illustrate the impact of even modest deviations from reliability (0.8 is taken as the ideal, acceptable lower limit), Table 8.4 shows how the confidence interval for estimating an individual's true score on the test gets wider and wider as test reliability decreases.

Table 8.4 The impact of different reliabilities on estimated true score

	Reliability		
	0.9	0.8	0.6
Observed score	100	100	100
Probable (95% confidence) range for candidate's true score	91–109	87–113	81–119

■ **KEY LEARNING POINT**
Studies with larger sample sizes are less prone to sampling error and more likely to give reliable results.

Even with good reliability (0.8) two apparently quite different observed scores such as 94 and 112 could, due to lack of measurement precision, have identical true scores. When data from unreliable tests are used to calculate correlation coefficients the effect is clear. An unreliable test (or any set of scores) contains a large amount of random error.

Obviously these random factors will not vary systematically (i.e. correlate) with any other factors; hence, as the reliability of a measure decreases, the opportunity for the measure to correlate with any other variable also decreases. Indeed, in technical terms the reliability of a measure sets a precise limit on the possible magnitude of its correlation with any other variable: the square root of the reliability is the maximum possible level of correlation (*see* Moser and Schuler, 1989). Similarly, the availability of only a restricted range of scores will set an artificially low ceiling on the magnitude of any observed correlation. Consider what may happen, for example, in a predictive validity study when the candidates who score badly on the selection tests are not offered employment. If these low-scoring candidates were offered jobs they would be expected to perform badly. This link between people with low selection test scores producing low job performance scores is an important element in producing high validity coefficients. When these low scorers are excluded from the sample the resulting validity coefficient can be based only on high and average scorers, where differences in job performance will be much less extreme. The resulting validity coefficient will thus be limited in magnitude. If the degree of range restriction in a study is known, then it is a simple matter to make a statistical correction for this range restriction (*see* Smith and Robertson, 1993, for the relevant formula).

> ■ **KEY LEARNING POINT**
> *Restriction of range in scores will artificially limit the magnitude of validity coefficients and give misleadingly low results.*

The statistical procedures of meta-analysis (Hunter and Schmidt, 1990) involve methods for estimating the amount of sampling error in a set of studies and hence calculating a more accurate estimate of the validity coefficient in question. More complex meta-analysis formulae also allow the estimation of validity coefficients corrected for unreliability and range restriction (Hunter and Schmidt, 1990). Notice that removing the effect of sampling error does not change the magnitude of the validity coefficient; it changes the estimated variance in observed coefficients and hence narrows the confidence interval around the mean coefficient. As expected from the discussion of these artefacts, correcting for unreliability and range restriction *will* increase the magnitude of the mean validity coefficients. The development and use of meta-analytic procedures has had a considerable impact on personnel selection research and has enabled investigators to get a much clearer picture of the validity of personnel selection methods. Meta-analysis techniques have been applied to the available research evidence on the validity of all major personnel selection procedures.

> ■ **KEY LEARNING POINT**
> *Meta-analysis provides a way of using the results from many individual studies to derive a more reliable estimate of the validity of personnel selection procedures.*

Table 8.5 provides a simplified summary of the results of meta-analytic investigations of the validity of selection procedures. The significant research evidence on each of the techniques listed in Table 8.5 is discussed below.

Table 8.5 A summary of meta-analytic studies of the validity of selection procedures

Selection method	Evidence concerning overall criterion-related validity
Work samples Trainability tests Assessment centres Cognitive tests Biodata	Good
Personality assessment	Promising
Interviews	Poor to good, depending on the type of interview
References	Poor
Handwriting	Nil

THE VALIDITY OF PERSONNEL SELECTION PROCEDURES

Interviews

Interviews have always been the most popular form of personnel selection. In their survey of selection practices in the UK, Robertson and Makin (1986) found that over 80 per cent of companies always used interviews. More recent surveys in the UK and other European countries have produced similar results (Shackleton and Newell, 1994) although there is clearly some variation; German companies, for example, make less use of interviews (only about 60 per cent use interviews always) than other European countries. The interview is not a uniform selection procedure and the available research shows that structured interviews, utilising job-related questions, are much better predictors of a candidate's subsequent performance than more open procedures. Several meta-analytic studies of interview validities (e.g. Weisner and Cronshaw, 1988; Huffcut and Arthur, 1994) have revealed the superiority of structured, job-related interviews. Although there is no clear proof of this, one of the benefits of getting interviewers to follow a predetermined structure and to ask only job-related questions is probably that of minimising the opportunity for irrelevant information, prejudice and bias to have an effect on the decision. When constrained by a structure and question strategy, interviewers are probably forced to pay more attention to job-related items of information.

The situational interviewing approach developed by Latham and colleagues (e.g. Latham and Saari, 1984) provides a good example of the structured, job-related interview approach. Like all good selection procedures this approach begins with a thorough analysis of the job. With the aid of job experts, critical situations involving examples of particularly good or poor performance in the job are identified. The critical-incidents approach (Flanagan, 1954) is sometimes useful at this stage. Job experts are also used to provide realistic behavioural examples of good and poor performance for each key situation; these examples are then used to provide benchmarks for interviewers to use when scoring the responses of interviewees. The overall format of situational interview development and use involves the following stages:

1 job analysis is used to identify key situations;

2 job experts produce benchmark behaviours;

3 using information gathered in the first two stages, situational questions and a behaviourally based scoring key for each question are developed;

4 interviewers are trained in observation, interpersonal and judgmental skills and given practice with the interview questions;

5 interviews are conducted by presenting interview questions one at a time (either orally or on cards) to candidates. Twelve or so questions may be used in a typical interview. Often these may be selected by interviewers from a larger bank or questions developed earlier in the process.

Table 8.6 gives an example question and scoring key taken from a study reported by Robertson *et al* (1990). In recent years situational interviews have probably been the most popular form of structured job-related interviews and in general they have produced good validity data (*see also* Weekley and Gier, 1987). Other structured, interview formats have also produced good results (e.g. Janz, 1982; Orpen, 1985).

Table 8.6 An example of a situational interview

EXAMPLE SITUATION AND HIGH-, MEDIUM- AND LOW-RESPONSE ANCHORS TO ASSESS ADAPTABILITY (FLEXIBILITY)

Two young people in their early twenties have approached the organisation for finance to set up a new venture making and selling equipment to enable home-computer users to translate games easily between different models of computer. They are enthusiastic and talented, but freely confess that they have no business, manufacturing or selling experience. What advice will you give them?

Scale points

Low   Contact someone else (e.g. accountant) for information on cash flows.
Tell them not to go ahead – too risky, no market.

Medium   Recommend information to them.
Tell them to recruit business person.
Tell them accountant will prepare cost report.
Arrange for them to see organisation's experts.
Ask them to talk more once they have thought some more about their business proposition.

High   Say the organisation is enthusiastic about them as customers.
Ask them about the legal side of game translation.
Do they have a prototype?
Contact Patent Office.
Seems a big area of growth at the moment.

Obtain information and recommend: Board of Trade, new business, offer organisation's own information accountants.

> ■ KEY LEARNING POINT
> *Situational interviews and other forms of structured interview produce good criterion-related validity.*

Psychometric tests

For personnel selection purposes psychometric tests may be divided into two categories: cognitive tests (e.g. general intelligence, spatial ability, numerical ability) and personality tests (*see* Chapter 6 for more information on specific tests). The personality tests used in selection and assessment activities are usually based on some kind of trait-factor analytic model of personality as discussed in Chapter 6. For more than two decades the status of personality tests as predictors of performance was low (*see*, for example, Guion and Gottier, 1965). Some authors (e.g. Adler and Weiss, 1988) have argued persuasively that personality is an important determinant of behaviour at work.

Personality tests may have several unique characteristics making them rather different from other predictors and perhaps providing some explanation of their strong appeal to many practitioners.

TASK *Think about some different jobs and the personality factors* (see *Chapter 6*) *which might help or hinder effectiveness. You may also like to think of how people with very different personalities could do a job equally well – but in very different ways.*

It may well be, for example, that for many jobs quite different personality profiles may be equally effective; furthermore, scores in the middle range on some personality traits may be preferable to scores at either extreme. Traditional validation procedures, with their strong emphasis on bivariate, linear correlational methods of analysis, may not be appropriate for personality testing. Despite these potential difficulties, recent research has produced quite promising validity coefficients for personality measures. Early meta-analytic research which cumulated the validity coefficients from many studies adopted an essentially exploratory approach (Schmitt *et al.*, 1984). In this research all available personality-criterion correlations were entered into the meta-analysis, regardless of whether or not the researchers expected there to be a relationship between the specific variables. The validities produced were disappointing. Tett *et al.* (1991) looked at all of the available research and found that the correlations between personality constructs and work criteria were much better in studies where specific hypotheses were being investigated. Other recent research has adopted hypothesis-driven procedures, in which relationships between specific personality constructs and work competencies were explored. This work (e.g. Barrick and Mount, 1991; Robertson and Kinder, 1993) has found some evidence that personality factors are correlated reasonably well with work criteria.

> ■ KEY LEARNING POINT
> *Validity coefficients for personality measures were much better in confirmatory studies, where specific hypotheses linking personality with work performance were tested.*

Unlike personality testing, cognitive ability testing has produced extremely good validity data across a wide range of occupational areas. Although the results have varied a little from study to study (partly due to the different corrections made by different authors) meta-analyses of the validity of cognitive tests (e.g. Hunter and Hunter, 1984) have consistently shown good validity for what most investigators now refer to as general mental ability, which seems analogous with general intelligence or 'g' (*see* Chapter 6). Perhaps even more remarkable is an argument first advocated, together with supporting data, in a very important and influential article by Schmidt *et al.* (1981) and since replicated by Burke *et al.* (1986). These investigators obtained validity data from five different job families and showed that the validity of apparently different classes of ability tests (e.g. verbal, perceptual, quantitative) did not vary substantially across jobs or job families. Schmidt *et al.* (1981) used these data to suggest that cognitive selection tests are equally valid across different jobs. Although the proponents of the use of cognitive tests have refrained from arguing to this extreme, the extreme form of this argument suggests that all cognitive tests are equally valid in all jobs and, more simply, that general mental ability tests are valid for all jobs! Ree *et al.* (1994) investigated the role of general mental ability, 'g' compared with specific mental ability, 's' (*see* Chapter 6). Their results showed that 'g' provided good criterion-related validity and that 's' provided only a small increase in validity. In other words general intelligence is the most useful predictor and specific abilities do not add much practically useful validity.

In the 1970s, particularly in the USA, cognitive ability testing became increasingly unpopular and it was common for people to argue that such tests had no useful role in personnel selection. The recent meta-analytic work and the evidence for validity generalisation (i.e. the generalisation of validity across job families) have caused personnel psychologists to revise these views. The scientific community may not support the view that cognitive tests are equally valid across all jobs, but equally no one doubts that such tests provide useful predictions of job performance across a wide range of occupational areas. Given their relatively low cost and good criterion-related validity, cognitive tests (general mental ability tests in particular) are likely to be used in selection procedures for some time to come.

■ **KEY LEARNING POINT**

Cognitive tests produce good criterion-related validities for a wide range of jobs.

This concentration by selection researchers on the use of general mental ability testing is something of a paradox in at least two ways. The first paradox is that while selection research is focusing on a unitary trait of general mental ability, research into intelligence itself is moving away from this simple conceptualisation of intelligence (Wolman, 1985; Sternberg and Wagner, 1986) and developing multifaceted models of intelligence. The second paradox is that despite the improved status of cognitive testing as a personnel selection procedure there has been relatively little development of new testing strategies or procedures. For example, advances in computerisation of tests and testing theory have had relatively little impact on cognitive testing procedures (*see* Robertson, 1988). In recent years there has been some limited evidence of the use of computer-based methods in selection and assessment procedures (*see* Bartram, 1994). Although the use of computers to generate narrative reports, based on conventional testing sessions, is widespread, computerisation has had no real impact on the use or development of more advanced applications of testing theory. Several computerised versions of existing tests have been developed and although a potentially useful step, this represents no more than a change in administration procedure. Within the UK, recently developed cognitive tests have improved face validity but are based on traditional psychometric testing theory (Gulliksen, 1950) and models of the intellect (*see* Chapter 6). The coverage of practical intelligence in Chapter 6 gave an indication of an alternative approach to cognitive ability, which concentrates much more on understanding and measuring the nature of real-world performance. The most exciting findings from this research show that tests of practical intelligence (Wagner and Sternberg, 1986) are predictive of work performance but do not correlate highly with traditional measures of cognitive ability. This suggests that a combination of evidence from both sources is likely to improve our ability to predict candidates' work performance. So far no empirical work has been done to confirm this view.

In the USA in the 1970s arguments against the use of cognitive tests in personnel selection were often based on the belief that such tests were unfair to ethnic minorities. The evidence on this issue is reviewed briefly in a separate section on fairness later in this chapter.

Work-sample tests

As noted earlier in this chapter, work-sample tests provide an example of an alternative to the 'sign-based' approach to personnel selection exemplified by psychometric testing. Two fundamental forms of work-sample testing may be identified. First, there is the work-sample test administered to the experienced candidate. Examples include the typing tests and in-tray tests mentioned earlier in this chapter. These kinds of tests have consistently produced good validity data (*see* Robertson and Kandola, 1982; Hunter and Hunter, 1984; Muchinsky, 1986). Trainability work-sample tests were originally developed in the UK by Sylvia Downs and are suitable for candidates who are not trained in the relevant job. Indeed, the main purpose of trainability work-sample tests is to assess whether an applicant is suitable for training or not. Trainability tests have been developed for several occupational areas and have also produced consistently good validity data (Robertson and Downs, 1989).

One problem which may apply to work-sample tests in general was identified by Robertson and Downs (1989) in their meta-analytic study of trainability testing. They showed that the validity of trainability tests attenuated over time. In other words, the longer the follow-up period involved in the validation study, the smaller the validity coefficient. This attenuation in validity may be because trainability tests, like all work-sample tests, are closely tied to the specific tasks of the job. As time passes these job-specific facets of performance may become less important.

Another issue of practical concern with respect to trainability tests is the extent to which these tests, which are costly and time consuming, measure something unique that cannot be assessed more cost-effectively by cognitive testing (*see* Robertson and Downs, 1989). Further research is needed to investigate the overlap between trainability tests and cognitive ability.

Assessment centres

Assessment centres seem to be an increasingly popular method of selection and assessment in organisational settings. As well as being used to choose between external candidates assessment centres are often also used in internal promotion/assessment schemes. Assessment centres were described briefly earlier in this chapter. As far as criterion-related validity is concerned assessment centres perform well (Gaugler *et al.*, 1987). There are, however, some problems with the construct validity of assessment centres. Beginning with the seminal study of Sackett and Dreher (1982), several other investigators (e.g. Robertson *et al.*, 1987; Reilly *et al.*, 1990) have shown that the convergent and discriminant validity of assessment centres is poor. Table 8.7 shows part of a typical dimension (i.e. individual psychological characteristic or construct by exercise matrix). Convergent validity would be apparent if ratings of a particular dimension (e.g. problem-solving ability) were strongly intercorrelated across different exercises.

Table 8.7 Part of an assessment centre dimension by exercise matrix

Dimension	Exercise			
	In-tray	Group discussion	Role play	Presentation exercise and report
Problem-solving skills	✓	✓	✓	✓
Interpersonal ability	–	✓	✓	–
Written skills	✓	–	–	✓

Similarly, discriminant validity would be shown if correlations of different dimensions within the same exercises were small. Examinations of the psychometric properties of assessment centres have consistently shown low convergent and discriminant validity. If the ratings of the same dimension across different exercises do not correlate (i.e. poor convergent validity) this suggests that the dimensions (constructs) being measured are not stable from one situation to another, or that the measurement procedure is inadequate. Either way, these are troubling results and show that although assessment centres clearly measure something of importance (since their criterion-related validity is good), there is considerable uncertainty about what they do measure.

■ KEY LEARNING POINT
There are problems with the construct validity of assessment centres.

Other methods

The use of biographical data as a selection procedure is an interesting and sometimes controversial topic. Like several of the other personnel selection procedures discussed in this chapter, biodata have several unique features that distinguish them from other approaches. The fundamentals of the biodata approach involve identifying correlations between items of biographical information and criterion measures (e.g. work performance, absenteeism). These correlations are established empirically by conducting a predictive or (more often) concurrent validation study.

Biodata items that predict the criterion are then combined into a questionnaire which may be administered to applicants. Information from the prior validation stage can then be used to provide a scoring procedure. For example, items may be assigned weights based on their ability to predict the relevant criterion (Guion, 1965). Weights may also be assigned by other procedures (see Drakeley, 1989). It should be stressed at this point that the correlations observed between biodata items and the criterion will be influenced by chance factors, and before using the results of a biodata validation study for selection purposes, cross-validation, preferably using a second sample, is needed. It is also clear from empirical research that the validity of biodata items is not always stable over time and it is advisable to revalidate periodically. Both Muchinsky (1986) and Drakeley (1989) have recommended revalidation every three to five years. Meta-analytic studies have revealed that biodata provide reasonably good criterion-related validity. Evidence for the criterion-related validity of biodata is strong (see Mumford and Stokes, 1992) and validity coefficients for biodata inventories are among the best that have been obtained for personnel selection methods (often 0.3 and upwards, uncorrected).

Most of the problems with the use of biodata arise from the uncritical use of empirically derived items. In other words, many biodata studies have involved the identification of items that predict the criterion, with no attempt to consider *why* the items are predictive. For example, why should it be that living in a particular area of town or having had a newspaper delivery round as a child is associated with job success? Two problems may be associated with this kind of empiricism. One problem is that the observed biodata item may be a surrogate for some other variable; for example, what if the area of town in question is predominantly inhabited by a particular social or ethnic group? The other, more general, problem is that while they may provide predictive value, such items provide no help in *understanding* the determinants of job success.

> ■ **KEY LEARNING POINT**
>
> *The uncritical use of empirically-derived items in biodata questionnaires leads to problems. Rationally-derived items are safer and less likely to lead to unforeseen problems.*

With these problems in mind the rational approach to the development of biodata has been utilised. This approach is in line with attempts by some authors (e.g. Owens and Schoenfeldt, 1979) to develop a theoretical rationale for the predictive validity of biodata. Using the rational approach involves clear hypotheses about specific job-relevant constructs such as ability to work in a team, which may be tapped by specific biodata items (e.g. membership of clubs and societies). Only items with a potential rational connection with the criterion will then be tried out, even in the pre-validation version of the biodata questionnaire. This approach is clearly much more appealing from the explanatory point of view, although evidence to date (Mitchell and Klimoski, 1982) suggests that it has slightly poorer validity than the empirical approach. Gains in fairness and understanding may, however, outweigh this loss of validity. Stokes and Reddy (1992), after reviewing the evidence, suggest that a combination of approaches might produce the best and most interpretable results.

Reference reports are widely used methods for obtaining information on candidates (Shackleton and Newell, 1991, 1994), although it seems likely that in many situations potential employers take up references only when they are about to make a job offer. This high level of usage is not, however, matched by a comparable amount of research on references. In general, the validity evidence for reference reports is not particularly good (Reilly and Chao, 1982; Hunter and Hunter, 1984) although some studies (e.g. Carroll and Nash, 1972; Williams and Dobson, 1987) have found useful criterion-related validity. One reason for the poor validity of references may be that they are not reliable and referees do not give consistent views on candidates (*see* Dobson, 1989). Given their high level of usage, further research into references would seem to be important. For example, although a study by Kryger and Shikiar (1978) touched on the issues, there are no studies that directly address the issue of fairness (i.e. unfair discrimination against specific subgroups of the population) of references. From the practical point of view Dobson (1989) has provided some example reference formats and suggestions on how to maximise the validity of references.

TASK   *Why is it that references do not show particularly good criterion-related validity?*

Self-assessment and peer assessment both have the potential to be used for selection decision making. Self-assessment is rarely used in practical selection settings and there are obvious problems with leniency and so forth (*see* Ash, 1980). Studies of the validity of self-assessment in personnel selection have rarely found encouraging results (*see* Reilly and Chao, 1982; Schmitt and Robertson, 1990). One possible promising line of research involves using ideas and measurement procedures from self-efficacy theory (Bandura, 1986). Recent research has shown that correlations between self-efficacy ratings and measures of job performance are reasonably good (e.g. Robertson and Sadri, 1993; Sadri and Robertson, 1993). Whether or not this can be made to pay off in practical selection contexts remains to be seen.

Peer assessments, by contrast to self-assessment, have been found to have consistently good validity (Reilly and Chao, 1982; Hunter and Hunter, 1984; Schmitt *et al.*, 1984). Their use is obviously limited to circumstances where peers are in a position to make an assessment of a candidate (e.g. internal promotion). Although peer assessment systems are used extensively in some settings (e.g. promotion in the university system), the use of such systems is likely to be limited by the lack of enthusiasm shown for such systems by participants (*see* Cederblom and Lounsbury 1980; Love 1981). Although in some circumstances, such as career counselling rather than assessment, peer assessment may be popular (Roadman, 1964), the use of peer assessment seems likely to be limited to specific kinds of organisations and circumstances.

Other potential selection methods not mentioned so far in this chapter include graphology (handwriting analysis), astrology and polygraphy (the use of the so-called lie detector test). In brief, none of these procedures is used to any great extent in the UK, although some continental European companies make extensive use of graphology (Shackleton and Newell, 1991; 1994). As far as validity is concerned there is relatively little research available on the use of these methods for personnel selection but the clear balance of available evidence is that none of the methods shows any useful criterion-related validity. Summaries of the evidence on graphology and polygraphy may be found in Ben-Shakhar (1989). Smith and Robertson (1993) provide a review of the relevant research on astrology and graphology.

■ **KEY LEARNING POINT**

There is no evidence for the criterion-related validity of graphology.

CASE STUDY 8.1

Organisation expansion and selection procedures

Although Dr Lyn Evans enjoyed computer science and her work in the Research and Development (R&D) division of GenFive Computers, she had realised that her future career progression was limited by the small number of senior technical posts in the company. With this in mind she registered for a part-time masters degree in management and broadened her grasp of managerial concepts and practices. Shortly after obtaining her MSc Lyn made a crucial career move and left the R&D division to join the Sales and Marketing division of GenFive.

In the next few years Lyn and GenFive were very successful and Lyn became marketing director. Shortly after her appointment as marketing director GenFive was poised to make a rapid expansion of its sales and marketing force and began to sell its products directly to retail stores and to approach small businesses directly (something it had never done before). An enormous expansion of the field sales force was needed, together with a restructuring of the current Sales and Marketing division into seven geographical regions, each with a semi-autonomous regional manager. Lyn had little over a year to achieve the necessary organisational changes, and three to four years to expand the sales force (from 20 to over 200). Her most important problem was the selection of her future regional managers (either from the existing team of 25 sales personnel or from outside recruitment). Next, and no less important, was the selection and recruitment of over 200 new sales personnel.

Suggested exercise

Use your knowledge of the material covered in Chapters 7 and 8 to prepare a plan for Lyn to achieve her goals over the next five years.

An opportunity for work psychology

Nicole Schneider was the first professionally qualified work psychologist that Milligans had ever employed. Milligans had a chain of family-fun theme parks throughout Europe, several bistro-type restaurants and three hotels. Almost all of the sites were in holiday resorts and the majority of sites were only fully active during the summer months. Several theme parks ran with only a skeleton staff during the winter and some closed completely. The hotels and restaurants, with varying success, remained open throughout the year but were much busier during the summer.

Milligans' staffing needs, particularly at more junior levels, were seasonal and they recruited large numbers of temporary employees to work during the peak summer months. Managers at almost all of the sites were constantly complaining about the quality of their temporary staff. In turn the staff themselves often resigned before their expected date of departure and complained about the behaviour of Milligans' customers.

Nicole made three interventions which, in the course of three years, brought about a dramatic improvement in the situation. First, after thorough job analyses of the relevant temporary jobs, she introduced a performance assessment system which included behaviourally anchored rating scales. The managers were trained in the usage of the system and it was implemented during Nicole's first summer with Milligans. The results of the assessment scheme, together with the prior job analysis data, gave her a much more precise grasp of the problems and why the managers complained about the quality of temporary staff.

During the next year Nicole and her two personnel assistants developed a set of structured, situational interview questions and scoring procedures. Several of the articles from the work psychology literature provided models of how to develop the questions and associated scoring procedures. In addition to the situational interviews Nicole and her colleagues developed trainability work-sample tests for the main temporary jobs involved.

During Nicole's second summer the tests and interviews were used at a selected set of Milligans' sites. They were administered by Nicole's assistants and a specially trained small group of Milligans' junior managers. The interview and test results were not used to take selection decisions – unless the site managers felt very strongly that they wanted to use the results immediately. The data collected at this stage, together with the end-of-season performance ratings, gave Nicole the basis for a predictive validity study.

Some simple utility calculations showed that despite the extra time needed to conduct the selection procedures, the new interviews and trainability tests would provide significant financial gain for Milligans.

Although not all of the site managers were convinced by Nicole's results, some were persuaded sufficiently to try the new procedures. From the next summer onwards there was a steady improvement in the quality of seasonal staff recruited, and more and more site managers began to use the selection procedures.

Suggested exercises

1 *Explain why the circumstances in this case study made it possible for Nicole to have such a quick and effective impact.*

2 *Consider other tactics and selection procedures that Nicole might have used. Explain whether or not you feel that these would have been equally successful.*

SOCIAL AND ECONOMIC FACTORS

The impact of personnel selection procedure on candidates

Iles and Robertson (1989) have pointed out that there has been relatively little work in personnel selection which has looked at the issues involved from the perspective of candidates. The only candidate-centred area of work which features extensively in the personnel selection research literature concerns the extent to which selection procedures are fair to different subgroups (usually ethnic minorities or women) of the population. A large amount of research material focused on this issue has been produced. A variety of terms such as bias, adverse impact, fairness and differential validity are used in the literature on this issue and a clear grasp of the meanings and definitions of some of these terms is crucial to an understanding of the research results.

First, it needs to be made clear that a test is not unfair or biased simply because members of different subgroups obtain different scores on the tests. Men and women have different mean scores for height; this does not mean that rulers are unfair measuring instruments. However, it would be unfair to use height as a selection criterion for a job, if the job could be done by people of any height, since it is important for selection criteria to be job-related. Normally, of course, the extent to which a selection method is related to job performance can be estimated by validation research, and it is clear therefore that fairness and validity are closely related.

Unfortunately, it is possible for tests to appear to be valid and yet be biased against some subgroups. This may happen if the relationship between the test score and job performance is not the same for the two subgroups. For example, it is possible to imagine that the link between job performance and certain personality or ability factors could be different for two subgroups of the population. A validity study based on a mixed sample of people would produce results that were somewhat incorrect for both subgroups; if the results were used to develop a selection procedure the predictions of candidates' work performance would be in error. Of course, the situation would be even worse if the validity study was based on only one subgroup but then used to select members of another. In this case the errors for the selected group would be much greater than for the validation group, resulting in obvious unfairness.

This description of possible unfairness leads to the definition of test bias (fairness) which is accepted by most work psychologists: 'A test is biased for members of a subgroup of the population if, in the prediction of a criterion for which the test was designed, consistent non-zero errors of prediction are made for members of the subgroup' (Clearly, 1968, p. 115). When, triggered by civil rights movements in the United States, fairness first became an issue in personnel selection research, it was felt that many selection procedures, including tests, were unfair. This was because of consistent differences in mean scores between different subgroups of the population (*see* Schmitt, 1989). As the discussion above makes clear, subgroup differences in mean scores are not the same as fairness. A procedure is biased or unfair when, in line with Cleary's (1968) definition, it shows different validity for different groups. In general, research on personnel selection has shown that, although there are examples of subgroup differences on selection instruments (e.g. black–white differences on aptitude tests or male–female differences on strength tests), there is little evidence for significant differences in subgroup validity coefficients.

179

The fact that the scientific research provides little evidence of differential validity for well-established selection procedures does not imply that all selection methods are unbiased, nor does it imply that unfair discrimination does not take place. It is clear, for example, that, despite the 1976 Race Relations Act, unfair discrimination still takes place in the UK. Brown and Gay (1985), for instance, showed that a disproportionate number of black applicants compared with similarly qualified white applicants were not invited for interview after applying for various jobs. In the UK a very thorough review of the impact of selection testing on the employment opportunities of men and women has been conducted by Pearn *et al.* (1987). One of the key lessons from the case studies conducted for this report is that a job analysis is a prerequisite for the development of fair selection procedures. The work of Tett *et al.* (1991) provides further support for this advice by revealing that the validity for personality tests is much better in settings where the use of such tests was preceded by a job analysis.

It is also clear that some personnel selection procedures provide more opportunity for unfairness than others and in some cases there is clear evidence of unfairness (*see* Reilly and Chao, 1982). In particular, unstructured procedures with poor reliability and validity provide recruiters with the opportunity to exercise their prejudices and biases. Well-researched selection procedures such as assessment centres, work-sample tests and structured interviews minimise the opportunity for bias and, as research has clearly shown, there is little, if any, evidence of unfairness with these methods. Such methods are a weapon against unfairness, rather than, as some ill-informed commentators have asserted, a cause of unfairness.

■ **KEY LEARNING POINT**
Most of the valid personnel selection procedures do not show evidence of bias or lack of fairness.

Recent research (e.g. Fletcher, 1991; Robertson *et al.*, 1991) has begun to focus on other important ways in which personnel selection procedures may have impact on candidates. This work has departed from the traditional view that selection and assessment procedures are neutral measuring devices that do not influence candidates. Anyone who has been through an unsuccessful assessment experience will recognise that there is the potential for powerful psychological impact on the person being assessed. Obviously this impact may not always be negative. It is quite possible to imagine that if someone is assessed fairly, with the use of valid and reliable methods, the overall impact, especially if sensitive feedback is given, will be beneficial. Equally, it is also possible to see that being unfairly dealt with by an inappropriate procedure may be very demotivating for a candidate. The potential for problems of this kind seems particularly strong when people are being assessed internally by their existing organisation. The research so far has not uncovered any very damaging effects but there is evidence that self-esteem may be damaged (Fletcher, 1991) and that the candidates' views of the adequacy of the procedure may help to determine the degree of impact (Robertson *et al.*, 1991). This is an area of research that may produce important findings for the practical application of selection and assessment procedures within organisations.

FINANCIAL UTILITY

Like many organisational practices, personnel selection procedures cost money to implement. Using selection procedures with good predictive validity is always important but, unfortunately, procedures with good predictive validity alone do not guarantee that a selection procedure will be cost effective. Two important factors determining cost effectiveness (usually referred to as utility) are:

1 selection ratio, i.e. $\dfrac{\text{number of jobs}}{\text{number of candidates}}$;

2 the financial benefit of improved job performance.

Let us now examine in a little more detail the role that validity, selection ratio and the other factors play in determining utility. Figure 8.1a shows the situation for a validity coefficient of 0.1. The shaded areas (B and C) identify people who will be hired by the organisation. Notice, however, that although all of these people achieve the minimum

**Fig. 8.1 The effect of different validity coefficients on the proportion hired:
(a) validity coefficient = 1; (b) validity coefficient = 0.5**

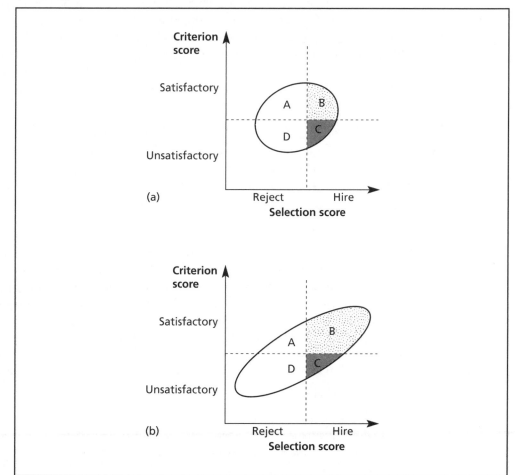

score on the predictor, only a proportion of them (B) also show satisfactory work performance. Similarly, although all of the people in the unshaded areas (A and D) fail to achieve the cut-off score on the predictor, some of them are capable of satisfactory work performance (those in area A). Areas B and D represent correct selection decisions; area D contains people who have been justifiably rejected, known as true negatives. Area C contains the false positives; that is, people who would be hired but produce unsatisfactory work performance. Area A contains the false negatives; that is, people who would not be hired but are capable of satisfactory work performance. Areas A and C represent errors in the selection process. Note that unless the validity coefficient is 1.0 there will *always* be errors of selection.

Validity

As Fig. 8.1b shows, when validity increases (0.5), the proportions in areas A and C decrease and the proportion of correct decisions (areas B and D) increases. Thus, as validity increases, the quality of selection decisions also increases.

If validity was perfect, error-free selection could be achieved and the relative performance of candidates on the selection method would be reproduced in their work performance. Thus, a group of candidates with selection scores in the top 10 per cent would deliver work performance scores at the same level (remember that in perfect selection, work performance is perfectly correlated with selection score).

If the assumption that candidates' scores are normally distributed is made, then it is possible to use statistical tables to calculate the average standard score (z-score; *see* Chapter 4) of any group of candidates (e.g. the top 10 per cent). With *perfect selection*, the average z-score of the selected candidates would also be their average work performance score:

Average selection score (zs) = average work performance score (zw)

Of course, in reality, selection is never perfect and the predictive accuracy of the selection score is proportional to the magnitude of the validity coefficient. The work performance that can be expected of selected candidates will be dependent on the accuracy of selection:

(zs)(validity coefficient) = zw

The next step in the process is to consider how much value can be assigned to different levels of work performance. Several investigators have tackled this problem, and although there is no accepted solution (*see* Boudreau, 1989), a very conservative rule of thumb is to assign a value of 40 per cent of salary to each standard deviation of performance. Once this step has been made it is a simple matter to derive an estimate of the financial gain that can be expected from different selection situations. Since z-scores are already expressed in standard score units, the estimate of zw gives a direct estimate of financial gain. The cost of the procedure needs to be subtracted and account taken of the expected tenure of recruits and the number of people selected. The final equation is:

(zs)(r)(T)(N) = financial benefit

where: zs = average z-score of selected group
      r = validity coefficient for the selection procedure
      T = number of years recruits will stay
      N = number of recruits taken in one year

This equation has many potential uses. It could be used, for instance, to calculate the gain to be derived from changing from one selection method to another. To make the relevant calculations it is often necessary to make some estimates of the various terms in the equation. For example, if a company was considering the use of assessment centres to replace a procedure that involved only unstructured interviews it would be necessary to make estimates of the likely validity for the new procedure. Given the wealth of research on most selection methods such estimates can be made with reasonable confidence. Similarly, the equation could be used to estimate the gain that could be derived from the attraction of a bigger field of candidates (e.g. by extensive advertising). The financial gain derived from the improved selection ratio (see below) may then be set against the cost of the advertising campaign.

> ■ **KEY LEARNING POINT**
>
> *Utility calculations can be used to address a variety of problems and assist organisations in determining recruitment advertising strategies etc., as well as indicating the direct benefits to be derived from selection procedures.*

Selection ratio

Clearly, when the selection ratio is greater than one (i.e. there are more available jobs than applicants), the use of any selection procedure is likely to be of relatively little benefit. In this situation the organisation may be forced to accept anyone who applies for a job. In practice, even with a selection ratio of more than one, it may still be sensible for an organisation to apply stringent selection criteria and leave jobs empty rather than hire totally unsuitable employees. When the selection ratio is less than one (i.e. more applicants than jobs), the organisation can gain obvious benefits from using selection. Consider the situation for two different selection ratios. If the selection ratio is 0.7 (i.e. seven jobs for every ten applicants), the organisation can afford to refuse jobs to people with the lowest 30 per cent of scores on the predictor. If, however, the selection ratio is 0.4, the bottom 60 per cent of applicants can be rejected and the group of applicants selected will have a much higher score. In turn, as the material presented above shows, this will translate into financial gain.

> ■ **KEY LEARNING POINT**
>
> *The cost effectiveness of a personnel selection procedure is not dependent on validity alone.*

Other factors

Studies where selection utility has been estimated have shown very clearly that, even with modest validity coefficients, striking financial gains may be made. Schmidt *et al.* (1984), for example, showed that gains of over $US1 million per annum could be expected if cognitive ability tests were used to select the large numbers of US Park

Rangers recruited each year. Schmidt *et al.* (1979) showed that even more dramatic gains could be obtained if the *computer programmer aptitude test* (Hughes and McNamara, 1959) was used to select computer programmers in the USA. With a selection ratio of 0.5 (i.e. two applicants per job), gains of between $US13 and 37 million could be expected!

Using research to improve staff selection

A major financial services company is seeking to improve the quality of its intake of new graduates. At the moment the company uses interviews for selection of the graduates. The interviews are conducted at the relevant university by a member of the HR staff and the manager of the nearest branch. Both interviewers are given training in interview techniques and are encouraged to take a flexible approach to the interview, adapting the questions and structure to each candidate. The graduates are placed on a three-year development programme and then appointed to positions in various different areas of the company, depending on their progress and experience.

The human resources team at the company has some knowledge of the occupational psychology literature, including an awareness of the results from meta-analysis on the main personnel selection methods. As part of the team, you have to prepare for a meeting to discuss the selection procedures. The human resources director has asked for advice on several specific issues:

1 Is it possible to improve on the selection procedures currently in use?

2 Can the results of meta-analysis be used to help the company decide which methods to use?

3 Will it be necessary for the company to set up its own criterion-related validity study?

4 Could there be any direct financial gain in using revised selection procedures?

Suggested exercise

Prepare a draft presentation, covering these issues, for the meeting.

SUMMARY

A variety of personnel selection procedures is available for use in organisational settings. Research over the past two decades has provided a much clearer picture of the criterion-related validity of these procedures. Some of the methods, such as cognitive ability tests, seem to have broad applicability across a range of situations. As well as examining the validity of personnel selection procedures, research has also concentrated on the impact of the procedures on candidates. One area that has been reasonably well researched involves an examination of the fairness (to different subgroups) of the various techniques. Preliminary research suggests that the assessment experience itself may have an impact on candidates' psychological characteristics. Developments in utility theory have enabled the estimation of the financial benefit that may be gained through improved personnel selection.

TEST YOUR LEARNING

Short-answer questions

1 What selection procedures are used in assessment centres?

2 How does sampling error distort validation studies?

3 Even with good reliability (0.8), how could two apparently quite different scores such as 94 and 112 have identical true scores?

4 What stages are involved in the situational interview format?

5 What problems may apply to work-sample tests?

6 What are unique features of biodata?

7 What are the main items of information needed in order to calculate the financial utility of a selection procedure?

Essay questions

1 Critically review the validity evidence for contemporary personnel selection procedures.

2 Discuss the impact of personnel selection and assessment on candidates.

GLOSSARY OF TERMS

Assessment centres A personnel assessment procedure that makes use of many different methods (e.g. interviews, work-sample tests and multiple sessions). Usually conducted over a period of 1–3 days.

Bias A psychological assessment procedure is biased if consistent errors of prediction (or classification) are made for members of a particular subgroup.

Biodata Life history information about candidates, usually collected with the aid of a structured questionnaire. Criterion-related validity for biodata is explored by examining statistical links between biodata items and criterion measures.

Cognitive ability Also referred to as intelligence or general mental ability. Refers to the capacity of individuals to process information and use the information to behave effectively (including the capacity to learn from experience).

Concurrent validity A form of criterion-related validity in which data on the predictor and criterion are obtained at the same time.

Construct validity An indication of the extent to which the test or procedure measures the psychological construct that it is intended to measure.

Correlation Usually expressed as a correlation coefficient, which can vary from −1 to +1. Positive correlations indicate that as one variable increases, so does the other. A correlation of zero indicates that there is no relationship between the variables.

Criterion-related validity The extent to which a predictor measure (e.g. a selection test score) is related to a criterion (e.g. work performance). In personnel selection, high criterion-related validity indicates that a selection measure gives an accurate indication of candidates' performance on the criterion.

Differential validity This would exist if there was conclusive evidence that a selection procedure had different levels of criterion-related validity for different subgroups of the population.

Fairness *See* **Bias.**

g *See* **Cognitive ability.**

Meta-analysis A statistical procedure for cumulating the results from many separate studies in order to obtain a more stable indication of the effect under investigation.

Practical intelligence A view of intelligent behaviour that focuses on real-world activity, rather than controlled behaviour assessed by conventional intelligence testing.

Predictive validity A form of criterion-related validity in which data on the criterion are obtained *after* data on the predictor.

Predictor A term sometimes used to refer to a selection procedure, on the grounds that a selection procedure is intended to *predict* candidates' job performance.

Psychometric tests Standardised procedures (often using pen and paper) embodying a series of questions (items) designed to assess key cognitive or personality dimensions. Must have acceptable levels of validity and reliability to be of value.

Range restriction This arises when a limited range of scores (rather than when the full population range) is present in a sample. It can occur when the sample is biased in some way, e.g. selection scores are available *only* for people who were given jobs.

Reliability An indicator of the consistency which a test or procedure provides. It is possible to quantify reliability to indicate the extent to which a measure is free from error.

Sampling error Fluctuations in observed results which arise when small samples are used. Any small sample may contain some unrepresentative cases, but if the sample is small these cases may have an unduly large influence on the results.

Selection ratio An indication of the number of positions available compared to the number of candidates. Ten candidates for every post would give a selection ratio of 1:10, i.e. 0.1.

Situational interviews A form of structured interview in which key work situations (identified through job analysis) are used to provide a basis for questioning and assessing job candidates.

Trainability tests A form of work-sample test which incorporates a systematic learning period for the candidate, who is then required to attempt the task unaided.

Utility (financial) A procedure for estimating the financial gain that may be derived from the improved job performance that is obtained from better personnel selection.

Validity A general term indicating the extent to which a test or procedure measures what it is intended to measure.

Work-sample tests Personnel assessment procedures that require candidates to conduct tasks that are sampled from the job(s) in question.

SUGGESTED FURTHER READING

1 Clive Fletcher's article in the *Journal of Occupational Psychology* (full reference in the list below) on candidates' reactions to assessment centres provides an example of a well-designed study in an emerging area of interest.

2 A special issue of the *International Journal of Selection and Assessment* (vol. 2, no. 2, 1994) includes the article by Shackleton and Newell on selection methods in Europe together with surveys from Australia and North America.

3 The text book on systematic personnel selection by Mike Smith and Ivan Robertson (full reference in the list below) provides more detail on all of the main topics covered in this chapter.

REFERENCES

Adler, S. and Weiss, H.M. (1988) 'Recent developments in the study of personality and organizational behaviour' in Cooper, C.L. and Robertson, I.T. (eds) *International Review of Industrial and Organizational Psychology*. Chichester: John Wiley.

Ash, R.A. (1980) 'Self-assessments of five types of typing ability', *Personnel Psychology*, vol. 33, pp. 2–73, 82.

Bandura, A. (1986) *Social Foundations of Thought and Action: A social cognitive theory*. Englewood Cliffs, NJ: Prentice Hall.

Barrick, M.R. and Mount, M.K. (1991) 'The big five personality dimensions and job performance: a meta-analysis', *Personnel Psychology*, vol. 44, pp. 1–26.

Bartram, D. (1994) 'Computer-based assessment' in Cooper, C.L. and Robertson, I.T. (eds) *International Review of Industrial and Organizational Psychology*, vol. 9. Chichester: John Wiley.

Ben-Shakhar, G. (1989) 'Non-conventional methods in personnel selection' in Herriot, P. (ed.) *Assessment and Selection in Organizations*. Chichester: John Wiley.

Boudreau, J.W. (1989) 'Selection utility analysis: a review and agenda for future research' in Smith, M. and Robertson, I.T. (eds) *Advances in Selection and Assessment*. Chichester: John Wiley.

Brown, E. and Gay, P. (1985) *Racial Discrimination 17 Years after the Act*, working paper no. 646. London: Policy Studies Institute.

Burke, M.J., Raju, N.S. and Pearlman, K. (1986) 'An empirical comparison of the results of five validity generalization procedures', *Journal of Applied Psychology*, vol. 71, pp. 349–53.

Carroll, S.J. and Nash, A.N. (1972) 'Effectiveness of a forced reference check', *Personnel Administration*, March/April, pp. 42–6.

Cederblom, D. and Lounsbury, J.W. (1980) 'An investigation of user acceptance of peer evaluation', *Personnel Psychology*, vol. 33, pp. 567–79.

Cleary, T.A. (1968) 'Test bias: prediction of grades of negro and white students in integrated colleges', *Journal of Educational Measurement*, vol. 5, pp. 115–24.

Dobson, P. (1989) 'Reference reports' in Herriot, P. (ed.) *Assessment and Selection in Organizations*. Chichester: John Wiley.

Drakeley, R.J (1989) 'Biographical data' in Herriot, P. (ed.) *Assessment and Selection in Organizations*. Chichester: John Wiley.

Flanagan, J.C. (1954) 'The critical incident technique', *Psychological Bulletin*, vol. 51, pp. 327–58.

Fletcher, C. (1991) 'Candidates' reactions to assessment centres and their outcomes: a longitudinal study', *Journal of Occupational Psychology*, vol. 64, pp. 117–27.

Gaugler, B., Rosenthal, D.B., Thornton, G.C. and Bentson, C. (1987) 'Meta-analysis of assessment center validity', *Journal of Applied Psychology*, vol. 72, pp. 493–511.

Guion, R. M. (1965) *Personnel Testing*. New York: McGraw-Hill.

Guion, R.M. and Gottier, R.F. (1965) 'Validity of personality measures in personnel selection', *Personnel Psychology*, vol. 18, pp. 135–64.

Gulliksen, H. (1950) *Theory of Mental Tests*. New York: John Wiley.

Huffcut, A.I. and Arthur, W.A. (1994) 'Hunter and Hunter revisited: interview validity for entry-level jobs', *Journal of Applied Psychology*, vol. 79, pp. 184–90.

Hughes, J.L. and McNamara, W.J. (1959) *Manual for the Revised Programmer Aptitude Test*. New York: Psychological Corporation.

Hunter, J.E. and Hirsh, H.R. (1987) 'Applications of meta-analysis' in Cooper, C.L. and Robertson, I.T. (eds) *International Review of Industrial and Organizational Psychology*. Chichester: John Wiley.

Hunter, J.E. and Hunter, R.F. (1984) 'Validity and utility of alternative predictors of job performance', *Psychological Bulletin*, vol. 96, pp. 72–98.

Hunter, J.E. and Schmidt, F.L. (1990) *Methods of Meta-analysis*. Newbury Park, CA: Sage.

Iles, P.A. and Robertson, I.T. (1989) 'The impact of personnel selection procedures on candidates' in Herriot, P. (ed.) *Assessment and Selection in Organizations*. Chichester: John Wiley.

Janz, T. (1982) 'Initial comparisons of patterned behavior description interviews versus unstructured interviews', *Journal of Applied Psychology*, vol. 67, pp. 577–80.

Kryger, B.R. and Shikiar, R. (1978) 'Sexual discrimination in the use of letters of recommendation', *Journal of Applied Psychology*, vol. 63, pp. 309–14.

Latham, G.P. and Saari, L.M. (1984) 'Do people do what they say? Further studies on the situational interview', *Journal of Applied Psychology*, vol. 69, pp. 569–73.

Love, K.G. (1981) 'Comparison of peer assessment methods: reliability, validity, friendship bias and user reactions', *Journal of Applied Psychology*, vol. 65, pp. 451–7.

Mitchell, T.W. and Klimoski, P.M. (1982) 'Is it rational to be empirical? A test of methods of scoring biographical data', *Journal of Applied Psychology*, vol. 71, pp. 311–17.

Moser, K. and Schuler, H. (1989) 'The nature of psychological measurement' in Herriot, P. (ed.) *Assessment and Selection in Organizations*. Chichester: John Wiley.

Muchinsky, P.M. (1986) 'Personnel selection methods' in Cooper, C.L. and Robertson, I.T. (eds) *International Review of Industrial and Organizational Psychology*. Chichester: John Wiley.

Mumford, M.D. and Stokes, G.S. (1992) 'Developmental determinants of individual action: theory and practice in the application of background data measures' in Dunnette, M.D. and Hough, L.M. (eds) *Handbook of Industrial and Organizational Psychology*, vol. 3. Palo Alto, CA: Consulting Psychologists Press.

Orpen, C. (1985) 'Patterned behavior description interviews versus unstructured interviews: a comparative validity study', *Journal of Applied Psychology*, vol. 70, pp. 774–6.

Owens, W.A. and Schoenfeld, L.A. (1979) 'Towards a classification of persons', *Journal of Applied Psychology*, vol. 64, pp. 569–607.

Pearn, M.A., Kandola, R.S. and Mottram, R.D. (1987) *Selection Tests and Sex Bias*. London: HMSO.

Ree, M.J., Earles, J.A. and Teachout, M.S. (1994) 'Predicting job performance: not much more than g', *Journal of Applied Psychology*, vol. 79, pp. 518–24.

Reilly, R.R. and Chao, G.T. (1982) 'Validity and fairness of some alternative employee selection procedures', *Personnel Psychology*, vol. 35, pp. 1–62.

Reilly, R.R., Henry, S. and Smither, J.W. (1990) 'An examination of the effects of using behavior checklists on the construct validity of assessment center dimensions', *Personnel Psychology*, vol. 43, pp. 71–84.

Roadman, H.E. (1964) 'An industrial use of peer ratings', *Journal of Applied Psychology*, vol. 48, pp. 211–14.

Robertson, I.T. (1988) 'Computer-assisted testing and assessment', *Guidance and Assessment Review*, vol. 4, pp. 1–3.

Robertson, I.T. and Downs, S. (1989) 'Work-sample tests of trainability: a meta-analysis', *Journal of Applied Psychology*, vol. 74, pp. 402–10.

Robertson, I.T. and Kandola, R.S. (1982) 'Work-sample tests: validity, adverse impact and applicant reaction', *Journal of Occupational Psychology*, vol. 55, pp. 171–83.

Robertson, I.T. and Kinder, A. (1993) 'Personality and job competences: the criterion-related validity of some personality variables', *Journal of Occupational and Organizational Psychology*, vol. 66, pp. 225–44.

Robertson, I.T. and Makin, P.J (1986) 'Management selection in Britain: a survey and critique', *Journal of Occupational Psychology*, vol. 59, pp. 45–57.

Robertson, I.T. and Sadri, G. (1993) 'Managerial self-efficacy and managerial performance', *British Journal of Management*, vol. 4, pp. 37–45.

Robertson, I.T., Gratton, L. and Sharpley, D. (1987) 'The psychometric properties and design of managerial assessment centres: dimensions into exercises won't go', *Journal of Occupational Psychology*, vol. 60, pp. 187–95.

Robertson, I.T., Gratton, L. and Rout, U. (1990) 'The validity of situational interviews for administrative jobs', *Journal of Organizational Behaviour*, vol. 11, pp. 69–76.

Robertson, I.T., Iles, P.A., Gratton, L. and Sharpley, D. (1991) 'The impact of personnel selection and assessment methods on candidates', *Human Relations*, vol. 44, pp. 963–82.

Sackett, P.R. and Dreher, G.F. (1982) 'Constructs and assessment centre dimensions: some troubling empirical findings', *Journal of Applied Psychology*, vol. 67, pp. 401–10.

Sadri, G. and Robertson, I.T. (1993) 'Self-efficacy and work-related behaviour: a review and meta-analysis', *Applied Psychology: An International Review*, vol. 42, pp. 139–52.

Schmidt, F.L., Hunter, J.E., McKenzie, R.C. and Muldrow, T. W. (1979) 'Impact of valid selection procedures on workforce productivity', *Journal of Applied Psychology*, vol. 64, pp. 609–26.

Schmidt, F.L., Hunter, J.E. and Pearlman, K. (1981) 'Task differences as moderators of aptitude test validity in selection: a red herring', *Journal of Applied Psychology*, vol. 66, pp. 166–85.

Schmidt, F.L., Mack, M.J. and Hunter, J.E. (1984) 'Selection utility in the occupation of US Park Ranger for three modes of test use', *Journal of Applied Psychology*, vol. 69, pp. 490–7.

Schmitt, N. (1989) 'Fairness in employment selection' in Smith, J.M. and Robertson, I.T. (eds) *Advances in Selection and Assessment*. Chichester: John Wiley.

Schmitt, N. and Robertson, I.T. (1990) 'Personnel selection', *Annual Review of Psychology*, vol. 41, pp. 289–319.

Schmitt, N., Gooding, R.Z., Noe, R.D. and Kirsch, M. (1984) 'Meta-analysis of validity studies published between 1964 and 1982 and the investigation of study characteristics', *Personnel Psychology*, vol. 37, pp. 407–22.

Shackleton, V.J. and Newell, S. (1991) 'Management selection: a comparative survey of methods used in top British and French companies', *Journal of Occupational Psychology*, vol. 64, pp. 23–6.

Shackleton, V.J. and Newell, S. (1994) 'European management selection methods: a comparison of five countries', *International Journal of Selection and Assessment*, vol. 2, pp. 91–102.

Smith, J.M. and Robertson, I.T. (1993) *The Theory and Practice of Systematic Personnel Selection*. London: Macmillan.

Sternberg, R.J. and Wagner, R.K. (eds) (1986) *Practical Intelligence*. Cambridge: Cambridge University Press.

Stokes, G.S. and Reddy, S. (1992) 'Use of background data in organizational decisions' in Cooper, C.L. and Robertson, I.T. (eds) *International Review of Industrial and Organizational Psychology*. Chichester: John Wiley.

Tett, R.P., Jackson, D.N. and Rothstein, M. (1991) 'Personality measures as predictors of job performance: a meta-analytic review', *Personnel Psychology*, vol. 44, pp. 703–42.

Wagner, R.K. and Sternberg, R.J. (1986) 'Tacit knowledge and intelligence in the everyday world' in Sternberg, R.J. and Wagner, R.K. (eds) *Practical Intelligence*. Cambridge: Cambridge University Press.

Weekley, J.A. and Gier, J.A. (1987) 'Reliability and validity of the situational interview for a sales position', *Journal of Applied Psychology*, vol. 72, pp. 484–7.

Weisner, W.H. and Cronshaw, S.F. (1988) 'A meta-analytic investigation of the impact of interview format and degree of structure on the validity of the employment interview', *Journal of Occupational Psychology*, vol. 61, pp. 275–90.

Williams, A.P. and Dobson, P. (1987) *The Validation of the Regular Commissions Board*. Farnborough, Hants.: Army Personnel Research Establishment.

Wolman, B. (1985) *Handbook of Intelligence*. New York: John Wiley.

9

Attitudes at work

LEARNING OBJECTIVES

After studying this chapter, you should be able to:

1 briefly describe two ways in which attitudes have been divided into three components;

2 specify two functions of attitudes for the person who holds them;

3 describe Thurstone and Likert scaling in attitude measurement;

4 describe four factors which affect the success of attempts to change attitudes;

5 explain why attitudes and behaviour are not always consistent;

6 describe three features of attitudes which increase the probability that they will influence behaviour;

7 describe the theory of planned behaviour;

8 define job satisfaction and identify three general propositions about what affects it;

9 describe one research study which has suggested that a person's job satisfaction is not simply a function of the nature of his or her work;

10 define organisational commitment and its component parts;

11 specify the factors which appear to strengthen a person's organisational commitment.

INTRODUCTION

This chapter examines attitudes and attitude change. In the first place, it provides a discussion of what an attitude is with particular reference to the work situation. Second, it briefly describes the ways in which attitudes can be measured. Then attention turns to the question of what factors affect the formation and change of attitudes at work. Attitude change might not be very important if it is not reflected in behaviour change, so the connection between attitudes and behaviour is then examined. Finally, we look at two important work attitudes: job satisfaction and organisational commitment. In each case we describe their nature, measurement, causes and consequences, and make links back to material earlier in the chapter.

WHAT IS AN ATTITUDE?

Attitudes were defined by Secord and Backman (1969) as 'certain regularities of an individual's feelings, thoughts and predispositions to act toward some aspect of his [sic] environment'. Feelings represent the *affective component* of an attitude, thoughts the *cognitive component*, and predispositions to act the *behavioural component*. Attitudes are evaluative; that is, they reflect a person's tendency to feel, think or behave in a positive or negative manner towards the object of the attitude. Attitudes can be held about the physical world around us (e.g. modern architecture), about hypothetical constructs (e.g. democracy) and about other people (e.g. the boss, mother-in-law, the Prime Minister). The general point is that attitudes refer to a particular *target* – e.g. person, group of people, object or concept. This is one way in which attitudes differ from personality, since personality reflects a person's predispositions across a range of situations. Attitudes at work can concern a person's work itself (including its characteristics; *see* Chapter 19), pay, supervision, employing organisation, colleagues, customers or physical work environment. They can even refer to quite specific things such as the quality of pencils one's employer provides.

The affective component of an attitude is reflected in a person's physiological responses (e.g. blood pressure), and/or in what the person says about how he or she feels about the object of the attitude. The cognitive component refers to a person's perception of the object of the attitude, and/or what the person says he or she believes about that object. The behavioural component is reflected by a person's observable behaviour toward the object of the attitude and/or what he or she says about that behaviour. In practice, the term 'attitude' is usually taken to mean the cognitive and/or affective components. Behaviour is most often construed as an outcome of attitudes (*see* below, 'Attitudes and behaviour').

■ **KEY LEARNING POINT**
Attitudes are a person's predisposition to think, feel or behave in certain ways towards certain defined targets.

Is it worth making distinctions between the three components of attitude? This is disputed (*see* Cacioppo *et al.*, 1989), but the answer seems to be yes. Breckler (1984) has shown that although our feelings, beliefs and behaviours towards an object do tend to be consistent with each other, they are not so highly consistent that they can be thought of as the same thing. Hence, for example, it is possible for a person to feel positive about his or her job (affective component) but to believe that the job has few attractive elements (cognitive component). Thus, a person can hold two different attitudes to his or her job simultaneously. Which attitude is expressed, and which one will influence behaviour on any given occasion, may therefore depend on whether the person is concentrating on emotions or on beliefs at that time (Millar and Tesser, 1989).

It is also important to distinguish attitudes from other related concepts. George and Jones (1997) analyse the relationships between attitudes, values and moods. Values are a person's beliefs about what is good or desirable in life. They are long-term guides for a person's choices and experiences. Moods, on the other hand, are 'generalized affective states that are not explicitly linked to particular events or circumstances which may have originally induced the mood' (George and Jones, 1997, p. 400). Values, attitudes and moods differ in terms of (i) whether they concern the past, present, or future; (ii) their stability over time; and (iii) whether they are general or specific. These differences are summarised in Table 9.1. In the long run, attitudes can change values. For example, being dissatisfied with one's job for a long time may change a person's beliefs about the importance of work in life. A consideration of values and moods also helps to explain why attitudes do not always predict behaviour at work. A person may have negative attitudes towards his or her job and colleagues but still help out others at work because he or she places a high value on being responsible and co-operative. The link (or lack of it) between attitudes and behaviour is discussed further later in this chapter.

■ **KEY LEARNING POINT**

Attitudes are related to, but distinguishable from, values, moods and personality.

Table 9.1 Values, attitudes and moods

	Values	Attitudes	Moods
Time perspective	Future (how things should be)	Past (my past experience of a target)	Present (how I feel right now)
Dynamism	Stable (little change over long periods)	Evolving (slow or steady change)	Fluctuating (substantial change over short periods)
Focus	General (guides approach to life)	Specific (directed towards a specific target)	General (how I feel about everything right now)

Source: Adapted from George and Jones (1997).

Another generally-agreed feature of attitudes is that they are *evaluative*. That is, they express whether we consider the target of our attitude to be broadly good or bad. This is likely to depend partly on our personality and values (*see* previous paragraph), but also on our past experiences of the target. Pratkanis and Turner (1994) have analysed attitudes from a social-cognitive perspective (*see* Chapter 2), and asked the important question of why we have attitudes – in other words, what purposes do they serve? There are two general answers to this:

1 attitudes help us to make sense of our environment and act effectively within it, so, for example, our attitudes can be a 'filter' through which we recall certain events but not others, and interpret events of unclear meaning. For example, people who are dissatisfied with their job are more likely than others to believe that ambiguous events are sure to end in disaster;

2 attitudes help us to define and maintain our sense of self-identity (who we are) and self-esteem (a sense of personal value). For example, by expressing our attitudes, we may be able to create certain impressions of ourselves in the minds of others. Also, knowing our own attitudes and those of others helps us to categorise people into groups.

Pratkanis and Turner (1994) argue that an attitude is stored in memory as a 'cognitive representation' which consists of three components:

1 an object label and rules for applying it. For example, if one is concerned about attitudes to colleagues, it is necessary to be clear about who counts as a colleague;

2 an evaluative summary of that object, i.e. whether it is broadly 'good' or 'bad';

3 a knowledge structure supporting the evaluative summary. This can be simple or complex, and may include technical knowledge about the domain, arguments for or against a given proposition, or a listing of the advantages and disadvantages of a target.

> ■ **KEY LEARNING POINT**
>
> *Attitudes are cognitive representations which help us to structure our social world and our place within it.*

As an initial example of some research on attitudes, let us take an article by Furnham *et al.* (1994). They used their academic contacts in 41 countries to obtain a total sample of more than 12 000 young people, who completed a questionnaire concerning their attitudes to work and economic issues. Furnham *et al.* assessed, among other things, the following attitudes, each of which was measured with several statements and a Likert response scale (*see* next section) asking the respondent to what extent he or she agreed or disagreed with each statement.

- *Work ethic*   Example statement: 'I like hard work.'
- *Competitiveness*   Example statement: 'I feel that winning is important in both work and games.'
- *Money beliefs*   Example statement: 'I firmly believe money can solve all my problems.'

They found quite marked differences between countries in the extent to which young people held these attitudes. Work ethic was higher in America than in Europe or the East and Asia. The reverse was true for competitiveness. Money beliefs were highest in the East and Asia, lower in America, and lower again in Europe. At the level of individual countries, those with high economic growth tended to score higher on both competitiveness and money beliefs. However, it is not clear whether the attitudes caused the economic growth, were caused by it, both, or neither. This illustrates one of the problems of the survey method, as discussed in Chapter 3.

HOW ARE ATTITUDES MEASURED?

Attitudes are almost always assessed using self-report questionnaires. In other words, attitude measurement depends upon what people say about their feelings, beliefs and/or behaviour towards the particular object in question. Attitude questionnaires are not just thrown together haphazardly. There are several fairly sophisticated techniques for ensuring that they measure the attitude in question properly. Two of these are Thurstone scaling and Likert scaling.

In the *Thurstone approach*, or the equal interval scale, the psychologist generates a number of potential questionnaire items, ranging from highly favourable about the topic in question to highly unfavourable – for example, in terms of one's attitude towards working overtime, from 'working overtime is the highlight of my week' to 'there is no conceivable justification for working overtime'. After collecting, say, about a hundred such statements, the psychologist asks a sample group of those ultimately to be assessed to rate each statement on a scale from (for example) one to eleven on the degree of favourableness of the attitude statement. The psychologist then includes in the final attitude questionnaire only those statements where (i) there is a high degree of agreement between evaluators on its degree of favourableness, and (ii) the average scale value of the item ranges up the eleven-point scale at equal intervals from one to eleven. Perhaps 20–22 statements are included in the final questionnaire, each of which is separated from the previous one by a scale value of, say, roughly half a point. A person's attitude score is the mean or median scale value of all the statements with which they express agreement.

The second approach is the *Likert technique*, which is sometimes known as the summated scale. This is generally much easier and quicker than Thurstone scaling. In this approach, the psychologist selects a large number of statements that relate to the attitude object concerned. They should either be clearly in favour of the object, or clearly against it. Unlike Thurstone scaling, there is no requirement to establish all points between the extremes. Respondents indicate their agreement or disagreement with each statement. Statements are included in the final scale only if they: (i) tend to be responded to in the same way as others covering apparently similar ground, and (ii) elicit the same responses on two occasions. Whereas in the Thurstone method the respondents might reply with 'yes', 'no' or 'not applicable', in the Likert method a five-, seven- or ten-point response scale is utilised for each statement, usually in terms of strongly agree to strongly disagree. For example, with a five-point response scale, respondents might have the options 'strongly agree' (score 4), 'agree' (score 3), 'neither agree nor disagree' (score 2), 'disagree' (score 1) and 'strongly disagree' (score 0). Scores are reversed (i.e. 4 changes to 0, 3 to 1, etc.) for statements worded negatively (e.g. 'overtime is a real nuisance'), and the person's overall attitude score is the sum or mean of their responses to the statements. Because the scores for negative statements have been reversed, a high score indicates a favourable attitude.

> ■ KEY LEARNING POINT
>
> *Attitude measurement is systematic and quantitative. In line with the positivist research philosophy (see Chapter 3), it is assumed that attitudes exist independently of attempts to articulate or measure them.*

One difficulty with both of these techniques is that they are subject to the *social desirability effect* – that is, to respondents giving the socially desirable answer, as, for instance, 'Of course I don't think war is glorious' when, in fact, they think just the opposite. There are techniques available to minimise this effect. For example, in the questionnaire in Table 9.2, one of the authors wanted to find out what people thought about male and female managers. Instead of asking them directly, he devised two questionnaires which

Table 9.2 Stereotyped attitudes towards male versus female managers

Description of a character you may know

    Is 20 years old
    Graduate
    Trainee manager
    Woman/man*
    Unmarried
    Enjoys films

Whereabouts on these scales would you place this character? Please put a tick in the appropriate box according to where you think she/he* would most probably be best described on the scale.

Will be a 'high flyer'					Will not necessarily be a 'high flyer'
Is inclined to be 'bossy'					Is inclined to be meek
Is a good mixer socially					Is rather shy socially
Is very studious					Is not very studious
Would assume leadership in groups					Would not assume leadership in groups
Contains emotions					Expresses emotions freely
Is self-confident					Is not self-confident
Is ambitious					Is not particularly ambitious
Is assertive					Is not particularly assertive

How much do you think he/she* will be earning   (a) when he/she* is 30? £ ...../p.a.
                                              (b) when he/she* is 60? £ ...../p.a.

* One or the other given on each form

were exactly alike, except that in each version a single line was different – 'male' and 'female'. The two versions of the questionnaire were distributed among a random sample of the general public and the differences between the two forms were assessed, without the issue of male versus female stereotypes ever being raised on the questionnaire.

Whatever the technique of attitude measurement, the result is normally a measure of how *extreme* a person's attitude is: for example, whether he or she strongly likes, mildly likes, is indifferent towards, mildly dislikes or strongly dislikes studying work psychology. Petty and Krosnick (1992) argue for the more general concept of attitude *strength*. As well as extremity, this includes the amount of certainty people feel about their attitude, its importance to them, how intensely they hold the attitude and how knowledgeable they are about it. Petty and Krosnick suggest that consideration of these factors will improve the predictability of behaviour from attitudes. Along the same lines, Pratkanis and Turner (1994) have referred to attitude *salience*, which concerns the extent to which an attitude is clearly relevant to the situation at hand. Their definition of a strong attitude is one which comes easily to mind.

■ **KEY LEARNING POINT**
As well as extremity, strength and certainty are important properties of attitudes.

ATTITUDE CHANGE THROUGH PERSUASION

Changing attitudes is an important part of many people's work. Sales staff try to persuade potential customers to hold a positive attitude to whatever they are selling. Politicians and others interested in social or economic change try to influence public attitudes concerning those issues (*see*, for example, Eiser and van der Pligt, 1988, chapter 7). Managers may seek to change the attitudes of colleagues and subordinates on issues such as marketing strategy or work practices. It should be noted that such attempts are ultimately aimed at changing behaviour, and/or the behavioural component of attitudes. The connection between attitudes and behaviour is examined further in the section on 'Attitudes and behaviour'. Now, however, let us examine some of the factors that determine the success or otherwise of attempts by one person to change the attitudes of another. Most of this material is drawn from social psychology. It is important to remember that attempts to change people's attitudes to something they experience personally and often (such as work) solely through verbal persuasion are unlikely to be successful.

Communicator credibility

The credibility of a communicator rests partly on his or her expertness and trustworthiness as perceived by the person on the receiving end of the communication (Hovland and Weiss, 1951). Expertness concerns how much the communicator knows about the subject of the communication. Trustworthiness usually depends mainly on whether the communicator has a record of honesty, and on whether he or she appears to be arguing against his or her own interests (Eagly *et al.*, 1978). For example, although BAT (the British American Tobacco Company) would be low in credibility if it argued that there was no relationship between smoking and lung cancer, it would have great credibility if it argued that smoking definitely leads to lung cancer. This highlights the fact that credibility depends not only on the communication source, but also on the particular issue and arguments presented.

However, the picture is not quite so simple. Sometimes a low-credibility communicator has as much persuasive effect as a high credibility one – but not immediately; not until a few weeks later. This has been termed the *sleeper effect*, and is thought to be due to the person remembering the message but forgetting the source (Cook *et al.*, 1979). So there is hope even for unpopular politicians and propagandists!

Communicator attractiveness

Tannenbaum (1956) and others since have found that the amount of attitude change is directly related to the degree of attractiveness of the change agent. In Tannenbaum's work, the attractiveness of the communicator was measured through the use of the semantic-differential technique. The ratings of the subjects on the following six evaluation scales were obtained: fair–unfair, dirty–clean, tasty–distasteful, good–bad, pleasant–unpleasant, worthless–valuable. The power of attractiveness may well rest on the desire of the message receiver to be like the communicator. There is also some evidence that attractiveness is especially useful when the message is likely to be unpopular (Eagly and Chaiken, 1975), though its power can be undone if the communicator is perceived to be deliberately exploiting his or her attractiveness.

> ■ **KEY LEARNING POINT**
> *The perceived integrity, expertise and attractiveness of the communicator of a persuasive message partly determine whether the recipients of the message are persuaded by it.*

One-sided versus two-sided arguments

Is it better to give both sides of an argument (though portraying the favoured one more convincingly), or is a one-sided message more persuasive? This issue was first examined by Yale University researchers (Hovland *et al.*, 1949) in their studies of training and indoctrination films used by the American armed forces during the Second World War. One-sided and two-sided communications were used to evaluate the effectiveness of messages in convincing the soldiers that a long, hard war was likely with Japan. They found:

1 that the two-sided presentation was more effective for men who initially held the opposite opinion that the war with Japan would be a short one (less than two years). For men who initially favoured the position of the communication (that war would last longer than two years) the one-sided presentation was more effective. This finding was subsequently replicated in a study by McGinnies (1966);

2 that better educated men were influenced less by the one-sided than by the two-sided presentation. Thus, persons who value their own independence of judgement and their own intellectual competence may view the acceptance of a one-sided communication as incompatible with maintaining self-esteem.

More recent research has suggested some reasons why one-sided or two-sided arguments might be more effective in different situations. For example, a number of studies have indicated that one-sided arguments may allow the individual more time to contemplate the arguments they receive (Chattopadhyay and Alba, 1988). This may be necessary to persuade people with limited cognitive ability and/or low familiarity with the issues. Also, as Tesser and Shaffer (1990) have contended, 'perhaps the need to decide the relative merits of two sides of an unfamiliar issue leads people to concentrate on receiving the message at the expense of thinking about its implications in detail'.

Use of fear

Is the use of threat effective in changing attitudes? Janis and Feshbach (1953) studied the effects of different intensities of fear-arousing messages in an illustrated lecture on dental hygiene. They found that change in attitude and behaviour tended to be greater when intensity of fear arousal was fairly low. Of subjects exposed to the mild fear appeal, 36 per cent followed the recommendations (e.g. tooth-brushing) of the lecture, but only 8 per cent of those who heard the high fear lecture did so.

However, fear arousal can in some circumstances be effective in changing attitudes and behaviour. For example, Dabbs and Leventhal (1966) used it successfully in persuading students to get themselves inoculated against tetanus. Rogers' (1983) *protection motivation theory* proposes that attempts to induce fear will be successful in changing behaviour when they convince a person that:

- the problem is serious
- the problem may affect the person
- he or she can avoid the problem by taking certain specific action
- he or she is capable of performing the behaviour required to avoid the problem.

This bears some resemblance to expectancy theory of motivation (*see* Chapter 11). Protection motivation theory has received considerable support in research (e.g. Mulilis and Lippa, 1990). But offering reliable strategies to avoid the feared fate is often difficult. Many insurance companies present fear-arousing messages (e.g. about having a disabling accident), and then suggest that buying one of their insurance policies is an effective strategy. They forget that, for most people, monetary reward neither avoids such an occurrence nor fully compensates for it.

Social pressures in persuasion

Requiring people to commit themselves publicly to a change in attitude has long been used by change agents (Kiesler, 1971). One might term this requirement the 'Billy Graham effect'. If people make their stand public, they will be less likely to change their position as a result of persuasion in the opposite direction. This is demonstrated by various religious groups that encourage public commitments in the hope of preventing public reconversion or a lapse in faith. As Krech *et al.* (1962) noted, 'Public commitment has been found to be an effective procedure; private commitment has been found to be ineffective'.

Research on group decision making (*see* Chapter 13) has sought to explain why groups tend to arrive at more extreme positions than those initially held by the individual members of the group, an effect that has been labelled *group polarisation*. It seems that people are persuaded to adopt more extreme positions by hearing arguments that they regard as both valid and novel (Isenberg, 1986). As Turner (1991, pp. 67–72) points out, though, it is likely that attitudes are also changed by repeated exposure to arguments that people have heard before and that are therefore not novel to them. For example, Arkes *et al.* (1991) showed that simply repeating a statement causes it to be judged more true by those who hear it. It is also possible that *social comparison processes* play a part. If a member of a group hears other group members advocating a certain position, he or she may draw two conclusions: first, that this position is socially acceptable, and second, that 'anything (s)he can do, I can do better', leading the person to adopt a position more extreme than the one he or she has just heard.

■ KEY LEARNING POINT

The social context in which the persuasive message is received can affect the extent to which it is successful.

Events before the persuasive message

If the recipients of a persuasive message have been forewarned about that message, they are more likely to resist it if they feel threatened or demeaned by that attempt. Generally, people tense up (both physically and psychologically) if they are led to expect a challenge (Cacioppo and Petty, 1979). But if the recipients are already amenable to being persuaded, forewarning can soften them up, and perhaps produce some attitude change even before they have heard the arguments (Hass, 1975).

Another relevant factor concerns what has sometimes been called inoculation. Some attitudes are widely held in our society. For example, it is commonly believed that fresh fruit is good for you. Such beliefs are never challenged or questioned, or only very rarely. In some classic research, McGuire and Papageorgis (1961) found that it was easier to change attitudes that had not earlier been challenged than those that had. Challenge leads the recipient to think of reasons why he or she was correct all along. These reasons act as 'antibodies' against subsequent attempts at persuasion.

Overview of attitude change: central versus peripheral routes to persuasion

Petty and Cacioppo (1985) have made a distinction between the central route to persuasion (which involves careful thought and weighing up of arguments) and the peripheral route, which relies more on emotional responses but relatively little thought. They argued that attitude change through the central route is longer lasting and more closely associated with behaviour than that through the peripheral route. Chaiken (1987) has come up with a similar distinction between systematic and heuristic processing of information.

Persuasive messages processed through the central route need to contain strong arguments that stand up to scrutiny. People who enjoy thinking, are able to concentrate, feel involvement in the issues in question and feel personally responsible for evaluating the message are most likely to process persuasive messages by the central route. For them, the fate of the persuasive message depends more on their weighing up of the arguments than simply remembering those arguments (Cacioppo and Petty, 1989), though the latter is also important when evaluating two-sided messages (Chattopadhyay and Alba, 1988; *see also* the section on 'One-sided versus two-sided arguments', above).

Peripheral processing of information occurs when the recipient of the persuasive message is unwilling or unable to pay it very much attention. When this is the case, the strength of the arguments matters less, and peripheral cues matter more, in determining the success or otherwise of the attempt at attitude change. These peripheral cues include communicator attractiveness and expertise, sheer length of the message (irrespective of the quality of its content), and reactions of other recipients of the message (*see*, for example, Wood and Kallgren, 1988). It seems that peripheral processing is likely when the recipient of the message is in a good mood. Good moods seem to reduce the extent to which messages are critically examined, and weak arguments are sometimes as convincing as strong ones (Eagly and Chaiken, 1992).

> ■ KEY LEARNING POINT
>
> *How persuasive a message is depends partly on which cognitive processes are used by the recipient when thinking about it.*

Clearly the distinction between central and peripheral processing is important for those who wish to change the attitudes of others. It gives some guidance about which aspects of the message, its contents and its context are important to different audiences in different situations. The relevant research tends to concern theory development rather than theory application (*see* Tesser and Shaffer, 1990; Olson and Zanna, 1993). But it promises much for future practice.

ATTITUDES AND BEHAVIOUR

It could be argued that attitudes only matter if they influence actual behaviour. For example, racial prejudice in the workplace is damaging to the extent that it finds expression in discrimination or other negative behaviour towards minority groups. To what extent do attitudes predict behaviour? The answer based on an early review of the research evidence seemed to be 'not very much' (Wicker, 1969). People's avowed feelings and beliefs about someone or something seemed only loosely related to how they behaved towards that person or object.

A number of possible reasons were suggested for this lack of correspondence. One was social pressures of various kinds: laws, societal norms and the views of specific people can all prevent a person behaving consistently with his or her attitudes. So can other attitudes, limitations on a person's abilities, and, indeed, a person's general activity levels. There was also some suggestion that the research on this issue was badly designed, and therefore failed to find correspondence that did in fact exist between attitudes and behaviour. In particular, it was argued that measures of attitude were often general (e.g. attitudes about law-breaking) whereas measures of behaviour were specific, reflecting only one of many elements of the attitude (e.g. committing motoring offences). Also, behaviour was assessed on only one occasion or over a short time period. Longer-term assessments of multiple instances of the behaviour would be a fairer test of whether attitudes predict behaviour.

In the article referred to earlier, Pratkanis and Turner (1994) summarised observations from earlier research and added some of their own in discussing when the link between attitudes and behaviour is likely to be strong. Here are four of the factors they suggest will increase the correspondence between attitudes and behaviour:

1 when the object of the attitude is both well-defined and salient. An example of a poorly defined object would be where a person was not sure whether his or her immediate supervisor should be classed as a member of management. This would make it uncertain whether that person's attitudes to management would affect his or her behaviour towards the supervisor. Salience concerns the extent to which the object of the attitude is perceived as relevant to the situation at hand;

2 when attitude strength is high – that is, when the attitude comes easily to mind;

3 when knowledge supporting the attitude is plentiful and complex. This increases a person's certainty about what he or she thinks, as well as his or her ability to act effectively towards the object of the attitude;

4 when the attitude supports important aspects of the self. For example, an accountant may have positive attitudes towards other accountants because he or she believes that accountants (and therefore by extension himself or herself) perform an important role in the national economy.

> ■ **KEY LEARNING POINT**
> *The lack of correspondence between attitudes and behaviour found in much research is partly due to poor research design, and partly to a neglect of cognitive processes concerning attitudes.*

Ajzen and Fishbein (1980) developed a model of the relationship between attitudes and behaviour designed to overcome these difficulties. This model was called the *theory of reasoned action*. It assumed that actions are best predicted by intentions, and that intentions are in turn determined by a person's attitude and his or her perception of social pressure.

The theory of reasoned action was then adapted by Ajzen and Madden (1986), and its name was changed to the *theory of planned behaviour* (Fig. 9.1). It now includes the concept of perceived behavioural control. This reflects the extent to which the person believes that he or she can perform the necessary behaviours in any given situation. It is therefore similar to the concept of *self-efficacy* and is in line with self-regulatory theories of motivation (*see* Chapter 11). Perceived behavioural control is thought to influence behaviour directly, and also indirectly through intentions. Some research (e.g. McCaul *et al.*, 1988) has indicated that the addition of concepts reflecting control does indeed further improve the extent to which behaviour can be predicted.

Fig. 9.1 Theory of planned behaviour

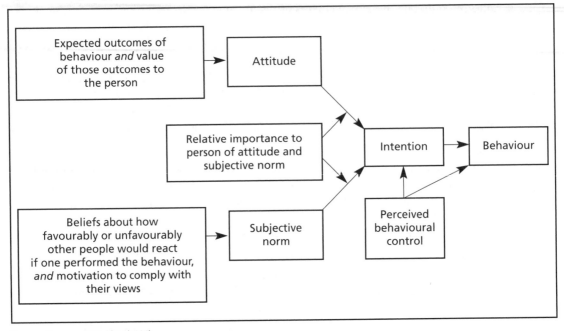

Source: Ajzen and Madden (1986)

Note that in the theory of planned behaviour, 'attitude' is defined in precise and rather unusual terms – it concerns beliefs about the consequences of behaviour, and not general beliefs or feelings about the object of the attitude. This is similar to expectancy theories of motivation (*see* Chapter 11). Note also that 'subjective norm' takes into account both the opinions of other people and the person's wish (or lack of it) to comply with those opinions. The theory of planned behaviour also acknowledges that people vary in the relative importance of attitude and subjective norm in determining their intentions. It has proved quite successful in predicting behaviour in a wide range of settings. However, relatively few of these directly concern work behaviour (though many concern consumer behaviour). This is perhaps an example of how work psychology sometimes neglects theoretical advances in social psychology. Sheppard *et al.* (1988) reported that research studies have typically found that the theory explains about half of the variance in behaviour. This is quite an impressive performance.

> ■ **KEY LEARNING POINT**
>
> *The theory of planned behaviour takes ideas from cognitive theories of motivation in proposing that actions are the product of attitudes, social pressures and intentions.*

Ajzen (1991) has provided a thorough account of the theory of planned behaviour and research on it. He points out that, as the theory suggests, intentions to perform particular behaviours are often accurately predicted by attitudes towards the behaviour, subjective norms and perceived behavioural control. Also, intentions, together with perceived behavioural control, are quite good at predicting a person's actual behaviour. Ajzen also draws attention to some additional points. First, the relative importance of the various factors in predicting intention might be expected to vary with different behaviours and different situations, but little is known beyond this very general proposition about how particular situations/behaviours might exert such an influence. Second, perceived behavioural control really does matter – so the theory of planned behaviour is an improvement on the theory of reasoned action. But the usefulness of perceived behavioural control will be limited if the perception is wildly inaccurate. If a person believes that he or she is in control of a situation, but is mistaken, then no amount of belief will translate an intention into behaviour. Third, the influence of subjective norms on intentions and behaviour is often quite weak. Ajzen suggests that some people may be more responsive to their own perceptions of moral obligations than to the opinions of other people. These observations suggest areas in which the theory of planned behaviour may be improved in future. Also, comparison of the theory of planned behaviour with material presented earlier in this chapter shows that it ignores factors like the salience of the attitude and the extent to which it is supported by knowledge.

CASE
STUDY
9.1

A lunchtime drink

Jerry Lander felt that there was nothing wrong with drinking a glass or two of beer during his lunchbreak. He could afford it easily enough. He claimed that he had never seen any evidence that a lunchtime drink harmed his work performance during the afternoon. He found that it helped him feel more relaxed and happy at work. Nevertheless, he could do without a drink without much difficulty if he had to. Jerry liked the friendship and approval of other people, and at lunchtime the nearby bar was full of acquaintances he could chat to. Work was an important part of Jerry's life and he was keen to gain promotion. Unfortunately his boss did not approve of alcoholic drink at lunchtime – or indeed at any other time. Nor did most of his colleagues, with whom he had to work closely. They seemed to view it as a sign of personal inadequacy.

Suggested exercise

Use the theory of planned behaviour to decide whether Jerry Lander is likely to drink a glass of beer during his lunchbreak on most working days.

So far in this chapter we have deliberately avoided discussing specific attitudes, in order to ensure that we cover the important general points. Now it is time to be more specific. We therefore conclude this chapter by looking at two concepts central to work psychology: job satisfaction and organisational commitment. The first concerns a person's evaluation and feelings about his or her job, while the second reflects how attached he or she is to the employing organisation. Both have been the subject of much research and practical interest over many years.

JOB SATISFACTION

Job satisfaction has been seen as important for two main reasons. First, it is one indicator of a person's psychological well-being, or mental health. It is unlikely (though not impossible) that a person who is unhappy at work will be happy in general. So psychologists and others who are concerned with individuals' welfare are keen to ensure that high job satisfaction is experienced. Second, it is often assumed that job satisfaction will lead to motivation and good work performance. We have already noted that such connections between attitudes and behaviour do not necessarily occur, and that in fact the link between job satisfaction and work performance is very weak (*see* Chapter 3).

What is job satisfaction?

Locke (1976) defined job satisfaction as a 'pleasurable or positive emotional state resulting from the appraisal of one's job or job experiences'. The concept generally refers to a variety of aspects of the job that influence a person's levels of satisfaction with it. These usually include attitudes toward pay, working conditions, colleagues and boss, career prospects, and the intrinsic aspects of the job itself. Judge and Hulin (1993), among others, have suggested that in the field of job satisfaction there are three different approaches. The first is that work attitudes such as job satisfaction are dispositional in nature; that is, they are 'stable positive or negative dispositions learned through experience' (Griffin and Bateman, 1986; Staw *et al.*, 1986), or based on a person's genetic inheritance. The second approach is the 'social information processing' model, which suggests that job satisfaction and other workplace attitudes are developed or constructed out of experiences and information provided by others at work (Salancik and Pfeffer, 1978; O'Reilly and Caldwell, 1985). In other words, at least in part, job satisfaction is a function of how other people in the workplace interpret and evaluate what goes on. The third approach is the information processing model, which is based on the accumulation of cognitive information about the workplace and one's job. In a sense, this is the most obvious approach – it argues that a person's job satisfaction is influenced directly by the characteristics of his or her job (Hackman and Oldham, 1976; *see also* Chapter 19), and the extent to which those characteristics match what that person wants in a job.

> ■ **KEY LEARNING POINT**
>
> *Job satisfaction can be seen in three ways – as a function of (i) the features of a person's job; (ii) the opinions of other people in the person's workplace; or (iii) his or her general personality or disposition.*

Measuring job satisfaction

There have been many measures of job satisfaction in the workplace, from the very widely used Job Description Index (JDI; Smith *et al.*, 1969) to the Job Satisfaction Scales of Warr *et al.* (1969) to the more recent job satisfaction scale of the Occupational Stress Indicator (OSI; Cooper *et al.*, 1987). They all involve questions or statements asking respondents to indicate what they think and/or feel about their job as a whole (so-called global job satisfaction) and/or specific aspects of it, such as pay, work activities, working conditions, career prospects, relationship with superiors and relationships with colleagues (so-called job facet satisfaction). Likert scaling (see earlier in this chapter) is usually employed. In Table 9.3 we provide an example of a measure of job satisfaction from the OSI, which contains all of the elements that usually make up a job satisfaction measure.

Table 9.3 A job satisfaction measure

How you feel about your job

Very much satisfaction	6	Much satisfaction	5
Some satisfaction	4	Some dissatisfaction	3
Much dissatisfaction	2	Very much dissatisfaction	1

1 Communication and the way information flows around your organisation	6 5 4 3 2 1
2 The relationships you have with other people at work	6 5 4 3 2 1
3 The feeling you have about the way you and your efforts are valued	6 5 4 3 2 1
4 The actual job itself	6 5 4 3 2 1
5 The degree to which you feel 'motivated' by your job	6 5 4 3 2 1
6 Current career opportunities	6 5 4 3 2 1
7 The level of job security in your present job	6 5 4 3 2 1
8 The extent to which you may identify with the public image or goals of your organisation	6 5 4 3 2 1
9 The style of supervision that your superiors use	6 5 4 3 2 1
10 The way changes and innovations are implemented	6 5 4 3 2 1
11 The kind of work or tasks that you are required to perform	6 5 4 3 2 1
12 The degree to which you feel that you can personally develop or grow in your job	6 5 4 3 2 1
13 The way in which conflicts are resolved in your company	6 5 4 3 2 1
14 The scope your job provides to help you achieve your aspirations and ambitions	6 5 4 3 2 1
15 The amount of participation which you are given in important decision making	6 5 4 3 2 1
16 The degree to which your job taps the range of skills which you feel you possess	6 5 4 3 2 1
17 The amount of flexibility and freedom you feel you have in your job	6 5 4 3 2 1
18 The psychological 'feel' or climate that dominates your organisation	6 5 4 3 2 1
19 Your level of salary relative to your experience	6 5 4 3 2 1
20 The design or shape of your organisation's structure	6 5 4 3 2 1
21 The amount of work you are given to do, whether too much or too little	6 5 4 3 2 1
22 The degree to which you feel extended in your job	6 5 4 3 2 1

Source: Cooper *et al.* (1987).

Studies of job satisfaction

The major determinants of job satisfaction seem to derive from all three of the theoretical approaches identified above. Thus, regarding the job itself, for most people the major determinants of global job satisfaction derive from the intrinsic features of the work itself. These are most commonly based on the Hackman and Oldham (1976) core constructs of skill variety, task identity, task significance, autonomy and feedback (*see also* Chapter 19). Hackman and Oldham (1976) defined their constructs as:

- *skill variety*: the extent to which the tasks require different skills;
- *task identity*: the extent to which the worker can complete a 'whole' piece of work, as opposed to a small part of it;
- *task significance*: the extent to which the work is perceived as influencing the lives of others;
- *autonomy*: the extent to which the worker has freedom within the job to decide how it should be done;
- *feedback*: the extent to which there is correct and precise information about how effectively the worker is performing.

In addition, as Griffin and Bateman (1986) have observed, 'in general, most studies find significant and positive correlations between leader behaviours such as initiating structure and consideration, and satisfaction'. So leader behaviour is also important in satisfaction at work. Other social factors have more subtle influences on job satisfaction, as predicted by the social information processing approach. For example, Agho *et al.* (1993) found that perceptions of distributive justice (the fairness with which rewards were distributed in the organisation) predicted job satisfaction. O'Reilly and Caldwell (1985) demonstrated that both task perceptions and job satisfaction of workers were influenced by the opinions of others in their workgroups.

Taber and Alliger (1995) have investigated the extent to which overall job satisfaction can be thought of as the total or average of people's opinions about each task in their job. They asked over 500 employees of a US medical college to describe the tasks of their job, and to rate each task according to its importance, complexity, level of supervision, level of concentration required, how much they enjoyed it, and the amount of time spent on it each week. Taber and Alliger found that the percentage of time spent in enjoyable tasks correlated 0.40 with satisfaction with the work itself, and 0.28 with global job satisfaction. The importance of the task, closeness of supervision and concentration required did not have much impact on job satisfaction. The correlations show that the accumulation of enjoyment across the various tasks involved in the job did, not surprisingly, say something about overall job satisfaction. But the correlations were also low enough to indicate that other factors also matter. As the authors noted (p. 118):

> Perhaps workers form a gestalt – a perception of pattern – about their jobs that is not a simple linear function of task enjoyment ... a worker might perform 15 different enjoyable tasks; nevertheless, the worker's global job satisfaction still could be low if the 15 tasks were so unrelated to one another that the total job was not meaningful, or did not relate clearly to the mission of the organization.

The coverage of attitudes earlier in this chapter suggests that job satisfaction is likely to be used by people to help make sense of their work, and to define who they are, or are not. So in a brief reply to Taber and Alliger, Locke (1995) pointed out that job satisfaction will depend partly on how well people's tasks fit their long-term purposes, how much their self-esteem depends on their job and which job experiences are processed most thoroughly in their memory. One could add that the opinions of others, as discussed by O'Reilly and Caldwell (1985), will also influence a person's overall feelings about his or her job.

> ■ **KEY LEARNING POINT**
> *Job satisfaction is more than how much the person enjoys the job tasks.*

The dispositional approach to job satisfaction has also received some support. In a review of research, Arvey *et al.* (1991) suggested that somewhere between 10 per cent and 30 per cent of the variation in job satisfaction depends on genetic factors. They argued that 'there is less variability in job satisfaction between genetically identical people [i.e. identical twins] who hold different jobs than there is among genetically unrelated people who hold the same job' (p. 374). However, it is difficult to be sure about what proportion of job satisfaction is a function of a person's disposition. Most research has construed it as what is left over when situational factors have been considered. But this assumes that all of the important situational factors have been taken into account – surely an optimistic assumption. According to Judge and Hulin (1993), research has also tended to use small samples and/or data originally collected for other purposes, and has been unclear about what aspects of a person's disposition might be expected to affect his or her job satisfaction.

Judge and Hulin (1993) obtained data from 255 people working in medical clinics, and for 160 of them they also got the opinions of other individuals who knew them well. The researchers wanted to examine the linkages between affective disposition (that is, a person's tendency to feel positive or negative about life), subjective well-being (how they feel about life right now), job satisfaction and job characteristics. Their data were most consistent with the causal model shown in Fig. 9.2. Affective disposition not surprisingly had a substantial effect upon subjective well-being. That is, a person's tendency to take an optimistic and happy approach to life influenced how optimistic and happy he or she felt day to day. Subjective well-being (and therefore, indirectly, affective disposition) had a substantial impact on job satisfaction, and job satisfaction had almost as much effect upon subjective well-being. Intrinsic job characteristics affected job satisfaction, as one would expect, but scarcely more strongly than subjective well-being. The research of Judge and Hulin suggests: (i) the nature of the job really does matter for job satisfaction; (ii) so, indirectly, does a person's disposition; and (iii) job satisfaction has an impact on more general well-being – work does spill over, psychologically, into other areas of life.

Another angle on the idea that job satisfaction is more a feature of the person than the job is expressed in research on sex differences in job satisfaction. A number of studies have, for example, found that on average women's job satisfaction is lower than men's. This has fuelled stereotypical views of women (*see* Chapter 12) as being less interested and involved in work than men. Often this is assumed to be because women's earnings are, or have been, the subsidiary income of the household, whereas men tend to be the main breadwinners. On the other hand, a less often considered possibility is that

Fig. 9.2 A causal model of job satisfaction reported by Judge and Hulan (1993)

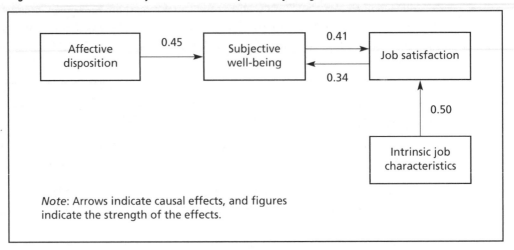

Note: Arrows indicate causal effects, and figures indicate the strength of the effects.

women might be less satisfied simply because they tend to have less good jobs than men. Indeed, this was what Lefkowitz (1994) found. Lefkowitz obtained a diverse sample of 371 men and 361 women from nine organisations. As predicted, men scored significantly higher on average than women on work satisfaction and pay satisfaction. However, these differences disappeared when variables such as actual income, occupational status, level of education and age were held constant.

Does job satisfaction change over the lifespan?

Some research has suggested that job satisfaction tends to increase fairly steadily through working life. If accurate, this could be for a variety of reasons. First, older people may be in objectively better jobs than younger ones, since they have had longer to find a job that suits them. Second, older people may have lowered their expectations over the years, so that they are more easily satisfied. Third, older people might always have been more satisfied than younger ones – a so-called *cohort effect*. Fourth, dissatisfied older people may be more likely than younger ones to opt for early retirement or voluntary redundancy, so that those remaining in employment represent a biased sample of older people. In the most thorough recent study of the relationship between job satisfaction and age, Clarke *et al.* (1996) found in a sample of over 5000 UK employees that job satisfaction started fairly high in a person's teens, then dipped in the 20s and 30s, then rose through the 40s (back to teenage levels) and further in the 50s and 60s. After controlling for various factors, Clarke *et al.* reckoned that, on average, job satisfaction bottomed-out at age 36. The dip and subsequent rise was more marked for men than for women. Because the study was cross-sectional, the researchers were, however, unable to rule out any of the first three possible explanations described above.

> ■ **KEY LEARNING POINT**
> *Job satisfaction is partly determined by a person's general disposition, but not so much so that it is constant over a person's working life.*

ORGANISATIONAL COMMITMENT

What is organisational commitment?

The concept of organisational commitment has generated huge amounts of research from the 1980s onwards. This is no doubt partly because it is what some employers say they want from employees – organisational commitment is a managerial agenda to a greater extent than job satisfaction. In recent years particularly, this can be seen as exceptionally one-sided: as Hirsh *et al.* (1995) have pointed out, what some employers now appear to want is totally committed but totally expendable staff. Exactly *why* employers should want committed staff is less obvious, partly because, as we shall see below, commitment does not guarantee high work performance.

Organisational commitment has been defined by Mowday *et al.* (1979) as 'the relative strength of an individual's identification with and involvement in an organisation'. This concept is often thought to have three components (Griffin and Bateman, 1986): (i) a desire to maintain membership in the organisation, (ii) belief in and acceptance of the values and goals of the organisation, and (iii) a willingness to exert effort on behalf of the organisation. If a person is committed to an organisation, therefore, he or she has a strong identification with it, values membership, agrees with its objectives and value systems, is likely to remain in it, and, finally, is prepared to work hard on its behalf. More recently, it has also been suggested that commitment will lead to so-called organisational citizenship behaviours, such as helping out others and being particularly conscientious.

Some work psychologists divided organisational commitment slightly differently from the way described above. For example, Allen and Meyer (1990) have distinguished between:

- *affective commitment*: essentially concerns the person's emotional attachment to his or her organisation;

- *continuance commitment*: a person's perception of the costs and risks associated with leaving his or her current organisation. There is considerable evidence that there are two aspects of continuance commitment: the personal sacrifice that leaving would involve, and a lack of alternatives available to the person;

- *normative commitment*: a moral dimension, based on a person's felt obligation and responsibility to his or her employing organisation.

There is good evidence for the distinctions between these forms of commitment (Dunham *et al.*, 1994). Interestingly, they approximate respectively to the affective, behavioural and cognitive components of attitudes identified at the start of this chapter.

Other observers have pointed out that people feel multiple commitments at work – not only to their organisation, but also perhaps to their location, department, work group or trade union (Reichers, 1985; Barling *et al.*, 1990). There is also a wider issue here: what exactly *is* the organisation? Complexities like parent companies and franchises can make it difficult to identify exactly which organisation one belongs to. But more than that, some psychologists (e.g. Coopey and Hartley, 1991) are critical of the whole notion of organisational commitment because it implies that the organisation is unitarist – that is, it is one single entity with a united goal. A moment's thought reveals that most organisations consist of various factions with somewhat different and possibly even contradictory goals. Faced with these ambiguities, it seems that most people think of the term organisation as meaning top management. This is clearly different from commitment to (for example) one's supervisor or work group, which employees may also feel (Becker and Billings, 1993). Further, it is possible to distinguish between (yet more!) different bases of commitment to the various constituencies in an organisation. Two such bases are identification and internalisation. As Becker *et al.* (1996, p. 465) have put it:

> Identification occurs when people adopt attitudes and behaviours in order to be associated with a satisfying, self-defining relationship with another person or group ... Internalization occurs when people adopt attitudes and behaviours because their content is congruent with their value systems.

■ KEY LEARNING POINT

Organisational commitment concerns a person's sense of attachment to his or her organisation. It has several components, and is only one of a number of commitments a person may feel.

Measuring organisational commitment

A number of questionnaires have been developed to measure the various aspects or theories of commitment discussed above. For example, a widely used scale is the Organizational Commitment Questionnaire (OCQ), which was developed by Mowday *et al.* (1979). It is a 15-item questionnaire which has been used as a total commitment scale, but has also been broken down into subscales by various researchers (Bateman and Strasser, 1984). The OCQ is comprised of items like 'I feel very little loyalty to this organization', 'I am willing to put in a great deal of effort beyond that normally expected in order to help this organization be successful', and 'I really care about the fate of this organization'. The OCQ was designed before the distinctions between affective, normative and continuance commitment were articulated in the literature. Subsequent research has clearly shown that the OCQ chiefly reflects affective commitment. There are other scales in use as well. For example, Warr *et al.* (1979) developed a nine-item scale. An example item is 'I feel myself to be part of the organization'. This measure also tends to concentrate on affective commitment. Allen and Meyer (1990) have developed their own questionnaire measure of affective, normative and continuance commitment, with each of the three components assessed by eight items. Although not perfect, this measure has stood up well to psychometric scrutiny, and is now commonly used. There are also plenty of other questionnaire measures designed to measure other components and concepts of commitment.

■ KEY LEARNING POINT

Like job satisfaction, organisational commitment is usually measured with questionnaires using Likert scaling.

Causes and consequences of organisational commitment

Much research has investigated how organisational commitment relates to other experiences, attitudes and behaviour at work. This is discussed below. Figure 9.3 represents our attempt to summarise what is known, and what seems likely.

As with job satisfaction, there are several distinct theoretical approaches to organisational commitment. One of these, the behavioural approach, sees commitment as being created when a person does things publicly, of his or her own free will, and which would be difficult to undo (Kiesler, 1971). Rather like Bem's (1972) self-perception approach, it is suggested that people examine their own behaviour and conclude that since they did something with significant consequences in full view of others, when they could have chosen not to do so, they really must be committed to it. So if a person freely chooses to join an organisation, and subsequently performs other committing behaviours (e.g. voluntarily working long hours), he or she will feel more committed to it. This is a neat theory. There is a certain amount of evidence in favour of it (Mabey, 1986).

More commonly, however, it has been suggested that people's commitment can be fostered by giving them positive experiences. This reflects a kind of social exchange

Fig. 9.3 A model of organisational commitment

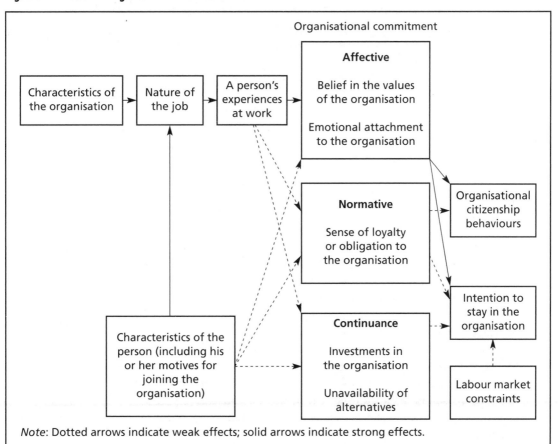

Note: Dotted arrows indicate weak effects; solid arrows indicate strong effects.

approach. The person is essentially saying 'if this work organisation is nice to me, I will be loyal and hardworking'. Many researchers have tried to identify exactly which pleasant experiences matter most for organisational commitment. On the whole, it seems that factors intrinsic to the job (e.g. challenge, autonomy) are more important in fostering commitment than extrinsic factors such as pay and working conditions (Mathieu and Zajac, 1990; Dunham *et al.*, 1994). This seems especially true for the affective component of commitment (i.e. commitment based on emotional attachment). On the other hand, continuance commitment (that is, the extent to which leaving would be costly for the person) is more influenced by the person's perception of his or her past contributions to the organisation and present likely attractiveness (or lack of it) to other employers (Meyer *et al.*, 1989). But there is also some suggestion that commitment is partly a function of the person rather than what happens to him or her at work (Bateman and Strasser, 1984). That is, perhaps some people are, through their personality or disposition, more prone to feel committed than others, just as some seem more likely than others to feel satisfied with their job. Given the research on job satisfaction, that looks like a reasonable proposition. However, research on organisational commitment has not yet gone down that route.

> ### ■ KEY LEARNING POINT
>
> *It is usually assumed that organisational commitment is fostered by positive experiences at work, and to a lesser extent by the circumstances in which the person joined the organisation. The possibility that some people may be more predisposed to be committed than others is less often investigated.*

The distinction between affective and continuance commitment may also be significant for work performance. Meyer *et al.* (1989, 1993) found that workers high on affective commitment to their organisation tended to be better performers than those low on affective commitment. But the opposite pattern of results was observed for continuance commitment. This makes sense: high continuance commitment is based partly on a perceived lack of employment options, and one reason for people lacking options may be that they are not much good at their work! On the other hand, some other research has failed to find these links between commitment and performance. As with job satisfaction, it seems that many factors intervene between attitude and behaviour. One of these might be ability. A person is unlikely to perform well at a task that he or she is not able to do, even if highly committed to the organisation. Therefore, one might expect a stronger link between commitment and performance for aspects of performance that depend more on motivation than ability. Consistent with this, Organ and Ryan (1995) reviewed relevant research and found a correlation between commitment and organisational citizenship behaviours of about 0.32, which is higher than usually found between commitment and overall job performance. Here again, it may also be worth taking into account commitment to other constituencies, since Becker *et al.* (1996) have found that commitment to the supervisor (especially commitment based on internalisation) is more highly correlated with job performance than is organisational commitment.

> ■ **KEY LEARNING POINT**
>
> *Organisational commitment has only very loose links with overall job performance. However, highly committed people are more likely than less committed people to help others in the organisation.*

As one would expect, a person who does not feel committed to his or her employing organisation is more likely to want to leave it, and actually to do so, than a person who feels more committed (Mathieu and Zajac, 1990). In fact, intention to leave the organisation is the strongest and most often reported correlate of low organisational commitment. This appears especially the case for affective commitment (Meyer, 1997). However, intention to leave does not necessarily translate into actual leaving. For example, if a person believes that it would be difficult to obtain another job (low perceived behavioural control in terms of the theory of planned behaviour), then low commitment is unlikely to lead him or her to leave the employing organisation. This once again illustrates how attitudes do not necessarily find expression in behaviour.

SUMMARY

In this chapter we have taken a close look at attitudes. In particular, we have focused on what they are, how they can be measured, how they can be changed, and their links with behaviour. Like most social psychological phenomena, attitudes are more complicated than they seem at first sight. They have several different components which may or may not fit together nicely. Changing attitudes is difficult, but it is not impossible – and easier if the persuader is aware of research findings on attitude change. A person's

CASE STUDY 9.2

Attitudes to job search

Imagine that you are a careers adviser at a university or college. You have become concerned at the number of students who do not seem to start thinking about what they will do after graduation until well into their final year of study. You know that it usually takes at least six months to obtain a job, and sometimes a lot longer. You also know that while some graduates seem happy enough to be unemployed or doing casual work for some months after graduation, many others are not. They regret not having begun to plan for their future early enough.

You decide that you should try to change students' approach to planning for their future career. You decide to compose a handout of not more than 200 words which will be distributed to students during their penultimate year of study.

Suggested exercise

Using the information in this chapter, compose a handout of not more than 200 words designed to persuade students to start their career planning earlier. Let someone else read your handout. Ask them to tell you whether or not they find it persuasive, and why. Justify your wording of the handout to that person.

attitudes may predict his or her behaviour quite well in some circumstances, if the right attitude is assessed, and if the person's perceptions of social pressures and his or her own capabilities are also taken into account. Two key work attitudes are job satisfaction and organisational commitment. Job satisfaction concerns a person's evaluation of his or her job, while organisational commitment refers to the extent to which a person feels attached to his or her employing organisation. They can both be measured satisfactorily, both are influenced by the nature of the person's job, and both appear to have quite complex connections with a range of behaviours and attitudes at work. However, neither is strongly associated with work performance.

TEST YOUR LEARNING

Short-answer questions

1 Define three aspects of an attitude.

2 Why are attitudes useful for a person?

3 Compare and contrast Likert and Thurstone attitude scaling.

4 List the features of the communicator of a persuasive message which affect the success of that message.

5 List the features of a persuasive message which affect the success of that message.

6 Draw a diagram to show the theory of planned behaviour, and define its key concepts.

7 Briefly describe three general phenomena that can influence job satisfaction.

8 Define organisational commitment and its component parts.

Essay questions

1 In what circumstances do attitudes determine behaviours at work?

2 Examine how much is known about what factors determine *either* job satisfaction *or* organisational commitment.

3 To what extent does the research evidence about organisational commitment suggest that managers in organisations should care about how committed their staff are?

GLOSSARY OF TERMS

Attitude A regularity in an individual's feelings, thoughts and predispositions to act towards some aspect of his or her environment.

Attractiveness of communicator The extent to which a person attempting to change the attitude of another is seen as the kind of person that the recipient of the message would like to be.

Central route to persuasion Attitude change which occurs as a result of a person carefully considering information and arguments relevant to that attitude.

Cohort effect Lasting differences in psychological functioning between people born in different eras.

Credibility of communicator The extent to which a person attempting to change the attitude of another is seen as expert and trustworthy.

Dispositional approach to attitudes An approach which views attitudes as determined by a person's genetic make-up or by other deep-seated stable personality characteristics.

Group polarisation The process by which groups of people tend to adopt positions that are more extreme than the initial opinions of the individuals who make up that group.

Job satisfaction A pleasurable or positive emotional state arising from the appraisal of one's job or job experiences.

Likert scaling A method of measuring attitudes where people respond by indicating their opinion on a dimension running from (for example) 'strongly agree' at one end to 'strongly disagree' at the other.

One-sided argument Attempt at persuasion where all of the points made support the direction of attitude change desired by the communicator. Contrast with two-sided arguments, where points for and against the desired change are presented.

Organisational commitment The relative strength of an individual's identification with and involvement in an organisation.

Perceived behavioural control In the theory of planned behaviour, perceived behavioural control concerns the extent to which a person believes that he or she can perform the behaviour required in a given situation.

Peripheral route to persuasion Attitude change which occurs as a result of 'surface' features of an attempt at persuasion such as communicator attractiveness or an easily-recalled slogan.

Planned behaviour A theory which attempts to explain how and when attitudes determine intentions and behaviour.

Protection motivation theory A theory proposed by Rogers (1983) to explain the effect of fear on attitude change and behaviour.

Sleeper effect Where an attempt at attitude change produces a delayed but not an immediate effect.

Socio-cognitive An approach to attitudes which stresses how they are encoded in a person's memory and what functions they serve for the person.

Subjective norm In the theory of planned behaviour, subjective norm is a combination of the (perceived) opinions of other people and the person's motivation to comply with them.

Thurstone scaling A method of measuring attitudes where statements are graded in terms of their extremity of agreement or disagreement with a particular attitude.

SUGGESTED FURTHER READING

1 John Meyer's chapter in the 1997 *International Review of Industrial and Organizational Psychology* (full reference in the list below) provides a very thorough analysis of the literature on organisational commitment.

2 Ajzen's 1991 article in the journal *Organizational Behavior and Human Decision Processes* (full reference in the list below) describes the influential theory of planned behaviour. Not an especially easy read, but very informative about attitude theory.

3 The paper by Pratkanis and Turner in the journal *Human Relations* is an excellent example of how the study of attitudes has profited from the social cognitive tradition in psychology. The full reference is listed below, and elements of the paper have been briefly summarised in this chapter.

REFERENCES

Agho, A.O., Mueller, C.W. and Price, J.L. (1993) 'Determinants of employee job satisfaction: an empirical test of a causal model', *Human Relations*, vol. 46, pp. 1007–27.

Ajzen, I. (1991) 'The theory of planned behavior', *Organizational Behavior and Human Decision Processes*, vol. 50, pp. 179–211.

Ajzen, I. and Fishbein, M. (1980) *Understanding Attitudes and Predicting Social Behavior*. Englewood Cliffs, NJ: Prentice Hall.

Ajzen, I. and Madden, J.T. (1986) 'Prediction of goal-directed behavior: attitudes, intentions, and perceived behavioral control', *Journal of Experimental Social Psychology*, vol. 22, pp. 453–74.

Allen, N.J. and Meyer, J.P. (1990) 'The measurement and antecedents of affective, continuance and normative commitment to the organization', *Journal of Occupational Psychology*, vol. 63, pp. 11–18.

Arkes, H.R., Boehm, L.E. and Xu, G. (1991) 'Determinants of judged validity', *Journal of Experimental Social Psychology*, vol. 27, pp. 576–605.

Arvey, R.D., Carter, W.G. and Buerkley, D.K. (1991) 'Job satisfaction: dispositional and situational influences' in Cooper, C.L. and Robertson, I.T. (eds) *International Review of Industrial and Organizational Psychology*, vol. 6. Chichester: John Wiley.

Barling, J., Wade, B. and Fullagar, C. (1990) 'Predicting employee commitment to company and union: divergent models', *Journal of Occupational Psychology*, vol. 63, pp. 49–61.

Bateman, T. and Strasser, S. (1984) 'A longitudinal analysis of the antecedents of organizational commitment', *Academy of Management Journal*, vol. 27, pp. 95–112.

Becker, T.E. and Billings, R.S. (1993) 'Profiles of commitment: an empirical test', *Journal of Organizational Behavior*, vol. 14, pp. 177–90.

Becker, T.E., Billings, R.S., Eveleth, D.M. and Gilbert, N.L. (1996) 'Foci and bases of employee commitment: implications for job performance', *Academy of Management Journal*, vol. 39, pp. 464–82.

Bem, D.J. (1972) 'Self-perception theory', *Advances in Experimental Social Psychology*, vol. 6, pp. 1–62.

Breckler, S.J. (1984) 'Empirical validation of affect, behavior and cognition as distinct attitude components', *Journal of Personality and Social Psychology*, vol. 47, pp. 1191–205.

Cacioppo, J.T. and Petty, R.E. (1979) 'Effects of message repetition and position on cognitive responses, recall, and persuasion', *Journal of Personality and Social Psychology*, vol. 37, pp. 97–109.

Cacioppo, J.T. and Petty, R.E. (1989) 'Effects of message repetition on argument processing, recall, and persuasion', *Basic and Applied Social Psychology*, vol. 10, pp. 3–12.

Cacioppo, J.T., Petty, R.E. and Green, T.R. (1989) 'From the tripartite to the homeostasis model of attitudes' in Pratkanis, A.R., Breckler, S.J. and Greenwald, A.G. (eds) *Attitude Structure and Functions*. Hillsdale, NJ: Lawrence Erlbaum.

Chaiken, S. (1987) 'The heuristic model of persuasion' in Zanna, M.P., Olson, J.M. and Herman, C.P. (eds) *Social Influence: The Ontario Symposium*. Hillsdale, NJ: Lawrence Erlbaum.

Chattopadhyay, A. and Alba, J.W. (1988) 'The situational importance of recall and inference in consumer decision making', *Journal of Consumer Research*, vol. 15, pp. 1–12.

Clark, A., Oswald, A. and Warr, P. (1996) 'Is job satisfaction U-shaped in age?', *Journal of Occupational and Organizational Psychology*, vol. 69, pp. 57–81.

Cook, T.D., Gruder, C.L., Hennigan, K.M. and Flay, B.R. (1979) 'History of the sleeper effect: some logical pitfalls in accepting the null hypothesis', *Psychological Bulletin*, vol. 86, pp. 662–79.

Cooper, C.L., Sloan, S. and Williams, S. (1987) *Occupational Stress Indicator*. Windsor: NFER/Nelson.

Coopey, J. and Hartley, J. (1991) 'Reconsidering the case for organizational commitment', *Human Resource Management Journal*, vol. 1, pp. 18–32.

Dabbs, J. and Leventhal, H. (1966) 'Effects of varying the recommendations in fear-arousing communication', *Journal of Personality and Social Psychology*, vol. 4, pp. 525–31.

Dunham, R., Grube, J.A. and Castañeda, M.B. (1994) 'Organizational commitment: the utility of an integrative definition', *Journal of Applied Psychology*, vol. 79, pp. 370–80.

Eagly, A.H. and Chaiken, S. (1975) 'An attribution analysis of the effect of communicator characteristics on opinion change: the case of communicator attractiveness', *Journal of Personality and Social Psychology*, vol. 33, pp. 136–44.

Eagly, A.H. and Chaiken, S. (1992) *The Psychology of Attitudes*. San Diego, CA: Harcourt Brace Jovanovich.

Eagly, A.H., Wood, W. and Chaiken, S. (1978) 'Causal inferences about communicators and their effect on opinion change', *Journal of Personality and Social Psychology*, vol. 36, pp. 424–35.

Eiser, J.R. and van der Pligt, J. (1988) *Attitudes and Decisions*. London: Routledge.

Furnham, A., Kirkcaldy, B.D. and Lynn, R. (1994) 'National attitudes to competitiveness, money and work among young people: first, second and third world differences', *Human Relations*, vol. 47, no. 1, pp. 119–32.

George, J.M. and Jones, G.R. (1977) 'Experiencing work: values, attitudes and moods', *Human Relations*, vol. 50, pp. 393–416.

Griffin, R.W. and Bateman, T.S (1986) 'Job satisfaction and organizational commitment' in Cooper, C.L. and Robertson, I.T. (eds) *International Review of Industrial and Organizational Psychology*. Chichester, John Wiley, pp. 157–88.

Hackman. J.R. and Oldham, G.R. (1976) 'Motivation through the design of work: test of a theory', *Organizational Behavior and Human Performance*, vol. 16, no. 2, pp. 250–79.

Hass, R.G. (1975) 'Persuasion or moderation? Two experiments on anticipatory belief change', *Journal of Personality and Social Psychology*, vol. 31, pp. 1155–62.

Hirsh, W., Jackson, C. and Jackson, C (1995) *Careers in Organizations: Issues for the Future*, IES Report 287. Brighton: Institute for Employment Studies.

Hovland, C. and Weiss, W. (1951) 'The influence of source credibility on communication effectiveness', *Public Opinion Quarterly*, vol. 15, pp. 635–50.

Hovland, C., Lumsdaine, A and Sheffield, F. (1949) *Experiments on Mass Communication*. Princeton, NJ: Princeton University Press.

Isenberg, D.J. (1986) 'Group polarization, a critical review and meta-analysis', *Journal of Personality and Social Psychology*, vol. 50, pp. 1141–51.

Janis, I. and Feshbach, S. (1953) 'Effects of fear arousing communications', *Journal of Abnormal and Social Psychology*, vol. 48, pp. 78–92.

Judge, T.A. and Hulin, C.L. (1993) 'Job satisfaction as a reflection of disposition: a multiple source causal analysis', *Organizational Behavior and Human Decision Processes*, vol. 56, pp. 388–421.

Kiesler, C.A. (1971) *The Psychology of Commitment*. New York: Academic Press.

Krech, D., Crutchfield, R.S. and Ballachey, E.L. (1962) *Individual in Society*. New York: McGraw-Hill.

Lefkowitz, J. (1994) 'Sex-related differences in job attitudes and dispositional variables: now you see them . . .', *Academy of Management Journal*, vol. 37, pp. 323–49.

Locke, E.A. (1976) 'The nature and causes of job satisfaction', in Dunnette, M.D. (ed.) *Handbook of Industrial and Organizational Psychology*. Chicago, IL: Rand McNally, pp. 1297–349.

Locke, E.A. (1995) 'The micro-analysis of job satisfaction: comments on Taber and Alliger', *Journal of Organizational Behavior*, vol. 16, pp. 123–5.

Mabey, C. (1986) *Graduates into Industry*. Aldershot: Gower.

Mathieu, J.E. and Zajac, D.M. (1990) 'A review and meta-analysis of the antecedents, correlates and consequences of organizational commitment', *Psychological Bulletin*, vol. 108, pp. 171–94.

McCaul, K.D., O'Neill, H.K. and Glasgow, R.E. (1988), 'Predicting the performance of dental hygiene behaviors: an examination of the Fishbein and Ajzen model and self-efficacy expectations', *Journal of Applied Social Psychology*, vol. 18, pp. 114–28.

McGinnies, E. (1966) 'Studies in persuasion: reactions of Japanese students to one sided and two sided communications', *Journal of Social Psychology*, vol. 70, pp. 62–74.

McGuire, W.J. and Papageorgis, D. (1961) 'The relative efficacy of various types of prior belief-defense in producing immunity against persuasion', *Journal of Abnormal and Social Psychology*, vol. 62, pp. 327–37.

Meyer, J.P. (1997) 'Organizational commitment' in Cooper, C.L. and Robertson, I.T. (eds) *International Review of Industrial and Organizational Psychology*, vol. 12. Chichester: John Wiley.

Meyer, J.P., Paunonen, S.V., Gellatly, I.R., Goffin, R.D. and Jackson, D.N. (1989) 'Organizational commitment and job performance: it's the nature of the commitment that counts', *Journal of Applied Psychology*, vol. 74, pp. 152–6.

Meyer, J.P., Allen, N.J. and Smith, C.A. (1993) 'Commitment to organizations and occupations: extension and test of a three-component conceptualization', *Journal of Applied Psychology*, vol. 78, pp. 538–51.

Millar, M.G. and Tesser, A. (1989) 'The effects of affective–cognitive consistency and thought on attitude–behavior relations', *Journal of Experimental Social Psychology*, vol. 25, pp. 189–202.

Mowday, R., Steers, R. and Porter, L. (1979) 'The measurement of organizational commitment', *Journal of Vocational Behavior*, vol. 14, pp. 224–47.

Mulilis, J. and Lippa, R. (1990) 'Behavioral change in earthquake preparedness due to negative threat appeals: a test of protection motivation theory', *Journal of Applied Social Psychology*, vol. 20, pp. 619–38.

Olson, J.M. and Zanna, M.P. (1993) 'Attitudes and attitude change' in Porter, L.W. and Rosenzweig, M.R. (eds) *Annual Review of Psychology*, vol. 44. Palo Alto, CA: Annual Reviews Inc.

O'Reilly, C.A. and Caldwell, D.F. (1985) 'The impact of normative social influence and cohesiveness on task perceptions and attitudes: a social information-processing approach', *Journal of Occupational Psychology*, vol. 58, pp. 193–206.

Organ, D.W. and Ryan, K. (1995) 'A meta-analytic review of attitudinal and dispositional predictors of organizational citizenship behavior', *Personnel Psychology*, vol. 48, pp. 775–802.

Petty, R.E. and Cacioppo, J.T. (1985) 'The elaboration likelihood model of persuasion' in Berkowitz, L. (ed.) *Advances in Experimental Social Psychology*, vol. 19. New York: Academic Press.

Petty, R.E. and Kronsnick, J.A. (1992) *Attitude Strength: Antecedents and Consequences*. Hillsdale, NJ: Lawrence Erlbaum.

Pratkanis, A.R. and Turner, M.E. (1994) 'Of what value is a job attitude? A socio-cognitive analysis', *Human Relations*, vol. 47, pp. 1545–76.

Reichers, A.E. (1985) 'A review and re-conceptualization of organizational commitments', *Academy of Management Review*, vol. 10, pp. 465–76.

Rogers, R.W. (1983) 'Cognitive and physiological processes in fear appeals and attitude change: a revised theory of protection motivation' in Cacioppo, J.T. and Petty, R.E. (eds) *Social Psychophysiology*. New York: Guilford.

Salancik, G.R. and Pfeffer, J.C. (1978) 'A social information processing approach to job attitudes and task design', *Administrative Science Quarterly*, vol. 23, pp. 224–53.

Secord, P.F. and Backman, C.W. (1969) *Social Psychology*. New York: McGraw-Hill.

Sheppard, B.H., Hartwick, J. and Warshaw, P.R. (1988) 'A theory of reasoned action: a meta-analysis of past research with recommendations for modifications and future research', *Journal of Consumer Research*, vol. 15, pp. 325–43.

Smith, P.C., Kendall, L.M. and Hulin, C.L. (1969) *The Measurement of Satisfaction in Work and Retirement*. Chicago, IL: Rand-McNally.

Staw, B.M., Bell, N.E. and Clausen, J.A. (1986) 'The dispositional approach to job attitudes: a lifetime longitudinal test', *Administrative Science Quarterly*, vol. 31, pp. 56–77.

Taber, T.D. and Alliger, G.M. (1995) 'A task-level assessment of job satisfaction', *Journal of Organizational Behavior*, vol. 16, pp. 101–21.

Tannenbaum, P. (1956) 'Initial attitude toward source and concept as factors in attitude change through communication', *Public Opinion Quarterly*, vol. 20, pp. 413–26.

Tesser, A. and Shaffer, D. (1990) 'Attitudes and attitude change' in Rosenzweig, M.R. and Porter, L.W. (eds) *Annual Review of Psychology*, vol. 41. Palo Alto, CA: Annual Reviews Inc.

Turner, J.C. (1991) *Social Influence*. Milton Keynes: Open University Press.

Warr, P., Cook, J. and Wall, T. (1979) 'Scales for the measurement of some work attitudes and aspects of psychological well-being', *Journal of Occupational Psychology*, vol. 52, pp. 129–48.

Wicker, A.W. (1969) 'Attitudes versus actions: the relationship of overt and behavioral responses to attitude objects', *Journal of Social Issues*, vol. 25, pp. 41–78.

Wood, W. and Kallgren, C.A. (1988) 'Communicator attributes and persuasion: recipients' access to attitude-relevant information in memory', *Personality and Social Psychology Bulletin*, vol. 14, pp. 172–82.

10

The analysis and modification of work behaviour

After studying this chapter, you should be able to:

1 describe the behaviourist view of psychology;

2 briefly summarise the two main types of conditioning in the behaviourist approach;

3 explain what is meant by reinforcement schedules and the reinforcement hierarchy;

4 explain what contiguity and contingency mean;

5 describe Luthans and Kreitner's five-step procedure for using OB Mod techniques;

6 state some of the rewards that might be used for reinforcement;

7 describe the effect on preceding behaviour of five different consequences;

8 state and define the main concepts involved in social cognitive theory.

INTRODUCTION

The scientific study of human *behaviour* has a central role in the development of psychological knowledge. The italics in the previous sentence stress the point that for many people the focus of attention in psychology is on what people actually do, rather than what they may be thinking or feeling. Indeed, it is obviously extremely difficult to form an impression of what anyone thinks or feels without attending to their behaviour, whether the behaviour involved is their speech, speed of movement, facial expression or whatever. This focus on behaviour as the crucial unit of analysis is particularly important in work psychology. What people actually do at work is critical to organisational success, and it is no accident that the field of organisational *behaviour* has become an important area of research and study within business and management schools.

In the early 1980s Davis and Luthans (1980, p. 281) made the following comment:

> There is today a jungle of theories that attempt to explain human behaviour in organizations. Unfortunately, many of the theoretical explanations have seemed to stray from behaviour as the unit of analysis in organizational behaviour. There is a widespread tendency for both scholars and practitioners to treat such hypothetical constructs as motivation, satisfaction and leadership as ends in themselves. We think it is time to re-emphasize the point that behaviours are the empirical reality, not the labels attached to the attempted explanation of the behaviours.

The viewpoint that Davis and Luthans proposed is derived from the ideas of behaviourist psychology (e.g. Skinner, 1974). Behaviourist ideas have a long and influential history within fundamental psychology (*see* Chapter 2) and in many areas of applied psychological research and practice. In rudimentary terms, the behaviourist view argues that a satisfactory and useful science of psychology must be based on the observation and analysis of external, observable behaviour. Behaviourists argue that to focus attention on internal psychological processes which cannot be directly observed is both unscientific and unlikely to provide a coherent and systematic understanding of human behaviour. Thus, internal psychological states, processes, emotions, feelings and many other aspects of human subjective experience are rejected as topics for study in favour of an examination of behaviour, the external conditions in which the behaviour is exhibited and the observable consequences of behaviour. For some this represents a limited and restricting view of human psychology, but for behaviourists it represents a philosophically clear and practical view from which to develop an understanding of behaviour. As this chapter demonstrates, the research of the behaviourists has produced a variety of interesting ideas, many of which have been applied with enthusiasm and some success in organisational settings. In some areas of applied research the pure form of behaviourism (which rejects any form of internal mental process as unscientific) has been diluted with the acceptance of ideas and techniques from other theoretical perspectives.

This chapter provides several examples of the use of behaviourist ideas in practice and also shows how behaviourist concepts may be incorporated into more general theories such as social cognitive theory (Bandura, 1977, 1986) to produce useful organisational applications.

> ■ **KEY LEARNING POINT**
> *The behavioural approach focuses on external behaviour.*

221

CONDITIONING AND BEHAVIOUR

The application of behaviourist ideas within organisations is explored later in this chapter, but first an outline of the major research findings and key concepts of behaviourism is provided (*see* Chapter 2 for a brief introduction to some of these). Two main types of conditioning provide the basis of the behaviourist approach: classical (respondent) conditioning and instrumental (operant) conditioning.

Classical conditioning

Classical conditioning is a simple but important form of learning first identified by the Russian physiologist Pavlov, who was studying the digestive and nervous system of dogs. He did in fact win a Nobel Prize in 1904 for this work, but it was a chance discovery resulting from this original research that earned him lasting fame. Like all dogs, the ones in Pavlov's laboratory would salivate when food was placed in their mouths. Pavlov noticed, however, that once the dogs had been in the laboratory for some time, the sight of their food dish arriving, or even the approaching footsteps of the attendant who fed them, would be enough to cause salivation. Pavlov recognised that the salivation which occurred in response to the dish or attendant's footsteps involved some form of very basic learning on the part of the animals. After his initial observations, Pavlov went on to investigate the phenomenon in a controlled, experimental setting. He arranged for the amount of saliva produced by the dogs to be measured. Then he sounded a tone slightly before food was placed in the animals' mouths. After several trials it was found that the tone by itself would produce salivation, therefore the dogs had been conditioned to respond to the tone.

The general form of classical conditioning involves an unconditioned stimulus (UCS), such as food, which produces an automatic unconditioned response (UCR), such as salivation. Conditioning occurs when the unconditioned stimulus becomes associated with a conditioned stimulus (CS), such as a bell. In fact, classical conditioning is an extremely widespread phenomenon and it is clear that Pavlov had discovered something of considerable importance and generality. Although we can only guess at the scope and variety of phenomena that can be explained in terms of classical conditioning, such conditioning is often closely involved in our emotional or 'gut reaction' to various experiences. Many people experience strong emotional reactions to certain situations, often because in the past these have been paired with particularly vivid, painful or pleasant experiences.

TASK *Review some of the typical strong emotional reactions of your own. Can you imagine how they could have been established through classical conditioning?*

In his original work Pavlov went on to pair other conditioned stimuli (e.g. a shape) with the tone. After several trials the dogs salivated to the shape alone. This procedure of introducing a second stimulus to which the organism can be conditioned to respond is known generally as higher-order conditioning. The specific example above would be referred to as second-order conditioning. Although Pavlov was only ever able to achieve third-order conditioning with his dogs, modern scientists accept that humans may be conditioned to higher orders. Such higher-order conditioning may play an important part in many of our emotional reactions.

Operant conditioning

The idea that certain basic phenomena such as classical conditioning may be used to explain the behaviour of a range of organisms, from laboratory rats, pigeons or dogs to humans, is one of the mainstays of the behaviourist tradition. The behaviourists began their work in the hope that by studying simple forms of learning in simple animals, it would be possible to uncover the basic laws and principles of learning. These could then be generalised and used to explain human learning and behaviour.

The most famous contemporary behaviourist, B. F. Skinner, is also often described as the most influential psychologist of this century. Skinner distinguished between two types of behaviour: respondent and operant. Respondent behaviour refers to the kind of behaviour shown during classical conditioning when a stimulus triggers a more or less natural reaction such as the salivation produced by Pavlov's dogs or other automatic responses like excitement, fear and sexual arousal. Operant behaviour (behaviour that operates on the environment) deals with the forms of behaviour that are not the result of simple, automatic responses. Most human behaviour, in fact, is operant behaviour – going to work, driving a car, solving a mathematical problem and playing tennis are all examples of operant behaviour. According to Skinner, such behaviour is learned and strengthened by a process of operant conditioning.

The key elements involved in operant conditioning are the stimulus, the response and reinforcement or reward. As an example of the operant conditioning process at work, consider an executive who is asked to speak at a management meeting. The stimulus is the request for the executive to speak. The executive responds by giving certain views, and this response may be reinforced (rewarded) by nods and smiles from a senior manager. The effect of reinforcement is to increase the likelihood that the executive will respond with the same or similar views at future meetings. The learning involved is sometimes described as instrumental conditioning because the response of the person or other organism involved is instrumental in obtaining the reinforcement.

Although the example given above involves human behaviour, much of the work on operant conditioning has been carried out with laboratory animals such as rats and pigeons. In some classic experiments, mostly with rats and pigeons, Skinner was able to show that by providing them with reinforcement (usually food) at appropriate points, animals could be taught to exhibit a wide range of behaviour. Many of the experiments were conducted with the aid of an operant chamber often called a 'Skinner box'. Reinforcement is provided when the animal in the box exhibits certain operant behaviour (e.g. pressing the lever or pecking a certain region of the box).

Operant techniques, unlike classical conditioning, can be used to produce behaviour that is not normally part of the organism's repertoire. For example, pigeons have been taught to play ping-pong and 'Priscilla the Fastidious Pig' was taught to turn on the radio, eat breakfast at table, drop dirty clothes in a washing hamper, vacuum the floor and select her sponsoring company's food in preference to brand X (Breland and

Breland, 1951). According to Skinner, the same fundamental processes of operant conditioning are involved regardless of whether we are concerned with a pigeon learning how to obtain food in an operant chamber, a child learning to talk and write, or a subordinate learning how to deal with a difficult manager. Operant behaviours (pecking in the right spot, pronouncing a difficult word correctly or saying the appropriate thing at a committee meeting) produce reinforcement (food, the praise of parents or the manager), and as a consequence the behaviour that produced the reinforcement is learned and strengthened. The process of operant conditioning is often described with the aid of a three-term framework: *antecedents* (A), *behaviour* (B) and *consequences* (C). Antecedents refer to the conditions or stimuli that precede the behaviour, and consequences refer to the reinforcing or punishing outcomes that the behaviour produces.

With animals, reinforcement often takes the form of food, but for humans, reinforcement may take a wide variety of forms – smiles, gifts, money, complimentary words – and a wide range of other things may provide reinforcement for behaviour. Broadly, reinforcement is anything which follows operant behaviour and increases the probability that the behaviour will recur. In many circumstances, of course, during our daily lives we administer reinforcement to others in a fairly unsystematic and uncontrolled fashion. Smiles, nods, praise and so on are all given with little thought for the consequences on the operant behaviour of others, or the learning that we are unwittingly encouraging. A common example occurs when parents say 'no' to a child's request for something and at first resist even when the child cries and makes them feel mean and unfair. Eventually, when they can stand it no longer, they give in and comply with the child's request, thus unwittingly reinforcing the child's persistent crying.

■ **KEY LEARNING POINT**

Operant conditioning can be used to shape behaviour and to produce behaviour that will not appear spontaneously.

The behaviourist research into operant learning has proved to be a rich source of information about certain types of learning experience; many of the basic principles have been applied in a wide range of organisational and other contexts. Over the next few pages some of the more important principles derived from behaviourist research are discussed.

Extinction

So far we have looked at the effect that reinforcement has on strengthening behaviour. What happens when reinforcement is not produced as a result of behaviour? When reinforcement is withdrawn or perhaps never given at all, the operant behaviour associated with it will gradually cease to occur. In technical terms, it is extinguished. Learned behaviour will continue only if the person is being reinforced. For many things we learn during formal education, at work and in everyday life, reinforcement is so frequent and common that we do not notice it. Nevertheless, as Zohar and Fussfeld (1981) point out, when operant techniques are used to change employees' behaviour in organisations, the new behaviour will sometimes extinguish quite rapidly if reinforcement is removed.

Schedules of reinforcement

Sometimes reinforcement takes place on a continuous basis. An employee who is rewarded every time a satisfactory piece of work is produced is being reinforced on a continuous basis. Most reinforcement at work and in everyday life, however, occurs on a partial basis: parents rarely praise their children every time they exhibit good manners; good work often goes unnoticed by superiors; people do not always laugh uproariously at our jokes! In general, behaviour that is based on a partial reinforcement schedule is much more persistent and likely to continue even when reinforcement is removed. This is true despite the fact that on partial reinforcement schedules less reinforcement is provided. In fact, the general rule is that the lower the percentage of correct responses that are rewarded, the more persistent the behaviour will be. An experiment reported by Lewis and Duncan (1956) helps to explain this apparent paradox. In the experiment people were allowed to gamble, using slot machines. The machines were 'rigged' so that some paid out on every trial (i.e. continous reinforcement). Other machines paid out on a partial bias (as real slot machines do). In the second part of the experiment everyone played on a second machine – rigged so that it would never pay out. People who had been trained on the partial schedules were much more resistant to extinction and they continued to play long after people on a continuous schedule had stopped. In fact, the overall results conformed well with the idea mentioned above, that the lower the percentage of responses rewarded, the more resistant to extinction is the behaviour concerned, demonstrating the powerful effect of partial reinforcement schedules compared with continuous reinforcement.

Partial reinforcement may be given on either an interval or ratio schedule. Interval reinforcement occurs when a specified amount of time has passed. The next response that occurs will then produce reinforcement. For example, a telephone salesperson might be told to take a break by the supervisor as soon as the last call in any 45-minute period is completed. Ratio reinforcement is based not on the passage of time, but on the number of responses that have occurred (e.g. a worker is given a break after every fifty components produced). Schedules of reinforcement can also be either fixed or occur regularly every so many minutes of responses, or they may be variable and occur, on average, every 'x' minutes of responses, but the actual gap between each reinforcement is varied (*see* Fig. 10.1).

> ■ **KEY LEARNING POINT**
> *Partial reinforcement produces more effective changes in behaviour than continuous reinforcement.*

The reinforcement hierarchy

Some ideas concerning reinforcement, which seem particularly valuable within the context of organisational behaviour, have been proposed and developed by Premack (1965), who demonstrated by experiment that an event which serves as a reinforcer for some behaviour may not have a reinforcing effect on other, different behaviour. In addition,

Fig. 10.1 Different schedules of reinforcement. (a) A fixed-interval (FI) schedule.
Reinforcement occurs on a regular, timed basis. Typically, responding slows down immediately
after reinforcement and begins to increase as the time for (b), the next reinforcement,
approaches. (b) A variable ratio (VR) schedule. Reinforcement occurs 'on average' every so
many responses (e.g. VR10 = every 10 responses on average), but the occurrence of each
specific reinforcement is irregular and unpredictable. Responding is frequent and regular.

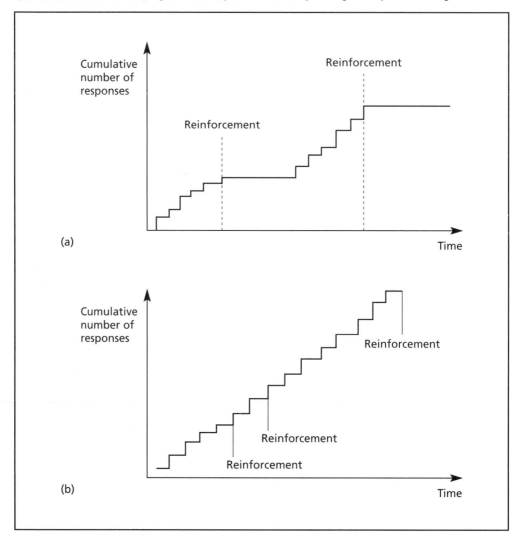

he demonstrated that reinforcers may sometimes change places with the behaviour
which produces them. For example, a thirsty laboratory animal will run to obtain water;
equally, an animal subjected to a long period of inactivity will drink in order to take an
opportunity to run. In other words, drinking may reinforce running, but in some circumstances running may reinforce drinking. This simple example demonstrates the fact
that the attraction of reinforcers may change as circumstances change. Premack has
argued that there is, in effect, a hierarchy of reinforcement. The order of reinforcers in
the hierarchy will change as circumstances change. Behaviours at the top of the hierar-

chy are things that we would like to engage in if given the opportunity – collecting £1 million from a bank, for instance. Behaviours at the bottom are those that we would rarely engage in even if the opportunity to do so were unlimited.

The reinforcement hierarchy may be used to influence or explain behaviours in many settings. Consider, for example, an employee who enjoys finishing work early and taking a long break from work at lunchtime. If the reinforcement provided by an early finish is further up the hierarchy than a lunchtime break, the employee may be persuaded to work through the lunch period for the reward of an early finish. In other words, one behaviour (early finish) may be used to reinforce another (work through lunch). Of course, if the employee in question had reason to attend a particularly important social event at lunchtime, the position of the two behaviours in the hierarchy might become reversed and the lunch-break might act as a reinforcer for working late. This general principle can be used to great advantage in a wide variety of settings.

> ■ **KEY LEARNING POINT**
> *The opportunity to engage in one behaviour can be used as a reinforcer for other behaviour (Premack principle).*

Makin and Hoyle (1993) used the Premack principle to understand and influence the behaviour of four engineers. The engineers were part of a department, recently taken over by a new manager. The manager was not happy with the performance of the department, which had a growing backlog of work and a number of dissatisfied customers. The engineers 'spent a considerable amount of time hopping from one job to another' and 'An air of crisis management pervaded' (Makin and Hoyle, 1993, p. 16). Makin and Hoyle found that all of the engineers were putting considerable effort into their work and overall motivation appeared to be high. The problem was that the engineers were directing their attention to tasks which they found reinforcing, rather than those necessary for production. The use of a combination of feedback, praise and recognition was linked to an increase in performance for the section of 73 per cent. The output of the indivdual engineers improved by between 31 per cent and 270 per cent!

TASK *Can you think of a way of using the Premack principle to improve your own study habits? For example, you could make a trip to the pub or a cup of coffee contingent on completing an item of work.*

Punishment

Just as reinforcement will increase the likelihood of a response, punishment (the use of aversive or unpleasant stimuli) will decrease the likelihood of the behaviour that immediately precedes it. At first sight, punishment may seem to be a useful means for suppressing or eliminating certain behaviours. It is – but only when used correctly.

Consider the case of a supervisor who always raises disciplinary problems at the company's weekly progress meetings and, in so doing, reveals that he has consistently made bad decisions and errors of judgement when supervising his staff. At first, at the meetings, his manager responds with tactful and diplomatic assistance and tries to point out the errors to the supervisor, suggesting how they might be avoided in future. Eventually, however, the manager becomes exasperated, loses her temper and punishes the supervisor with strong words and a public dressing-down. For the next few months there are no more reports of discipline problems and the manager begins to feel that the 'short, sharp shock' has worked. Suddenly, however, the manager is confronted with a deputation of employees from the supervisor's department who claim that discipline has grown progressively worse and that their working conditions are now intolerable. What went wrong? Had the punishment not worked? The punishment had worked, but inevitably – as anticipated above – it had decreased the likelihood of the behaviour immediately preceding it, which in this case was the *reporting* of problems by the supervisor at the weekly meetings. The supervisor had learned that this was not a successful thing to do. Consequently, he deliberately neglected raising the issue at meetings and thus avoided the possibility of punishment occurring, which was not the outcome the manager had intended. On the contrary, the behaviour the manager had tried to punish had continued unchecked and the supervisor continued making errors of judgement.

In many cases it is impractical to give punishment at the appropriate time. For this and many other reasons (e.g. a classically conditioned aversion to the punisher, and the fact that avoiding punishment may provide a form of reinforcement and therefore encourage avoidance behaviour), most people feel that punishment is not a very effective means of controlling behaviour. Incidentally, punishment – the presentation of an aversive stimulus – should not be confused with negative reinforcement. Negative reinforcers are stimuli that have the effect of increasing the probability of occurrence of the response that precedes them when they are *removed* from the situation.

■ **KEY LEARNING POINT**
Punishment is not a very effective way of changing behaviour.

FUNDAMENTALS OF CONDITIONING: CONTIGUITY AND CONTINGENCY

The general overview of the work of the behaviourists given above has illustrated their use of certain key concepts such as response, stimulus, reinforcement and extinction. The research on punishment mentioned immediately above illustrates two important concepts, one of which is contiguity – that is, for conditioning to occur there should be only a small delay between behaviour and reinforcement (or punishment). In broad terms, the longer the gap between these two events, the less likely it is that the target behaviour will be strengthened or diminished. The other fundamental concept, not mentioned explicitly so far, is the idea of contingency. This emphasises that reinforcement is contingent on the response; in other words, for conditioning to occur, reinforcement should be provided only when the desired behaviour occurs.

Reinforcing other behaviour makes it likely that this will be influenced and that the intended behaviour will not be affected. Contiguity and contingency are seen as fundamental elements involved in understanding how conditioning takes place and, taken together, with concepts of stimulus, response, reinforcement and extinction, represent the core of the behaviourist position.

ORGANISATIONAL BEHAVIOUR MODIFICATION

The principle of operant conditioning and systematic procedures of behaviour analysis have been applied in educational and clinical settings for some time (Ulrich *et al.*, 1974; Rimm and Masters, 1979). More recently, they have also been used within organisational settings to modify behaviour. Comprehensive coverage of the application of operant techniques to *organisational behaviour modification* (OB Mod) has been presented by Luthans and Kreitner (1975). The essence of the OB Mod approach involves focusing on critical behaviours that are important for satisfactory work performance and the application of reinforcement principles attempting to strengthen appropriate behaviour patterns. Luthans and Kreitner describe a five-step procedure for using OB Mod techniques:

1 identify the critical behaviours

2 measure the critical behaviours

3 carry out a functional analysis of the behaviours

4 develop an intervention strategy

5 evaluate.

Critical behaviours represent the activities of the personnel within the organisation that are influencing organisational performance and are to be strengthened, weakened or modified in some way. Such behaviour might be identified in a variety of ways, including discussion with relevant personnel, systematic observation or tracing the cause of performance or production deficiencies. An important point, however, is that only specific, observable behaviour is used. To say that it is critical to have a 'positive attitude' would not be acceptable and the behaviour that demonstrated such qualities (low absenteeism, prompt responses to requests, instructions etc.) would need to be identified.

Once the critical behaviours are identified, a baseline measure of their frequency of occurrence is obtained, either by direct observation or recording, or perharps from existing company records. This baseline measure is important in two main ways. It provides an objective view of the current situation, indicating, for example, that the scale of a problem is much bigger or smaller than it was at first thought to be, and it provides a basis for examining any change that might eventually take place as a result of intervention.

Functional analysis involves identifying:

1 the cues or stimuli in the work situation (antecedent conditions) that trigger the behaviour;

2 the contingent consequences (i.e. the consequences in terms of reward, punishment etc.) that are maintaining the behaviour.

These can be examined using the A-B-C (*antecedents–behaviour–consequence*) framework mentioned earlier. This stage is critical for the success of any programme of OB Mod, since it is essential to have an accurate picture of the antecedents and consequences that may be maintaining the behaviour in question. For example, an OB Mod programme may be considered by a sales manager as a means of encouraging sales personnel to make fewer visits to base – visits that are spent in unproductive chats with colleagues. The sales manager may be concerned about the behaviour because of the time-wasting involved and because the sales director keeps making comments about large numbers of the sales force 'sitting at base together doing nothing'. The apparently rewarding consequences of returning to base may be the opportunity to relax and avoid the pressures of being on the road. It could be, however, that the important consequence for the sales staff is the opportunity for social interaction with colleagues and that it is the reinforcing effect of this social interaction which is maintaining their undesirable behaviour. Any attempt to modify their behaviour by providing opportunities for relaxation away from base, or by staggering their visits to base so that only small numbers are there at any time, would be founded on an inaccurate view of the behaviour – consequence contingencies.

Once the functional analysis has been conducted an intervention strategy designed to modify the behaviour concerned must be developed. The purpose of the intervention strategy is to strengthen desirable behaviour and weaken undesirable behaviour. A central feature of human behaviour is the range and variety of rewards that might be used to provide reinforcement. Money provides an obvious example, but many other potential rewards can be identified; Table 10.1 provides some examples. It is worth noting that not all of the rewards involve the organisation in direct costs, such as friendly greetings and compliments. Various intervention strategies may be used, but most involve the use of

Table 10.1 Possible rewards for use in organisational behaviour modification

Contrived on-the-job-rewards				Natural rewards	
Consumables	Manipulatables	Visual and auditory	Tokens	Social	Premack
Coffee-break treats	Desk accessories	Office with a window	Money	Friendly greetings	Job with more responsibility
Free lunches	Wall plaques	Piped-in music	Stocks	Informal recognition	Job rotation
Food baskets	Company car	Redecoration of work environment	Stock options	Formal acknowl-edgement of achievement	Early time off with pay
Easter hams	Watches		Passes for films		Extended breaks
Christmas turkeys	Trophies	Company literature	Trading stamps		Extended lunch period
Dinners for the family on the company	Commendation	Private office	Paid-up insurance policies	Invitations to coffee/lunch	
	Rings/tie-pins		Dinner and theatre tickets	Solicitations of suggestions	Personal time off with pay
Company picnics	Appliances and furniture for the home	Popular speakers or lecturers	Holiday trips	Solicitations of advice	Work on personal project on company time
After-work wine and cheese parties	Home shop tools	Book club discussions	Coupons redeemable at local stores	Compliment on work progress	Use of company machinery or facilities for personal projects
	Garden tools	Feedback about performance	Profit-sharing	Recognition in house organ	
Beer parties	Clothing			Pat on the back	Use of company recreation facilities
	Club privileges			Smile	
	Special assignments			Verbal or non-verbal recognition or praise	

positive reinforcement in some way. Punishment appears to have had a lesser role in most studies, although it has received some attention (*see* Arvey and Ivancevich, 1980). It is also possible to make use of Premack's reinforcement hierarchy principle mentioned earlier, whereby employees are rewarded for engaging in behaviour low down in the hierarchy (e.g. working at a job until it is finished, even if it means staying late) by being allowed to engage in behaviours higher up it (e.g. being given more challenging and responsible work). The choice of appropriate reinforcers is crucial for successful interventions, since the effects of specific potential rewards vary according to the people involved. To some people, for instance, the allocation of more challenging and responsible work would not be as rewarding as the opportunity to leave work on time every evening; some people would find money more attactive than time off, and so on.

> ■ **KEY LEARNING POINT**
> *OB Mod is based on the systematic analysis of the antecedent conditions and the consequences of behaviour.*

OB Mod in practice

Table 10.2 illustrates the primary consequences that can follow behaviour and gives references to some illustrative OB Mod studies. Although it is not an exclusively behaviourist concept, feedback is included in Table 10.2 because of its widespread usage in OB Mod studies, often in conjunction with reinforcers such as praise (Alavosius and Sulzer-Azaroff, 1986) or money and free gifts (Haynes *et al.*, 1982). Feedback is an important aspect of many other theoretical positions and behaviour change strategies, such as goal setting (Locke and Latham, 1990). Within the behaviourist framework feedback is construed as a consequence of behaviour, and since behaviour may be influenced by adjusting consequences, feedback may be used to help to shape behaviour. Despite this, feedback and its role in helping to shape behaviour is a troublesome concept for pure behaviourism since it is difficult to see how it can have any influence on subsequent behaviour without the informational (i.e. cognitive) component of feedback being important (*see* Bandura 1986; Locke and Henne, 1986).

Behaviour modification has been used in a wide variety of settings to produce changes in many aspects of organisational behaviour. One of the earliest and best-known studies (although it is not methodologically rigorous) was the Emery Air Freight study in 1973. One of the remarkable things about this study is that marked changes in behaviours related to work quality were brought about with the use of feedback and praise only.

The study and several other early studies focusing on work quality, absenteeism, supervisory training and other aspects of work behaviour showed that the operant-based systematic application of OB Mod techniques could produce important changes in behaviour (*see* O'Brien *et al.*, 1982; Luthans and Martinko, 1987, for further examples). An illustrative study involving the application of behaviourist principles is that of Zohar and Fussfeld (1981). This study was conducted in a textile factory in which noise levels were extremely high (106 dBA). Despite these dangerously high levels of noise the employees were reluctant to wear ear defenders and only 35 per cent were normally wearing them. Zohar and Fussfeld first made contact with the personnel involved and

Table 10.2 Consequences of behaviour and organisational behaviour modification

Consequence	Effect on preceding behaviour	Usage in OB Mod	Illustrative studies
Positive reinforcement	A consequence which, when introduced, increases the frequency of immediately preceding behaviour recurring	Widely used, although praise and social reinforcers are more common than monetary reinforcers	Komaki et al. (1978) used feedback to safety. Geller et al. (1983) used incentives (free dinners) to improve the usage rates of seat belts
Negative reinforcement	A consequence which, when removed, increases the frequency of the immediately preceding behaviour recurring	Not used explicitly very often, but may be a side effect of intervention in some studies	Luthans et al. (1981) used cash awards and paid vacations to change behaviour Fox et al. (1987) used a token economy to reduce lost work and lost time in open-pit coal mines
Extinction	The absence of any rewarding or punishing consequence. Causes the subsequent frequency of the preceding behaviour to decrease. Often difficult to differentiate from punishment (e.g. if a reinforcer is deliberately withdrawn in order to extinguish some specific behaviour)	Often explicitly or implicitly used in conjunction with positive reinforcement to strengthen desirable behaviour and weaken undesirable behaviour	Karan and Kopelman (1987) used feedback to reduce the vehicle accidents in a packaging forwarding facility
Feedback	Providing information about the outcomes of behaviour – or actual behaviour (e.g. how close behaviour is to a target behaviour)	One of the most frequently used intervention strategies	

established some reinforcers that the personnel found attractive (consumer durables, such as radios and TV sets). After taking baseline measures of the frequency of ear defender usage, Zohar and Fussfeld then introduced a variable ratio token economy system. Under this scheme, tokens were secondary reinforcers, since they had no direct rewarding value themselves, but they could be exchanged for the consumer durables, when an operative had collected enough tokens. The tokens were given to operatives by supervisors, who distributed them on an irregular basis only to operatives who were wearing ear defenders. The token economy had the almost immediate effect of increasing ear defender usage from 35 to 90 per cent. Furthermore, when the investigators collected follow-up data nine months after the token economy (which ran for only two months) had been discontinued, ear defender usage was still at 90 per cent. This study is a good example of OB Mod at work since it shows how a previously intractable problem – the company had already tried poster campaigns and other means to improve ear defender usage – may be resolved permanently at relatively little cost.

> ■ **KEY LEARNING POINT**
> *Research has shown a wide variety of reinforcers to be effective in changing behaviour. These include financial reward, praise and the use of secondary reinforcers, such as tokens.*

EVALUATING THE EFFECT OF OB MOD

Evaluation is an important element in the application of any OB Mod programme. Various designs can be used to conduct the evaluation phase of an OB Mod programme. The primary aim of the evaluation is, of course, to examine if, and to what extent, the intervention has modified the target behaviours. The most widely used designs are the reversal or ABAB design and the multiple baseline design. The reversal (ABAB) design involves alternating use of the OB Mod programme and removal of the programme over a period of time (*see* Fig. 10.2). In such a design the frequency of the target behaviour is assessed before the programme begins. This provides a baseline (the A phase). The next phase involves intervening and using reinforcement, punishment and so forth to modify behaviour (the B phase). After the intervention has produced stable new rates for the behaviour, it is removed (the reversal) and conditions revert to baseline. Usually the behaviour will also revert, or at least show some return towards baseline levels.

Fig. 10.2 The reversal (ABAB) design for evaluating an OB Mod programme

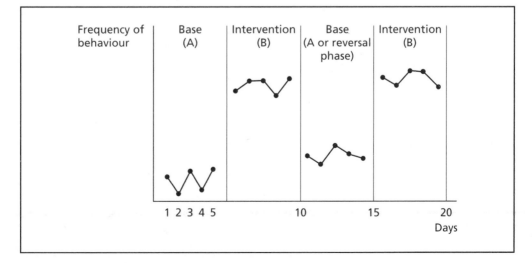

Although this design can provide impressive evidence of the effect of the intervention, there are obvious problems. The return to baseline may not always be desirable. Furthermore, the intervention may have been deliberately designed to ensure lasting behaviour change so that even when the specific reinforcers used in the intervention phase are removed, the behaviour should not revert to baseline levels (Zohar and Fussfeld, 1981).

The multiple baseline design can help to deal with these problems. In this design baseline data are collected across two or more behaviours, then a specific intervention strategy to change each behaviour in turn is introduced (*see* Fig. 10.3). Each behaviour should change only when the relevant intervention strategy is used. If this happens it provides convincing evidence (without the need for reversals) that the intervention is causing the change. Further details on these and other methods may be found in Kazdin (1980), Luthans and Martinko (1987) and Komaki and Jensen (1986).

PUTTING MORE THOUGHT INTO OB MOD

Despite its obvious success in bringing about useful behaviour change, traditional OB Mod has frequently been criticised (e.g. Locke, 1977) and its potential for theoretical growth and conceptual development has been constrained by the rigorous emphasis, in pure behaviourism, on directly observable and measurable phenomena. The difficulties encountered in trying to incorporate such obviously cognitive concepts as feedback into such a resolutely anti-mentalistic framework have already been mentioned. Problems such as this, together with the theoretical developments which have extended behaviourist theory into the cognitive domain (Bandura, 1986), have led to an integration of OB Mod with more cognitive approaches.

The cognitive approaches of most relevance to contemporary organisational behaviour and analysis are social cognitive theory (Bandura, 1986) and goal-setting theory (Locke and Latham, 1990). Goal setting is discussed in Chapter 11. Essentially, goal setting is a cognitively based theory which proposes that specific, difficult goals, when they are accepted by the individual, will lead to effective performance. Goals influence cogni-

Fig. 10.3 The multiple baseline design for evaluating an OB Mod programme

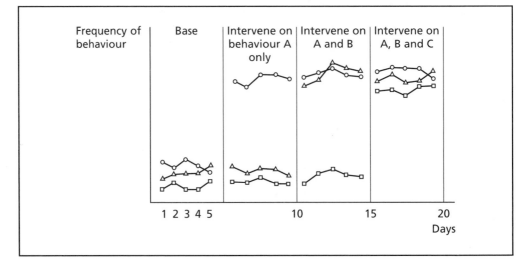

234

tions by directing attention. Feedback on goal attainment is necessary for goal setting to be maximally effective. Many behaviour-change studies have made use of both goal setting and feedback, and extremely effective interventions have been produced (e.g. Chokkar and Wallin, 1984). A behaviourist interpretation of goals would see them as antecedent conditions. It has, however, become increasingly accepted by researchers that cognitive states concerning goal commitment, acceptance and attributions are important concepts in understanding how goal setting works.

■ KEY LEARNING POINT

More recent approaches to behaviour change emphasise the causal role of mental processes or the interaction of person and situation variables.

CASE STUDY 10.1

Improving attendance with OB Mod

Absenteeism at SJR Foods' plant had been getting steadily worse for many years. Radha El-Bakry, the production manager, felt that it would be worth investing some money in solving the problem. In consultation with the company unions she developed and installed a lottery scheme which involved the issuing of free tickets to employees who attended work. Each full day's attendance entitled the employee to one free lottery ticket. Full attendance for a week produced a bonus of two extra tickets. The lottery was drawn every Friday evening and prizes were available for collection on the spot. Within two weeks of its introduction the scheme was more than paying for itself in improved attendance (*see* Fig. 10.4).

Fig. 10.4 Attendance rates at SJR Foods

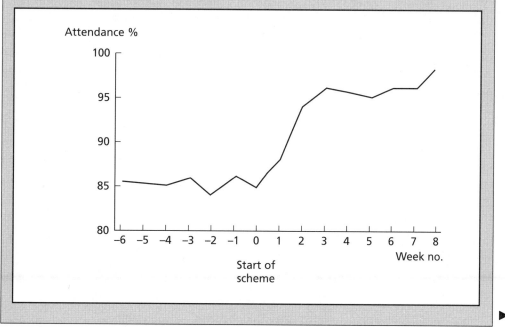

CASE
STUDY
10.1

At the same time as she introduced the lottery system, Radha had agreed a goal with the employee representatives of 90 per cent attendance. At the end of each week a chart in the canteen (similar to Fig. 10.4) was completed, which showed the attendance rate for that week.

Suggested exercises

1 *Using the terminology and concepts of OB Mod, explain what had been done at SJR Foods.*

2 *Discuss the extent to which this intervention adopted a pure behaviourist approach.*

Social cognitive theory does not reject the operant-based view of behaviour development which is at the heart of behaviourism. This theory does, however, extend the operant view and makes use of important additional cognitive concepts. The essence of social cognitive theory (formerly called social learning theory) is that the role of cognitive processes in determining behaviour is given prominence.

Social cognitive theory accepts the basic tenets of the behavioural approach (i.e. reinforcement, contingency and contiguity and the impact of schedules of reinforcement) but goes on to add further novel concepts. Some of these novel concepts involve significant departures from traditional operant approaches to behaviour. The overall framework within which these concepts are developed involves the concept of 'reciprocal determinism' (*see* Fig. 10.5).

Social learning theory emphasises that the interaction of situation and person factors may be a better theoretical basis for organisational behaviour than the purely situational view based on operant conditioning only. Social learning theory differs from the traditional operant approach in many ways.

One of the important differences concerns the acceptance that internal cognitive processes are important determinants of behaviour. For example, whereas traditional reinforcement theory argues that behaviour is regulated by its immediate, external consequences only, social learning theory suggests that internal psychological factors such as expectancies about the eventual consequences of behaviour have a role in controlling behaviour. Bandura (1977, p. 18) expresses it as follows:

Fig. 10.5 Reciprocal determinism

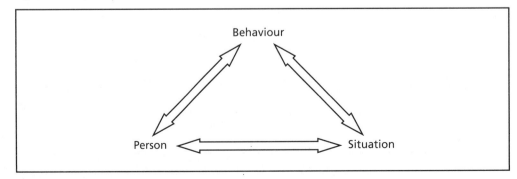

> Contrary to the mechanistic view, outcomes change behaviour largely through the intervening influence of thought ... Anticipatory capacities enable humans to be motivated by prospective consequences. Past experiences create expectations that certain actions will bring valued benefits, and that still others will avert future trouble ... Homeowners, for instance, do not wait until they experience the distress of a burning house to purchase fire insurance.

Social learning theorists also argue that, as well as responding to the influence of reinforcement in the environment, people often control and develop behaviour patterns through the use of self-reinforcement: 'Self-appraisals of performance set the occasion for self-produced consequences. Favourable judgements give rise to rewarding self-reactions, whereas unfavourable appraisals activate punishing self-responses' (Bandura, 1977, p. 133). Bandura and other social learning theorists argue that internal psychological events and processes such as self-reinforcement and expectancies help to determine behaviour. This behaviour will, to some extent, influence the situation surrounding the person, and in turn external situational factors, such as the behaviour of others, and help to determine expectancies and the other internal cognitive factors. In other words, there is a constant cycle of interaction between person and situation factors, a process described by Bandura as reciprocal determinism. This view is quite different from the traditional operant view that: 'A person does not act upon the world, the world acts upon him' (Skinner, 1971, p. 211).

Another important aspect of social learning theory is the proposal that people often develop their own patterns of behaviour by observing and then copying or modelling the behaviour of others. The concept of observational learning or modelling is difficult for those holding the traditional, operant behavioural view to explain. For example, the act of copying a model provides no direct reinforcement in itself. Social learning theorists argue that this sort of action can, however, be explained if we accept that the modelling occurred because the learner had expectancies about what might eventually occur as a consequence of modelling. Thus, junior members of an organisation model their dress, attitudes and behaviours on those of successful senior personnel, based on expectancies, goals and plans that they have about the eventual consequences of their behaviours. Luthans and Kreitner (1975) have provided a framework for OB Mod which is rooted firmly in the concepts of social cognitive theory.

In keeping with this convergence of behavioural and cognitive theories, more recent studies have often incorporated behavioural interventions within a cognitive framework. A study by Pritchard et al. (1988), for example, used a mixture of goal setting, feedback and incentives. Their study, conducted in a military setting, involved a baseline period of eight to nine months followed by feedback (five months); this was followed by the addition of goal setting (five months); finally, incentives were used (five months). The results indicated an improvement in productivity over baseline of 50 per cent for feedback, 75 per cent for group goal setting and 76 per cent for incentives. Although the study did not provide conclusive proof of the different effects of the various interventions, the authors felt that incentives added little to the improvements brought about by feedback and goal setting. This finding from one study must, however, be set against the results obtained by Guzzo et al. (1985) in their meta-analytic (see Chapter 8) investigation of many studies, which showed that incentives do generally improve performance, although the effect depends on the method of application and circumstances.

TASK   *Why is it that the effectiveness of feedback is so difficult for behaviourists to explain – without reference to internal mental processes?*

It is clear from other work (e.g. Duff *et al.*, 1994) that behaviour change may be brought about very effectively without the use of incentives. In their study Duff *et al.* (1994) focused on the safety behaviour of operatives on construction sites in the north of England. The design for the study used many of the features mentioned earlier in this chapter, including a multiple baseline, with reversal. As an integral part of the study the investigators developed a comprehensive measure of safety on construction sites. This measure was then used by trained observers to record safety levels on the specific sites involved in the study. Feedback and goal-setting procedures were then introduced and safety levels were monitored regularly (three times per week). Two features of this study illustrate important points. The first is that, as already noted, no incentives were offered nor were any rewards given. Some would argue that rewards were implicit in the feedback, which, when positive, could impact on factors such as self-esteem and feelings of greater security or job satisfaction. Whatever mechanism is involved, feedback (*see* Algera, 1990) and goals (*see* Locke and Latham, 1990), even without reward, can provide a base for behaviour change. The second point to note is that the measures and feedback information did not focus on behaviour only. Some of the items in the safety measure did indeed focus on behaviour (e.g. wearing and use of safety equipment); others focused on the *consequences* of behaviour (e.g. evidence of objects thrown down from height, ladders not tied off properly). In behaviour-change studies it is often impossible to observe behaviour as it happens but this does not preclude the use of the methods described in this chapter.

■ **KEY LEARNING POINT**
Even without reward, goal setting and feedback can bring about substantial behaviour change.

Saari and Nasanen (1989) used feedback to reduce accidents in a shipyard, achieving a reduction of 70–90 per cent in accidents, persisting to a three-year follow-up. This study is interesting in another sense since, like that of Duff *et al.* (1994), it was conducted outside the USA, in this case in Finland. Most of the research on behaviour change cited in this chapter has been conducted in the USA, and some authors (e.g. Hale and Glendon, 1987) have expressed the view that feedback techniques may not work as effectively in European cultures as they have done in the USA. One consistent champion of the operant approach in organisational settings is Komaki who, in her work, has extended the operant approach well beyond the straightforward attempts to manipulate behaviour into a variety of interesting and important areas, such as leader behaviour and supervision (e.g. Komaki *et al.*, 1989); and performance measurement (Komaki *et al.*, 1987).

SUMMARY

In many ways what people do (i.e. their behaviour) at work is the most important aspect of work psychology. Behaviourally-orientated psychologists have developed concise and powerful frameworks which have been shown to be effective in changing behaviour in organisational settings. The work of Luthans and Kreitner (1975) and others has provided a range of examples of the use of behavioural techniques. Despite its success, even the major exponents of behaviour modification (based on purely behavioural frameworks) recognise that there are also theoretical and practical shortcomings. More recent work has shown that the inclusion of ideas from social cognitive theory provides a theoretically more advanced, yet still practical, basis for bringing about behavioural change.

CASE STUDY 10.2

The effects of punishment on behaviour

Barry Cavanagh's new job as safety manager with Castell Construction was extremely challenging. The construction industry in general had one of the worst accident records of all industries in the country and although Castell's safety record was better than some companies it was still a source of great concern. Barry felt that he understood the general causes of accidents very well: it was easier and quicker to take short cuts when it came to safety. For example, when a small number of breeze blocks needed cutting down to a smaller size with a power cutter, it was inconvenient and time consuming to get protective goggles, gloves and face mask from the stores. So the job would be done without protection. To make matters worse, because they were often under intense pressure from senior managers to work to agreed production targets, site managers and supervisors were often prepared to turn a blind eye to unsafe practices, if it meant that the job would get done on time.

Barry was a direct, no-nonsense kind of person and felt sure that it was a waste of time to try to educate the construction workers and to change their underlying attitudes to safety. He knew that to have any impact their behaviour needed to change. He also knew that various previous attempts to improve safety, initiated by his predecessor, had failed. These had included poster campaigns and talks from medical staff.

Barry decided that the best approach was to come down very heavily and severely on any examples of unsafe behaviour. Barry and his site managers began a campaign in which unsafe acts were punished severely with reprimands and other more severe forms of punishment such as loss of earnings. Most of their reprimands were given to accident victims or (when it was not the victim's fault) others involved in causing the accident.

At first Barry's policy seemed to be working. He maintained a close watch on accident reports and even within the first weeks of the campaign there was a clear decrease, particularly in minor accidents. After a routine meeting with site managers Barry had been a little disappointed that they did not share his pleasure at the decrease in accident rates. After the meeting one of the site managers took Barry to one side and explained why this was so, and, furthermore, that the scheme was doing more harm than good. There had actually been no change in accident rates – but to avoid punishment operatives were covering up and not reporting all but the most serious and noticeable incidents! Not only was there no improvement in accidents but the relationships between site managers and operatives had deteriorated. Site personnel were angered by the behaviour of managers, who were reprimanding operatives who were often still shaken and in pain after an accident.

Suggested exercises

1 *Using the concepts and terminology of behaviour modification, explain what went wrong and why.*

2 *Make suggestions about how Barry might have gone about achieving his goal by a more successful route, using OB Mod techniques.*

Short-answer questions

1 Give an example of classical conditioning.

2 Give an example of operant conditioning.

3 Why is behaviour based on partial reinforcement more persistent than behaviour based on continuous reinforcement?

4 Explain why punishment does not work under some circumstances.

5 What are the two items that need to be identified when functional analysis of behaviour is carried out?

6 Give details of the study carried out by Zohar and Fussfeld (1981), involving the application of behaviourist principles.

7 What is the reversal or ABAB design?

8 Outline the concept of 'reciprocal determinism'.

9 What is modelling behaviour?

Essay questions

1 Critically evaluate the OB Mod approach to work performance and discuss its ethical basis.

2 Show how behaviourist concepts may be incorporated into more general theories such as social cognitive theory.

Antecedents Events that precede the occurrence of behaviour. In (non-behaviourist) approaches they may be seen to *cause* the behaviour.

Behaviourism An approach to psychology which concentrates on the external (to the person) conditions under which behaviour is exhibited and the observable consequences of behaviour.

Classical conditioning A form of conditioning in which a previously neutral stimulus such as a tone (the conditioned stimulus) is repeatedly linked with the presentation of an unconditioned stimulus (such as food) so that the conditioned stimulus will, after repeated pairings, produce the unconditioned response (e.g. salivation) normally associated with the unconditioned stimulus. In other words (using this example) an animal could be conditioned to salivate at the sound of a tone.

Conditioned stimulus *See* **Classical conditioning**.

Contiguity The existence of only a small delay between behaviour and reinforcement (or punishment).

Contingency This is present if reinforcement (or punishment) is given *only* when specific behaviour precedes it.

Extinction This occurs when behaviour is not followed by reinforcement (or punishment). Under these circumstances operant behaviour will cease to occur.

Negative reinforcement This is *not* punishment. Negative reinforcers *increase* the probability of the preceding behaviour when they are *removed* from the situation (for example, putting up an umbrella takes away the rain).

Operant conditioning A form of conditioning that shapes (operant) behaviour by the application of reinforcement, punishment or extinction.

Organisational behaviour modification (OB Mod) A systematic approach to influencing the behaviour of people in organisations which is based on the principles of conditioning.

Premack principle The principle that there is a hierarchy of behaviour in which opportunity to engage in behaviour further up the hierarchy may be used to reinforce behaviour lower down.

Punishment The application of an aversive stimulus.

Reciprocal determinism The complex interaction between situational, personal and behavioural variables.

Reinforcement A consequence (or outcome) which increases the probability that the behaviour preceding it will recur.

Respondent conditioning Another term for classical conditioning.

Unconditioned response *See* **Classical conditioning**.

Unconditioned stimulus *See* **Classical conditioning**.

SUGGESTED FURTHER READING

Note: full references for all three pieces of suggested further reading are given in the reference list below.

1 The review of behavioural approaches in organisations by Luthans and Martinko (1987) covers the background to OB Mod and gives a scholarly account of its use and development.

2 Edwin Locke's 1977 paper in the *Academy of Management Review* gives a vigorous critique of the behaviourist view – which at the time was the dominant approach. The article is useful in providing an understanding of the criticisms that later socio-cognitive approaches were designed to avoid.

3 An easy to read illustration of the use of OB Mod is given in Makin and Hoyle's (1993) application of it to four underperforming engineers.

REFERENCES

Alavosius, M.P. and Sulzer-Azaroff, B. (1986) 'The effects of performance feedback on the safety of client lifting and transfer', *Journal of Applied Behavior Analysis*, vol. 19, pp. 261–7.

Algera, J.A. (1990) 'Feedback systems in organisations' in Cooper, C.L. and Robertson, I.T. (eds) *International Review of Industrial and Organizational Psychology*, vol. 5. Chichester: John Wiley.

Arvey, R.D. and Ivancevich, J.M. (1980) 'Punishment in organizations: a review, propositions and research suggestions', *Academy of Management Review*, vol. 5, pp. 123–32.

Bandura, A. (1977) *Social Learning Theory*. Englewood Cliffs, NJ: Prentice Hall.

Bandura, A. (1986) *Social Foundations of Thought and Action: A social cognitive theory*. Englewood Cliffs, NJ: Prentice Hall.

Breland, K. and Breland, M. (1951) 'A field of applied animal psychology', *American Psychologist*, vol. 6, pp. 202–4.

Chokkar, J.S. and Wallin, J.A. (1984) 'A field study of the effect of feedback frequency on performance', *Journal of Applied Psychology*, vol. 69, pp. 524–30.

Davis, T.R. and Luthans, F. (1980) 'A social learning approach to organizational behavior', *Academy of Management Review*, vol. 5, pp. 281–90.

Duff, A.R., Robertson, I.T., Phillips, R.A. and Cooper, M.D. (1994) 'Improving safety by the modification of behaviour', *Construction Management and Economics*, vol. 12, pp. 67–78.

Fox, D.K., Hopkins, B.L. and Anger, W.K. (1987) 'The long-term effects of a token economy on safety performance in open-pit mining', *Journal of Applied Behavior Analysis*, vol. 20, pp. 215–24.

Geller, E.S., Davis, L. and Spicer, K. (1983) 'Industry-based incentives for promoting seat belt use: differential impact on white-collar versus blue-collar employees', *Journal of Organizational Behavior Management*, vol. 5, pp. 17–29.

Guzzo, R.A., Jette, R.D. and Katzell, R.A. (1985) 'The effects of psychologically based intervention programmes on worker productivity: a meta-analysis', *Personnel Psychology*, vol. 38, pp. 275–91.

Hale, A.R. and Glendon, A.I. (1987) *Individual Behavior in the Control of Danger*. Amsterdam: Elsevier.

Haynes, R.S., Pine, R.C. and Fitch, H.G. (1982) 'Reducing accident rates with organizational behavior modification', *Academy of Management Journal*, vol. 25, pp. 407–16.

Karan, B.S. and Kopelman, R.E. (1987) 'The effects of objective feedback on vehicular and industrial accidents: a field experiment using outcome feedback', *Journal of Organizational Behavior Management*, vol. 8, pp. 45–56.

Kazdin, A.E. (1980) *Behavior Modification in Applied Settings*, rev. edn. Homewood, IL: Dorsey Press.

Komaki, J. and Jensen, M. (1986) 'Within group designs: an alternative to traditional control-group designs' in Cataldo, M.F. and Coates, T.J. (eds) *Health and Industry: A behavioral medicine perspective*. New York: John Wiley.

Komaki, J., Barwick, K. and Scott, L. (1978) 'A behavioural approach to occupational safety: pinpointing and reinforcing safe performance in a food manufacturing plant', *Journal of Applied Psychology*, vol. 63, pp. 434–45.

Komaki, J.L., Collins, R.L. and Temlock, S. (1987) 'An alternative performance measurement approach: applied operant measurement in the service sector', *Applied Psychology: An International Review*, vol. 38, pp. 71–86.

Komaki, J.L., Desseles, M.L. and Bownam, E.D. (1989) 'Definitely not a breeze: extending an operant model to effective supervision to teams', *Journal of Applied Psychology*, vol. 74, pp. 522–9.

Lewis, D.J. and Duncan, C.P. (1956) 'Effects of different percentages of money reward on extinction of a lever pulling response', *Journal of Experimental Psychology*, vol. 52, pp. 23–7.

Locke, E.A. (1977) 'The myths of behavior modification in organizations', *Academy of Management Review*, vol. 4, pp. 543–53.

Locke, E.A. and Henne, D. (1986) 'Work motivation theories' in Cooper, C.L. and Robertson, I.T. (eds) *International Review of Industrial and Organizational Psychology*. Chichester: John Wiley.

Locke, E.A. and Latham, G.P. (1990) *A Theory of Goal-Setting and Task Performance*. Englewood Cliffs, NJ: Prentice Hall.

Luthans, F. and Kreitner, R. (1975) *Organizational Behavior Modification*. Glenview, IL: Scott-Foresman.

Luthans, F. and Martinko, M. (1987) 'Behavioral approaches to organizations' in Cooper, C.L. and Robertson, I.T. (eds) *International Review of Industrial and Organizational Psychology*. Chichester: John Wiley.

Luthans, F., Paul, R. and Baker, D (1981) 'An experimental analysis on salespersons' performance behaviours', *Journal of Applied Psychology*, vol. 66, pp. 314–23.

Makin, P.J. and Hoyle, D.J. (1993) 'The Premack principle: professional engineers', *Leadership and Organization Development Journal*, vol. 14, pp. 16–21.

O'Brien, R.M., Dickinson, A.M. and Rosow, M.P. (1982) *Industrial Behavior Modification*. New York: Pergamon Press.

Premack, D. (1965) 'Reinforcement theory' in Levine, D. (ed.) *Nebraska Symposium on Motivation*. Lincoln, NE: University of Nebraska Press, Ch. 14.

Pritchard, R.D., Jones, S.D., Roth, P.L., Stuebing, K.K. and Ekeberg, S.E. (1988) 'Effects of group feedback, goal-setting, and incentives on organizational productivity', *Journal of Applied Psychology*, vol. 73, pp. 337–58.

Rimm, D.C. and Masters, J.C. (1979) *Behavior Therapy: Techniques and empirical findings*. 2nd edn. New York: Academic Press, Ch. 14.

Saari, J. and Nasanen, M. (1989) 'The effect of positive feedback on industrial housekeeping and accidents; a long-term study at a shipyard', *International Journal of Industrial Ergonomics*, vol. 4, pp. 201–11.

Skinner, B.F. (1971) *Beyond Freedom and Dignity*. New York: Knopf.

Skinner, B.F. (1974) *About Behaviourism*. New York: Knopf.

Ulrich, R., Strachnik, T. and Mabry, J. (eds) (1974) *Control of Human Behavior*. Glenview, IL.: Scott-Foresman.

Zohar, D. and Fussfeld, N.A. (1981) 'A systems approach to organizational behaviour modification: theoretical considerations and empirical evidence', *International Review of Applied Psychology*, vol. 30, pp. 491–505.

Approaches to work motivation

INTRODUCTION

In this chapter we examine the concept of motivation and explore some of its implications. We look at some conflicting 'common-sense' ideas about motivation. The chapter then turns to a description and evaluation of some key approaches to motivation, including need theories, the motivation to manage, expectancy theory, justice theories, and goal setting and its recent extensions. Both theoretical and practical issues are covered. Theoretical developments have now started to integrate what seemed to be contradictory approaches to motivation. Goal-setting theory has acted as a trigger for such developments, which have also encompassed ideas not previously applied to motivation. This chapter therefore concludes with an examination of such integration. Behaviourist theories are also relevant to motivation, and are covered in Chapter 10. Attempts to enhance motivation through the careful design of people's jobs are examined in Chapter 19.

OVERVIEW OF MOTIVATION

As with many important concepts in psychology, there is no single universally accepted definition of motivation. Nevertheless, the word itself gives us some clues. To use a mechanical analogy, the motive force gets a machine started and keeps it going. In legal terms, a motive is a person's reason for doing something. Clearly, then, motivation concerns the factors that push us or pull us to behave in certain ways. Specifically, it is made up of three components:

1 *direction*: what a person is trying to do

2 *effort*: how hard a person is trying

3 *persistence*: how long a person continues trying.

In a study of bank tellers (cashiers) Gary Blau (1993) assessed *effort* by filming each teller for a day and calculating the proportion of the time they were engaged in work behaviours. He assessed *direction* using a questionnaire which asked tellers to indicate how often they engaged in each of twenty different behaviours. Blau found that both the overall effort and the type of behaviours tellers engaged in (i.e. direction) predicted the quality of their work performance. This suggests that effort and direction are indeed separable, and that both are important.

Some key points should be remembered:

1 people are usually motivated to do *something*. A person may try hard and long to avoid work – that is motivated behaviour! Hence we should always remember the 'direction' component (*see above*);

2 it is easy to make the mistake of thinking that motivation is the only important determinant of work performance. Other factors, such as ability, quality of equipment and co-ordination of team members' efforts also affect performance;

3 research on motivation occasionally uses persistence as the outcome of interest. More often it uses effort, and more often again, performance. But, as noted in point 2, performance depends on other factors too. Increasingly, research on motivation focuses

on *what* people choose to do rather than their overall job performance. This is partly due to a recognition that in many jobs there is more than one behaviour or set of behaviours that can lead to good job performance (Kanfer, 1992).

One often-made distinction is between *content* theories and *process* theories of motivation. The former focus on *what* motivates human behaviour at work. The latter concentrate on *how* the content of motivation influences behaviour. In fact, most theories have something to say about both content and process, but they do vary considerably in their relative emphasis.

■ **KEY LEARNING POINT**

Motivation concerns what drives a person's choice of what to do, how hard to try, and how long to keep trying. It is not *the only factor which influences work performance.*

'COMMON-SENSE' APPROACHES TO MOTIVATION

McGregor (1960), Argyris (1964), Schein (1988) and others have collectively identified three broad 'common-sense' approaches to motivation which are endorsed by different individuals or even by the same individual at different times. McGregor (1960) termed two of the three *theory X* and *theory Y*, though the reader should be clear that in neither case is the word 'theory' used in its formal academic sense. Schein (1988) added what can be called the *social* approach. In all three cases, we are essentially uncovering a general perspective on human nature. Briefly, they are as follows:

- *theory X*: people cannot be trusted. They are irrational, unreliable and inherently lazy. They therefore need to be controlled and motivated using financial incentives and threats of punishment. In the absence of such controls, people will pursue their own goals, which are invariably in conflict with those of their work organisation;

- *theory Y*: people seek independence, self-development and creativity in their work. They can see further than immediate circumstances and are able to adapt to new ones. They are fundamentally moral and responsible beings who, if treated as such, will strive for the good of their work organisation;

- *social*: a person's behaviour is influenced most fundamentally by social interactions, which can determine his or her sense of identity and belonging at work. People seek meaningful social relationships at work. They are responsive to the expectations of people around them, often more so than to financial incentives.

As you can probably see, theory X and theory Y are in most respects opposites, with the social approach different from both. Which of these 'common-sense' approaches do you find most convincing? The authors' experience with business/management undergraduates is that, if forced to choose one, about half go for the social approach, about 40 per cent for theory Y and about 10 per cent for theory X. Interestingly, most of that 10 per cent can usually be found right at the back of the lecture theatre!

> ■ **KEY LEARNING POINT**
> *Common-sense views of motivation contradict each other but all have some truth.*

None of these three 'common-sense' accounts is universally correct. But, as Schein (1988) points out, over time people may be socialised into their organisation's way of thinking about motivation. Ultimately, managers can influence their staff to see motivation their way. Of course they may also attract and select staff who are already inclined to see things their way. Nevertheless, none of the approaches can be forced on all of the people all of the time. Indiscriminate use of any could have disastrous results. Hence, although each of these approaches finds some expression in theories of motivation, the match between theory and common sense is not particularly close. So what are the theories? Let us now examine some of the most widely known and extensively researched.

NEED THEORIES

What are they?

Need theories are based on the idea that there are psychological needs, probably of biological origin, which lie behind human behaviour. When our needs are unmet, we experience tension or disequilibrium which we try to put right. In other words, we behave in ways which satisfy our needs. Clearly the notion of need reflects the *content* of motivation as opposed to process. But most need theories also make some propositions about how and when particular needs become salient – i.e. process. The notion of need has a long history in general psychology. It has, for example, formed the basis of at least one major analysis of personality (Murray, 1938). Two major traditions have been evident in the work setting. First, there are models based on the notion of psychological growth. Second, there are various approaches which focus on certain quite specific needs.

Need theories based on psychological growth

Easily the best known of these theories is that of Abraham Maslow (1943). Maslow was a humanistically-orientated psychologist (*see* Chapter 2) who offered a general theory of human functioning. His ideas were applied by others to the work setting.

Maslow proposed five classes of human need. Briefly, these are:

1 *physiological*: need for food, drink, sex etc., i.e. the most primitive and obviously biological needs;

2 *safety*: need for physical and psychological safety, i.e. a predictable and non-threatening environment;

3 *belongingness*: need to feel a sense of attachment to another person or group of persons;

4 *esteem*: need to feel valued and respected, by self and significant other people;

5 *self-actualisation*: need to fulfil one's potential – to develop one's capacities and express them.

Maslow proposed that we strive to progress up the hierarchy shown in Fig. 11.1. When one need is satisfied to some (unspecified) adequate extent, the next one up the hierarchy becomes the most important in driving our behaviour.

Other psychologists produced rather similar analyses. For example, Alderfer (1972) proposed three classes of need: existence, relatedness and growth. Existence equated to Maslow's physiological and safety needs. Relatedness can be matched to belongingness and the esteem of others. Growth is equivalent to self-esteem and self-actualisation. Both Maslow and Alderfer made propositions about how particular needs become more or less important to the person (i.e. process), but need theories are often thought of as examples of content theories because of their emphasis on describing needs.

For some years, need theories (especially Maslow's) dominated work motivation. Unfortunately, evaluations of them (e.g. Wahba and Bridwell, 1976; Salancik and Pfeffer, 1977; Rauschenberger *et al.*, 1980) revealed a number of significant flaws, such as:

- needs did not group together in the ways predicted;

- the theories were unable to predict when particular needs would become important;

- there was no clear relationship between needs and behaviour, so that (for example) the same behaviour could reflect different needs, and different behaviours the same need;

Fig. 11.1 Maslow's hierarchy of needs

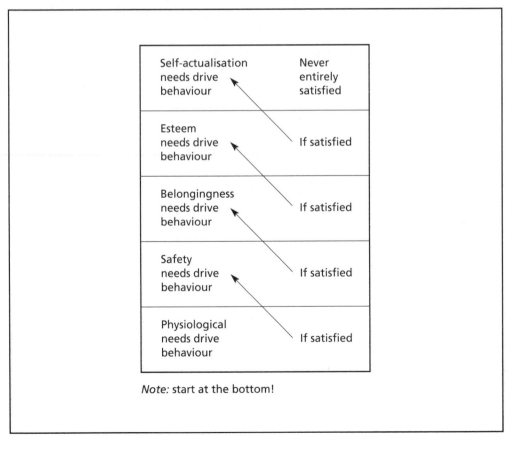

Note: start at the bottom!

- needs were generally described with insufficient precision;
- the whole notion of need as a biological phenomenon is problematic. It ignores the capacity of people and those around them to construct their own perceptions of needs and how they can be met.

> ■ **KEY LEARNING POINT**
> *Need theories have intuitive appeal and provide possible explanations for some human behaviour, but research suggests that they are difficult to use at work.*

Hence these accounts of motivation based on needs have only limited value in understanding and managing work behaviour. They offer interesting and intuitively compelling ways of thinking about human functioning, but their theoretical foundation is doubtful and they have offered no clear guidance to managers about how to motivate individuals. That is not to say that needs are unimportant or nonexistent. Baumeister and Leary (1995) have reviewed a wide range of literature and concluded that the need to belong is powerful and pervasive. People seem strongly driven to form social bonds and are reluctant to break them. Deprivation of frequent interactions of a positive or at least non-conflictual nature has consequences for mental and physical health. Our interpersonal relationships affect the way we think, and how we interpret the situations we encounter. Moreover, Maslow's work has provided a clear picture of the self-actualising person. Maslow regarded self-actualisation as the pinnacle of human growth and adjustment, but argued that few of us operate at that level. Examine Table 11.1 to see whether you do, and whether Maslow's description of a fully-functioning person matches yours. To what extent do work organisations need self-actualising people?

Achievement, power and motivation to manage

Rather more success has been enjoyed by need-based approaches to motivation which concentrate on a small number of more specific needs. Need for achievement was one of the twenty needs underlying behaviour proposed by Murray (1938). It concerns the desire 'to overcome obstacles, to exercise power, to strive to do something difficult as well and as quickly as possible' (Murray, 1938, pp. 80–1, quoted by Landy, 1985, p. 322). Typically, people with high need for achievement seek fairly difficult, but not impossible, tasks. They like to take sole responsibility for them, and want frequent feedback on how well they are doing. Need for achievement formed the basis of McClelland's (1961) theory of work motivation. McClelland argued that a nation's economic prosperity depends partly on the level of need for achievement in its population. He also believed that people could be trained to have high need for achievement. As for personal success, Parker and Chusmir (1991) found that people with high need for achievement tend to feel more successful regarding status/wealth, professional fulfilment and contribution to society than those with lower need for achievement.

Need for achievement has attracted considerable attention in both theoretical and applied contexts (e.g. *see* Beck, 1983). It is not a simple construct, however, and several attempts have been made to identify its components (e.g. Cassidy and Lynn, 1989).

Table 11.1 The self-actualising person

1 *Perceives people and events accurately*, without undue interference from his or her own preconceptions.

2 *Accepts self and others*, including imperfections, but seeks improvement where possible.

3 *Is spontaneous* – especially in thoughts and feelings.

4 *Focuses on problems outside self*, rather than being insecure and introspective.

5 *Is detached*, so that he or she is not unduly thrown off course by awkward events.

6 *Is autonomous*, and remains true to self in spite of pressure to conform.

7 *Appreciates good and beautiful things*, even if they are familiar.

8 *Has peak experiences* of intense positive emotions of a sometimes mystic quality.

9 *Has close relationships*, but only with a few carefully chosen people.

10 *Respects others*, avoids making fun of people and evaluates them according to their inner qualities rather than race or social class.

11 *Has firm moral standards*, and sense of right and wrong, though these may be different from those of many other people.

12 *Is creative.* This is perhaps the most fundamental aspect of self-actualisation, and is seen as the result of the other aspects listed above. By being open-minded and open to experience, the self-actualising person sees things in novel ways and can draw novel conclusions from established information.

Source: Based on Sugarman (1986, pp. 31–44)

Sagie *et al.* (1996) argue that it is important to restrict analysis to the level of tasks, as opposed to wider considerations of status and power. They propose six task preferences that signal high need for achievement:

1 tasks involving uncertainty rather than sure outcomes;
2 difficult tasks rather than easy ones;
3 tasks involving personal responsibility, not shared responsibility;
4 tasks involving a calculated risk, rather than no risk or excessive risk;
5 tasks requiring problem solving or inventiveness, rather than following instructions;
6 tasks which gratify the need to succeed, rather than ensuring the avoidance of failure.

Sagie *et al.* report a five-country study of levels of achievement motivation. People from America generally scored highest on most components, followed by people from the Netherlands and Israel, with those from Hungary lower and those from Japan lower again, except on the first component, where Japanese people scored close to Americans. Given the economic success of Japan as a country, and Japanese organisations, it is important to remember two points:

1 need for achievement is not the only route to successful work performance;

2 need for achievement may be a very Western concept, of little relevance to some other cultures.

A person's need for achievement is often assessed using *projective* tests, which involve the person interpreting ambiguous stimuli such as making up a story about what is happening in a short series of pictures. It is assumed that people *project* their personality onto the stimuli through their interpretations. This general technique is derived from psychoanalytic theory (*see* Chapter 2). Need for achievement can also be assessed in a more straightforward manner using questions about the person's behaviour, thoughts and feelings as in a personality questionnaire. Spangler (1992) reviewed the relevant literature and found that scores on most assessments of need for achievement are indeed correlated with outcomes like career success. Also, despite the generally poor record of projective tests in psychology, projective measures of need for achievement correlated more highly with outcomes than did questionnaire measures.

Other needs, such as affiliation and autonomy, have also been proposed (e.g. Steers and Braunstein, 1976). Need for dominance or power is sometimes included within need for achievement (*see above*), but sometimes treated separately.

John Miner (1964) developed the concept of *motivation to manage*. He also devised a measure of it, called the Miner Sentence Completion Scale (MSCS), which requires people to complete 35 half-finished sentences. Their responses are then scored by a carefully-trained expert on the various components of motivation to manage. These are shown in Table 11.2. The need for power and self-control, and low need for affiliation probably underlie motivation to manage. So do some of the components of need for achievement.

Table 11.2 Components of motivation to manage

Component	Meaning
Authority figures	A desire to meet managerial role requirements in terms of positive relationships with superiors
Competitive games	A desire to engage in competition with peers involving games or sports
Competitive situations	A desire to engage in competition with peers involving occupational or work-related activities
Assertive role	A desire to behave in an active and assertive manner involving activities which are often viewed as predominantly masculine
Imposing wishes	A desire to tell others what to do and to utilise sanctions in influencing others
Standing out from group	A desire to assume a distinctive position of a unique and highly visible nature
Routine administrative functions	A desire to meet managerial role functions requirements of a day-to-day administrative nature

Source: Miner and Smith (1982, p. 298). Copyright © 1982 by the American Psychological Association. Adapted with permission.

251

> ■ KEY LEARNING POINT
>
> *Need for achievement is a sufficiently specific and valid construct to explain some aspects of work behaviour, including managerial behaviour, at least in Western contexts.*

Miner believes that levels of managerial motivation have a substantial effect on a nation's economic performance, and few have disagreed with that. Carson and Gilliard (1993) report that over a number of research studies, the higher a manager's motivation to manage as assessed by the MSCS, the higher his or her work performance, status and salary, other things being equal. So motivation to manage is associated with personal success in managerial occupations. There have been some disputes about whether average levels of motivation to manage have been falling in Western societies (Miner and Smith, 1982; Bartol and Martin, 1987). Whether or not that is the case, Carson and Gilliard (1993) show that, as one would expect, people who opt for management careers have higher motivation to manage than those who do not.

CASE
STUDY
11.1

The motivation to manage

Marie Herzog is an administrative assistant at a large packaging factory in Lyons. She had previously been promoted from the factory floor and is keen to go higher. Her boss, Simone Trouchot, is not so sure – how keen is Marie? Simone made the following observations. Marie seemed rarely to impose her will on her clerical subordinates, even when they were obviously in the wrong. She got on well with the higher managers at the factory, and seemed willing to work closely to the remit they gave her. On the other hand, Marie rarely volunteered her department for trying out experimental new ideas. She seemed uncomfortable when the spotlight was turned on her and her department, even if the attention was congratulatory. Marie seemed happiest dealing with the routine administrative tasks she knew well. She was an accomplished athlete, and had recently been Lyons 400 metres champion two years in succession. Marie was extremely keen to get her department working better than other similar ones, and to ensure that she dealt with problems faster and better than others in similar jobs at the factory.

Suggested exercise

Consult Table 11.2 to judge the extent and nature of Marie Herzog's motivation to manage. Are there particular kinds of managerial roles in which she would feel particularly motivated?

EXPECTANCY THEORY: WHAT'S IN IT FOR ME?

Whereas need theories place heavy emphasis on the content of motivation, expectancy theory concentrates on the process. Originally proposed by Vroom (1964), expectancy theory (also sometimes called VIE theory or instrumentality theory) aims to explain how people choose which of several possible courses of action they will pursue. This choice process was seen as a cognitive, calculating appraisal of the following three factors for each of the actions being considered:

1 *expectancy*: if I tried, would I be able to perform the action I am considering?

2 *instrumentality*: would performing the action lead to identifiable outcomes?

3 *valence*: how much do I value those outcomes?

Vroom (1964) proposed that expectancy and instrumentality can be expressed as probabilities, and valence as a subjective value. He also suggested that force to act is a function of the product of expectancy, instrumentality and valence: in other words, V, I and E are multiplied together to determine motivation. This would mean that if any one of the components was zero, overall motivation to pursue that course of action would also be zero. This can be seen in Fig. 11.2, where, for example, the instrumentality question is not even worth asking if a person believes he or she is incapable of writing a good essay on motivation.

If correct, VIE theory would therefore have important implications for managers wishing to ensure that employees were motivated to perform their work duties. They would need to ensure that all three of the following conditions were satisfied:

1 employees perceived that they possessed the necessary skills to do their jobs at least adequately (expectancy);

2 employees perceived that if they performed their jobs well, or at least adequately, they would be rewarded (instrumentality);

3 employees perceived the rewards offered for successful job performance to be attractive (valence).

How many managers can honestly claim that these conditions hold in their organisation?

Fig. 11.2 Example of VIE theory in action

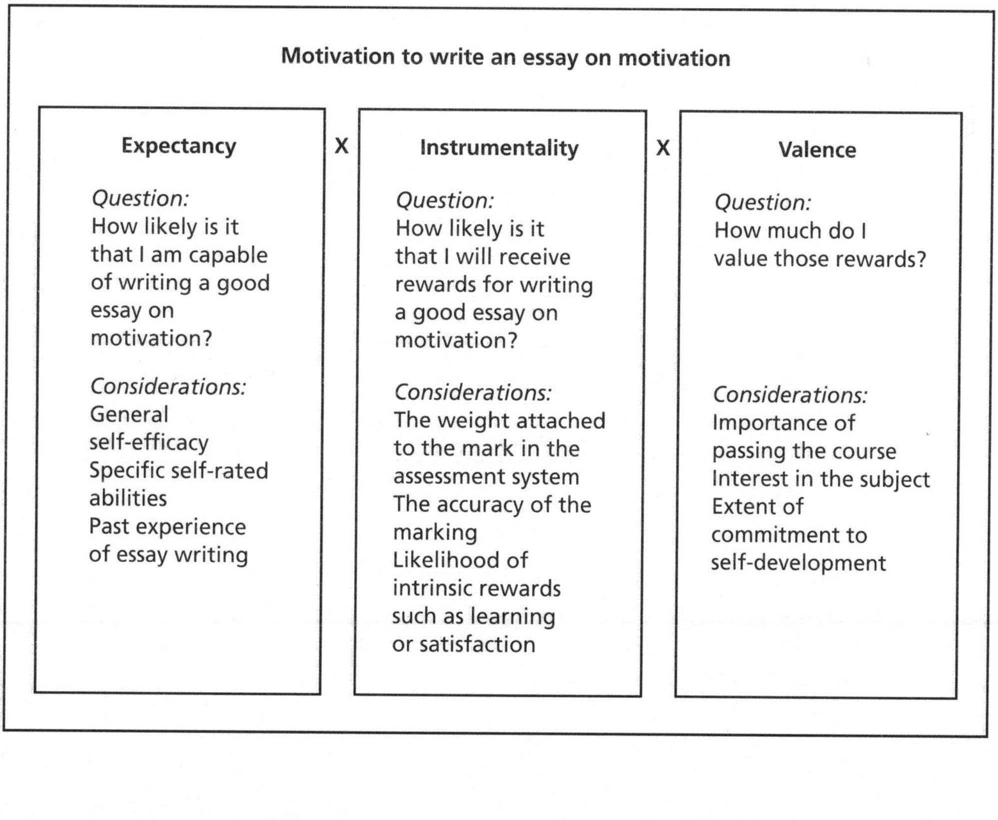

Motivation to write an essay on motivation				
Expectancy	X	**Instrumentality**	X	**Valence**
Question: How likely is it that I am capable of writing a good essay on motivation?		*Question:* How likely is it that I will receive rewards for writing a good essay on motivation?		*Question:* How much do I value those rewards?
Considerations: General self-efficacy Specific self-rated abilities Past experience of essay writing		*Considerations:* The weight attached to the mark in the assessment system The accuracy of the marking Likelihood of intrinsic rewards such as learning or satisfaction		*Considerations:* Importance of passing the course Interest in the subject Extent of commitment to self-development

Although it looks attractive, VIE theory has not done especially well when evaluated in research (e.g. Schwab *et al.*, 1979). The following points can be made:

- research studies which have not measured expectancy, or have combined it with instrumentality, have accounted for effort and/or performance better than studies which assessed expectancy and instrumentality separately;
- behaviour is better predicted by adding the components rather than multiplying them;
- the theory does not work where any of the outcomes have negative valence (i.e. are viewed as undesirable) (Leon, 1981);
- the theory works better when the outcome measure is objective performance, or self-reported effort and performance, rather than effort or performance reported by another person;
- VIE theory works best where the person is choosing between not fewer than ten and not more than fifteen outcomes;
- self-report measures of V, I and E have often been poorly constructed;
- most research has compared different people with each other, rather than comparing different outcomes for the same person. The latter would enable a better test of VIE theory.

Only the first three of these points reflect badly on VIE theory as a whole. The next two demonstrate some boundaries of its effectiveness, and the last two are limitations of research design rather than the theory itself. Nevertheless, as Schwab *et al.* (1979, p. 146) stated:

> there is a nagging suspicion that expectancy theory overintellectualizes the cognitive processes people go through when choosing alternative actions (at least insofar as choosing a level of performance or effort is concerned). The results of the present review are consistent with this suspicion.

But it is still useful to identify the potential determinants of the motivation process, even if they do not combine as predicted by VIE theory. As Landy (1985, pp. 336–7) has put it:

> The cognitive nature of the approach does a good job of capturing the essence of energy expenditure ... A manager can understand and apply the principles embodied in each of the components of the model. Instrumentalities make sense. The manager can use this principle to lay out clearly for subordinates the relationships among outcomes (e.g. promotions yield salary increases, four unexcused absences yield a suspension of one day). Similarly, the manager can affect effort – reward probabilities by systematically rewarding good performance.

■ **KEY LEARNING POINT**

Instrumentality theory may over-complicate the cognitive processes involved in motivation, but is a helpful logical analysis of key factors.

Finally, notice how little attention VIE theory pays to explaining *why* an individual values or does not value particular outcomes. No concepts of need are invoked to address this question. VIE theory proposes that we should ask someone how much they value something, but not bother about *why* they value it. This is another illustration of VIE theory's concentration on process, not content.

JUSTICE THEORIES: AM I BEING FAIRLY TREATED?

Justice theories are like expectancy theory in that they focus on the cognitive processes which govern a person's decision whether or not to expend effort. But unlike expectancy theory they suggest that people are motivated to obtain what they consider fair return for their efforts rather than to get as much as they can. This strains the credulity of some students and managers, but let us suspend disbelief for the moment and consider the propositions of equity theory.

Equity theory was derived from work by Adams (1965), originally in the context of interpersonal relationships. Huseman *et al.* (1987, p. 222) have described the propositions of equity theory like this:

1 individuals evaluate their relationships with others by assessing the ratio of their outcomes from and inputs to the relationship against the outcome/input ratio of a comparison other;

2 if the outcome/input ratios of the individual and comparison other are perceived to be unequal, then inequity exists;

3 the greater the inequity the individual perceives (in the form of either over-reward or under-reward), the more distress the individual feels;

4 the greater the distress an individual feels, the harder he or she will work to restore equity ... Equity restoration techniques include altering or cognitively distorting inputs or outcomes, acting on or changing the comparison other, or terminating the relationship.

In other words, a person is motivated to maintain the same balance between his or her contributions and rewards as that experienced by salient comparison person or persons.

Laboratory experiments generally provided reasonable support for equity theory. Because rewards and availability of comparison others are closely controlled by the experimenter, the only way that people participating in the experiment could establish equity was to increase or decrease the quantity or quality of their work. And this they did, on the whole (Pritchard, 1969). But in the 'real world' things are of course more complicated. People have much more choice of strategy to establish equity and choice of comparison other. They often, but not always, choose similar workers in other organisations (Dornstein, 1988).

Equity theory has been broadened into theories of organisational justice in the late 1980s and 1990s (*see*, for example, Greenberg, 1987). A distinction is made between *distributive justice* and *procedural justice*. The former concerns whether people believe they have received or will receive fair rewards. The latter reflects whether people believe that the procedures used in an organisation to allocate rewards are fair (Folger and Konovsky, 1989). For example, is the reward system impartial, not favouring one group above another? Does it take into account all of the appropriate information? Is there a way of noticing and correcting errors? So if people believe that they are poorly paid relative to people doing similar jobs in other organisations, they may perceive distributive injustice. But if at the same time they think their employing organisation is making available as much reward as possible, and operating fair systems to distribute them, then they may perceive procedural justice. Their satisfaction with pay would probably be low, but their commitment to their employer (*see* Chapter 9) might well be high (McFarlin and Sweeney, 1992).

■ KEY LEARNING POINT

The role of fairness and justice in motivation is becoming more prominent, and increasingly concerns a person's perceptions of the fairness of organisational systems.

The possible role of justice in motivation has become more apparent in recent years. The downsizing, delayering and other changes that have occurred in many work organisations have meant that the deal, or psychological contract, that many employees felt they had with their organisation has been broken (*see also* Chapters 1 and 16). Some people feel a strong sense of injustice about this. To the extent that they can, they are likely to reduce their contribution to their organisation both in terms of their own work performance and other 'good citizen' behaviours such as helping others and attending functions on behalf of their employer (Parks and Kidder, 1994). Figure 11.3 shows how this process might work. It suggests that justice, especially procedural justice, plays a large part in determining reactions to a broken psychological contract, and so does a person's perception of the reasons why the organisation fell short of his or her expectations. There is some evidence for elements of this process (Daly and Geyer, 1994). But it is still likely that people's perceptions of what is fair are heavily influenced by self-interest, so that, for example, you or I tend to believe that we are less fairly treated than other people think we are.

Fig. 11.3 Justice and motivation

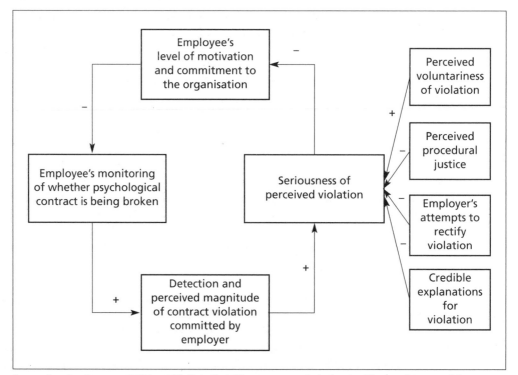

Source: Based on Rousseau (1995, p. 118). Note that this same process is depicted to illustrate features of the psychological contract in Fig. 16.2.

GOAL-SETTING THEORY

The theory

This approach to motivation was pioneered in the USA by Ed Locke and his associates, starting in the 1960s and continuing with increasing strength and sophistication ever since – so much so, that by the 1990s, well over half the research on motivation published in leading academic journals reported tests, extensions or refinements of goal-setting theory.

As Locke *et al.* (1981, p. 126) put it, 'A goal is what an individual is trying to accomplish; it is the object or aim of an action. The concept is similar in meaning to the concepts of purpose and intent'. Locke drew on both academic writing on intention (Ryan, 1970) and the much more practical 'management by objectives' literature in formulating his ideas. Figure 11.4 represents goal-setting theory, and shows that the characteristics of a goal and attitudes towards it are thought to be influenced by incentives, self-perceptions and the manner in which goals are set. In turn, those goal characteristics and attitudes are thought to determine behavioural strategies, which lead to performance within the constraints of ability. Knowledge of results (also called feedback) is thought to be essential to the further refinement of behavioural strategies.

What does research say about goal setting? Reviews by Locke and Latham (1990) and Mento *et al.* (1987) arrive at a number of conclusions, most of which fully or substantially support goal-setting theory. Most fundamental has been overwhelming confirmation of the following phenomena:

Fig. 11.4 Goal-setting theory

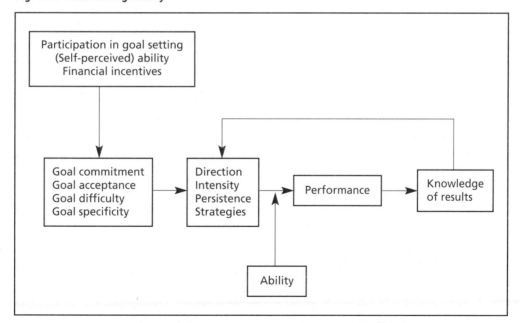

Source: Adapted from *Psychology of Work Behavior* by F. Landy. Copyright © 1989, 1985, 1980, 1976 Brooks/Cole Publishing Company, a division of International Thomson Publishing Inc. By permission of the publisher.

- difficult goals lead to higher performance than easy goals, so long as they have been accepted by the person trying to achieve them. This follows from the fact that people direct their behaviour towards goal achievement, so that difficult goals produce more effective behaviour than easy ones;

- specific goals lead to higher performance than general 'do your best' goals. Specific goals seem to create a precise intention, which in turn helps people to shape their behaviour with precision;

- knowledge of results (feedback) is essential if the full performance benefits of setting difficult and specific goals are to be achieved. Locke *et al.* (1981) have pointed out that although feedback may exert its main effect through providing a person with information, it may also itself have motivating properties. The optimal timing, frequency and amount of feedback are at present somewhat uncertain;

- the beneficial effects of goal setting depend partly on a person's goal commitment: that is, his or her determination to try to achieve it, and unwillingness to abandon or reduce it (Hollenbeck *et al.*, 1989).

These findings establish the core of goal setting and make it probably the most consistently supported theory in work and organisational psychology. Locke *et al.* (1981) observed that 90 per cent of laboratory and field research studies produced results supporting the fundamental elements of goal-setting theory. Mento *et al.* (1987) reinforced that conclusion, and further commented (pp. 74–5) that:

> If there is ever to be a viable candidate from the organizational sciences for elevation to the lofty status of a scientific law of nature, then the relationships between goal specificity/difficulty and task performance are most worthy of serious consideration. [There is also] clear support of the efficacy of coupling feedback with hard specific goals. Both knowledge and motivation, it would seem, are necessary for enhanced performance.

Some further comments can be made on the basis of research evidence. First, financial incentives can indeed enhance performance. Locke *et al.* (1981) report that this occurs either through raising goal level, or through increasing commitment to a goal. Second, and unsurprisingly, ability also affects performance. Third, research on goal setting has been carried out in a range of contexts. Much work has been in laboratories using students who tackle tasks such as solving anagrams or brainstorming, but much has been conducted with groups such as truck drivers and lumberjacks in their work settings. Fourth, goal setting is magnificently clear about how managers can enhance the performance of their employees. Research results also show that goal setting is worth doing – Locke *et al.* (1981) reported that in goal-setting field experiments, the median improvement in work performance produced by goal setting was 16 per cent.

A continuing issue in goal setting concerns participation. Locke *et al.* (1981) concluded that there was no evidence from published research that participation in goal setting by the person attempting to achieve the goal produced better performance than if the goal was assigned to him or her by someone else. Mento *et al.* (1987) reported some evidence that participation was superior but added that the evidence was far from conclusive. Latham *et al.* (1988) conducted a series of experiments designed to investigate whether participation in goal setting is desirable. Over earlier years, Gary Latham (working in the USA) had consistently found no effect of participation on performance. But Miriam Erez, who worked mainly in Israel, consistently found that participation in goal setting enhanced greater goal commitment (and sometimes performance) than simply assigning goals. So Latham and Erez, using Locke as an arbiter, put their heads together and designed a series of experiments that would settle the matter. As they proudly pointed out, it is most unusual for scientific adversaries to work together in this manner.

■ **KEY LEARNING POINT**

The setting of difficult and specific goals often improves a person's work performance by focusing his or her strategies and intentions.

Latham and Erez identified several differences in how they had conducted their earlier experiments. They tested the impact of each difference in their collaborative experiments. One in particular turned out to be important. In Latham's experiments, where a goal was assigned to subjects, an attempt was also made to 'sell' the goal by encouraging them to believe it was attainable. But in Erez's work, subjects were simply told what the goal was. Latham *et al.* (1988) found that this made all the difference. The goal commitment and self-efficacy of 'tell and sell' subjects were very similar to those of subjects who participated in goal setting, and higher than those of subjects in the 'tell only' condition. A similar pattern, though less pronounced, was also evident for task performance. Thus it seems that (at least in laboratory experiments) participation in goal setting is better than simply telling people their goal, but not better than assigning people a goal and attempting to justify it to them.

The notion of goal commitment has been mentioned several times in this section. It can be defined as an unwillingness to abandon or lower the goal (Wright *et al.*, 1994). It is usually treated as a moderator variable – that is, one which affects how much impact goals have on performance. The more committed a person is to the goal, the better he or she will do, other things being equal (*see also* Chapter 9 for more on commitment). But it could be argued that commitment is itself motivation – if I am committed to a goal, then that could be another way of saying I am motivated to achieve it. Tubbs (1994) suggests that one way of looking at it is to say that goal commitment is a function of (i) the closeness of one's personal goals to the goal that has been assigned, and (ii) the importance of that personal goal. Goal commitment is influenced by factors such as goal difficulty and participation in goal setting, and influences a person's persistence in pursuing his or her goal and the formation of strategies to achieve it.

Possible limits to the effectiveness of goal setting

Austin and Bobko (1985) identified four respects in which goal-setting theory had not been properly tested. First, goals which reflect quality of work (as opposed to quantity) were rarely set in goal-setting research. Yet in many people's work, quality is more important than quantity. Second, real jobs often have conflicting goals: achieving one may mean neglecting another. This could complicate or even undermine the application of goal setting. Third, goal-setting research has used goals for individual people and assessed performance of individuals. In the world of work, however, group goals and group performance often matter more. Fourth, Austin and Bobko argued that goal setting had not adequately demonstrated its effectiveness outside laboratory settings. Since Austin and Bobko published their work, evidence suggests that the latter two of their concerns are in fact dealt with by goal-setting theory (*see*, for example, Pritchard *et al.*, 1988). Goal setting does work for groups and it does work outside the laboratory. But the first two of Austin and Bobko's concerns do still carry some force. For example, Yearta *et al.* (1995) found some evidence that setting difficult goals may have actually impaired the work performance of the research scientists they studied. They suggest that goal setting distorted the scientists' choices of work activities, so that they paid too much attention to short-term tasks on which they could obtain clear feedback.

Some other research has directly investigated specific potential limitations of goal setting. Meyer and Gellatly (1988) argued that one function normally served by an assigned goal is to signal what constitutes an appropriate level of performance, or *performance norm*. They manipulated subjects' beliefs about performance norms on a brainstorming (i.e. creative idea generation) task so that they were sometimes different from the goal set. They found that this affected performance and reduced the impact of goal setting. The practical implication is that goal setting may be undermined in the workplace where people already have clear ideas (perhaps widely held within a workgroup) about what constitutes acceptable performance. This is consistent with the findings of the Hawthorne studies 60 years earlier (*see* Chapter 3).

Earley *et al.* (1989) suggested that goal setting may be harmful where a task is novel and where a considerable number of possible strategies are available to tackle it. They asked students to undertake a stock market prediction task, and, sure enough, they found that people who were assigned specific, difficult goals performed *worse* than those assigned a 'do your best' goal. They also changed their strategy more. It seems, then, that when people are tackling unfamiliar and complex tasks, goal setting can induce them to pay too much attention to task strategy and not enough to task perfor-

CASE
STUDY
11.2

Goal setting in a car repair shop

Giovanni Ronto was dissatisfied with the performance of the mechanics at his car repair workshop. He did not keep detailed records, but in his opinion too many customers brought their cars back after repair or servicing, complaining they were still not right. Others found that their cars were not ready by the agreed time. The garage had recently become the local dealer for one of the smaller car manufacturers. The mechanics had been relatively unfamiliar with cars of that make, and were still often unsure how to carry out certain repairs without frequently checking the workshop manual. Giovanni had decided to introduce performance targets for the mechanics as a group. He told them that complaints and delays must be 'substantially reduced', and to sweeten the pill he immediately increased the group's pay by 8%. The increase would continue as long as performance improved to what he regarded as a satisfactory extent. He promised to let the mechanics know each month whether he regarded their collective performance as satisfactory.

Suggested exercise

Use goal-setting theory and research to decide whether Giovanni Ronto's attempt at goal setting is likely to succeed.

mance itself. A major innovative piece of work by Kanfer and Ackerman (1989), which combined motivation theories with cognitive ability theories, has produced a similar conclusion. Kanfer and Ackerman focused on skill acquisition as opposed to performance of established skills, and concluded (p. 687):

> Our findings indicate that interventions designed to engage motivational processes may impede task learning when presented prior to an understanding of what the task is about. In these instances, cognitive resources necessary for task understanding are diverted towards self-regulatory activities (e.g. self evaluation). Because persons have few spare resources at this phase of skill acquisition, these self-regulatory activities can provide little benefit for learning.

Kanfer *et al.* (1994) got students to attempt a simulated air traffic control task and repeated the findings that goal setting can harm performance of unfamiliar complex tasks. But they also found that giving people time to reflect on their performance between repeated attempts at similar tasks eliminated that effect. The breaks enabled them to devote attentional resources to their strategies without having simultaneously to tackle the task itself.

■ **KEY LEARNING POINT**
Goal setting harms work performance when it takes attention away from learning the task.

GOAL SETTING AND SELF-REGULATION

Goal setting could be criticised in its early days for being a technology rather than a theory. It successfully described how goals focus behaviour, without really addressing why or through what processes goals influenced behaviour. During the 1980s and 1990s, developments within the goal-setting tradition (e.g. Latham and Locke, 1991) and outside it have helped progress on these issues. For example, VIE theory predicts that (other things being equal) people will tend to be motivated by tasks where they feel certain they can succeed. Goal setting, on the other hand, suggests that people are most motivated by difficult tasks where success is (presumably) not certain. In fact Mento *et al.* (1992) showed that most people perceive trying for difficult goals as more likely to bring benefits such as a sense of achievement, skill development and material rewards (instrumentality) than trying for easy goals. This more than offsets the lower expectancy of success associated with difficult compared to easy goals.

Other motivation theories can also be integrated with goal setting in order to explain further how people choose, change and implement strategies for achieving and reviewing goals (Kanfer, 1992). Social learning and social cognitive theories of *self-regulation* (*see* Chapter 2) suggest some processes through which people do these things. Bandura (1986) points out that goals provide a person with a cognitive representation (or 'image') of the outcomes they desire. Depending on the gap between goal and the current position, the person experiences *self-reactions*. These include emotions (e.g. dissatisfaction) and self-efficacy expectations (that is, perceptions of one's ability to achieve the goal). These reactions, together with other factors, affect the level and direction of a person's future effort as well as his or her self-concept. For example, suppose a student is attempting to achieve the difficult task of writing a good essay in one evening's work, but by midnight only half the essay has been written. The student's self-efficacy expectations are likely to be reduced somewhat, especially if high to begin with. But if self-efficacy is still fairly high, and so is dissatisfaction, the student is likely to persist until the essay is finished. If his or her self-efficacy has dropped a lot, or was low to start with, the student may give up even if dissatisfied with the lack of progress.

Other work relevant to the processes involved in goal setting has been reported by Dweck (1986). She has developed a theory of motivation and learning which distinguishes between *learning goal orientation* and *performance goal orientation*. Farr *et al.* (1993, p. 195) describe these as follows:

> When approaching a task from a learning goal perspective, the individual's main objective is to increase his or her level of competence on a given task ... Alternatively, when a task is approached from a performance goal orientation, individuals are primarily concerned with demonstrating their competency either to themselves or to others via their present level of task performance.

Farr *et al.* (1993) argue that people who adopt a performance goal orientation will tend to be more fearful of failure, less willing to take on difficult goals, and perhaps less effective in using thought processes to achieve them, than those who adopt a learning goal orientation. They are also less likely to feel they have control over whether they achieve their goals, because by definition the goals of a performance goal orientated person depend partly on what other people are doing. In short, Farr and his colleagues suggest that goal setting as a theory may be more applicable to, and useful for, learning goal orientated people than performance goal orientated ones. They also believe that in the long-run, learning goal orientation is more likely to produce high performance and competence than performance goal orientation. They suggest that there is an increasing and ironic tendency in work organisations for goals to be set which are defined in terms of performance relative to other people, thus encouraging performance goal orientation rather than learning goal orientation.

■ **KEY LEARNING POINT**

A person's characteristic tendencies to be concerned (or not) with learning, performance and goal achievement influence the extent to which goal setting affects his or her work behaviour.

Another theory concerning self-regulation which is also applicable to goal setting has been put forward by Kuhl (1992). Kuhl is concerned to explain how we regulate our behaviour in order to achieve goals, and stop ourselves going to do other things before our goals have been achieved. Kuhl distinguishes between *action orientation*, in which people use self-regulatory strategies to achieve desired goals, and *state orientation*, where they do not. He argues that (i) clear intentions, and (ii) moderate discrepancies between current and desired situation both encourage an action orientation. In other words, we 'swing into action' when we think there is a significant but not hopelessly large gap between where we are and where we want to be, and where we can establish a clear picture of what we are trying to do. The similarity with difficult, specific goals should be obvious!

Kuhl has argued that various self-regulatory strategies are part of action orientation. These include *selective attention* to information relevant to current intention, and *emotion control*, which prevents feelings blocking the implementation of intentions. In contrast, state orientation is characterised by *preoccupation* (with past experiences), *hesitation* (in initiating new behaviour), and *volatility* – frequent impulsive switching between different activities.

Action versus state orientation is probably partly a characteristic of individuals, and partly induced by the situation. If so, there are two ways in which Kuhl's ideas contribute to goal setting. First, goal setting is likely to encourage action orientation. Second, goal-setting motivational techniques are more likely to work for people who characteristically have an action orientation than for those with a state orientation.

Klein (1989) has proposed that *control theory* forms the most appropriate basis for providing a 'meta-theory', or general framework within which more specific theories can address particular motivation issues. Control theory proposes that behaviour is governed by a system where an organism's current state is compared with a referent standard (i.e. desired state), and if there is a discrepancy, behavioural strategies are employed to reduce it. Klein's 'integrated control theory model of work motivation' is shown in Fig. 11.5.

Figure 11.5 needs a little explanation, but is simpler than it might at first seem. A goal (box 1) is a desired standard which elicits behaviour and performance. Feedback on the results of performance is compared with the standard by the so-called compactor (box 5). If there is no discrepancy, or error (box 6), the previous behaviour is continued in order to keep things that way. If there *is* an error, two things can happen. If the situation is familiar to the person, he or she is likely to engage in an 'unconscious scripted response' (box 8), which routinely produces more already learned behaviour so that the error can be reduced. The notion of script was briefly introduced in Chapter 2. It refers to cognitive structures that specify familiar sequences of events and behaviours. Many work behaviours follow scripts or sometimes 'plans', which are more general descriptions of slightly less familiar situations. If it is not immediately obvious why there is a discrepancy between actual and desired states, the person seeks to attribute a reason for it (box 9). The person considers questions like whether the cause of the discrepancy is internal or external to self (*see* Chapter 12), whether the cause is long term or short term, and whether it is controllable.

Klein argues that the results of the attribution process determine the perceived attractiveness of the goal and the person's expectancy of achieving it. These are said to be multiplied to produce the subjective expectancy utility (SEU) of goal attainment (box 10). Personal characteristics (e.g. abilities, needs) also influence SEU, as do situational ones (such as time available). Decisions about SEU can lead both to behaviour change (box 13) and change of goal, which brings us back to the start.

Klein's work is still the best example of how diverse approaches in psychology are now being brought to bear on work motivation. Klein has combined ideas from attribution theory, control theory, expectancy theory, feedback theory, goal-setting theory and information-processing theory. Much of recent psychology is here. Like the other work

Fig. 11.5 Klein's integrated control theory of work motivation

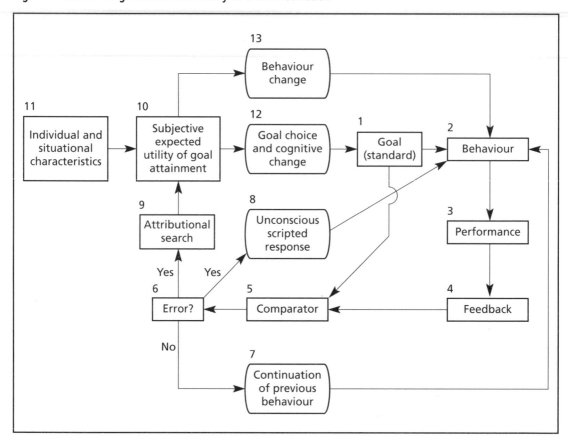

Source: Reproduced with permission from Klein (1989)

on self-regulation described above, Klein has tried to describe and explain how people form and implement intentions to achieve goals. Compared with Dweck and Kuhl, Klein focuses more on the *processes* of self-regulation and less on the *content* (recall the distinction between process and content theories made earlier in this chapter). His work is part of the trend towards integration of theories concerning self-regulation and goal setting.

PAY AND MOTIVATION

Do pay increases affect motivation? Pay is certainly used in many attempts to increase motivation. Performance-related pay (PRP) has been tried in many organisations. PRP involves attempts to link pay directly to work performance of individuals or (occasionally) groups. Often there is only a certain amount of pay available in total, so individuals compete to win greater increases (or smaller decreases) than their colleagues (Torrington and Hall, 1991, chapter 35).

What do the theories presented in this chapter say about pay and motivation? For Maslow, pay would be a motivator only for people functioning at the lower levels of the hierarchy of needs. Advocates of need for achievement point to the fact that pay and other material rewards often signal that a person is successful. So from this perspective pay is a motivator if and when it indicates that the person has succeeded in his or her work tasks. In expectancy theory, pay will be an effective motivator to the extent that it is desired by the person, *and* he or she can identify behaviours that will lead to high payment, *and* he or she feels capable of performing those behaviours. From the perspective of organisational justice, people will be concerned with whether their pay is a fair reward relative to the rewards received by others. They will also want to see fair procedures for allocating pay. A common problem for PRP is that these procedures are *not* seen as fair.

Goal-setting theory normally involves goals that are defined in terms of a person's behaviour and/or accomplishments, not pay. Nevertheless, if there is a very clear and direct link between a person's accomplishments and pay, then specific, difficult goals defined in terms of earnings may be motivating. On the other hand, when pay is an indicator of how well a person is doing *compared with others*, we can expect it to encourage a performance goal orientation rather than a learning goal orientation. As noted above, this might be seen as a 'bad thing'.

Studies have found that, when asked what motivates them at work, the majority of people give answers like variety, responsibility, interesting work or challenge rather than pay (e.g. Herzberg, 1966; *see also* Chapter 19). The recent interest in empowerment is in line with these findings. This leads us to a broad distinction between *intrinsic motivation* and *extrinsic motivation*. The former is based on rewards *intrinsic* to the task itself (e.g. interest, sense of achievement). The latter concerns rewards that are separate from, or *extrinsic* to, the task. Clearly, pay falls into the latter category. Intrinsic motivation has clear links with Maslow's esteem and self-actualisation needs. Some research in the 1970s suggested that high pay actually undermined intrinsic motivation by focusing a person's attention on extrinsic rewards (Deci and Ryan, 1980). More recently, however, it appears that pay can enhance intrinsic motivation, or at least not damage it, if the level of pay provides a person with information about his or her competencies.

SUMMARY

Work motivation is a wide-ranging topic of considerable practical and theoretical importance. It concerns the direction, intensity and persistence of work behaviour. Some psychologists view motivation as a product of innate human needs. Others see it as a calculation based on the question 'how can I maximise my gains?'. Still others take the view that we are motivated to achieve what we perceive as a fair situation relative to that experienced by other people. But the most effective approach to motivation is goal setting. It is based on the premise that intentions shape actions. If work goals (e.g. target levels of performance) are specific and difficult, and if they are accompanied by feedback on how well one is doing, work performance is usually enhanced. There are some circumstances, however, in which goal setting is less effective. The most recent analyses of motivation use ideas from other theories to account for these limitations and thus further develop our understanding of motivation. They focus on how people allocate their cognitive resources such as attention, thinking and problem solving to tasks, and how their self-concepts influence their thought processes.

An unmotivated building inspector

Nobody at Kirraton Council planning department knew what to do about Simon Lucas. Simon was a building inspector. It was his job to approve proposals for small alterations to buildings (such as extensions and loft conversions) which did not need formal planning permission, and to check that the building work carried out was consistent with the approved plans. The trouble was, he didn't – at least, not often and not quickly. There had been a number of complaints about delays in approval of plans that were Simon's responsibility. He did not seem to keep up with the frequent changes in building regulations, which meant that he sometimes made decisions that contradicted them. He only rarely carried out site inspections. This meant that some of the less scrupulous builders got away with unauthorised changes to plans, and others who genuinely wanted his advice did not get it. However, it was difficult to pin Simon down. Council guidance was vague: plans should be dealt with 'within a few weeks'; site inspections conducted 'as and when necessary', and decisions made 'within the spirit', not the letter, of some of the less vital regulations.

Simon's boss, Katherine Walker, decided that she would check his records and unobtrusively observe him at work – it was an open-plan office, so this was feasible. She discovered that he was 26 years old, and had qualified as a building inspector two years earlier. Simon had been recruited by Katherine's predecessor, apparently partly because Simon had 'come up the hard way'. Rather than attending college full-time to obtain the necessary qualifications, he had worked for several years as an architect's draughtsman and attended college night classes. In fact, he had been one of the last people to qualify in that way. The building inspectors' professional institute had subsequently decided that part-time study could not develop the necessary skills and knowledge for work as a qualified building inspector. Katherine knew it was true that the part-time route was often seen as 'second class'. She heard it said that this had prevented Simon from getting a job in another area of the country where he very much wanted to live. Few senior building inspectors held the view of Katherine's predecessor that Simon's route into the profession was superior to full-time study.

Katherine observed that Simon often seemed not to be doing very much. He sat at his desk doodling quite a lot. He sometimes had to phone people more than once because he had forgotten to check something the first time. It took him a long time to find things on his shelves and desk. As far as she could tell, his home life was not a particular problem. Simon was married, apparently happily, and seemed to participate in many social and leisure activities judging from his lunchtime conversations, not to mention his phone calls to squash clubs, campsites etc. during work time!

Simon's job was relatively secure. Ultimately he could be sacked if he demonstrated continuing incompetence, but he had successfully completed his probationary period (Katherine wasn't sure how). Because Kirraton Council covered only a small area, and because Simon's job was a specialist one, he could not be moved to another town or department. Building inspectors' pay depended on age and length of service, with slightly higher rates for those with a relevant college degree. Outstanding performance could only be rewarded with promotion, and this was extremely unlikely for anyone with less than ten years' service.

The other four building inspectors were quite a close-knit group of building sciences graduates who had worked together for several years before Simon's arrival. He had found it hard to establish a relationship with them, and now it was even harder because they felt his apparently poor performance reflected badly on them all. They did not involve him much in their activities, nor did they appear to respect him. Katherine knew something had to be done, but what, and how?

Suggested exercises

1 *What can (i) need theories, (ii) expectancy theory, (iii) organisational justice theory and (iv) goal-setting theory contribute to our understanding of this situation?*

2 *What does each theory suggest about what Katherine Walker should do? What further information would she need in each case?*

TEST YOUR LEARNING

Short-answer questions

1 Describe the key features of the theory X and theory Y 'common-sense' views of motivation.

2 Define the needs in Maslow's hierarchy. According to Maslow, what determines which needs govern our behaviour at any given time?

3 List five features of the 'self-actualising' person as described by Maslow.

4 What are the components of the motivation to manage?

5 Describe valence, instrumentality and expectancy. According to Vroom, how do they combine to determine motivation?

6 Draw a simple diagram which shows the key elements of goal setting.

7 What are the key differences between performance goal orientation and learning goal orientation?

8 What self-regulatory strategies are features of an action orientation?

Essay questions

1 Examine the usefulness of need theories in understanding and predicting behaviour at work.

2 It is often claimed that goal setting is a theory of motivation which works. Examine the evidence for and against that claim.

3 Assess whether insights on self-regulation drawn from social-cognitive psychology can improve our understanding of the motivational impact of goal setting.

4 When and how is pay a motivator?

GLOSSARY OF TERMS

Action orientation A psychological state in which a person uses self-regulatory strategies in order to achieve desired goals. Contrast with **State orientation** (*see below*).

Belongingness need The psychological need to feel part of a group, organisation or other collective endeavour.

Content theories of motivation Theories which concentrate on *what* motivates people, rather than *how* motivation works. Contrast with **Process theories of motivation** (*see below*).

Control theory An approach to motivation which focuses on the psychological processes involved when people compare their actual situation with their desired state, and decide what to do about any discrepancy.

Equity theory An approach to motivation which argues that people are motivated to achieve an equitable (fair) return for their efforts in comparison with other people.

Esteem need The psychological need to feel respected by others and also by oneself.

Expectancy In expectancy theory, expectancy is the extent to which a person believes that he or she has the ability to perform certain behaviours.

Expectancy theory An approach to motivation which focuses on the rational decision-making processes involved in choosing one course of action from alternatives.

Extrinsic motivation The motivation to perform a task derived from rewards that are not part of the task itself (e.g. money, status). Contrast with **Intrinsic motivation** (*see below*).

Goal commitment In goal-setting theory, goal commitment is the extent to which a person is determined to achieve a goal.

Goal-setting theory This approach to motivation concentrates on how goals (performance targets) can affect a person's work strategies and performance.

Instrumentality In expectancy theory, instrumentality is the extent to which a person believes that performing certain behaviours will lead to a specific reward.

Intrinsic motivation The motivation to perform a task for rewards that are part of the task itself (e.g. interest, challenge). Contrast with **Extrinsic motivation** (*see above*).

Learning goal orientation An approach people may take to a task where their main concern is to increase their level of competence on the task. Contrast with **Performance goal orientation** (*see below*).

Motivation The factors which determine the effort, direction and persistence of a person's behaviour.

Motivation to manage The needs and values which underlie the effort and persistence a person devotes to management tasks.

Need A biologically-based desire that is activated by a discrepancy between actual and desired states.

Need for achievement The desire to carry out a task as well and as quickly as possible.

Organisational justice An approach to motivation which focuses on the extent to which people perceive that rewards are distributed fairly in their organisation, and that the process of deciding reward allocation is fair.

Performance goal orientation An approach to a task where people's main concern is to demonstrate their competence to themselves and other people. Contrast with **Learning goal orientation** (*see above*).

Physiological needs The desire to avoid hunger, thirst and other unpleasant bodily states.

Process theories of motivation Approaches to motivation which focus on *how* motivation works, rather than *what* motivates behaviour. Contrast with **Content theories of motivation** (*see above*).

Safety needs The desire to avoid physical or psychological danger.

Self-actualisation The need to fulfil one's potential: to develop and express one's capacities.

Self-regulation The strategies a person uses to monitor and direct his or her behaviour in pursuit of a goal.

Social approach A 'common-sense' approach to motivation which argues that a person is motivated to establish and maintain meaningful social relationships.

State orientation A psychological state in which a person does *not* use self-regulatory strategies to achieve goals. Contrast with *Action orientation* (*see above*).

Theory X A 'common-sense' approach to motivation which views people as untrustworthy, to be motivated by financial reward and punishment.

Theory Y A 'common-sense' approach to motivation which views people as inherently trustworthy and responsible, to be motivated by challenge and responsibility.

Valence In expectancy theory, valence is the subjective value a person attaches to a particular reward.

SUGGESTED FURTHER READING

1 Ruth Kanfer (1992; full reference in the list below) provides a good account of how motivation theory is developing to take account of ideas from other areas of psychology. It is quite a technical article, but worth the effort of reading carefully.

2 Ivan Robertson, Mike Smith and Dominic Cooper (1992) *Motivation: Strategies, theory and practice*, 2nd edn, Institute of Personnel and Development. An accessible analysis of theories of work motivation, explored in more detail than is possible here.

3 Rick Steers and Lyman Porter (1991) *Motivation and Work Behaviour*, published by McGraw-Hill, gives a detailed North American perspective on the theory and practice of motivation.

REFERENCES

Adams, J.S. (1965) 'Inequity in social exchange' in Berkowitz, L. (ed.) *Advances in Experimental Social Psychology*, vol. 2. New York: Academic Press.

Alderfer, C.P. (1972) *Existence, Relatedness and Growth: Human needs in organizational settings*. New York: Free Press.

Argyris, C. (1964) *Integrating the Individual and the Organization*. Chichester: John Wiley.

Austin, J.T. and Bobko, P. (1985) 'Goal-setting theory: unexplored areas and future research needs, *Journal of Occupational Psychology*, vol. 58, pp. 289–308.

Bandura, A. (1986) *Social Foundations of Thought and Action: A social cognitive theory*. Englewood Cliffs, NJ: Prentice Hall.

Bartol, K.M. and Martin, D.C. (1987) 'Managerial motivation among MBA students: a longitudinal assessment', *Journal of Occupational Psychology*, vol. 60, pp. 1–12.

Baumeister, R.F. and Leary, M.R. (1995) 'The need to belong: desire for interpersonal attachments as a fundamental human motivation', *Psychological Bulletin*, vol. 117, pp. 497–529.

Beck, R.C. (1983) *Motivation: Theory and principles*. Englewood Cliffs, NJ: Prentice Hall.

Blau, G. (1993) 'Operationalizing direction and level of effort, and testing their relationships to individual job performance', *Organizational Behavior and Human Decision Processes*, vol. 55, pp. 152–70.

Carson, K.P. and Gilliard, D.J. (1993) 'Construct validity of the Miner Sentence Completion Scale', *Journal of Occupational and Organizational Psychology*, vol. 66, pp. 171–5.

Cassidy, T. and Lynn, R. (1989) 'A multifactorial approach to achievement motivation: the development of a comprehensive measure', *Journal of Occupational Psychology*, vol. 62, pp. 301–12.

Daly, J.P. and Geyer, P.D. (1994) 'The role of fairness in implementing large-scale change: employee evaluations of process and outcome in seven facility relocations', *Journal of Organizational Behavior*, vol. 15, pp. 623–38.

Deci, E.L. and Ryan, R.M. (1980) 'The empirical exploration of intrinsic motivational processes' in Berkowitz, L. (ed.) *Advances in Experimental Social Psychology*, vol. 13. New York: Academic Press.

Dornstein, M. (1988) 'Wage reference groups and their determinants: a study of blue-collar and white-collar employees in Israel', *Journal of Occupational Psychology*, vol. 61, pp. 221–35.

Dweck, C.S. (1986) 'Motivational processes affecting learning', *American Psychologist*, vol. 41, pp. 1040–8.

Earley, P.C., Connolly, T. and Ekegren, G. (1989) 'Goals, strategy development and task performance: some limits on the efficacy of goal-setting', *Journal of Applied Psychology*, vol. 74, pp. 24–33.

Farr, J.L., Hofman, D.A. and Ringenbach, K.L. (1993) 'Goal orientation and action control theory: implications for industrial and organizational psychology' in Robertson, I.T. and Cooper, C.L. (eds) *International Review of Industrial and Organizational Psychology*, vol. 8. Chichester: John Wiley.

Folger, R. and Konovsky, M.A. (1989) 'Effects of procedural and distributive justice on reactions to pay rise decisions', *Academy of Management Journal*, vol. 32, pp. 115–30.

Greenberg, J. (1987) 'A taxonomy of organizational justice theories', *Academy of Management Review*, vol. 12, pp. 9–22.

Herzberg, F. (1966) *Work and the Nature of Man*. Cleveland, OH: World Publishing.

Hollenbeck, J.R., Williams, C.R. and Klein, H.J. (1989) 'An empirical examination of the antecedents of commitment to difficult goals', *Journal of Applied Psychology*, vol. 74, pp. 18–23.

Huseman, R.C., Hatfield, J.D. and Miles, E.W. (1987) 'A new perspective on equity theory: the equity sensitivity construct', *Academy of Management Review*, vol. 12, pp. 222–34.

Kanfer, R. (1992) 'Work motivation: new directions in theory and research' in Robertson, I.T. and Cooper, C.L. (eds) *International Review of Industrial and Organizational Psychology*, vol. 7. Chichester: John Wiley.

Kanfer, R. and Ackerman, P.L. (1989) 'Motivation and cognitive abilities: an integrative/aptitude–treatment interaction approach to skill acquisition', *Journal of Applied Psychology*, vol. 74, pp. 657–90.

Kanfer, R., Ackerman, P.L., Murtha, T.C. and Dugdale, B. (1994) 'Goal-setting, conditions of practice, and task performance: a resource allocation perspective', *Journal of Applied Psychology*, vol. 79, pp. 826–35.

Klein, H.J. (1989) 'An integrated control theory model of work motivation', *Academy of Management Review*, vol. 14, pp. 150–72.

Kuhl, J. (1992) 'A theory of self-regulation: action versus state orientation, self-discrimination and some applications', *Applied Psychology: An International Review*, vol. 41, pp. 97–129.

Landy, F.J. (1989) *Psychology of Work Behavior*. 4th edn. Homewood, IL: Brooks/Cole Publishing Co.

Latham, G.P. and Locke, E.A. (1991) 'Self-regulation through goal-setting', *Organizational Behavior and Human Decision Processes*, vol. 50, pp. 212–47.

Latham, G.P., Erez, M. and Locke, E.A. (1988) 'Resolving scientific disputes by the joint design of crucial experiments by the antagonists: application to the Erez–Latham dispute regarding participation in goal setting', *Journal of Applied Psychology*, vol. 73, pp. 753–72.

Leon, F.R. (1981) 'The role of positive and negative outcomes in the causation of motivational forces', *Journal of Applied Psychology*, vol. 66, pp. 45–53.

Locke, E.A. and Latham, G.P. (1990) *A Theory of Goal-Setting and Task Performance*. Englewood Cliffs, NJ: Prentice Hall.

Locke, E.A., Shaw, K.N., Saari, L.M. and Latham, G.P. (1981) 'Goal setting and task performance 1969–1980', *Psychological Bulletin*, vol. 90, pp. 125–52.

Maslow, A.H. (1943) 'A theory of motivation', *Psychological Review*, vol. 50, pp. 370–96.

McClelland, D.C. (1961) *The Achieving Society*. Princeton, NJ: Van Nostrand.

McFarlin, D.B. and Sweeney, P.D. (1992) 'Distributive and procedural justice as predictors of satisfaction with personal and organizational outcomes', *Academy of Management Journal*, vol. 35, pp. 626–37.

McGregor, D. (1960) *The Human Side of Enterprise*. New York: McGraw-Hill.

Mento, A.J., Locke, E.A. and Klein, H.J. (1992) 'Relationship of goal level to valence and instrumentality', *Journal of Applied Psychology*, vol. 77, pp. 395–405.

Mento, A.J., Steel, R.P. and Karren, R.J. (1987) 'A meta-analytic study of the effects of goal setting on task performance: 1966–1984', *Organizational Behavior and Human Decision Processes*, vol. 39, pp. 52–83.

Meyer, J.P. and Gellatly, I.R. (1988) 'Perceived performance norm as a mediator in the effect of assigned goal on personal goal and task performance', *Journal of Applied Psychology*, vol. 73, pp. 410–20.

Miner, J.B. (1964) *Scoring Guide for the Miner Sentence Completion Scale*. Atlanta, GA: Organizational Measurement Systems Press.

Miner, J.B. and Smith, N.R. (1982) 'Decline and stabilization of managerial motivation over a 20-year period', *Journal of Applied Psychology*, vol. 67, pp. 297–305.

Murray, H.J. (1938) *Explorations in Personality*. Oxford: Oxford University Press.

Parker, B. and Chusmir, L.H. (1991) 'Motivation needs and their relationship to life success', *Human Relations*, vol. 44, pp. 1301–12.

Parks, J.M. and Kidder, D.L. (1994) '"Till death us do part ...": changing work relationships in the 1990s' in Cooper, C.L. and Rousseau, D.M. (eds) *Trends in Organizational Behaviour*, vol. 1. Chichester: John Wiley, pp. 111–36.

Pritchard, R.D. (1969) 'Equity theory: a review and critique', *Organizational Behavior and Human Performance*, vol. 4, pp. 176–211.

Pritchard, R.D., Jones, S.D., Roth, P.L., Stuebing, K.K. and Ekeberg, S.E. (1988) 'Effects of group feedback, goal-setting and incentives on organizational productivity', *Journal of Applied Psychology*, vol. 73, pp. 337–58.

Rauschenberger, J., Schmitt, N. and Hunter, J.E. (1980) 'A test of the need hierarchy concept by a Markov model of change in need strength', *Administrative Science Quarterly*, vol. 25, pp. 654–70.

Rousseau, D. (1995) *Psychological Contracts in Organizations*. London: Sage.

Ryan, T.A. (1970) *Intentional Behavior*. New York: Ronald Press.

Sagie, A., Elizur, D. and Yamauchi, A. (1996) 'The structure and strength of achievement motivation: a cross-cultural comparison', *Journal of Organizational Behaviour*, vol. 17, pp. 431–44.

Salancik, G.R. and Pfeffer, J. (1977) 'An examination of need satisfaction models of job attitudes', *Administrative Science Quarterly*, vol. 22, pp. 427–56.

Schein, E.H. (1988) *Organizational Psychology*. 3rd edn. Englewood Cliffs, NJ: Prentice Hall.

Schwab, D.P., Olian-Gottlieb, J.D. and Heneman, H.G. (1979) 'Between subjects expectancy theory research: a statistical review of studies predicting effort and performance', *Psychological Bulletin*, vol. 86, pp. 139–47.

Spangler, W.D. (1992) 'Validity of questionnaire and TAT measures of need for achievement: two meta-analyses', *Psychological Bulletin*, vol. 112, pp. 140–54.

Steers, R.M. and Braunstein, D.N. (1976) 'A behaviorally-based measure of manifest needs in work settings', *Journal of Vocational Behavior*, vol. 9, pp. 251–66.

Sugarman, L. (1986) *Life-Span Development*. London: Methuen.

Torrington, D.P. and Hall, L.A. (1991) *Personnel Management: A new approach*. 2nd edn. London: Prentice Hall.

Tubbs, M. (1994) 'Commitment and the role of ability in motivation: comment on Wright, O'Leary-Kelly, Cortina, Klein and Hollenbeck (1994)', *Journal of Applied Psychology*, vol. 79, pp. 804–11.

Vroom, V.H. (1964) *Work and Motivation*. Chichester: John Wiley.

Wahba, M.A. and Bridwell, L.B. (1976) 'Maslow reconsidered: a review of research on the need hierarchy theory', *Organizational Behavior and Human Performance*, vol. 15, pp. 212–40.

Wright, P.M., O'Leary-Kelly, A.M., Cortina, J.M., Klein, H.J. and Hollenbeck, J. (1994) 'On the meaning and measurement of goal commitment', *Journal of Applied Psychology*, vol. 79, pp. 795–803.

Yearta, S.K., Maithis, S. and Briner, R.B. (1995) 'An exploratory study of goal-setting in theory and practice: a motivational technique that works?', *Journal of Occupational and Organizational Psychology*, vol. 68, pp. 237–52.

12

Perceiving people

After studying this chapter, you should be able to:

1 specify two underlying reasons why people may be biased in their perception of other people;

2 define the term stereotype and specify two reasons why a stereotype may be inaccurate;

3 describe the circumstances in which people are most likely to use stereotypes;

4 describe the key features of social identity theory;

5 define the assimilation and contrast effects in person perception;

6 define the term implicit personality theory;

7 describe how people may unintentionally confirm their initial impression of another person;

8 describe the primacy and recency effects in person perception;

9 describe the halo and horns effects in person perception;

10 define impression management;

11 define distinctiveness, consistency and consensus information in attribution theory;

12 describe three biases in the attribution process.

INTRODUCTION

How do we make judgements about other people? Do we do it well, and could we do it better? Although not often defined as a topic area in work and organisational psychology, person perception is clearly crucial to a wide range of activities in the workplace. That is why it is given its own chapter here. This chapter aims to introduce the reader to some common phenomena in person perception and to apply them to work situations. It also aims to enable the reader to become as aware as possible of his or her own person perception. A brief introduction to the field is followed by coverage of stereotypes, implicit personality theories, impression management and attribution, as well as other more specific phenomena. The emphasis throughout is on how findings from social psychology can be used to understand and improve interpersonal communication in the workplace.

OVERVIEW OF PERSON PERCEPTION

Person perception concerns how we obtain, store and recall information about other people in order to make judgements about them. In the 1980s, it became increasingly apparent that advances in person perception made by social psychologists were being largely ignored by work and organisational psychologists (Ilgen and Klein, 1989). There were some exceptions, such as selection interviewing (*see* Chapter 8) and leadership (*see* Chapter 14). But person perception is clearly relevant to many more work situations than these, including meetings, sales presentations, conferences, telephone conversations and even written material such as memos or reports.

Person perception can be considered at three levels:

1 perceiving the *behaviour* of other people
2 perceiving the *personality* of other people
3 perceiving the *causes* of events involving people.

Clearly, people who do these things well are at an advantage in the workplace, other things being equal. They will be more likely to relate well to others, get the best out of them, and manage social situations with skill. But aren't we all quite good at person perception? Isn't it just common-sense stuff that comes naturally? No. We frequently succumb to various biases and distortions which can impair our perception of others. There are two general sources of such problems:

1 *motivation or emotion*: for reasons such as the protection of our own self-esteem, we may not even attempt to achieve accuracy in our perception of others. We may however *believe* that we are trying to be accurate;
2 *information-processing limitations*: we may seek the truth, but lack the cognitive resources to weigh up information about other people in an optimal manner.

> ■ KEY LEARNING POINT
> *Person perception concerns how we perceive and interpret the behaviour and characteristics of other people, and the causes of events involving them.*

The first of these is loosely derived from psychoanalytic approaches to psychology, and the second from social cognitive approaches (*see* Chapter 2). Social psychologists working in both these traditions have spent thirty years or more concentrating on our imperfections when we perceive others. As Higgins and Bargh (1987, p. 371) put it:

> It sometimes appears as though the burden of proof is on demonstrating that people take environmental information into account, rather than on showing that they dismiss, discount or distort it in line with their prior theories.

But now the pendulum is swinging back. As we shall see, more recent work tends to show that although we are not perfect, we are not nearly as bad at perceiving others as has sometimes been claimed. The amount of effort and skill we use in our perception of other people seems to depend on our aims. When we need to be accurate in our impression of another person, we are relatively likely to be, even if it takes us some time. When we need to be quick, or when our perception of another person is simply not very important, we are less systematic (Fiske, 1993). But it is equally clear that we need to be aware of possible pitfalls in order to overcome them. To quote Higgins and Bargh (1987, p. 415) again:

> recognizing that one's own beliefs, inferences and memory are limited promotes the realization, 'I could be wrong' – a first step in tolerance, open-mindedness, and prudence.

Two additional points should be made before we look further. First, much of the above discussion depends on the notion of accuracy in person perception – that there is a right answer to the question 'what is (s)he like?' if only we can find it. This seems a reasonable assumption when we are perceiving people's *behaviour*. It is less straightforward when applied to judgements of *personality* and personal responsibility. Neither of these can be observed directly (Forgas, 1985, chapter 2).

The second point concerns method in social psychology. Most of what social psychologists know about person perception comes from experimental laboratory studies. People are often asked to make judgements about others which do not usually have significant consequences for either the perceiver or the perceived. The judgements are normally made using dimensions provided by the psychologist, which are not necessarily those the observer would have chosen. They are usually made by students because students are easily accessible to most experimenters. Of course, these are all common features of laboratory research in psychology, and there are some compensatory advantages (*see* Chapter 3). But perhaps it is not surprising that some work psychologists have been reluctant to take the practical implications of that research at face value.

The remainder of this chapter is devoted to outlining some common phenomena in person perception. Guidance is offered about how to recognise them, avoid mistakes, and use them to good effect.

STEREOTYPES

What are stereotypes and how do they arise?

Stereotypes are generalised beliefs about the characteristics, attributes and behaviours of members of certain groups (Hilton and Von Hippel, 1996, p. 240). Groups can be defined on any number of criteria. Obvious possibilities are race, sex, occupation and age, but research suggests that most people do not have a stereotype of all women or all men or all old people. Stereotypes tend to be based on rather more specific groups, such as old men or old white women (Stangor *et al.*, 1992). Some stereotypes held by a person refer to quite specific groups, as in the following examples:

- trade union officials are mostly militant ideologues
- most police are violent authoritarians
- managers in this company are honest
- accountants are more stimulating than anybody else
- production managers usually speak their mind.

Clearly, then, stereotypes vary in their favourability. They also differ in their extremity. The third and fourth above do not allow for any exceptions, but the others do because they refer to 'most' rather than 'all'. Often stereotypes have some validity, in the sense that *on average* members of one group differ from members of another. On average, middle managers are doubtless more intelligent in some respects than building site labourers. But there is equally certainly a large overlap – some building site labourers are more intelligent than some middle managers (*see* Chapter 6 for a discussion of what intelligence is). In fact, formation of stereotypes may lead to overestimation of the differences between groups (Krueger, 1991).

We may develop stereotypes of groups based on very limited information about them – perhaps confined to what we see on television. Other stereotypes can arise when a generalisation is true of a very few people in one group and practically none in another group. Suppose for a moment that one in five hundred shop stewards are members of revolutionary left-wing political groups, compared with one in three thousand of the general population. Would it be a good idea to expect that a shop steward you were about to meet for the first time would be a revolutionary left-winger? Clearly not. It is more probable that he or she holds such views than someone who is not a shop steward, but still not at all likely.

> ■ KEY LEARNING POINT
> *Stereotypes are generalised beliefs about what people in a particular group are like. They are often inaccurate.*

Stereotypes and group identity

Stereotypes are often thought to derive from a need to establish a clear 'map' of our social world where our identity and that of others is defined in terms of group memberships. This is a fundamental premise of *social identity theory* (Tajfel and Turner, 1985), which has become enormously influential in European social psychology. This theory proposes that not only do we wish to create a social map, we also wish to uphold the value of our own group (and thereby of ourselves too) relative to other groups. Some remarkable experimental work has shown that this happens even where groups are short term, and defined on the basis of some apparently innocuous criterion such as preference for one painting rather than another, or even random allocation. Further, it seems that group members seek to maximise the *difference* between the rewards received by their own group and another group, even at the expense of absolute gain. Thus a reward of (say) eight pounds for own-group members and three for members of another group is usually preferred to ten pounds for each group.

Principles of social identity theory have been applied to work organisations by Ashforth and Mael (1989). They point out a danger that people in different groups (e.g. departments, functions, levels) will perceive each other in terms of negative stereotypes, and use this to justify attempts to maintain or enhance their own superiority while minimising collaborative activities. This tendency is especially marked where groups are in fact relatively similar because that is when people most feel the need to establish their own distinctiveness. Groups of relatively low status are also more concerned than others to establish an identity, and the relative unconcern of higher status groups simply serves to frustrate them.

> ■ KEY LEARNING POINT
> *We sometimes use stereotypes to devalue other groups relative to our own.*

So are stereotypes dangerous?

They can be. As some of the above discussion demonstrates, they can serve to handicap intergroup understanding with potentially negative consequences for work organisations and society in general. More optimistically, if group members feel that differences between groups in resources or status are legitimate, they form less negative views of members of other groups. Also, group members often arrive at a 'compromise' where they see themselves and members of another group as possessing complementary virtues (Van Knippenberg, 1984). Thus the accountant may acknowledge that the marketer has valuable creative flair, but argue that flair needs careful costing and control which only the accountant can provide. Fostering such beliefs about complementary strengths is an important task for managers who wish their organisations to function in an integrated fashion.

The so-called *self-fulfilling prophecy* is one way in which stereotypes can be harmful. For example, if a manager thinks that shop-floor workers tend to be surly and unco-operative, he or she is likely to treat them in exactly the dismissive or aggressive way which will elicit a surly and unco-operative response. Worse, this will strengthen the manager's stereotype of shop-floor workers.

Another problem with stereotypes is that, once formed, they may be hard to change. In some ingenious experimental work, Hill *et al.* (1990) showed subjects photographs of people with brief personality descriptions. This was rigged so that subtle variations in nose positioning were associated with personality description. They found that the subjects learned the associations between facial features and personality unconsciously. What was more, that association continued to gain strength in the subjects' minds, even when it no longer applied to subsequent photographs they were shown.

A number of social psychology experiments have shown that we require more and stronger evidence to abandon a stereotype than to stick with it. So, if a person behaves inconsistently with stereotype on one occasion, an observer is unlikely to abandon the stereotype. But if that person behaves consistently with stereotype, the observer is likely to think 'oh yes, just as I would expect', and thus be re-confirmed in his or her stereotypic thinking. On the other hand, there is also good evidence that we remember information inconsistent with stereotype *better* than consistent information (Stangor and McMillan, 1992). This might be assumed to undermine stereotypes, but apparently this is not so. Hilton and Von Hippel (1996) point out that our memory for stereotype-inconsistent behaviour prompts us to think harder about the reasons why that behaviour occurred. Often, we draw the conclusion that it wasn't so inconsistent after all – perhaps because the person was in an unusual situation, or for some other reason was prompted to behave in an uncharacteristic manner. Also, it seems that when we are busy, the tendency to remember stereotype-incongruent information is reversed. People with a lot on their minds remember things that are consistent with their stereotypes *better* than those which are not.

■ **KEY LEARNING POINT**

Stereotypes can be learned outside our awareness. For various reasons (see Fig. 12.1) they are then often quite resistant to change.

It seems that we are more likely to use stereotypes in some situations than in others. When we are at the low point of our daily circadian rhythm (Bodenhausen, 1990), or under time pressure (Heaton and Kruglanski, 1991) we are more likely to use stereotypes than at other times. This is because using a stereotype can save us the trouble of concentrating on what people are actually doing and saying when we are forming impressions of them. When we are tired or rushed, we have less capacity and perhaps less motivation to take that trouble – though having other things to think about can also inhibit our use of stereotypes in certain circumstances. Whether or not we are busy, threats to our self-esteem or sense of security encourage stereotyped perception as a means of protecting our identity. So in organisations where (for example) people feel overworked and insecure in their jobs, we can expect more stereotyping in person perception, with probable negative consequences for work performance and interpersonal relationships at work.

Overcoming inappropriate use of stereotypes

Perhaps most of us like to think that we are free of stereotypes. If so, we are probably fooling ourselves. At the university where two of the authors are employed, a small number of students come each year from Norway. One of us (who shall remain nameless!) still catches himself feeling slightly surprised that many of these students are *not* blond and tall – his stereotype of Scandinavians. Devine (1989) argues that we cannot avoid starting out with stereotypes. The difference between prejudiced and non-prejudiced individuals is that the latter deliberately inhibit the automatically activated stereotype and replace it with more open-minded thoughts (Devine, 1989, p. 15).

Fig. 12.1 Some causes and consequences of stereotypes

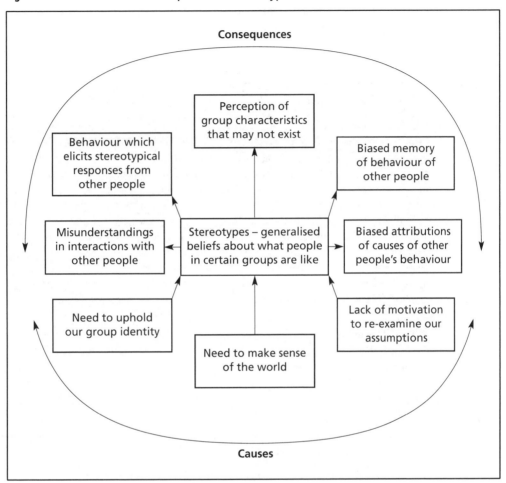

[This] can be likened to the breaking of a bad habit ... The individual must (a) initially decide to stop the old behavior; (b) remember the resolution, and (c) try repeatedly and decide repeatedly to eliminate the habit before the habit can be eliminated.

Other work has shown that simply instructing people to try to suppress stereotypic thoughts can actually be counterproductive. Ironically, the instruction itself leads people to be more conscious of the stereotype they are trying to suppress (Bodenhausen and Macrae, 1996). As Devine implied, what matters seems to be a personal commitment to changing one's perception or behaviour. Often this will involve changing one's assumptions about why a particular person is the kind of person they are – for example, poor because of lack of opportunity, not laziness.

One other catch is worth noting. It seems that we interpret information about a person – a particular action, for example – as consistent with our stereotype if that action reaches a certain 'threshold' level of consistency with the stereotype. In other words, we then exaggerate the extent to which the action matches the stereotype – a so-called *assimilation effect*. But if the action does not quite reach that threshold, the opposite happens. We interpret it as inconsistent with the stereotype, and in fact overemphasise the inconsistency

– a *contrast effect* (Manis *et al.*, 1988). So if we are not careful, as observers we can actually end up perceiving someone as *more* different from our stereotype than he or she really is. From the viewpoint of the person being observed, this brings the hope that we do not have to behave in an extreme fashion in order to alter somebody's stereotypical perception of us.

CASE STUDY 12.1

Stereotyping and social identity

Stig Kornstadt works in the medical records department of a large hospital. He takes a dim view of doctors: 'The trouble is they are all so arrogant. They walk in here and expect me to find patients' case notes immediately. It's not as simple as that – they could be almost any place in the hospital. They couldn't do their job properly if it wasn't for me, but they seem to forget that. One doctor actually comes in here and threatens to report me if I don't do what he wants right away. Another always finds me in the canteen during my lunch break and makes me come back here for an urgent file she needs. They don't all do things like that, but I bet they would if they thought they could get away with it. And of course I never get invited onto the wards to see what goes on there. I can only remember one doctor being really nice to me – and he had just been promoted! People say they notice doctors being friendly to me sometimes but I can't say I do. So I just do what they ask without wasting my time being pleasant.'

Suggested exercise

Go through the section on 'Stereotypes' above and find as many phenomena as you can which are reflected in this case study. Are there any others? Is there any hope of changing Stig's view of doctors?

■ **KEY LEARNING POINT**

Overcoming inappropriate use of stereotypes requires a personal commitment, and a willingness to consider the causes of people's behaviour, as well as the nature of it.

IMPLICIT PERSONALITY THEORIES AND PROTOTYPES

What are they?

Stereotypes are not the only way we form expectations about people. We also carry around our own 'theories' about which personality characteristics tend to go with which others. We do not usually articulate these to ourselves: they are implicit rather than explicit – hence the term 'implicit personality theories'. Prototypes refer to our idea of what a 'typical x' is like, where x is a personality type. Hence we probably have our own ideas about what a 'typical extrovert' 'typical worrier' or 'typical snob' is like. In each case, of course, a prototype represents a partial summary of our implicit personality theories. Prototypes differ from stereotypes in that the latter concern perceived characteristics of externally-defined groups, whereas prototypes concern personality types, as noted above.

The use of the 'big five' personality characteristics (*see* Chapter 6) in perceiving others seems to generalise across cultures. That is, the dimensions extroversion, agreeableness, conscientiousness, emotional stability and openness to experience are used by people all around the world. On the other hand, the frequency of use and importance ascribed to each of the 'big five' varies between cultures (Ip and Bond, 1995). An example of this is that Chinese people place greater emphasis on conscientiousness than people in Western cultures.

To some extent even people within the same culture have different implicit personality theories. To take a simple example, one of the authors presents students with the following dimensions drawn from the 16PF personality questionnaire (*see* Chapter 6):

Outgoing	–	Reserved
Stable	–	Emotional
Imaginative	–	Practical
Bold	–	Timid
Tender-minded	–	Tough-minded
Self-sufficient	–	Group-tied
Tense	–	Relaxed

He invites the students to assume that a particular individual is outgoing as opposed to reserved. Then the students are asked: 'does your knowledge that the person is outgoing lead you to infer anything about their scores on any of the other personality dimensions shown here? If so, what?'. Most students feel able to make some inferences. They feel they can identify certain personality characteristics which, in their own implicit personality theories, are associated with being outgoing. But to the students' surprise, they disagree a lot about which dimensions, and which ends of particular dimensions, are associated with being outgoing. For example, some students assume that an outgoing person is likely to be emotional, whereas others believe that person will probably be stable. So some aspects of implicit personality theories are quite specific to individual perceivers.

Other aspects of implicit personality theories are more widely shared. A classic experiment by Kelley (1950) showed that the dimension warm–cold seems to influence our judgements of people on many other dimensions, even after we have interacted with them. Kelley gave university students a description of a visiting lecturer. It consisted of a brief paragraph about him. For half of the students, the last sentence read 'People who know him consider him to be a rather cold person, industrious, critical, practical and determined'. For the other half of the class, the words 'rather cold' were replaced with 'very warm'. The students did not know that they had received different descriptions.

The visiting lecturer then took the class for a short discussion. After he had left, the students completed anonymous evaluations of him. Relative to the 'very warm' group, the 'rather cold' group rated the lecturer considerably less sociable, and considerably more ruthless, self-centred and irritable, among other things. And this was after they had all participated in the same class! The 'rather cold' group also contributed less to the group discussion than the 'very warm' group.

■ **KEY LEARNING POINT**

Our expectations of what a person will be like can affect the way we perceive his or her subsequent behaviour.

Apart from highlighting the centrality of warm–cold in our implicit personality theories, this demonstrates again how our expectations of a person can influence our subsequent impressions of him or her. Where we have formed clear expectations, and where we do not seek to challenge them, we are in danger of forming biased judgements of others.

Confirming what we already believe

The students in Kelley's experiment had only a very limited opportunity to influence the behaviour of their visiting lecturer. In less formal situations there is often more opportunity – so much so that some people have wondered whether we simply use our interaction with somebody to confirm our expectations about them. Snyder and Swann (1978) conducted some research which appeared to show exactly that. They asked women students to choose questions they would ask another person in order to determine whether that person matched an already-supplied personality profile. The students received either an 'introvert' or an 'extrovert' profile. They were given a choice of 26 questions to ask. These varied according to whether they were considered (by independent judges) to be the sort asked by someone who already knows the target person to be extrovert (11), introvert (10) or neither (5). The results were clear. The students showed a *confirmatory bias*; that is, a strong tendency to choose questions which could only confirm the personality description they had already been given, especially for the extrovert description. Snyder and Swann also demonstrated that people who listened to tapes of the chosen questions being put to an interviewee judged the interviewee in ways consistent with the questions asked.

If generalisable, these results would have serious implications in the world of work. They would mean that we are rarely capable of proving our own expectations wrong. Fortunately, it has subsequently been shown that we rise well above the depths suggested by Snyder and Swann, although a preference for so-called 'hypothesis matching' questions is clear enough. Other work (e.g. Pennington, 1987) indicates that:

- people almost never ask leading questions of the kind provided by Snyder and Swann when they can devise the questions themselves;
- people usually prefer questions which are capable of testing their expectation, even if they are framed in a way which is consistent with that expectation;
- where people are able to choose their questions as their interaction with someone proceeds (rather than beforehand) they soon depart from a confirmatory strategy.

Are implicit personality theories accurate?

The possibility that we might after all be quite good at person perception was reinforced by Rothstein and Jackson (1984), who argued that an interviewer's implicit personality theories are typically used appropriately in judging interviewees. Borkenau and Ostendorf (1987) arrived at somewhat similar conclusions. In their experimental research, people estimated the extent to which they expected various categories of behaviour to occur together in a group discussion. Observation of real group discussions showed that the estimates were generally accurate, as were observers' recollections of what happened in the discussions. One persistent mistake was noted, however. Estimates ignored the base-rate frequency of behaviour. For example, let us take two behaviours:

stealing a pencil from work, and stealing a word processor from work. We might expect these behaviours to be associated. But presumably the second is rarer than the first – at least one hopes so! This means that someone who steals a word processor from work is also likely to steal a pencil. But the reverse is less true, simply because fewer people steal word processors than pencils from work. We seem to forget such 'base-line' information when we form our expectations about what people are likely to do. This mirrors the earlier point about shop stewards made in the section on stereotypes.

CASE
STUDY
12.2

Expectations and social reality

The manufacturing firm where Brian Hall was personnel officer was looking for a new part-time industrial chaplain for their main factory. One of the local vicars, Peter Hinde, was interested. Brian took him for a thorough tour of the factory, chatting as they went. Brian had previously heard from one of Hinde's parishioners that he could be rather secretive, which was bad news because in his opinion a chaplain needed to be open, honest and sincere. On the way round the factory, he observed that Hinde laughed only occasionally and rarely cracked jokes though when he did they were good ones. He talked to people in an intense way, but not for long. Each time he quickly moved on. Hinde commented a lot to Brian on the people they met on their tour and seemed to feel they were straightforward, open and honest. Especially in the early part of the tour, Hinde did not give much away about his religious beliefs, concentrating instead on *their* lives and points of view. He listened to what they had to say and never interrupted. Brian asked him some questions about how he handled situations where parishioners wanted him to give more information than he wanted to. After Hinde left, Brian sat in his chair and sighed. Peter Hinde probably wasn't right for the factory. Just his luck! As if he wasn't fed up enough already, having only yesterday been turned down for a promotion that would have meant he could say goodbye to tasks like this.

Suggested exercises

1 *What conclusions do you think Brian Hall drew about Peter Hinde as they toured the factory? Why did he come to those conclusions?*

2 *Supposing Brian had got his promotion, and had heard that Peter Hinde was quite open in his dealings with people. How might he then have assessed Hinde's behaviour in the factory?*

SOME OTHER PHENOMENA IN PERSON PERCEPTION

So far, much of this chapter has concerned how our prior expectations can colour our subsequent perceptions of people. But this of course neglects social interaction itself. Surely what actually happens must have some effect!

One important phenomenon is the so-called *primacy effect*. If we are not careful, first impressions are lasting impressions, and we place too much weight on early information about a person. If your first encounter with a new colleague is in the bar one evening when she is loud and excited, and she knocks a drink over you, it will take a great deal of sober and careful behaviour on her part over the following weeks to change your initial impression of her – too much, in fact: we tend not to revise that initial impression readily enough. This is analogous to the finding (Springbett, 1958) that selection interviewers often make up their mind about a candidate's suitability within the first few minutes of the interview. It is relatively easy to train people to avoid the primacy effect, though it then becomes important to guard against the *recency effect* – a tendency to give too much weight to the *last* information received about a person. In the context of training assessors for performance appraisal, it is possible to pay so much attention to such 'technicalities' that basic accuracy suffers (Bernardin and Pence, 1980).

> ■ **KEY LEARNING POINT**
>
> *If we are unaware of the danger, our first impressions of a person can be very hard to change.*

So-called *halo and horns effects* are also important. The halo effect refers to our tendency to assume that one desirable characteristic in a person means that they will also possess other desirable characteristics, even if we have no direct evidence for them. The horns effect refers to the same phenomenon, but concerns undesirable characteristics. Clearly the halo and horns effects are close relatives of implicit personality theories. They are also undesirable in themselves, but like primary and recency effects, too much concentration on avoiding them can deflect attention from accuracy in person perception (Bernardin and Pence, 1980).

What are the relative importances of *verbal* and *non-verbal behaviour* in determining our impression of a person? The answer to this depends partly on what impressions are involved, but often non-verbal behaviour is considerably more important: it's not what we say, it's the way we say it. Factors like eye contact, limb movement and positioning, body posture and voice intonation (this counts as non-verbal behaviour) all matter here (Argyle *et al.*, 1971). Often as observers we are not aware that our impressions are being affected by such factors, but they are. Some such impressions seem to be universal, across all cultures. For example, people who walk in a youthful manner are perceived as more sexually attractive than those who do not (Montepare and Zebrowitz, 1993). Presumably this stems from the biological reality that mating with young people as opposed to older ones increases the chances of one's genes being transmitted to subsequent generations.

Are perceptions of other people affected by the perceiver's *mood*? We would hope that the perceiver can take his or her own mood into account, but apparently this is not so. Baron (1987) among others has found that an interviewer's mood affects the positiveness of his or her judgement of an interviewee. This finding could not be attributed to the interviewer's mood affecting the candidate's behaviour, since this was held constant. It is worrying to think that when we are judged by someone who happens to be in a bad mood, they may well take it out on us! On the other hand, this may not necessarily apply where perceiver and perceived already know each other well.

THE TARGET STRIKES BACK

It is easy to forget that the person being perceived (the 'target person', to use social psychologists' terminology) is not necessarily passive in the person perception process. Presenting a certain image of ourselves to the world is important to most of us, and is of course central to many jobs. This is often termed *impression management* (Rosenfeld *et al.*, 1995). To some extent, then, the perceiver only perceives what the target wants him or her to perceive. Through techniques such as ingratiation, positive descriptions of self, apologies and selective description of events, we seek to create and maintain desired impressions of ourselves. Some impression management techniques involve fairly direct and open attempts to persuade other people of our virtues, but others are more subtle and covert. Table 12.1 shows some of the techniques available. For a fuller analysis *see*, for example, Feldman and Klich (1991). Some of the techniques are often referred to as organisational politics, the effects of which can be quite harmful (*see* Chapter 13).

Snyder (1974) has coined the term 'self-monitoring' to express the extent to which a person notices the self-presentation of others and uses that information to guide his or her own self-presentation. People who score high on self-monitoring are better able to change

Table 12.1 Some impression management techniques

Technique	Description	Intended outcome
Disclosing obstacles	The person reveals or makes up obstacles or barriers that have been overcome in an already successful performance	What a motivated and competent person this must be!
Playing dumb	The person pretends he or she is unable to carry out certain tasks	The freedom to concentrate solely on the tasks the person prefers
Playing safe	The person avoids situations where he or she might be shown in an unfavourable light	The maintenance of a reputation for not making mistakes
Expert-citing	The use of the opinions of high status people to support one's own position	The impression of expertise and good contacts
Opinion conformity*	Agreeing with a person one wishes to influence	Winning the liking and respect of the other person
Flattery*	Telling a person one wishes to influence good things about himself or herself	Winning the liking and respect of the other person
Doing favours*	Putting oneself out (or appearing to do so) on behalf of a person one wishes to influence	Winning the liking and respect of the other person

* These three tactics are aspects of *ingratiation* – attempting to make oneself more liked by, and attractive to, other people.

Note: Part of this table is based on Rosenfeld *et al.* (1995, pp. 149–50).

their behaviour to suit the situation or audience. They are therefore often better performers in jobs which require communication with a variety of people (Gardner and Martinko, 1988).

There are of course limits to the power of impression management. We cannot be 'all things to all people' for very long without being found out. Kenny and De Paulo (1993) have examined a lot of research evidence and conclude that our perceptions of what other people think of us are actually more a product of our self-perception than anything else. Although we have a reasonably accurate idea of what people in general think of us, we are not at all good at perceiving what any particular *individual* thinks of us. Furthermore, this matters because different observers *do* tend to have considerably different opinions of a target person. We seem to assume that people's opinion of us is the same as our opinion of ourself. But this is not necessarily the case, and our attempts at impression management are likely to fail if we are incorrect in our judgement of what somebody thinks of us.

Nevertheless, it is clear that if our self-presentation is true to our self-concept, an observer may be swayed by it (Swann and Ely, 1984). Some other experimental work has also shown that observers tend to be more influenced by a target person's claims about their own virtues than by what other people think of the target (Jones *et al.*, 1984). This phenomenon may depend partly on the perceived credibility and motives of those other people, but nevertheless it is interesting that what is probably the most biased source of information (the target) can be seen as reasonably credible.

> ■ **KEY LEARNING POINT**
> *Many different tactics are available to us if we wish to manipulate the extent to which other people regard us as competent, and/or like us. Collectively, these tactics are called impression management.*

It is therefore sometimes necessary for observers to 'see through' not only their own expectations but also the overt behaviour of a person they are trying to weigh up. This brings us to the final theme of the chapter: how do we decide what causes people to behave as they do?

WHY DID THEY DO THAT?

Some principles of attribution theory

In the 1960s and 1970s, a school of thought developed in social psychology that has become known as *attribution theory*. Many people have pointed out that nowadays it is really too fragmented to be called a theory, but this should not detract from the value of its principles. Beginning with the observation that we are often more interested in the causes of events than the events themselves (Heider, 1958), attribution theorists have sought to uncover the principles we use in deciding why something happened. Naturally enough, psychologists have been most interested in events involving human action, which are in any case the sort of events we encounter most often in our day-to-day lives.

People are normally viewed as 'naive scientists' who seek the truth by weighing up all the evidence surrounding an event in order to establish a 'theory' of what caused it. The most obvious possible causes are (i) the actor – the person whose behaviour was the event; (ii) the entity – the person or thing towards which the actor's behaviour was directed; and (iii) the situation in which the behaviour took place.

Several attribution frameworks have been proposed, but perhaps the most useful is that of Kelley (1971). An adaptation of his proposals is described in Table 12.2. This model assumes that the observer already has some familiarity with the actor. It is also clearly not the whole story. Deciding whether the actor, entity or situation caused the actor's behaviour does not in itself establish *what* about the actor, entity or situation was responsible. Even if we conclude that a sales assistant is rude to customers because of something about the assistant herself or himself, we could still choose between impatience, intolerance, lack of social skill, lack of motivation, a persistently painful back problem, and plenty of other possibilities.

Let us take an example. Suppose a factory-floor supervisor, Sarah, notices one of the shop-floor workers, Dave, becoming angry and frustrated with the machine he is working on. Before deciding what, if anything, to do about this, Sarah asks herself why Dave is behaving in this manner. If she follows the attributional principles shown in Table 12.2, she will address the following questions:

- Have I seen Dave reacting this way when working on other similar machines on the shop floor? (*distinctiveness*)
- Have I seen Dave getting angry with this machine on other occasions? (*consistency*)
- Do other people get angry with this machine when they work on it? (*consensus*)

Suppose that Sarah *has* seen Dave reacting this way with this and other machines, but has not seen other people react in that way to that machine. She will feel confident in attributing the behaviour to Dave himself – that's the way he is. On the other hand, if

Table 12.2 Attributing causes of behaviour

> Any behaviour involves:
> An *actor* – the person performing the behaviour
> An *entity* – the person or thing towards whom/which the behaviour is directed
>
> An observer examines the extent to which the actor's behaviour demonstrates:
>
> 1 *Distinctiveness* – does the actor do this only in the presence of that entity?
> 2 *Consistency* – does the actor do this repeatedly with this entity over time and different situations?
> 3 *Consensus* – do other people behave in the same way towards that entity?
>
> We decide that a relatively stable feature of the *actor* was responsible (i.e. make an *internal attribution*) when the answers to these questions are:
>
> 1 No 2 Yes 3 No
>
> We hold the *entity* responsible when the answers to these questions are:
>
> 1 Yes 2 Yes 3 Yes
>
> Other combinations of answers produce less certain attributions often to some feature of the situation (other than the entity), especially where the answer to question 2 is 'no'

Sarah recalls that both Dave and other people get angry with this machine, and that Dave does not react that way to other machines, she will attribute his reaction to the machine. She may conclude that it is not working properly and ask one of the maintenance engineers to check it over.

We can see that the conclusions Sarah draws have real implications for her, Dave and the factory's productivity. The distinctiveness, consistency and consensus questions look like sensible ones to ask, though perhaps not the only ones. And, indeed, research has shown that people do consider these issues, albeit not necessarily in quite the way they are framed here. But is it that simple? Not quite. As ever, we introduce various biases and emphases into the attribution process. Some can be put down to faulty information processing. Others have more to do with our desire to see the world in certain ways.

> ■ KEY LEARNING POINT
>
> *The conclusions we draw about the causes of other people's behaviour are based on what we know about them, their situation, and the person or thing towards which their behaviour is directed.*

Some biases in the attributional process

There is considerable evidence that people in Western cultures show a tendency to attribute the cause of behaviour to the actor. A lot of research has demonstrated that even where an actor's behaviour is clearly constrained, observers are inclined to conclude that the behaviour reflects the actor's own attitudes or personality (although research by Fleming and Darley, 1989, also suggests that observers do look for evidence about the actor's emotional reactions to what he or she is having to do).

This tendency to attribute responsibility to the actor too readily is often termed the *fundamental attribution error*. Perhaps it is not a surprising phenomenon in cultures which emphasise individual responsibility for actions. On the other hand, we do not apply the same rules when explaining our own behaviour! When considering our own actions we more often look to the situation for an explanation. Although in some respects we like to think of ourselves as distinct from others, when it comes to explaining our own behaviour we seem included to believe that we did what any reasonable person would have done in the circumstances.

The fundamental attribution error is predominantly a Western phenomenon. Morris and Peng (1994) found that people from non-Western cultures were more likely to make external and situational attributions than those from Western cultures. Specific cultures also tend to emphasise certain causal attributions at the expense of others. For example, in Chinese culture the constructs of effort and fatedness carry high weight in understanding the causes of human behaviour (Leung, 1995).

Another related phenomenon is our apparent tendency to under-use consensus information and indeed most other cues not immediately evident in the actor's behaviour. One such cue mentioned earlier in this chapter is the baseline frequency of different behaviours. Nevertheless, where consensus information is available and/or brought to the attention of the observer, it is used (Krosnick *et al.*, 1990).

A motivational bias in attribution can also be observed. Children tend to hold someone responsible for an act to the extent that it has important consequences. It seems that adults have something of the same tendency. For example, one experiment (Walster, 1966) showed that more blame is attributed to a car driver whose parked car rolls down a hill and causes lots of damage than to one whose car rolls down but fortuitously does little damage. Such scapegoating seems to be based on a desire to believe that serious events must happen for a reason, and preferably one that we can control. Related to this is the tendency to believe in a 'just world' where people get what they deserve (Lerner, 1965).

> ■ **KEY LEARNING POINT**
> *There are often biases in the attribution process. Like stereotypes, they arise both from motivation and from cognitive limitations.*

Let us finally return to the case of the factory supervisor and the machine worker. If Sarah and Dave fit the phenomena described in this section, Sarah will tend to start from the position that Dave is responsible for his action, while Dave is likely to see things quite differently. Sarah may forget to ask herself whether other workers react in the same way to that machine (consensus) and find Dave accusing her of picking on him and ignoring others when they do the same as him. Sarah is more likely to hold Dave responsible if in his frustration he happens to break the machine than if the same actions happen not to cause a breakage.

SUMMARY

The way we perceive somebody is usually influenced by our prior expectations of them. Those expectations may or may not be particularly accurate. We need to be aware of them, and consciously seek evidence that they are wrong rather than only seeing what we expect to see. We should also examine what our expectation is based on, and consider whether that is a sound foundation. Stereotypes of others based on their group membership are probably inevitable, but it is important to remember that other groups may have complementary virtues to our own. Our ideas about which personal characteristics are associated with which others may well be reasonably accurate. However, we cannot take this for granted. We must be careful to notice and remember behaviour which violates our assumptions, and avoid 'remembering' behaviour which never actually occurred. It is necessary to guard against giving too much weight to first impressions of someone. Persons being perceived by others can often manage the impression they give, and cannot be considered 'sitting targets' just waiting to be perceived. Their own beliefs about what they are like are often adopted by the perceiver. In deciding causes of a person's behaviour, we should also find out as much about the situation as possible, and about what other people generally do in the same situation. We should also try to consider the behaviour independently of its consequences.

An interpersonal conflict at Homebuy

Stephanie Barnes had a problem. She was one of the two supervisors of a large team of clerks at the headquarters of Homebuy mail order shopping company. One of the clerks who reported to Stephanie, Martin Warner, was being very disruptive. He seemed to have a grudge against her. On checking her records, Stephanie was surprised to find that his timekeeping was as good as anybody's, and so was his work. But he could be very rude and abrupt toward Stephanie. She found conflict hard to handle at the best of times, and could not understand why Martin apparently disliked her so much. None of the other clerks seemed to find it necessary to behave like that toward her.

As far as Stephanie could see from observing Martin unobtrusively at his desk and in the canteen, he was perfectly civil and friendly to other people. He was however rather cold towards Michael Butcher, who was the other supervisor of Stephanie's grade. Interestingly, Martin seemed to be at his worst when she was trying to check a query about his work. At other times (for example when Stephanie was assigning him work or answering a question he asked) he didn't seem so bad.

Things looked different from Martin's point of view. This was the third job he had held since leaving school at the age of 17. In each of the previous two he had had trouble with his supervisor. In his experience, first-line managers were interfering bullies whose main aim was to make their subordinates feel small using all kinds of devious methods. It didn't help that in his first few weeks at Homebuy, Stephanie Barnes had repeatedly checked his work even though the tasks were quite straightforward and did not in his opinion need checking.

She seemed to do it less now, but still more often than he would like, and for all the types of work he handled, even the simple ones. She did not check up on the other clerks so often, and when she checked up on him she would pretend to be giving him a helping hand when she was really snooping. Michael Butler had supervised Martin for a few weeks when Stephanie had been on holiday or ill, but Martin had formed no particular impression of his supervisory style.

After almost a year of this, Stephanie had had enough. She felt that Martin was probably simply an aggressive young man with a chip on his shoulder. Yet somehow it did not all quite add up. Perhaps a quiet chat to show him she was not a threat would help. So Stephanie called Martin into her office. After carefully explaining what she saw as the problem, Stephanie asked Martin whether there was any particular reason why he was such an aggressive person. This provoked an angry response from Martin, so she tried a different tack. She asked him to describe his past experiences with bosses, and his relationships with people more generally. They parted an hour later with Stephanie feeling she had learned a little about Martin and sowed the seeds of a somewhat better relationship.

Suggested exercises

1 *Use attribution theory to predict how Stephanie and Martin might see the causes of each other's behaviour. Are there any special problems where (to use attribution terminology) the observer is also the entity?*

2 *Examine the significance in this case study of: (i) expectations based on stereotypes, (ii) the primacy effect, (iii) the 'horns' effect and (iv) self-fulfilling hypotheses.*

TEST YOUR LEARNING

Short-answer questions

1 What are stereotypes, and when are we likely to use them?

2 In what ways can inaccurate stereotypes be created?

3 What is an implicit personality theory?

4 Define confirmatory bias and describe its impact on person perception.

5 Describe the primacy and recency effects in person perception.

6 Describe the halo and horns effects in person perception.

7 Name and define four impression management techniques.

8 According to attribution theory, what three types of information are used by people when trying to understand the causes of events?

9 What is the fundamental attribution error?

Essay questions

1 Discuss the proposition that we process information about other people to the extent required to achieve our purpose at the time: no more and no less.

2 Examine the role of stereotypes in person perception.

3 Before meeting a person, we may have some expectations about what that person may be like. What are the sources of those expectations, and to what extent might they affect our subsequent interactions with that person?

4 To what extent does attribution theory accurately describe how people understand the causes of events?

GLOSSARY OF TERMS

Assimilation effect The process where person A perceives the behaviour of person B as more similar to A's stereotype than it actually is.

Attribution theory A branch of social psychology which analyses how people construct explanations for events.

Confirmatory bias A tendency for a person to behave in ways which confirm his or her existing beliefs.

Consensus information In attribution theory, consensus information refers to the extent to which people in general perform a specific behaviour toward a specific object.

Consistency information In attribution theory, consistency information refers to the extent to which a person performs a particular behaviour repeatedly over time and different situations.

Contrast effect The process where person A judges person B to be more different from A's expectations than he or she really is because B violates some of A's expectations.

Distinctiveness information In attribution theory, distinctiveness information refers to the extent to which a person performs a particular behaviour only in quite specific circumstances.

Fundamental attribution error The tendency to explain a person's behaviour in terms of some feature of them rather than their situation.

Halo effect The tendency to assume that one desirable characteristic exhibited by a person generalises to other (perhaps unrelated) desirable characteristics.

Horns effect The tendency to assume that one undesirable characteristic exhibited by a person generalises to other (perhaps unrelated) undesirable characteristics.

Implicit personality theory The assumptions (perhaps unconscious) a person makes about which personality characteristics tend to go together.

Impression management The strategies a person adopts in order to present a desired image of himself or herself to other people.

Mood A short-term generalised affective state.

Non-verbal behaviour All aspects of behaviour other than the words a person speaks; includes the intonation, speed etc. of speech.

Person perception The impressions and judgements formed by a person about other individuals or groups, and the processes underlying those impressions and judgements.

Primacy effect The tendency for information presented early in a sequence to dominate subsequent memory and judgement.

Prototype The set of characteristics a person assumes that a particular kind of person possesses.

Recency effect The tendency for information presented late in a sequence to dominate subsequent memory and judgement.

Social identity theory A theory which emphasises how a person uses concepts of social groups to clarify his or her identity and uphold its value.

Stereotype The set of characteristics a person believes are possessed by a particular social group.

SUGGESTED FURTHER READING

Note: details of all three items below are given in the reference list.

1 James Hilton and William Von Hippel's chapter on stereotypes in the 1996 *Annual Review of Psychology* presents a very informative review of a large and important area of person perception. It is written in quite a technical style (as is usual for articles in the *Annual Review* series) but nevertheless is not *too* hard to follow.

2 Paul Rosenfeld and colleagues' 1995 book entitled *Impression Management in Organizations* is an entertaining and straightforward but nevertheless scholarly analysis of how people in the workplace can manipulate the judgements made by others about them.

3 Although fairly old now, Blake Ashforth and Fred Mael's 1989 article in *Academy of Management Review* on the applications of social identity theory to work organisations provides a welcome attempt to establish more links between social psychology and work psychology.

REFERENCES

Argyle, M., Alkema, F. and Gilmour, R. (1971) 'The communication of friendly and hostile attitudes by verbal and nonverbal signals', *European Journal of Social Psychology*, vol. 1, pp. 385–402.

Ashforth, B.E. and Mael, F. (1989) 'Social identity theory and the organization', *Academy of Management Review*, vol. 14, pp. 20–39.

Baron, R.A. (1987) 'Interviewer's moods and reactions to job applicants: the influence of affective states on applied social judgements', *Journal of Applied Social Psychology*, vol. 17, pp. 911–26.

Bernardin, H.J. and Pence, E.C. (1980), 'Effects of rater training: creating new response sets and decreasing accuracy', *Journal of Applied Psychology*, vol. 65, pp. 60–6.

Bodenhausen, G.V. (1990) 'Stereotypes as judgmental heuristics: evidence of circadian variations in discrimination', *Psychological Science*, vol. 1, pp. 319–22.

Bodenhausen, G.V. and Macrae, C.N. (1996) 'The self-regulation of intergroup perception: mechanisms and consequences of stereotype suppression' in Macrae, C.N., Hewstone, M. and Stangor, C. (eds) *Foundations of Stereotypes and Stereotyping*. New York: Guildford Press.

Borkenau, P. and Ostendorf, F. (1987) 'Fact and fiction in implicit personality theory', *Journal of Personality*, vol. 55, pp. 415–43.

Devine, P.G. (1989) 'Stereotypes and prejudice: their automatic and controlled components', *Journal of Personality and Social Psychology*, vol. 56, pp. 5–18.

Feldman, D.C. and Klich, N. (1991) 'Impression management and career strategies' in Giacalone, R.A. and Rosenfeld, P. (eds) *Applied Impression Management*. London: Sage.

Fiske, S.T. (1993) 'Social cognition and social perception' in Porter, L.W. and Rosenzweig, M.R. (eds) *Annual Review of Psychology*, vol. 44. Palo Alto, CA: Annual Reviews Inc.

Fleming, J.H. and Darley, J.M. (1989) 'Perceiving choice and constraint: the effects of contextual and behavioral cues on attitude attribution', *Journal of Personality and Social Psychology*, vol. 56, pp. 27–40.

Forgas, J.P. (1985) *Interpersonal Behaviour*. Oxford: Pergamon Press.

Gardner, W.L. and Martinko, M.J. (1988) 'Impression management: an observational study linking audience characteristics with verbal self-presentations', *Academy of Management Journal*, vol. 31, pp. 42–65.

Heaton, A.W. and Kruglanski, A.W. (1991) 'Person perception by introverts and extraverts under time pressure: effects of need for closure', *Personality and Social Psychology Bulletin*, vol. 17, pp. 161–5.

Heider, F. (1958) *The Psychology of Interpersonal Relations*. New York: John Wiley.

Higgins, E.T. and Bargh, J.A. (1987) 'Social cognition and social perception', *Annual Review of Psychology*, vol. 38, pp. 369–425.

Hill, T., Lewicki, P., Czyzewska, M. and Schuller, G. (1990) 'The role of learned inferential encoding rules in the perception of faces: effects of nonconsious self-perpetuation of a bias', *Journal of Experimental Social Psychology*, vol. 26, pp. 350–71.

Hilton, J.L. and Von Hippel, W. (1996) 'Stereotypes', *Annual Review of Psychology*, vol. 47, pp. 237–71.

Ilgen, D.R. and Klein, H.J. (1989) 'Organizational behavior', *Annual Review of Psychology*, vol. 40, pp. 327–51.

Ip, G.W.M. and Bond, M.H. (1995) 'Culture, values and the spontaneous self-concept', *Asian Journal of Psychology*, vol. 1, pp. 30–6.

Jones, E.E., Schwartz, J. and Gilbert, D.T. (1984) 'Perceptions of moral expectancy violation: the role of expectancy source', *Social Cognition*, vol. 2, pp. 273–93.

Kelley, H.H. (1950) 'The warm–cold variable in first impressions of persons', *Journal of Personality*, vol. 18, pp. 431–9.

Kelley, H.H. (1971) *Attribution in Social Interaction*. Morristown, TN: General Learning Press.

Kenny, D.A. and De Paulo, B.M. (1993) 'Do people know how others view them? An empirical and theoretical account', *Psychological Bulletin*, vol. 114, pp. 145–61.

Krosnick, J.A., Li, F. and Lehman, D.R. (1990) 'Conversational conventions, order of information acquisition, and the effect of base rates and individuating information on social judgements', *Journal of Personality and Social Psychology*, vol. 59, pp. 1140–52.

Krueger, J. (1991) 'Accentuation effects and illusory change in exemplar based category learning', *European Journal of Social Psychology*, vol. 21, pp. 37–48.

Lerner, M.J. (1965) 'Evaluation of performance as a function of performer's reward and attractiveness', *Journal of Personality and Social Psychology*, vol. 3, pp. 355–60.

Leung, K. (1995) 'Beliefs in Chinese culture' in Bond, M.H. (ed.) *Handbook of Chinese Psychology*. Oxford: Oxford University Press.

Manis, M., Nelson, T.E. and Shedler, J. (1988) 'Stereotypes and social judgement: extremity, assimilation and contrast', *Journal of Personality and Social Psychology*, vol. 55, pp. 28–36.

Montepare, J.M. and Zebrowitz, L.A. (1993) 'A cross-cultural comparison of impressions created by age-related variations in gait', *Journal of Nonverbal Behavior*, vol. 17, pp. 55–68.

Morris, M.W. and Peng, K.P. (1994) 'Culture and cause: American and Chinese attributions for social and physical events', *Journal of Personality and Social Psychology*, vol. 67, pp. 949–71.

Pennington, D.C. (1987) 'Confirmatory hypothesis-testing in face-to-face interaction: an empirical refutation', *British Journal of Social Psychology*, vol. 26, pp. 225–36.

Rosenfeld, P., Giacalone, R.A. and Riordan, C.A. (1995) *Impression Management in Organizations*. London: Routledge.

Rothstein, M. and Jackson, D.N. (1984) 'Implicit personality theory and the employment interview' in Cook, M. (ed.) *Issues in Person Perception*. London: Methuen.

Snyder, M. (1974) 'Self-monitoring of expressive behavior', *Journal of Personality and Social Psychology*, vol. 30, pp. 526–37.

Snyder, M. and Swann, W.B. (1978) 'Hypothesis-testing processes in social interaction', *Journal of Personality and Social Psychology*, vol. 36, pp. 1202–12.

Springbett, B.M. (1958) 'Factors affecting the final decision in the employment interview', *Canadian Journal of Psychology*, vol. 12, pp. 13–22.

Stangor, C. and McMillan, D. (1992) 'Memory for expectancy-congruent and expectancy-incongruent information, a review of the social and social developmental literatures', *Psychological Bulletin*, vol. 111, pp. 42–61.

Stangor, C., Lynch, L., Duan, C. and Glass, B. (1992) 'Categorization of individuals on the basis of multiple social features', *Journal of Personality and Social Psychology*, vol. 62, pp. 207–18.

Swann, W.B. and Ely, R.J. (1984) 'A battle of wills: self-verification versus behavioral confirmation', *Journal of Personality and Social Psychology*, vol. 46, pp. 1287–302.

Tajfel, H. and Turner, J.C. (1985) 'The social identity theory of intergroup behaviour' in Worchel, S. and Austin, W.G. (eds) *Psychology of Intergroup Relations*. 2nd edn. Chicago, IL: Nelson-Hall.

Van Knippenberg, A.F.M. (1984) 'Intergroup differences in group perceptions' in Tajfel, H. (ed.) *The Social Dimension: European Developments in Social Psychology*, vol. 2. Cambridge: Cambridge University Press.

Walster, E. (1966) 'The assignment of responsibility for an accident', *Journal of Personality and Social Psychology*, vol. 5, pp. 508–16.

Decisions, teams and groups at work

After studying this chapter, you should be able to:

1 describe factors which affect how information is processed when a person is making a decision involving risk;

2 explain how individuals or groups can become over-committed to a poor decision, and suggest how this can be prevented;

3 describe alternative styles of decision making;

4 describe four reasons why groups sometimes make poor decisions;

5 define group polarisation and explain why it occurs;

6 explain the stages of development some teams go through;

7 describe Belbin's nine team roles;

8 define the key elements of power and politics in organisations;

9 define negotiation and distinguish between different types of negotiator behaviour;

10 describe likely influences on negotiators outside the negotiating situation;

11 identify the issues psychologists have concentrated on within the field of industrial relations.

INTRODUCTION

Decisions concern choices between more than one possible course of action. For many people, work involves frequent decisions. Some are perhaps made almost automatically – so much so, that some writers (e.g. Hunt, 1989) have argued that the whole notion of deliberate, conscious choice has been taken too seriously by work psychologists. Others disagree, contending that understanding how decisions (conscious or otherwise) are made in the workplace, and how they might be improved, is crucial to enhancing the performance of organisations and even national economies. This chapter therefore examines decision making by individuals and groups in the workplace from a psychological perspective. Important insights can indeed be gained. Because teamwork is increasingly important in the workplace, some more general issues concerning team effectiveness are also analysed. In some cases, psychologists have simply demonstrated particular phenomena, leaving it to individuals to work out what, if anything, to do about them. In other instances, psychologists have designed interventions aimed at improving decision making or more general team functioning. This chapter also discusses decisions made in conditions of potential conflict: that is, negotiations. What happens in negotiations, and can the outcomes of a negotiation be predicted? Negotiations in the workplace often involve trade union representatives, and this chapter ends with a brief consideration of some industrial relations issues.

DECISION MAKING BY INDIVIDUALS

Information processing in decision making

Much of psychologists' work on individual decision making has focused on how we deviate from strictly 'rational' processes. 'Rationality' is often defined as choosing the option that has the *highest expected value* among those potentially open to us. For example, suppose you can choose between a 40 per cent chance of winning £2000 (with a 60 per cent chance of winning nothing) and the certainty of winning £600. The expected value of the first option is £800 (40 per cent × £2000), and that of the second is £600 (100 per cent × £600). The 'rational' decision would therefore be the 40 per cent chance of winning £2000. Much research on decision making has used problems of this general kind. It is true, of course, that the first option is preferable, *other things being equal*. But suppose you had no money at all, and your bank manager had written telling you that your debts would be called in, thus causing your business to fail, unless you paid at least £500 into your account immediately. In such circumstances, the 'rational' decision could be argued to be the less attractive. This illustrates the general point that it can make more sense to consider total assets than gains or losses. It also brings to mind the adage 'don't bet if you can't afford to lose'. Further, it is important to recognise that the attractiveness, or expected utility, of various possible outcomes of decisions varies between people – that is, it is *subjective*. Using this notion of subjective expected utility (SEU), psychological research has uncovered some interesting phenomena, some of which will be described shortly. Much of this research has been conducted (often with students in laboratories) by Kahneman, Tversky and colleagues (Kahneman and Tversky, 1979, 1981, 1984; Tversky and Kahneman, 1981, 1986).

■ KEY LEARNING POINT

What is a rational decision from a strictly logical viewpoint may not be the most appropriate one for a particular person given his or her values and/or circumstances.

There are many systematic strategies for decision making apart from a thorough search for the maximum gain. For example, one can evaluate alternatives on a very limited range of important criteria. Ignoring less crucial criteria may not have important costs, but it is of course possible that the cumulative effect of those criteria would be significant. Another possible strategy is to search for an alternative which one considers good enough, and stop the search as soon as one is found. This approach has been termed *satisficing* and can be contrasted with *maximising*, where a thorough search is conducted for the best possible solution. Clearly, strategies like satisficing cut corners. But they may be justified if a person does not have the time and/or ability to use more thorough ones, or if the decision is not particularly important.

Frisch and Clemen (1994) have argued that SEU is not an entirely redundant concept. Once people know what the decision is that they are trying to make, it is logical to try to maximise SEU. But they also argue that the earlier stages of decision making are of great importance. These include generating options, deciding which consequences to consider and identifying the relevant risks. So, in line with many other writers, they argue that more attention must be paid to the *process* of decision making. This should normally involve:

1 *consequentialism*: making decisions on the basis of expected personal consequences rather than habit or tradition;

2 *thorough structuring*: more than one option must be considered, and the likely consequences thought through carefully;

3 *compensation*: most decisions involve trade-offs of one benefit against another, and this should be recognised.

Despite the limitations of the notion of expected utility (subjective or otherwise), some interesting phenomena in decision making have been uncovered by research on it.

Certainty versus uncertainty

We seem to give high weight in our decisions to the difference between, for example, a 95 per cent chance of a particular outcome, and a 100 per cent chance of it, or that between a 5 per cent chance and 0 per cent. In other words, when something is 95 per cent certain, we are very aware of the 5 per cent chance that it will not happen. And when there is only a 5 per cent chance of something happening, we are very conscious that 'there's a chance'. In both examples, this reflects the difference between absolute certainty and near certainty. We give less weight to a difference of similar magnitude between intermediate probabilities (e.g. 60 per cent versus 55 per cent). As Kahneman and Tversky (1984) point out, this means that we tend to find a highly likely (but not certain) pleasant outcome *less* attractive than we should. Similarly, we are likely to find a highly unlikely pleasant outcome *more* attractive than we should. Hence we tend to be less inclined to take a small risk for a gain, and more inclined to bet on a long shot, than is indicated by objective probability. The popularity of the recently introduced National Lottery in the United Kingdom is a good example of this.

Gains versus losses

As Kahneman and Tversky put it, the attractiveness of a possible gain is less than the aversiveness of a loss of the same amount. This leads to risk-averse decisions concerning gains and risk-seeking decisions concerning losses. Thus, Kahneman and Tversky have pointed out that while most people prefer the certainty of winning £800 over an 85 per cent chance of winning £1000, a large majority of people prefer an 85 per cent chance of *losing* £1000 (with a 15 per cent chance of losing nothing) over a certain loss of £800. Such risk-seeking over losses has also been found in (laboratory) studies where non-monetary outcomes such as hours of pain or loss of human lives are at stake. This has some interesting implications. For example, an unpopular government facing an election may be more inclined to risk a new policy initiative which could lose votes than a popular government in the same position. Firms in financial difficulties may take more risks (because they are trying to eliminate losses) than firms doing well (which are dealing with gains) (Fiegenbaum and Thomas, 1988). Singh (1986) reported that among 64 American and Canadian companies, the performance of a firm was indeed negatively related to risk-taking organisational decisions. But the picture was not that simple, because poor-performing companies tended to centralise their decision making, which militated against risk taking, thus masking the relationship between performance and riskiness of decisions.

Framing

The same information can be presented in different ways. This can affect decisions made on the basis of that information. Thus, for example, organisers of conferences often advertise a special low fee for people who register early rather than expressing it as a surcharge for people who register late. The organisers may privately think in terms of the latter, but use the label 'discount' rather than 'surcharge' in order to keep customer goodwill, and hopefully increase the number of attenders. There are also links here with the previous subsection, because some choices can be framed in terms of either gains or losses. An often-used scenario in laboratory experiments concerns the choice of medical programmes to combat a killer disease. The potential benefits of these programmes are presented either in terms of the number of people who will be saved (equivalent to gains), or the number who will die (equivalent to losses). According to Kahneman and Tversky (1981) when the options are presented in terms of number of deaths, people tend to prefer a programme which might succeed completely or fail completely (i.e. a risk) over one with a guaranteed moderate success level. The reverse is true when the same figures are presented in terms of number of lives saved. However, Fagley and Miller (1987) found no such effect, and questioned its generality. Although their hypothetical scenario was not exactly like that of Kahneman and Tversky, the results of Fagley and Miller do indeed cast doubt on this particular aspect of framing.

> ■ KEY LEARNING POINT
>
> *The way situations requiring decisions are described, and whether they involve gains or losses, can significantly influence the decision that is made.*

Escalation of commitment

Some approaches to commitment (*see* Kiesler, 1971; *see also* Chapter 9) emphasise that if a decision is made freely and explicitly, the person making it feels a need to justify it to self and others. The person is *committed* to it, and seeks retrospectively to find reasons why he or she 'did the right thing'. There is some evidence for this concerning choice of organisation to work in (e.g. Mabey, 1986). It also seems to happen in political decisions, such as American involvement in the Vietnam war, and in some managerial decisions (Staw, 1981; Bazerman *et al.*, 1984). In laboratory simulations, people who are told that their own earlier financial investment decisions have so far been unsuccessful tend to allocate more additional funds to that investment than if the earlier decisions were made by another member of their (imaginary) organisation. They feel compelled to prove that ultimately their own wisdom will be demonstrated, but observers are more likely to think they are 'pouring good money after bad'. This escalation of commitment phenomenon is now well established. The next question is therefore how it can be reduced or eliminated. In a laboratory study of a simulated marketing decision, Simonson and Staw (1992) asked decision makers to specify in advance minimum outcome levels that would have to be achieved for the decision to be considered successful. If their decisions did not achieve that level, they were less likely to invest further in it than decision makers who did not specify a minimum outcome level. Simonson and Staw also found that further investment in a losing course of action was less likely if decision makers were told that their performance on this task did not reflect their managerial abilities, since the task was rather artificial – in other words, some of the threat to decision makers' dignity was removed. Finally, escalation of commitment was also reduced if decision makers were told that their performance would be evaluated on the quality of decision-making processes, not the outcomes (which in the real world depend partly on factors outside the decision maker's control). While the second strategy is rather laboratory-specific, the first and last strategies can and should be used by decision makers and those who appraise their performance at work.

Heuristics

Heuristics are 'rules of thumb' that people use to simplify information processing and decision making (Eiser, 1986, p. 220). These can be social – for example, 'I will ignore everything person x tells me' – or abstract – such as, 'Never do anything without checking the production figures first'. In their early work, Tversky and Kahneman (1974) identified three particularly common heuristics. The *representativeness* heuristic is analogous to the finding in person perception (*see* Chapter 12) that we ignore base-rate information. We judge someone or something purely according to how representative it appears of a particular category, and we ignore the naturally occurring probability of belonging to that category in the first place. So if we meet a young person wearing a tracksuit and looking fit, we might be inclined to believe he or she is a professional athlete, even though statistically the probability of any individual (even a young, fit one) being an athlete is low. We are swayed by the person's appearance. The *anchoring* bias refers to our failure to change our views as much as we should in the light of new information. We seem 'anchored' by our starting point. This too finds expression in person perception, in the same sense that first impressions can be hard to dislodge. Finally, the *availability* heuristic concerns our tendency to consider an event more probable if it can easily be imagined than if it cannot. Hence an industrial relations manager contemplating policy changes might overestimate the risk of a strike (vivid event), and underestimate the risk of a persistently resentful and not particularly co-operative workforce (less vivid).

> ■ **KEY LEARNING POINT**
>
> *Some of the ways in which we habitually think about decisions are bad in the sense that they distort the real situation.*

CASE STUDY 13.1

An upmarket move?

Three years ago, Harry Milento gave up a highly-paid job in insurance in order to opt for a 'quieter life' running his own guest house in a scenic coastal location. Redecoration and improvements to the large old house he purchased proved more expensive and time consuming than he had expected. Business was not good: a difficult economic climate had adversely affected the holiday trade, and a new guest house like Harry's inevitably had trouble getting established. The result was that he was certain to make a loss for the third successive year, albeit one which would not exhaust his financial reserves. An established traditional hotel nearby had recently gone upmarket with some success, and Harry was considering the same strategy. After all, he could relate well to successful and wealthy people, having once been one himself. The area had historically offered middle-to-low budget family holidays rather than more luxurious ones, but maybe things were changing, Harry thought. But, for him, a move upmarket would need extensive further alterations to his premises, and these would swallow up his remaining reserves.

Suggested exercise

Use psychological findings about decision making to suggest what Harry Milento is likely to do. Is this what he should do?

Decision-making style

People differ in the way they go about making decisions, and the same person may make decisions in different ways in different circumstances. Arroba (1978) identified six decision-making styles from her sample of managers and manual workers:

1 *no thought*
2 *compliant* – with expectations from outside
3 *logical* – careful, objective evaluation of alternatives
4 *emotional* – decision made on basis of wants or likes
5 *intuitive* – the decision simply seemed right and/or inevitable
6 *hesitant* – slow and difficult to feel committed.

Arroba found that the logical style was much more often used for work-related decisions than for personal ones. The 'no thought' style was used more for unimportant decisions than for others, the emotional style for quite important decisions, and the intuitive style for very important decisions. Overall, the logical style was used most often, with no thought a distant second, and emotional third. Perhaps the use of intuitive style for very important issues is due to a lack of complete information on which to base a decision. Some other (experimental) research has, however, produced rather different results. As decisions become more important and irreversible, people are more likely to adopt a logical approach, especially where they expect to be held responsible for the decision (McAllister *et al.*, 1979).

Janis and Mann (1977, 1982) identified five styles which are directly related to decision quality. They argued that decisions by definition involve psychological conflict, and people have different ways of dealing with that. Specifically, these are:

1 *unconflicted adherence*: the decision maker continues with the existing course of action, ignoring potential risks

2 *unconflicted change*: the decision maker embarks on whatever new course of action is in his or her mind at the time without evaluating it

3 *defensive avoidance*: the decision maker avoids the decision by delaying it or denying responsibility

4 *hypervigilance*: the decision maker desperately searches for a solution, and seizes on the first one that seems to offer quick relief

5 *vigilance*: the decision maker searches carefully for relevant information and weighs it up in an unbiased fashion.

Underlying these five coping strategies are three factors:

1 awareness or otherwise of risks associated with any alternative

2 optimism or otherwise about finding an acceptable alternative

3 belief that there is (or is not) enough time in which to make the decision.

Clearly vigilance is seen as the optimal strategy, and Frisch and Clemen (1994) felt that their recommendations reflected a vigilant decision-making strategy. Janis and Mann (1982) have argued that defensive avoidance is both the most common defective strategy for making major decisions, and also the hardest to correct. They have made a number of suggestions about how to encourage proper gathering and processing of information. Techniques include preparation for dealing with the negative aspects of a decision, forcing a person to attend to unwelcome information, and role-playing to explore situations likely to result from a particular decision. Janis and Mann examined these techniques in the context of counselling, but a determined person could probably use them without the assistance of a counsellor.

> ■ **KEY LEARNING POINT**
> *Some ways of making decisions are better than others, but probably no single method is the best for all individuals in all situations.*

GROUP DECISION MAKING

Groups versus individuals

Although many people are very cynical about the value of meetings and committees, the fact is that their work tends to involve a lot of them. In work organisations most major decisions and many lesser ones are made by groups of people, not individuals. Hence groups have attracted a lot of interest, an increasing proportion of which is from organisational psychologists (Guzzo and Dickson, 1996). If handled in the right way, a decision made by groups can evoke greater commitment than those made by individuals because more people feel a sense of involvement in it. On the other hand, group decisions usually consume more time (and more money) than individual ones, so they need to justify the extra costs. One often-asked question over many years is whether individual or group decisions are superior (Davis, 1992). At one extreme is the 'many heads are better than one' school of thought, which holds that, in groups, people can correct each other's mistakes and build on each other's ideas. On the other hand there is the 'too many cooks spoil the broth' brigade, which contends that problems of communication, rivalry and so on between group members more than cancel out any potential advantage of increased total available brain power. In fact it is not possible to generalise about whether individuals or groups are universally better. It depends on the abilities and training of the individuals and groups, and also on the kind of task being tackled (Hill, 1982).

McGrath (1984) has identified eight different types of task that groups can face: four of these directly concern decision making. These are:

1 generating plans

2 generating ideas

3 solving problems with correct answers

4 deciding issues with no identifiably correct answer at the time the decision is made.

The second and third of these provide the best opportunities for comparing group and individual performance. *Brainstorming*, for example, is a technique for generating ideas with which many readers will already be familiar. It was originally advocated by Osborn (1957), who argued that if a group of people agree that (i) the more ideas they think of the better, and (ii) members will be encouraged to produce even bizarre ideas, and not be ridiculed for them, then individuals can think up twice as many ideas in a group as they could on their own. In fact, research indicates that lone individuals encouraged to think of as many ideas as possible generate almost twice as many ideas per individual than groups do (e.g. Lamm and Trommsdorf, 1973) – quite the reverse of Osborn's claim! A number of possible explanations have been suggested for this phenomenon. These include *evaluation apprehension*, where a person feels afraid of what others will think, despite the brainstorming instructions, and *free-riding*, where group members feel that other group members will do the work for them. Diehl and Stroebe (1987) devised experiments to test alternative explanations, and came out in favour of a third explanation: *production blocking*. Simply, only one person at a time in a group can talk about their ideas, and in the meantime other members may forget or suppress theirs. In a related vein, it seems that groups linked by computer produce more ideas than those meeting face to face, and also have greater equality of participation (Hollingshead and McGrath, 1995), although they also tend to make more extreme decisions and have some hostile communications.

> ■ KEY LEARNING POINT
>
> *The production of new ideas tends to be greater when individuals brainstorm alone rather than in groups.*

Psychologists have conducted a number of experiments comparing individual and group performance on problems with correct answers. For example Vollrath *et al.* (1989) found that groups recognised and recalled information better than individuals. However, McGrath (1984) has pointed out that the extent to which the correct answer can be shown to be correct varies. On one hand there are 'Eureka' tasks – when the correct answer is mentioned, everyone suddenly sees that it must be right. There are also problems where the answer can be proved correct with logic, even though its correctness is not necessarily obvious at first sight. Then there are problems where the correct (or best) answer can only be defined by experts, whose wisdom may be challenged by a layperson.

An example of the second kind of problem, often used in research, is the so-called 'horse-trading task'. A person buys a horse for £60 and sells it for £70. Then he or she buys it back for £80 and again sells it for £90. How much money does the person make in the horse-trading business? Many people say £10, but the answer is £20 – though strictly this assumes that the person does not have to borrow the extra £10 to buy back the horse, and it ignores the opportunity cost of using the £10 in that way rather than another.

Some early research with problems of this kind (e.g. Maier and Solem, 1952) produced several important findings. First, lower status group members had less influence on the group decision than higher status ones, even where they (the lower status people) were correct. Second, even where at least one person in the group knew the correct answer, the group decision was by no means always correct. Third, group discussion made people more confident that their consensus decision was correct, but unfortunately the discussion did not in fact make a correct decision more likely! For problems like the horse-trading one, it typically needs two correct people, not one, to convince the rest of the group. Put another way, on average *the group is as good as its second-best member*. This could be taken to mean that, for solving problems with correct answers, groups are on average better than individuals, but inferior to the best individuals.

> ■ KEY LEARNING POINT
>
> *For problems with demonstrably correct answers, groups are on average as good as their second-best member. However, groups can do better or worse than this average according to their membership and process.*

However, conclusions of this kind cannot easily be generalised. Many decisions in organisations do not have a provable correct answer, or even an answer which experts can agree on. Also, even if groups typically do badly, perhaps they can be improved. This latter issue has been the subject of much popular and academic debate, and we now turn to it.

Group deficiencies and overcoming them

Some social scientists have concentrated on identifying the context within which groups can perform well (e.g. Larson and LaFasto, 1989). They point out necessities such as having group members who are knowledgeable about the problem faced, having a clearly-defined and inspiring goal (*see* Locke's goal-setting theory in Chapter 11), having group members who are committed to solving the problem optimally, and support and recognition from important people outside the group. Other work has attempted to identify the roles that group members should adopt in order to function effectively together. Perhaps the most influential has been Belbin (1981, 1993), who identified the roles required in a team. Other observers of groups have concentrated more on procedural factors (e.g. Rees, 1984, chapter 12). Prominent here are the practices of the chairperson in facilitating discussion and summing it up, ensuring that everyone has their say and that only one person speaks at a time, and making sure that votes (if taken) are conducted only when all points of view have been aired, and with clearly-defined options, so that group members know what they are voting for and against.

Social psychologists have noted many features of the group decision-making process which can impair decision quality. Many of these underlie the practical suggestions noted above. Hoffman and Maier (1961) noted a tendency to adopt 'minimally acceptable solutions', especially where the decision task is complex. Instead of seeking the best possible solution, group members often settle on the first suggested solution which everyone considers 'good enough'. In certain circumstances this might be an advantage, but on most occasions it is probably not a good idea. Hackman and Morris (1975) pointed out that groups rarely discuss what strategy they should adopt in tackling a decision-making task (i.e. how they should go about it), but that when they do, they tend to perform better. In these authors' experience, simply telling groups to discuss their strategy before they tackle the problem itself is usually not enough – strategy discussion has to be treated as a separate task if it is to be taken seriously.

Motivational losses in groups can also be a problem. Experimental research has repeatedly shown that as the number of people increases, the effort and/or performance of each one often decreases – the so-called *social loafing* effect (e.g. Latane *et al.*, 1979). On the other hand, this motivational loss can be avoided if individuals in the group feel that their contribution can be identified, *and* that their contribution makes a significant difference to the group's performance (Williams *et al.*, 1981; Kerr and Bruun, 1983). Hence a group leader would be well advised to ensure that each group member can see the connection between individual efforts and group performance both for themselves and other group members.

Interestingly, there is some evidence that social loafing does not occur in collectivist societies. Earley (1989) found that while American management trainees exhibited this effect in a laboratory-based management task, trainees from the People's Republic of China did not. In collective societies, one's sense of shared responsibility with others (in contrast with individualistic Western cultures) is perhaps the source of this difference. Once again, this is a reminder of the culture-specific nature of some phenomena in applied psychology. More than that, Erez and Somech (1996) found that subcultural differences in individualism–collectivism even within one country (Israel) made a difference to the social loafing effect. But even then, groups in an individualistic subculture only showed social loafing when they lacked specific goals. As Erez and Somech pointed out, most groups in the workplace have members who know each other, who communicate, have team goals that matter to them, and whose individual performance can be identified. So social loafing may be the exception not the rule in the real world, even in individualistic cultures.

> ■ KEY LEARNING POINT
>
> *Group members tend to reduce their efforts as group size increases, at least in individualistic cultures. This problem can, however, be overcome.*

It seems that groups may be even more likely than individuals to escalate their commitment to a decision even if it does not seem to be working out well (Whyte, 1993). This can occur even if the majority of group members start off with the opinion that they will not invest any further resources in the decision. The essentially risky decision of the group may be even more marked if it is framed in terms of avoiding losses rather than achieving gains. As noted earlier in this chapter, most people are more inclined to accept the risk of a big loss in the hope of avoiding a moderate loss than they are to risk losing a moderate profit in pursuit of a big profit.

Janis (1972, 1982a,b) has arrived at some disturbing conclusions about how some real-life policy-making groups can make extremely poor decisions which have serious repercussions around the world. He analysed major foreign policy errors of various governments at various times in history. One of these was the Bay of Pigs fiasco in the early 1960s. Fidel Castro had recently taken power in Cuba, and the new American administration under President John F. Kennedy launched an 'invasion' of Cuba by 1400 Cuban exiles, who landed at the Bay of Pigs. Within two days they were surrounded by 20 000 Cuban troops, and those not killed were ransomed back to the USA at a cost of $53 million in aid. Janis argued that this outcome was not just bad luck for the USA. It could and should have been anticipated. He suggested that in this and other fiascos, various group processes could be seen, which collectively he called *groupthink*.

According to Janis, groupthink occurs when group members' motivation for unanimity and agreement override their motivation to evaluate carefully the risks and benefits of alternative decisions. This usually occurs in 'cohesive' groups – i.e. those where group members are friendly with each other, and respect each other's opinions. In some such groups disagreement is construed (usually unconsciously) as a withdrawal of friendship and respect. When this is combined with a group leader known (or believed) to have a position on the issues under discussion, an absence of clear group procedures, a difficult set of circumstances, and certain other factors, the group members tend to seek agreement. This leads to the symptoms of groupthink shown in Fig. 13.1. The symptoms can be summarised as follows:

1 *overestimation of the group's power and morality*: after all, group members have positive opinions of each other

2 *closed-mindedness*: including efforts to downplay warnings and stereotype other groups as inferior

Fig. 13.1 The groupthink model (after Janis and Mann, 1977)

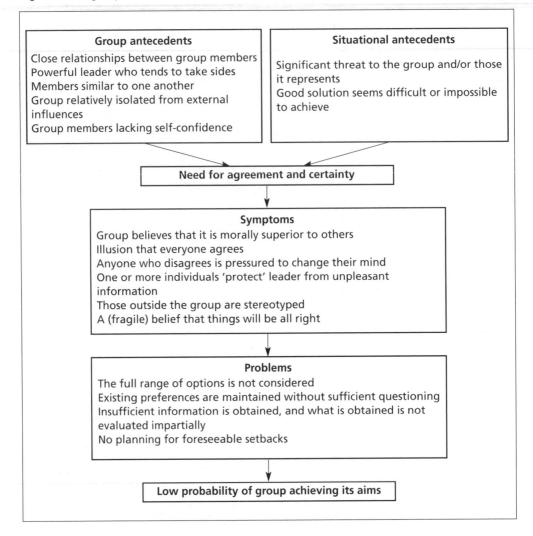

3 *pressures towards uniformity*: including suppression of private doubts, leading to the illusion of unanimity and 'mindguards' to shield group members (especially the leader) from uncomfortable information.

> ■ **KEY LEARNING POINT**
> *Groupthink is a set of group malfunctions which occurs when group members are more concerned to achieve unanimity and agreement than to find the best available solution to a problem or situation.*

Janis (1982b) has argued that certain measures can be taken to avoid groupthink. These include:

- impartial leadership (so that group members are not tempted simply to 'follow the leader');
- each person in the group should be told to give high priority to airing doubts and objections;
- experts should be in attendance to raise doubts;
- 'second chance' meetings should be held where members express their doubts about a previously made but not yet implemented decision.

One might add the necessity of fostering a group norm that disagreement does *not* signal disrespect or unfriendliness.

> ■ KEY LEARNING POINT
>
> *It is possible for groups to use formal procedures to combat groupthink, though these may be tiresome and time consuming.*

Janis' work has not gone unchallenged (Aldag and Fuller, 1993). It has been argued that the groupthink syndrome is really simply a collection of phenomena which do not occur together as neatly as Janis claims, and which anyway have already been investigated by other social scientists. Also, Janis obtained much of his information from published retrospective accounts, which (some argue) may be much too inaccurate and/or incomplete. On the other hand, most research investigating groupthink has been carried out in laboratories, where groups do not have the history implied by some of the antecedents listed in Fig. 13.1. Whyte (1989) has argued that so-called groupthink is not itself a unitary phenomenon. Instead, it is a product of groups seeking risks when they perceive that losses are at stake (*see* 'Information processing in decision making', above), and of group polarisation (*see below*).

Aldag and Fuller (1993) point out that some research has found that group cohesiveness actually helps open discussion of ideas, rather than inhibiting it as Janis has argued. In fact, Mullen and Copper (1994), in a review of 66 tests of the relationship between group cohesiveness and group performance, found that cohesiveness was on average a significant though not large aid to performance, especially when groups were small. They also found that successful group performance tended to foster cohesiveness more than cohesiveness fostered performance. This is not surprising. If we think of cohesiveness as a combination of interpersonal attraction, commitment to the task and group pride, we would expect all of these to increase when the group succeeds in its tasks. In an attempt to reflect the research findings Aldag and Fuller (1993) present their *general group problem-solving model* (GGPSM), which is shown in Fig. 13.2. It includes some of the groupthink concepts, but also adds many others. Among other things, the GGPSM makes the point that decision quality is not the only outcome that may be important.

All of the criticisms of groupthink have some force. Nevertheless, Janis has provided rich case studies which graphically illustrate many potential problems in group decision making, and which should dispel any belief we might cling to that really important decisions are always made rationally.

Fig. 13.2 The general group problem-solving model

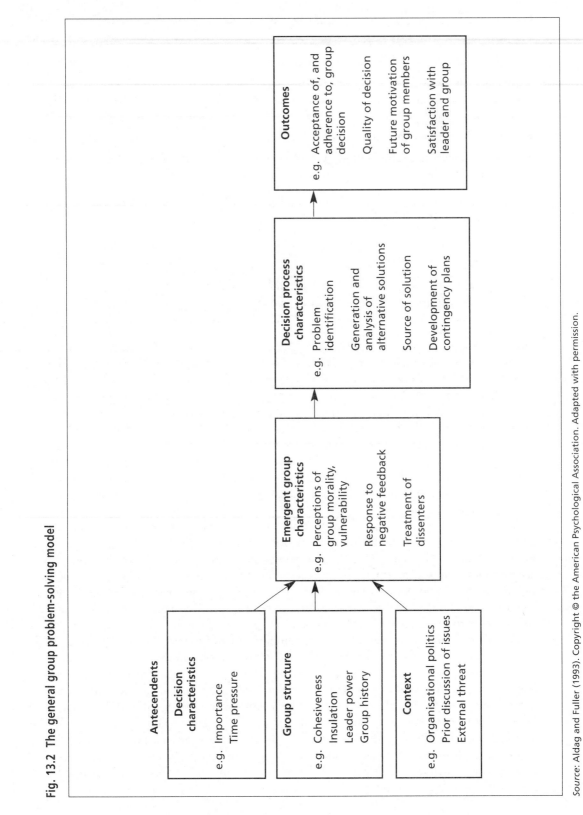

Source: Aldag and Fuller (1993). Copyright © the American Psychological Association. Adapted with permission.

Some other features of group decision making

Group polarisation

One often-voiced criticism of groups is that they arrive at compromise decisions. But in fact this is often not so. Instead, it seems that groups tend to make more extreme decisions than the initial preferences of group members (Myers and Lamm, 1976). This has most often been demonstrated with respect to risk. If the initial tendency of the majority of group members is to adopt a moderately risky decision, the eventual group decision is usually more risky than that. Conversely, somewhat cautious initial preferences of group members translate to more cautious eventual group decisions.

Psychologists have reduced no fewer than eleven possible explanations of group polarisation down to just two, using systematic research (Isenberg, 1986). The *social comparison* explanation is that we like to present ourselves in a socially desirable way, so we try to be like other group members, only more so. The *persuasive argumentation* explanation is that information consistent with the views held by the majority will dominate discussion, and (so long as that information is correct and novel) have persuasive effects. Both explanations are valid, though the latter tends to be stronger. While polarisation is not in itself inherently good or bad, clearly group members need to ensure that they air all relevant information and avoid social conformity – back to groupthink!

> ■ **KEY LEARNING POINT**
> *Contrary to popular opinion, groups often produce more extreme decisions, and fewer compromises, than individuals.*

Minority influence

Minorities within groups only rarely convert the majority to their point of view. But how can they maximise their chances? Many people say that they should gain the acceptance of the majority by conforming wherever possible, and then stick out for their own point of view on a carefully chosen crucial issue. Moscovici and colleagues have argued otherwise (Moscovici and Mugny, 1983; Moscovici, 1985). They have found that, if it is to exert influence, a minority needs to disagree consistently with the majority, including on issues other than the one at stake. Minorities do not exert influence by being liked or being seen as reasonable, but by being perceived as consistent, independent and confident. Much debate has centred on why and how minorities in groups exert influence (Latane and Wolf, 1981; Nemeth, 1986; Kruglanski and Mackie, 1989). The predominant view is that minorities and majorities exert influence in different ways. Nemeth (1986) suggested that majorities encourage convergent, shallow and narrow thinking, while consistent exposure to minority viewpoints stimulates deeper and wider consideration of alternative perspectives. Nemeth (1986, p. 28) concluded from experimental data that:

> Those exposed to minority viewpoints ... are more original, they use a greater variety of strategies, they detect novel solutions, and importantly, they detect correct solutions. Furthermore, this beneficial effect occurs even when the minority viewpoints are wrong.

This emphasises again that groups need to encourage alternative points of view, not suppress them.

■ **KEY LEARNING POINT**

Minority views may be tiresome, but their expression typically leads to better group functioning.

Wood *et al.* (1994) reviewed 143 studies of minority influence, and found that minorities do indeed have some capacity to change the opinions of people who hear their message. This effect is stronger if recipients of the message are not required to publicly acknowledge their change of opinion to the minority. Opinion change is also much greater on issues indirectly related to the message than on those directly related to it. Indeed, although the opinion of the majority usually has more effect than that of the minority, this seems not to be the case on issues only indirectly related to the message.

CASE STUDY 13.2

A soft drink product decision

Rudi Lerner was managing director of a medium-size soft drinks company. His father had founded and then managed the business for nearly thirty years before handing over to his son four years ago. Rudi felt he knew much more about the business than his colleagues on the top management team. They agreed about that, and they liked and respected their boss as well as each other. They usually went out of their way to avoid contradicting him. On the rare occasions they did so, they received a friendly but firm reminder from the chairman that he had been in the business much longer than they had. That was true, but the team membership had not changed for five years now, so nobody was exactly ignorant. However, it was hard to argue – after all, the company had been successful relative to its competitors over the years. Rudi attributed this to frequent takeovers of competitors by people from outside the business. He rarely commissioned market research, relying instead on his 'gut feeling' and extensive prior experience. Now a new challenge faced the company: should it go into the low-calorie 'diet' drinks market, and if so, with what products? The demand for diet drinks was recent but might be here to stay.

Suggested exercise

How likely is it that Rudi and the rest of the management team will make a good decision about entering the 'diet' market?

DEVELOPMENT AND DIVERSITY IN TEAMS

Much of the previous section focused on the effectiveness of teams, mainly in so far as they make decisions. Chapter 14, on leadership, has a lot to say about how to manage teams. In this section we look at team functioning from a broader perspective. Teams are increasingly common in organisations as functional boundaries break down and work is increasingly based on projects requiring input from people with different expertise and experience.

It is quite difficult to distinguish between groups and teams at work. Indeed, Guzzo and Dickson (1996) think it is more or less impossible, and probably pointless. They argue that a work group is made up of individuals who:

- see themselves and are seen by others as a social entity;
- are interdependent because of the tasks they perform;
- are embedded in one or more larger social systems;
- perform tasks that affect others such as co-workers or customers.

Perhaps teams differ from groups in the extent to which (i) members are interdependent (more so in teams) and (ii) the team as a whole (rather than the individuals in it) has performance goals.

Teams are not constant. As well as changes in personnel, they change over time in terms of how they approach their tasks and how team members relate to each other. One early analysis (Tuckman, 1965) suggested that teams tend to go through a series of stages in their development:

1 *forming*: there is typically ambiguity and confusion when a team first forms. The members may not have chosen to work with each other. They may be guarded, superficial and impersonal in communication, and unclear about the task;

2 *storming*: this can be a difficult stage when there is conflict between team members and some rebellion against the task as assigned. There may be jockeying for positions of power and frustration at a lack of progress in the task;

3 *norming*: it is important that open communication between team members is established. A start is made on confronting the task in hand, and generally-accepted procedures and patterns of communication are established;

4 *performing*: having established how it is going to function, the group is now free to devote its full attention to achieving its goals. If the earlier stages have been tackled satisfactorily, the group should now be close and supportive, open and trusting, resourceful and effective.

Most teams have a limited life, so it is probably appropriate to add another stage called something like disbanding. It would be important for team members to analyse their own performance and that of the group, to learn from the experience, and agree whether to stay in touch, and if so what that might achieve.

Not everyone agrees that these stages are either an accurate description or a desirable sequence. Teams composed of people who are accustomed to working that way may jump straight to the norming stage. The members may already know each other. Even if they don't, they may be able quickly to establish satisfactory ways of interacting without conflict. In any case, many teams are required to perform right from the start, so they need to bypass the earlier stages, at least partially. West (1994, p. 98) argues that key tasks in team start-up concern the establishment of team goals and individual tasks which are meaningful and challenging, and of procedures for performance monitoring and review.

> ■ KEY LEARNING POINT
> *Some teams go through stages in their development, but many need to achieve high performance straight away.*

Teams at work sometimes use people from outside the team to help them improve their effectiveness. This is usually called team-building, and it can focus on some or all of the following:

- the team's goals or priorities
- the work required and its distribution between team members
- the team's deliberate and accidental procedures, processes and norms
- relationships with other groups and teams.

One particularly influential tool used in team-building has been developed by Belbin (1981, 1993a). He identified the roles that team members need to fulfil if the team is to be successful. These are shown in Fig. 13.3.

Of course, not all teams are composed of exactly nine people, each of whom takes one role. Usually it is necessary for each person to fill more than one role. Most individuals are capable of doing this, though each of us have roles we would find it very difficult to fill effectively. An important part of team-building using Belbin's roles

Fig. 13.3 Belbin's nine team roles

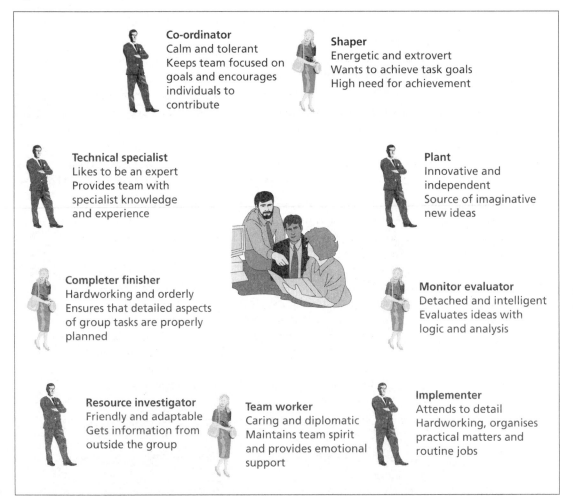

Co-ordinator
Calm and tolerant
Keeps team focused on goals and encourages individuals to contribute

Shaper
Energetic and extrovert
Wants to achieve task goals
High need for achievement

Technical specialist
Likes to be an expert
Provides team with specialist knowledge and experience

Plant
Innovative and independent
Source of imaginative new ideas

Completer finisher
Hardworking and orderly
Ensures that detailed aspects of group tasks are properly planned

Monitor evaluator
Detached and intelligent
Evaluates ideas with logic and analysis

Resource investigator
Friendly and adaptable
Gets information from outside the group

Team worker
Caring and diplomatic
Maintains team spirit and provides emotional support

Implementer
Attends to detail
Hardworking, organises practical matters and routine jobs

involves assessing the preferred roles of each team member and encouraging all members to appreciate the characteristics and strengths of the others. Belbin has developed a self-assessment questionnaire for identifying individuals' preferred team roles. It is a useful tool for raising awareness but has a number of psychometric weaknesses which cast doubts on its ability to measure stable aspects of personality (Furnham *et al.*, 1993). But if the scores can be taken at face value, in my experience many management teams are over-supplied with Shapers and Implementers, but lacking Plants and Team Workers. This means that plans are formulated and fleshed out quite quickly, but that they are often insufficiently creative, and are discussed in a combative fashion which can leave some team members upset or alienated.

> ■ KEY LEARNING POINT
> *Team members need to adopt different roles and to appreciate the value of all the roles, not just those they personally feel comfortable with.*

Belbin is one of many people who stress the importance of diversity in teams. That is, it is important for an effective team to have people with differing outlooks and strengths. The problem is, of course, that we may devalue characteristics we happen not to possess ourselves. While diversity in terms of occupational or organisational role is expected in a team, diversity in terms of gender, nationality, ethnicity, age or personality is often less readily accepted. It is also hard to manage well, since team members may have quite different values and expectations of how to behave. So although teams with diverse members have the *potential* to be highly effective because of the varied outlooks they possess, they often fail to achieve that potential (Kandola, 1995). Maznevski (1994) has argued that teams need integration, and that this is more difficult to achieve as they become more diverse. Integration relies on:

- a social reality shared by group members;
- the ability to decentre – that is, see things from others' points of view;
- the motivation to communicate;
- the ability to negotiate and agree on norms of behaviour within the team;
- the ability to identify the true causes of any difficulties which arise (e.g. not blaming people for things that are not their fault);
- self-confidence of all group members.

These are good guidelines for any team, but are harder to achieve in a diverse one. Teams with diverse members must be especially careful to establish integration.

THE WIDER ORGANISATIONAL CONTEXT

Guzzo and Dickson (1996) point out that improved group performance does not guarantee improved organisational performance. It depends on the appropriateness of what the group is being asked to do, and how well the efforts of different groups are co-ordinated. However, there is plenty of evidence that teams are being used more and more in organisations (Applebaum and Blatt, 1994). Macy and Izumi (1993) found that organisational financial performance improves most when a range of change initiatives (*see* Chapter 20) are used, such as organisational structure, technology and human resource management techniques. But team development interventions were among the more effective of those initiatives. So group interventions do appear to be useful in the wider organisational context.

Decisions in organisations can be divided into various types, and each decision has various phases (Mintzberg *et al.*, 1976; Heller and Misumi, 1987). As regards types, there are (i) operational decisions (usually with short-term effects and of a routine nature); (ii) tactical decisions (usually with medium-term effects and of non-routine nature but not going so far as reviewing the organisation's goals); and (iii) strategic decisions (usually with long-term effects and concerning the organisation's goals). In line with leadership research (*see* Chapter 14), it is also possible to distinguish between people-orientated and task-orientated decisions within each type. Phases of decision making include (i) start-up, when it is realised that a decision is required; (ii) development, when options are searched for and considered; (iii) finalisation, when a decision is confirmed; and (iv) implementation, where the finalised decision is put into operation or fails (Heller *et al.*, 1988).

Much attention has been focused on who in organisations really makes decisions, and how their influence is distributed across the decision types and phases described above (French and Raven, 1959; Pfeffer, 1981; Mintzberg, 1983; Heller *et al.*, 1988). The concept of *power* is frequently invoked. Power concerns the ability of an individual or group to ensure that another individual or group complies with its wishes. Power can be derived from a number of sources, including the ability to reward and/or punish; the extent to which a person or group is seen as expert; and the amount of prestige or good reputation that is enjoyed by a person or group. These sources of power are distinct, though they tend to go together (Finkelstein, 1992). Especially if these sources of power are in short supply, individuals and groups often use *organisational politics* to maximise their chances of getting their way. Politics consists of tactics like enlisting the support of others, controlling access to information, and creating indebtedness by doing people favours for which reciprocation is expected. In extreme forms politics can also involve more deceitful activities such as spreading rumours. In general, however, the effectiveness and morality of power and politics depend on their intended goals. The distinction between the two goals of self-aggrandisement and organisational effectiveness is often blurred. After all, most of us probably construe ourselves as playing important and legitimate roles in our work organisations, and it is easy to jump from there to a belief that what is good for us must therefore also be good for the organisation.

Several large studies over the years have examined who participates in organisational decisions. Heller *et al.* (1988), for example, conducted a detailed longitudinal study of seven organisations in three countries (the Netherlands, the UK and the former Yugoslavia). Not surprisingly, they found that most decision-making power was generally exercised by top management. The lower levels and works councils typically were merely informed or at best consulted. The distribution of power did, however, vary considerably between organisations and also somewhat between countries, with Yugoslavia (as it then was) generally having the highest degree of participation by bottom organisational levels, and the UK the lowest. There was also some variation between types and phases of decision making. Top management were most influential in strategic decisions. Within tactical decisions, workers had quite high influence at the start-up phase of people-orientated decisions but little thereafter. This led to frustration. But for tactical task-orientated decisions, they had much influence in the finalisation phase. This was often less frustrating, since the right of management to initiate decisions of this kind was rarely challenged (i.e. high legitimate power). Effective decisions about who to involve in the decision-making process, and how, are more likely if those involved are clear about the nature of the situation they are facing (*see* Fig. 13.4). It is likely that different people will need to be involved in different situations, and for different reasons. Decisions about who to involve may appropriately be based on criteria proposed by Vroom in his theory of leadership (*see* Chapter 14) which revolve primarily around the needs for decision quality and decision acceptance.

■ **KEY LEARNING POINT**

The amount and type of workforce participation in organisational decision making varies between countries and between phases of the decision-making processs.

Finally, examinations of strategic decision making by management have been undertaken (e.g. Hickson *et al.*, 1986). Some interesting findings have emerged. For example, Frederickson and Iaquinto (1989) found that comprehensive information search and

Fig. 13.4 Organisational decision situations

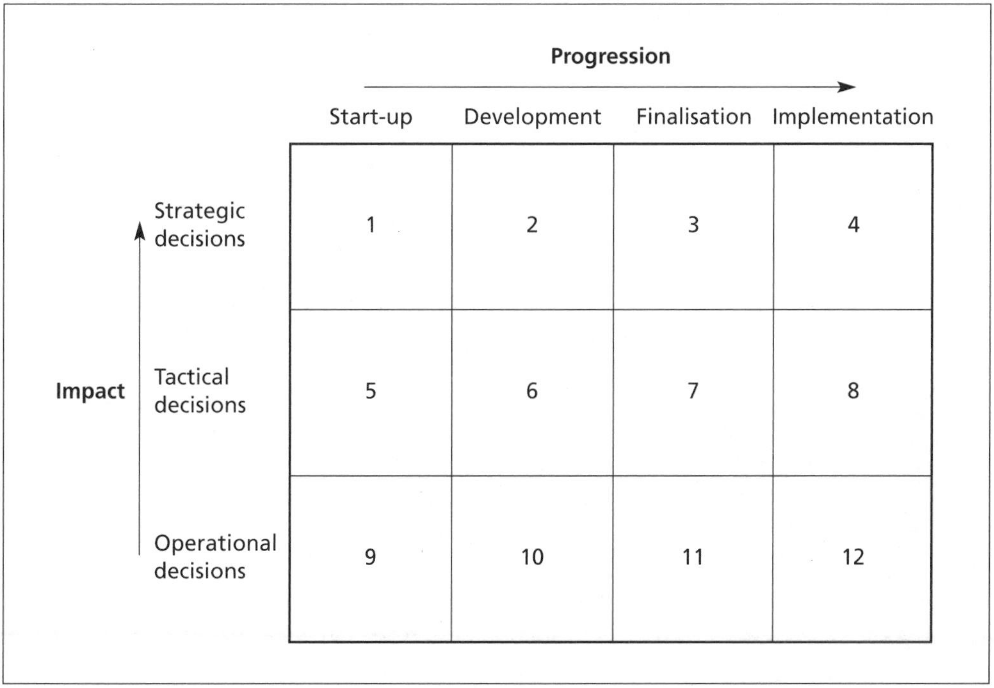

		Progression			
		Start-up	Development	Finalisation	Implementation
Impact	Strategic decisions	1	2	3	4
	Tactical decisions	5	6	7	8
	Operational decisions	9	10	11	12

Source: Heller *et al.* (1988)

option consideration assisted effective strategic decision making in stable economic environments, but the reverse was true in unstable environments. Participating firms were drawn from the American paint industry (said to be stable) and forest products industry (unstable). Similarly, Eisenhardt (1989), working with firms in the unstable (or, as she called it, 'high velocity') environment of microcomputers, found that fast decisions were superior to slow ones. More surprisingly, perhaps, fast decision makers seemed to use *more* information and consider *more* alternatives than slow ones. It could be that decision-making speed is simply an aspect of general competence.

Dean and Sharfman (1996) have investigated the process and outcomes of 52 strategic decisions in 24 companies. The most common types of strategic decision concerned organisational restructuring, the launch of a new product and organisational change. Dean and Sharfman used multiple in-depth interviews with senior managers involved in the decisions. Their findings are summarised in Fig. 13.5. The procedural rationality of the decision-making process (that is, the extent to which relevant information was sought, obtained and evaluated) had a significant impact on decision effectiveness, particularly when the business environment was changeable, requiring careful monitoring of trends. But even more important was the thoroughness and care with which the decision was implemented. This is an important reminder that managers cannot afford simply to make decisions – the decisions must be followed through. However, not everything is under decision makers' control. Dean and Sharfman found that the favourability of the business and industrial environment also had an impact on decision effectiveness. Political behaviour by those involved was bad for decision effectiveness. So, behaviour such as disguising one's own opinions and negotiations between factions of the decision-making group should not be accepted as an inevitable part of organisational life. They impair organisational performance, though of course they may serve the interests of individuals or subgroups.

Fig. 13.5 Influences on the effectiveness of strategic decisions

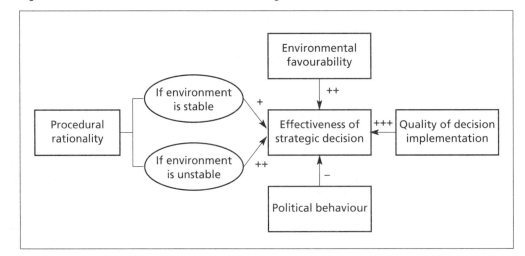

Source: Adapted from Dean and Sharfman (1996)

NEGOTIATION

Some decisions involve discussion between two or more individuals or groups who have different opinions about what the decision should be, at least at the outset. The process of attempting to resolve these differences through discussion is called *negotiation*. The most obvious form of negotiation in the workplace is that between management and employees in organisations, the latter often represented by a trade union. Rather like group decision making, psychologists have tried to describe what happens in negotiations and also in some cases to recommend strategies for success as a negotiator. They have tended to concentrate on what happens in the negotiation itself, and placed less emphasis on the economic and political context in which a negotiation takes place (Lewicki *et al.*, 1992). Although some research has involved real negotiations, much has been conducted in laboratories with students tackling standard tasks under varying conditions.

As Pruitt (1981) has pointed out, at certain key decision points during a negotiation, a negotiator can choose between three types of behaviour:

1 *unilateral concession*: the negotiator lowers his or her demands, or agrees to something desired by an opposing negotiator;

2 *standing firm, or contention*: the negotiator restates his or her demands, or refuses to give something desired by an opposing negotiator. This can also involve strong uncompromising arguments in support of one's own position, and even threats;

3 *collaboration*: the negotiator tries to work with, rather than against, opposing negotiators to find a mutually acceptable solution.

In an early and influential piece of work, Walton and McKersie (1965) drew a distinction between *distributive bargaining* and *integrative bargaining*, which are similar to Pruitt's competition and collaboration, respectively. In distributive bargaining the negotiators assume that there is a fixed amount of reward available, so that one negotiator's gain is another's loss. But integrative bargaining involves an attempt to increase the size of the overall reward available to both sides. One phenomenon often observed in research is that negotiators tend to treat the task as distributive even though they could gain more by taking an integrative approach. For example, suppose that negotiators A and B are trying to reach an agreement over the sale of A's house, which B wishes to buy. A wants £100 000, and B begins by offering £90 000. After some discussion, A agrees to accept £98 000 and B increases the offer to £95 000. Neither side is prepared to shift further on the price so it looks like a deal will not be struck. However, if A and B then search together for other ways of viewing the problem, they may reach an agreement. Perhaps A has little use for the carpets and curtains in the house because the one she is moving to has them fitted already. In fact, she would prefer to avoid the hassle of removing them. B on the other hand very much wants A to leave the carpets and curtains because he likes them and is too busy to arrange new ones. So A and B may agree a price of £98 000 including carpets and curtains. B considers the extra £3000 a fair price for the carpets and curtains, and A is also happy because the carpets and curtains are of no value to her, and she has got the price she wanted.

This kind of outcome, sometimes referred to as 'win–win' (Pruitt and Rubin, 1986), often depends on the negotiators having complementary priorities so that each can make concessions over issues where their subjective loss is smaller than the corresponding gain experienced by another negotiator. To engage in problem solving implies that a negotiator has some concern for the other party's outcomes as well as his or her own. Indeed, a negotiator's predominant negotiating style can be predicted on the basis of the extent of his or her concern about outcomes of the participating parties. This is shown in Fig. 13.6.

Although quite simple, Fig. 13.6 has three important lessons. First, a negotiator has more options than conceding or not conceding. Second, a negotiator may not only be concerned with his or her own outcomes. Especially if one negotiator anticipates having to work with another in the future, he or she would be wise to pay attention to the other's wishes because this helps to maintain their relationship. Third, compromise is not in the middle of Fig. 13.6 as one might expect. Instead it is near the top. This indicates that compromise requires a strong concern about the other party's outcomes. A contentious negotiator is almost as unlikely to compromise as to make a concession (Van de Vliert and Prein, 1989).

> ■ **KEY LEARNING POINT**
>
> *Effective negotiators pay attention to the interests of the other side as well as their own.*

As Carnevale and Pruitt (1992) point out, whatever a negotiator's preferred or typical style, the state of the negotiation may dictate his or her behaviour. This is another illustration of the fact that situation sometimes overrides personality (*see* Chapter 3).

Fig. 13.6 Negotiator concerns and characteristic strategies

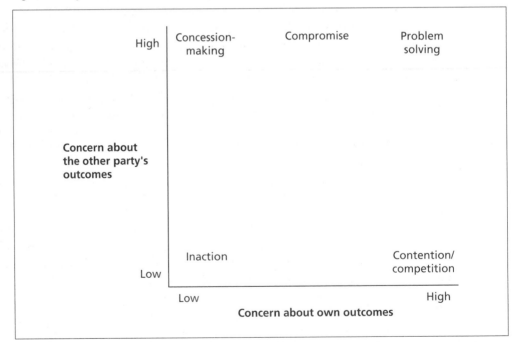

Source: Adapted from Carnevale and Pruitt (1992), with permission from the *Annual Review of Psychology*, vol. 43. © 1992 by Annual Reviews Inc.

Indeed, some research has suggested that negotiators typically behave in a contentious fashion early in a negotiation, adopting a problem-solving approach only when their position has been stated clearly and repeatedly. Up to a point this seems to be a sensible strategy. Research suggests that early in negotiation, uncompromising statements by one negotiator may produce concessions, or at least a rather lower opening bid, from the other than would otherwise have been the case (Pruitt and Syna, 1985). However, making high initial demands *and* sticking to most of them is a high-risk strategy because it is likely that no agreement at all will occur. In most work settings, failing to reach agreement is unsatisfactory for both or all parties – a so-called 'lose–lose' outcome. On the other hand making low initial demands and making many concessions produces a quick agreement but a rather one-sided one! It may also be a mistake to start with moderate demands and then refuse to move – the moderation raises the expectations of the other negotiator(s) but then the inflexibility frustrates them and leaves them unable to point to concessions they have won for their supporters (Hamner, 1974). The best approach may often be to start with high demands and make frequent concessions. But this assumes a distributive as opposed to integrative bargaining situation, and also that failure to reach agreement is costly.

As well as integrative and distributive bargaining, Walton and McKersie (1965) proposed two other processes: *attitudinal structuring* and *intra-organisational bargaining*. The former refers to negotiators' attempts to influence the quality and nature of their relationships, and the 'climate' in which a negotiation takes place. For example, a well-timed joke, perhaps at one's own expense, can improve the level of trust between negotiators.

Intra-organisational bargaining refers to negotiators' relationships with other negotiators on their own side, and with the people they represent. As Lewicki *et al.* (1992) point out, much research on negotiation seems to rest on the assumption that the only negotiation worth considering occurs at the negotiating table. Yet Walton and McKersie (1965) argued that much significant negotiation occurs when negotiators try to persuade their constituents to accept a deal as the best that can be achieved, and when negotiators on the same side discuss with each other how they should respond to a certain situation. Negotiators tend to believe (sometimes correctly) that their constituents are more anxious to win than they are themselves. This makes them more inclined to engage in contentious negotiation tactics, perhaps in the real hope of getting a good deal, or perhaps just to impress their constituents even if there is no hope of further progress. On the other hand, when negotiators have to justify their behaviour to their constituents *and* when they want a continuing relationship with the other side, they are quite likely to engage in problem solving tactics. This is presumably because problem solving is the strategy most likely to maintain their credibility with both their constituents and opposing negotiators.

> ■ **KEY LEARNING POINT**
> *Negotiators often have to persuade their own side that a deal is acceptable. This requirement can influence their behaviour during the negotiation itself.*

Ideas from cognitive and social psychology have also contributed to our understanding of negotiator behaviour. For example, we have already seen in this chapter how people are more inclined to take a risk in the hope of avoiding a loss than in the hope of making a gain. When applied to negotiation, this means that a negotiator who perceives that he or she is trying to avoid a loss will be more inclined to resist concessions (thus risking failure to reach agreement) than a negotiator who construes the position as trying to make a gain (Bazerman *et al.*, 1985). Negotiators also run the risk of escalating commitment to their initial position, especially if they are inexperienced.

A negotiator may develop his or her own schema (*see* Chapter 2) for the negotiation situation. For example, a negotiation might be perceived as a 'fixed-pie' exercise (i.e. distributive bargaining), where one party's gain is equal to another's loss. Thompson (1990) found that negotiators whose first negotiation experiences really were of the 'fixed-pie' type tended to develop a schema of negotiation as necessarily of that kind. They failed to spot win–win possibilities in subsequent episodes because they were not alert to them. Negotiators also have expectations or scripts (*see* Chapter 2) concerning how negotiations will unfold. One common element of such a script is that a concession, once made, is not withdrawn. This expectation means that such a withdrawal is less likely to happen, and that if it does happen it will be viewed with outrage.

Finally, one frequent feature of negotiation is the need to maintain good relationships with other negotiators while disagreeing with them. Some practical guidelines to negotiation (e.g. DuBrin, 1994, chapter 7) suggest ways of achieving this. One is separating the people from the problem, and being gentle with the former but tough on the latter. Another is focusing on the other party's interests, not their position, which avoids forcing them into defending their claims, even if they don't want to any longer.

CASE STUDY 13.3

A negotiation at Micro

Industrial relations at the Micro electronics company had reached a critical point. The company was performing well in its markets and making a good profit. In order to maintain this, managers wanted to abandon one of the company's products, for which demand was declining. This might mean some compulsory redundancies. At the same time, the employees who remained would undertake more varied and sometimes more skilled work. Managers had underestimated the strength of opposition to their plans for implementing the changes they desired. Although there had not yet been industrial action, it was a clear possibility in the near future. New pay discussions were also due. The union negotiator, Nils Gunderson, was generally felt by union members to have achieved a poor deal in the last pay discussions two years ago. He was keen to move out of his job at Micro into a full-time union post. He had had a cordial relationship with the previous managing director, but his few encounters with the new one, Stephanie Viken, had not been so pleasant during the six months she had been in post. For her part, Stephanie was anxious to secure active union co-operation (as opposed to passive compliance) with company plans. She knew that she would need the employees on her side, and was also worried by the possibility that many might change to another, more militant, union.

Suggested exercise

On the basis of (i) the issues to be negotiated and (ii) the concerns of Nils Gunderson and Stephanie Viken, what approach to the forthcoming negotiation is each person likely to take? How might this affect the outcome of the negotiation?

INDUSTRIAL RELATIONS

Negotiation is often conducted by representatives of owners and/or managers on one side and representatives of employees on the other. But negotiation is only one aspect of *industrial relations*, which have been defined by Walker (1979, p. 11) as being to do with 'the accommodation between the various interests that are involved in the process of getting work done'. This definition does not assume that the parties involved are necessarily management and other employees, nor that the latter are represented by trade unions, nor that there is necessarily conflict between the parties. It should also be remembered that the word 'industrial' can be extended to other sectors of the economy.

Hartley (1992) has provided a helpful account of many aspects of industrial relations. Figure 13.7 is an adaptation of her picture of the field. The first point to note about it is that the wider political and economic context (such as government policies and product markets) affects parties, processes and outcomes in industrial relations. So, for example, legislation introduced during the 1980s in the United Kingdom meant that the conditions in which employees could take strike action were narrowed. The balloting procedures required before a strike could legally be mounted were extended. This may well have had far-reaching effects on how parties involved in industrial relations relate to each other, how individuals relate to the parties of which they are a member, and

Fig. 13.7 Psychology in industrial relations

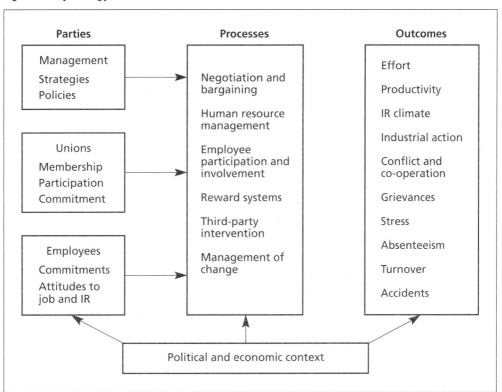

Source: Adapted from J. Hartley (1992), 'The psychology of industrial relations' in C.L. Cooper and I.T. Robertson (eds) *International Review of Industrial and Organizational Psychology*, vol. 7. Copyright John Wiley and Sons Ltd. Reproduced with permission.

whether particular processes (such as downsizing of an organisation) lead to conflict. Differences between countries in the way industrial relations are organised are well documented and frequently cited as a good illustration of how difficult it is to generalise about industrial relations (International Labour Office, 1984).

Figure 13.7 reflects trends in many Western countries during the 1980s and 1990s. The references to HRM (human resource management) and employee participation and involvement reflect a decreasing emphasis on collective, formal employment relationships. Instead, there is an increasing tendency for workplace-specific employment agreements; more emphasis on management for quality; training and flexibility of employees; and a greater concern with the commitment of individuals to their employing organisation (Guest, 1991). Attempts to increase employee commitment and performance include share ownership, quality circles (where groups of employees jointly review the quality of output), and empowerment. The last of these involves trusting people to recognise and solve problems themselves rather than referring them to someone 'higher up', or not noticing them at all. Kelly and Kelly (1991) conclude that while many employees react positively to such interventions, they do not change their fundamental attitudes to managers. This is because employees often believe, rightly or wrongly, that powerful groups in the organisation are still in control and might at any time choose to exert their control in a more draconian manner.

■ **KEY LEARNING POINT**

The ways in which different power blocs in organisations relate to each other depend partly on the wider legal of cultural context in which the organisation operates.

Although the influence and membership of trade unions has been declining in many countries, much research of industrial relations still focuses on them. In a way this makes good sense: it is more interesting and useful to discover what encourages people to join a union and participate in its activities in such conditions than when everyone takes union membership for granted.

Joining and participating in a trade union

Research suggests that there is no predominant single reason why people join a trade union. Certainly relatively few people join because of a strong ideological commitment to trade unionism. General dissatisfaction with one's employer is not necessarily enough either (Klandermans, 1986) though it can be important (Guest and Dewe, 1988). A specific intense dispute seems likely to strengthen employees' sense of belonging to a trade union, but for some people the most important factor in joining one is 'insurance' against difficult circumstances that might arise in the future, even if they are not obvious now. In other words, a fairly common reason for joining a union is 'just in case' I need protection. Of course, this implies that employees see unions as capable of offering useful protection should the need arise. Variants of expectancy theory (*see* Chapter 11) have been useful here in understanding union joining. According to this the person asks what benefits are potentially available, whether union membership will help to obtain them, and whether the benefits sufficiently exceed the costs of membership (e.g. membership fees). Hartley (1992) acknowledges the potential usefulness of this, but criticises it for a lack of attention to the potential social influence of families, friends and work-mates.

Aspects of social identity have been used more in understanding who participates in union activities. Kelly and Kelly (1994) studied 350 union members in a UK local government organisation. They divided participation into 'easy' (e.g. reading union journals, attending union meetings) and 'difficult' (e.g. being a union delegate, speaking at branch meetings). Perhaps not surprisingly, the extent to which people engaged in either form of participation was predicted by the extent to which they identified with the union. In addition, 'easy' participation was affected by the extent to which union members had stereotypical 'us and them' perceptions of management – the more stereotypical the perceptions, the more the 'easy' participation. Interestingly, these aspects of social identity were better predictors of participation than the extent to which members felt they were badly off relative to comparison groups.

Union commitment

Being a member of a union does not necessarily signal feelings of commitment towards it. We have examined aspects of organisational commitment in Chapter 9, and many of these have been extended to the investigation of union commitment. Two issues have formed the focus of attention: first, what predicts the extent to which people are committed to their union, and second, whether those who are highly committed to their union tend also to be highly committed to their employing organisation. Both of these issues are related to that of union joining described above, because it seems plausible to suggest that whatever impels people to join a union will also affect how committed they are to it. So if a person joins a union because he or she thinks it can offer protection from disciplinary action, his or her commitment to the union may subsequently depend on continuing to believe that. Also, if a person joins a union because of a perceived threat from his or her employer, it seems likely that high commitment to the union will be accompanied by low commitment to the employer. On the other hand, if commitment to a union reflects an underlying personality trait of being an enthusiastic joiner and participator, then the kind of person who feels highly committed to the union will also tend to feel highly committed to his or her employer. In fact, psychological research has not yet managed to clarify these issues very much, due partly to poor conceptualisation and measurement of commitment (Gordon and Ladd, 1990).

Conflict and industrial action

A number of ideas from social psychology have been applied to the analysis of conflict in organisations. Some of these are covered in Chapter 12 on person perception. They have in common the notion that people tend to value themselves and other members of groups to which they belong more highly than members of other groups. This may be engendered by groups having conflicting goals (Sherif, 1966) or simply because our group memberships define our identity, and we are motivated to uphold the value of that identity relative to others (Tajfel, 1972). The implication of these theories is that industrial action such as strikes and overtime bans occur either when the goals of differ-ent groups are very much in conflict and cannot readily be resolved (Sherif), or when members of a group feel that their identity is so threatened that they must make a stand (Tajfel). Note that this does not take into account an assessment of whether industrial action is likely to improve their material or psychological state, nor does it say much about how a group of people could (or should) organise and conduct industrial action. Given that industrial action is an unpleasant experience for most people involved in it, it is important for a group taking industrial action to maintain cohesion and a sense of purpose without undue escalation of commitment to an unwinnable battle. Hartley *et al.* (1983) showed how committees of union members set up to organise the conduct of a strike can help to maintain solidarity. In attempting to keep the support of other members, leaders can use techniques of persuasion (*see* Chapter 9), as can representa-tives of the 'opposition' who wish to appeal to people taking industrial action over the heads of their leaders.

The quality of inter-group relations in the workplace, and whether poor relations lead to industrial action, depends partly on the extent to which members of the different groups have accurate perceptions of each other (*see* Chapter 9). Allen and Stephenson (1984) have shown that when members of groups overestimate differences in attitudes and beliefs between their own group and other groups, industrial action is more likely than when the differences are underestimated. This is another illustration of the impor-tance of social factors: not only the real difference in views, but also the perceived difference, can influence whether industrial action occurs.

Stress and industrial relations

Involvement in industrial action is stressful (Barling and Milligan, 1987). But stress is not confined to times of industrial action. It is easy to see how people with trade union or other representative duties might experience stress from role conflict, role ambiguity, interpersonal conflict, split loyalties and work overload (*see* Chapter 17), especially per-haps if they are working in an 'ordinary' job and not as a full-time union official. Nandram and Klandermans (1993) found that much of union officials' stress was induced by role ambiguity *within* the union role rather than ambiguity about whether they should be acting as an employee or a union representative at any given time. That is, they were not clear what they, or their union, were trying to achieve. More optimisti-cally, Shirom and Mayer (1993) reported that although trade union officials among teachers experienced high role overload and conflict, they did not experience more stress. This suggests that union activities have some compensatory advantages which might cancel out some of the unpleasant features. These advantages may include greater job challenge, a sense of being useful to one's colleagues, and perhaps also the esteem and gratitude of those colleagues.

> ■ **KEY LEARNING POINT**
> *For individuals, union participation can depend on their social
> identity, and can lead to significant stress related to conflicts
> between union and employee roles.*

SUMMARY

Decisions by individuals and groups are influenced by many psychological phenomena. For individuals, the subjective evaluation of risk and rewards is rarely the same as an objective mathematical calculation. This does not necessarily imply that people are typically mistaken, although some features of decision making can be construed as biased or ineffective in certain circumstances. Groups are typically more effective than the average individual but less so than the best individual in decision-making tasks. Groups can make terrible decisions, especially if characterised by the 'groupthink' syndrome. However, the typical effectiveness of groups should not be viewed as the best they could do. Possible ways in which groups and teams can improve include more consideration in advance of the problem-solving strategy they wish to adopt, a clear expectation that members should challenge each other, and an understanding that such challenges do not signal hostility or disrespect. Members of groups and teams need to fulfil a wide range of roles and to respect diversity. The nature of decision-making tasks, their importance and their subject matter all have implications for the way they are handled. Some decisions require negotiation with other parties. Negotiations are often perceived as 'fixed-pie' or 'zero sum' scenarios where one party's gain is equal to another's loss. However, this is not necessarily the case, and negotiations which produce an agreement satisfactory to both (or all) parties usually involve some collaborative problem solving, which may uncover a solution that gives all involved rewards that they value. Negotiations are just one part of industrial relations, which concern the adjustments groups make to each other in the workplace. Theories from social psychology help to explain how industrial action arises as well as why people do or do not participate in trade union activities.

CASE STUDY 13.4

To expand or not to expand?

The management team of the Fastsave retail chain store company had a decision to make. Should they build a new store in Danesville, a medium-size town in which the company owned a suitable patch of land? Fastsave was doing quite well, and had more than enough financial resources to make the necessary investment in a town which did not currently have a major supermarket. On the other hand, there were two existing large superstores within 25 kilometres. It was agreed that there was no significant danger of substantial losses: the question was more whether the time and effort involved in expansion would be worth the return.

The management team consisted of the general manager (GM), finance manager (FM), marketing manager (MM), operations manager (OM), personnel manager (PM) and company secretary (CS). Each member of the team had been supplied with reports on the demographic make-up of the town, a market research survey, detailed costings of building the store, and the likely attitude of the local council planning authority.

Group members were accustomed to working together and there was rivalry (at present friendly) between them about which of them if any would succeed GM when she retired in about three years. At the outset of the meeting, GM made it clear that she would act as an impartial chairperson, and not reveal her own opinions until the end. In the past, however, she had usually been cautious about business expansions. The following extract is representative of the group's deliberations:

CASE
STUDY
13.4

FM: I suspect the time is not right. We are currently upgrading six other stores, and to start a completely new one would run the risk of spreading our resources too thin. In purely financial terms we can do it, but would we do a good job?

OM: Yes, we've certainly got our hands full at present. In fact, I would be in favour of reviewing two of our already-planned store upgradings because I'm not sure they are really worth it either. Generally we're doing all right as we are – let's consolidate our position.

MM: I can't believe I'm hearing this! According to our market research report, the population of Danesville wants its own big supermarket, and what's more the 45+ age group particularly likes our emphasis on low price rather than super de luxe quality.

CS: Come on, as usual you're taking an approach which could possibly pay off but could land us in trouble ...

MM: Like what?

CS: Well, there has been a lot of housing development in Danesville, and the local council is under pressure to preserve what it sees as the charm of the town. It would be very bad public relations to be perceived as undermining that. And having a planning application refused wouldn't be much better.

FM: That's right, and being seen as an intruder would probably reduce sales too.

PM: I can't comment on that last point, but as a general principle we should not stand still. Our competitors might overtake us. If resources are spread too thin, we can recruit more staff: we have the money, and experience suggests that the labour force in the region has the necessary skills.

FM: You've had a rush of blood to the head, haven't you? You're normally telling us how difficult it is to manage expansion of staff numbers. I must say I share the concern about a couple of our existing upgrading plans, let alone building an entirely new store. Do those stores really need refitting yet? They are doing all right.

CS: I notice that Danesville has an increasingly young, mobile population these days. In spite of the market research report, will they really be interested in a local store, especially with our position in the market?

MM: They can be made to be. Anyway, who says that a Danesville store should not go slightly more upmarket? Tesco seem to manage to have both upmarket and downmarket stores.

OM: Well yes, but I don't think we are big enough to be that versatile ...

Suggested exercises

1 *Examine this case study from the following perspectives:*

   (a) the likely attitude to risk

   (b) group polarisation

   (c) minority influence.

2 *Given this examination, what do you think the group is likely to decide? What is your evaluation of that decision?*

Short-answer questions

1 Explain the distinction between satisficing and maximising in decision making.

2 Define escalation of commitment to a decision and briefly describe the circumstances in which it is likely to occur.

3 Describe the decision-making styles identified by Janis and Mann (1977).

4 List three key features of effective strategic decision making by organisations.

5 What strategies should minorities in groups use in order to maximise their chances of influencing a group decision?

6 What is group polarisation and why does it happen?

7 List the team roles identified by Belbin and explain why they are needed for team effectiveness.

8 Briefly outline three reasons why groups sometimes make poor decisions.

9 Define power and politics in organisations.

10 Distinguish between distributive and integrative bargaining.

11 Briefly describe the topics within industrial relations studied by psychologists.

Essay questions

1 Examine the importance of the work of Tversky and Kahneman for understanding decision making by individuals.

2 Discuss the proposition that Janis' groupthink model adequately accounts for failures in group decision making.

3 Examine the potential benefits and problems of diversity in teams.

4 What factors affect the occurrence of industrial action and how it is resolved?

5 Critically assess the proposition that compromise in negotiation is not the same as weakness.

GLOSSARY OF TERMS

Brainstorming A technique for generating ideas which involves people thinking of as many things as possible that might be relevant to a given problem, however far-fetched their ideas may seem.

Decision-making style A person's normal or habitual way of going about making decisions.

Distributive bargaining A form of negotiation characterised by an assumption by the negotiators that the total rewards available are fixed, so that one negotiator's gain is another's loss.

Escalation of commitment A process whereby a person makes further investments in a course of action in order to justify to self and others his or her original decision to pursue that action.

Framing effect The impact on decision making of the way the problem is expressed – for example either in terms of its potential losses or its potential gains.

Group Two or more people who are perceived by themselves and others as a social entity.

Group polarisation A phenomenon where the decision of a group after discussion is more extreme than the original preferences of individual group members.

Groupthink A failure of group decision making identified by Irving Janis, where the motivation of group members to seek agreement with each other exceeds their motivation to conduct a thorough and open analysis of the situation.

Heuristic General rules that people use to guide their decision making about complex problems.

Industrial relations The accommodations made by the various parties involved in getting work done.

Intra-organisational (or intra-party) bargaining The negotiations that occur between members of the same party.

Integrative bargaining A form of negotiation characterised by collaborative problem solving and attempts by the negotiators to find a mutually beneficial solution.

Organisational politics Interpersonal processes used by people in an organisation to enhance or maintain their reputation.

Organisational power The capacity of an individual or group within an organisation to make other individuals or groups do what they want them to do.

Social loafing The process where some members of a group do not contribute their share of effort, but still obtain the rewards of group membership.

Strategic decision A decision which affects the overall goals, aims or mission of an organisation.

Team A group of people who work together towards group objectives.

Team-building Techniques designed to enhance the effectiveness of a new or established team.

Team roles The functions that need to be fulfilled by team members if the team is to be effective.

SUGGESTED FURTHER READING

Note: All four suggested readings are listed in detail in the reference list below.

1 Michael West's book *Effective Teamwork* (published in 1994 by the British Psychological Society) is an accessible and wide-ranging introduction to how groups and teams function in the workplace.

2 Richard Guzzo and Marcus Dickson have provided an up-to-date (1996) review of research on teams in organisations in the *Annual Review of Psychology*. It is not a particularly easy read, but is packed with useful findings and ideas.

3 Jean Hartley's 1992 chapter on the psychology of industrial relations in the *International Review of Industrial and Organizational Psychology* is a good demonstration of how psychological theories can be integrated with other disciplines and applied to wide-ranging social-structural phenomena.

4 Although now quite old, the 1984 article in *American Psychologist* by Daniel Kahneman and Amos Tversky provides a good summary of research on the psychological processes involved in decision making by individuals.

REFERENCES

Aldag, R.J. and Fuller, S.R. (1993) 'Beyond fiasco: a reappraisal of the groupthink phenomenon and a new model of group decision processes', *Psychological Bulletin*, vol. 113, pp. 533–52.

Allen, P.T. and Stephenson, G.M. (1984) 'The relationship of inter-group understanding and inter-party friction in industry', *British Journal of Industrial Relations*, vol. 23, pp. 203–13.

Applebaum, E. and Blatt, R. (1994) *The New American Workplace*. Ithaca, NY: ILR.

Arroba, T.Y. (1978) 'Decision-making style as a function of occupational group, decision content and perceived importance', *Journal of Occupational Psychology*, vol. 51, pp. 219–26.

Barling, J. and Milligan, J. (1987) 'Some psychological consequences of striking: a six month longitudinal study', *Journal of Occupational Behaviour*, vol. 8, pp. 127–38.

Bazerman, M.H., Giuliano, T. and Appelman, A. (1984) 'Escalation of commitment in individual and group decision making', *Organizational Behavior and Human Performance*, vol. 33, pp. 141–52.

Bazerman, M.H., Magliozzi, T. and Neale, M.A. (1985) 'Integrative bargaining in a competitive market', *Organizational Behavior and Human Decision Processes*, vol. 35, pp. 94–313.

Belbin, R.M. (1981) *Management Teams: Why they succeed or fail*. London: Heinemann.

Belbin, R.M. (1993) *Team Roles at Work: A strategy for human resource management*. Oxford: Butterworth-Heinemann.

Carnevale, P.J. and Pruitt, D.G. (1992) 'Negotiation and mediation', *Annual Review of Psychology*, vol. 43, pp. 531–82.

Davis, J.H. (1992) 'Some compelling intuitions about group consensus decisions, theoretical and empirical research, and interpersonal aggregation phenomena: selected examples, 1950–1990', *Organizational Behavior and Human Decision Processes*, vol. 52, pp. 3–38.

Dean, J.W. Jr and Sharfman, M.P. (1996) 'Does decision process matter? A study of strategic decision-making effectiveness', *Academy of Management Journal*, vol. 39, pp. 368–96.

Diehl, M. and Stroebe, W. (1987) 'Productivity loss in brainstorming groups: toward the solution of a riddle', *Journal of Personality and Social Psychology*, vol. 53, pp. 497–509.

DuBrin, A.J. (1994) *Contemporary Applied Management*. 4th edn. Boston, MA: Irwin.

Earley, P.C. (1989) 'Social loafing and collectivism: a comparison of the United States and the People's Republic of China', *Administrative Science Quarterly*, vol. 34, pp. 565–81.

Eisenhardt, K.M. (1989) 'Making fast strategic decisions in high-velocity environments', *Academy of Management Journal*, vol. 32, pp. 543–76.

Eiser, J.R. (1986) *Social Psychology: Attitudes, cognition and social behaviour*. Cambridge: Cambridge University Press.

Erez, M. and Somech, A. (1996) 'Is group productivity loss the rule or the exception? Effects of culture and group-based motivation', *Academy of Management Journal*, vol. 39, pp. 1513–37.

Fagley, N.S. and Miller, P.M. (1987) 'The effects of decision framing on choice of risks vs. certain options', *Organizational Behavior and Human Decision Processes*, vol. 39, pp. 264–77.

Fiegenbaum, A. and Thomas, H. (1988) 'Attitudes toward risk and the risk return paradox: prospect theory explanations', *Academy of Management Journal*, vol. 31, pp. 86–106.

Finkelstein, S. (1992) 'Power in top management teams: dimensions, measurement and validation', *Academy of Management Journal*, vol. 35, pp. 505–38.

Fredrickson, J.W. and Iaquinto, A.L. (1989) 'Inertia and creeping rationality in strategic decision processes', *Academy of Management Journal*, vol. 32, pp. 516–42.

French, J.R.P. and Raven, B. (1959) 'The bases of social power' in Cartwright, D. (ed.) *Studies in Social Power*. Ann Arbor, MI: Institute for Social Research.

Frisch, D. and Clemen, R.T. (1994) 'Beyond expected utility: rethinking behavioral decision research', *Psychological Bulletin*, vol. 116, pp. 46–54.

Furnham, A., Steele, H. and Pendleton, D. (1993) 'A psychometric assessment of the Belbin Team-Role Self-Perception Inventory', *Journal of Occupational and Organizational Psychology*, vol. 66, pp. 245–57.

Gordon, M.E. and Ladd, R.T. (1990) 'Dual allegiance: renewal, reconsideration and recantation', *Personnel Psychology*, vol. 43, pp. 37–69.

Guest, D.E. (1991) 'Personnel management: the end of orthodoxy?', *British Journal of Industrial Relations*, vol. 29, pp. 149–76.

Guest, D.E. and Dewe, P. (1988) 'Why do workers belong to a trade union? A social psychological study in the UK electronics industry', *British Journal of Industrial Relations*, vol. 26, pp. 178–94.

Guzzo, R.A. and Dickson, M.W. (1996) 'Teams in organizations: recent research on performance and effectiveness', *Annual Review of Psychology*, vol. 47, pp. 307–38.

Hackman, J.R. and Morris, C. (1975) 'Group tasks, group interaction process and group performance effectiveness: a review and proposed integration' in Berkowitz, L. (ed.) *Advances in Experimental Social Psychology*, vol. 8. London: Academic Press.

Hamner, W.C. (1974) 'Effects of bargaining strategy and pressure to reach agreement in a stalemated negotiation', *Journal of Personality and Social Psychology*, vol. 30, pp. 458–67.

Hartley, J.F. (1992) 'The psychology of industrial relations' in Cooper, C.L. and Robertson, I.T. (eds) *International Review of Industrial and Organizational Psychology*, vol. 7. Chichester: John Wiley.

Hartley, J.F., Kelly, J.E. and Nicholson, N. (1983) *Steel Strike*. London: Batsford.

Heller, F.A. and Misumi, J. (1987) 'Decision making' in Bass, B., Drenth, P. and Weissenberg, P. (eds) *Advances in Organizational Psychology*. London: Sage.

Heller, F.A., Drenth, P., Koopman, P. and Rus, V. (1988) *Decisions in Organizations: A three-country comparative study*. London: Sage.

Hickson, D., Butler, R., Gray, D., Mallory, G. and Wilson, D. (1986) *Top Decisions: Strategic decision-making in organizations*. Oxford: Basil Blackwell.

Hill, G.W. (1982) 'Group versus individual performance: are N+1 heads better than one?', *Psychological Bulletin*, vol. 91, pp. 517–39.

Hoffman, L.R. and Maier, N.R.F. (1961) 'Quality and acceptance of problem solutions by members of homogeneous and heterogeneous groups', *Journal of Abnormal and Social Psychology*, vol. 62, pp. 401–7.

Hollingshead, A.B. and McGrath, J.E. (1995) 'Computer-assisted groups: a critical review of the empirical research' in Guzzo, R.A. and Salas, E. (eds) *Team Effectiveness and Decision-making in Organizations*. San Francisco, CA: Jossey-Bass.

Hunt, R.G. (1989) 'On the metaphysics of choice, or when decisions aren't' in Cardy, R.L., Puffer, S.M. and Newman, J.M. (eds) *Information Processing and Decision-Making in Organizations*. Greenwich, CT: JAI Press.

International Labour Office (1984) *Collective Bargaining: A response to the recession in industrial market economy countries*. Geneva: ILO.

Isenberg, D.J. (1986) 'Group polarization: a critical review and meta-analysis', *Journal of Personality and Social Psychology*, vol. 50, pp. 1141–51.

Janis, I.L. (1972) *Victims of Groupthink*. Boston, MA: Houghton Mifflin.

Janis, I.L. (1982a) *Groupthink*. Boston, MA: Houghton Mifflin.

Janis, I.L. (1982b) 'Counteracting the adverse effects of concurrence – seeking in policy planning groups: theory and research perspectives' in Brandstatter, H., Davis, J.H. and Stocker-Kreichgauer, G. (eds) *Group Decision Making*. London: Academic Press.

Janis, I.L. and Mann, L. (1977) *Decision-Making: A psychological analysis of conflict, choice and commitment*. New York: Free Press.

Janis, I.L. and Mann, L. (1982) 'A theoretical framework for decision counseling' in Janis, I.L. (ed.) *Counseling on Personal Decisions*. New Haven, CT: Yale University Press.

Kahneman, D. and Tversky, A. (1979) 'Prospect theory: an analysis of decisions under risk', *Econometric*, vol. 47, pp. 263–91.

Kahneman, D. and Tversky, A. (1981) 'The framing of decisions and the psychology of choice', *Science*, vol. 211, pp. 453–8.

Kahneman, D. and Tversky, A. (1984) 'Choices, values and frames', *American Psychologist*, vol. 39, pp. 341–50.

Kandola, R. (1995) 'Managing diversity: new broom or old hat?' in Cooper, C.L. and Robertson, I.T. (eds) *International Review of Industrial and Organizational Psychology*, vol. 10. Chichester: John Wiley, pp. 131–67.

Kelly, C. and Kelly, J.E. (1994) 'Who gets involved in collective action? Social psychological determinants of individual participation in trade unions', *Human Relations*, vol. 47, pp. 63–88.

Kelly, J.E. and Kelly, C. (1991) '"Them and us": social psychology and the "new industrial relations"', *British Journal of Industrial Relations*, vol. 29, pp. 25–48.

Kerr, N.L. and Bruun, S.E. (1983) 'Dispensability of member effort and group motivation losses: free-rider effects', *Journal of Personality and Social Psychology*, vol. 44, pp. 78–94.

Kiesler, C.A. (1971) *The Psychology of Commitment*. New York: Academic Press.

Klandermans, B. (1986) 'Psychology and trade union participation: joining, acting, quitting', *Journal of Occupational Psychology*, vol. 59, pp. 189–204.

Kruglanski, A. and Mackie, D.M. (1989) 'Majority and minority influence: a judgmental process analysis' in Stroebe, W. and Hewstone, M. (eds) *Advances in European Social Psychology*. Chichester: John Wiley.

Lamm, H. and Trommsdorf, G. (1973) 'Group versus individual performance on tasks requiring ideational proficiency (brainstorming)', *European Journal of Social Psychology*, vol. 3, pp. 361–87.

Larson, C.E. and LaFasto, F.M.J. (1989) *Teamwork: What must go right/what can go wrong*. London: Sage.

Latane, B. and Wolf, S. (1981) 'The social impact of majorities and minorities', *Psychological Review*, vol. 88, pp. 438–53.

Latane, B., Williams, K. and Harkins, S. (1979) 'Many hands make light the work: the causes and consequences of social loafing', *Journal of Personality and Social Psychology*, vol. 37, pp. 822–32.

Lewicki, R.J., Weiss, S.E. and Lewin, D. (1992) 'Models of conflict, negotiation and third party intervention: a review and synthesis', *Journal of Organizational Behavior*, vol. 13, pp. 209–52.

Mabey, C. (1986) *Graduates into Industry*. Aldershot: Gower.

Macy, B.A. and Izumi, H. (1993) 'Organizational change, design, and work innovations: a meta-analysis of 131 North American field studies 1961–1991' in Passmore, W. and Woodman, R. (eds) *Research in Organizational Change and Development*, vol. 7. Greenwich, CT: JAI Press, pp. 235–313.

Maier, N.R.F. and Solem, A.R. (1952) 'The contribution of a discussion leader to the quality of group thinking: the effective use of minority opinions', *Human Relations*, vol. 5, pp. 277–88.

Maznevski, M.L. (1994) 'Understanding our differences: performance in decision-making groups with diverse members', *Human Relations*, vol. 47, no. 5, pp. 531–52.

McAllister, D.W., Mitchell, T.R. and Beach, L.R. (1979) 'The contingency model for the selection of decision strategies: an empirical test of the effects of significance, accountability and reversibility', *Organizational Behavior and Human Performance*, vol. 24, pp. 228–44.

McGrath, J.E. (1984) *Groups: Interaction and performance*. Englewood Cliffs, NJ: Prentice Hall.

Mintzberg, H. (1983) *Power in and around Organizations*. Englewood Cliffs, NJ: Prentice Hall.

Mintzberg, H., Raisinghani, D. and Theoret, A. (1976) 'The structure of "unstructured" decision processes', *Administrative Science Quarterly*, vol. 21, pp. 246–75.

Moscovici, S. (1985) 'Social influence and conformity' in Lindzey, G. and Aronson, E. (eds) *The Handbook of Social Psychology*. 3rd edn. New York: Random House.

Moscovici, S. and Mugny, G. (1983) 'Minority influence' in Paulus, P.B. (ed.) *Basic Group Processes*. New York: Springer-Verlag.

Mullen, B. and Copper, C. (1994) 'The relation between group cohesiveness and performance: an integration', *Psychological Bulletin*, vol. 115, pp. 210–27.

Myers, D.G. and Lamm, H. (1976) 'The group polarization phenomenon', *Psychological Bulletin*, vol. 83, pp. 602–27.

Nandram, S.S. and Klandermans, B. (1993) 'Stress experienced by active members of trade unions', *Journal of Organizational Behavior*, vol. 14, pp. 415–32.

Nemeth, C.J. (1986) 'Differential contributions of majority and minority influence', *Psychological Review*, vol. 93, pp. 23–32.

Osborn, A.F. (1957) *Applied Imagination*, rev. edn. New York: Scribner.

Pfeffer, J. (1981) *Power in Organizations*. London: Pitman Publishing.

Pruitt, D.G. (1981) *Negotiation Behavior*. New York: Academic Press.

Pruitt, D.G. and Rubin, J.Z. (1986) *Social Conflict: Escalation, stalemate and settlement*. New York: Random House.

Pruitt, D.G. and Syna, H. (1985) 'Mismatching the opponent's offers in negotiations', *Journal of Experimental Social Psychology*, vol. 21, pp. 103–13.

Rees, W.D. (1984) *The Skills of Management*. Beckenham: Croom Helm.

Sherif, M. (1966) *Group Conflict and Co-operation*. London: Routledge and Kegan Paul.

Shirom, A. and Mayer, A. (1993) 'Stress and strain among union lay officials and rank and file members', *Journal of Organizational Behavior*, vol. 14, pp. 401–14.

Simonson, I. and Staw, B.M. (1992) 'De-escalation strategies: a comparison of techniques for reducing commitment to losing courses of action', *Journal of Applied Psychology*, vol. 77, pp. 419–26.

Singh, J.V. (1986) 'Performance, slack, and risk-taking in organizational decision making', *Academy of Management Journal*, vol. 29, pp. 562–85.

Staw, B.M. (1981) 'The escalation of commitment to a course of action', *Academy of Management Review*, vol. 6, pp. 577–87.

Tajfel, H. (1972) *Differentiation between Social Groups: Studies in the social psychology of intergroup relations*. London: Academic Press.

Thompson, L.L. (1990) 'The influence of experience on negotiation performance', *Journal of Experimental Social Psychology*, vol. 26, pp. 528–44.

Tuckman, B.W. (1965) 'Development sequence in small groups', *Psychological Review*, vol. 63, pp. 384–99.

Tversky, A. and Kahneman, D. (1974) 'Judgement under uncertainty: heuristics and biases', *Science*, vol. 185, pp. 1124–31.

Tversky, A. and Kahneman, D. (1981) 'The framing of decisions and the psychology of choice', *Science*, vol. 211, pp. 453–8.

Tversky, A. and Kahneman, D. (1986) 'Rational choice and the framing of decisions', *Journal of Business*, vol. 59, pp. 251–78.

Van de Vliert, E. and Prein, H.C.M. (1989) 'The difference in the meaning of forcing in the conflict management of actors and observers' in Rahim, M.A. (ed.) *Management Conflict: An interdisciplinary approach*. New York: Praeger.

Vollrath, D.A., Sheppard, B.H., Hinsz, V.B. and Davis, J.H. (1989) 'Memory performance by decision-making groups and individuals', *Organizational Behavior and Human Decision Processes*, vol. 43, pp. 289–300.

Walker, K.F. (1979) 'Psychology and industrial relations: a general perspective' in Stephenson, G.M. and Brotherton, C.J. (eds) *Industrial Relations: A social psychological approach*. Chichester: John Wiley.

Walton, R. and McKersie, R. (1965) *A Behavioral Theory of Labor Negotiations: An analysis of a social interaction system*. New York: McGraw-Hill.

West, M. (1994) *Effective Teamwork*. Leicester: British Psychological Society.

Whyte, G. (1989) 'Groupthink reconsidered', *Academy of Management Review*, vol. 14, pp. 40–56.

Whyte, G. (1993) 'Escalating commitment to individual and group decision making: a prospect theory approach', *Organizational Behavior and Human Decision Processes*, vol. 54, pp. 430–55.

Williams, K., Harkins, S. and Latane, B. (1981) 'Identifiability as a deterrent to social loafing: two cheering experiments', *Journal of Personality and Social Psychology*, vol. 40, pp. 303–11.

Wood, W., Lundgren, S., Ouellette, J.A., Busceme, S. and Blackstone, T. (1994) 'Minority influence: a meta-analytic review of social influence processes', *Psychological Bulletin*, vol. 115, pp. 323–45.

14

Leadership

After studying this chapter, you should be able to:

1 identify various criteria of leader effectiveness;

2 explain why a leader's personality traits do not in themselves ensure good group performance;

3 define consideration and structure;

4 name and define four aspects of transformational leadership and two aspects of transactional leadership;

5 define the key concepts and propositions of Fiedler's contingency theory of leadership;

6 define the key concepts and propositions of Fiedler's cognitive resource theory of leadership;

7 name and define five leader styles varying in participativeness, and ten features of the problem situation, identified by Vroom and Jago in their theory of leadership;

8 describe how concepts of leadership held by subordinates and in society generally give an alternative perspective on leadership;

9 explain why effective leader behaviour may differ between countries and cultures.

INTRODUCTION

Leadership is a topic of great importance to people who are leaders, who aspire to be leaders, or who are on the receiving end of leadership. That includes nearly everybody in work! This chapter examines what leaders in the workplace are like, what they do, and what they *should* do in order to be effective. It also looks at the different kinds of situation facing leaders, the various strategies leaders can adopt, and the relationships between leaders and followers. It ends with a discussion of whether the concept of leadership is, in fact, helpful. The main aim throughout is to show the reader the essential factors in effective leadership, in so far as they can be identified. No current approach to leadership is substantially better than all of the others, but several approaches offer useful insights. These are, however, usually confined to advising the leader *what* to do, and have less to say about how to do it *well*. Aspects of that latter issue tend to crop up more in motivation (*see* Chapter 11) and group decision making (*see* Chapter 13). This is not surprising, since much of leadership is ultimately about motivating and deciding.

SOME IMPORTANT QUESTIONS ABOUT LEADERSHIP

A leader can be defined as the 'person who is appointed, elected, or informally chosen to direct and co-ordinate the work of others in a group' (Fiedler, 1995, p. 7). This definition acknowledges the important truth that the formally appointed leader is not always the real leader. But it also confines the notion of leader to a group context. If we take the word 'group' literally, this definition excludes leaders of nations, large corporations and so on, except in so far as they lead a small group of senior colleagues. Nevertheless, psychologists have also taken an interest in top leaders of organisations and nations.

So much for the leader. Leader*ship* can be considered to be the personal qualities, behaviours, styles and decisions adopted by the leader. In other words, it concerns how the leader carries out his or her role. Hence while the role of leader can be described in a job description, leader*ship* is not so easily pinned down.

> ■ **KEY LEARNING POINT**
> *The real leader of a group may not be the person who was formally appointed to the role.*

Over the years several distinct but related questions have been asked about leaders and leadership. These include:

- who becomes a leader?
- how do leaders differ from other people?
- how can we describe their leadership?

It is in fact difficult to consider these questions without bringing in the notion of effectiveness. So we can also ask:

- what are effective leaders like?
- how do effective leaders differ from ineffective ones?
- what characteristics of situations help and hinder a leader's effectiveness?

At this point it is worth pausing to consider how we can tell whether or not a leader is effective. The most obvious method is to assess the performance of his or her group relative to other similar groups with different leaders. Quite apart from the assumption that such comparison groups will be available, there is also the problem that performance is often determined by many things other than leadership. The reader can probably think of several straight away. Sometimes grievance rates against the leader, and/or group members' satisfaction with the leader, have been used as a measure of leader effectiveness. But who is to say that, for example, low grievance rates are a good thing? Perhaps a group needs 'shaking up', and it could be argued that a good leader should ruffle a few feathers. Similar considerations apply to voluntary turnover among group members as a measure of leader effectiveness. In short, there is no perfect measure of leader effectiveness. Group performance is used most often, probably correctly. But we must remember not to expect an especially strong association with leadership: too many other factors come into play.

> ■ **KEY LEARNING POINT**
> *There is no one perfect indicator of leadership effectiveness.*

In recent years further questions about leadership have been raised. When and why is leadership seen as being important? How do leaders come to be perceived as such? These two questions emphasise that leadership is an interpersonal issue as well as a personal one. The social psychology of relationships between pairs of people, and within groups, is seen as crucial. There is also a perception that theories which concentrate on leader effectiveness have tended to neglect adequate description of interactions between leader and subordinates. Hence this more recent approach is to some extent returning to a descriptive rather than an evaluative orientation. However, its sophistication ensures that it does not simply cover old ground.

LEADER-FOCUSED APPROACHES TO LEADERSHIP

It seems reasonable to look for the simple before resorting to the complex. This has indeed been the case in leadership research. Most theory and practice up to the 1960s, and plenty since then, has had two key features:

1 description of the leader rather than the dynamics of the leader's relationship with subordinates;

2 attempts to identify the characteristics/behaviour of a 'good leader' regardless of the situation.

Leader characteristics

Some early work (reviewed by Stogdill, 1974; House and Baetz, 1979) found that leaders tended to be higher than non-leaders on:

- intelligence
- dominance/need for power
- self-confidence
- energy/persistence
- knowledge of the task.

Many other personality characteristics (for example adjustment, extroversion) have also been found in some studies to be more characteristic of leaders than non-leaders. In addition, intelligence and sociability seem characteristic of emergent (as opposed to appointed) leaders. Characteristics which help leaders to reach the top may subsequently prove their undoing. For example, a high level of dominance and need for *personal* power (as opposed to power exercised on behalf of others) may prevent a leader maintaining good relationships with his or her team or superiors, and this may precipitate his or her removal (Conger, 1990).

Most writers (*see*, for example, Yetton, 1984) used to assert that there was little conclusive evidence for an association between specific characteristics and leadership, let alone *effective* leadership. House and Baetz (1979) were, however, more optimistic. They point out that many of the early studies which produced inconclusive findings involved leadership in children's groups. Research with adults has produced more clear-cut results. They argue that the very nature of the leadership role must mean that sociability, need for power and need for achievement are relevant. However, House and Baetz also acknowledge two insights which are nowadays accepted by many people involved in leadership:

1 a leader's personal characteristics must be expressed in his or her *behaviour* if those characteristics are to have an impact on performance;
2 different types of tasks will require somewhat different leader characteristics and behaviours.

Of course, one of the most obvious and difficult-to-change personal characteristics is one's gender. It can be argued that most leadership roles are typically described in stereotypically masculine terms, which might mean that women have more difficulty in being selected for them, and being seen as good leaders when they are. On the other hand, one might expect women to do better precisely because only the most able ones make it to leadership roles. In a meta-analysis of 96 studies, Eagly *et al.* (1995) found no overall difference in leadership performance between men and women. However, men had an advantage in military and outdoor pursuits (ie. stereotypically masculine settings), while there was no difference or a slight advantage for women in business, education and government settings.

> ■ **KEY LEARNING POINT**
> *Personality characteristics in themselves do not make leaders effectove. What matters is how those characteristics are expressed in their behaviour.*

Task orientation and person orientation

In the 1950s, attention turned from leader traits to leader behaviours. Just as traits had been assumed to be quite stable, so were leader behavioural styles. One research team at Ohio State University and another at Michigan University launched major projects on leadership. They worked more or less independently of each other, and approached the task in opposite directions. The Ohio group sought to uncover the central features of leader behaviour by asking subordinates, and to a lesser extent leaders themselves, to describe the leader's behaviour. From an initial list of almost 2000 questions, ten dimensions of leader behaviour were identified. It was then discovered that two more general dimensions underlay the ten. These two have consistently emerged in subsequent work, and have been described as follows (Fleishman, 1969):

1 *consideration*: the extent to which a leader demonstrates trust of subordinates, respect for their ideas, and consideration of their feelings;

2 *structure*: the extent to which a leader defines and structures his or her own role and those of subordinates toward goal attainment. The leader actively directs group activities through planning, communicating information, scheduling, criticising and trying out new ideas.

The Michigan team started by classifying leaders as effective or ineffective. They then looked for behaviours which distinguished between the two groups. One distinction was that effective managers seemed concerned about their subordinates whereas ineffective ones were concerned only with the task. Clearly this bears considerable resemblance to the distinction between consideration and structure described above. It seemed that consideration was a good thing, and structure a bad one if it was not accompanied by consideration. Blake and Mouton's (1964) much-used Managerial Grid encourages leaders to examine their own style on these two dimensions. It assumes that leaders can be high on both, low on both or high on one and low on the other. Blake and Mouton proposed that it is best to be high on both.

How realistic is all this? It seems that leaders see consideration and structure as quite separate when describing their own behaviour. However, subordinates tend to report that their leader is *either* person-orientated *or* task-orientated, not both (Weissenburg and Kavanagh, 1972). Research suggests that in many situations a certain level of consideration is essential for maintenance of satisfactory relations between leader and group. However, where group performance is the outcome measure, it is far from clear whether consideration and structure are always good, bad or indifferent.

■ **KEY LEARNING POINT**

Consideration and structure are useful concepts which have stood the test of time in analysing leader behaviour.

Participation and democracy

Another dimension of behavioural style which has received much attention is participativeness. This concerns the extent to which the leader is democratic or autocratic. It is clearly related to the dimensions already discussed, but arguably not identical. For example, the definition of structure given earlier does not necessarily exclude subordinates from influencing the direction given by the leader. Gastil (1994) has discussed the nature of democratic leadership, and made the general point that it is certainly not just a case of letting the subordinates get on with their work. According to Gastil, the three key elements of democratic leadership are:

1 *distributing responsibility*: ensuring maximum involvement and participation of every group member in group activities and setting of objectives;

2 *empowerment*: giving responsibility to group members, setting high but realistic goals, offering instruction but avoiding playing the role of the 'great man'. Keller and Dansereau (1995) have found that use of empowerment by leaders can both help them get the performance they want from subordinates and increase subordinates' satisfaction with their leadership;

3 *aiding deliberation*: by playing an active part in the definition and solution of group problems, without dictating solutions.

In the aftermath of the Second World War it was hoped and believed that democratic or participative leadership was superior to autocratic. In fact, the evidence is that on the whole participation has only a small positive effect on performance and satisfaction of group members (Wagner, 1994). As Filley *et al.* (1976) observed, where the job to be done is clearly understood by subordinates, and within their competence, participation is not going to make much difference because there is little need for it. On the other hand, in many less straightforward situations, participation does aid group performance. We will return to that theme later in this chapter.

> ■ **KEY LEARNING POINT**
> *A democratic leader is active in group affairs: he or she does not just sit back and let the rest of the group sort everything out.*

Charisma and transformational leadership

Much of the early research on leadership viewed the leader as a strategist, not as an inspirational figure. Yet real leaders in business and politics (not to mention fictional leaders in films and literature) are frequently portrayed as heroes and heroines. They unite and motivate their followers by offering shared visions and goals usually based on a better tomorrow. Leaders deemed to be non-charismatic (for example, former American president George Bush and former British prime minister John Major) are often seen as lacking what it takes, though of course that did not prevent their rise to the top. Psychologists have therefore turned their attention to charisma and related concepts.

A currently influential approach to leadership makes a distinction between so-called transactional and transformational leadership (Burns, 1978). *Transactional* leaders try to motivate subordinates by observing their performance, identifying the rewards they desire and distributing rewards for appropriate behaviour. Komaki *et al.* (1986) have analysed in detail some of the leader behaviours involved in transactional leadership, though they did not use that label. *Transformational* leaders, on the other hand, go beyond the skilled use of inducements by developing, inspiring and challenging the intellects of followers in order to go beyond their self-interest in the service of a higher collective purpose, mission or vision. Leaders encourage this by setting a personal example (Bass, 1990).

Bass (1985) has developed a questionnaire called the Multifactor Leadership Questionnaire (MLQ) to assess the extent to which subordinates feel that their leader exhibits transformational and transactional leadership. Questions in the MLQ assess four components of transformational leadership, two of transactional leadership and also a 'laissez-faire' (i.e. do nothing) approach to leadership. Transformational and transactional leadership are described in Table 14.1.

These two forms of leadership are not entirely mutually exclusive: leaders are not necessarily one or the other – or indeed either! Needless to say, research has been done, and is being done, to evaluate whether transforming leaders exist, and if so whether they really do get better results. It has been shown that transformational leadership is not confined to the top levels of organisations. There is also evidence that leaders who use transformational leadership are viewed more positively by their subordinates than those who do not. The same is true of transactional leadership, but to a lesser extent. Leaders who use transformational techniques seem to be more successful in their own careers (Hater and Bass, 1988).

A summary of relevant research by Bryman (1992) suggests that idealised influence (i.e. charismatic leadership) and inspirational motivation seem to be the components of transformational leadership which have the greatest impact on work performance and effort. Contingent reward, which is an aspect of transactional leadership, is also associated with positive outcomes. The non-interventionist strategies of laissez-faire and

Table 14.1 Components of transformational and transactional leadership

The four components of transformational leadership

1 *Individualized consideration*: the leader treats each follower on his or her own merits, and seeks to develop followers through delegation of projects and coaching/mentoring

2 *Intellectual stimulation*: the leader encourages free thinking, and emphasises reasoning before any action is taken

3 *Inspirational motivation*: the leader creates an optimistic, clear and attainable vision of the future, thus encouraging others to raise their expectations

4 *Idealised influence, or charisma*: the leader makes personal sacrifices, takes responsibility for his or her actions, shares any glory and shows great determination

The two components of transactional leadership

1 *Contingent reward*: the leader provides rewards if, and only if, subordinates perform adequately and/or try hard enough

2 *Management by exception*: the leader does not seek to change the existing working methods of subordinates so long as performance goals are met. He or she intervenes only if something is wrong. This can be active, where the leader monitors the situation to anticipate problems, or passive, where the leader does nothing until a problem or mistake has actually occurred

passive management by exception generally produce poor results. But of course that is not the whole story. Contingent reward can be negatively correlated with desired outcomes, and the impact of transformational leadership depends at least partly on subordinates' support for the general idea of seeking new ways of doing and seeing things (Howell and Avolio, 1993).

So the distinction between transactional and transformational leadership looks like an important one. More evidence is needed on just how useful transformational leadership is, how it works, and whether leaders can be trained to use it. But it looks as though it matters. Even in our sophisticated modern world (perhaps *especially* in our sophisticated modern world) we need a leader we can believe in.

> ■ KEY LEARNING POINT
> *Transformational leadership is about inspiring and challenging subordinates and setting a personal example. It is often successful in eliciting high group performance.*

American psychologist Robert House has conducted research specifically on charisma (House, 1977; House *et al.*, 1991). House defines charisma as the ability of a leader to exercise diffuse and intense influence over the beliefs, values, behaviour and performance of others through his or her own behaviour, beliefs and personal example. He argues that although charisma is defined as a relationship between leader and followers, it is partly a function of the leader's personality, particularly need for power (*see also* Chapter 11).

House *et al.* (1991) conducted an interesting study of presidents of the USA right back to George Washington, in which aspects of their charisma were related to their personality and to their success as president. Personality was measured by rating material such as speeches by the presidents and biographies of them for signs of motives like need for power. Charisma was assessed with similar material, rated for features such as strong ideological conviction, high expectations of followers, showing confidence in subordinates and extra involvement/effort on the part of subordinates. House *et al.* called these *behavioural charisma*. Another assessment of charisma was derived from newspaper editorials (*editorial charisma*) about them immediately after their election. Presidential performance was measured in several ways, including ratings by historians and analyses of specific presidential actions and their consequences for international relations, economic performance and social issues. As House *et al.* expected, a president's need for power predicted his charisma, and his charisma predicted his performance. The link between charisma and performance occurred for both behavioural and editorial charisma.

Despite the very thorough and ingenious ways in which House *et al.* conducted their study, there must be some suspicion that they were reflecting observers' interpretations and accounts of presidential behaviour based on the observers' implicit theories of leadership (*see* Chapter 12; *see also* 'Perceiving leadership', below). Nevertheless, taken at face value their results provide a powerful confirmation that a leader's charisma does matter. They also help to extend psychologists' studies of leadership well beyond small workgroups to whole nations.

CASE
STUDY
14.1

Transactional and tranformational leadership

Marc LeBlanc is manager of the claims department of a medical insurance company. The department's job is to process claims by clients who have spent time in hospital. Marc considers himself scrupulously fair with his staff of 17 administrative and clerical staff. He thinks that if something (such as a training course) is good for one of them, then it is good for all. He has successfully resisted senior management's wish for performance-related pay, arguing that group solidarity will ensure that everyone pulls their weight. Marc thinks of his job as making sure that the members of the department know where it is going and why. In contrast to his predecessor, he never tires of telling his staff that their job is to 'play a proper part in the client's return to good health' rather than contest every doubt, however tiny, about a client's claim. He has a noticeboard for displaying complimentary letters from clients grateful for prompt and trouble-free processing of their claims. He frequently emphasises the need to look at things from the client's point of view. He tells his staff to focus on certain key aspects of the long and complicated claim form, and only briefly inspect most of the rest of it. Marc checks on whether they are doing this, but only when a complaint is received from a client or the company's own internal claims auditors. In such cases he defends his staff, provided they have conformed to the department's way of doing things. He is less sympathetic if they have taken decisions about claims on other criteria, even if those claims have some unusual features.

Suggested exercises

1 *Marc LeBlanc scores high on just one aspect of transformational leadership. Which one?*

2 *He scores high on one aspect of transactional leadership. Which one?*

3 *The performance of the claims department could be measured with more than one criterion. Think of one respect in which Marc's style* enhances *the department's performance, and one respect in which his style* hinders *performance.*

FROM LEADER-FOCUSED APPROACHES TO CONTINGENCY THEORIES

The above approaches to leader behaviour vary in their sophistication. They have all left their mark, and each contributes something to our understanding of what leaders actually do and what it is best for them to do. In their original forms they have an important feature in common. They all seek to describe leader behaviour without considering the wider context. In essence, they are stating that in order to be effective, leaders need to perform certain behaviours and do so whatever the situation.

In fact, concepts like consideration, structure, participation, and transactional and transformational leadership can all be used more flexibly. Indeed, some of them have been. The key idea is that some situations demand one kind of behaviour from leaders, while other situations require other behaviours. Do we really need a leader high on consideration and low on structure in an emergency such as a bomb scare? Probably not – we need someone who will quickly tell us where to go, and what to do. We can do without a leader who asks us, at that moment, how we feel about the bomb scare.

On the other hand, if a leader is responsible for allocating already well-defined tasks to a group of junior managers, we might hope for some sensitive consideration of the managers' preferences, career development plans etc.

This brings us to contingency theories; so-called because they assume that optimal leader behaviour is contingent upon (i.e. depends upon) the situation. Contingency theories are necessarily fairly complex and they reflect very clearly the different elements of psychological theory described in Chapter 3. Their task is not easy. They have to specify not only which leader behaviours are crucial, but also which aspects of the situation matter most, and how leader and situation interact. Needless to say, there is plenty of room for disagreement about this. We will now take a look at the most influential and controversial contingency theories.

> ■ KEY LEARNING POINT
>
> *Contingency theories of leadership propose that different situations demand different leader behaviours.*

Fiedler's contingency theory of leadership

Fred Fiedler put forward his first theory of leadership in the 1960s (Fiedler, 1967). He built his theory from data collected over the previous decade. Fiedler argued that leaders have fairly stable personal characteristics which in turn lead to a characteristic style which they (and their subordinates) are stuck with. For Fiedler, the key personal characteristic concerns how positively the leader views his or her *least preferred co-worker*. He has developed a questionnaire measure of this concept called LPC (which stands for least preferred co-worker). The measure consists of sixteen dimensions, such as pleasant–unpleasant, boring–interesting and insincere–sincere. The leader describes his or her least preferred co-worker on these dimensions. A high LPC score signifies a positive view of the least preferred co-worker. A low LPC score indicates a negative opinion.

There is some dispute about exactly what a leader's LPC score means. It could be quite similar to consideration (high LPC) and structure (low LPC), though this assumes that consideration and structure are opposite ends of the same continuum rather than independent constructs. Indeed, high LPC leaders are often referred to as person-orientated – after all, they must be if they can be nice even about people they do not like! Low LPC leaders are often thought of as task-orientated. There is no doubt considerable overlap between LPC on the one hand and consideration and structure on the other. But Fiedler and others have argued that LPC also reflects the leader's deeper pattern of motivation. Some have suggested that LPC involves cognitive complexity. High LPC leaders are sometimes said to be more cognitively complex than low LPC leaders because they can differentiate between a person's inherent worth and his or her work performance.

> ■ KEY LEARNING POINT
>
> *Fiedler assumes that a leader's perception of his or her least preferred co-worker indicates how person-orientated the leader is.*

Whatever LPC is, Fiedler argued that in some situations it is best to have a high LPC leader at the helm, while in others a low LPC leader is preferable. Specifically, Fiedler proposed three key aspects of the situation which together define its favourableness to the leader. In descending order of importance, these are:

1 *leader–member relations*: whether or not the subordinates trust and like their leader;
2 *task structure*: the extent to which the group's tasks, goals and performance are clearly defined;
3 *position power*: the extent to which the leader controls rewards and punishments for subordinates.

If we divide each of these three into high and low, we arrive at $2 \times 2 \times 2 = 8$ types of situation. The most favourable is where leader–member relations are good, and task structure and position power are high. The least favourable is where leader–member relations are poor, and task structure and position power are low.

The key features of Fiedler's theory are shown in Table 14.2. From his early data, he concluded that in highly and fairly favourable situations, and in very unfavourable ones, group performance was better if the leader had a low LPC score (i.e. was task-orientated). In situations of moderate to low favourability, high LPC scores were best (i.e. person-orientated).

It is not altogether clear why this should be. One common-sense explanation is, however, plausible. Where the situation is good, the leader does not *need* to spend time on interpersonal relationships. Where the situation is bad, things are so difficult that it is not *worth* spending time on interpersonal relationships. In both cases, forging ahead with the task is best. But where the situation falls between the two extremes, keeping group members happy becomes more important. A leader needs high LPC to hold the group together so that its tasks can be tackled. One problem with this explanation arises from its emphasis on leader–member relations. Inspection of Table 14.2 shows that the switch from low LPC to high LPC occurs between situations III and IV, in both of which leader–member relations are good.

Table 14.2 Fiedler's Theory of Leadership

	Situation highly favourable I	II	III	IV	V	VI	VII	Situation highly unfavourable VIII
Leader–member relations	Good	Good	Good	Good	Poor	Poor	Poor	Poor
Task structure	Structured	Structured	Unstructured	Unstructured	Structured	Structured	Unstructured	Unstructured
Leader position power	Strong	Weak	Strong	Weak	Strong	Weak	Strong	Weak
Desirable leader LPC score	Low	Low	Low	High	High	High	High	Low

Fiedler's theory asserts that because leaders have a fairly stable LPC score, there is little point trying to train them to cope with different situations. They cannot change their style. Instead, he has argued (Fiedler and Chemers, 1984) that it is important to match leader to situation. Placement is more useful than training. So if you are a high LPC leader, you cannot expect to be placed in the most favourable leadership situations!

> ### ■ KEY LEARNING POINT
> *Fiedler proposes that task-orientated leaders are best in very favourable and unfavourable situations, and that people-orientated leaders are best in moderately favourable or moderately unfavourable situations.*

Many problems with Fiedler's theory have been pointed out. Apart from the unclear nature of LPC, there is doubt about whether the LPC score is as stable as Fiedler assumes. Perhaps it depends too much on just how undesirable the leader's least preferred co-worker really is – that is, the LPC score may say more about the co-worker than the leader. Another issue concerns Fiedler's concept of the situation. For example, in the medium and long term, leader–member relations are perhaps a function of the leader and subordinates themselves. Is it therefore valid to treat leader–member relations as part of the situation? This has important implications. Suppose for a moment that a leader and group find themselves in situation V (*see* Table 14.2). If they succeed in improving their relationship, the situation becomes I. This in turn would mean that a different kind of leader is required. Would moving the leader to another group be an appropriate reward for the improvement in leader–member relations? Surely not.

Despite these doubts, it is clear that Fiedler is on to something. Peters *et al.* (1985) report a thorough meta-analysis of tests of Fiedler's theory. They observe that the data on which the theory was originally based support it very well. Hence the theory was appropriately constructed given the data then available. Subsequent research testing the theory gives it partial support. Laboratory-based studies have produced results more consistent with the theory than field studies. Situation II seems to be a particular problem because some research has found that a high LPC score is best, rather than a low one. Peters *et al.* (1985) conclude that the theory fits moderately well with research data, but more features of the situation probably need to be taken into account. For example, Bryman *et al.* (1987) suggest organisational transience. In a study of construction sites, they found that low LPC leaders were an advantage on short-term sites, but not on longer-term ones. The longer a team is together, the more person-orientation is needed. Schriesheim *et al.* (1994) reviewed only the research studies which compared leader performance in different situations. They too found general support for Fiedler, but with some caveats. Low LPC leaders did better in the two most favourable situations and the one least favourable one. High and low LPC leaders were about equal in the third most favourable situation. High LPC leaders did better in situations IV to VII (*see* Table 14.2), and their advantage in situations V and VI was enormous. The authors point out that if we assume that most leadership situations are moderately favourable, we can simply say that high LPC leaders are better, rather than going to the trouble of engineering situations to fit different leader styles.

Cognitive resource theory

Fiedler himself has built on his earlier work (e.g. Fiedler and Garcia, 1987). His more recent *cognitive resource theory* (CRT) examines how the cognitive resources of leaders and subordinates affect group performance. As Fiedler (1995, p. 7) has put it:

> the relationship between cognitive resources and leadership performance is strongly dependent on such factors as the leader's situational control over the group's processes and outcomes, and the stressfulness of the leadership situation.

The reference to situational control demonstrates the links between CRT and Fiedler's earlier contingency theory, since situational control is presumably determined by leader–member relations, position power and task structure. The stressfulness of the situation is also partly tied up with this: less favourable situations are presumably more stressful. But Fiedler (1995) also sees stress as coming from the leader's own boss, if he or she is unsupportive, hostile or over-demanding.

Some of the key predictions of CRT are shown in Fig. 14.1. Fiedler argues that cognitive performance is inhibited in high-stress situations. That is, when leaders feel anxious or overloaded, they are unable to think clearly. In difficult situations they are likely to fall back on well-learned patterns of behaviour which result from their experience. Hence, in high-stress situations experience is a more important attribute of leaders than intelligence – indeed, high intelligence seems actually to be a small *dis*advantage.

■ **KEY LEARNING POINT**

Fiedler's cognitive resource theory introduces new factors about the leader and the situation. It proposes that, in difficult situations, leaders use their experience rather than their intelligence.

Fig. 14.1 Predictions of leader performance in Fiedler's cognitive resource theory

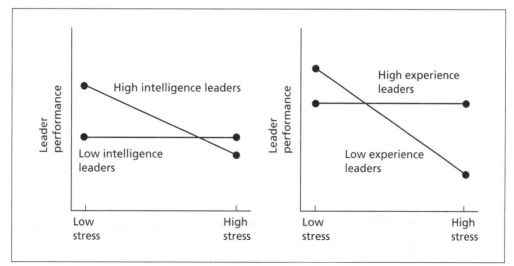

Sternberg (1995) makes the point that experience is in fact a disguised measure of so-called crystallised intelligence; that is, our store of know-how and knowledge about the world. This contrasts with fluid intelligence, which is relatively context-free logic and problem solving, and which is essentially what Fiedler is referring to when he uses the word intelligence. When a lot of our cognitive resources are being used in coping with a difficult situation, we use 'automatic' behaviour, which we can do without having to think. That behaviour is more likely to be appropriate if it is based on long experience.

Not all psychologists are very convinced by CRT. Vecchio (1990, 1992) has argued that there is not much support for it, but Fiedler et al. (1992) claim that this is because it has not been tested properly. Fiedler (1995) reports a number of studies consistent with his predictions, and most of the commentators on his article (in the same issue of the journal *Applied Psychology: An International Review*) do not challenge them fundamentally.

Thus, Fiedler is now introducing more characteristics of the leader over and above LPC. As he points out, experience and intelligence are often key criteria in selecting leaders. His recent work suggests that the concept of matching leader to situation must be based on the leader's intelligence and experience as well as LPC and situational characteristics. Stress-reduction programmes are now thought to have a role in helping leaders to utilise their cognitive resources. But one important practical implication of Fiedler's work remains the same: try to determine the characteristics of the situation you are selecting a leader for, and thereby specify the characteristics you most desire in the leader.

CASE STUDY 14.2

Using Fiedler's theories of leadership

For the last year, Debbie Walsh has been head of the ten staff of the market analysis department of a garden furniture company. The company sells its produce through selected garden centres and do-it-yourself shops. The department's tasks are well established. For example, it monitors sales of each product at each outlet. It evaluates the viability of potential alternative outlets. It checks the products and prices of competitors. Debbie is a 'high-flyer' academically, having obtained a first-class honours degree and an MBA with Distinction. The managing director has great faith in her, and has given her complete discretion over awarding salary increases to her staff and most other aspects of people management in the marketing department. This is Debbie's first marketing job: most of her previous four years' work experience were spent in general management at a knitwear company. Other staff do not resent Debbie. They feel her appointment demonstrates the truth of the company's pledge to put ability ahead of experience in promotion decisions. They may in future benefit from that policy themselves, since most of them are young and well qualified. Debbie takes a 'no-nonsense' approach to her work and colleagues. She responds well to businesslike people who come straight to the point. She has little patience with those who are slower to get to the heart of a problem, or who do not share her objectives. Most of her present staff have a similar approach to hers. But in one of Debbie's previous jobs her hostility toward several slow and awkward colleagues was a major factor in her decision to leave.

Suggested exercises

1 *Which of Fiedler's eight situation types is portrayed here?*

2 *Using Fiedler's contingency and cognitive resources theories, decide whether Debbie is well suited to her situation.*

Vroom and Jago's theory of leader decision making

Vroom and Yetton (1973) proposed a contingency theory of leader decision making. This has been updated and extended by Vroom and Jago (1988). Contrary to Fiedler, they suggest that leaders are perfectly capable of changing their behaviour from situation to situation. Certainly, most leaders say they do. The theory identifies five styles of leader decision making, ranging from the most autocratic to the most democratic (*see also* 'Participation and democracy', above). These are:

- AI: the leader decides what to do, using information already available;
- AII: the leader obtains required information from subordinates, and then makes the decision himself or herself. The leader may or may not tell the subordinates what the problem is;
- CI: the leader shares the problem with each subordinate individually, and obtains their ideas. The leader then makes the decision;
- CII: the leader shares the problem with subordinates as a group, and obtains their ideas. The leader then makes the decision;
- GII: the leader shares the problem with subordinates as a group. They discuss alternatives together and try to reach collective agreement. The leader accepts any decision supported by the group as a whole.

Vroom and Jago (1988) have also identified some key features of problem situations that leaders should consider. Taken together, these features indicate the style a leader should adopt in that particular situation. The situational features are shown in Fig. 14.2.

Also, Vroom and Jago (1988) argue that two further factors are relevant if the situational factors shown in Fig. 14.2 allow more than one recommended style. These are the importance to the leader of (i) minimising decision time and (ii) maximising opportunities for subordinate development. Computer software has been developed which allows a leader to input his or her answers to the questions listed above, and then calculates an overall 'suitability score' for each possible style. The formulae used are too complex to examine here, but some general rules of thumb governing use of the leader styles in the Vroom and Jago model include the following:

- where subordinates' commitment is important, more participative styles are better;
- where the leader needs more information, AI should be avoided;
- where subordinates do not share organisational goals, GII should be avoided;
- where both problem structure and leader information are low, CII and GII tend to be best.

It should, however, be apparent that, in some cases, other factors, such as time constraints or staff development needs, can override these rules of thumb.

> ■ **KEY LEARNING POINT**
> *Vroom and Jago assume that leaders are able to alter their style to fit the decision-making situation they are in. The nature of the situation is determined by many factors identified by Vroom and Jago.*

Fig. 14.2 Vroom and Jago's features of leadership situations

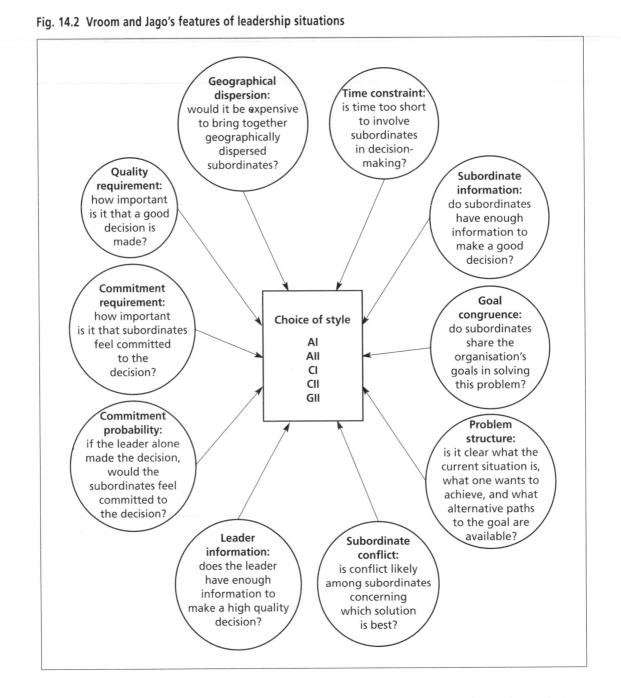

There is some evidence that the skill with which the leader puts his or her style into action is at least as important as choosing a style deemed appropriate in the first place (Tjosvold *et al.*, 1986). The Vroom and Jago model has not been examined much in published literature, but looks promising. It is based on fifteen years of research and development by its originator and on an earlier version of the model, so it should have considerable value. On the other hand, its complexity makes it difficult for leaders to use quickly and easily, even with computer support. Vroom and Jago (1988) have expressed the hope that knowledge of its general principles, including those presented here, will often be sufficient.

Other contingency approaches: is a leader really necessary?

In their Situational Leadership Theory (SLT), Hersey and Blanchard (1982) have argued that leader effectiveness depends on the interplay between leader style and follower maturity. They considered two leader styles: relationship orientation and task orientation. These are more or less equivalent to consideration and structure, respectively. Follower maturity refers to the subordinates' understanding of the job and commitment to it, but length of time in the job is often used to measure it.

Vecchio has explained the theory as follows (1987, p. 444):

> During the early stages of an employee's tenure, a low level of relationship orientation coupled with high task orientation is considered to be ideal. As an employee (or group of employees) gains in maturity, the need for supervisory social–emotional support increases, while the need for structuring declines. At the highest levels of employee maturity, supervisory task and social behaviours become superfluous to effective employee performance.

In other words, employees first need to be introduced to their tasks. Then as they are coping with tasks they need sympathetic help and advice. After that they should have come to grips with both task and social relationships, and are best left to get on with it.

Vecchio (1987) declared that SLT is much used by managers but rarely tested. He found that among 303 teachers in America, the theory's predictions were fairly accurate for subordinates with low maturity, reasonably accurate for those with moderate maturity, and not at all accurate for those with high maturity. His measure of maturity was school principals' ratings of teachers' task-relevant and psychological maturity.

Perhaps the crucial message of Vecchio's results is that even when subordinates are mature, it is not a good idea for their leader to neglect both task and relationships. This rather argues against an extension of SLT principles proposed by Kerr and Jermier (1978). They developed the idea that in some circumstances leaders are unnecessary. Their approach has been termed *substitutes for leadership*, though it also includes the notion that some factors can neutralise the impact of leadership (as opposed to substitutes, which do the leadership job for the leader). Examples of proposed substitutes for leadership are: intrinsically interesting tasks; ability, experience, training and knowledge of subordinates; and availability of senior staff other than subordinates' own leader.

Consistent with Vecchio (1987), research has tended to find that the presence of substitutes for leadership does not eliminate effects of leadership style on subordinate satisfaction and performance. This may be partly because measures of substitutes for leadership are not very good (Williams *et al.*, 1988). However, it is hard to escape the conclusion that leadership *does* matter. The apparent lack of efficacy of substitutes for leadership suggests either that leadership tasks cannot easily be distributed around a group, or that we have an in-built psychological need for a leader. We now turn to further consideration of that latter possibility.

PERCEIVING LEADERSHIP

In recent years increasing attention has been paid to how and when we perceive leadership to be important. A related issue is how we identify someone as leader. Many of the principles of person perception apply here (*see* Chapter 12).

In an article appropriately entitled 'The romance of leadership', Meindl *et al.* (1985, p. 79) argued that:

> we may have developed highly romanticized, heroic views of leadership – what leaders do, what they are able to accomplish, and the general effects they have on our lives. One of the principal elements in this romanticized conception is the view that leadership is ... the premier force in the scheme of organizational processes and activities.

Meindl *et al.* (1985) further argued that our conception of leadership as important and influential should lead us to consider leadership a key factor where performance is *either* very good *or* very bad. When things go really well, we attribute it to the leader's skill. When things go really badly, we blame the leader's ineptitude. But when things go averagely well, we are unlikely to say it was primarily due to average leadership. This is because we see leadership as a big concept which has big effects, not moderate ones.

Meindl *et al.* (1985) produced support for their point of view in a number of interesting ways. First, they searched the *Wall Street Journal* (WSJ) between 1972 and 1982 for articles about 34 firms representing a range of American industries. They then related the proportion of WSJ articles about each company which mentioned the leadership of top management to the company's performance. Sure enough, they found that a higher proportion of 'leadership' articles appeared when firms were doing especially well or especially badly – particularly the former. Second, they surveyed dissertations by postgraduate students and related that to overall American economic performance. Increasing numbers of dissertations about leadership were associated with *downturns* in the USA economy two to four years earlier (it usually takes two to four years to produce a dissertation). Third, they conducted a similar analysis with business journals, where the articles generally take less time to produce than dissertations. In this case *upturns* in the USA economy were associated with increasing numbers of articles about leadership. Perhaps academics want to understand what goes wrong whereas business people want to understand (and presumably copy) what goes right. Finally, Meindl *et al.* conducted a series of laboratory experiments where case studies of corporate success and failure were presented, and students were asked to rate the importance of various possible causes, including leadership. Again, leadership was seen as a more important cause of extreme (especially good) performance than of medium performance. Alternative causes were generally seen as less important than leadership, and at a fairly constant level of importance across the range of performance outcomes. Pillai and Meindl (1991) expanded on this by finding that the charisma of the chief executive officer in a hypothetical case study of a fast food company was indeed very high if the case described a crisis followed by success for the company, and very low if the crisis was followed by decline.

Gemmill and Oakley (1992) have argued that leadership is indeed a culturally defined concept which has no objective existence. We use it to protect ourselves from anxiety brought about by uncertainty concerning what we should do ('no need to worry, the leader will decide'), and from various uncomfortable emotions and wishes that arise when people try to work together. One cost of using the concept of leadership to organise our social world is *alienation* – that is, feeling distant from our true self and devoid of authentic relationships with others. Because we give too much responsibility to people we label leaders, we find it difficult to lead purposeful lives, or to view ourselves as purposeful, self-managing individuals. This radical view of leadership draws partly on psychoanalytic theory (*see* Chapter 2). It challenges both 'common sense' and academic theories of leadership. Most people working in organisations would probably find it difficult to agree that leadership is illusory, or that it is a harmful concept. Yet Gemmill and Oakley do convincingly make the point that as individuals we may try to transfer tasks to leaders that it would be better to do ourselves. This brings us back to a point made by Gastil (1994): democratic leaders may have to insist that their subordinates take a share of the responsibility.

All of this seems like very good evidence for a 'romanticised' view of leadership, where we grossly overestimate its importance. Meindl has argued that current interest in charisma and transformational leadership shows even more clearly just how romanticised it is. Meindl essentially argues that we are fooling ourselves. But this is not necessarily true. Meindl *et al.* (1985) did not demonstrate that we are wrong to make these attributions about leadership, only that we do make them. Others, such as Yukl (1994), argue forcefully that the quality of leadership really does make a difference to outcomes that matter in the real world.

> ■ **KEY LEARNING POINT**
> *Leadership is partly in the eye of the beholder. We may be inclined to overestimate the impact of leaders, particularly when performance is very good or very bad.*

GLOBAL LEADERSHIP

The globalisation of markets brought about by communications technology and the mobility of production resources mean that more and more people work in countries and cultures that are novel to them. For many managers, this means leading people of different backgrounds and outlooks to their own. There has been much recent interest in identifying the cultural dimensions along which countries can differ. The work which started it all was carried out by Hofstede (1980), who collected data from employees of IBM across many countries. He identified four cultural dimensions:

Power distance: The extent to which members of a society accept that there should be an unequal distribution of power between its members.

Uncertainty avoidance: The extent to which members of a society wish to have a predictable environment, and have set up institutions and systems designed to achieve this.

Masculinity v. femininity: A masculine society values assertion, success and achievement, while a feminine one is orientated more towards nurturing and caring.

Individualism v. collectivism: The former reflects a belief that individuals should be self-sufficient while the latter emphasises people's belongingness to groups in which there is mutual support.

It would be strange if there were *not* differences between countries in the most used and most effective leadership styles. Using Hofstede's cultural dimensions we might expect autocratic styles to be more effective in high power–distance cultures than in low ones. Leaders whose style is high on structure will probably be more appreciated in high uncertainty–avoidance cultures than others.

There is also the general issue of whether leader behaviour is interpreted differently in different cultures and countries. Some research (Smith *et al.*, 1989; Peterson *et al.*, 1993) has sought to discover whether leader styles are described using the same dimensions across different cultures. Using data from electronics firms in the UK, the USA, Japan and Hong Kong, Smith *et al.* (1989) concluded that what they call maintenance and performance leadership styles (approximately equivalent to the consideration and structure dimensions described earlier in this chapter) do indeed exist in different cultures. However, they also stated that 'the specific behaviours associated with those styles differ markedly, in ways which are comprehensible within the cultural norms of each setting' (p. 97). For example, one of the questions asked by Smith *et al.* was: 'When your superior learns that a member is experiencing personal difficulties, does your superior discuss the matter in the person's absence with other members?'.

In Hong Kong and Japan, this behaviour is seen as highly characteristic of maintenance (consideration). In the UK and the USA it is not – probably most Western subordinates would regard this as 'talking about me behind my back'. Not that all other British and American perceptions were identical: as Smith *et al.* (1989) note, in Britain, consideration can be expressed by talking about the task, but this is not so in the USA.

Political changes in some countries, for example in Eastern Europe, also have implications for the way managers are expected to lead. Maczynski (1997) has shown that Polish leaders' preferred problem-solving styles shifted towards more participation between 1988 and 1994, during which time communism was toppled. Smith *et al.* (1997) have recently found some differences between Eastern European countries which, at least in the late 1980s, had similar cultural emphases on acceptance of hierarchies coupled with high individualism (Trompenaars, 1993). Smith *et al.* (1997) found that managers in the Czech Republic and Hungary tend to report that they make great use of their own experience and those of others around them. This is an individualistic style consistent with those countries' long-standing links with Western Europe, and contrasts with Romanian and Bulgarian managers' self-reported reliance on widespread beliefs held in their country to guide their behaviour.

These insights are very important as work organisations become increasingly international. Assuming that leaders can identify which style they wish to adopt, they need to make sure they behave in ways which are interpreted as consistent with that style. Those behaviours differ somewhat between countries and cultures.

■ KEY LEARNING POINT

Both long-standing cultural differences and major social and political change can influence actual leader behaviour and the behaviour desired by subordinates.

SUMMARY

This chapter has explored many approaches to leadership. Consideration, structure, cognitive complexity/intelligence, participativeness and charisma have been identified as some key leader behaviours. There is considerable overlap between these concepts, and some tidying up and increased precision is needed. The same is true of the various situational variables proposed by contingency theorists. For example, take another look at the Vroom and Jago decision questions (Fig. 14.2). At least two relate closely to Fiedler's notions of leader–member relations and task structure. The theories are in some respects more similar than they might seem. It is therefore not surprising that several of them are equally (and moderately) good at explaining leadership phenomena. Several approaches, especially that of Vroom and Jago, and transformational leadership, contain useful practical guidance about how to go about being a leader. Future theory and practice in leadership need to combine concepts from the better theories in a systematic way. Greater attention must also be paid to whether and how leaders can be trained or selected not only to do the desirable things, but to do them well.

CASE STUDY 14.3

Leadership and policy implementation

It was a turbulent time in the health and safety department of Super Chem's Hamburg plant. The multinational chemical company had recently adopted a policy of developing managers by giving them international experience. A consequence of this policy had been that a 32-year-old Spaniard, José Alonso, had been put in charge of the department. José's German was more than adequate for the task, but this was his first assignment outside Spain, a country seen by many in the company as peripheral to its operations. He had much to learn when he first arrived, especially about German health and safety legislation. He was, however, an experienced health and safety manager, having been head of health and safety at two smallish plants in Spain for two years each.

Almost as soon as he arrived, José was pitched into an interesting situation. Two major accidents at other plants had caused a high-level health and safety policy review. The resulting report had come out in favour of more stringent inspection and a tougher approach from company health and safety departments. The recommendations were clear and specific.

José knew that his presence was resented by his six staff, who had worked together for some time and tended to think alike. They felt they had more specialist knowledge than he did. Most were older than him, and they could not understand why the deputy head, Gunter Koenig, had not been promoted. Koenig himself was understandably especially bitter. José felt that he could not follow his staff around as they inspected the plant: it would look too much like snooping. On the other hand, he needed to tap into his staff's knowledge of the plant and of how things had always been done there. Existing policy documents were too vague to be much help.

José had reason to believe that his staff typically adopted a collaborative approach with the managers whose areas they inspected. They preferred to use friendly persuasion and gentle hints rather than the precise written reports and threats for non-compliance required by the new policy. It had always worked at that plant, they said, and it would continue to do so. Yet José knew that exactly the same had been said at the plants where major accidents occurred. What was worse for José, it was fairly clear that the plant

▶

manager privately agreed with José's staff. José's position was all the more difficult because he was known to be on a two-year secondment, after which the previous head (who had herself been seconded elsewhere) was expected to return in his place. Therefore he was not in a position to exert a long-term influence on the careers of his staff. But José himself was answerable not only to the plant manager but also to the company health and safety chief, who was the chief proponent of the new policy.

José knew that he was not a particularly creative or imaginative individual. He enjoyed the precision and rules and regulations of health and safety work. He was usually inclined to draw up detailed plans of work for himself and others, and to keep a careful check on implementation of those plans. At the same time, he could understand how his staff felt: he had been landed with an unwelcome boss himself a few years earlier. He did not blame them for their attitude, and, characteristically, he was always keen to emphasise what he genuinely saw as the many strengths of his subordinates.

Despite the complicated situation, José felt that his task was clear enough. A decision had to be made about how, if at all, the department's practices would need to change in order to implement the new health and safety policy. Also, it had to be made in time for a visit by the health and safety chief six weeks later.

Suggested exercises

1 *Analyse this case study using Fiedler's theories. What kind of situation is it? How well suited to it is José Alonso? What should he do next? What important features of this case study, if any, are neglected by Fiedler's ideas?*

2 *Analyse this case study using the Vroom and Jago theory. What kind of situation is it? What should José Alonso do next? What important features of this case study, if any, are neglected by Vroom and Jago?*

TEST YOUR LEARNING

Short-answer questions

1 Describe the strengths and weaknesses of alternative measures of leader effectiveness.

2 Briefly, what factors other than the leader's personality traits influence his or her effectiveness?

3 Define consideration and structure.

4 Describe the key features of democratic leadership.

5 Name and define four aspects of transformational leadership and two aspects of transactional leadership.

6 Outline the main features of Fiedler's contingency theory. Suggest two strengths and two weaknesses of the theory.

7 Outline the main features of Fiedler's cognitive resource theory.

8 List the leadership styles and problem-situation features identified in Vroom's theory of leadership.

Essay questions

1 Discuss the proposition that all of the aspects of leadership style identified in research essentially amount to person-orientation and task-orientation.

2 Examine the extent to which different contingency theories of leadership share the same key ideas.

3 Examine the implications for leadership of research which views leadership as a socially constructed phenomenon.

4 Discuss how and why leaders need to adjust their behaviour to different cultures.

GLOSSARY OF TERMS

Alienation A state of being where a person does not feel that he or she is in touch with his or her true self, nor does he or she experience fulfilling relationships with others.

Charisma A set of attributes of leaders and/or their relationships with subordinates where the leader demonstrates and promotes a sense of pride and mission through personal example.

Cognitive resource theory A theory of leadership proposed by Fred Fiedler which focuses on how the cognitive resources (e.g. intelligence, knowledge) of leaders influence group performance in situations of varying stress and leader control.

Consideration An aspect of leadership style which reflects the extent that the leader demonstrates trust of subordinates, respect for their ideas and consideration of their feelings.

Contingency theories These are theories of leadership which focus on how features of the situation determine what is the most effective leadership style.

Democratic leadership A leader style which encourages self-determination, equal participation and active deliberation by group members.

Leader The person who is appointed, elected or informally chosen to direct and co-ordinate the work of others in a group.

Leader–member relations Defined as a feature of the situation in Fiedler's contingency theory of leadership, this refers to the extent to which leader and subordinates have relationships characterised by respect and mutual trust.

Least preferred co-worker (LPC) In Fiedler's contingency theory, LPC refers to the leader's attitude towards the subordinate he or she likes least. This attitude is assumed to reflect the leader's general orientation towards others at work.

Managerial grid Put forward by Blake and Mouton, this is a simple aid to assessing leadership style, based on the leader's person- and task-orientation.

Participativeness The extent to which a leader includes his or her subordinates in, and allows them control over, decision making.

Position power In Fred Fiedler's contingency theory, position power refers to the extent to which a leader is able, by virtue of his or her position in the organisation, to influence the rewards and punishments received by subordinates.

Situational leadership theory A theory of leadership which proposes that the maturity of subordinates dictates the style a leader should adopt.

Structure Sometimes called initiating structure, this is an aspect of leadership style which reflects the extent to which the leader plans, organises and monitors the work of his or her group.

Substitutes for leadership This term, coined by Kerr and Jermier, reflects the idea that in some circumstances the resources of a group are sufficient to make a leader unnecessary.

Transactional leadership A leadership style originally identified by Burns (1978), in which the leader uses rewards for good performance and tends to maintain existing work methods unless performance goals are not being met.

Transformational leadership Another leadership style originally identified by Burns (1978), this refers to the extent to which a leader articulates a clear vision and mission, while treating individuals on their merits and encouraging free thinking.

Vroom–Jago theory of leadership This theory assumes that leaders can vary the participativeness of their decision-making style according to the situation, and identifies key aspects of the situation.

SUGGESTED FURTHER READING

1 *Business Leadership* by Viv Shackleton, published by Routledge in 1995, is a readable overview of leadership theory and practices which expands on many of the themes of this chapter.

2 Alan Bryman's 1992 book *Charisma and Leadership in Organizations*, published by Sage, provides an in-depth, constructively critical analysis of the currently dominant approaches to leadership.

3 Gary Yukl has produced a thorough text called *Leadership in Organizations*. The third edition was published in 1994 by Prentice Hall.

REFERENCES

Bass, B.M. (1985) *Leadership and Performance: Beyond expectations*. New York: Free Press.

Bass, B.M. (1990) *Bass and Stogdill's Handbook of Leadership: Theory, research and managerial application*. 3rd edn. New York: Free Press.

Blake, R.R. and Mouton, J.S. (1964) *The Managerial Grid*. Houston, TX: Gulf Publishing.

Bryman, A. (1992) *Charisma and Leadership in Organizations*. London: Sage.

Bryman, A., Bresnen, M., Ford, J., Beardsworth, A. and Keil, T. (1987) 'Leader orientation and organizational transience: an investigation using Fiedler's LPC scale', *Journal of Occupational Psychology*, vol. 60, pp. 13–19.

Burns, J.M. (1978) *Leadership*. New York: Harper & Row.

Conger, J.A. (1990) 'The dark side of leadership', *Organizational Dynamics*, Autumn, pp. 44–5.

Eagly, A.H., Karau, S.J. and Makhijani, M.G. (1995) 'Gender and the effectiveness of leaders: a meta-analysis', *Psychological Bulletin*, vol. 117, pp. 125–45.

Fiedler, F.E. (1967) *A Theory of Leadership Effectiveness*. New York: McGraw-Hill.

Fiedler, F.E. (1995) 'Cognitive resources and leadership performance', *Applied Psychology: An International Review*, vol. 44, pp. 5–28.

Fiedler, F.E. and Chemers, M.M. (1984) *Improving Leadership Effectiveness: The leader match concept*. 2nd edn. New York: John Wiley.

Fiedler, F.E. and Garcia, J.E. (1987) *New Approaches to Effective Leadership: Cognitive resources and organizational performance*. New York: John Wiley.

Fiedler, F.E., Murphy, S.E. and Gibson, F.W. (1992) 'Inaccurate reporting and inappropriate variables: a reply to Vecchio's (1990) examination of Cognitive Resource Theory', *Journal of Applied Psychology*, vol. 77, pp. 372–4.

Filley, A.C., House, R.J. and Kerr, S. (1976) *Managerial Process and Organizational Behavior*. Glenview, IL: Scott, Foresman and Co.

Fleishman, E.A. (1969) *Leadership Opinion Questionnaire Manual*. Henley-on-Thames: Science Research Associates.

Gastil, J. (1994) 'A definition and illustration of democratic leadership', *Human Relations*, vol. 47, pp. 953–75.

Gemmill, G. and Oakley, J. (1992) 'Leadership: an alienating social myth?', *Human Relations*, vol. 45, pp. 113–29.

Hater, J. and Bass, B.M. (1988) 'Superiors' evaluations and subordinates' perceptions of transformational and transactional leadership', *Journal of Applied Psychology*, vol. 73, pp. 695–702.

Hersey, P. and Blanchard, K. (1982) *Management of Organizational Behavior*. 4th edn. Englewood Cliffs, NJ: Prentice Hall.

Hofstede, G. (1980) *Culture's Consequences*. Beverley Hills: Sage Publications.

House, R.J. (1977) 'A 1976 theory of charismatic leadership' in Hunt, J.G. and Larson, L.L. (eds) *Leadership: The cutting edge*. Carbondale, IL: Southern Illinois Press.

House, R.J. and Baetz, M.L. (1979) 'Leadership: some empirical generalizations and new research directions' in Staw, B.M. (ed.) *Research in Organizational Behavior*, vol. 1. Greenwich, CT: JAI Press.

House, R.J., Spangler, W.D. and Woycke, J. (1991) 'Personality and charisma in the US presidency: a psychological theory of leader effectiveness', *Administrative Science Quarterly*, vol. 36, pp. 364–96.

Howell, J.M. and Avolio, B.J. (1993) 'Transformational leadership, transactional leadership, locus of control, and support for innovation: key predictors of consolidated-business-unit performance', *Journal of Applied Psychology*, vol. 78, pp. 891–902.

Keller, T. and Dansereau, F. (1995) 'Leadership and empowerment: a social exchange perspective', *Human Relations*, vol. 48, pp. 127–46.

Kerr, S. and Jermier, J.M. (1978) 'Substitutes for leadership: their meaning and measurement', *Organizational Behavior and Human Performance*, vol. 22, pp. 375–403.

Komaki, J.L., Zlotnick, S. and Jensen, M. (1986) 'Development of an operant-based taxonomy and observational index of supervisory behaviour', *Journal of Applied Psychology*, vol. 71, pp. 260–9.

Maczynski, J. (1997) 'A comparison of leadership style of Polish managers before and after market economy reforms', paper presented at the Eighth European Congress of Work and Organisational Psychology, Verona, April.

Meindl, J.R., Ehrlich, S.B. and Dukerich, J.M. (1985) 'The romance of leadership', *Administrative Science Quarterly*, vol. 30, pp. 78–102.

Peters, L.H., Hartke, D.D. and Pohlmann, J.T. (1985) 'Fiedler's contingency theory of leadership: an application of the meta-analysis procedures of Schmidt and Hunter', *Psychological Bulletin*, vol. 97, pp. 274–85.

Peterson, M.F., Smith, P.B. and Tayeb, M.H. (1993) 'Development and use of English versions of Japanese PM leadership measures in electronics plants', *Journal of Organizational Behavior*, vol. 14, pp. 251–67.

Pillai, R. and Meindl, J.R. (1991) 'The impact of a performance crisis on attributions of charismatic leadership: a preliminary study', paper presented at the Eastern Academy of Management, Hartford, Connecticut.

Schriesheim, C.A., Tepper, B.J. and Tetrault, L.A. (1994) 'Least preferred coworker score, situational control, and leadership effectiveness: a meta-analysis of contingency model performance predictions', *Journal of Applied Psychology*, vol. 79, pp. 561–73.

Smith, P.B., Misumi, J., Tayeb, M., Peterson, M. and Bond, M. (1989), 'On the generality of leadership style measures across cultures', *Journal of Occupational Psychology*, vol. 62, pp. 97–109.

Smith, P.B., Kruzella, P., Czegledi, R., Tsvetanova, S., Pop, D., Groblewska, B. and Halasova, D. (1997) 'Managerial leadership in Eastern Europe: from uniformity to diversity' in Pepermans, R., Buelens, A., Vinkenburg, C.J. and Jansen, P.G.W. (eds) *Managerial Behaviour and Practices: European Research Issues*. Leuven: Acco.

Sternberg, R.J. (1995) 'A triarchic view of "Cognitive resources and leadership performance"', *Applied Psychology: An International Review*, vol. 44, pp. 29–32.

Stogdill, R.M. (1974) *Handbook of Leadership: A survey of theory and research*. New York: Free Press.

Tjosvold, D., Wedley, W.C. and Field, R.H.G. (1986) 'Constructive controversy, the Vroom–Yetton model, and managerial decision-making', *Journal of Occupational Behaviour*, vol. 7, pp. 125–38.

Trompenaars, F. (1993) *Riding the Waves of Culture*. London: Brealey.

Vecchio, R.P. (1987) 'Situational leadership theory: an examination of a prescriptive theory', *Journal of Applied Psychology*, vol. 72, pp. 444–51.

Vecchio, R.P. (1990) 'Theoretical and empirical examination of Cognitive Resource Theory', *Journal of Applied Psychology*, vol. 75, pp. 141–7.

Vecchio, R.P. (1992) 'Cognitive Resource Theory: issues for specifying a test of the theory', *Journal of Applied Psychology*, vol. 77, pp. 375–6.

Vroom, V.H. and Jago, A.G. (1988) *The New Leadership: Managing participation in organizations*. Englewood Cliffs, NJ: Prentice Hall.

Vroom, V.H. and Yetton, P.W. (1973) *Leadership and Decision Making*. Pittsburgh, PA: Pittsburgh Press.

Wagner, J.A. (1994) 'Participation's effects on performance and satisfaction: a reconsideration of research evidence', *Academy of Management Review*, vol. 19, pp. 312–30.

Weissenburg, P. and Kavanagh, M.J. (1972) 'The independence of initiating structure and consideration: a review of the evidence', *Personnel Psychology*, vol. 25, pp. 119–30.

Williams, M.L., Podsakoff, P.M., Todor, W.D., Huber, V.L., Howell, J.P. and Dorfman, P.W. (1988) 'A preliminary analysis of the construct validity of Kerr and Jermier's "substitutes for leadership" scales', *Journal of Occupational Psychology*, vol. 61, pp. 307–34.

Yetton, P.W. (1984) 'Leadership and supervision' in Gruneberg, M. and Wall, T. (eds) *Social Psychology and Organizational Behaviour*. Chichester: John Wiley.

Yukl, G.A. (1994) *Leadership in Organizations*. 3rd edn. Englewood Cliffs, NJ: Prentice Hall.

15

Training and learning at work

After studying this chapter, you should be able to:

1 state the main stages involved in the training and development process;

2 describe the main levels of analysis for the assessment of training need;

3 give brief definitions of job analysis and skills analysis;

4 state the three components that make up a learning objective;

5 describe how hierarchical task analysis is carried out and used to develop training;

6 state the main stages involved in skill development;

7 distinguish between declarative and procedural knowledge;

8 identify the six principal types of learning capabilities defined by Gagné;

9 outline a framework for the evaluation of training;

10 give examples of study designs for the evaluation of training.

INTRODUCTION

The capacity to learn very effectively is one of the most distinctive attributes of humans. Within organisational settings, just as in other settings, people develop and change as time passes. Some of this development occurs in a rather unsystematic fashion and takes place as people learn from each other and learn how to integrate themselves into the organisation. Other development and change take place in a more controlled and planned fashion, when programmes of planned training and development are organised in attempts to improve the knowledge and skills that people have. In most modern organisations such programmes represent an important component in their success and have significant cost–benefit implications. Figure 15.1 represents an outline of the most important elements involved in the training and development process, and during the remainder of this chapter each of the elements will be described in some detail. This chapter concentrates on the contribution of work psychology to training. To obtain a comprehensive overview of the training function it would be important to consult texts that concentrate, more heavily than this book does, on the administrative and organisational issues of relevance (e.g. Goldstein, 1993).

As Fig. 15.1 shows, the training and development process moves from an assessment of need, through the development of programmes, to evaluation of what has taken place. It is important to recognise that although Fig. 15.1 presents the elements involved in an orderly sequence, in practice there are many links and interactions between these elements, and often parts of various elements will be taking place in parallel or in a different order from the one shown.

Fig. 15.1 A systematic approach to training

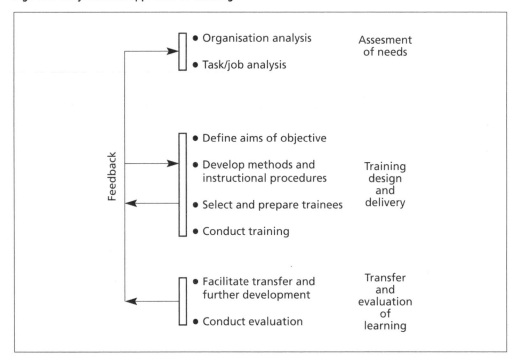

Although this chapter covers the primary factors involved in the training process itself, other chapters present material of considerable importance to the training process including, in particular, job analysis and personnel selection (Chapters 7 and 8).

> ■ **KEY LEARNING POINT**
> *Although there is a systematic approach to training, in practice things are not always done in a set order.*

ASSESSING NEEDS

Before setting in motion any systematic training or development within an organisation, those responsible should satisfy themselves that such activity is going to produce worthwhile results and is therefore necessary. On occasions, in some organisations, it is clear that programmes of training and development can take on a more or less independent 'life of their own' and various activities will take place regardless of any clear and established need for them. Without adequate systems for staff training and development, an organisation cannot function effectively, but as Davies (1972) pointed out, both too little and too much training can cause problems. Assessing training needs is not a mechanistic procedure, and a significant amount of judgement is involved. The most convenient way of viewing needs assessment is to consider three basic levels of analysis: organisation, occupation and person. Although this classification has been used for some time (McGhee and Thayer, 1961), it still provides a valuable perspective (Latham, 1988) for the analysis of training needs.

At the organisational level, the first step in the assessment of need is to examine and identify the aims and objects of the organisation. These can often be identified in general terms by examining plans and statements of policy and by discussion with senior personnel in the organisation. Very broadly, organisational training needs exist when there is, or is likely to be, some sort of barrier hindering the achievement of organisational aims and objectives (either now or at some predicted future occasion). Symptoms might include output problems caused by bottlenecks in production, excessive errors or wastage, or stress and related problems caused by lack of ability in some people or overload on other fully trained individuals. It is important to stress, however, that such problems represent training needs only if the barrier to the achievement of aims and objectives might be best removed by training rather than by some other activity. Production problems, for example, might well be solved more effectively by redesigning the job or equipment, improving recruitment and selection procedures, or providing job aids. Recent emphasis in organisational level training needs assessment has stressed the kind of system-wide thinking embodied in the above description, or organisational analysis, in which consideration of the link between training activities and organisational goals is important (e.g. Goldstein, 1993). This systems view is also evident in more general work on strategic human resources management.

To bring about any form of training it is important to have a clear understanding of the target behaviour that is to be developed, and in most organisational settings this means a clear grasp of the main job components or activities involved. The closely related techniques of job analysis, skills analysis and task analysis have an important role here.

> ■ KEY LEARNING POINT
> *Training needs can be assessed at three levels: organisation, occupation and person.*

Job analysis

A great deal of job analysis is carried out in organisations in order to produce job descriptions. Such descriptions include information about the conditions of work, salary, physical surroundings and so on, but provide only a general description of the tasks involved in the job and of the skills required; as such, they are of very limited value in a training context. Some of the methods for job analysis can be useful for training purposes – for example, the *position analysis questionnaire* (PAQ) (*see* Chapter 7). However, even techniques such as the PAQ provide information that, although comprehensive, is often not detailed enough to allow for the construction of specific exercises and programmes of planned training.

Skills analysis

This term is usually reserved for procedures and methods of analysis similar to the technique described by Seymour (1966). Essentially, such techniques call for detailed analysis of the skilled physical movements involved in manual operations, and although they are useful in some training situations, their range of application is limited.

Task analysis

This is probably the most important form of analysis for training purposes. The technique focuses on the objectives or outcomes of the tasks that people perform and provides an extremely flexible and useful method of analysis. The main unit of analysis is the operation. An operation is defined by Annett *et al.* (1971) as 'Any unit of behaviour, no matter how long or short its duration and no matter how simple or complex its structure, which can be defined in terms of its objective'.

One of the important features of the procedures developed by Annett *et al.* (1971) is that tasks are analysed and broken down into increasingly specific operations in a hierarchical fashion. Because of this approach to analysis the technique is known as *hierarchical task analysis* (HTA). The starting point for HTA involves a general description of the main operation(s) involved in the job or job components being analysed. These operations are then divided into suboperations and, in turn, the suboperations themselves may be subdivided. Consider an example of a task that many of us have had to contend with, that of 'knock-flat' furniture. Figure 15.2 shows how this may be described in task analysis terms.

The analysis begins with a fairly high-level description of the main operation involved (i.e. assemble table), which is then subdivided into further operations at increasingly specific levels of analysis. It is important to remember that an operation is a very flexible unit, and at the beginning of the process the analyst will not have any fixed ideas about how many operations are involved nor about the number of levels of analysis that will

Fig. 15.2 Part of a task analysis for the assembly of a 'knock-flat' table

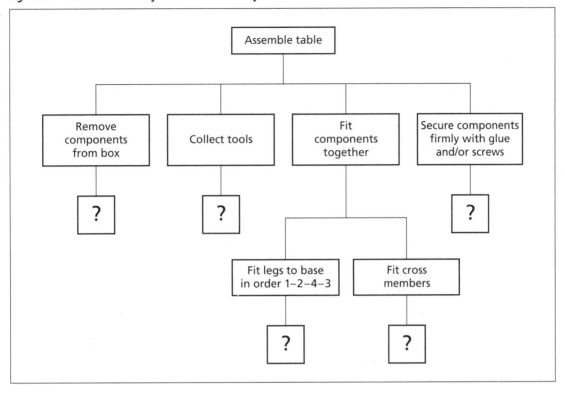

be needed. An analysis conducted in this way could continue to break down the operations involved until they are describing very tiny units of behaviour, and obviously at some point it is necessary to be able to decide that the analysis has reached a sufficiently specific level of detail. Two factors may be taken into account to help with this decision. The first of these is the probability that an untrained person would fail to carry out the operation successfully (P). The second is the cost to the system that would be incurred if the operation was carried out inadequately (C). Each operation in the analysis is examined with these two factors in mind in order to determine whether it needs to be divided further.

> ■ **KEY LEARNING POINT**
> *The P × C rule in hierarchical task analysis provides a signal about how much detail is necessary.*

An operation needs to be analysed in more detail if the product of P × C is unacceptably high. The rationale for this is fairly straightforward. If the probability of failure is high, the operation will probably need to be described in more detail before the analysis can be used as a basis for developing training, unless the cost of failure is minimal. If the cost of failure (C) for a particular operation is high, more detail will be needed, unless the operation is easy for even an untrained person to perform. In other words, difficult operations with important cost consequences need to be analysed further until P × C becomes acceptably low. Additional information about the analytical techniques and recording procedures for HTA may be found in Annett *et al.* (1971), Duncan (1972) and Shepherd (1976).

As well as the approaches mentioned above, there are several other analytical procedures that are useful in the training needs assessment phase. It is often helpful to employ questionnaires to collect relevant information. Such questionnaires may be targeted at any level of analysis and derive information from various people, or groups of people. Interviews or discussion-based data collection procedures also come in useful, and in many settings, some detailed observation of relevant jobs and job holders is essential. Goldstein (1993) lists and evaluates nine basic needs assessment techniques. Patrick (1992) gives a review of the various techniques that are of use for training analysis; he also provides a consideration of general methodological issues relevant to the use of such techniques.

Person analysis essentially involves identifying who needs training and what kind of training they need. Methods available for answering these questions are not particularly sophisticated and most rely on the administration of interviews or questionnaires to collect the opinions of key individuals. A note of caution on the interpretation of such surveys is in order in view of the findings of studies comparing the perceived needs of job holders and their supervisors. Both McEnery and McEnery (1987) and Staley and Shockley-Zalabak (1986) found little agreement between job incumbents and their supervisors. McEnery and McEnery (1987) also found that supervisors' assessments of their subordinates' needs correlated more closely with their (the supervisors) assessment of their own needs than the subordinates' own need assessment!

TASK   *Why is it the case that people apparently project their own training needs on to others?*

TRAINING DESIGN

Training and development activities are designed to bring about changes in people's behaviour, and the success of such endeavours is determined by how effectively these changes are instituted. Developing a clear grasp of the operations involved in the relevant jobs by the use of techniques such as HTA is an essential step in the process. Before training begins, however, the results of such analyses need to be used in order to provide a clear statement of the outcomes, or targets, of training. As Mager (1962) put it: 'If you don't know where you're heading you'll probably end up some place else'.

A useful distinction can be made between the aims and the objectives of training. Aims involve general statements of intent: examples might be that a programme sets out to provide participants with 'a grasp of the basic principles of management accountancy' or 'an awareness of the relevance of industrial psychology to the management process'. By contrast, objectives are much more specific and precise. In their most explicit form, objectives are sometimes expressed in the following, three-component form:

1 *the terminal behaviour:* a statement of what the trainee should be able to do at the end of training. Because of this emphasis on terminal behaviour, objectives expressed in this way are often referred to as behavioural objectives;

2 *the conditions* under which the behaviour is to be exhibited;

3 *the standard of performance* of the behaviour.

It is important to recognise that objectives specify what the person will be able to do at the end of training; they do not describe what will happen during training. The statement that participants will gain experience of various personnel selection interviewing techniques would not be acceptable as an objective. It says what will happen on the course but not what the outcomes will be.

> ■ KEY LEARNING POINT
> *Objectives give a clear description of what the trainee should be capable of doing at the end of training.*

In many practical training situations a full description of the expected outcomes of training is not provided in the form described above. Sometimes competence at the end of training is assessed by the use of various tests, or job simulation exercises. The behaviour that will produce satisfactory performance on these exercises represents the targets for the programme of training. Regardless of whether behavioural objectives or other methods are used to define these targets, it is important that the desired outcomes of training are clear at an early stage so that programmes can be designed to enable trainees to reach the targets. Of course, in some circumstances it is legitimate for the objectives of a programme to be relatively general and not expressed in the precise way described above. For example, many experiential learning exercises, such as T-groups, are conducted within organisations and have quite general aims concerned with the psychological awareness and growth of participants. To attempt to express precise objectives for such experiences would be completely counter to their purpose, since the learning that takes place for each individual is of a highly personal and often emotional nature and each person acquires different things from such experiences.

Training methods

One of the more frequent problems which arises with training programmes is that the method of instruction to be used is the first decision that is taken. It should be obvious from the previous pages that methods should be chosen or developed as a consequence of the desired targets of training and not the other way round. An enormous range of possible training methods is available.

To discuss training methods as if they were separate and clearly defined techniques is inappropriate, since even the most widely used and well-known methods such as lectures, case studies, demonstration and practice show wide variation in use depending on factors such as the instructors and trainees involved and the task being learnt. Methods are adapted and combined in an almost infinite variety of ways. The use of closed-circuit television (CCTV) as a training method provides a good illustration. CCTV is often used to provide trainees with feedback on their own behaviour so that, with the aid of a trainer, they can observe their own behaviour and assess their strengths and weaknesses. Recently, however, a number of researchers using social learning theory (Bandura, 1986) as a basis have shown that such training might be carried out more effectively by using films or CCTV to present model behaviour that the trainees should attempt to emulate. Thus, although both approaches use CCTV as 'the method', because of developments in underlying ideas about how learning takes place the two approaches are quite different. From the training and development viewpoint, understanding of the general process involved in learning and some grasp of the theoretical background are likely to provide a much more useful framework than detailed examination of specific methods.

Models of learning

Although there is no single, universally accepted model for the learning process there are several widely accepted underlying principles and points of agreement among psychologists. Within the history of psychology the most prominent approach to learning originates in the work of the behaviourist school (*see* Chapter 10). Although, as Chapter 10 makes clear, the behavioural approach to psychology has been replaced by approaches that give a more central role to cognitive processes, the evidence, compiled by the behaviourists, about the processes of classical and operant conditioning, is still of some value. These processes are, however, neither neither comprehensive nor sophisticated enough to explain the full complexity of human learning, nor are they sophisticated enough to serve as a basis for the development of training programmes. The more recent approaches to learning have focused increasingly on the cognitive processes that are involved, rather than looking only at the external, behavioural manifestations of these processes. Behaviourism explained learning as a trial and error process, in which behaviour was strengthened or weakened by the direct effects of the environment. Social learning theory added to this view by providing a bigger role for internal, mental processes. In the social learning view, key cognitive processes, such as expectancies about what might happen and the capacity of individuals to learn without direct experience, had a crucial role to play in learning (Bandura, 1986). For a significant period the views of behaviourists and social–cognitive theorists had a significant influence on the development of training, and until quite recently text books providing an outline of the 'principles of learning' would draw very heavily on such approaches. More recently, the theories of cognitive psychologists have become increasingly relevant and influential.

One of the central theoretical problems in the cognitive psychology of learning has been to explain the development that takes place as a person moves from being an unskilled novice to becoming an expert. This is a significant question because it holds the key to understanding how skilled performance develops. Fitts (1962) proposed a theory that has been well regarded by psychologists with an interest in training. In essence, Fitts suggested that skill development progressed through three distinct phases: cognitive, associative and autonomous. Although the phases can be separated conceptually, Fitts recognised that there might well be some practical overlap between them. In the cognitive phase the learner is attempting to get some intellectual understanding of the tasks involved. Actions are deliberate and in the forefront of consciousness during the cognitive stage as the learner concentrates on the key features of skilled performance. During this stage a novice golfer will, for example, concentrate on which club to select, how to stand, how to hold the club, and so on. For skills that are not trivially easy to learn, practice is the key feature of the next (associative) phase as the learner attempts to reproduce skilful performance. During this phase there is less and less ponderous concentration on the steps involved and, usually through practice and feedback, a gradual improvement in the smoothness and accuracy of performance. The autonomous stage is reached as the skill becomes more and more automatic. In this phase performance of the skill requires less in the way of psychological resources, such as memory or attention, and is increasingly resistant to interference from distractions or competing activities. The skilled driver can drive a car and talk, the novice is safer not to attempt this!

> ■ KEY LEARNING POINT
> *In developing a skill, the learner passes through a series of stages, with each one producing performance that is more and more automatic.*

Anderson (1983, 1987) has proposed a very influential theory which, in some ways, reflects the ideas put forward by Fitts (1962) within the context of contemporary cognitive psychology. Anderson's theory also has three stages, which can be related quite well to the three phases proposed by Fitts (*see* Table 15.1). A central feature of Anderson's (1983, 1987) approach is the distinction between *declarative* and *procedural* knowledge. Declarative knowledge is essentially factual knowledge that may be stated (declared) and made explicit. So, a skilled counsellor may be able to provide a definition of clinical depression and list the chief symptoms. By contrast, procedural knowledge may be involved when the counsellor deals with a client who is threatening self-harm. Procedural knowledge is the basis for knowing how to do something, whereas declarative knowledge is knowing that something is or is not the case. For example many people know *that* to ride, and stay on, a horse involves gripping with the knees, sitting upright, holding the reins in a particular way and maintaining balance as the horse

Table 15.1 Phases of skill development

Fitts	Anderson
Cognitive phase: learning the basic ingredients that make up skilled performance. Performance is prone to error and some lack of understanding of how to conduct task(s) may be apparent	*Declarative stage*: establishing the basic 'facts' about the tasks. The trainee is beginning to grasp what is involved in the task(s) (i.e. declarative knowledge)
Associative phase: establishment of the appropriate patterns of behaviour, underpinned by the knowledge acquired in the first phase. Initially rather a lot of errors but improvement with repeated practice	*Knowledge compilation stage*: physical mechanisms are developed for transforming the declarative knowledge into procedural knowledge (i.e. knowing how to accomplish the task(s))
Autonomous phase: the task(s) are performed increasingly smoothly with relatively low demands on memory or attention. Performance is very resistant to interference or stress	*Tuning stage*: performance strengthens and generalises across tasks within the relevant skill domain

Sources: Fitts (1962), Anderson (1983, 1987).

moves. Not all of the people who know this have the procedural knowledge to know *how* to stay on a difficult horse for any length of time. Anderson proposes that as the development of a new skill begins people move into the declarative stage, where important facts are learnt and the learner attempts to use them in working out how to conduct the tasks involved. In this stage demands on attention and memory are considerable. During the knowledge compilation stage the trainee develops better and better specific procedures for conducting the tasks. By the end of this stage the procedural knowledge, usually incorporating the application of guiding rules, is in place. As the tuning stage is reached the underlying rules are refined and streamlined so that performance is increasingly efficient and automatic.

TASK *Think about some of the skills that you have developed and the phases you passed through. Learning to talk is probably impossible to remember (why is this?) but learning to ride a bike or drive a car should be easier to recall.*

It is generally accepted that skilled performance is often organised in a hierarchical fashion, much as the software for computer programmes is organised. The learning process and the development of skill and knowledge are complex and depend on a variety of related aspects of an individual's psychological functioning. Perception, memory, motivation, cognitive ability and personality are all of some importance in understanding how and what any individual might learn. Detailed coverage of these issues and of other psychological theories of learning are beyond the scope of this chapter but much of the relevant material is dealt with elsewhere in this book. The interested reader should also consult a text that deals with the psychology of training and skill acquisition in some detail (e.g. Patrick, 1992).

The type of learning that takes place as a result of training and development programmes is quite varied and it is traditional to make distinctions between the development of knowledge, skills and attitudes. Rather confusingly, contemporary American industrial/organisational psychologists use the term KSAs to refer to knowledge, skills and *abilities*. According to this distinction, knowledge is concerned with the recall and understanding of facts and other items of information. Skills may be used with reference to the psychomotor movements involved in practical activities such as operating equipment or machinery but may also incorporate higher-order cognitive or interpersonal processes. Attitudes refer primarily to the emotional or affective feelings and views that a person has, although attitudes also have other components (*see* Chapter 9). For example, a person might be able to operate a drilling machine (skill) and might also be aware that certain safety procedures should be observed (knowledge) but feel that observing such procedures is time wasting and unnecessary (attitude).

This very simple distinction between knowledge, skills and attitudes is a useful starting point for identifying different types of learning but is inadequate in many ways. For example, the distinction between knowledge and skill is not as clear as it might at first seem. At first sight the job of a car mechanic might seem to be largely skill-based and that of a medical practitioner largely knowledge-based. Consider what happens, however, when the car mechanic is confronted with a car that is making a peculiar noise. The mechanic will make use of various fault-finding strategies in an attempt to establish what is causing the noise. These strategies are based on the application of various rules for finding faults, probably developed from direct experience and training. In much the same way, the medical practitioner will attempt to diagnose the cause of a patient's symptoms. Both of them are exhibiting a form of skill, but the skill in question is not dependent on co-ordinated physical movements, though the mechanic may need these as well; rather, it is an intellectual skill involving the use of rules and analysis to guide behaviour.

■ **KEY LEARNING POINT**
The apparently clear distinction between knowledge, skills and attitudes is difficult to maintain.

The categories of different types of learning developed by Gagné (1977) provide a much more comprehensive description than the knowledge/skills/attitudes distinction. Gagné identifies the following six types of learning, which he calls capabilities:

1 *basic learning*: stimulus–response associations and chains. This represents the formation of simple associations between stimuli and responses such as those that occur during classical conditioning (*see* Chapter 10);

2 *intellectual skills*: divided into the following hierarchy:
   a *discriminations*: being able to make distinctions between stimulus objects or events;
   b *concrete concepts*: classification of members of a class, by observation (e.g. red, circular);
   c *defined concepts*: classification by definition (e.g. mass, square roots);
   d *rules*: use of a relation or association to govern action;
   e *higher-order rules*: generation of new rules (e.g. by combining existing rules);

3 *cognitive strategy*: skills by which internal cognitive processes such as attention and learning are regulated (e.g. learning how to learn or learning general strategies for solving problems);

4 *verbal information*: ability to state specific information;

5 *motor skills*: organised motor acts;

6 *Attitude*.

The benefit to be gained from identifying learning capabilities involved in a training programme is that they can often provide guidance on the methods or sequences of training that might be most useful. Guidance about training methods and sequence can thus be arrived at by moving from task analysis, to learning capabilities, to sequence and method of instruction.

The theoretical ideas about skill development are also extremely useful when it comes to the selection or development of training methods. The training method may be selected on the basis of the kind of learning outcome that is intended: motor skills, for example, require repeated practice to develop adequately. The training needed will also depend on the stage of skill development that the trainees are likely to have reached. It would be pointless to design a series of high-speed practice exercises for trainees who were still at the first (declarative knowledge) stage of skill development. Another illustration of the link between training outcome and training method is the design of training to produce attitude change. The training here is not designed to bring about skill development, so text books, lectures and other cognitively based approaches would not be appropriate.

One serious problem in providing an overview of the effectiveness of different training methods is that much of the literature on training is atheoretical, rather than based on sound concepts. The literature is descriptive, rather than evaluative and much of it is contained in various practitioner-orientated magazines and books. The scientific literature of work psychology does not contain such an extensive array of material but, in general, the material is more rigorous and analytical. Within this narrower range of literature there are relatively few studies that provide a thorough evaluation of the effectiveness of a training method or methods.

PARTICIPATION IN TRAINING

A variety of factors seem to be involved in determining who participates in training. Obviously, more or less everyone who works needs some initial training for the job in question. This initial training may be very lengthy (for example, for professional jobs such as lawyers or doctors) or quite brief (for example, fork-lift truck drivers can be trained in a few days). Beyond initial training, the host organisation can be very influential in determining the degree of training available to its employees. Organisations may have a significant influence on participation in training by developing policies and regulations that facilitate or encourage employees to take part in training (Maurer and Tarulli, 1994).

It seems likely that training should be more frequent in more complex jobs where a high level of skill development is involved. This point of view is supported by the evidence available which shows that managers and professionals participate in more training than clerks, technical personnel and non-managers (Ralphs and Stephan, 1986; Noe and Wilk, 1993).

Management training and development

There is a great diversity of approaches available for management training and development. Some of these are rather mundane and make use of fairly standard classroom training techniques. Many of the management development techniques focus on the individual manager and try to develop his or her abilities in a bespoke fashion. One approach – mentoring – makes minimal use of formal classroom learning and links the manager with an experienced colleague, who offers support and assistance during the development process. In some cases mentoring is a long-term relationship designed to provide the protégé with a range of career advice, psychological support, social support and assistance (e.g. through feedback on performance) in the development of key competencies. In other cases the mentoring is more focused.

Increasingly the management training and development process begins with an obtained assessment of the manager's current competencies and career goals. This is often during a 'development centre'. Development centres are defined by Lee and Beard

(1994) as 'workshops which measure the abilities of participants against agreed criteria for a job or role' (p. 3). The approach has its origins in assessment centres (*see* Chapter 8) which are multi-assessor, multi-exercise events designed to assess the competencies of candidates for entry into the organisation, or for promotion. Development centres make use of the assessment techniques embodied in assessment centres but use the information to deliver feedback to candidates and help them to develop, rather than to select them for a job or promotion. Managers who participate in development centres often have mentors assigned to help them to benefit from the experience.

The unique feature of the development centre approach is the combination of initial assessment and subsequent development. A variety of other techniques take a similar approach and 'assessment based development' is becoming the predominant approach to management training. As Table 15.2 shows, such techniques are widely used, at least among the sample of UK MBA managers surveyed by Mabey and Iles (1994).

Table 15.2 Assessment and career development techniques: reported usage by MBA managers in the UK (Mabey and Illes, 1994)

Technique	Used in present organisation (%)
Career reviews	77
Informal mentors	43
Career-path information	35
Fast-track programmes	34
Assigned mentors	26
Psychometrics with feedback	22
Self-assessment materials	19
Development centres	18
Career planning workshops	14

TRAINING TRANSFER AND EVALUATION

It has already been emphasised that the development of successful programmes of training and development is a difficult and uncertain process, and frequently programmes will need to be modified or redesigned as a result of experience. Techniques for the validation and evaluation of training provide a means of examining the success of programmes and identifying areas where change is needed. Examining the validity of a training programme involves assessing the extent to which trainees have reached the objectives of the training and can be established properly only by examining trainees' capabilities after training. The evaluation of training is usually taken to be a much broader concept than validation, dealing with the overall benefits of a training programme (often including validity).

Probably the most popular framework for training evaluation studies is that of Kirkpatrick (1967), which involves four main levels of data collection: reaction, learning, behaviour and results (Fig. 15.3). Collecting reaction data represents the minimal level of evaluation for a training programme. Reaction data in Kirkpatrick's (1967) scheme are concerned with trainees' views of the training. Obviously trainees' views are valuable but may easily give a misleading impression of the value of a training programme. Trainees' views inevitably provide an incomplete view of training effectiveness. Trainees may, for example, be very enthusiastic about a training programme because it was fun and an interesting break from routine. Equally, they may give poor reports on a training programme during which they had to work extremely hard or one which involved an unpopular instructor. None of these items of feedback tells us whether the training was actually effective in promoting new learning or not.

Reaction evaluation involves gaining and using information about trainees' reactions. Many training designers collect this sort of information, sometimes without asking for it! It is undoubtedly useful to collect trainees' comments, but unfortunately in many cases this is the only information that is collected (*see*, for example, Cantalanello and Kirkpatrick, 1968).

■ **KEY LEARNING POINT**

In many cases training evaluation is limited to the collection of reaction data.

Fig. 15.3 Levels of training evaluation

REACTION

This involves collecting data directly from trainees about their *reactions* to the training. It might focus on issues such as the length of training (did trainees feel it was too long?), the depth, pace, difficulty level etc.

LEARNING

Data at this level are concerned with new knowledge acquired by trainees. Information is often collected with the aid of some test or assessment process. An actual assessment is needed – merely asking trainees if they feel more knowledgeable or skilful is not sufficient.

BEHAVIOUR

A direct test of new skills is usually what is involved here – can the trainee perform to the appropriate standard?

RESULTS

This level of evaluation focuses on the extent to which the training produces results in the workplace.

The collection of learning data represents a considerable improvement over the use of reaction data only. Learning criteria are concerned with whether or not the trainees show evidence that they have attained the immediate learning objectives of the programme. To examine this question may, for example, involve administering pre- and post-programme written tests to check participants' understanding of the material covered during training. Learning results are usually collected immediately after training is over. Like reaction data, learning data are useful but incomplete. Trainees may react well to material and understand it perfectly well but may not behave effectively when they return to work. This problem of the transfer of learning from the training course to the workplace is the focus of the next level of evaluation: behaviour. Trainees may perform well at the end of training but fail to transfer their learning to the workplace for a variety of reasons, including a fear of looking foolish (in the eyes of their established work colleagues who may not have been exposed to the training) or a belief that the old methods are more effective. Behaviour evaluation involves assessing the impact of the training on behaviour. Trainees' behaviour may be examined in a variety of ways but the main point of concern, for evaluation purposes, is to gain a clear indication of trainees' post-training behaviour. This, after all, is the reason for training in the first place. If trainees' behaviour does not change, then positive views about the training (reaction) and abundant new knowledge (learning) will count for nothing. The methods and procedures used to examine behaviour are similar to the methods described for examining job performance in Chapter 6.

TASK *How would you go about evaluating the educational programme that you are currently undertaking?*

Levels of evaluation that go beyond the reaction or learning level are concerned with the transfer of new skills to external settings. The best ways of bringing about effective training transfer have been of interest to trainers and psychologists for many years. A very wide set of factors is involved in determining the effectiveness of training transfer. At the most general level, the environment into which the trainee returns after training is crucially important. An unsupportive setting, where attempts to behave differently are not rewarded, or perhaps even ridiculed, will minimise the transfer that takes place. From the point of view of theories of skill acquisition, it is also possible to identify certain important features of training that will enhance transfer. Skills developed to the point where they are largely autonomous and rely very little on conscious processes for execution are much more resistant to deterioration. This suggests that some degree of overlearning during training will provide a better base for transfer than if training is concluded when trainees have only just reached the 'tuning' stage of skill development.

> ■ **KEY LEARNING POINT**
> *Overlearning produces skills that are more likely to transfer from the training setting to the job.*

Baldwin and Ford (1988) have produced a model of the key elements in the transfer process, which includes: trainee characteristics (ability, personality and motivation); training design (use of sound principles of learning, appropriate sequencing and content); and work environment (support and opportunities to use).

Results level evaluation involves assessing the extent to which the training has had an impact on the organisation's effectiveness. In other words, the focus here is on the organisational needs identified during the initial training needs assessment. Results criteria, although conceptually clear, are extremely difficult to assess in a controlled fashion and it is often more or less impossible to be certain whether or not changes in organisational effectiveness have been brought about by the effect of training, or whether some other factors may also be partly or entirely responsible. Sales figures, for example, may be improved as a consequence of improved sales training or by events in the external economic situation. Productivity can be improved by operator training, better equipment, improved industrial relations, social factors on the factory floor, and so on.

■ **KEY LEARNING POINT**

Although important, results level evaluation data are often very difficult to collect.

Threats to accurate evaluation

The problem of whether training is actually responsible for observed changes is one that makes the effective evaluation of training a technically complex and extremely time-consuming endeavour. The most thorough consideration of experimental designs that can be used by evaluators to examine the effectiveness of training programmes has been presented by Cook *et al.* (1990). Fundamentally, the goal of training evaluation is to provide the training designer with information about effectiveness that can be *unambiguously* interpreted and is *relevant* to the question of training effectiveness. To illustrate the problems involved in conducting good evaluation work we will consider some of the common difficulties that may arise. These difficulties are usually referred to as internal or external threats to *validity*, since they affect (or threaten to affect) the validity of conclusions that can be drawn from the evaluation. The validity of training may be divided into two broad types: internal validity is concerned with the extent to which the training has brought about new learning; questions of external validity are to do with the extent to which the training will generalise to subsequent groups of trainees and settings.

Threats to internal validity are concerned with the factors or problems which can make it appear that a training programme has been responsible for changes in learning, behaviour or results, when in fact the changes were caused by some other factors. For example, a group of new entrants to an organisation may be given a pre-training test of knowledge of the organisation's rules and procedures. After a period of induction training (one hour per day for their first week) they may be tested again. If their test scores have improved, does this mean that the induction training was responsible? Of course not – the improved knowledge could have been gained in the six or seven hours per day spent in the organisation outside the induction training course. An obvious solution to this problem is to administer the tests immediately before and after training. Would any differences now be attributable to the training? It seems more likely now, but, for example, there is the possibility that trainees might benefit from the formal training only when they have spent some of the previous day doing their normal duties in the organisation. This could be important, for instance, if, for any reason, the organisation wanted to run the induction training in one block all at once, instead of spreading it over the first week. The question here is partly one of internal validity: did the training bring about the change? It is also partly a question of external validity: will the programme be effective for different trainees in different circumstances?

Evaluation designs

In an attempt to control various threats to the validity of training, evaluation investigators will often make use of experimental designs. Most training evaluation has to be conducted within real organisational settings, and under these circumstances it is often not possible to obtain the conditions necessary for perfect experimental designs. In such circumstances it is common for what Campbell and Stanley (1963; *see also* Cook *et al.*, 1990) have called quasi-experimental designs to be utilised. Campbell and Stanley (1963) also described what they term pre-experimental designs. Such designs are unfortunately commonplace in the training world, although they produce results with so many threats to validity that they are uninterpretable and not capable of providing clear findings about training effectiveness (*see* Wexley, 1984, pp. 538–9). Two of the best-known pre-experimental designs are shown in Fig. 15.4, together with more complex designs which overcome some of the problems inherent in the pre-experimental designs.

Fig. 15.4 Pre-experimental, experimental and quasi-experimental designs for training evaluation studies

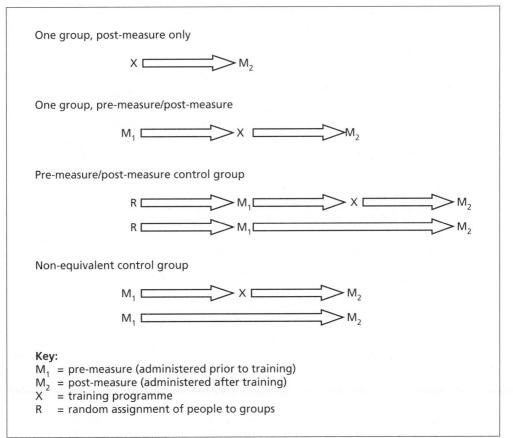

CASE
STUDY
15.1

Assessing the effectiveness of training

The Midland Provincial Bank was going through a difficult period. Changes in the status and aims of many financial services organisations, such as building societies, meant that competition for business was getting tougher and tougher. Like many banks, Midland Provincial was a fairly traditional organisation and most of its longer-serving employees had spent their careers in an industry where competition was restrained and relationships with customers were of less significance than financial acumen. In recent years this had all changed, and attracting and holding customers was of increasing importance. Interpersonal skills, customer care programmes and sales and marketing know-how were crucial qualities for the bank's employees to develop.

The bank's senior management team decided that the only way forward was to invest heavily in training in order to develop the required characteristics in their staff. Several commercial training consultancies were invited to discuss the situation with the board, and three were invited to tender for the job of retraining the bank's personnel. The board of the bank were impressed with all of the proposals and found it very difficult to choose between the two consultants who submitted the best tenders.

Eventually the decision was delegated to a small working group involving the personnel director, the controller of training and the head of human resources. The working group invited each consultant to prepare and run one pilot training course for branch managers in two different regions of the country. The personnel director visited both courses and at the end of the course conducted private (i.e. without the consultants) interviews with the course participants. He felt that the branch managers trained by one of the consultants had gained much more from the course and eventually the steering group awarded the contract to this consultancy.

Suggested exercise

Decide whether or not you feel that the steering group adopted a suitable procedure for choosing between the consultants. Explain why. Suggest ways in which the choice could have been made more effectively.

Clearly, the single-group, post-test-only design controls for none of the possible threats to internal or external validity and it is quite impossible to interpret the data. It is impossible to tell whether scores are better after training than before – let alone whether training or some other factor is responsible for any changes. The one-group, pre–post measure design goes some way towards resolving the problems by making it possible to measure change. Nevertheless, it is not possible with this design to assess whether training may have caused any difference. This may only be done if there is also an untrained control group, who are similar to the trained group and whose performance has also been measured at the appropriate times. To conduct a true experiment, trainees should be assigned to the experimental and control groups on a random basis since systematic differences between groups before the experiment could bias the results. Often this degree of control is impossible in field research and the kind of quasi-experimental design shown in the non-equivalent control group example of Fig. 15.4 is the best that can be done. Typically pre-existing groups in the organisation, such as all of the members of a particular job group, region or unit, form the groups. This is obviously administratively much more convenient than random assignment and does control for some of the main threats to validity. Even the pre–post measure control group design is subject to some threats to validity, and for totally unambiguous results more complex designs are needed (*see* Campbell and Stanley, 1963).

Evaluation research findings

The procedures for training evaluation described above are complex and difficult to administer, and it is therefore not surprising that there are so few thorough evaluation studies available; some very good examples do, however, exist (*see,* for example, Latham and Saari, 1979).

Training evaluation research has tended to concentrate on a limited set of training procedures which have been of theoretical importance or felt to have significant promise. The procedures in this category include Fiedler's *leader match training* (Fiedler, 1967) – a self-instructional programmed text (Fiedler *et al.*, 1976). Rater learning (i.e. training people to improve their ability to make accurate ratings of others) has also attracted quite a lot of attention – presumably because of the ubiquitous use of ratings in many areas of work psychology.

One approach to training that has attracted a great deal of attention in recent years is *behaviour-modelling training* (BMT), which is based on the theoretical ideas of *social learning theory* (SLT) (Bandura, 1977), more recently referred to as social cognitive theory (SCT) (Bandura, 1986); *see also* Chapter 10. Behaviour-modelling may be more promising than other training 'fads' because of its strong theoretical base. Ideas from SCT concerning how the vicarious learning process takes place form the basis for behaviour-modelling training. Vicarious learning is one of the notable ways in which SCT differs from classical ideas of operant conditioning and allows for the fact that, in addition to learning from direct experience, people may learn from observing the behaviour of others (i.e. second-hand or vicariously). In other words, trainees may learn new ways of behaving from observing the behaviour of models, hence the term behaviour-modelling training.

Early work in BMT was conducted in clinical settings (e.g. treating people with phobias). In 1974 Goldstein and Sorcher published a book describing their procedures for applying SLT and developing industrial behaviour-modelling programmes. Essentially BMT involves using Bandura's ideas about the component processes of vicarious learning as the basis for a training sequence. According to Bandura (1977), the main components of vicarious learning are: (i) attention (to a model); (ii) retention and mental organisation of the model's behaviour, (iii) motor reproduction of the model's behaviour; and (iv) motivation processes which serve to reinforce and strengthen the modelled behaviour. More succinctly: (i) notice the model; (ii) remember the behaviour; (iii) try it out; and (iv) the trainee needs to have some reason to adopt the model's behaviour (*see* Decker and Nathan, 1985).

Early research on BMT in industry laid the foundations for using the approach but did not provide the systematic control and experimental rigour necessary to evaluate the effectiveness of the technique. Some classic well-designed studies have subsequently examined the overall effectiveness (using all four of Kirkpatrick's levels) of BMT in industrial settings (e.g. Latham and Saari, 1979). More recent work (Russell *et al.*, 1984) suggests that factors concerned with the post-training work environment are crucial to the effectiveness of BMT. Several studies have examined the effectiveness of particular aspects of BMT. Most research has focused on retention processes and the use of various techniques designed to aid retention (e.g. Decker, 1982; Hogan *et al.*, 1986; Robertson *et al.*, 1991). Research on other features of the vicarious learning process (e.g. motor reproduction or motivation) is less extensive. Taken overall, BMT has a record of reasonable success. It is clear that trainees are enthusiastic about the approach and can learn from it; nevertheless the extent to which BMT can cause real changes in behaviour at work is in need of further confirmation. Robertson (1990) has provided a review and summary of much of the industrial behaviour-modelling work.

The uncertain conclusions concerning the effectiveness of BMT are reflected in many other areas of research into training effectiveness. Burke and Day (1986) conducted a quantitative analysis of 70 managerial training studies involving a variety of content areas and instructional techniques. In general, the results showed that management training techniques were effective but the authors warn that further well-designed research is essential before more conclusive statements can be made.

> ■ **KEY LEARNING POINT**
> *In general, research offers support for the effectiveness of training.*

SUMMARY

Constant social and technological change provides the context for organisational life. This, coupled with individual growth and career development, means that training has a key role in many organisations. The adequate analysis of training needs (at organisation, task and personal levels) provides the basis for training activities. Although the analysis of needs, together with a clear statement of training aims and objectives, is important, there is still a certain degree of judgement involved in choosing appropriate training methods. This essential subjectivity can be checked and assessed by the application of systematic procedures for evaluating the effectiveness of training. Evaluation at reaction, learning, behaviour and results levels provides a way of determining the overall value of training and assessing necessary improvements. In general, research has shown that training is an effective way of bringing about behaviour change, although there are often problems in ensuring that the potential for change provided by training activities actually transfers to the work setting.

CASE
STUDY
15.2

Training and organisational change

Premier TV had undergone enormous changes in the last few years. The most important of these concerned the new agreement that had been reached between management and unions. This provided a much more flexible rostering system so that unit managers could use people's time more effectively. The previous system had involved fixed rosters and set numbers of personnel for specific tasks. All this was now history and managers (in consultation with programme makers) could decide who should work on which job and how many people were needed. However, the new agreement had been achieved at a cost and it was only after severe management pressure, which included threats of compulsory redundancy, that the unions agreed to the new agreement. This had left smouldering bad feeling between many employees and the company's senior managers.

Other changes in the organisational structure of the company had also taken place. Financial controls on what was spent to make programmes were now much tighter and each department or unit was accounted for as a separate cost centre and was expected to operate at a profit by selling its services to other units within Premier TV or to outside companies.

During the period of change the human resources staff at Premier had had little opportunity to assess training needs or to organise training events – so, apart from induction training and some specialist technical training nothing had taken place for the last five years. Kathy Lamb, the human resources manager, was well aware that this could not continue and resolved to take some positive action.

Suggested exercise

Decide what Kathy Lamb should do. Explain why.

TEST YOUR LEARNING

Short-answer questions

1 What are the three key phases in the training system?

2 Explain the function of learning objectives in the design of training.

3 Describe Anderson's three stages of skill development.

4 Explain the role of probability of success (P) and cost of failure (C) in hierarchical task analysis.

5 Explain how a consideration of learning capabilities can help in training design.

6 Name and explain (briefly) four main types of evaluation data.

7 Explain what is meant by internal and external validity.

8 Give a brief critical explanation of two designs that might be used for an evaluation study.

Essay questions

1 Discuss the extent to which it is possible to obtain an unambiguous evaluation of the effectiveness of any specific training programme.

2 Explain how you would review the training needs of an organisation and design relevant training programmes.

3 Consider what value and understanding the psychology of learning has for a training manager.

GLOSSARY OF TERMS

Associative phase The second phase of skill acquisition, when the learner begins to combine the actions needed to produce skilled performance.

Autonomous phase The final phase of skill acquisition, when performance becomes increasingly polished. To some degree performance is automatic and control relies less and less on memory or attention.

Behaviour-modelling training An approach to training in which models are reinforced for engaging in the intended behaviour.

Cognitive phase The first phase of skill acquisition, when the learner is developing knowledge about the task but lacks the procedural skill to carry it out.

Development centres Events, based on the assessment centre approach (*see* Chapter 8), in which a participant is assessed through a series of tests and exercises and then given developmental feedback.

Declarative knowledge Factual knowledge that may be stated or made explicit.

External validity The extent to which one can be sure that some specific training will generalise and bring about results for subsequent groups of trainees or settings.

Hierarchical task analysis A procedure for identifying the tasks involved in a job, which proceeds to increasingly detailed task units. Task breakdown ceases when predetermined criteria are satisfied, ensuring that the analysis is sufficiently detailed for the purpose in mind.

Internal validity The extent to which one can be confident that a specific training programme (rather than some other possible cause) has brought about changes in trainees.

Job analysis Procedures (there is more than one way to do a job analysis) for producing systematic information about jobs, including the nature of the work performed, position in the organisation, relationships of the job holder with other people.

Learning data Data that are concerned with the extent to which specific skills and knowledge have been attained.

Mentoring An approach to development in which an experienced mentor is paired with a less experienced colleague to offer career advice, support and assistance in the development of new skills.

Pre-experimental design Study design (e.g. one-shot, post-only data) that does not control for major threats to validity. The results of such designs cannot be interpreted with any certainty since many factors could have been involved in causing the observed outcomes. This design may be useful for case studies.

Procedural knowledge The kind of knowledge that provides a basis for skilful performance; knowledge of how to do something which may be difficult to articulate.

Quasi-experimental design Study design that has some, but not all, of the features needed for a perfect experimental design. Such designs are often used in field settings.

Reaction data Data that are concerned with how trainees react to the training they have been given.

Terminal behaviour A statement of what the trainee should be able to do at the end of training.

Training transfer Transfer occurs when new learning is used in new settings (e.g. on-the-job) beyond those employed for training purposes.

SUGGESTED FURTHER READING

1 John Patrick's (1992) book *Training: Research and practice* provides thorough coverage of the psychology of learning and the whole area of training. He covers operative training particularly well.

2 Several, varied approaches to management development are explored in *Managing Learning*, edited by Mabey and Iles, published by Routledge in 1993.

3 Burke and Day's (1986) meta-analysis gives an insight into the range of studies done into training effectiveness. Some of the statistical analysis may prove difficult but Chapter 4 of this book should help.

REFERENCES

Anderson, J.R. (1983) *The Architecture of Cognition*. Cambridge, MA: Harvard University Press.

Anderson, J.R. (1987) 'Skill acquisition: compilation of weak-method problem solutions', *Psychological Review*, vol. 94, pp. 192–210.

Annett, J., Duncan, K.D., Stammers, R.B. and Gray, M.J. (1971) *'Task Analysis'*, Training Information Paper No. 6. London: HMSO.

Baldwin, T.T. and Ford, J.K. (1988) 'Transfer of training: a review and directions for future research', *Personnel Psychology*, vol. 41, pp. 63–105.

Bandura, A. (1977) *Social Learning Theory*. Englewood Cliffs, NJ: Prentice Hall.

Bandura, A. (1986) *Social Foundations of Thought and Action: A social cognitive theory*. Englewood Cliffs, NJ: Prentice Hall.

Burke, M.J. and Day, R. (1986) 'A cumulative study of the effectiveness of managerial training', *Journal of Applied Psychology*, vol. 71, pp. 232–45.

Campbell, D.T. and Stanley, J.C. (1963) *Experimental and Quasi-Experimental Designs for Research*. Chicago, IL: Rand McNally.

Cantalanello, R.F. and Kirkpatrick, D.L. (1968) 'Evaluating training programmes: the state of the art', *Training and Development Journal*, May 9.

Cook, T.D., Campbell, D.T. and Peracchio, L. (1990) 'Quasi experimentation' in Dunnette, M.D. and Hough, L.M. (eds) *Handbook of Industrial and Organizational Psychology*. Palo Alto, CA: Consulting Psychologists Press.

Davies, I.K. (1972) *The Management of Learning*. London: McGraw-Hill.

Decker, P.J. (1982) 'The enhancement of behavior medeling training of supervisory skills by the inclusion of retention processes', *Personnel Psychology*, vol. 35, pp. 323–32.

Decker, P.J. and Nathan, B.R. (1985) *Behavior Modeling Training*. New York: Praeger.

Duncan, K.D. (1972) 'Strategies for analysis of the task' in Hartley, R. (ed.) *Strategies for Programmed Instruction: An educational technology*. London: Butterworth.

Fiedler, F. (1967) *A Theory of Leadership Effectiveness*. New York: McGraw-Hill.

Fielder, F., Chemers, M.M. and Mahar, L. (1976) *Improving Leadership Effectiveness: The leader match concept*. New York: John Wiley.

Fitts, P.M. (1962) 'Factors in complex skill training' in Glaser, R. (ed.) *Training Research and Education*. New York: John Wiley.

Gagné, R.M. (1977) *The Conditions of Learning*. 3rd edn. New York: Rinehart and Winston.

Goldstein, A.P. and Sorcher, M. (1974) *Changing Supervisory Behavior*. New York: Pergamon Press.

Goldstein, I.L. (1993) *Training in Organizations: Needs assessment, development and evaluation*. Pacific Grove, CA: Brooks/Cole.

Hogan, P.M., Hakel, M.D. and Decker, P.J. (1986) 'Effects of trainee-generated versus trainer-provided rule codes on generalization in behavior-modeling training', *Journal of Applied Psychology*, vol. 71, pp. 469–73.

Kirkpatrick, D.L. (1967) 'Evaluation of Training' in Craig, R.L. and Bittel, L.R. (eds) *Training and Development Handbook*. New York: McGraw-Hill.

Latham, G.P. (1988) 'Human resource training and development', *Annual Review of Psychology*, vol. 39, pp. 545–82.

Latham, G.P. and Saari, L.M. (1979) 'Application of social learning theory to training supervisors through behavioral modeling', *Journal of Applied Psychology*, vol. 64, pp. 239–46.

Lee, G. and Beard, D. (1994) *Development Centres*. London: McGraw-Hill.

McEnery, J. and McEnery, J.M. (1987) 'Self-rating in management training needs assessment: a neglected opportunity', *Journal of Occupational Psychology*, vol. 60, pp. 49–60.

McGhee, W. and Thayer, P.W. (1961) *Training in Business and Industry*. New York: John Wiley.

Mabey, C. and Iles, P. (1994) 'Career development practices in the UK: a participant perspective' in Mabey, C. and Iles, P. (eds) *Managing Learning*. London: Routledge.

Mager, R.F. (1962) *Preparing Objectives for Instruction*. Belmont, CA: Fearon.

Maurer, T.J. and Tarulli, B.A. (1994) 'Investigation of perceived environment, perceived outcome and person variables in relationship to development activity by employees', *Journal of Applied Psychology*, vol. 79, pp. 3–14.

Noe, R.A. and Wilk, S.A. (1993) Investigation of the factors that influence employees' participation in development activities', *Journal of Applied Psychology*, vol. 78, pp. 291–302.

Patrick, J. (1992) *Training: Research and practice*. London: Academic Press.

Ralphs, L.T. and Stephan, B. (1986) 'HRD in the Fortune 500', *Training and Development Journal*, vol. 10, pp. 69–76.

Robertson, I.T. (1990) 'Behaviour modelling training: its record and potential in training and development', *British Journal of Management*, vol. 1, pp. 117–25.

Robertson, I.T., Bell, R. and Sadri, G. (1991) 'Behaviour modelling training: variations in retention processes', *Personnel Review*, vol. 20, pp. 25–8.

Russell, J.S., Wexley, K.E. and Hunter, J.E. (1984) 'Questioning the effectiveness of behavior modeling training in an industrial setting', *Personnel Psychology*, vol. 37, pp. 465–81.

Seymour, W.D. (1966) *Industrial Skills*. London: Pitman Publishing.

Shepherd, A. (1976) 'An improved tabular format for task analysis', *Journal of Occupational Psychology*, vol. 47, pp. 93–104.

Staley, C.C. and Shockley-Zalabak, P. (1986) 'Communication proficiency and future training needs of the female professionals: self assessment vs. supervisors' evaluations', *Human Relations*, vol. 39, pp. 891–902.

Wexley, K.N. (1984) 'Personnel training', *Annual Review of Psychology*, vol. 35, pp. 519–51.

16

Careers and career management

LEARNING OBJECTIVES

After studying this chapter, you should be able to:

1 define career and list three significant features of that definition;

2 list six ways in which careers are changing;

3 define the psychological contract and explain briefly its significance;

4 name and define Holland's six vocational personality types, and draw a diagram to show their relationship to each other;

5 identify four conclusions that can be drawn from research on Holland's theory;

6 describe three styles of career decision making;

7 name and describe the stages in two developmental theories;

8 name and describe the stages of the transition cycle proposed by Nigel Nicholson;

9 describe the psychological processes associated with each stage of the transition cycle;

10 name and describe the career anchors identified by Schein;

11 name and briefly describe eight career management interventions that can be used in organisations;

12 explain the circumstances in which career management interventions are most likely to be successful.

INTRODUCTION

Individuals and organisations are paying increasing attention to planning and managing careers. This is partly because the fast pace of economic change makes careers much less clearly defined and predictable than they once were. Ideas and perspectives from psychology play a central part in understanding and managing careers. In this chapter we examine definitions of career, alternative approaches to career choice and career development, and some of the practical applications arising from them. We also cover starting work and subsequent work-role transitions; and techniques available to help manage careers in organisations. The chapter aims to help readers to understand career theory and practice, and to apply key concepts to their own careers and also the careers of other people.

THE CONTEXT OF CAREERS

Definitions

Many definitions of career have been proposed. Like many concepts in applied psychology, there is not complete agreement about what a career is. For our purposes, we can consider a career as: *the sequence of employment-related positions, roles, activities and experiences encountered by a person*. This definition reflects ideas from several sources (e.g. Greenhaus and Callanan, 1994). Several points can be made about it:

- the notion of *sequence* means 'more than one'. Instead of looking at a person's present job in isolation, we are interested in how it relates to his or her past and future;

- the inclusion of *experiences* emphasises that careers are subjective as well as objective. Hence, for example, a person's feeling of having been successful in his or her own career may differ from an 'objective' assessment of success such as status or salary. One person may regard reaching deputy managing director as a great success, another as a disappointment. Some people may be more concerned about how effectively they integrate work and home life than about promotion (Peluchette, 1993);

- careers are *not* confined to professional and managerial occupations, nor to 'conventional' career paths involving increasing seniority within a single occupation and/or organisation;

- the term *employment-related* means that activities such as training, education and voluntary work, as well as *un*employment, can be considered elements of a person's career. Employment includes self-employment and short-term contracts.

Psychological approaches to careers can be divided between *career choice* and *career development*. The former concerns the nature and process of choice by (usually) young people, while the latter involves subsequent changes and adjustment. The distinction between career choice and career development is somewhat artificial because choices made in early adulthood nowadays often become obsolete, and have to be re-made in the light of subsequent developments. Also, career choices themselves often reflect a person's earlier changes and adjustments. Ironically, given our earlier discussion, career choice is still usually construed as choice of a type of work. Another relevant concept is *career management*, which refers to attempts to influence the nature of a career – one's own or someone else's. We have already noted that these days there is an increasing need for people to take an active part in managing their own careers. Some employing organisations also play a role in managing the careers of their staff.

> ■ KEY LEARNING POINT
> *Careers include* any *sequence of work experiences, not just conventional or orderly ones.*

Current trends in careers

The changing employment scene described in Chapter 1 has major implications for careers (*see also* Arnold, 1997, chapter 2). Briefly, features of the changing labour market in the UK and most other Western countries include:

- *increasing workload for individuals*, both in terms of hours worked per week, and the intensity of effort required during each working hour;
- *organisational changes*, particularly the elimination of layers of management (delayering) and reductions in the number of people employed (downsizing);
- *more global competition*, which means that organisations in Western countries need to control costs and also make maximum use of employees' skills and ideas;
- *more team-based work*, where individuals with different types of expertise are brought together for a limited period to work on a specific project with clear goals, such as the development of a new product;
- *more short-term contracts*, where the length of a person's employment is specified at the outset. Renewal of the contract when that time has expired is the exception, not the norm;
- *increasingly frequent changes in the skills required in the workforce*, because of the changing requirements of work partly brought about by new technology (*see* Chapter 19);
- *more part-time jobs*. Most part-time jobs are occupied by women, and many part-time workers have two or more part-time jobs;
- *changing workforces*. Relatively low birth rates and increasing longevity mean that the average age of people in work or available for it is increasing quite rapidly in most Western countries. Historic patterns of immigration and other factors mean that the workforce is more diverse in terms of ethnicity, values and gender;
- *more self-employment and employment in small organisations*. One might cynically say that a small organisation is a big one after downsizing, but in reality most small organisations have never been big. Nearly half of the people in work in the United Kingdom are either self-employed or work in organisations with fewer than 20 employees;
- *working at or from home*. Advances in communications technology and cost-cutting by employers mean that more people, currently around 3–5 per cent of those in employment, either work at home or are permanently based there;
- *increasing pressure on occupational and employer-based pension schemes*, due to the ageing population and more mobility between occupations and organisations.

It is pretty clear that these labour market changes mean significant changes in the nature of jobs and careers. Careers are different from what they were, and also on the whole more difficult to manage. Figure 16.1 illustrates this. The differences include:

- a greater need for individuals to look ahead and ensure that they update their skills and knowledge in order to remain employable. One consequence is the necessity of viewing learning as lifelong, not confined to childhood and early adulthood;

- organisations, too, need to look ahead in order to develop the skills and knowledge required for future survival;

- less frequent promotions within organisations, and (because of delayering) bigger increases in status and responsibility when promotions do happen;

- less time (and often energy) is left over for a person to consider his or her future. This is ironic because, as already noted, the need to do so is increasing;

Fig. 16.1 The changing context of careers

Changes in:	Lead to:	Changes in careers and their management:
Organisations Greater competitive pressures Fewer levels Fewer employees Smaller size More dispersed (e.g. working at home)		More need to look ahead and develop staff, but less time or resources to do it
		Less frequent promotion
		More need for networking by individuals
		More need for individuals to tolerate ambiguity
		Greater need for lifelong learning by individuals
Jobs More teamworking More short-term More part-time Changing skill requirements Harder work		More need for individuals to look ahead
		Less time/energy for individuals to look ahead
		More skills of entrepreneurship required
People Older on average More women More diverse More mobile		Everyone must be able to cope with change
		More personal financial management skills required
		Greater need to understand others' values and cultures
		Greater need to understand one's own values, skills, interests

- a greater need for individuals to make an effort to build up and maintain their networks of contacts;
- a greater need for older people, as well as younger ones, to initiate and cope with change;
- a greater need for skills of entrepreneurship, self-management and small business management;
- a greater need for individuals to be able to handle uncertainty;
- a greater need for individuals to be flexible in terms of the work they are prepared to do, and the people with whom they are able to work constructively;
- an increasing need for effective management of one's personal finances.

> ■ KEY LEARNING POINT
> *Careers are becoming more varied and more difficult to manage for both individuals and organisations.*

It is still tempting to view careers in the narrow sense of predictable moves to jobs of increasing status, usually within a single occupation or organisation. This is what Kanter (1989) has called the bureaucratic career, and indeed many people do see career in that narrow way. Consequently, there is a tendency to believe that the notion of career is becoming outdated. In line with our broader definition of career given earlier, we argue the contrary – careers are becoming more diverse and more difficult to handle, but that makes it *more* important to consider the various sequences a person experiences. As Jackson *et al.* (1996, p. 7) argue:

> Whatever soothsayers about the future of careers may assert, individual men and women remain passionately interested in ... their personal development through work experience over the course of their lifetime. People are more concerned about their skills, competencies, future roles and opportunities for self-determination than they are about most other areas of their work experience.

In recognition of the changing nature of careers, Arthur has referred to the *boundaryless career*. Careers are boundaryless in the sense that, either by choice or necessity, people move across boundaries between organisations, departments, hierarchical levels, functions and sets of skills. Movement across these boundaries is made easier by the fact that they are tending to dissolve anyway. Such movement is necessary for individuals to maintain their employability and for organisations to maintain their effectiveness. Careers are also becoming more like a sequence of short-term episodes rather than a long drawn-out systematic accumulation of experience. Hall and Mirvis (1995, p. 277) have expressed this very well:

> Careers too are becoming more complex. We would argue that what we are seeing now, instead of one set of career stages spanning a lifespan ... is a series of many shorter learning cycles over the span of a person's work life ... As a result, people's careers will become increasingly a succession of 'mini-stages' (or short-cycle learning stages) of exploration–trial–mastery–exit, as they move in and out of various product areas, technologies, functions, organizations and other work environments. ... Thus, the half-life of a career stage would be driven by the half-life of the competency field of that career work.

The psychological contract

The *psychological contract* is a concept which is proving very useful in explaining people's responses to the changing context of careers. A quite large research literature on the psychological contract has been produced in only a short time, with the key players being, in the USA, Denise Rousseau (e.g. Rousseau, 1995) and in the UK, Peter Herriot and Carole Pemberton (Herriot and Pemberton, 1995). Although much of the interest in the psychological contract is recent, its roots go back a long time, it having originally been discussed by Argyris (1960).

The psychological contract has been defined in several slightly different ways. We will use the following definition (Robinson and Rousseau, 1994, p. 246):

> An individual's belief regarding the terms and conditions of a reciprocal exchange agreement between that focal person and another party ... a belief that some form of a promise has been made and that the terms and conditions of the contract have been accepted by both parties.

So, in the context of careers, the psychological contract represents informal, unwritten understandings between employer and employee(s). From the employees' point of view, the psychological contract is the agreement that they think they have with their employer about what they will contribute to the employer via their work, and what they can expect in return. This matters for one very simple reason. During the last part of the twentieth century, and especially since around the mid-1980s, the trends described earlier in this chapter and in Chapter 1 have changed the careers landscape, and for the worse in many people's opinions. The deal many employees thought they had with their employer has turned out to be worth less than the paper it wasn't written on. As Herriot and Pemberton (1995, p. 58) put it in their book entitled *New Deals*, captains of industry 'have set in motion a revolution in the nature of the employment relationship the like of which they never imagined. For they have shattered the old psychological contract and failed to negotiate a new one'.

So what was the old psychological contract that has been broken? Herriot and Pemberton draw on a well-established distinction between a relational and a transactional contract. The former refers to a long-term relationship based on trust and mutual respect. The employees offered loyalty, conformity to requirements, commitment to their employer's goals, and trust in their employer not to abuse their goodwill. In return, the organisation supposedly offered security of employment, promotion prospects, training and development, and some flexibility about the demands made on employees if they were in difficulty. But global competition, new technology, downsizing, delayering and the rest of it have put an end to all that. Many employers no longer keep their side of the bargain. The new deal is imposed rather than agreed; it is transactional rather than relational. Instead of being based on a long-term relationship, it is much more like a short-term economic exchange. The employee offers longer hours, broader skills, tolerance of change and ambiguity, and willingness to take more responsibility. In return the employer offers (to some) high pay, rewards for high performance and, simply, a job.

According to Herriot and Pemberton (1995), many people have understandably responded very negatively to these changes. This might be particularly the case for managers, many of whom identify with the organisation rather than a profession. Their sense of identity and self-worth is therefore particularly threatened when their organisation 'rats' on the deal. Reactions vary, but include outrage, disappointment, anger, sullen conformity, fear, anxiety and probably lots of other negative things besides. The new psychological contract results from changes principally directed towards cost-cutting for increased competitiveness. However, this has gone about as far as it can go, and indeed even further if some of the research described earlier in this chapter is to be believed. Now and in the future, the UK economy will rely upon the knowledge, skills, creativity and perhaps most of all the goodwill of its workforce rather than further cost competitiveness. Unfortunately, relationships between employers and employees are not currently conducive to that. Herriot and Pemberton describe typical reactions to violation of the psychological contract as get out, get safe or get even – or, to put it another way: to leave, to stay and keep your head below the parapet, or to stay and take your revenge.

It is clear that many employees feel that their psychological contract has been violated by their employer. For example, Robinson and Rousseau (1994) found that 70 of their sample of 128 managers thought that their employer had violated their psychological contract (i.e. what they thought they had been promised) in the first two years of employment. Violations most commonly concerned training and development, pay and benefits, and promotion opportunities. When employees felt that their employer had violated the psychological contract, they were not surprisingly inclined to feel less sense of obligation and less commitment (*see* Chapter 9) to their employing organisation.

The apparent frequency with which psychological contracts are violated has led psychologists to try to clarify what is coming to be called the 'violation process'. Figure 16.2 illustrates this. Contract violation does not necessarily lead to reduced employee loyalty and

Fig. 16.2 The process of psychological contract violation

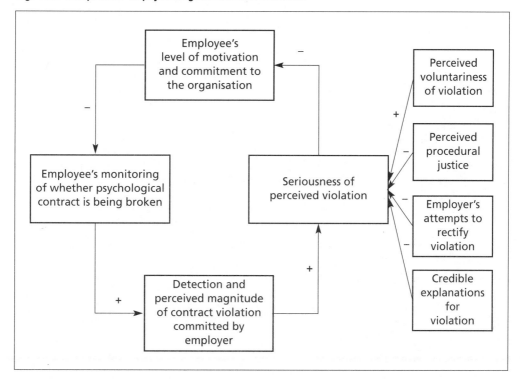

Source: Adapted from Rousseau (1995, p. 118). Note that this same process is depicted to illustrate features of motivation in Fig. 11.3.

commitment. If it is felt that the violation was neither the employer's fault, nor intended, then the impact on the employee's loyalty is likely to be small, particularly if the violation is put right quickly. Further, there is of course a lot of scope for individual interpretation in this process. For example, a person who starts out favourably disposed towards his or her employer might be less likely to notice violations than somebody who already mistrusts the employer.

> ■ **KEY LEARNING POINT**
>
> *The psychological contract concerns an individual employee's perceptions of his or her rights and obligations with respect to the employing organisation. In the eyes of individuals, employers frequently break their side of the contract.*

The psychological contract is perhaps in danger of overuse, and it does have some limitations (Arnold, 1996). Briefly, the following points can be made:

- if the psychological contract exists purely in the mind of an employee, it is no sort of contract at all. There is no agreement, written or unwritten, with any other party;
- an organisation is not a person, and therefore cannot be a party to a psychological contract. Organisations consist of many different individuals and groups, and each employee may have quite specific expectations about his or her rights and obligations vis-à-vis those individuals (e.g. supervisor) and groups (e.g. departments);
- violation of the psychological contract carries a clear implication of a broken promise. This is more emotionally charged than the more neutral notion of unmet expectations, and more complicated than simply asking how pleasant a person's experiences have been within a work organisation. It is not yet clear whether the psychological contract explains people's work behaviour any better than more neutral and simpler concepts.

CAREER CHOICE

The basic requirements of effective career choice were identified long ago by Frank Parsons (1909, p. 5, described in Sharf, 1992, chapter 2):

1 a clear understanding of ourselves, our attitudes, abilities, interests, ambitions, resource limitations and their causes;
2 a knowledge of the requirements and conditions of success, advantages and disadvantages, compensation, opportunities and prospects in different lines of work;
3 true reasoning on the relations of these two groups of facts.

This nicely describes the nature of the task, but does not in itself help people to do it well. We now examine psychologists' attempts to take things further.

Holland's theory

John Holland (1985a) has developed over many years an influential theory of career choice. In the course of his earlier work as a careers counsellor in the USA, he thought he could discern six pure types of vocational personality. He also felt that he could see the roots of these types in traditional personality theory. Throughout the 1960s he developed his concepts and measures of them. Subsequent work has sought to validate these, and to test Holland's hypotheses about career choice (*see below*). Very briefly, Holland's six personality types are:

1 *realistic*: outdoor-type. Tend to like, and be good at, activities requiring physical strength and/or co-ordination. Not keen on socializing;

2 *investigative*: interested in concepts and logic. Tend to enjoy, and be good at, abstract thought. Often interested in the physical sciences;

3 *artistic*: tend to use their imagination a lot. Like to express their feelings and ideas. Dislike rules and regulations; enjoy music, drama, art;

4 *social*: enjoy the company of other people, especially in affiliative (i.e. helping, friendly) relationships. Tend to be warm and caring;

5 *enterprising*: also enjoy the company of other people, but mainly to dominate or persuade rather than help them. Enjoy action rather than thought;

6 *conventional*: like rules and regulations, structure and order. Usually well organised, not very imaginative.

Holland proposed that the types can be arranged in a hexagon in the order described above to express their similarity to each other (*see* Fig. 16.3). Each type is placed at a corner of the hexagon. Types on opposite corners of the hexagon (i.e. three corners apart) are in many senses opposites. Types on adjacent corners (e.g. *realistic* and *conventional*) are quite similar to each other. No single type exactly matches any individual,

Fig. 16.3 Holland's six types of vocational personality

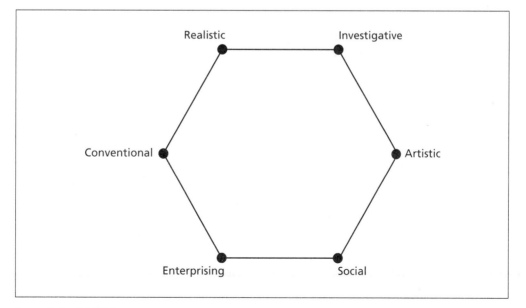

Source: Holland (1985a)

but nevertheless any given person resembles some types more than others. In fact, Holland suggests that people are most usefully described in terms of three types they resemble most, in descending order of similarity. Hence, for example, for an ISE person, the *investigative* type comes closest to describing him or her, the *social* type comes next and *enterprising* third. Holland proposed that occupations can also be described in terms of the six types. He has argued that any environment exerts its influence through the people in it. Hence occupations are described in terms of the people in them, again using the three most prevalent types in descending order. In the USA, Holland's classification of occupations has been widely applied in, for example, the *Dictionary of Occupational Titles* (US Department of Labor, 1977).

> ■ KEY LEARNING POINT
> *John Holland has identified six vocational personality types. These types map on to different occupations.*

Holland's fundamental hypothesis is that people will be most satisfied, and most successful, in occupations which are congruent with (i.e. match) their personality. Thus Holland's theory reflects a well-established tradition in work psychology: the matching of person and work, with the assumption that both are fairly stable over time. The large volume of research on this and other aspects of Holland's theory has been reviewed by Spokane (1985) and Tranberg *et al.* (1993), among others. Several conclusions can be drawn:

- Holland's vocational personality types are a reasonably good reflection of basic personality dimensions identified in more general psychology, as indeed they should be. The match is not perfect though (Tokar and Swanson, 1995). Also, the hexagonal arrangement, while not a perfect representation of the relative similarities of the types, is nevertheless a good approximation (Tracey and Rounds, 1993);

- there is some evidence that congruence is correlated with satisfaction and success, but it is surprisingly weak. Even when the correlation is observed we cannot be sure that congruence *leads* to satisfaction and success;

- using three types in establishing a person's personality may be unnecessary. The one or two types the person most strongly resembles may well be enough;

- some research has examined the congruence between a person and his or her career *choice*, rather than the person and his or her actual career or educational environment. A choice is not an environment, and is therefore an inappropriate basis for assessing congruence;

- much research has relied entirely on pencil-and-paper measures rather than behavioural ones. Thus, people often complete one questionnaire about their personality, another about their occupational or educational preferences and yet another about (for example) their satisfaction. Behavioural outcomes like absence, rate of promotion and performance should be examined more often.

Holland's approach to personality assessment is a little unusual. He has developed the *Self-Directed Search* (SDS) (Holland, 1985b), which asks the respondent about his or her preferred activities, reactions to occupational titles, abilities, competencies and even daydreams. People can score their own SDS, establish their three-letter code, and then examine an 'occupations finder' to check which occupations might be appropriate for them. There is also a 'leisure activities finder' for people who are seeking congenial spare-time pursuits. They are encouraged to try various permutations of their three-letter code, especially if their three highest scores are of similar magnitude. All of this is unusual in a number of respects. First, it is rare for questions about both abilities and interests to be included in a vocational guidance instrument. Second, the SDS is deliberately transparent – people can see what it is getting at (Holland and Rayman, 1986). Third, it is rare for psychologists to allow the people they assess to score and interpret their own data. Holland feels that most people simply need reassurance that their career ideas are appropriate, and that the SDS generally provides this much more quickly and cheaply than careers counselling.

More generally, there are many tests of occupational interests on the market – some paper-and-pencil, others computerised. Few have such a strong theoretical and empirical basis as Holland's. One that does is the *Strong–Campbell Interest Inventory* (Hansen and Campbell, 1985), which has been revised to reflect the Holland types. Data from it have contributed to the classification of occupations in Holland's terms.

> ■ KEY LEARNING POINT
> *Holland's Self-Directed Search makes it easy for a person to see for him or herself what occupations seem to be most suitable.*

Even if research on congruence has not always supported Holland's hypotheses, his approach is very valuable because it provides a structure for understanding and assessing individuals and occupations. Even so, some have suggested that alternative structures are even better. Prediger and Vansickle (1992) complained that Holland's hexagon does not allow placement of a person or occupation in two- or three-dimensional space. They proposed instead two dimensions, *data–ideas* and *things–people*. So any person could be described by his or her position on each of these dimensions, the relationships of which with Holland's hexagon are shown in Fig. 16.4. There has been a lively debate about the relative merits of the Holland and Prediger structures. Holland and Gottfredson (1992) complained that Prediger's system can produce strange or uninformative descriptions of individuals and occupations. Dawis (1992) criticised the Holland hexagon for the assumption that there are six clusters, even though eight or ten are equally plausible. On the other hand, Dawis said that Prediger's approach is based too much on vocational interests as opposed to abilities or values. The debate is likely to continue, but Holland's hexagon will certainly remain prominent in career theory and practice.

Making career decisions

Theories such as Holland's describe the *content* of actual and ideal decisions, but not the *process*. How can a person make an effective career decision? Several factors are relevant.

Fig. 16.4 Prediger and Vansickle's career dimensions in relation to Holland's types

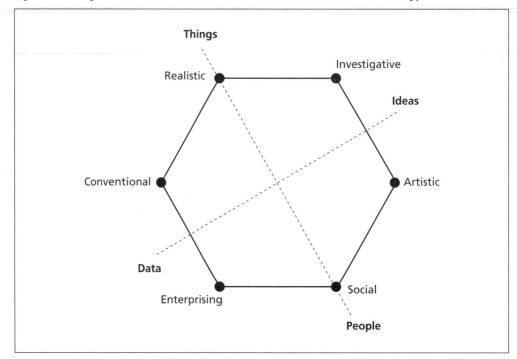

Source: Adapted form Prediger and Vansickle (1992)

Self-awareness

First, a person needs to have an accurate appraisal of his or her own strengths and weaknesses, values, likes and dislikes. Numerous exercises and techniques are available for this, some in published books (e.g. Hopson and Scally, 1991; Ball, 1996) and others homegrown in (for example) college careers advisory services. Most are designed to help people to examine systematically their experiences in the work setting and outside it, in order to arrive at the most accurate and complete self-assessment that their past experience allows. The importance of examining emotions as well as thoughts, and negative experiences as well as positive ones, is usually stressed. Careful self-assessment is important because research (e.g. Farh and Dobbins, 1989) has shown that self-assessments often fail to agree with assessments by objective tests or by other people. Mabe and West (1982) did, however, find that if people have previous experience of self-assessment and if they think carefully about how they compare with other people, their self-assessment is more likely to be accurate or at least plausible.

Knowledge of occupations

Again, there are many workbooks that give guidance on how to find out about occupations (e.g. Hopson and Scally, 1991; Bolles, 1993). Apart from reading published information, methods include talking to a person in that occupation, and 'shadowing' such a person for a period of time in order to see what he or she actually does. Emphasis is placed on avoiding stereotypes of occupations, and ensuring that one pays attention not only to positions one might ultimately occupy in an occupation, but also to those one will have to fill on the way.

Putting self-knowledge and occupational knowledge together

Often it is surprisingly difficult for people to relate what they know about occupations to what they know about self (Yost and Corbishley, 1987, chapter 5). This is especially the case when a person is trying to choose between fairly similar occupations. One advantage of the better-developed vocational measures is that they do describe people and occupations in the same language, but even then there are usually several occupations to which the person seems well suited. It is the choice between these which is often difficult. Computer-based packages, some interactive and quite sophisticated, can help people to organise their knowledge about self and world of work, and suggest possible avenues for future exploration (Jackson, 1993).

Decision-making styles

Much relevant work on decision making is described in Chapter 13. Specifically regarding *career* decision making, Phillips *et al.* (1985) identified three styles: *rational*, where advantages and disadvantages of various options are considered logically and systematically, *intuitive*, where various options are considered and the decision is made on 'gut feeling', and *dependent*, where the person essentially denies responsibility for decision making and waits for other people or circumstances to dictate what he or she should do. Not surprisingly, it seems that the dependent style is least successful. The other two are about equally successful when aggregated across large numbers of individuals, though one or the other may suit any particular person best.

CASE
STUDY
16.1

> # Your own career decision making
>
> 1 How clear are you about your abilities and interests? How specific can you be about this? For example, it is not much good simply saying you like being with people. In what situations, and for what purposes do you like being with people? If you are not clear, you might like to reflect further on your past experiences, or seek new ones to find out more about yourself.
>
> 2 How much do you know about different occupations? How clear are you about what people in particular occupations actually do, and the conditions (hours, pay, environment) in which they work? If you are not clear, you might like to read more about certain occupations, and/or ask people working in them to tell you what they know.
>
> 3 What is your typical decision-making style – rational, intuitive or dependent? How successful have your decisions been in the past? If you tend to make decisions in a dependent manner, you might try to develop one of the other styles, perhaps by practising with small decisions.

CAREER AND LIFE STAGE APPROACHES TO CAREER DEVELOPMENT

Many social scientists have sought to map out human development in adulthood (*see*, for example, Perlmutter and Hall, 1992). They have often identified age-linked stages of development, each with its own specific concerns and tasks for the person. For example, Erikson (1968), working originally from a psychoanalytic perspective, identified four stages of adult life, each with its own task that had to be satisfactorily resolved before the person could move on to the next stage:

1 *adolescence*: the key task is achieving a sense of identity. Dangers are either remaining unclear about one's self-concept, or, at the opposite extreme, developing a rigid, inflexible sense of self. Typical ages: 15–24;

2 *young adulthood*: the key task is to develop intimacy and involvement with (for example) another person, an organisation or a cause. Dangers are on the one hand being lonely and isolated due to failure to get involved, and on the other hand losing one's individuality through being too reliant upon another person or people. Typical ages: 25–34;

3 *adulthood*: the key task is to accomplish something of lasting value, preferably something that will remain after the person has gone. The main danger is achieving nothing lasting. Typical ages: 35–64;

4 *maturity*: the key task here is to feel satisfied with one's life, choices and actions. The main danger is having too many regrets about things it is too late to rectify. Typical ages: 65+.

Donald Super (1957) identified four career stages in his early work. They are similar but not identical to Erikson's life stages:

1 *exploration* of both self and world of work in order to clarify the self-concept and identify occupations which fit it. Typical ages: 15–24;

2 *establishment*: perhaps after one or two false starts, the person finds a career field, and makes efforts to prove his or her worth in it. Typical ages: 25–44;

3 *maintenance*: the concern now is to hold onto the niche one has carved for oneself. This can be a considerable task, especially in the face of technological changes and vigorous competition from younger workers. Typical ages: 45–64;

5 *disengagement*: characterised by decreasing involvement in work: a tendency to become an observer rather than a participant. Typical ages: 65+.

Clearly there are some parallels between Erikson and Super. Both saw the late teens and twenties as a time of exploration and self-concept clarification. Both viewed the following years as a time when people 'get stuck in' and make themselves indispensable. But there are differences too. Super saw this 'getting stuck in' as achievement-orientated, whereas Erikson thought more in terms of involvement. Super's view of middle-age essentially concerns hanging on, while Erikson's emphasised creative striving.

Some research has examined whether people's career concerns do indeed match Super's stages (e.g. Veiga, 1983; Isabella, 1988). The results suggest some distinction between stages, but they are not very clear cut. As Hall (1986, chapter 4) pointed out, it is difficult to identify what career stage a person is in, especially if, for example, he or she enters a career relatively late in life. Also, of course, the changing nature of careers makes it much more difficult to link stages with ages. In fact, Super (1980, 1990) acknowledged this, and developed a much more flexible framework for mapping a person's life and career. He identified six roles people typically perform in Western societies: homemaker, worker, citizen, leisurite, student and child. The importance of each of these roles in a person's life can rise and fall over time. Also, at any given time, a person can be at different stages (exploration, establishment etc.) in different roles. In other words, the career stages have now become priorities, or concerns, that an individual may have at any point in his or her adult life. These insights do not in themselves create a theory, but they do help people to consider their lives in a systematic way (Super, 1990). Some self-assessment devices such as the *Adult Career Concerns Inventory* (Super *et al.*, 1985) and the *Salience Inventory* (Super and Nevill, 1985) have been developed to assist in this process.

> ■ **KEY LEARNING POINT**
> *Erikson and Super both proposed stage theories of career and life-span development. Super in particular later loosened the connection between ages and stages.*

Of the many other attempts to map out adult life, that of Levinson and colleagues (1978) is perhaps the most influential. This influence is perhaps surprising, given that Levinson and his colleagues conducted interviews (albeit in-depth ones) with only 40 American-born men between the ages of 35 and 45. Nevertheless, Levinson came up with some interesting conclusions. He proposed that in each of three eras of adulthood (early, middle and late) there are alternating stable and transitional periods (Fig. 16.5). For example, early adulthood (ages 17–40) begins with the *early adult transition* (ages 17–22), where the person seeks a niche in the adult world. Then comes a stable phase *entering the adult world* (ages 22–28), where the task is to explore various roles while keeping one's options open. Next, between 28 and 33, comes the *age 30 transition*, where the person appraises his or her experiences and searches for a satisfactory lifestyle. This is followed by a stable settling down phase, when that lifestyle is implemented. This was called Boom (Becoming One's Own Man) by Levinson, who felt that it was a key time for men to achieve in their occupational lives.

Fig. 16.5 Phases of development in adulthood

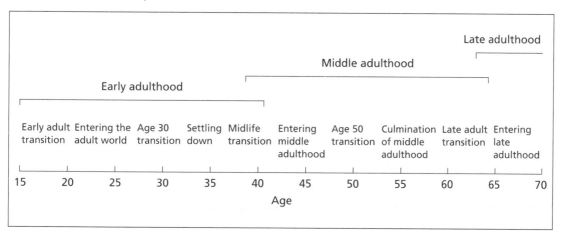

Source: Adapted from Levinson and colleagues (1978)

The *midlife transition* (ages 40–45) identified by Levinson has often been considered the most significant aspect of his work. He argued that the lifestyle is re-appraised at this age, often with considerable urgency and emotion – so much so, that some people refer to the 'midlife crisis'. People realise that their life is probably at least half over and this concentrates their minds on what they should be doing with the rest of it. In the eyes of their children they are now symbols of authority, old-timers, rather than the up-and-coming young adults that the parents would prefer to see. Physical signs of ageing become unmistakable. There are by now clear indications of whether or not earlier career ambitions will be achieved. These factors can lead to substantial life changes: for example, a change of career or a change of spouse. Alternatively, a commitment to the current lifestyle may be reaffirmed, and increased effort put into it.

After the midlife transition comes *entering middle adulthood* (45–50), then the *age 50 transition* (50–55), then the *culmination of middle adulthood* (55–60). These all concern implementing and living with midlife decisions. The *late adult transition* and *late adulthood* follow. Here, as at some other stages, Levinson's theory bears considerable similarity to Erikson's. There are also parallels with Super's work, particularly during the earlier part of adult life. But more than Erikson and Super, Levinson was very clear that his stages were closely linked with age. He argued that the lives of particular individuals may look very different on the surface, but underlying them are similar personal issues (Levinson, 1986).

■ **KEY LEARNING POINT**

Levinson proposed a closely age-linked series of phases in adult life. The phases were alternately transitional and stable in terms of tasks facing the person.

These approaches to adult development have implications for career management in organisations. If people are going to work effectively, the needs and concerns of their life stage should be taken into account. Therefore, in early adulthood, people must be given the opportunity to integrate themselves into an organisation and/or career, and demonstrate their worth to themselves and others. This may involve special efforts to give the newcomer significant work assignments and social support. In mid-career, it may be necessary to provide opportunities for some people to retrain, perhaps in the light of a midlife re-appraisal. They could also be given opportunities to allow them to keep up to date in their chosen field. It may also be helpful to give people in their mid to late career a chance to act as mentor or guide to younger employees (*see* 'Mentoring', below) – this is, after all, a way of handing on one's accumulated wisdom and thereby making a lasting impression. But these developmental theories are all vulnerable to the accusation that they really only reflect the lives of middle class males in Western countries in the mid- to late-twentieth century.

WORK-ROLE TRANSITIONS

Since the start of the 1980s, increasing attention has been paid to the processes involved in changing jobs (e.g. Sokol and Louis, 1984). This has included international job moves, which can make particularly severe demands on the person (Black *et al.*, 1991).

CASE
STUDY
16.2

Career stages

Jenny Peterson was 36 years old and had been working in the sales function of a large retailer since she was 18. She had found her early years quite difficult, and for a time wondered how she had ended up in the job. During those years, however, she gradually found that she could handle the tasks, and that some of them were quite enjoyable. By the time she was 23, she felt confident that she could cope with anything that came her way, but wondered whether she really wanted to work for the company. She thought a great deal about whether or not she liked its people and philosophy. Over the next decade, she slowly but surely found herself feeling more attached to both. Now a different matter was bothering her. Some of the younger staff seemed to know more than she did about sales techniques and marketing strategies. Was she already obsolete at age 36, she wondered?

Suggested exercise

Consider the extent to which Jenny Peterson's career so far is consistent with Super's and Erikson's stages.

Such attention is much needed. In their study of managers in the United Kingdom, Nicholson and West (1988) showed that the frequency of job moves was increasing, with three years the average time a manager spent in any single job. Equally important, the most common job moves involved changes in both status and function (27.6 per cent of job changes) or all three of employer, status and function (24.6 per cent). In other words, job changes were frequently quite dramatic. Furthermore, it appeared that many managers were unable to predict correctly whether they would change jobs even only a few months ahead. More recent evidence from Inkson (1995) has reinforced these findings, and showed that the increasing frequency of managerial job changes was not slowed by economic recession in the early 1990s. More and more job changes involve *decreases* in status.

> ■ KEY LEARNING POINT
> *Moves between jobs are happening with increasing frequency.*

Nicholson (1990) proposed a *transition cycle* model of job change. The cycle consists of four stages undergone by a person making a job change: *preparation, encounter, adjustment* and *stabilisation*. These are described in Fig. 16.6, along with some of the problems often encountered at each stage, and strategies for dealing with them. Nicholson (1990) pointed out that there is *disjunction* between stages – or put another way, each stage has its own characteristics that differentiate it from the others. At the same time, the stages are *interdependent*: that is, what happens in one stage has implications for the next. Successfully managing one stage makes it easier to manage the next successfully, and vice versa.

Fig. 16.6 The transition cycle

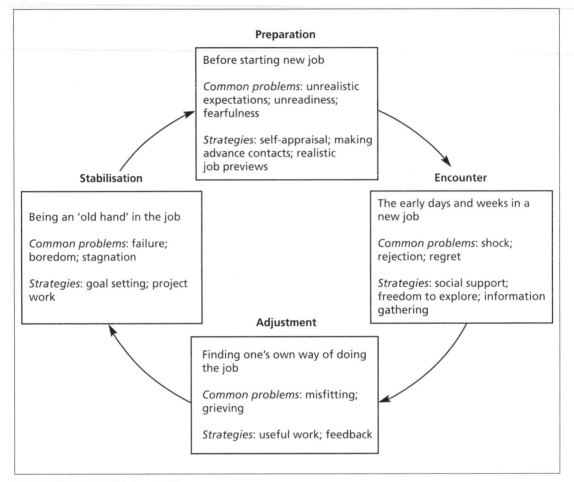

Source: Adapted from Nicholson (1990)

Preparation

The preparation stage concerns what both individual and future employer can do before the individual starts the job. From the individual's perspective some of this involves making an effective career or job choice through techniques such as self-appraisal and gathering information. Both sides have a responsibility to paint an accurate picture of themselves in order to ensure that there is no mismatch of expectations. Yet in the selection process this is not what usually happens. Both sides try to make themselves seem as attractive as possible: the individual so that he or she will be offered the job and the organisation so that the person to whom they offer the job is likely to accept it. This creates the likelihood that each side will have unrealistically high expectations about how wonderful the other is.

One technique for helping an applicant have accurate expectations of the job and organisation is to use a *realistic job preview* (RJP) during the selection process. An RJP can be a written booklet, a videotape, or a chance to do the job for a day or two. It represents an attempt to describe the job and organisation as seen by those in it. Crucially, it includes bad points as well as good ones. Although managers often fear that good applicants will be deterred by hearing about the disadvantages as well as the advantages, research suggests that RJPs succeed in reducing the number of people who leave their jobs quickly, in increasing positive work attitudes among those who experience an RJP, and in increasing the number of people who voluntarily drop out of the selection process, presumably because they realise the job is not suitable for them (Premack and Wanous, 1985). There is also some evidence that the work performance of people who experience a videotape RJP is improved, possibly because they see people doing the job, modelling effective work behaviour.

The benefits of RJPs probably depend partly on factors like whether job candidates can afford to turn down a job offer, and also whether the RJP presents an optimal amount of negative information – it is possible to be *too* negative (Wanous *et al.*, 1992). Overall, though, it seems that RJPs can reduce recruitment and training costs, and perhaps increase productivity. The exact reasons why these effects occur are still a matter of some debate. But this has not stopped Wanous (1989) offering some well-informed practical advice about how to install an RJP that works.

Encounter

RJPs are a good example of how what happens at one stage of the transition cycle can affect subsequent ones. RJPs occur at the preparation stage, but their benefits are seen at the encounter and adjustment stages. The task at the encounter stage is for the new-comer to establish a 'mental map' of his or her new environment: to understand who's who, what 'social rules' operate, what is expected of him or her, and so on. If any of this is not what the newcomer was led to expect, or if the newcomer feels it is in some sense wrong, then he or she may regret taking the job (and those who employed him or her may regret it too).

Perhaps a more common problem at the encounter stage is simply that the newcomer is not able, or enabled, to explore the new environment optimally. This may be because other people do not welcome the newcomer's questions, or because they are too busy to show the newcomer the way things are done. Alternatively, it may be because the new-comer is not very good at gathering information. How the newcomer goes about gathering information has been the subject of some research. Ostroff and Kozlowski (1992) pointed out four types of information a newcomer needs to seek out:

1 *task*: information about work duties and routines
2 *role*: information about boundaries of authority and responsibility
3 *group*: information about group norms and values
4 *organisation*: information about organisational politics, power and style.

Research by Morrison (1993), among others, has shown that active attempts by new-comers to find this information tend to be successful, and that this leads to better satisfaction, performance and commitment. A particularly useful strategy seems to be *monitoring* – that is, observing and listening to what goes on. It tends to work better than asking direct questions or consulting written documents.

> ■ **KEY LEARNING POINT**
>
> *Realistic job previews provided by the organisation and effective information seeking by the newcomer both help to integrate the newcomer quickly.*

Adjustment

Adjustment is the stage when the person has already developed an understanding of the work environment and seeks to use it to establish how to go about doing the job in the long term. Clearly, how individual and organisation have dealt with each other up to this point will influence the mode of adjustment adopted by the individual. Of importance here is research on *innovation*. For example, Schein (1971) identified three orientations a person may adopt in a job:

1 *custodianship*: where the person accepts the role requirements as given;

2 *content innovation*: where the person accepts the goals of the role but adopts his or her own ways of achieving them;

3 *role innovation*: where the person redefines the goals of the job and probably the methods too.

In the long run, role innovators are probably vital for societal advance. In the short term, many work organisations claim to value content innovators (though they would not use that term) but probably in truth they reward custodians more highly because they conform to the existing organisational culture.

Van Maanen and Schein (1979) specified some key aspects of organisational 'people-processing' strategies which would, they proposed, influence whether a person became a custodian or an innovator. These dimensions all concerned the extent to which the newcomer's socialisation was *institutionalised* or *individualised*. Institutionalised socialisation involves sending newcomers on structured training courses together as a group, and separate from other members of the organisation, with a clearly defined timetable and career plan. Individualised socialisation involves ambiguous timings of assignments, on-the-job learning in the company with established members of the organisation, and relative isolation from other newcomers (perhaps because there aren't any). The institutionalised approach tends to lead to a custodial orientation (Ashforth and Saks, 1996). This is because institutionalised socialisation exposes all newcomers to similar and quite narrow experiences. On the other hand, it gives newcomers a comforting feeling of predictability and being 'looked after' by the organisation, which leads them to feel committed to it (Allen and Meyer, 1990). The challenge is now to find ways of socialising newcomers which foster *both* innovation and commitment.

> ■ **KEY LEARNING POINT**
>
> *The ways in which newcomers to an organisation are socialised can significantly affect how they subsequently go about their work.*

Stabilisation

Nicholson (1990) has commented that much of work psychology seems to be built on the assumption that people are in the stabilisation stage. Yet the pace of change as we approach and enter a new century is such that many people spend little or no time in this stage before moving on. On the other hand, for a few people, the effect of organisations reducing the number of levels in their management hierarchy and disbanding well-established career routes is to keep them in a job for much longer than they had anticipated. This is sometimes termed a *career plateau*, which Feldman and Weitz (1988) defined as the point in a person's career where the likelihood of additional increases in responsibility is very low.

It is often assumed that the plateaued person is unhappy about this situation and that this unhappiness is likely to produce negative work attitudes and poor performance. This pattern does indeed sometimes happen (Goffee and Scase, 1992). But plateauing can occur for many reasons, and produce many reactions, not all negative (Nicholson, 1993). A person may have all the responsibility he or she wants already. Howard and Bray's (1988) longitudinal research over twenty years showed that people are often able to reduce their ambitions quite painlessly. Plateauing may therefore be something that some people are reconciled to by the time it happens. Indeed, they may *choose* not to take on additional responsibility even though they are seen as capable of handling it. Even if this is not the case, it is important to consider exactly why an individual is plateaued in order to determine what should be done about it. A lack of ability may be rectifiable by retraining. A lack of experience can be made good by a sideways move to another job which will provide the required experience, or by project work within the existing job. In some cases of possible discrimination on the basis of (for example) ethnicity or gender, senior members of the organisation may need urgently to review organisational career management practices.

Transitions into and out of the employment market

Aside from the transition cycle, there are certain transitions and aspects of transitions that have received some special attention. The first is the transition into work from education. For some years there has been a tendency to assume that this transition is likely to be difficult for young people because they are entering an unfamiliar world, making important decisions about their future, and simultaneously making the transition from childhood to adulthood. But in fact most young people who enter employment do so without undue stress (Arnold, 1990). They are often pleasantly surprised by the friendliness and informality of their workplace, and sometimes their work is actually better than they expected (Arnold, 1985). Unpleasant surprises include the political and apparently irrational ways in which decisions are made in work organisations. As Schein (1978) observed, a key task for young people entering the world of work is to accept that this is the way things are, and to decide how to handle it rather than merely complaining about it.

At the other end of the career, the transition out of work – *retirement* – has also received some attention. Just as the transition into work is becoming less clearcut than it was due to the increasing number of part-time jobs, work experience schemes in schools etc., so the same is happening to the transition out of it. Retirement is often a gradual *disengagement* (to use Super's term) from the labour force rather than a sudden change in status. Also, there is sometimes a gap between subjective and objective retirement. A person may not consider himself or herself retired even if classified as retired on the basis of the (small) number of hours worked and being in receipt of a pension (Feldman, 1994). As is the case for the transition into work, retirement is often experienced quite positively, though not always. Good health, retiring voluntarily as opposed to compulsorily, adequate income and personal preparation for retirement all help a person adjust well to being retired (Bosse *et al.*, 1991).

> ■ KEY LEARNING POINT
> *Transitions at the start and end of working life are, for most people, less difficult than is often assumed.*

Relocation

The management by organisations of people transferring from one job to another within that organisation is often covered under the label *relocation*. Brett *et al.* (1992) have identified three main forms of relocation:

1 *job transfer*: a within-country move between jobs in the same organisation;

2 *international transfer*: an international move between jobs in the same organisation;

3 *group moves*: a relocation of a relatively large group of employees who normally work together.

Employees have become more reluctant to relocate in recent years. This is partly because relocation affects the whole family. Lawson and Angle (1994), among others, have found that disruption to children's education and friendships, and difficulties of house buying and selling were more important to relocating employees and their partners than work concerns. Other research suggests that relocation has more disruptive effects on teenagers than on younger children because teenagers find it harder to break into circles of established friends in their new environment (Munton and Forster, 1990).

Of course, increasing numbers of relocations involve moves between countries. Brett and Stroh (1995) found that managers' willingness to relocate internationally was (not surprisingly) principally a product of their general attitude to moving and their spouse's willingness to relocate. Biographical variables such as age, education and number of children at home were less significant. For many reasons, including cultural and language differences, international relocation is likely to present more problems of management and adjustment than domestic relocation. In a wide-ranging review, Black *et al.* (1991) estimated that somewhere between 16 and 40 per cent of American employees sent overseas return early, and between 30 and 50 per cent stay in their assignments but are considered ineffective or only marginally effective. There is no particular reason to think that the figures for expatriates from many other countries would be much different, so it looks as if international relocation almost qualifies as a disaster zone!

Even more clearly than for domestic relocation, recent research has demonstrated the importance of non-work factors in adjustment to international relocation. In particular, the adjustment of family members seems crucial to the work and general adjustment of the relocatee. Nicholson and Imaizumi (1993, p. 130) have referred to this as 'a significant flow of adjustment from the domestic to the employment sphere' in their study of Japanese managers working in the United Kingdom. Consistent with this, Arthur and Bennett (1995) found that the family situation was perceived by a sample of 338 international relocators in 45 multinational companies as very important in determining the success of an international relocation. In fact, it was seen as more important than job knowledge and motivation, relational skills, flexibility/adaptability and even extracultural openness.

It seems that many employing organisations are rather poor at managing relocations, particularly international ones. There is often uncertainty about who is responsible for what – for example, how the assignee will be found a role on his or her return. Although training and orientation to different national cultures for international assignees are becoming more common, it is still not unusual for employees to receive only a few weeks' notice of their relocation, and this greatly increases the stress they experience. Relocation can and should be managed better than it typically is, and should form part of an organisation's strategic human resource development (Forster, 1990).

> ■ **KEY LEARNING POINT**
> *The management of relocation requires great attention to family-related concerns.*

CAREER ANCHORS

Edgar Schein (1993) has used some research he carried out many years earlier to develop the concept of *career anchors*. This has become very popular in recent years. Schein defined a person's career anchor as an area of the self-concept that is so central that he or she would not give it up even if forced to make a difficult choice. He felt that people's anchors develop and become clear during their early career, as a result of experience and learning from it. Schein's list of alternative anchors people hold is shown in Table 16.1 We might look at the list of anchors and feel that several or even all of them are important to us, but which would win if we had to choose? That is our real anchor. Career anchors consist of a mixture of abilities, motives, needs and values. They therefore reflect quite deep and far-reaching aspects of the person. It is perhaps the career anchor that a person questions when he or she is in the transitional periods identified by Levinson (*see* earlier in this chapter).

> ■ **KEY LEARNING POINT**
> *Career anchors are areas of the self-concept that a person would not give up, even if faced with a difficult choice.*

Being able to identify one's career anchor is clearly important for the effective management of one's own career. It is also important that people in organisations responsible for managing careers are aware of the prevalence of the various anchors in their organisation.

Table 16.1 Career anchors

1 *Managerial competence*. People with this anchor are chiefly concerned with managing others. They wish to be generalists, and they regard specialist posts purely as a short-term means of gaining some relevant experience. Advancement, responsibility, leadership and income are all important.

2 *Technical/functional competence*. These people are keen to develop and maintain specialist skills and knowledge in their area of expertise. They build their identity around the content of their work.

3 *Security*. People with a security anchor are chiefly concerned with a reliable, predictable work environment. This may be reflected in security of tenure – i.e. having a job – or in security of location – wanting to stay in a particular town, for example.

4 *Autonomy and independence*. These people wish most of all to be free of restrictions on their work activities. They refuse to be bound by rules, set hours, dress codes and so on.

5 *Entrepreneurial creativity*. Here people are most concerned to create products, services and/or organisations of their own.

6 *Pure challenge*. This anchor emphasises winning against strong competition or apparently insurmountable obstacles.

7 *Service/dedication*. This anchor reflects the wish to have work which expresses social, political, religious or other values that are important to the individual concerned, preferably in organisations that also reflect those values.

8 *Lifestyle integration*. People who hold this anchor wish most of all to keep a balance between work, family, leisure and other activities, so that none is sacrificed for the sake of another.

This might inform human resource policies such as job placement and transfer, promotion hierarchies and control systems. For example, problems are likely if there is an attempt to impose standard working hours and methods on people who most value the autonomy/independence anchor. Also, a common issue in organisations is how far up the hierarchy specialists such as scientists and engineers can rise without becoming general managers. Often the answer is not very far, which may create a problem for some talented staff who subscribe to the technical/functional competence career anchor. Given the labour market changes described earlier in this chapter and in Chapter 1, people with a security anchor are likely to have quite a difficult time because security is now harder to attain than it was. The technical/functional competence anchor could be a problem in organisations with project-based multidisciplinary teams, while the lifestyle integration anchor is increasingly difficult to honour when workloads are increasing.

CAREER MANAGEMENT IN ORGANISATIONS

Some organisations have responded to the trends described earlier in this chapter by giving up any attempt to manage the careers of employees. Because traditional career paths have disappeared, and organisational structures are continually changing, there does not seem much point in managing careers. The term 'self-development' is now frequently used. As the words suggest, it means that individual employees are responsible for identifying their own development needs, and doing something about them. But self-development seems to mean slightly different things in different places. On the one hand, it can be quite an aggressive message: 'You're on your own; look after yourself'. Alternatively, it can be more supportive: 'Don't expect the organisation to tell you how you need to develop, but we can play a part in helping you to make and implement your own decisions'.

Table 16.2 describes some of the interventions that can be used in organisations to manage careers. It is difficult to obtain accurate figures on which interventions are used most, though evidence from Iles and Mabey (1993) and Gutteridge *et al.* (1993) is helpful. It looks as if internal vacancy advertising is nearly universal. Mentoring seems to be becoming increasingly common, with perhaps 50 per cent of medium to large-size organisations either running organised schemes or actively encouraging the formation of informal mentor–protégé pairings. Formal career path information is (or is said to be) provided in about one-third of organisations, which is perhaps surprising given the disappearance of career paths in many organisations. Self-assessment materials, development centres, career planning workshops and career counselling probably feature in one in four or one in six organisations.

> ■ **KEY LEARNING POINT**
> *There are many different career management interventions available to organisations.*

Several of the career management interventions shown in Table 16.2 (for example, mentoring, career action centres) can be used to support self-development rather than organisational control of careers. But on the whole, the interventions are used to pursue organisational goals, and in some organisations the notion of managing careers has rather come back into fashion. This is a reaction to the fact that the choices people make about their self-development do not necessarily serve the needs of the organisation. For example, a company's IT specialists may tend to seek training on a popular software package which helps them to maintain their employability, but which happens to be of little use to that company.

It is neither possible nor desirable to use all of the interventions in the same organisation at the same time. Hirsh *et al.* (1995) point out that it is much better to do a few things well than a lot badly. It is also necessary to be clear about what an intervention is designed to achieve, and on whose behalf. Possible purposes are:

- filling vacancies – that is, selecting one or more people for specific posts;
- assessment of potential, competencies, skills or interests – this might help an organisation to assess its human resources, or individuals to know how well placed they are to obtain specific jobs inside or outside the organisation;
- development of skills and competencies – in order to help an organisation to function effectively in its markets, or individuals to be more effective in future jobs;
- identification of career options – that is, what types of work or specific posts might be obtainable for one or more individuals;
- action to implement career plans.

Table 16.2 Career management interventions in organisations

1 *Internal vacancy notification.* Information about jobs available in the organisation, normally in advance of any external advertising, with a job description and some details of preferred experience, qualifications.

2 *Career paths.* Information about the sequences of jobs that people can do, or competencies they can acquire, in the organisation. This should include details of how high in the organisation any path goes, the kinds of interdepartmental transfers that are possible, and perhaps the skills/experience required to follow various paths.

3 *Career workbooks.* These consist of questions and exercises designed to guide individuals in determining their strengths and weaknesses, identifying job and career opportunities, and determining necessary steps for reaching their goals.

4 *Career planning workshops.* Cover some of the same ground as workbooks, but offer more chance for discussion, feedback from others, information about organisation-specific opportunities and policies. They may include psychometric testing.

5 *Computer assisted career management.* Various packages exist for helping employees to assess their skills, interests and values, and translate these into job options. Sometimes those options are customised to a particular organisation. A few packages designed for personnel or manpower planning also include some career-relevant facilities.

6 *Individual counselling.* Can be done by specialists from inside or outside the organisation, or by line managers who have received training. May include psychometric testing.

7 *Training and educational opportunities.* Information and financial support about, and possibly delivery of, courses in the organisation or outside it. These can enable employees to update, retrain or deepen their knowledge in particular fields. In keeping with the notion of careers involving sequences, training in this context is not solely to improve performance in a person's present job.

8 *Personal development plans (PDPs).* These often arise from the appraisal process and other sources such as development centres. PDPs are statements of how a person's skills and knowledge might appropriately develop, and how this development could occur, in a given timescale.

9 *Career action centres.* Resources such as literature, videos and CD-ROMS and perhaps more personal inputs such as counselling available to employees on a drop-in basis.

10 *Development centres.* Like assessment centres in that participants are assessed on the basis of their performance in a number of exercises and tests. However, development centres focus more on identifying a person's strengths, weaknesses and styles for the purpose of development, not selection.

11 *Mentoring programmes.* Attaching employees to more senior ones who act as advisors, and perhaps also as advocates, protectors and counsellors.

12 *Succession planning.* The identification of individuals who are expected to occupy key posts in the future, and who are exposed to experiences which prepare them appropriately.

13 *Job assignments/rotation.* Careful use of work tasks can help a person to stay employable for the future, and an organisation to benefit from the adaptability of staff.

14 *Outplacement.* This may involve several interventions listed above. Its purpose is to support people who are leaving the organisation to clarify and implement plans for their future.

15 *Secondment.* Individuals work temporarily in another organisation, or in another part of the same one.

> ■ **KEY LEARNING POINT**
>
> *It is important that the purpose(s) of career management interventions are clearly defined and stated.*

Any intervention might achieve more than one purpose, but it is important to be clear about what purpose(s) it is designed for. It is also necessary, according to Hirsh *et al.* (1995), to be clear about who in the organisation is eligible to participate in interventions – preferably everyone. The operation of a career management intervention must be consistent with its goals. So, for example, it would be inappropriate for feedback about performance in a development centre to be withheld from participants if an aim of the development centre was to help people identify their career options.

We will now briefly describe three career management interventions that are of particular interest to work psychologists.

Career counselling

This has been defined by Nathan and Hill (1992) as 'a process which enables people to recognise and utilise their resources to make career-related decisions and manage career-related problems'. One might add that this process is an interpersonal one, in order to distinguish counselling from (for example) computer-aided guidance.

There are several different approaches to career counselling, some of which draw very directly on specific traditions in psychology (*see* Chapter 2; *see also* Walsh and Osipow, 1990). One approach relies heavily on the use of psychometric tests and here the counsellor tends to give advice on the basis of the test results. However, the most common approach to counselling can be described as person-centred, based loosely on Carl Rogers' humanist ideas (*see* Chapter 2). The counsellor does not generally give advice, but helps the client clarify his or her ideas about self and world of work by offering unconditional positive regard and asking open-ended questions. Reddy (1987), among others, has adapted the work of Egan (1990 and earlier editions), and identified three phases in a counselling episode:

1 *understanding*: the counselling focuses on listening to what the client is saying, and observing the associated non-verbal behaviour. The counsellor seeks to show no more than understanding. Listening requires concentration. Normal everyday conversation often involves surprisingly little listening, so a person who is being a counsellor needs to work on it;

2 *challenging*: as Reddy (1987) points out, listening helps for a lot longer than one might think, but not for ever. The aim of this second phase is to help a client shift his or her thinking by probing for further information, challenging apparent inconsistency, summarising what the counsellor thinks the client has said, and perhaps by giving information. Suggesting interpretations and picking out themes are other possible counsellor techniques of this stage, *but not before*;

3 *resourcing*: having clarified the feeling (phase 1) and thinking (phase 2), possible decisions and plans of action often emerge. Here the counsellor's role is often to help the client to fine-tune plans, perhaps by giving coaching in job-seeking techniques, and suggesting sources of further information.

> ■ KEY LEARNING POINT
> *Career counselling is more about listening than giving advice.*

Career counselling is offered by a number of individuals and agencies in education and private practice. It can also occur much more informally through work colleagues, friends or relatives. Some organisations offer (and pay for) career counselling for staff, normally delivered by an independent consultant who has no stake in the organisation and who can therefore work purely in the client's interest. Perhaps understandably, it is common for organisations to offer career counselling only when there is an immediate and obvious need, such as when people are being made redundant. Whatever the situation in which counselling occurs, it is important that the counsellor maintains confidentiality. Nothing that is said or done in the counselling sessions can normally be revealed to anyone else, except with the client's permission.

Career planning workshops

A small but growing number of organisations use career planning workshops for employees. These can take a variety of forms, but normally involve a group of four to ten people spending three or four days together in the presence of a leader. The days are normally spread over several weeks, and there may be 'homework' for group members between meetings.

A common pattern is for participants to discuss their strengths and weaknesses, exchange feedback about each other's ideas, engage in self-assessment exercises and perhaps make plans for future career moves which they present to the group. This requires considerable trust on the part of group members that information they reveal will not be fed back to people in the organisation who can influence their career prospects. Care is required in selecting members of the group, and in establishing a clear understanding that even if some members of the group are more senior in the organisation than others, seniority does not count for anything in the workshop.

The managers of people who attend careers workshops are often worried that their subordinates may be trying to change career or at least move to another part of the organisation. This is sometimes true, but more often it is a case of workshop attenders clarifying their commitment to their current career and perhaps developing ways of managing their current situation better (Jackson, 1990).

Mentoring

Mentoring has been defined in a number of ways, but perhaps the most widely accepted definition is that of Kram (1985): 'a relationship between a young adult and an older, more experienced adult that helps the younger individual learn to navigate in the adult world and the world of work. A mentor supports, guides and counsels the young adult as he or she accomplishes this important task'.

Mentoring can fulfil a number of specific functions for the person being mentored (who is normally called the protégé). Kram (1985) divided these into *career functions* and *psychological functions*. The *career functions* include sponsorship, where the mentor promotes the interests of the protégé by putting him or her forward for desirable projects or job moves; exposure and visibility to high-ranking people; coaching the protégé by sharing ideas and suggesting strategies; protecting the protégé from risks to his or her reputation; and (if the mentor is in a position to do so) providing challenging work assignments for the protégé. The *psychological functions* include acting as a role model for the protégé; providing acceptance and confirmation; frank discussion of the protégé's anxieties and fears; and friendship.

Mentoring is becoming a popular technique for developing younger employees; so much so that claims like 'everyone needs a mentor' (Clutterbuck, 1991) are taken seriously. It is potentially an effective way of socialising new employees and passing on accumulated wisdom. It also offers some people in mid or late career the chance to be a mentor, which may appeal to their needs for generativity (*see* Erikson, 1968) and can introduce a motivating new element to their job. On the other hand, there is not yet very much research demonstrating that people who participate in organised mentoring schemes receive benefits that other people do not. What evidence there is suggests that they enjoy better salaries and promotion rates, at least under some circumstances (Whitely *et al.*, 1991; Scandura, 1992). But it is less clear whether receiving mentoring is actually what produces the benefits. Perhaps the people who experience mentoring tend to have certain characteristics (for example, ability to get themselves noticed by effective mentors, or to be selected by organisations offering mentoring) which would have brought them success even without mentoring.

It is likely that some mentoring schemes work better than others. It is probably important that mentors and protégés want the relationship, and they may well need training and orientation in order to make the most of it. The goals of the mentoring scheme should be clear and specific. The mentor's work performance should be assessed and rewarded partly on the basis of how effectively he or she is carrying out the mentoring role. The culture of the organisation should be one which values personal and professional development. Even then there is a danger that mentors will hand on outdated knowledge and skills to protégés, especially in times of rapid change.

> ■ **KEY LEARNING POINT**
> *Mentoring has potential benefits for all parties involved, but it is not easy to achieve those benefits with a managed scheme.*

GENDER AND CAREERS

Much research on careers has focused on males, and often white, middle-class ones at that. This is not a satisfactory state of affairs. Since the 1980s there have been some attempts to rectify the imbalance (*see*, for example, Larwood and Gutek, 1987; Davidson and Burke, 1994). There is no doubt that women are at a disadvantage relative to men in the labour market (Davidson and Cooper, 1992; *see also* Chapter 5) so to what extent do existing theory and practice reflect women's needs and career problems? Not very much, many would answer.

The life-span theories of Levinson and Erikson described earlier in this chapter have been particularly heavily criticised for focusing on the experiences and personal concerns of men to the exclusion of those of women. For example, Bardwick (1980) and Gallos (1989), among others, have argued that women focus more on attachment and affiliation in their development, in contrast to men, who emphasise separateness and achievement. Nevertheless, although some developmental issues are more problematic for women than for men, Levinson would argue that the same underlying concerns arise at the same ages for both sexes. So whereas for a man the age 30 transition might focus mainly on occupational concerns, for a woman it might concern whether and when to have children. The issues are different but the theme of fine-tuning the direction of one's life is the same (Roberts and Newton, 1987).

A number of psychologists have developed theories concerning aspects of women's career development. For example, Fassinger (1985) has developed a model of college women's career choice. Betz and Hackett (1981) have examined how self-efficacy influences women's career choices and aspirations. Gattiker and Larwood (1988) have discussed what career success means for women. These and other analyses have in common a recognition that the socialisation of girls and societal expectations of women's and men's roles are likely to have profound effects on the way women think about their careers. The same is true for men, but this is less often recognised because of the temptation to take male socialisation and values as an unquestioned norm.

When women's career success is assessed on the basis of conventional criteria of salary progression and promotion, there is generally bad news. Stroh *et al.* (1992) found that women members of a large sample of American managers, who were comparable to men in education, qualifications, experience, proportion of family income generated and willingness to relocate, still suffered from slightly less good salary progression than the men. Schneer and Reitman (1995) found that women MBA graduates, up to 18 years after obtaining their degree, earned on average 19 per cent less than men, and that only a small part of this could be explained by possibly legitimate factors such as years of work experience. But perhaps the most significant evidence comes from Schein *et al.* (1989), who found that most people's stereotype of the characteristics of a manager was much more similar to their stereotype of a typical man than a typical woman. This trend was slightly less strong than it had been in the 1970s, but still suggested that women have difficulty in being taken seriously as candidates for management jobs.

> ■ **KEY LEARNING POINT**
> *Women and men tend to have different developmental paths. Career theory and practice reflect men's perspectives better than women's.*

One way in which women's careers have traditionally differed from men's is, of course, their likelihood of being interrupted by child-bearing and child-rearing, and by the fact that in most households a woman does more of the childcare and housework than a man, no matter what her employment situation. The presence of two people in a household pursuing careers (usually called dual-career couples) adds extra stresses for both partners, but again these seem to fall more on the woman than on the man (Cooper and

Lewis, 1993). A variety of measures designed to help people with family responsibilities are used by some employers, though not very many. One of these is flexible working patterns, such as total annual working hours which people can distribute through the year as they wish (within certain fairly broad limits). Career breaks have been used relatively extensively, most notably by financial services organisations. People can suspend their career with the organisation for several years, normally in order to make a start on raising a family. During that time they must report for refresher training for a small number of weeks per year. These may look like expensive schemes, but what evaluation evidence there is suggests that they are cost effective for organisations because they help to retain skilled labour. On the other hand, there is some feeling that people who make use of them may find that their subsequent progress is handicapped by others perceiving that they are not really serious about their career (Schwartz, 1996).

SUMMARY

Careers concern the sequence of jobs people hold, and the attitudes and behaviours associated with them. Labour market and organisational changes have made the careers experienced by many people less predictable than they once were, and a sense of injustice and broken promises is quite common among employees in work organisations. It is increasingly recognised that choices frequently have to be re-made later in careers, and that between choices many significant developments can occur. Much career development theory and practice therefore attempts to identify people's concerns at different stages of their lives, though research on career choice tends to treat it as choice of a type of work based on relatively static personal characteristics. Theory tends to reflect men's perspectives better than women's. Given the increasing frequency of job changes, there is also a lot of attention paid to how individuals and organisations can manage transitions from one job to another. Some organisations attempt to manage the career development of their employees. A number of techniques can be used to achieve this, including mentoring, careers counselling and development centres. Current trends are towards increasing flexibility of career structures, and towards identifying how career development systems can be implemented and maintained successfully within organisations.

CASE
STUDY
16.3

A successful laboratory technician

Pauline Ware was deputy chief laboratory technician at the main factory of a medium size agrochemicals company. She had been there eleven years, ever since joining from school. This is her story:

'When I left school I didn't really know exactly what I wanted to do. I took my exams, mainly in sciences. I passed but did less well than I had hoped. I had really wanted to be a science teacher, but I wasn't sure whether my grades were good enough to get into a teacher training course, and somehow I never got round to finding out. Also, I wasn't very confident about my abilities at that time, and wondered whether I could really handle lots of youngsters. Mind you, I had helped one of my teachers with one of his classes of younger children a few times, and that seemed to go quite well.

▶

Anyway, I saw an advert in the local paper for a trainee lab technician job here. It sounded good. They said the person selected would be able to choose which project they wanted to work on, and that in the long term there would be chances to take extra courses and get promotion to a job as development scientist. I was also told that most of my work would be quite skilled, and that other people were employed to do the most boring bits. Well, they offered me the job and I took it. I soon found out that things weren't quite as I'd imagined. There was no choice of project at that time, the budget for technician education was small, nobody could remember anyone being promoted from technician to scientist, though it was possible in theory, and I found I *was* expected to do many unskilled tasks like sweeping the floor. I complained to Personnel or Human Resources as they are called these days. They were quite surprised, and said that the laboratory must have failed to implement the changes in technician's job descriptions agreed several months earlier.

So I was quite fed up, but I didn't leave. That was partly because I couldn't think of anything better, and partly because I was planning to get married, and somehow work didn't seem very important. And I did learn quite a lot in that first job. I got little training, and there were no other new technicians joining at the same time as me, so it was a bit scary at first, but I learned my own way of doing things. That stood me in good stead four years later when I was moved to another lab. I soon found out that my predecessor there had not been very effective. Although it was a different lab, I knew more or less what to do. I changed a lot of things for the better, and that got me noticed. In the next six years I was promoted three times. So now here I am as deputy chief technician.

You'd think that was fine, but actually I'm not so sure. I don't really know where to go next. I wouldn't want the chief's job. She has to go to lots of meetings, argue over financial allocations, draw up five-year plans and all that. Myself, I have to make sure we are getting the right equipment at the right time, and I look after the training of the technicians – so in a way I'm a teacher after all! The point is that I'm still using my scientific know-how.

In the last five years three chiefs have left because the chief's job does not involve technical work. So have two deputies who can't see any future for them in the chief's work. I have the same problem: I like my work, but I think in a couple of years I will have done all I can in this role. Then what? Nobody knows, least of all me. I want to prove I can handle a higher job because nowadays I feel confident about my abilities. Yet this company has never said anything about where you can go from here. In fact, I'm seeing Human Resources about it next week. Mind you, I still haven't forgotten how out of touch they were when they advertised my job.'

Suggested exercises

1 *Examine the role in this case study of (i) Pauline's self-concept, (ii) realistic job previews, (iii) socialisation and innovation, and (iv) career anchors.*

2 *If you were the human resources manager, what provision, if any, would you be making to support the career development of laboratory technicians in the company?*

Short-answer questions

1 Describe the reasons why careers are more difficult to manage than they used to be.

2 What vocational personality types have been identified by John Holland, and how are they related to each other?

3 What stages of adult life were identified by Erik Erikson, and what are the main characteristics of each stage?

4 Describe the transition cycle and for each stage suggest one problem that might arise for a person experiencing a work-role transition.

5 What is a 'realistic job preview'?

6 According to Schein, what is a career anchor? List at least six of the anchors Schein proposed.

7 What is a career plateau? List five reasons why a person may become plateaued.

8 Define mentoring and outline its potential benefits.

9 What three stages can be identified in a counselling relationship?

Essay questions

1 Examine how labour market changes are affecting the careers that people experience.

2 Examine the extent to which John Holland's theory has improved our understanding of careers.

3 In what ways, if any, does the transition cycle help us to understand and manage job change?

4 What, if anything, can career/life stage theories contribute to effective career management?

5 How much is known about the effectiveness of career management interventions in organisations?

GLOSSARY OF TERMS

Career The sequence of employment-related positions, roles, activities and experiences encountered by a person.

Career anchor The set of self-perceived skills, interests, motives and values that form a basis for a person's career preferences, and which he or she would not give up even if required to make a difficult choice.

Career choice The selection made by a person of an area of work or sequence of work roles which they intend to pursue.

Career counselling An interpersonal process which enables people to recognise and utilise their resources to make career-related decisions and manage career-related problems.

Career decision making The psychological processes involved in making a career choice.

Career development The changes and adjustments experienced by a person as a consequence of a career choice.

Career management The techniques and strategies used by individuals and organisations in seeking to optimise careers.

Career planning workshops Meetings of groups of people who, through discussion, exercises and information, seek to clarify their career plans.

Career plateau The point in a person's career when the likelihood of additional increases in responsibility is very low.

Career stage A period of time in a person's career characterised by a particular set of concerns or motives.

Congruence In John Holland's theory, congruence is the extent to which a person's vocational personality matches his or her work environment.

Life stage A period of time in a person's life characterised by a particular set of concerns or motives.

Mentoring A relationship between a young adult and an older, more experienced adult that helps the younger individual learn to navigate in the adult world and world of work.

Psychological contract An individual employee's beliefs about the rights and obligations of both sides in the employment relationship.

Realistic job preview A technique used in recruitment where an organisation presents a balanced view of a job to applicants rather than only its good points. This can be done using written materials, videos or even a day or two's experience of the job.

Relocation A job move within an organisation to a different location which requires a move of home.

Retirement There is no single accepted definition of retirement. For most people it is the time when, having experienced a number of years of work, they withdraw from the labour market and do not intend to re-enter it.

Role innovation The extent to which a person seeks to change the nature of his or her job.

Self-development An approach to staff development which places primary responsibility for identifying development needs and taking action to deal with them on the individual employee.

Socialisation The processes by which the person learns and adopts the behaviours, attitudes and values expected in his or her role.

Transition cycle In Nigel Nicholson's research on work-role transitions, the transition cycle is the sequence of stages a person goes through in adjusting to a new job.

Work-role transition Any move between jobs, into a job or out of one, or any substantial change in work duties.

SUGGESTED FURTHER READING

1 John Arnold's (1997) book *Managing Careers into the 21st Century*, published by Paul Chapman, provides a more detailed analysis of all of the topics covered in this chapter.

2 Peter Herriot and Carol Pemberton (1995) wrote a superbly readable account of what is happening to managers' careers, and what should be done about it. The book is called *New Deals*, and is published by Wiley.

3   In *The Workplace Revolution*, published by Kogan Page, Cary Cooper and Suzen Lewis (1993) have provided a wide-ranging and practical book concerning how individuals and organisations can deal with problems afflicting dual-career families.

REFERENCES

Allen, N.J. and Meyer, J.P. (1990) 'Organizational socialization tactics: a longitudinal analysis of links to newcomers' commitment and role orientation', *Academy of Management Journal*, vol. 33, pp. 847–58.

Argyris, C.P. (1960) *Understanding Organizational Behavior*. Homewood, IL: Dorsey.

Arnold, J. (1985) 'Tales of the unexpected: surprises experienced by graduates in the early months of employment', *British Journal of Guidance and Counselling*, vol. 13, pp. 308–19.

Arnold, J. (1990) 'From education to job markets' in Fisher, S. and Cooper, C.L. (eds) *On the Move: The psychological effects of change and transition*. Chichester: John Wiley.

Arnold, J. (1996)'The psychological contract: a concept in need of closer scrutiny?', *European Journal of Work and Organizational Psychology*, vol. 5, pp. 511–20.

Arnold, J. (1997) *Managing Careers into the 21st Century*. London: Paul Chapman.

Arthur, W. and Bennett, W. (1995) 'The international assignee: the relative importance of factors perceived to contribute to success', *Personnel Psychology*, vol. 48, pp. 99–114.

Ashforth, B.E. and Saks, A.M. (1996) 'Socialization tactics: longitudinal effects on newcomer adjustment', *Academy of Management Journal*, vol. 39, pp. 149–78.

Ball, B. (1996) *Assessing Your Career: Time for a change?* British Psychological Society, Leicester.

Bardwick, J. (1980) 'The seasons of a woman's life' in McGuigan, D. (ed.) *Women's Lives: New theory, research and policy*. Ann Arbor, MI: University of Michigan.

Betz, N.E. and Hackett, G. (1981) 'The relationship of career-related self-efficacy expectations to perceived career options in college women and men', *Journal of Counseling Psychology*, vol. 28, pp. 399–410.

Black, J.S., Mendenhall, M. and Oddou, G. (1991) 'Toward a comprehensive model of international adjustment: an integration of multiple theoretical perspectives', *Academy of Management*, vol. 16, pp. 291–317.

Bolles, R.N. (1993) *What Color is your Parachute?* Berkeley, CA: Ten Speed Press.

Bosse, R., Aldwin, C., Levenson, M. and Workman-Daniels, K. (1991) 'How stressful is retirement? Findings from a normative aging study', *Journal of Gerontology*, vol. 46, pp. 9–14.

Brett, J.M. and Stroh, L.K. (1995) 'Willingness to relocate internationally', *Human Resource Management*, vol. 34, pp. 405–24.

Brett, J.M., Stroh, L.K. and Reilly, A.H. (1992) 'Job transfer' in Cooper, C.L. and Robertson, I.T. (eds) *International Review of Industrial and Organizational Psychology*, vol. 7. Chichester: John Wiley.

Clutterbuck, D. (1991) *Everyone Needs a Mentor*. Wiltshire, UK: Cromwell Press.

Cooper, C.L. and Lewis, S. (1993) *The Workplace Revolution: Managing today's dual career families*. London: Kogan Page.

Davidson, M.J. and Burke, R.J. (eds) (1994) *Women in Management – Current research issues*. London: Paul Chapman.

Davidson, M.J. and Cooper, C.L. (1992) *Shattering the Glass Ceiling – The woman manager*. London: Paul Chapman.

Dawis, R.V. (1992) 'The structure(s) of occupations: beyond RIASEC', *Journal of Vocational Behavior*, vol. 40, pp. 171–8.

Egan, G. (1990) *The Skilled Helper*. 4th edn. Monterey, CA: Brooks/Cole.

Erikson, E.H. (1968) *Identity: Youth and Crisis*. New York: Norton.

Farh, J. and Dobbins, G.H. (1989) 'Effects of comparative performance information on the accuracy of self-ratings and agreement between self and supervisor ratings', *Journal of Applied Psychology*, vol. 74, pp. 606–10.

Fassinger, R. (1985) 'A causal model of college women's career choice', *Journal of Vocational Behavior*, vol. 27, pp. 123–53.

Feldman, D.C. (1994) 'The decision to retire early: a review and reconceptionization', *Academy of Management Review*, vol. 19, pp. 285–311.

Feldman, D.C. and Weitz, B.A. (1988) 'Career plateaux reconsidered', *Journal of Management*, vol. 14, pp. 69–80.

Forster, N.S. (1990) 'A practical guide to the management of job changes and relocations', *Personnel Review*, vol. 19, pp. 26–35.

Gallos, J.V. (1989) 'Exploring women's development: implications for career theory, practice and research' in Arthur, M.B., Hall, D.T. and Lawrence, B.S. (eds) *Handbook of Career Theory*. Cambridge: Cambridge University Press.

Gattiker, U. and Larwood, L. (1988) 'Predictors for managers' career mobility and satisfaction', *Human Relations*, vol. 41, pp. 569–91.

Goffee, R. and Scase, R. (1992) 'Organizational change and the corporate career: The restructuring of managers' job aspirations', *Human Relations*, vol. 45, pp. 363–86.

Greenhaus, J.H. and Callanan, G.A. (1994) *Career Management*. 2nd edn. Orlando, FL: Harcourt Brace.

Gutteridge, T.G., Leibowitz, Z.B. and Shore, J.E. (1993) *Organizational Career Development*. San Francisco, CA: Jossey-Bass.

Hall, D.T. (1986) 'Breaking career routines: midcareer choice and identity development' in Hall, D.T. (ed.) *Career Development in Organizations*. London: Jossey-Bass.

Hall, D.T. and Mirvis, P.H. (1995) 'Careers as lifelong learning' in Howard, A. (ed.) *The Changing Nature of Work*. San Francisco, CA: Jossey-Bass.

Hansen, J.C. and Campbell, D.P. (1985) *The Strong Manual*. Palo Alto, CA: Consulting Psychologists Press.

Herriot, P. and Pemberton, C. (1995) *New Deals*. Chichester: John Wiley.

Hirsh, W., Jackson, C. and Jackson, C. (1995) *Careers in Organizations: Issues for the Future*, IES report 287. Brighton: Institute for Employment Studies.

Holland, J.L. (1985a) *Making Vocational Choices*. 2nd edn. Englewood Cliffs, NJ: Prentice Hall.

Holland, J.L. (1985b) *The Self-Directed Search: Professional manual*. Odessa: Psychological Assessment Resources Inc.

Holland, J.L. and Gottfredson, G.D. (1992) 'Studies of the hexagonal model: an evaluation', *Journal of Vocational Behavior*, vol. 40, pp. 158–70.

Holland, J.L. and Rayman, J.R. (1986) 'The Self-Directed Search' in Walsh, W.B. and Osipow, S.H. (eds) *Advances in Vocational Psychology*, vol. 1. London: Lawrence Erlbaum.

Hopson, B. and Scally, M. (1991) *Build your own Rainbow*. London: Mercury.

Howard, A. and Bray, D.W. (1988) *Managerial Lives in Transition*. New York: Guilford Press.

Iles, P. and Mabey, C. (1993) 'Managerial career development programmes: effectiveness, availability and acceptability', *British Journal of Management*, vol. 4, pp. 103–18.

Inkson, K. (1995) 'Effects of changing economic conditions on managerial job changes and careers', *British Journal of Management*, vol. 6, pp. 183–94.

Isabella, L.A. (1988) 'The effect of career stage on the meaning of key organizational events', *Journal of Organizational Behavior*, vol. 9, pp. 345–58.

Jackson, C. (1990) *Careers Counselling in Organizations: The way forward*, IMS Report, 198. Brighton: Institute of Manpower Studies.

Jackson, C. (1993) 'The case of diversity in computer-aided careers guidance systems: a response to Watts', *British Journal of Guidance and Counselling*, vol. 21, no. 2, pp. 189–95.

Jackson, C., Arnold, J., Nicholson, N. and Watts, A.G. (1996) *Managing Careers in 2000 and Beyond*, IES Report 304. Brighton: Institute for Employment Studies.

Kanter, R.M. (1989) *When Giants Learn to Dance*. New York: Simon & Schuster.

Kram, K.E. (1985) *Mentoring at Work: Developmental relationships in organizational life*. Glenview, IL: Scott Foresman.

Larwood, L. and Gutek, B.A. (1987) 'Working toward a theory of women's career development' in Gutek, B.A. and Larwood, L. (eds) *Women's Career Development*. Beverly Hills, CA: Sage.

Lawson, M.B. and Angle, H. (1994) 'When organizational relocation means family relocation: an emerging issue for strategic human resource management', *Human Resource Management*, vol. 33, pp. 33–54.

Levinson, D.J. (1986) 'A conception of adult development', *American Psychologist*, vol. 41, pp. 3–13.

Levinson, D.J. with Darrow, C.N., Klein, E.B., Levinson, M.H. and McKee, B. (1978) *Seasons of a Man's Life*. New York: Knopf.

Mabe, P.A. and West, S.G. (1982) 'Validity of self-evaluation of ability: a review and meta-analysis', *Journal of Applied Psychology*, vol. 67, pp. 280–96.

Morrison, E.W. (1993) 'Newcomer information-seeking: exploring types, modes, sources and outcomes', *Academy of Management Journal*, vol. 38, pp. 557–89.

Munton, A.G. and Forster, N. (1990) 'Job relocation: stress and the role of the family', *Work and Stress*, vol. 4, pp. 75–81.

Nathan, R. and Hill, L. (1992) *Career Counselling*. London: Sage.

Nicholson, N. (1990) 'The transition cycle: causes, outcomes, processes and forms' in Fisher, S. and Cooper, C.L. (eds) *On the Move: The psychology of change and transition*. Chichester: John Wiley.

Nicholson, N. (1993) 'Purgatory or place of safety? The managerial plateau and organizational age grading', *Human Relations*, vol. 46, pp. 1369–90.

Nicholson, N. and Imaizumi, A. (1993) 'The adjustment of Japanese expatriates to living and working in Britain', *British Journal of Management*, vol. 4, pp. 119–34.

Nicholson, N. and West, M.A. (1988) *Managerial Job Change: Men and women in transition*. Cambridge: Cambridge University Press.

Ostroff, C. and Kozlowski, S.W.J. (1992) 'Organizational socialization as a learning process: the role of information acquisition, *Personnel Psychology*, vol. 45, pp. 849–74.

Parsons, F. (1909) *Choosing a Vocation*. Boston, MA: Houghton Mifflin.

Peluchette, J. (1993) 'Subjective career success: the influence of individual difference, family and organizational variables', *Journal of Vocational Behavior*, vol. 43, pp. 198–208.

Perlmuter, M. and Hall, E. (1992) *Adult Development and Aging*, 2nd edn. New York: John Wiley.

Phillips, S.D., Friedlander, M.L., Pazienza, N.L. and Kost, P.P. (1985) 'A factor analytic investigation of career decision-making styles', *Journal of Vocational Behavior*, vol. 26, pp. 106–15.

Prediger, D.J. and Vansickle, T.R. (1992) 'Locating occupations on Holland's hexagon: beyond RIASEC', *Journal of Vocational Behavior*, vol. 40, pp. 111–28.

Premack, S.L. and Wanous, J.P. (1985) 'A meta-analysis of realistic job preview experiments', *Journal of Applied Psychology*, vol. 70, pp. 706–19.

Reddy, M. (1987) *The Managers' Guide to Counselling at Work*. Leicester: British Psychological Society.

Roberts, P. and Newton, P.M. (1987) 'Levinsonian studies of women's adult development', *Psychology and Ageing*, vol. 2, pp. 154–63.

Robinson, S.L. and Rousseau, D.M. (1994) 'Violating the psychological contract: not the exception but the norm', *Journal of Organizational Behavior*, vol. 15, pp. 245–59.

Rousseau, D.M. (1995) *Psychological Contracts in Organizations*. London: Sage.

Russell, J.E.A. (1991) 'Career development interventions in organizations', *Journal of Vocational Behavior*, vol. 38, pp. 237–87.

Scandura, T. (1992) 'Mentoring and career mobility: an empirical investigation', *Journal of Organizational Behavior*, vol. 13, pp. 169–74.

Schein, E.H. (1971) 'Occupational socialization in the professions: the case of the role innovator', *Journal of Psychiatric Research*, vol. 8, pp. 521–30.

Schein, E.H. (1978) *Career Dynamics: Matching individual and organizational needs*. Reading, MA: Addison-Wesley.

Schein, E.H. (1993) *Career Anchors: Discovering your real values*, rev. edn. London: Pfeiffer & Co.

Schein, V.E., Mueller, R. and Jacobson, C. (1989) 'The relationship between sex role stereotypes and requisite managerial characteristics among college students', *Sex Roles*, vol. 20, pp. 103–10.

Schneer, J.A. and Reitman, F. (1995) 'The impact of gender as managerial careers unfold', *Journal of Vocational Behavior*, vol. 47, pp. 290–315.

Schwartz, D (1996) 'The impact of work–family policies on women's career development: boon or bust?', *Women in Management Review*, vol. 11, no. 1, pp. 5–19.

Sharf, R.F. (1992) *Applying Career Development Theory to Counseling*. Los Angeles: Brooks/Cole.

Sokol, M. and Louis, M.R. (1984) 'Career transitions and life event adaptation: integrating alternative perspectives on role transition' in Allen, V.L. and Van de Vliert, E. (eds) *Role Transitions*. New York: Plenum Press.

Spokane, A.R. (1985) 'A review of research on person–environment congruence in Holland's theory of careers', *Journal of Vocational Behavior*, vol. 26, pp. 306–43.

Stroh, L.K., Brett, J.M. and Reilly, A.H. (1992) 'All the right stuff: a comparison of female and male managers' career progression', *Journal of Applied Psychology*, vol. 77, pp. 251–60.

Super, D.E. (1957) *The Psychology of Careers*. New York: Harper & Row.

Super, D.E. (1980) 'A life-span, life-space approach to career development', *Journal of Vocational Behavior*, vol. 13, pp. 282–98.

Super, D.E. (1990) 'A life-span, life-space approach to career development' in Brown, D. and Brooks, L. (eds) *Career Choice and Development*. 2nd edn. San Francisco, CA: Jossey-Bass.

Super, D.E. and Nevill, D.D. (1985) *The Salience Inventory*. Palo Alto, CA: Consulting Psychologists Press.

Super, D.E., Thompson, A.S. and Lindeman, R.H. (1985) *The Adult Career Concerns Inventory*. Palo Alto, CA: Consulting Psychologists Press.

Tokar, D.M. and Swanson, J.L. (1995) 'Evaluation of correspondence between Holland's vocational personality typology and the five-factor model of personality', *Journal of Vocational Behavior*, vol. 46, pp. 89–108.

Tracey, T.J. and Rounds, S.B. (1993) 'Evaluating Holland's and Gati's vocational-interest models: a structural meta-analysis', *Psychological Bulletin*, vol. 113, pp. 229–46.

Tranberg, M., Slane, S. and Ekeberg, S.E. (1993) 'The relation between interest congruence and satisfaction: a meta-analysis', *Journal of Vocational Behavior*, vol. 42, pp. 253–64.

US Department of Labor (1977) *Dictionary of Occupational Titles*. 4th edn. Washington, DC: US Government Printing Office.

Van Maanen, J. and Schein, E.H. (1979) 'Toward a theory of organizational socialization' in Staw, B.M. (ed.) *Research in Organizational Behavior*, vol. 1. Greenwich, CT: JAI Press.

Veiga, J.F. (1983) 'Mobility influences during managerial career stages', *Academy of Management Journal*, vol. 26, pp. 64–85.

Walsh, W.B. and Osipow, S.H. (eds) (1990) *Career Counseling*. Hillsdale, NJ: Lawrece Erlbaum.

Wanous, J.P. (1989) 'Installing a realistic job preview: ten tough choices', *Personnel Psychology*, vol. 42, pp. 117–33.

Wanous, J.P., Poland, T.D., Premack, S.L. and Davis, K.S. (1992) 'The effects of met expectations on newcomer attitudes and behaviors: a review and meta-analysis'. *Journal of Applied Psychology*, vol. 77, pp. 288–97.

Whitley, W., Dougherty, T.W. and Dreher, G.F. (1991) 'Relationship of career mentoring and socioeconomic origin to managers' and professionals' early career progress', *Academy of Management Journal*, vol. 34, pp. 331–51.

Yost, E.B. and Corbishley, M.A. (1987) *Career Counseling*. London: Jossey-Bass.

Work, stress and psychological well-being

After studying this chapter, you should be able to:

1 define what stress is;

2 highlight the costs of stress to industry and society;

3 identify the sources of workplace stress;

4 identify the stress of being unemployed;

5 identify your own Type A stress-prone behaviour.

INTRODUCTION

Stress at work is costing industry a great deal of money. It has been estimated that nearly 10 per cent of the UK's GNP is lost each year due to job-generated stress in the form of sickness absence, high labour turnover, lost productive value, increased recruitment and selection costs and medical expenses. This chapter looks at what stress is, how you can identify it, what it costs industry, what its sources in the workplace are and what we can do about it. In identifying organisational sources of stress we will focus on factors intrinsic to a job, role problems, relationships at work, career development, organisational climate and structure, and the work–home interface (*see* Cooper *et al.*, 1988, for a more detailed account). We close this chapter with an examination of the stressful effects of being without work, i.e. unemployed.

WHAT IS STRESS?

Stress is a word derived from the Latin word *stringere*, meaning to draw tight. Early definitions of strain and load used in physics and engineering eventually came to influence one concept of how stress affects individuals. Under this concept, external forces (load) are seen as exerting pressure upon an individual, producing strain. Proponents of this view argue that we can measure the stress to which an individual is subjected in the same way that we can measure physical strain upon a machine (Hinkle, 1973).

While this first concept looked at stress as an outside stimulus, a second concept defines stress as a person's response to a disturbance. The idea that environmental forces could actually cause disease rather than just short-term effects, and that people have a natural tendency to resist such forces, was seen in the work of Walter B. Cannon in the 1930s. Cannon studied the effects of stress upon animals and people, and in particular the 'fight or flight' reaction. Through this reaction, people, as well as animals, will choose whether to stay and fight or try to escape when confronting extreme danger. Cannon observed that when his subjects experienced situations of cold, lack of oxygen, and excitement, he could detect physiological changes such as emergency adrenalin secretions. Cannon described these individuals as being 'under stress'.

One of the first scientific attempts to explain the process of stress-related illness was made by physician and scholar Hans Selye (1946), who described three stages an individual encounters in stressful situations:

1 alarm reaction, in which an initial phase of lowered resistance is followed by counter-shock, during which the individual's defence mechanisms become active;

2 resistance, the stage of maximum adaptation and, hopefully, successful return to equilibrium for the individual. If, however, the stress agent continues or the defence mechanism does not work, the individual will move on to a third stage;

3 exhaustion, when adaptive mechanisms collapse.

Newer and more complete theories of stress emphasise the interaction between a person and his or her environment. By looking at stress as resulting from a misfit between an individual and his or her particular environment, we can begin to understand why one person seems to flourish in a certain setting, while another suffers. Cummings and Cooper (1979) have designed a way of understanding the stress process:

- individuals, for the most part, try to keep their thoughts, emotions and relationships with the world in a 'steady state';
- each factor of a person's emotional and physical state has a 'range of stability', in which that person feels comfortable. On the other hand, when forces disrupt one of these factors beyond the range of stability, the individual must act or cope to restore a feeling of comfort;
- an individual's behaviour aimed at maintaining a steady state makes up his or her 'adjustment process', or coping strategies.

A stress is any force that pushes a psychological or physical factor beyond its range of stability, producing a strain within the individual (Cooper, 1996). Knowledge that a stress is likely to occur constitutes a threat to the individual. A threat can cause a strain because of what it signifies to the person. This description is summarised in Fig. 17.1.

As stress begins to take its toll on the body and mind, a variety of symptoms can result. Doctors have identified the physical and behavioural symptoms of stress listed in Table 17.1, as commonly occurring before the onset of serious stress-related illness. They have also identified those ailments having a stress background, meaning that they may be brought on or aggravated by stress.

> ■ **KEY LEARNING POINT**
> *When pressure exceeds the individual's ability to cope, he or she enters the stress arena.*

Fig. 17.1 The Cooper-Cummings framework

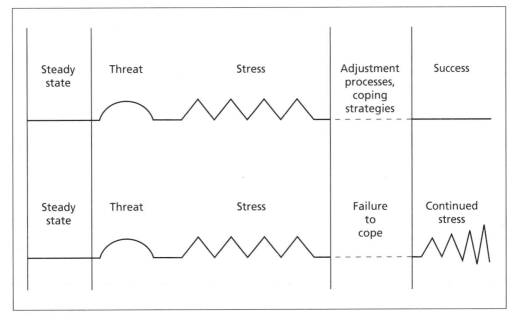

Source: Cummings and Cooper (1979)

Table 17.1 Physical and behavioural symptoms of stress

Physical symptoms of stress	Behavioural symptoms of stress	Ailments with stress aetiology
Lack of appetite	Constant irritability with people	Hypertension: high blood pressure
Craving for food when under pressure	Feeling unable to cope	Coronary thrombosis: heart attack
Frequent indigestion or heartburn	Lack of interest in life	Migraine
Constipation or diarrhoea	Constant or recurrent fear of disease	Hayfever and allergies
Insomnia	A feeling of being a failure	Asthma
Constant tiredness	A feeling of being bad or of self-hatred	Pruritus: intense itching
Tendency to sweat for no good reason	Difficulty in making decisions	Peptic ulcers
Nervous twitches	A feeling of ugliness	Constipation
Nail-biting	Loss of interest in other people	Colitis
Headaches	Awareness of suppressed anger	Rheumatoid arthritis
Cramps and muscle spasms	Inability to show true feelings	Menstrual difficulties
Nausea	A feeling of being the target of other people's animosity	Nervous dyspepsia: flatulence and indigestion
Breathlessness without exertion	Loss of sense of humour	Hyperthyroidism: overactive thyroid gland
Fainting spells	Feeling of neglect	Diabetes melitus
Frequent crying or desire to cry	Dread of the future	Skin disorders
Impotency or frigidity	A feeling of having failed as a person or parent	Tuberculosis
Inability to sit still without fidgeting	A feeling of having no one to confide in	Depression
High blood pressure	Difficulty in concentrating	
	The inability to finish one task before rushing on to the next	
	An intense fear of open or enclosed spaces, or of being alone	

THE COSTS OF STRESS

To the individual whose health or happiness has been ravaged by the effects of stress, the costs involved are only too clear. Whether manifested as minor complaints of illness, serious ailments such as heart disease, or social problems such as alcoholism and drug abuse, stress-related symptoms exact a heavy payment. It has also long been recognised that a family suffers indirectly from the stress problems of one of its members – suffering that takes the form of unhappy marriages, divorces, and spouse and child abuse. But what price do organisations and nations pay for a poor fit between people and their environments? Only recently has stress been seen as contributing to the health costs of companies and countries. But as studies of stress-related illnesses and deaths show, stress is taking a devastatingly high toll on our combined productivity and health (Watts and Cooper, 1992).

Costs to society

Heart and circulatory diseases

Today in the UK coronary heart disease remains the leading cause of death and kills more than 150 000 people each year – one person every three to four minutes. One man in eleven dies of a heart attack before he is 65 years old.

Almost half of all Americans die of cardiovascular disease, which includes heart attack and stroke. The resulting economic cost, including medical services and lost productivity, reached an estimated $78.6 billion in 1986. Heart attack is the leading cause of death in the USA, followed by cancer and stroke. It is also estimated that more than $700 million a year is spent by American employers to replace the 200 000 men aged 45–65 who die or are incapacitated by coronary heart disease. However, the US has succeeded in reversing the long prevailing upward trend in heart and vascular diseases. From the early 1960s to the 1980s, deaths of American men due to ischaemic heart disease fell by 20–30 per cent, while in England and Wales, male deaths increased by 3 per cent. Correspondingly, deaths of American women dropped by 31 per cent, while deaths of women in England and Wales increased by 11 per cent.

In the UK coronary heart disease is generally twice as prevalent in men as in women, but the disease's rate of increase over the years has been even greater in women. Further, as Table 17.2 shows, days lost from work by UK women between 1982–3 and 1984–5 increased dramatically due to causes of heart disease and cerebrovascular disease over a two-year period.

Table 17.2 Days lost in Britain from work for certain mental and stress-related causes

Cause	Male female	1982–83	1984–85	Change over two years (%)
Psychoses	M	7 098 538	8 138 000	+16.04
	F	3 253 344	3 275 080	+0.66
Neuroses	M	17 432 981	17 083 743	+2.90
	F	9 951 749	10 162 450	+2.18
Personality disorders	M	160 100	162 200	+1.31
	F	153 600	131 600	−14.32
Mental retardation	M	1 312 400	1 310 286	−0.17
	F	786 000	823 300	+4.74
Migraine	M	158 529	136 300	−14.02
	F	177 683	62 800	−64.65
Hypertensive diseases	M	9 477 164	9 890 527	+4.36
	F	1 997 336	2 060 400	+3.16
Ulcers	M	2 212 132	2 088 828	−1.75
	F	294 295	312 659	+6.24
Depressive disorder	M	6 439 698	6 134 613	−4.47
	F	4 276 919	4 201 100	−1.77
Alcohol dependence	M	896 600	895 401	−0.13
	F	79 600	38 800	−51.26
Ischaemic heart disease	M	29 092 909	32 912 455	+13.13
	F	1 908 911	2 389 044	+25.15
Cerebrovascular disease	M	6 222 500	7 011 600	+12.68
	F	529 800	920 700	+73.78
Total days lost in above causes	M	80 417 551	86 618 953	+7.71
	F	23 409 237	24 377 933	+4.14
Total number of days lost	M	271 715 438	253 562 397	−6.68
	F	89 229 711	74 546 812	−16.52

Source: Department of Health and Social Security (1986).

Another disease increasingly linked to stress is high blood pressure (hypertension). In 1983, it was estimated that nearly 55 million adult Americans – nearly one in four – suffered from hypertension. Hypertension, like heart disease and cerebrovascular disease, has increased as a cause of absence from work in the UK between 1982–3 and 1984–5 (see Table 17.2).

White versus blue collar

It is commonly believed that executives and other white-collar workers suffer the most from stress-related illnesses. Intense office situations with demanding deadlines, the required attention to detail and complex interpersonal relations are often believed to produce high levels of stress and strain.

Yet the frequencies of deaths due to major causes in the working population increase as we move from professional and white-collar jobs down to the unskilled. This applies both to stress-related illnesses such as ischaemic heart disease and to other illnesses such as pneumonia and prostate cancer. In addition, this pattern extends not only to deaths but to illnesses as well. Many blue-collar workers show a greater number of restricted activity days and consultations with general practitioners than do white-collar workers.

Mental illness*

The breakdown of an individual's mental health has been increasingly linked by medics and stress researchers to the level of stress he or she experiences. A look at work days lost due to mental health problems indicates the magnitude of the problem. Of the 328 million days lost from work in the UK in 1984–5, 53 million, or 16 per cent, were due to mental health causes. A look at the reasons given by British men for days off due to stress-related illness shows a huge increase over a 25-year period in the category of 'nervousness, debility and headache'.

In one effort to determine how widespread mental health problems are in the US, 17 000 people were interviewed at five regional sites as part of a government study. Results showed that over a six-month period, between 17 and 23 per cent of those interviewed had experienced at least one major psychological disorder. Between 7 and 15 per cent reported having had at least one anxiety disorder. When questioned about a lifetime's incidence of mental health problems, between 29 and 38 per cent said that they had suffered one or more major disorders. As the government study stated, 'psychological disorders were most common during the prime working ages of 25 to 44 years' (President's Commission on Mental Health, 1978).

Costs in the workplace

All of the potential stress costs outlined so far combine both to lessen the satisfaction obtained from work and to reduce on-the-job performance. Later in this chapter, we look more closely at how work influences stress levels, but it is relevant here to mention the ways in which stress is reflected in the workplace.

Job satisfaction

At least one study shows that job satisfaction among US workers fell during the 1970s (Quinn and Staines, 1979). The US experience was reinforced in other industrialised countries. For example, between a quarter and a third of Swedish workers described their work as often stressful (Bolinder and Ohlstram, 1971).

* Some of the material from this section comes from NIOSH (1986).

Differing stress levels in various occupations

Certain occupations, such as mining, piloting, police work, advertising and acting, are believed to provide the highest stress levels (Cooper *et al.*, 1988). Stress on the job becomes an occupational hazard for certain 'helping' professionals, such as physicians, dentists, nurses and health technologists, who have higher than expected rates of suicide and alcohol/drug abuse. 'Burnout', or the premature retirement from one's career due to stress, appears particularly common among nurses. Nurses and others in the health field suffer from mental ill health to the extent that more of them are being admitted to hospitals and clinics for the treatment of mental disorders than in previous years.

Job performance

Experiments and studies have shown that, within certain limits, an individual's performance actually improves with increased levels of stress. After a point, however, stress clearly results in reduced performance. The Yerkes–Dodson law, as shown in Fig. 17.2, reflects this phenomenon in medical terms. As Melhuish (1978) suggested:

> the portion of the graph between B and C represents pressures which the individual can tolerate: within these limits his health and quality of life improve with increased pressure (challenge). At C, however, increased pressure loses its beneficial effect and becomes harmful. Pressure becomes stress and in the portion C–D, health and quality of life decrease. C is the threshold (as is B, for boredom is also a potent stress and the portion B–A also represents increasing risk of stress illness).

Absenteeism and turnover of labour force

Absenteeism is one of the most obvious costs of stress to employers. In general, indications are that absenteeism is a widespread and accelerating problem in many occupations. By the 1970s, it was recognised that time lost from work due to stress-

Fig. 17.2 Medical extension of Yerkes–Dodson law

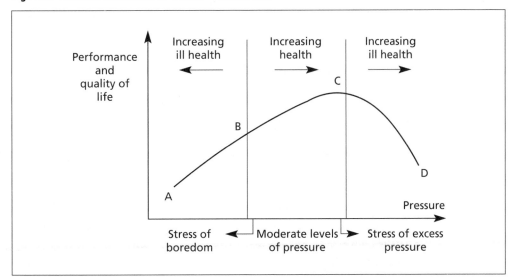

Source: Melhuish (1978)

related illnesses cost the UK far more than losses due to work stoppages and strikes. The Confederation of British Industry (CBI, 1970) reported that absenteeism 'has risen alarmingly in recent years in spite of improvements in social and working conditions, income levels, and family health'. In 1984–5, 328 million days of work were lost in the UK. In at least one occupation, nursing, short-term absences among nurses are increasingly being blamed on clinical anxiety and depression believed to result from occupational strain (Hingley and Cooper, 1986).

High rates of employee turnover can become quite expensive to a company – they raise training costs, reduce overall efficiency and disrupt other workers. Although it is hard to estimate the actual costs of labour turnover, it is thought that they often equal about five times an employee's monthly salary (Quick and Quick, 1984).

Litigation and health care costs

Employers are paying directly for stress-related illnesses through workers' compensation claims: 'In general, claims for psychological disorders suffered as the result of job experiences have multiplied over the decade of the '70s ... in 1979, the State of California alone received more than 3,000–4,000 "psychiatric" injury claims, half of which resulted in monetary awards' (Lubin, 1980). Ivancevich et al. (1985) have reviewed landmark court cases which have resulted in American corporations increasingly being held responsible for workplace stress. For example, in 1955, an iron worker named Bailey saw a fellow scaffolding worker fall to his death. Bailey returned to work, but gradually he began to have frequent blackouts and became paralysed. He also suffered from sleeping difficulties and extreme sensitivity to pain. In the resulting court case, Bailey v. American General, a Texas court ruled in Bailey's favour. The physical accident and psychological trauma were held responsible for the onset of the subsequent paralysis and other problems. Although not a radical decision, it paved the way for compensation cases under existing laws. Many employers are being held responsible for employee stress due to the belief that they are doing little to cut down the stressful aspects of many jobs. This may help to explain the growth in corporate health and stress management programmes in America. Those employers who are at least seen to be doing something about workplace stress may be able to put forward a better defence in the courts.

According to a US government report (NIOSH, 1993), one specific type of compensation claim, 'gradual mental stress', has shown significant growth in recent years. As the report explained, this type of claim refers to 'cumulative emotional problems stemming mainly from exposure to adverse psychosocial conditions at work ... Emotional problems related to a specific traumatic event at work, or to work-related physical disease or injury, such as witnessing a severe accident, are not included'. According to the report, about 11 per cent of all occupational disease claims involve gradual mental stress.

■ **KEY LEARNING POINT**

Stress costs industrialised economics around 10 per cent of GNP, through sickness absence, ill health and labour turnover.

WHAT ARE THE SOURCES OF STRESS AT WORK?

Stress-related illness is not confined to either high or low status workers (Smith *et al.*, 1978; McLean, 1979). Regardless of how one job may compare to another in terms of stress, it is helpful to recognise that every job has potential stress agents. Researchers have identified five major categories of work stress (Cooper *et al.*, 1988). Common to all jobs, these factors vary in the degree to which they are found to be causally linked to stress in each job. The five categories (Fig. 17.3) are:

1 factors intrinsic to the job
2 role in the organisation
3 relationships at work
4 career development
5 organisational structure and climate.

Fig. 17.3 Dynamics of work stress

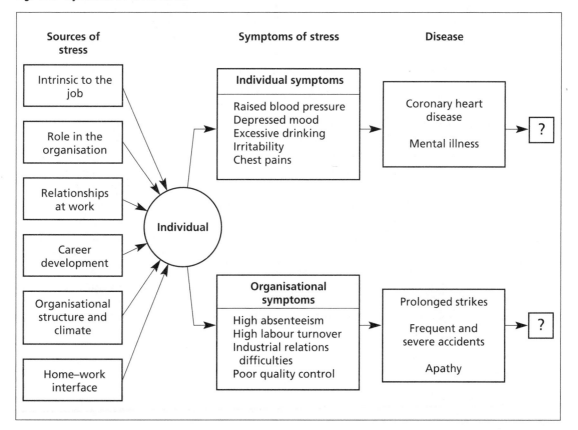

FACTORS INTRINSIC TO THE JOB

As a starting point to understanding work stress, researchers have studied those factors which may be intrinsic to the job itself such as: poor working conditions, shift work, long hours, travel, risk and danger, new technology, work overload and work underload.

Working conditions

Our physical surroundings – noise, lighting, smells and all the stimuli which bombard our senses – can affect our moods and overall mental state, whether or not we find them consciously objectionable. Considerable research has linked working conditions to mental health. Kornhauser (1965) suggested that 'poor mental health was directly related to unpleasant working conditions, the necessity to work fast and to expend a lot of physical effort, and to excessive and inconvenient hours'. Others have found that physical health is also adversely affected by repetitive and dehumanising work settings, such as fast-paced assembly lines (Cooper and Smith, 1985). In one study of stress factors associated with casting work in a steel manufacturing plant, poor working conditions such as noise, fumes and to a lesser extent heat, together with the social and psychological consequences, including isolation and tension among workers, had significant impact (Kelly and Cooper, 1981).

Health workers, too, often face a variety of noxious stimuli. Hospital lighting, for example, is usually artificial, monotonous, and too bright or garish. One study of the problems experienced by nurses working in intensive care units in the US found that an oppressive visual environment became particularly stressful to nurses over a period of time (Hay and Oken, 1972). This factor, combined with the incessant routine nature of many of the activities, led to feelings of being trapped, claustrophobia and dehumanisation. Poor ventilating systems worsen the problems in many hospitals. In addition, the high noise level of a busy ward adds to the stress factors faced by health professionals. All of this, of course, is in addition to the stress encountered in dealing daily with death and pain.

Each occupation has its own potential environmental sources of stress. For example, in jobs where individuals are dealing with close detail work, poor lighting can create eye strain. On the other hand, extremely bright lighting or glare presents problems for air traffic controllers. Similarly, as Ivancevich and Matteson (1980) stated, 'noise, in fact, seems to operate less as a stressor in situations where it is excessive but expected, than in those where it is unexpected, or at least unpredictable. The change in noise levels more than absolute levels themselves, seems to be the irritant. This, of course, is simply another way of saying that noise, like any stressor, causes stress when it forces us to change'.

The physical design of the workplace can be another potential source of stress. If an office is poorly designed, with personnel who require frequent contact spread throughout a building, poor communication networks can develop, resulting in role ambiguity and poor relationships.

Shift work

Many workers today have jobs requiring them to work in shifts, some of which involve working staggered hours. Studies have found that shift work is a common occupational stress factor. It has been demonstrated that shift work affects blood temperature, metabolic rate, blood sugar levels, mental efficiency and work motivation, not to mention sleep patterns and family and social life. In one study of air traffic controllers, shift work was isolated as a major problem area, although other major job stress agents were also present (Cobb and Rose, 1973). These workers had four times the prevalence of hypertension, and also more mild diabetes and peptic ulcers than did a control group of US Air Force personnel.

In a study of offshore oil rig workers, the third most important source of stress found was a general category labelled 'work patterns', such as shift work, physical conditions and travel (Sutherland and Cooper, 1987). The longer the work shift – for example '28 days on, 28 days off' versus '14 days on, 14 days off' – the greater the stress. The shift work patterns were a predictor of mental and physical ill health, particularly when the oil rig workers were married and had children.

A major study of American nurses (Tasto *et al.*, 1978) identified shift work as a major problem. The study, which compared nurses working fixed shifts with those working rotating shifts, found that the rotating nurses fared the worst, followed closely by night-shift workers. Shift rotators reported a greater use of alcohol, a higher frequency of problems with their health and their sex lives, and less satisfaction in their personal lives than other shift workers. Rotating shift nurses were significantly more confused, depressed and anxious than those nurses on non-rotating shifts. The investigators concluded that 'rotation was a scheduling system that imposes excessive physical and psychological costs to the workers'. The study also found that, unlike fixed shift workers, those on rotating shifts showed little or no tendency to adapt over time.

Long hours

The long working hours required by many jobs appear to take a toll on employee health. One research study has made a link between long working hours and deaths due to coronary heart disease (Breslow and Buell, 1960). This investigation of light industrial workers in the US found that individuals under 45 years of age who worked more than 48 hours a week had twice the risk of death from coronary heart disease than did similar individuals working a maximum of 40 hours a week.

Another study of 100 young coronary patients revealed that 25 per cent of them had been working at two jobs, and an additional 40 per cent worked for more than 60 hours a week (Russek and Zohman, 1958). Many individuals, such as executives working long hours and some medics who might have no sleep for 36 hours or more, may find that both they and the quality of their work suffer. It is now commonly recognised that beyond 40 hours a week, time spent working is increasingly unproductive and can create ill health (Sparks and Cooper, 1997).

Risk and danger

A job which involves risk or danger can result in higher stress levels. When someone is constantly aware of potential danger, he or she is prepared to react immediately. The individual is in a constant state of arousal, as described in the 'fight or flight' syndrome. The resulting adrenalin rush, respiration changes and muscle tension are all seen as potentially threatening to long-term health. On the other hand, individuals who face physical danger – such as police, mine workers, firefighters and soldiers – often appear to have reduced stress levels, particularly those who are adequately trained and equipped to deal with emergency situations.

New technology

The introduction of new technology into the work environment has required workers, particularly blue-collar workers, to adapt continually to new equipment, systems and ways of working. Having a boss trained in the 'old ways' may be an extra burden for the new employee trained in the latest methods, and raises questions about the adequacy of supervision and about those in senior positions.

In a study of causes of stress among executives in ten countries (Cooper, 1984), Japanese executives suffered particularly from pressure to keep up with new technology, that is, to maintain their technological superiority. Managers in 'developing countries' felt pressure due to the increasing emphasis on new technology, the need to deal with an adequately trained workforce and the imposition of deadlines. Also, in the UK a high percentage of managers (second only to Japan) said that keeping up with new technology was a great source of pressure at work. This is not surprising in a nation that many people feel is beginning to slip behind competitors in the race to grab new export markets. In addition, these UK managers described a high level of stress due to the amount of travel required by their work.

Work overload

Two different types of work overload have been described by researchers. Quantitative overload refers simply to having too much work to do. Qualitative overload refers to work that is too difficult for an individual (French and Caplan, 1972). In the first case, too much work often leads to working long hours with the attendant problems described above. Too heavy a work burden has also been connected with increased cigarette smoking.

In a 1973 study, 22 white-collar workers were observed for two or three hours a day for three days (French and Caplan, 1972). Two observers recorded data on events occurring in the job environment, and heart rate responses to these events. The workers also wore pocket-sized devices which assessed their heart rates without interfering with their activities. The workers also filled out questionnaires describing their workload over the three-day period. The researchers found that those people who admitted to feeling work pressure were observed to suffer more interruptions from visitors and phone calls. These workers also suffered significantly more physiological strain through higher heart rates and higher cholesterol levels.

Work underload

Cox (1980) has described the problem of not being sufficiently challenged by work. Job underload associated with repetitive routine, boring and understimulating work has been associated with ill health. Certain workers, such as pilots, air traffic controllers and nuclear power workers, face a special aspect of work underload. They must deal with long periods of time in which they have little to do, while facing the possibility that they may suddenly be required to spring into action in a crisis.

ROLE IN THE ORGANISATION

When a person's role in an organisation is clearly defined and understood, and when expectations placed upon the individual are also clear and non-conflicting, stress can be kept to a minimum. But as researchers have clearly seen, this is not the case in many workplaces. Three critical factors – role ambiguity, role conflict and the degree of responsibility for others – are seen to be major sources of stress.

Role ambiguity

Role ambiguity arises when individuals do not have a clear picture about their work objectives, their co-workers' expectations of them, and the scope and responsibilities of their job. Often this ambiguity results simply because a supervisor does not lay out to the employee exactly what their role is. As Warshaw (1979) has stated, 'The individual just doesn't know how he or she fits into the organization and is unsure of any rewards no matter how well he or she may perform'.

A wide range of activities can create role ambiguity. Ivancevich and Matteson (1980) highlighted the following: the first job, a promotion or transfer, a new boss, the first supervisory responsibility, a new company, or a change in the structure of the existing organisation – all of these events, and others, may serve to create a temporary state of role ambiguity. The stress indicators found to relate to role ambiguity are depressed mood, lowered self-esteem, life dissatisfaction, low motivation to work and the intention to leave a job.

Role conflict

Role conflict exists when an individual is torn by conflicting job demands or by doing things that he or she does not really want to do, or things which the individual does not believe are part of the job. Workers may often feel themselves torn between two groups of people who demand different types of behaviour or who believe the job entails different functions (*see* Fig. 17.4).

Conflict situations can clearly act as stress factors upon the individuals involved. Research has indicated that role conflict leads to reduced job satisfaction and higher anxiety levels. Other research has shown that role conflict can lead to cardiovascular ill health risks, such as elevated blood pressure and abnormal blood chemistry (Ivancevich and Matteson, 1980).

Personality variables

As might be expected, studies have shown that people with high anxiety levels suffer more from role conflicts than do people who are more flexible in their approach to life. Anxiety prone individuals experience role conflict more acutely and react to it with greater tension than people who were less anxiety prone; and more flexible individuals respond to high role conflict with lesser feeling of tension than their more rigid counterparts (Warr and Wall, 1975). In other studies, when the individual has had stronger needs for cognitive clarity or lower levels of tolerance for ambiguity, job-related stress has been found to be higher and more prolonged.

Responsibility

Responsibility has been found to be another organisational role stress agent. In an organisation, there are basically two types of responsibility: responsibility for people, and responsibility for things, such as budgets, equipment and buildings. Responsibility for people has been found to be particularly stressful. Studies in the 1960s found that this was far more likely to lead to coronary heart disease than was responsibility for things (Wardwell *et al.*, 1964). Being responsible for people usually requires spending more time interacting with others, attending meetings and attempting to meet deadlines.

Fig. 17.4 Source of role stress at work

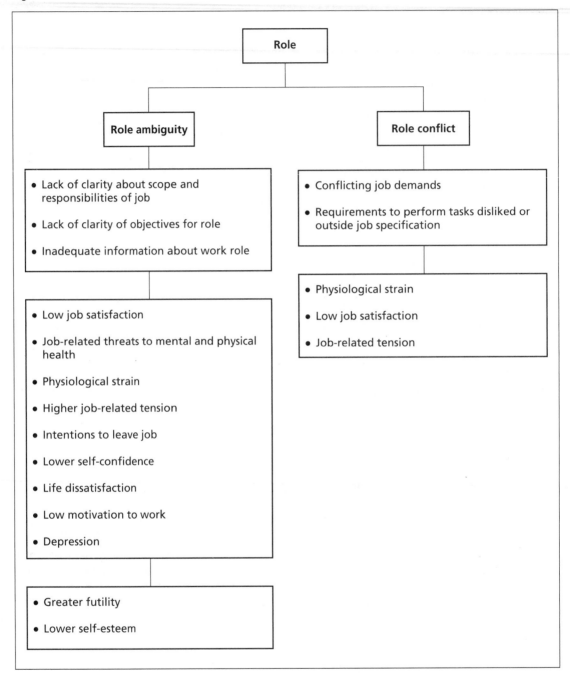

An investigation in the United Kingdom of 1200 managers sent by their companies for annual medical examinations linked physical stress to age and level of responsibility (Pincherle, 1972). The older the executive and the greater his or her responsibility, the greater the probability of coronary heart disease risk factors.

As Ivancevich and Matteson (1980) stated, 'Part of the reason responsibility for people acts as a stressor undoubtedly results from the specific nature of the responsibility, particularly as it relates to the need to make unpleasant interpersonal decisions. Another part of the reason ... is that people in responsibility positions lend themselves to overload, and perhaps role conflict and ambiguity as well'.

■ **KEY LEARNING POINT**

Workplace stress today is caused by overload, job insecurity, information overlead and a management style which punishes rather than praises.

RELATIONSHIPS AT WORK

Other people – and our varied encounters with them – can be major sources of both stress and support (Makin *et al.*, 1996). At work, especially, dealings with bosses, peers and subordinates can dramatically affect the way we feel at the end of the day. Selye (1974) suggested that learning to live with other people is one of the most stressful aspects of life.

It is an interesting fact, however, that little research has been done in this area. Lazarus (1966) suggested that supportive social relationships with peers, supervisors and subordinates at work are less likely to create interpersonal pressures, and will directly reduce levels of perceived job stress. Poor relationships were defined by researchers at the University of Michigan as those which include low trust, low supportiveness, and low interest in listening and trying to deal with problems that confront the organisational member.

Most studies (e.g. Cartwright and Cooper, 1997) have concluded that mistrust of fellow workers is connected with high role ambiguity, poor communications, and psychological strain in the form of low job satisfaction and to feelings of job-related threat to one's well-being. There are three critical relationships at work: relationships with superiors, relationships with subordinates and relationships with colleagues or co-workers.

Relationships with superiors

Physicians and clinical psychologists support the idea that problems of emotional disability often result when the relationship between a subordinate and a boss is psychologically unhealthy for one reason or another. Buck (1972) focused on the relationship of workers to an immediate boss and found that when the boss was perceived as 'considerate', there was 'friendship, mutual trust, respect and a certain warmth between boss and subordinate' (*see also* Chapter 13). Workers who said their boss was low on 'consideration' reported feeling more job pressure. Workers who were under pressure reported that their bosses did not give them criticism in a helpful way, played favourites, and pulled rank and took advantage of them whenever they had a chance.

To understand how to *manage* the boss, it is important to be able to identify different species of boss. Cooper *et al.* (1993) found that there were various boss prototypes: the bureaucrat, the autocrat, the wheeler-dealer, the reluctant manager and the open manager. Each has to be dealt with differently if the stress is to be minimised.

Relationships with subordinates

The way in which a manager supervises the work of others has always been considered a critical aspect of his or her work. For instance, the inability to delegate has been a common criticism levelled against some managers. It now appears that managers face a new challenge: learning to manage by participation. Today's emphasis on participation can be a cause of resentment, anxiety and stress for the managers involved.

Relationships with colleagues

Stress among co-workers can arise from the competition and personality conflicts usually described as 'office politics'. Adequate social support can be critical to the health and well-being of an individual and to the atmosphere and success of an organisation. Because most people spend so much time at work, the relationships among co-workers can provide valuable support or, conversely, can be a huge source of stress. French and Caplan (1972) found that strong social support from co-workers eased job strain. This support also mediated the effects of job strain on cortisone levels, blood pressure, glucose levels and the number of cigarettes smoked.

CAREER DEVELOPMENT

A host of issues can act as potential stress factors throughout one's working life. Lack of job security, fear of redundancy, obsolescence or retirement, and numerous performance appraisals can cause pressure and strain. In addition, the frustration of having reached one's career ceiling or having been over-promoted can result in extreme stress. Ivancevich and Matteson (1980) suggested that individuals suffering from 'career stress' often show high job dissatisfaction, job mobility, burnout, poor work performance, less effective interpersonal relationships at work and so on (*see also* Chapter 16).

Job security

For many workers, career progression is of overriding importance. Through promotion, people not only earn more money, but enjoy increased status and new challenges. In the early years in a job, the striving and ability required to deal with a rapidly changing environment is usually rewarded by a company through monetary and promotional rewards. At middle age, however, many people find their career progress has slowed or stopped. Job opportunities may become fewer, available jobs can require longer to master, old knowledge may become obsolete, and energy levels can flag. At the same time, younger competition threatens (*see also* Chapter 15).

Retirement

The transition to retirement can in itself be a stressful event. While a job is a socially defined role, retirement has been described as the 'roleless role'. The vagueness and lack of structure of retirement can provide problems for the ill prepared. For some individuals, becoming 'pensioners' or 'senior citizens' presents a situation in which they are uncertain about how to obtain the social rewards they value. In contrast, those individuals who have maintained balance in their lives by developing interests and friends outside their work can find retirement a liberating period in their lives.

Job performance

The process of being evaluated and appraised can be a stressful experience for all of us. It must be recognised that performance appraisals can be anxiety provoking, for both the individual being examined and the person doing the judging and appraising. The supervisor making performance judgements faces the threat of union grievance procedures in some cases, as well as interpersonal strains and the responsibility of making decisions affecting another person's livelihood.

The way in which an evaluation is carried out can affect the degree of anxiety experienced. For example, taking a written examination can be a short-term stress factor, while continuous and confidential appraisals by supervisors can have a more long-term effect, depending on the structure and climate of the organisation.

> ■ KEY LEARNING POINT
> *The concept of career is changing, with more and more people pursuing short-term contracts and freelance careers as organisations outsource more and more.*

ORGANISATIONAL STRUCTURE AND CLIMATE

Just being part of an organization can present threats to an individual's sense of freedom and autonomy. Organisation workers sometimes complain that they do not have a sense of belonging, lack adequate opportunities to participate, feel their behaviour is unduly restricted and are not included in office communications and consultations.

As early as the 1940s, researchers began reporting that workers who were allowed more participation in decision making produced more and had higher job satisfaction (Coch and French, 1948). They also found that non-participation at work was a significant predictor of strain and job-related stress, relating to general poor health, escapist drinking, depression, low self-esteem, absenteeism and plans to leave work. Participation in the decision-making process on the part of the individual may help increase his or her feeling of investment in the company's success, create a sense of belonging and improve communication channels within the organisation. The resulting sense of being in control seems vital for the well-being of the workforce (Sauter *et al.*, 1989).

THE STRESS OF BEING UNEMPLOYED

With relatively high levels of unemployment in the UK throughout the 1980s and into the 1990s, the stress of being unemployed has been a major topic of concern. It is a problem faced by many, from the unskilled to the professional worker. In a review of all the research on the psychological experience of being unemployed, Fryer and Payne (1986) suggested that people who experience unemployment can suffer from lower levels of personal happiness, life satisfaction, self-esteem and psychological well-being. They also tend to report increased depression, difficulty in concentrating and other minor to severe behavioural problems.

In addition, there is a growing literature which suggests a strong link between physical illness and unemployment stress. In Australia, one study found that the unemployed, in contrast to the employed, reported significantly more symptoms of bronchitis, ear, nose, and throat problems, and allergies. In a similar British study, similar results were found, with the added complications of obstructive lung disease and coronary heart disease (Hayes and Nutman, 1981).

Although there is a difference of opinion about the relationship of unemployment and mortality, evidence is emerging of a positive association, with studies indicating that long-term unemployment may adversely affect the longevity of the unemployed by as much as two to three years, depending on when the person had been made redundant.

It is clear, then, that people who are unemployed do not have an easy time. But how, exactly, does unemployment affect people? Some psychologists have proposed a stage model of reactions to unemployment (e.g. Eisenberg and Lazarsfeld, 1938). At first, people react with shock – an emotional response which may include surprise, anger or even relief. They then enter the optimism stage, when they still feel it is likely they will obtain another job, and often spend time catching up with jobs around the house. After a time, this is said to give way to pessimism as job applications meet with no success, and then to fatalism, when people feel a sense of hopelessness, become resigned to their fate, and stop trying to obtain another job. This stage model may be a reasonably accurate description of how many people react to unemployment, but it is very imprecise about when and why one stage gives way to the next (Kelvin and Jarrett, 1985).

Other psychologists have tried to identify exactly what it is about unemployment which leads people to feel psychologically bad. Jahoda (1979) wrote of the manifest function of employment (income), but also its latent functions – structuring of time, social contact outside the family, linkage to wider goals/purposes, personal status/identity and enforced activity. A person who becomes unemployed is deprived of both the manifest and the latent functions of employment, and it is this, Jahoda argued, that leads to negative psychological states.

Others have seen Jahoda's approach as too limited. Warr (1983) pointed out that not all employment fosters mental health, and identified features of 'psychologically good' employment. These included money, variety, goals, opportunity for decision making, skill use/development, security, interpersonal contact and valued social position. This pays more attention than Jahoda to characteristics of the job itself. Warr argued that becoming unemployed would have negative psychological effects to the extent that it led to loss of these features in day-to-day life. Fryer (Fryer and Payne, 1986) has taken a rather different approach. He has criticised conventional treatments of unemployment for taking an overly passive view of the person. The psychological effects of unemployment are, he has argued, the result of frustrated attempts to create a better future rather than memories and regrets about loss of a more satisfying past.

SUMMARY

Stress in the workplace has become the black plague of the twentieth century. This is likely to get worse as international competition increases with the advent of the European Union, the Pacific Basin and the economic and political liberation of Eastern Europe. These pressures at work are also likely to lead to less rather than more concern for the 'people management' aspects of the workplace. Much of the stress at work is caused not only by work overload and time pressures, but also by a lack of rewards and praise, and, more importantly, by not providing individuals with the autonomy to do their jobs as they would like (Makin *et al.*, 1996). We shall see, therefore, an increasing army of human resource professionals, such as stress counsellors, entering the arena of work over the next decade (Berridge, Cooper and Highley, 1997). We will need them, but they are only part of the answer. Organisations must begin to manage people at work differently, treating them with respect and valuing their contribution, if we are to enhance the psychological well-being and health of workers in the future.

CASE STUDY 17.1

Type A behavioural pattern

Many managers and other white collar and professional people who may be vulnerable to stress at work seem to display a pattern of behaviour termed Type A stress-prone behaviour (Rosenman, Friedman and Straus, 1964). The following questionnaire was developed by Bortner (1969) to assess an individual's Type A behaviour. We thought it might be useful for readers to assess their own stress-prone behaviour. Fill in the following questionnaire and then score it as suggested. If you are a high Type A it means that you are very competitive, high achieving, aggressive, hasty, impatient, time conscious and hard driving. Type B, which is the other end of the continuum, is the opposite of this characterisation.

Type A behaviour

Circle one number for each of the statements below which best reflects the way you behave in your everyday life. For example, if you are generally on time for appointments, for the first point you would circle a number between 7 and 11. If you are usually casual about appointments you would circle one of the lower numbers between 1 and 5.

Casual about appointments	1 2 3 4 5 6 7 8 9 10 11	Never late
Not competitive	1 2 3 4 5 6 7 8 9 10 11	Very competitive
Good listener	1 2 3 4 5 6 7 8 9 10 11	Anticipates what others are going to say (nod, attempts to finish for them)
Never feels rushed (even under pressure)	1 2 3 4 5 6 7 8 9 10 11	Always rushed
Can wait patiently	1 2 3 4 5 6 7 8 9 10 11	Impatient while waiting
Takes things one at a time	1 2 3 4 5 6 7 8 9 10 11	Tries to do many things at once, thinks about what will do next
Slow deliberate talker	1 2 3 4 5 6 7 8 9 10 11	Emphatic in speech, fast and forceful
Cares about satisfying him/herself no matter what others may think	1 2 3 4 5 6 7 8 9 10 11	Wants good job recognised by others
Slow doing things	1 2 3 4 5 6 7 8 9 10 11	Fast (eating, walking)

▶

Easy going	1 2 3 4 5 6 7 8 9 10 11	Hard driving (pushing yourself and others)
Expresses feelings	1 2 3 4 5 6 7 8 9 10 11	Hides feelings
Many outside interests	1 2 3 4 5 6 7 8 9 10 11	Few interests outside work/home
Unambitious	1 2 3 4 5 6 7 8 9 10 11	Ambitious
Casual	1 2 3 4 5 6 7 8 9 10 11	Eager to get things done

Plot total score below:

```
Type B                              Type A
14                  84              154
 |------------------|----------------|
 |                  |                |
```

Source: Cooper's adaptation of the Bortner Type A scale scoring

The higher the score received on this questionnaire, the more firmly an individual can be classified as Type A. For example, 154 points is the highest score and indicates the maximum Type A stress-prone personality. It is important to understand that there are no distinct divisions between Type A and Type B. Rather, people fall somewhere on a continuum leaning more towards one type than the other. An average score is 84. Anyone with a score above that is inclined towards Type A behaviour, and below that towards Type B behaviour.

Sources of stress on male managers at work and home

See if you can see yourself in Herbert Greenberg's (1980) description of a stressed manager: 'George's week hadn't been going too well. Last night he'd been up late. He and his wife had had another talk about their fifteen-year old son, a talk that had degenerated into a blaming argument. When he awoke, he was weary and unrested. He felt restless, and during breakfast he was clearly irritable and not very pleasant to be around. When he finally got off to work, the traffic was heavy. He impatiently changed lanes a lot and honked his horn several times. Later, when he arrived at work, his desk seemed overflowing with unfinished business. Today was no exception – problems and headaches. Several people, too, were waiting with dissatisfactions and complaints. He wasn't able to listen to them very patiently – he certainly wasn't particularly tolerant of their points of view. Throughout the morning, he found his mind wandering as other people talked to him. He just couldn't focus on several big projects he had planned to tackle.

He drank five or six cups of coffee during the morning and stuffed in a doughnut or two with each cup. When lunch time arrived, he felt a need for a drink and wanted nothing more than to escape – get away from it all. But he had an early afternoon meeting, so he gulped a quick lunch and went back to his office to get ready for it. All he remembered of the meeting was his indigestion. The rest of the afternoon was quieter but not much better. He snapped at his secretary once or twice and was curt with colleagues. He felt weary, tense, and tight. He again postponed several decisions. He finished one report but wasn't pleased with it.

When he arrived at home he wanted nothing more than a drink and a chance to spout off about how hard he worked and how lousy his job was.'

Suggested exercise

If you were a colleague of George's, how would you cope with him on this day? Carry out a role play, to illustrate your technique.

TEST YOUR LEARNING

Short-answer questions

1 What are Hans Selye's three stages of stress?

2 How does the Yerkes–Dodson law apply to workplace stress?

3 Which workplace stressor, in your view, is the most pernicious and damaging to the individual employee?

4 Define the following: role ambiguity, role conflict and type A behaviour.

5 Can bosses be managed, and how?

Essay questions

1 What are the major sources of stress at work?

2 Assess the case for employee litigation for stress at work.

3 What is the impact of job loss on the individual?

GLOSSARY OF TERMS

Alarm reaction When an individual's defence mechanisms become active.

Autonomy at work When individuals feels that they have some influence and control over their jobs.

Cumulative trauma The gradual build up of stress which leads to some stress-related illness or event; a term also applied to stress litigation cases.

Exhaustion When one's adaptive mechanisms collapse.

Flight–fight reaction Individuals will choose whether to stay and fight or try to escape when confronting extreme danger or stress.

Locus of control The degree to which the individual feels that he or she has substantial control over events (internality) or little control over events (externality).

Qualitative overload Work that is too difficult for an individual.

Quantitative overload Having too much work to do.

Role conflict When an individual is torn by conflicting job demands.

Role ambiguity Unclear picture of the nature of the job, its objectives, responsibilities etc.

Type A behaviour A hard-driving, time-conscious, aggressive, impatient lifestyle.

SUGGESTED FURTHER READING

1 *Managing Workplace Stress* by Susan Cartwright and Cary Cooper, published by Sage in 1996, explores the various stressful events in the workplace that create difficulties for employees, such as mergers, downsizing, reorganisations etc., with attempts at reducing their negative impacts.

2 *Handbook of Stress, Medicine and Health* by Cary Cooper, published by CRC Press in 1996, highlights all of the research linking stress with various forms of ill health. It also explores the various work and life precursors to ill health, from the top researchers in the field.

3 *Professionals on Workplace Stress* by Alex Roney and Cary Cooper, published by John Wiley & Sons in 1997, is an attempt to highlight the problems associated with workplace stress as viewed by lawyers, occupational physicians, human resource professionals and academics.

REFERENCES

Berridge, J., Cooper, C.L. and Highley, C. (1997) *EAPs and Workplace Counselling*. Chichester: John Wiley & Sons.

Bolinder, E. and Ohlstrom, B. (1971) *Stress pa Svenska Arbetsplatser: en Enkatstudie Bland LO-Medlemmasrna*. Prima/LO: Lund.

Bortner, R.W. (1969) 'A short rating scale as a potential measure of pattern A behaviour', *Journal of Chronic Diseases*, vol. 22, pp. 87–91.

Breslow, L. and Buell, P. (1960) 'Mortality from coronary heart disease and physical activity of work in California', *Journal of Chronic Diseases*, vol. 11, pp. 615–25.

Buck, V. (1972) *Working under Pressure*. London: Staples Press.

Cannon, W.B. (1939) *The Wisdom of the Body*. New York: Norton.

Cartwright, S. and Cooper, C.L. (1997) *Managing Workplace Stress*. London: Sage Publications.

CBI (1970) *Absenteeism: An analysis of the problem*. London: CBI.

Cobb, S. and Rose, R.H. (1973) 'Hypertension, peptic ulcer and diabetes in air traffic controllers', *Journal of the Australian Medical Association*, vol. 224, pp. 489–92.

Coch, L. and French, J.R.P. (1948) 'Overcoming resistance to change', *Human Relations*, vol. 1, pp. 512–32.

Cooper, C.L. (1984) 'Executive stress: a ten country comparison', *Human Resource Management*, vol. 23, pp. 395–407.

Cooper, C.L. (1996) *Handbook of Stress, Medicine and Health*. Boca Raton, FL: CRC Press.

Cooper, C.L. and Smith, M.J. (1985) *Job Stress and Blue Collar Work*. Chichester: John Wiley.

Cooper, C.L., Cooper, R.D. and Eaker, L.H. (1988) *Living with Stress*. Harmondsworth: Penguin.

Cooper, C.L., Makin, P. and Cox, C. (1993) 'Managing the boss', *Leadership and Organizational Development Journal*, vol. 19, no. 5, pp. 28–32.

Cox, T. (1980) 'Repetitive work' in Cooper, C.L. and Payne, R. (eds) *Current Concerns in Occupational Stress*. Chichester: John Wiley.

Cummings, T. and Cooper, C.L. (1979) 'A cybernetic framework for the study of occupational stress', *Human Relations*, vol. 32, pp. 395–419.

Department of Health and Social Security (1986) *Employment Gazette*, August. London: DHSS.

Eisenberg, P. and Lazarsfeld, P.F. (1938) 'The psychological effects of unemployment', *Psychological Bulletin*, vol. 35, pp. 358–90.

French, J.R.P. and Caplan, R.D. (1972) 'Organizational stress and individual strain' in Marrow, A. (ed.) *The Failure of Success*. New York: AMACOM.

Fryer, D. and Payne, R. (1986) 'Being unemployed' in Cooper, C.L. and Robertson, I.T. (eds) *International Review of Industrial and Organizational Psychology*. Chichester: John Wiley.

Greenberg, H. (1980) *Coping with Job Stress*. Englewood Cliffs, NJ: Prentice Hall.

Hay, D. and Oken, D. (1972) 'The psychological stresses of intensive care nursing', *Psychosomatic Medicine*, vol. 34, pp. 109–18.

Hayes, J. and Nutman, P. (1981) *Understanding the Unemployed*. London: Tavistock.

Hingley, P. and Cooper, C.L. (1986) *Stress and the Nurse Manager*. Chichester: John Wiley.

Hinkle, L.E. (1973) 'The concept of stress in the biological social sciences', *Stress Medicine*, vol. 1, pp. 31–48.

Ivancevich, J.M. and Matteson, M.T. (1980) *Stress and Work*. Glenview, IL: Scott, Foresman and Co.

Ivancevich, J.M., Matteson, M.T. and Richards, E.P. (1985) 'Who's liable for stress on the job?', *Harvard Business Review*, March/April, 1985.

Jahoda, M. (1979) 'The impact of unemployment in the 1930s and the 1970s', *Bulletin of the British Psychological Society*, vol. 32, pp. 309–14.

Kelly, M. and Cooper, C.L. (1981) 'Stress among blue collar workers', *Employee Relations*, vol. 3, pp. 6–9.

Kelvin, P. and Jarrett, J.E. (1985) *Unemployment: Its social psychological effects*. Cambridge: Cambridge University Press.

Kornhauser, A. (1965) *Mental Health of the Industrial Worker*. New York: John Wiley.

Lazarus, R.S. (1966) *Psychological Stress and Coping Process*. New York: McGraw-Hill.

Lubin, J.S. (1980) 'On-the-job stress leads many workers to file, and win, compensation awards', *Wall Street Journal*, 17 September.

Makin, P., Cooper, C.L. and Cox, C. (1996) *Organizations and the Psychological Contract*. Leicester: British Psychological Society.

McLean, A. (1979) *Work Stress*. Boston, MA: Addison-Wesley.

Melhuish, A. (1978) *Executive Health*. London: Business Books.

NIOSH (1986) *National Strategy on the Prevention of Work-related Psychological Disorders*. Cincinnati, OH: NIOSH.

NIOSH (1993) *A National Strategy for the Prevention of Psychological Disorders in the Workplace*. Cincinnati, OH: NIOSH.

President's Commission on Mental Health (1978) Stock no. 040-000-00390-8. Washington, DC: US Government Printing Office.

Pincherle, A. (1972) 'Fitness for work', *Proceedings of the Royal Society of Medicine*, vol. 65, pp. 321–4.

Quick, J.C. and Quick, J.D. (1984) *Organizational Stress and Preventive Management*. New York: McGraw-Hill.

Quinn, R.P. and Staines, G.L. (1979) *The 1977 Quality of Employment Survey*. Ann Arbor, MI: University of Michigan.

Rosenman, R.H., Friedman, M. and Straus, R. (1964) 'A predictive study of CHD', *Journal of the Medical Association*, vol. 189, pp. 15–22.

Russek, H.I. and Zohman, B.L. (1958) 'Relative significance of heredity, diet and occupational stress in CHD of young adults', *American Journal of Medical Sciences*, vol. 235, pp. 266–75.

Sauter, S., Hurrell, J.T. and Cooper, C.L. (1989) *Job Control and Worker Health*. Chichester: John Wiley.

Selye, H. (1946) 'The General Adaptation Syndrome and the diseases of adaptation', *Journal of Clinical Endocrinology*, vol. 6, p. 117.

Selye, H. (1974) *Stress without Distress*. Philadelphia, PA: J.B. Lippincott.

Smith, M., Colligan, M., Horning, R. and Hurrell, J. (1978) *Occupational Comparison of Stress-Related Disease Incidence*. Cincinnati, OH: NIOSH.

Sparks, K. and Cooper, C.L. (1997) 'Hours of work and health', *Journal of Organizational Psychology*, in press.

Sutherland, V. and Cooper, C.L. (1987) *Man and Accidents Offshore*. London: Lloyd's.

Tasto, D., Colligan, M., Skjei, E. and Polly, S. (1978) *Health Consequences of Shiftwork*. Washington, DC: NIOSH.

Wardwell, W., Hyman, I.M. and Bahnson, C.B. (1964) 'Stress and coronary disease in three field studies', *Journal of Chronic Disease*, vol. 17, pp. 73–4.

Warr, P. (1983) 'Work, jobs and unemployment', *Bulletin of the British Psychological Society*, vol. 36, pp. 305–11.

Warr, P. and Wall, T. (1975) *Work and Well-Being*. Harmondsworth: Penguin, pp. 197–205.

Warshaw, L.J. (1979) *Managing Stress*. Reading, MA: Addison-Wesley.

Watts, M. and Cooper, C.L. (1992) *Relax: Dealing with stress*. London: BBC Books.

Managing stress at work

LEARNING OBJECTIVES

After studying this chapter, you should be able to:

1 develop an understanding of primary, secondary and tertiary stress interventions;

2 understand the role of the employee assistance programme;

3 appreciate the significance of intervening at the primary or organisational level source of stress;

4 acquire a problem-solving framework for dealing with occupational or organisational stress.

INTRODUCTION

As we have seen in the previous chapter, stress at work is costly to the individual and the organisation. In this chapter, we explore how stress might be managed in the workplace to minimise its dysfunctional impact on individuals and organisations.

A MODEL OF STRESS MANAGEMENT INTERVENTION

We will examine the role of stress management training and stress counselling in the workplace and the likely effect. In addition, we will highlight organisation-directed strategies to reduce stress, interventions that get at the root of the job or organisational problem or stressor (e.g. changing an autocratic management style, redesigning a job, introducing more flexible working arrangements etc.).

DeFrank and Cooper (1987) suggest that stress interventions can focus on the individual, the organisation or the individual–organisational interface. Murphy (1988) emphasises three levels of intervention: (i) primary, or reducing the *sources* of organisational stress, (ii) secondary, or stress management training, and (iii) tertiary, or health promotion and workplace counselling.

Table 18.1 Levels of stress management interventions and outcomes

Interventions	*Outcomes*
Focus on individual	*Focus on individual*
Relaxation techniques	Mood states (depression, anxiety)
Cognitive coping strategies	Psychosomatic complaints
Biofeedback	Subjectively experienced stress
Meditation	Physiological parameters (blood pressure,
Exercise	catecholamines, muscle tension)
Employee assistance programmes (EAPs)	Sleep disturbances
Time management	Life satisfaction
Focus on individual/organisational interface	*Focus on individual/organisational interface*
Relationships at work	Job stress
Person–environment fit	Job satisfaction
Role issues	Burnout
Participation and autonomy	Productivity and performance
	Absenteeism
	Turnover
	Health-care utilisation and claims
Focus on organisation	*Focus on organisation*
Oganisational structure	Productivity
Selection and placement	Turnover
Training	Absenteeism
Physical and environmental characteristics of job	Health-care claims
Health concerns and resources	Recruitment/retention success
Job rotation	

Source: DeFrank and Cooper (1987).

As Cooper and Cartwright (1994) highlight, most workplace initiatives operate at the secondary or tertiary levels, which focus on stress management training or counselling and health promotion. Health promotion/education programmes aim to modify behaviourial risk factors that lead to disease and poor health, whereas health screening is concerned with the diagnosis and detection of existing conditions. In a recent survey of some 3000 worksites, the US Department of Health and Human Services found that more than 60 per cent of worksites with 750 or more employees now offer some form of stress management or health promotion activity. The form these activities take varies widely. They may involve the provision of keep fit facilities on site, dietary control, cardiovascular fitness programmes, relaxation and exercise classes, stress management training or psychological counselling, or some combination of these packages as part of a multimodular employee assistance programme (EAP). Such initiatives by their definition – EAP – have tended to be 'employee' rather than 'organisation' directed strategies, whereby the focus is directed at changing the behaviours of individuals and improving their lifestyles and/or stress management skills.

EMPLOYEE ASSISTANCE PROGRAMMES AND STRESS MANAGEMENT TRAINING

While organisation-directed interventions are attempting to eliminate the source of job or organisational stress, the focus of most workplace stress initiatives has been directed at helping employees as individuals learn to cope with any stressors, be they job or organisational, that occur at work. This is achieved by improving the adaptability of individuals to their environment by changing their behaviour and improving their lifestyle or stress management skills. Such an approach is commonly described as the Band-Aid or inoculation treatment. Inherent in this approach is the notion that the organisation and its working environment will not change, therefore the individual has to learn ways of coping which help him or her to 'fit in' better (Cartwright and Cooper, 1994).

Increasingly, these initiatives have been in the form of employee assistance programmes (Berridge et al., 1997). In the US, it has been estimated that over 75 per cent of all Fortune 500 companies, together with about 12 000 smaller companies, now have such programmes (Feldman, 1991). The introduction of such programmes in the UK is also showing a rapid upward trend. Berridge and Cooper (1993) define an EAP as:

> a programmatic intervention at the workplace, usually at the level of the individual employee, using behaviourial science knowledge and methods for the control of certain work related problems (notably alcoholism, drug abuse and mental health) that adversely affect job performance, with the objective of enabling the individual to return to making her or his full contribution and to attaining full functioning in personal life.

An EAP can take various forms. It may involve the provision of on-site fitness facilities, dietary control, cardiovascular fitness programmes, relaxation classes, or stress and health education, but most often psychological counselling. EAPs have proved more popular with organisations than primary-level interventions or dealing with the sources of the job/organisational stress, for several reasons:

1 the cost–benefit analysis of such programmes has produced some impressive results. For example, the New York Telephone Company's 'wellness' programme designed to improve cardiovascular fitness saved the organisation $2.7 million in absence and treatment costs in one year alone (Cooper, 1985);

2 the professional 'interventionists' – the counsellors, physicians and clinicians responsible for health care – feel more comfortable with changing individuals than changing organisations (Ivancevich et al., 1990);

3 it is considered easier and less disruptive to business to change the individual than to embark on an extensive and potentially expensive organisational development programme, the outcome of which may be uncertain (Cooper and Cartwright, 1994);

4 they present a high-profile means by which organisations can 'be seen to be doing something about stress' and taking reasonable precautions to safeguard employee health. This is likely to be important, not only in terms of the message which it communicates to employees, but also to the external environment. This latter point is particularly important, given the increasing litigation fears which now exist among employers throughout the US and Europe. It is not difficult to envisage that the existence of an EAP, regardless of whether or not an individual chooses to use it, may become an effective defence against possible legal action.

Evidence as to the success of stress management training, frequently a component of EAPs, is generally confusing and imprecise (Elkin and Rosch, 1990), which possibly reflects the idiosyncratic nature of the form and content of this kind of training. Recent studies, which have evaluated the outcomes of stress management training, have found a modest improvement in self-reported symptoms and psychophysiological indices of strain (Sallis et al., 1987; Reynolds et al., 1993), but little or no change in job satisfaction, work stress or blood pressure. Similarly, studies which have assessed the impact of psychological counselling (Allison et al., 1989; Cooper and Sadri, 1991) have shown significant improvements in the mental health and absenteeism of counselled employees, but little change in levels of organisational commitment and job satisfaction. Counselling and stress management training may have short-term effects, particularly if employees return to an unchanged work environment and its indigenous stressors. If, as has been discussed, such initiatives have little impact on improving job satisfaction, then it is more likely that the individual will adopt a way of coping which may have positive individual outcomes, but possibly negative implications for the organisation.

Health promotion activities are another key feature of most stress management and EAP initiatives. Research findings which have examined the impact of lifestyle and health habits provide further support that any benefits may not necessarily be sustained. Lifestyle and health habits appear to have a strong direct effect on strain outcomes, in reducing anxiety, depression and psychosomatic distress, but do not necessarily moderate the stressor–strain linkage (Baglioni and Cooper, 1988). Cardiovascular fitness programmes, such as the New York Telephone Company's 'wellness' programmes, have been shown to dramatically improve employee health, but, again, any benefit may be relatively short term, particularly, if as suggested (Ivancevich and Matteson, 1988), after a few years, 70 per cent of individuals fail to maintain a long-term commitment to exercise habits and are likely to revert to their previous lifestyle.

> ■ KEY LEARNING POINT
>
> *The way to view stress management is to think of* primary *(e.g. dealing with the source of the stress),* secondary *(e.g. training) and* tertiary *(e.g. EAPs) prevention.*

CHANGING THE *SOURCES* OF WORKPLACE STRESS

Although there is considerable activity at the stress management, counselling and health promotion level, the organisational-level strategies are comparatively rare (Murphy, 1984). It has been argued that the simplistic philosophy of 'one size fits all' (Elkin and Rosch, 1990), implicit in the current stress management interventions, may be appropriate for smoking cessation programmes, but is less appropriate for workplace stressor reduction. Cardiovascular fitness programmes may be successful in reducing the harmful effects of stress on the high-pressured executive, but such programmes will not eliminate the job stressor itself, which may be 'overpromotion' or a poor relationship with a boss. Identifying and recognising the source itself, and taking steps to tackle it, might arguably arrest the whole 'stress process' (Cartwright and Cooper, 1997).

Elkin and Rosch (1990) summarise a useful range of possible organisation-directed strategies to reduce stress:

- redesign the task
- redesign the work environment
- establish flexible work schedules
- encourage participative management
- include the employee in career development
- analyse work roles and establish goals
- provide social support and feedback
- build cohesive teams
- establish fair employment policies
- share the rewards.

Many of these strategies are directed at increasing employee participation and autonomy. It is recognised that social support, control/job discretion or autonomy (Karasek, 1989) and coping behaviour play an important role in moderating the stress response. Tertiary- and secondary-level interventions may be useful in improving and extending an individual's coping strategies and social support, but they do not directly address the important issue of control in the workplace.

Indirectly, many strategies which focus on changing the style of work organisation are often a vehicle for culture change moving the organisation towards a more open and 'employee empowered' culture. Previous reviews of the organisation behaviour literature have demonstrated that employee participation has a positive impact upon productivity and quality control (Guzzo *et al.*, 1985). Quality circle programmes, which it has been suggested represent the ultimate form of employee involvement, have been shown to impact favourably upon productivity and employee attitudes (Dale, Cooper and Wilkinson, 1998).

A healthy organisation, therefore, can be defined as an organisation characterised by both financial success (i.e. profitability) and a physically and psychologically healthy workforce, which is able to maintain over time a healthy and satisfying work environment and organisational culture, particularly through periods of market turbulence and change. Healthy work environments are those in which (Cartwright and Cooper, 1994):

- levels of stress are low;
- organisational commitment and job satisfaction are high;
- sickness, absenteeism and labour turnover rates are below the national average;
- industrial relations are good and strikes/disputes are infrequent;
- safety and accident records are good;
- fear of litigation is absent (i.e. professional negligence, worker compensation, product liability claims etc. are rare and insurance premiums generally are below the sector average).

Therefore, it could be argued that the truly 'healthy' organisation, which has been successful in creating and maintaining a healthy and relatively stress-free environment, will be an organisation in which stress management and counselling interventions are unnecessary. Such an organisation will have effectively targeted its interventions at reducing or eliminating job and organisational stressors before their longer-term consequences on employee and organisational health adversely affect the bottom line. Indeed, although organisations have recognised the benefits of providing regular health screening for employees, they have been less concerned or slower to recognise the potential diagnostic benefits of conducting regular 'stress audits' to ascertain the current state of health of their organisation as a whole (and its constituent parts), through occupational/organisational stress screening.

> ■ **KEY LEARNING POINT**
> *Dealing with the job and organisational sources of stress requires job redesign, flexible working arrangements, a supportive corporated culture and better organisational communications.*

DEALING WITH WORKPLACE STRESS: A PROBLEM-SOLVING FRAMEWORK

If the constructs and framework of problem solving are applied to the problem of workplace stress, then both the individual and the organisation need to:

1 be aware and accept that a problem exists;

2 be able to identify and isolate the problem/stressor;

3 attempt to change the problem/stressor in a way that provides a solution which is mutually beneficial;

4 if the problem/stressor cannot be changed, then find a way of coping with the problem;

5 monitor and review the outcome.

Cartwright and Cooper (1994) suggest the following steps:

Step 1: Being aware and accepting that a problem exists

It is widely accepted that recognising that one has a problem is the crucial first step towards solving it. Ownership of the problem is considered to be the most significant factor in the clinical treatment of problems such as alcoholism, drug abuse or a damaging relationship. The first step in dealing with stress, therefore, requires an awareness by the individual and the organisation that stress is a feature of modern working life, which at some time or other everybody is likely to experience, irrespective of their position in the organisation and, furthermore, that *it is not necessarily a reflection of their incompetence.*

It is important that the individual is able to 'tune in' to the problem and recognise his or her own stress symptomatology early in the stress process, and that the organisation seeks to create a climate which is perceived to be openly supportive rather than punitive.

Organisations can tune into the problem of stress by monitoring a variety of behaviourial indices. Aside from the more obvious indices such as rate of labour turnover, sickness and absence data, other more subtle indices might include error and accident rates, insurance claims, tardiness, levels of job satisfaction and industrial relations generally. Organisations can also provide training in symptom recognition and basic counselling skills for their supervisors and managers to help them to be more responsive to employee stress. It would seem desirable, if not essential, that this first step in the coping process requires an organisational initiative in demonstrably acknowledging and communicating to employees that stress has a legitimate place on the organisation agenda alongside other more traditional issues that fall into the category of health and safety at work.

Steps 2 and 3: Identifying the problem/stressor and attempting to eliminate it or change it

At the individual level, stressor identification can be achieved by the maintenance of a stress diary. By recording on a daily basis the incidents, types of situation, person(s) involved, which cause distress, over a period of time (e.g. four weeks), this information will reveal any significant themes or common stressor patterns and help the individual to identify specific problems or problem areas. It is also useful if the individual records show how they responded to the situation at the time, whether the strategy was successful in both the short and longer term, and how, on reflection, they might have handled it better.

On the basis of this information, the individual can then move towards developing an action plan as to how they could either eliminate the source of stress or change or modify it. For example, if a boss consistently undermines you at work, you can either confront or avoid him or her, or consider the options for employment elsewhere. If the stressor cannot be changed, however, then the individual has to accept the situation and explore ways of coping with the situation as it is. By cataloguing current responses and ways of coping and reviewing these with the benefit of retrospection, the individual can (i) identify areas where his or her coping skills could be improved and (ii) develop a repertoire of successful contingency-based coping methods which can be applied to similar situations in the future. The review process is particularly important, as has been suggested, when cognitive processes are frequently impaired under stress to the extent that the range of possible alternative strategies for coping is unlikely to be fully considered or poorly evaluated. An awareness of potential stressors can also help the individual to develop anticipatory coping strategies (i.e. pre-stressor).

At the organisational level, an employee survey or organisational stress audit can be used to assess and monitor employee health and well-being, and identify the source of stress which may be operating at an organisation-wide, departmental or work group level. Instruments such as the Occupational Stress Indicator (Cooper *et al.*, 1988) can be used, which also incorporate personality measures of Type A behaviour, locus of control and employee coping strategies. Different stressors are likely to suggest different organisational solutions. For example, eliminating or reducing stressors relating to factors intrinsic to the job may involve ergonomic solutions to the problem of poorly designed equipment, whereas if a significant source of stress among employees relates to career issues, then this may possibly be addressed by the introduction of regular appraisals, career counselling or retraining opportunities. Diagnostic stress audits can be advantageous in terms of directing organisations to areas when they can engage in anticipatory coping strategies and so arrest the stress process before its negative impact on employee health manifests itself, for example, in circumstances where the currently reported stress levels among employees are high, but the previous baseline outcome measures of physical and mental health and job satisfaction are comparable with normative data. At the more local workgroup level, there are less formal means by which potential stress-related problems can be identified through the introduction of regular workgroup review meetings or quality circle type initiatives.

Step 4: If the problem/stressor cannot be changed, then find ways of coping with it

There are likely to be certain stressors which neither the individual nor the organisation is able to change, but which have to be 'coped with' in the conventional sense of the word. It is in relation to stressors of this nature that secondary and tertiary levels of intervention have a definite role to play. It is also important to recognise that all of the stress which impacts on the workplace is not necessarily or exclusively caused by the work environment. Financial crisis, bereavement, marital difficulties and other personal life events create stress, the effects of which often spill over into the workplace. Tertiary-level interventions, such as the provision of counselling services, can be extremely effective in dealing with non-work-related stress, as evidenced by the experiences of the UK Post Office (Cooper and Sadri, 1991).

Step 5: Monitoring and reviewing the outcome

The final stage in any problem-solving process involves the evaluation of the implemented solution. As already discussed, the discipline of maintaining a stress diary can help the individual to review the efficacy of his or her own coping strategies. Similarly, stress audits can provide a baseline measure whereby the introduction of any subsequent stressor reduction technique implemented by an organisation can be evaluated. If, as has been argued, stressor reduction provides the most effective means of tackling the problem of occupational stress, the criteria by which an organisation may also assess its effectiveness would be in terms of the extensiveness of its secondary- and tertiary-level programmes, for one would expect that the more successful the organisation is in eliminating or modifying environmental stressors, the less demand there would be for stress management training and employee assistance programmes.

■ **KEY LEARNING POINT**

Managing stress at work requires a stage by stage approach: identifying a problem, intervening to change it or find ways of coping with it, and monitoring and reviewing progress.

Managing your time

7.30 a.m. The day starts badly. You forgot to set the alarm and you're running late. You have an important client meeting at 9.30 a.m. and you intended to get into the office early to reread the papers in preparation for the meeting. You have to stop for petrol on the way in, which further delays you. Traffic is heavy and there are roadworks on the motorway. You find yourself in a tailback of slow-moving traffic and it's at least four miles until the next exit. As you're crawling along, you suddenly become aware that you have developed a flat tyre. You limp on to the hard shoulder and look at your watch. It's 8.50 a.m. and you're still some eight miles from your office. You're not going to make that meeting!

Assuming a typical response to the previous scenario, the day might continue as follows:

9.45 a.m. You eventually arrive at your office. You go to collect the file for the client meeting and the phone rings. A subordinate is having some problems accessing information on the computer; brusquely, you give hasty instructions. You then spend a further ten minutes wading through the huge piles of paper stacked on your desk, searching for the right file. You notice a new pile of correspondence and phone messages on the desk, some marked 'urgent'. You contemplate dealing with these but you're now already 30 minutes late for this meeting. Suddenly, you realise that before you left last night your boss popped in and suggested a meeting at 10.30 a.m. You're going to be late for that one too.

Suggested exercise

What is the most effective way of handling the various problems in the above scenario? Discuss in small groups how you would have coped with each of the problems as they occurred.

TEST YOUR LEARNING

Short-answer questions

1 What is an EAP?

2 What are the range of organisation-directed strategies to reduce stress?

3 What is a stress audit?

4 What is the Occupational Stress Indicator, and what is it used for?

Essay questions

1 Why might stress management programmes be less effective than organisational ori-entated interventions?

2 Describe the steps found in the Cartwright and Cooper (1994) problem-solving framework for occupational stress.

GLOSSARY OF TERMS

EAP Employee assistance programme, usually referring to a counselling service provided for employees, most often by outside providers.

Employee empowerment The degree to which employees have a say in their jobs or the organisation they work for.

OSI Occupational Stress Indicator, a measure that assesses an individual's and organisation's stress profile.

Social support networks Refers to informal and formal relationships which can help the individual to explore and deal with stress.

Stressor Means the source of the stress, the cause or underlying reasons why an employee may show stress symptoms or disease.

Wellness programme A company-wide programme to promote employee health, both physi-cal and psychological.

SUGGESTED FURTHER READING

1 *Employee Assistance Programmes and Workplace Counselling* by John Berridge, Cary Cooper and Carolyn Highley-Marchington, published by John Wiley in 1997, is a comprehensive review of all research on EAPs, as well as a guide for human resource professionals about how to choose one, how to evaluate them and the costs/benefits of EAPs for organisations.

2 *Creating Healthy Work Organizations* by Cary Cooper and Steve Williams, published by John Wiley in 1994, highlights a number of good practice examples of what companies are doing to manage stress at work. The companies include Zeneca, Scottish and Newcastle, and Nestlé Rowntree, and the examples range from stress audits to managing mental health at work.

REFERENCES

Allison, T., Cooper, C.L. and Reynolds, P. (1989) 'Stress counselling in the workplace – the Post Office experience', *The Psychologist*, vol. 2, pp. 384–8.

Baglioni, A.J., Jr and Cooper, C.L. (1988) 'A structural model approach toward the development of a theory of the link between stress and mental health', *British Journal of Medical Psychology*, vol. 61, pp. 87–102.

Berridge, J. and Cooper, C.L. (1993) 'Stress and coping in US organizations: the role of the Employee Assistance Programme', *Work and Stress*, vol. 7, no. 1, pp. 89–102.

Berridge, J., Cooper, C.L. and Highley-Marchington, C. (1997) *Employee Assistance Programmes and Workplace Counselling*. Chichester: John Wiley.

Cartwright, S. and Cooper, C.L. (1997) 'Coping in occupational settings' in Zeidner, M. and Endler, N. (eds) *Handbook of Coping*, in press.

Cartwright, S. and Cooper, C.L. (1998) *Managing Workplace Stress*. London: Sage Publications.

Cooper, C.L. (1985) 'The road to health in American firms', *New Society*, pp. 335–6.

Cooper, C.L. and Cartwright, S. (1994) 'Healthy mind; healthy organization – a proactive approach to occupational stress', *Human Relations*, vol. 47, no. 4, pp. 455–71.

Cooper, C.L. and Sadri, G. (1991) 'The impact of stress counselling at work' in Perrewe, P.L. (ed.) *Handbook of Job Stress (Special Issue), Journal of Social Behavior and Personality*, vol. 6, no. 7, pp. 411–23.

Cooper, C.L., Sloan, S. and Williams, S. (1988) *Occupational Stress Indicator: The manual*. Windsor: NFER-Nelson.

Dale, B.D., Cooper, C.L. and Wilkinson, A. (1998) *Managing Quality and Human Resources: a guide to continious improvement*. Oxford: Blackwell.

DeFrank, R.S. and Cooper, C.L. (1987) 'Worksite stress management interventions: their effectiveness and conceptualization', *Journal of Managerial Psychology*, vol. 2, pp. 4–10.

Elkin, A.J. and Rosch, P.J. (1990) 'Promoting mental health at the workplace: the prevention side of stress management', *Occupational Medicine: State of the Art Review*, vol. 5, no. 4, pp. 739–54.

Feldman, S. (1991) 'Today's EAPs make the grade', *Personnel*, vol. 68, pp. 3–40.

Guzzo, R.A., Jette, R.D. and Katzell, R.A. (1985) 'The effects of psychologically-based intervention programs on worker productivity: a meta-analysis', *Personnel Psychology*, vol. 38, pp. 275–92.

Ivancevich, J.M. and Matteson, M.T. (1988) 'Promoting the individual's health and well being' in Cooper, C.L. and Payne, R. (eds) *Causes, Coping and Consequences of Stress at Work*. Chichester: John Wiley.

Ivancevich, J.M., Matteson, M.T., Freedman, S.M. and Phillips, J.S. (1990) 'Worksite stress management interventions', *American Psychologist*, vol. 45, pp. 252–61.

Karasek, R. (1989) 'Control in the workplace and its health related aspects' in Sauter, S.L., Hurrell, J.J. and Cooper, C.L. (eds) *Job Control and Worker Health*. Chichester: John Wiley.

Murphy, L.R. (1984) 'Occupational stress management: a review and appraisal', *Journal of Occupational Psychology*, vol. 57, pp. 1–15.

Murphy, L.R. (1988) 'Workplace interventions for stress reduction and prevention' in Cooper, C.L. and Payne, R. (eds) *Causes, Coping and Consequences of Stress at Work*. Chichester: John Wiley.

Reynolds, S., Taylor, E. and Shapiro, D.A. (1993) 'Session impact in stress management training', *Journal of Occupational and Organizational Psychology*, vol. 66, pp. 99–113.

Sallis, J.F., Trevorrow, T.R., Johnson, C.C., Hovell, M.F. and Kaplan, R.M. (1987) 'Worksite stress management: a comparison of programmes', *Psychology and Health*, vol. 1, pp. 237–55.

Job redesign and new technology

LEARNING OBJECTIVES

After studying this chapter, you should be able to:

1 describe the key features of scientific management (Taylorism);

2 list four techniques of job redesign;

3 list six reasons why various constituencies within an organisation might be interested in job redesign;

4 define the five core job characteristics identified by Hackman and Oldham;

5 describe two general forms of new technology in the workplace;

6 describe the 'task and technology' and 'organisation and end-user' approaches to the introduction of new technology;

7 evaluate the effects of new technology on the characteristics of people's work;

8 describe the features of jobs specified by Wall *et al.* (1990) as highly relevant to new technology;

9 describe some of the possible effects of new technology on the wider organisation.

INTRODUCTION

The term *job redesign* refers to attempts to increase the amounts of variety and autonomy experienced by people in their jobs. This increase has been deemed desirable by many managers in recent years because of a need to devolve responsibility in 'downsized' organisations, and is a contrast to the trend throughout the twentieth century for jobs to become increasingly monotonous and controlled. The first half of this chapter therefore elaborates on this perceived need, and evaluates theoretical and practical attempts to meet it. The second half of the chapter covers *new technology*, which is the general term given to computer-controlled equipment of various kinds. Such equipment is not really so new, since it became much more widely available and affordable from the 1970s onwards due to advances in microelectronics. The introduction of new technology into the workplace often has important implications for the nature of jobs. That is why job redesign and new technology are covered in the same chapter. The process of introducing new technology and the effects of new technology on organisations are also examined.

JOB REDESIGN

Job simplification and job enrichment

Surveys (e.g. Taylor, 1979) have identified the following key factors in the design of most jobs:

- minimising skill requirements
- maximising management control
- minimising the time required to perform a task.

These may appear to make good sense, especially against economic criteria. Unskilled or semi-skilled labour costs less than skilled labour, and productivity is enhanced if tasks are done quickly. But, as we shall see, jobs designed in this way frequently have human costs, and perhaps economic ones too.

This 'traditional' approach to job design stems from a philosophy called 'scientific management', or 'Taylorism', after its creator, F. W. Taylor. Taylor formulated his ideas in the USA in the early twentieth century. As a machine-shop foreman, he felt that workers consistently underproduced, and that the way to prevent this was to:

- systematically (or 'scientifically') compile information about the work tasks required;
- remove workers' discretion and control over their own activities;
- simplify tasks as much as possible;
- specify standard procedures and times for task completion;
- use financial (and *only* financial) incentives;
- by the above methods, ensure that workers could not deceive managers, or hide from them.

This of course bears a strong resemblance to the 'Theory X' view of human nature (*see* Chapter 11). Observers agree that jobs in many, perhaps most, organisations are implicitly or explicitly based on Taylorism.

> ■ KEY LEARNING POINT
>
> *Scientific management, also known as Taylorism, emphasises*
> *standardised methods and minimisation of costs in the design of work.*

Taylorism might make for a well-ordered world, but is it a happy and productive one? During the 1960s, a number of studies seemed to show that work organised along Scientific Management principles was associated with negative attitudes towards the job, as well as poor mental and/or physical health (e.g. Kornhauser, 1965; Turner and Lawrence, 1965). It was also often assumed that poor productivity would accompany such outcomes, though of course in Chapter 3 we have already seen that the maxim 'a happy worker is a productive worker' does not always apply. Another assumption was that simplified work actually *caused* poor mental health etc., rather than the reverse causal direction.

These studies of simplified work led to considerable concern about what came to be called *quality of working life* (QWL). Several theoretical perspectives were brought to bear on QWL. One was *job enrichment* – a concept developed through the work of Herzberg (1966). Herzberg proposed a basic distinction between *hygiene factors* and *motivators*. Hygiene factors included pay, conditions of employment, the work environment and other features extrinsic to the work activities themselves. Motivators included job challenge, recognition, and skill use – that is, features appealing to growth needs (*see* Chapter 11). On the basis of his data, Herzberg proposed that hygiene factors could not cause satisfaction, but that dissatisfaction could result if they were not present. On the other hand, motivators led to satisfaction: their absence produced not dissatisfaction, but a lack of satisfaction. Although Herzberg's data and conclusions can be criticised on several grounds, his recommendation that motivation and/or satisfaction can be enhanced by increasing skill use, job challenge etc. is consistent with much subsequent work.

Another relevant theoretical tradition is *socio-technical systems* (Cherns, 1976, 1987; Davis, 1982; Heller, 1989). Arising from studies in the immediate post-war years, socio-technical theory emphasises the need to integrate technology and social structures in the workplace. Too often, technology is introduced with scant regard for existing friendship patterns, work groups and status differentials (*see also* the 'New technology' section, below). Socio-technical theory attempts to rectify this, but it also makes wider propositions. For example, it states that job activities should be specified only in so far as necessary to establish the boundaries of that job. It also emphasises that boundaries should be drawn so that they do not impede transmission of information and learning. Such principles may seem self-evident, but close examination of many organisations will demonstrate that they are not adhered to. Socio-technical job design therefore emphasises autonomy, decision making and the avoidance of subordinating people to machines.

Interest in job redesign has been stimulated in recent years by concerns about the quality of products and services, the need for customer responsiveness, and the increasing use of teams. Another factor is the need for staff who can fulfil more than one function in the organisation – so-called functional flexibility (Cordery *et al.*, 1993). In other words, job redesign is part of hard-headed business strategy rather than (or as well as) a philanthropic concern with the quality of working life. This is well illustrated by a survey of 181 human resource managers in the United States reported by McCann and

Buckner (1994). From a list of twelve statements about work redesign, the one most often agreed with (by 69 per cent of the managers) was 'Work redesign is part of an overall quality/productivity improvement effort – all parts of our organization are being examined and changed'.

Whatever their exact theoretical origin, most attempts to redesign jobs centre on increasing one or more of the following (Wall, 1982):

- *variety* (of tasks or skills)
- *autonomy* (freedom to choose work methods, scheduling and occasionally goals)
- *completeness* (extent to which the job produces an identifiable end result which the person can point to).

This may be attempted in one or more of the following ways:

- *job rotation*: people rotate through a small set of different (but usually similar) jobs. Rotation is frequent (e.g. each week). It can increase variety;
- *horizontal job enlargement*: additional tasks are included in a person's job. They are usually similar to tasks already carried out. This too can increase variety;
- *vertical job enlargement*: additional decision-making responsibilities and/or higher level challenging tasks are included in the job. This increases autonomy, variety and possibly completeness. An increasingly commonly used term for this is *empowerment*: a person does not necessarily achieve an increase in formal status, but he or she is given more freedom to take decisions and implement them according to the needs of the situation at the time (Conger and Kanungo, 1988);
- *semi-autonomous work groups*: similar to vertical job enlargement, but at the level of the group rather than the individual. In other words, a group of people is assigned a task and allowed to organise itself to accomplish it. Semi-autonomous workgroups have been introduced in some car factories;
- *self-managing teams*: more often composed of managers and professionals than semi-autonomous work groups, these teams are often given considerable freedom to accomplish a group task, and perhaps even to define the task in the first place.

> ■ **KEY LEARNING POINT**
>
> *Job redesign can take a variety of forms and arise for many reasons (see Fig. 19.1), but it normally involves an attempt to increase the amount of variety, autonomy and/or completeness inherent in the work of one or more people.*

Another aspect of job redesign is discussed by Campion and McClelland (1993). They distinguish between *knowledge enlargement*, where there is an increase in the amount of understanding required of procedures relating to the different parts of an organisation's operation, and *task enlargement*, where further tasks relating to the same part of an organisation's operation are added to a job. Campion and McClelland found some evidence that knowledge enlargement had a more positive effect than task enlargement on work performance and satisfaction.

Fig. 19.1 Concerns leading to job redesign

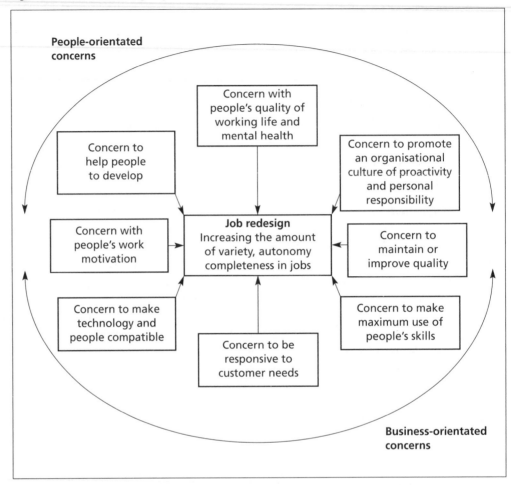

Wall (1982) reviewed earlier work on job redesign. He concluded that attempts to redesign jobs usually had some effect as long as they did not confine themselves to increasing variety. Redesign often succeeded in improving job satisfaction, motivation, employee mental health and performance. However, Wall also acknowledged that this conclusion was not definitive. Redesign rarely occurred in the absence of other changes, such as pay rates and staffing levels. It was therefore impossible to be sure what caused any change in employee attitudes and behaviour. More recently, there has been some scepticism about the genuineness of attempts to empower employees at lower levels of the organisation. It might be considered exploitation, in so far as it means that staff take on more responsibility without an increase in pay. There is also some suggestion that managers only really give away control over things they regard as unimportant, thus rendering empowerment something of a sham.

The job characteristics model

One theory has dominated the scene in job redesign since the late 1970s. This is the *job characteristics model* of Hackman and Oldham (1976, 1980). It is depicted in Fig. 19.2, which shows that Hackman and Oldham identify five 'core job characteristics':

1 *skill variety* (SV): the extent to which the job requires a range of skills;

2 *task identity* (TI): the extent to which the job produces a whole, identifiable outcome;

3 *task significance* (TS): the extent to which the job has an impact on other people, either inside or outside the organisation;

Fig. 19.2 Hackman and Oldham's job characteristics model

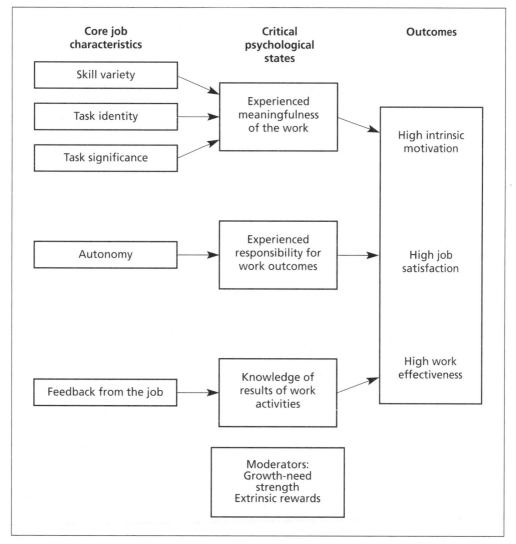

Source: Adapted from J.R. Hackman and G.R. Oldham (1980), *Work Redesign* © 1980 by Addison-Wesley Publishing Co, Inc. Reprinted by permission of Addison Wesley Longman Inc.

4 *autonomy* (Au): the extent to which the job allows the job holder to exercise choice and discretion in his or her work;

5 *feedback from job* (Fb): the extent to which the job itself (as opposed to other people) provides information on how well the job holder is performing.

The core job characteristics are said to produce 'critical psychological states'. The first three core job characteristics are believed to influence *experienced meaningfulness of the work*. Autonomy affects *experienced responsibility for outcomes of the work*, and feedback from the job impacts on *knowledge of the actual results of the work activities*. Collectively, the critical psychological states are believed to influence three outcomes: motivation, satisfaction and work performance. But this whole process is said to be moderated by several factors (*see* Fig. 19.2). The most often investigated of these is growth-need strength. This refers to the importance to the individual of Maslow's growth needs (*see* Chapter 11). The model is said to apply more strongly to people with high growth needs than to those with low ones.

> ■ **KEY LEARNING POINT**
> *The job characteristics model specifies five features of jobs which tend to make them intrinsically motivating and satisfying.*

The job characteristics model has provoked a huge amount of research, especially in the USA. This is not surprising, since it provides specific hypotheses about exactly which job characteristics matter, how they affect people's psychological states, what outcomes they produce, and which individual differences affect the whole process. Also, Hackman and Oldham have produced a questionnaire called the Job Diagnostic Survey (JDS) which assesses the constructs shown in Fig. 19.2. The JDS is completed by job holders. Hackman and Oldham also propose an overall motivating potential score (MPS), which is computed as follows:

$$\text{MPS} = \frac{\text{SV} + \text{TI} + \text{TS}}{3} \times \text{Au} \times \text{Fb}$$

Scores on the JDS for each core job characteristic can vary between 1 and 7, so the overall MPS can range from 1 to 343. As one would expect, typical scores vary somewhat between jobs, but a score of around 150 is common. Interestingly, MPS scores for the 'job' of student are often quite low. This is frequently because feedback from the job is very limited: students say they can rarely tell how well they have done without feedback from other people. Another reason is low task significance – usually students' work scarcely affects other people at all. This leads to one potential omission from the job characteristics model: despite a low TS score on the JDS, students often say that their role feels significant, because of its impact on *them*, as opposed to other people.

Roberts and Glick (1981) voiced a number of criticisms of the job characteristics model (JCM). These included the following:

● although research on the JCM had found many of the predicted relationships, this may have been due to *common method variance*. That is, in many research studies all the information about core job characteristics, critical psychological states and outcomes came from questionnaires, and all from the same people;

- few evaluations of the JCM had tested the model properly. For example, most omitted any examination of the moderator variables (*see* Fig. 19.2);

- few evaluations of the JCM had involved attempts to *redesign* jobs. Instead, most had looked for relationships between the variables of interest in unchanged jobs;

- the model says little about *how* to change a job in order to increase the amount of core job characteristics it offers;

- the model says little about how to redesign jobs for people low in growth need strength.

Roberts and Glick's points were well made, and some (especially the last three above) remain valid now. However, other psychologists have subsequently examined the JCM (e.g. Loher *et al.*, 1985; Fried and Ferris, 1987; Hogan and Martell, 1987; Champoux, 1991). The following conclusions can be drawn:

- people's descriptions of their jobs on the JDS correlate fairly highly with descriptions of those same jobs by supervisors and expert job analysts;

- JDS responses suggest that there are indeed several core job characteristics, but perhaps not as many as five. Specifically, it seems that skill variety, task significance and autonomy may all be part of the same dimension. In other words, they may go together closely enough to be thought of as reflecting the same underlying concept;

- the core job characteristics are generally correlated with outcomes as predicted. This is more consistently the case for motivation and satisfaction than for performance. But the core job characteristics do not always produce the specific psychological states that the JCM predicts;

- nevertheless, the critical psychological states correlate more highly with motivation/satisfaction outcomes than do the core job dimensions. But the reverse is true for the work performance outcome;

- the overall MPS score is often better at predicting outcomes than any individual core job characteristic, as indeed it should be if it represents a meaningful summary of a job. On the other hand, it often seems that simply adding scores on the five core characteristics is at least as good as the way of calculating MPS devised by Hackman and Oldham;

- as predicted, the relationships between core job characteristics, critical psychological states and outcomes are stronger for people with high growth-need strength than for those with low growth-need strength;

- the JCM fits the available research data better than models using similar variables but in different configurations. There is nevertheless a nagging suspicion that scores on many of the JCM variables stem *from* (rather than lead to) a person's general satisfaction with his or her work;

- there are probably additional job characteristics, as yet unidentified, which also predict the outcomes. Warr (1987) has suggested availability of money, physical security, interpersonal contact and valued social position as likely contenders.

CASE
STUDY
19.1

Bicycle assembly at Wheelspin

The Wheelspin bicycle company produces a range of bicycles for adults and children. At their factory, already-manufactured components are painted and assembled. Assembly is carried out on assembly lines which move at constant speeds. The factory manager decides which line will assemble which bicycle. Each member of staff has a specific part or parts which they screw, weld or otherwise fix onto the basic frame at a specified point on the assembly line. They carry out the same tasks about 80 times a day. Staff are recruited to a specific job: they generally remain on the same assembly line and deal with the same parts. Once every two or three months, the model being assembled changes, but generally the assembly tasks required are more or less constant. Noise levels are low enough to allow staff to chat to immediate neighbours as they work. Work quality is assessed at the end of the production line, where performance of the assembled bicycle is examined by quality control staff.

Suggested exercise

Examine the characteristics of the assembly jobs at Wheelspin. How might those characteristics be changed?

■ **KEY LEARNING POINT**

Research suggests considerable support for the job characteristics model, but also that it needs some refinement.

All in all, then, the JCM has stood empirical test reasonably well, especially considering the relatively large number of connections between specific variables it proposes. However, it is not the whole story, and paradoxically it still has not often been tested much in the context of job redesign. Further well-focused investigations are needed to build on the existing foundations.

Beyond the job characteristics model

The JCM is a very tightly defined theory which focuses on a limited range of variables. Kelly (1993) argues that job redesign not only affects job characteristics, and that research has failed to establish that changes in job characteristics lead to changes in motivation, satisfaction and performance. Part of the reason for this may be poor research design (Kelly, 1993, p. 754):

> Control groups are rare and measurement of post-redesign change has often been carried out within a relatively short time-span of around 12 months. Longitudinal studies spanning several years are still the exception.

Out of several hundred research reports on job redesign, Kelly found only 31 that were sufficiently rigorous and well designed to warrant his attention. Of these, 17 reported that job redesign led to improved perceptions of job content, but 8 reported no change (the other 6 did not investigate this). Job redesign by no means always led to improvements in satisfaction or motivation; and even when it did, increases in job performance did not necessarily follow. However, improvements in job performance *did* tend to happen when pay rises and/or job losses occurred along with job redesign.

On the basis of his review of research, Kelly (1993) has proposed what he calls the twin-track model of job redesign (*see* Fig. 19.3). One track concerns satisfaction/motivation and the other job performance. He argues that changes in work methods, pay rates, job security, goals (*see* Chapter 11) and individual rewards can occur as a result of job redesign, as well as (or instead of) changes in job characteristics. Changes in job characteristics affect satisfaction and motivation, but the other changes have a more direct impact on job performance, Kelly argues.

> ■ KEY LEARNING POINT
> *Improvements in* job performance *do not usually occur as a direct consequence of changes in job characteristics.*

Job redesign can also have knock-on effects which are often overlooked. For example, Cordery and Wall (1985) have examined what happens to supervisory roles if the work-

Fig. 19.3 Kelly's twin-track model of job redesign

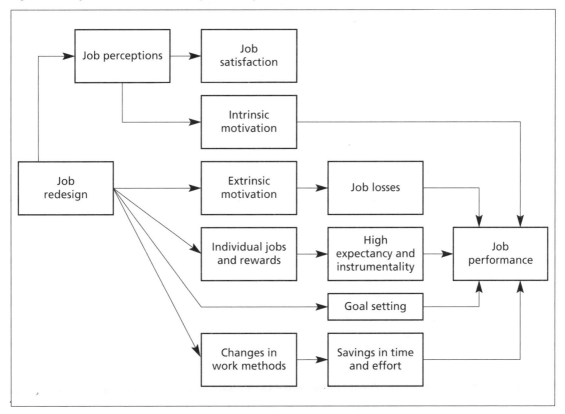

Source: Kelly (1993)

force is given more autonomy. They argue that supervisors must be helped to change from an overseeing and controlling orientation to an enabling one. Among other things, this requires them to take *more* control over defining the nature and boundary of their workgroup's task, while *relinquishing* control over how the task is carried out. Traditional approaches to leadership, and probably most supervisors, do not typically make that distinction (*see* Chapter 14). There is also a heightened need for the supervisor to provide feedback to the group on how things are going, so that the group members can adjust their work strategies if necessary.

Finally, it should be remembered that other quite different approaches to job (re)design exist. Campion and Thayer (1985) and Campion (1988) have pointed out that an *engineering approach* (in essence Scientific Management), a *biological approach* (focusing on human physiology) and a *perceptual/motor approach* (focusing on human information processing) also exist. Their data indicated that the motivational (i.e. JCM) approach does enhance satisfaction, but not work efficiency or reliability. The Scientific Management approach fostered efficiency and the perceptual/motor approach related to reliability. There were problems with some of the measures (for example, efficiency was defined as a low amount of training, education and experience being needed for effective job performance). Nevertheless, Campion's work demonstrates that quite different approaches can also contribute to job redesign, especially perhaps in enhancing some aspects of work performance.

As noted earlier, there have been relatively few attempts actually to redesign jobs reported in the literature. There have been even fewer long-term investigations to see whether any effects of job redesign are maintained over a long period. The few studies that have appeared (e.g. Griffin, 1991; Campion and McClelland, 1993) suggest that the impact of job redesign on attitudes and behaviour may wane over time. Also, jobs that become too complex may not be motivating because employees perceive a low probability of achieving satisfactory performance (*see* Chapter 11).

NEW TECHNOLOGY

What is new technology?

Technological change in the workplace has, of course, been a continuing process over the centuries. The term 'new technology' usually refers to a particular set of changes which have occurred from the 1970s onwards, so they are not so very new now. They have been brought about by the invention and development of *microchips*, which are tiny components of electrical circuits that can be combined to form much larger and more complex electronic systems. Microchips have made it possible to build such systems simply, cheaply and in only a tiny fraction of the weight and size that would formerly have been required (Wall, 1987). Although microchips have been around for some time now, what can be done with them continues to advance rapidly, producing a continuing high rate of technological change in the workplace (Clegg, 1994). There are two general forms of new technology in the workplace:

1 *advanced manufacturing technology* (AMT): this includes a wide range of equipment which contributes to the manufacturing process, usually by working on already-made

materials. One example is industrial 'robots', which can do tasks such as welding and spray-painting, or even playing snooker. Another is automatic guided vehicles (AGVs) which take components from one part of a factory to another. A third is computer numerically controlled (CNC) machine tools. These conduct precision cutting, drilling or grinding of materials, usually metal, to produce components of larger products. All of these examples are underpinned by microchip technology which allows computer control of the often precise and complex tasks they undertake (*see* Wall *et al.*, 1987a).

2 *office technology*: here the emphasis is on the storage, retrieval, presentation and manipulation of information usually in verbal and/or numerical forms (Pava, 1983). The most obvious example is perhaps word processing equipment, which during the 1980s rapidly became a prominent feature of most offices (Oborne, 1985, chapter 9). Another common manifestation is electronic 'point of sale' equipment in shops. This uses the bar codes on goods to produce a cumulative account of what has been purchased, not only to the customer but also to the retailing organisation for ordering and stock control. A further manifestation is expert and decision-support systems which compile information relevant to managerial decisions and also work on that information in order to contribute to the decision itself.

> ■ KEY LEARNING POINT
> *New technology concerns office or factory manufacturing and information processing equipment based upon microelectronics.*

Organisations in most Western countries have frequently been exhorted to invest quickly in new technology or face dire consequences in competitive international markets. This perceived need has rarely been challenged, but, interestingly, the uptake of some forms of new technology was not particularly quick, at least in the earlier years of its availability, perhaps partly due to high costs of initial purchase and installation. More controversial has been the impact of new technology on the total number of jobs available, with estimates varying from significant increases to huge decreases (*see* Burnes, 1989, pp. 5–8). Clearly, part of the point of introducing new technology is often to save on labour costs. But jobs may be saved or created by the fact that new technology can lead to new products or services, or to lower costs and therefore increased demand. Also, new technology does not always do all the things claimed by those who market it.

New technology is intended to improve both the short-term productivity of an organisation and its long-term flexibility in response to market demands. In reality, these benefits seem to occur quite rarely. Clegg *et al.* (1996) estimate that only 25–50 per cent of projects successfully integrate new technology with business goals. Lyytinen and Hirschheim (1987) reckoned that more than 50 per cent of systems development projects are partial or complete failures. Zammuto and O'Connor (1992, p. 703) comment as follows concerning AMT:

> Overall, the literature shows mixed results regarding the outcomes of implementing AMTs. A significant proportion of adopting organizations have experienced increased productivity; fewer appear to have increased their flexibility. And many report implementation failure, gaining neither AMT's productivity nor flexibility benefits.

One reason for this high failure rate may be that organisations cannot afford to buy a whole system of new technology – they buy only bits of it (Wall and Davids, 1992). Some other reasons for the high failure rate are discussed later in this chapter.

Psychologists and other social scientists have investigated a number of issues concerning new technology. Some ergonomists have worked to improve its compatibility with human information-processing capacities. A fair amount is now known about questions like how to design easily-learned word-processing software. However, ergonomists' influence in organisations is often very limited (Blackler, 1988), partly because ergonomics is based principally upon experimental studies of the cognitive psychology of individuals, and neglects the unpredictable, constrained and political nature of behaviour at work (Clegg, 1994). Ergonomic issues will not be covered further here. Instead, we will examine (i) how and why new technology is introduced into organisations; (ii) the impact of new technology on job characteristics, linking with the first part of this chapter; and (iii) the implications of new technology for organisations.

> ■ **KEY LEARNING POINT**
> *New technology often does not bring the intended benefits. This is often because its integration with organisational systems has not been properly considered.*

Introduction of new technology

Organisations may introduce new technology for a wide variety of reasons (Blackler and Brown, 1986; Burnes, 1989). Among these are:

- to reduce costs
- to increase productivity
- to increase quality
- to reduce dependence on skilled labour
- because it always seems a good idea to be up to date
- because competitor organisations are also introducing new technology
- because new technology is interesting
- to change the power relations between various groups in the organisation.

Few managers would confess to the last four as *key* reasons for introducing new technology, yet they often are. For example, Keen (1985) has pointed out that organisational power politics play a crucial role in determining whether and how new technology is introduced. Burnes (1989) found that none of the nine engineering companies he studied had seriously considered any alternative to introducing CNC machines, and several had carried out no financial assessment at all. While the first four reasons cited above were important, Burnes concluded that the main motive for introducing CNCs was a general belief that new technology was 'the future'.

Langley and Truax (1994) found that the adoption of new technology in small companies seemed to involve three interrelated processes:

1 the strategic commitment process: an 'incubation period' during which managers' commitment to new technology fluctuates according to changes in information, context and other decisions. Key events or information are usually needed to trigger the second process;

2 the technology choice process: this involves defining the technological needs and priorities through investigation and analysis;

3 the financial justification process: the preparation of formal proposals for the choice of new technology, emphasising financial results and market potential. Political factors such as the credibility and power of those who make the formal proposals are important.

The authors commented that political factors may play a more prominent part in larger organisations. They also noted that each of the three processes could be carried out in many different ways, and with varying skill and thoroughness.

Blackler and Brown (1986) focused more on the thought-processes and behaviours involved in introducing new technology. They identified three ways in which new technology can be introduced. These are summarised in Table 19.1. They argued that the 'muddle-through approach' is alarmingly common. It stems from management teams which have no long-term goals, and a very limited understanding of technology and organisational design. There are typically considerable problems at the system implementation stage, made worse by their unexpectedness.

The 'task and technology approach' reflects what is seen in many quarters as good management practice. This is because it focuses on control, careful planning, cost–benefit analysis and evaluation of new technology. But it also takes a limited view of the scope of the technology – wider issues of how it might affect organisation design are typically not addressed. Also, new technology is seen as a substitute for staff, not a way of using them better. All this is not universally a good or a bad thing. Blackler and Brown argued that the task and technology approach probably works best 'where a straightforward automation of existing practices is a realistic aim for the new work system' (p. 303).

The 'organisation and end-user approach' typically produces less tidy and predictable solutions than the task and technology orientation. Underlying this approach is a positive view of people and their value ('Theory Y'; *see* Chapter 11) as well as a determination to avoid choosing the most up to date and/or 'clever' technology unless it meets wider organisational needs. Indeed, the introduction of new technology is embraced as an excellent opportunity to review and perhaps change existing organisation structures and practices. This approach requires considerable effort to ensure that there is sufficient staff involvement.

■ **KEY LEARNING POINT**

New technology can be introduced in three ways: with no planning; with planning about the characteristics of the technology; or with planning about how the technology and people using it can work in harmony.

Table 19.1 Three ways of introducing new technology into work organisations

Phase	Muddle-through approach	Task and technology approach	Organisation and end-user approach
1 Initial awareness	Vague awareness that new technologies are available	Staff viewed as costly resource to be reduced if possible. Concern with operating costs, flexibility and operational control. Mainly top management involved	Staff viewed as costly resource which should be better utilised. Concern with operating costs, quality, flexibility, and organisational integration. Initial involvement from any part of organisation, then with top management
2 Feasibility analysis	Fascination with the technology. Short-term returns sought. Expectation that technology can be introduced into existing organisational systems	Mainly management project team but includes technical experts and is approved by top management. Search for most modern equipment. Priority given to technical and operational matters, which are reviewed in light of new technology. Precise objectives formulated	Diverse and representative project team, approved by top management. Search for ways to use and involve staff better. Priority given to system potential, rather than machine capability. General objectives formulated
3 System design	Reliance on technical experts. Technology seen as controlled by inherent laws. Technology to economise on staff	Tasks broken down into their constituent parts. Engineers and technical consultants seek technically neat final design. Consideration of ergonomic issues and staffing levels	Ways sought to enrich jobs and improve team working. Variety of experts and representatives seek designs which are compatible with individuals and groups. Consideration of ergonomic issues, staffing levels and likely social and psychological impact of systems
4 System implementation	Unexpected problems with system bugs, staff motivation, industrial relations. Unexpected need for staff training	Minor modifications only are expected. One-off skill training for operators. Union negotiates over conditions of employment. Operational responsibility passes to line management	Continuing staff and organisation development expected. Union negotiates over conditions of employment, staffing levels, training, grading etc. Continuing review of system operation

Source: Adapted from Blackler and Brown (1986, pp. 298–9).

The organisation and end-user approach implies considerable participation in system design by potential users of the new technology. Much theory and research has focused on such participation (e.g. Eason, 1982). The idea is that staff can contribute at all stages of the process. These include specification of system objectives, criteria against which to evaluate the new technology, pilot schemes, evaluation studies and user support. This is, needless to say, difficult to achieve. Although people working at the 'sharp end' often have a valuable perspective on what will and will not work, technical experts may feel threatened by such a potential challenge to their way of seeing things. In any case, experts often have a well-defined product to sell which can be modified only very slightly to fit varying circumstances. A further potential problem is that many technical experts have difficulty explaining new technology in language that non-specialists can understand. This further reduces the opportunity for non-specialists to influence systems design. All in all, then, it is difficult to implement successfully a participative approach to new technology (Blackler, 1988). The same applies to the organisation and end-user approach, in which participation plays a key role.

It should be clear from Table 19.1 that the way in which new technology is implemented can substantially affect the nature of jobs and organisations. We now turn to these considerations.

New technology and job characteristics

Some commentators see job simplification as an inevitable consequence of new technology. Job simplification means a reduction in the core job characteristics identified by Hackman and Oldham (1980), mentioned earlier in this chapter, especially perhaps skill variety and autonomy. 'Labour process' theorists such as Braverman (1974) see introduction of new technology as a standard strategy of the capitalist system to increase productivity while reducing costs and the power of organised labour, thereby increasing profits and managerial control. This Marxist perspective has enjoyed considerable popularity, but has also been challenged. As we have already seen, it is possible to use the introduction of new technology to empower staff and enrich jobs. Some European writers have argued that managements are now increasingly keen to use the flexibility, skills and knowledge of workers because they see that this can enhance productivity and help the organisation to respond to changing market demands (Dankbaar, 1988).

Especially in the 1980s, researchers tried to resolve this disagreement by investigating how, in practice, the introduction of new technology affects job characteristics (*see*, for example, Buchanan and Boddy, 1983; Patrickson, 1986; Wall *et al.*, 1987b; Carlopio, 1988; Dankbaar, 1988; Wilson and Buchanan, 1988). General conclusions are as follows:

- new technology sometimes enriches jobs and sometimes simplifies them. Both effects can occur within one workplace;

- simplification is probably rather more common than enrichment, at least for shop-floor manufacturing jobs;

- concerted and well-developed management strategies to influence job characteristics via new technology are rarely apparent;

- concerted worker resistance to new technology in itself is rare, and worker adjustment to new circumstances is often easier than anticipated. Resistance to perceived exploitation by management is, however, more likely;

- although new technology can produce enriched jobs, some individuals can nevertheless experience simplified jobs. For example, Dankbaar (1988, p. 43) commented that in a car factory he studied, 'production jobs have been upgraded, compared to the situation before the new technologies were introduced, but the old workers didn't move into these new jobs and for the skilled workers these jobs mean a degradation of work';

- jobs are usually changed in some respects by new technology. New skills, such as abstract thinking, computer programming and understanding of the organisation's systems are often required (Wall, 1987).

> ### ■ KEY LEARNING POINT
> *New technology almost always has a significant impact on the skills and activities required in jobs. Managers often have choices concerning the nature and extent of that impact.*

An example from one of the above-mentioned studies illustrates some of these points. Wall *et al.* (1987b) investigated work with old and new technologies at a plant of a large electronics company. Staff at the factory assembled printed circuit boards for computers. This involved inserting appropriate components into boards, which were made to a wide variety of specifications, often in small batches. There were many different components, and each board had to have them all in exactly the correct place. There were two 'traditional' technologies where circuit boards were assembled by hand. The main difference was that in one ('bench assembly') employees could work at their own pace, whereas in the other ('flowline') a kind of assembly line operated where employees had to keep up with each other. One of the new technologies ('manusert/logpoint') involved machines which indicated exactly where which component should go, and supplied that component. All the person had to do was insert it. In the other ('automatics') the machine inserted the components but the employee loaded the appropriate ones into the machine, set it up, checked its operation and made minor modifications if necessary.

Wall *et al.* (1987b) discovered that one old technology (bench assembly) and one new technology (automatics) were superior in perceived skill use, intrinsic job satisfaction and intrinsic job characteristics to the other old technology and other new technology. Bench assembly offered staff more freedom than flowline to pace work and insert components in the order they desired. Automatics took away some dexterity requirements but replaced them with new activities and responsibilities. In contrast, manusert/logpoint took away the choice element of assembly and put nothing in its place. The authors concluded (p. 248):

> The critical issue does not revolve around advanced manufacturing technology per se: it concerns the job design principles underlying a particular job. A well designed job is well designed whether it involves computers or not and the same is true for badly designed jobs.

Wall *et al.* (1990) and Jackson *et al.* (1993) have proposed a set of job characteristics which they see as particularly relevant to the introduction of new technology. Drawing on earlier work, they identify the following features which could have an impact on performance of the new system (i.e. technology *and* people), and on the job satisfaction and job-related strain of workers:

- timing control: over when tasks are done
- method control: over how tasks are done

- cognitive demand: to pay close, constant attention; to diagnose and solve problems
- responsibility: for the technology and output
- social interaction: amount and quality.

> ■ KEY LEARNING POINT
> *Research on new technology has focused attention on somewhat different job characteristics from those identified by Hackman and Oldham.*

Wall and Davids (1992) point out that from the stress literature (*see* Chapter 17), one would predict that where new technology creates high cognitive demand for monitoring (as opposed to problem solving) it will tend to reduce mental health. They also suggest that in many cases *control* is the key. If the introduction of new technology gives machine operators control over their job (including the responsibility and opportunity to rectify problems or even to prevent them occurring), improvements in both productivity and work attitudes can be expected. Control often gives people the opportunity to diagnose and solve problems, and the responsibility for output is theirs. Jackson *et al.* (1993) have developed questionnaire measures of the five job characteristics. The measures have good reliability and construct validity. They should assist further progress in understanding and managing the impact of new technology on people at work.

The job design choices available with new technology are not limitless (Blackler, 1988), but they are often considerable (Burnes, 1989). New technology itself does not necessarily simplify or enrich jobs: the approach of those who introduce it is what matters. As noted above, it is relatively rare for that approach to be clearly thought out in advance.

Implications of new technology for whole organisations

Several writers have noted how many organisations fail to get the best out of their new technology because they attempt to integrate it into existing structures rather than changing those structures (Child, 1987). Some social scientists have attempted to describe the actual and potential impact of new technology on organisations. Prominent among these have been Child (1987) and Huber (1990). These and other sources identify the following issues.

Centralisation of power

One often-voiced fear about new technology is that it will tend to place power in the hands of a small group of elite people within an organisation. This is said to occur through the deskilling of most jobs and the increased availability of information to top management which allows centralised decision making. On this latter point, some writers (e.g. Carlopio, 1988) have argued that lower and middle managers have most to fear from new technology, because its information compiling and processing capacity takes over their roles. On the whole, evidence suggests that new technology does tend to centralise power, but not to the extent originally feared by some (Blackler, 1988), and not when the production process is complex, with many interdependent operations. In this latter case, decisions still need to be made close to 'the sharp end' (Child, 1987). Huber (1990) has made the interesting proposition that new information technology will have an 'equalising' effect on power distribution. Highly centralised organisations will become less so as people at lower levels receive more information which allows them to challenge decisions. Highly decentralised organisations will become more centralised as top managers have better access to information previously unavailable (or denied) to them.

Bloomfield and Coombs (1992) argue that the power of information technology lies in its capacity to redefine the roles and relationships of people in organisations. They give the example of doctors in the British National Health Service (NHS), who found that they were increasingly being expected to work within, and manage, a fixed budget. Some resisted this (preferring the old expectation that their medical decisions should be made without regard to cost), but others were quite keen. The increasing usage of computerised information systems in the NHS supplied doctors with much of the information they needed in order to manage their budgets. In turn, this gave them the opportunity to *think of themselves* as budget holders, and negotiate with non-medical managers accordingly. Bloomfield and Coombs conclude that power is not something a person *has*. Instead, it is expressed in relationships between people. The nature of these relationships is influenced by the self-concepts and identities of the people concerned. In turn, these personal identities are affected by wider organisational practices and resources, including information technology.

Social interactions

New technology can affect greatly the amount and nature of social interaction experienced by staff in an organisation. Some of the ways this happens are easy to imagine. Well-established work groups may be broken up, redundancies may occur, communication may become less face-to-face and more computer-mediated, and the sheer amount of information conveyed by the new technology may reduce the need for interpersonal communication of any kind. More subtle effects are also possible. The arrival of new technology frequently changes the relative status of different workers. For example, workers whose jobs are deskilled by new technology may find that their needs and wishes are taken less seriously, and that they are less often consulted by managers. Some forms of new technology may in fact help people at lower levels of the organisation have a greater say than before. For example, Sproull and Kiesler (1991) have argued that electronic mail (e-mail) gives unprecedented access to the top people in an organisation and facilitates communication and information flow within it. By eliminating non-verbal cues, e-mail is also said to reduce people's inhibitions about saying what they mean. On the other hand, Mantovani (1994) has queried all this, suggesting that in reality most e-mail messages flow between people of similar status in close geographical proximity, and that e-mail may simply reflect and even reinforce the existing organisational culture. Whatever the truth of this, it is clear that social interaction patterns during and after the introduction of new technology do have consequences for people. Burkhardt (1994) studied this with a sample of 40 government office workers who were required to work with a new computer network. She found that the workers' belief in their ability to use the new network was affected by communications with the people they encountered most frequently. Their attitudes to using computers and how much they used them were influenced most strongly by people in similar jobs within the organisation, whether or not they met very frequently.

■ **KEY LEARNING POINT**
Social–psychological phenomena such as self-identity and interpersonal communication play a major role in determining the impact of new technology on organisations.

Working patterns

Computing technology undoubtedly makes it possible for more people to spend more time working at home. It is easier nowadays to obtain information at home, and to communicate with the workplace. So-called telecommuting, where people work predominantly at or from home and stay in touch using phone, personal computer, fax, e-mail, Internet or videoconferencing, is becoming increasingly common. Exact figures are hard to establish, but in both the UK and the US probably around 5 per cent of those in employment work in this way (*see* Chapman *et al.*, 1995). Huber (1990) proposed that information technology will increase the number of people who contribute information to decision making. But it will probably decrease the number of people and organisational levels involved in actually *making* decisions, because the necessary information and decision-support systems are more readily available. Huber also proposes that fewer face-to-face meetings will be necessary – a change that would no doubt be welcomed by many managers so long as it did not mean that they were being excluded from decision making.

Integration of work roles

New technology often integrates previously separate tasks. This could mean that people too will need to learn a more diverse set of skills than hitherto in order to work effectively with the new technology. It could, alternatively, mean that people with specialised skills will have to work together more in project teams, often for quite short periods of time (Child, 1987). Either way, there is likely to be less need for functional specialists working relatively independently of other parts of the organisation. Child proposes that whichever course is best for any particular organisation, the necessary changes are likely to be resisted by groups who wish to preserve their established areas of knowledge and skill.

Organisational performance

Whether performance gains result from new technology depends partly on some of the factors already discussed in this chapter. Huber (1990) also pointed out that some basic assumptions about new technology remain to be confirmed, and for the most part this remains true now. Does it lead to more accurate and rapid identification of problems and opportunities? Does it produce more accurate, timely and accessible information? Does it lead to quicker and more accurate decisions? Huber thought so, but argued that we do not yet know for sure. Zammuto and O'Connor (1992) argue that AMT is more likely to improve an organisation's productivity if that organisation already has a *flexibility-orientated culture* – that is, an emphasis on decentralisation, with different parts of the organisation given some freedom to do things their own way. Such organisations will find it easier to benefit from new technology than those with a *control-orientated culture*. This is because flexibility-orientated cultures encourage people to think of solutions that fit their needs (rather than accepting solutions dictated by senior management), and are more open to change. Kolodny *et al.* (1996) show that new technology can be used to help organisations obtain and process information about their rapidly changing environments more flexibly, and in ways which do justice to the complexity of that information. Used in this way, new technology can support flexible and customer-responsive forms of organisation. Such organisations avoid oversimplifying or distorting information to make it fit into existing organisational structures and practices. On the other hand, Kolodny *et al.* also found that new technology was sometimes used in ways which preserved that inflexibility – for example, to create ever more complex sales forecasts or planning projections based upon dubious assumptions about future business conditions.

> ■ **KEY LEARNING POINT**
>
> *New technology can either help organisations to be flexible and responsive, or preserve inflexibility.*

SUMMARY

Jobs are often designed in such a way as to minimise skill requirements, decision making and labour costs, but this also often minimises potential for human satisfaction and development at work. Attempts to increase skill use and meaningfulness in work are often termed job redesign. Psychologists have tried to specify the characteristics of psychologically healthy jobs, and have investigated the importance of these characteristics. Job redesign often, but not invariably, has beneficial outcomes for individual and organisation, though other factors such as wage levels may also influence those outcomes. New technology is based on microelectronics and has the potential to deskill jobs further. It is sometimes, but by no means always, introduced with that aim in mind. New technology can alternatively maintain or even enhance skill requirements, though the *nature* of the skills usually changes. New technology is sometimes introduced very haphazardly, with little appreciation of its consequences. Other times it is introduced systematically with heavy reliance on technical specialists. Alternatively, it can be introduced with wider organisational systems and staffing issues in mind. It can have a profound effect on such matters, whether anticipated or not.

CASE STUDY 19.2

New technology at Topspec Engineering

Topspec Engineering is a medium-size company specialising in the manufacture of metal components for the motor industry: not for the cars themselves, but for the machines involved in their manufacture. The components must be very precisely made – any errors will mean that the machines of which they form a part will function suboptimally or not at all. Normally the components are produced in small batches of between 20 and 50 to a particular specification.

Two years ago, Topspec invested in new computer numerically controlled (CNC) machine tools for manufacturing the components. These machines are programmed to cut or grind metal to the exact specification required. Before their introduction,

Topspec employed 45 skilled machinists who operated the traditional machine tools using levers, cranks etc. to do the necessary metalwork. This required an apprenticeship of several years and was a relatively high status job within the factory. The machinist used his or her (almost invariably his) expertise to ensure that the finished product met the required specification.

The managers at Topspec had noted that many competitors were introducing CNC machines. The sales literature from the CNC machine tool manufacturer indicated that CNCs should reduce labour costs and skill requirements as well as increasing productivity and product quality. Industrial relations had been poor in the preceding years and management felt they had been forced to concede over-generous pay claims. They had also lost one or two orders to companies with CNCs, apparently on grounds of cost.

The CNCs were introduced only after the union had ensured that there would be no redundancies or pay rate cuts among the existing machinists (but the same protection did not apply to staff hired subsequently). The managers were, however, relying on natural wastage as a means of reducing staffing levels – they hoped and expected that some machinists would leave as a result of the CNC machines. With the new technology, the machinists were required to load the raw materials, unload the machined product, and monitor the operation of the machine against the product specification. Five specialist programmers were recruited to program the necessary cutting and grinding operations (i.e. the operations formerly carried out manually by the machinists). The programmers also set up each CNC machine for each batch, and proved (i.e. checked) the operation of the programme, small but significant modifications to which were often necessary.

The CNC machines were expensive. So were the specialist programmers. Due to difficult local economic conditions, few of the machinists left and those who remained were not needed all the time. The machinists themselves became less co-operative, their absence and grievances rates increased, and they made more mistakes than their training and experience warranted. Taking into account the investment cost of the CNC machines, unit production costs increased significantly, and looked set to remain high for several years to come. Management wanted to introduce performance standards for the machinists' CNC jobs but nobody knew what standards were reasonable and in any case the agreement with the union specifically excluded any pay reductions – management had not expected production quality problems with their previously reliable machinists. To make matters worse, the specialist programmers were not familiar with the types of components manufactured. They therefore made more errors than management had expected. Programmers and machinists seemed unwilling or unable to share their skills and knowledge in order to improve this state of affairs.

Suggested exercise

Consider what went wrong when Topspec introduced the CNCs. How might the process have been better managed?

Short-answer questions

1 What are the main features of scientific management (Taylorism)?

2 What are the core job characteristics identified by Hackman and Oldham? According to Hackman and Oldham, what critical psychological states and outcomes do these core job characteristics lead to?

3 Apart from the motivational approach to job redesign favoured by psychologists, what other approaches have been identified by Campion and his colleagues? What are the possible benefits of those approaches?

4 List three weaknesses of much research evaluating the effects of job redesign.

5 List three conclusions about the job characteristics model suggested by research testing it.

6 What is advanced manufacturing technology (AMT)?

7 What are the differences between the task and technology approach and the organisation and end-user approach to the introduction of new technology?

8 List three conclusions suggested by research evaluating the impact of new technology on job characteristics.

9 Describe four ways in which new technology can affect how an organisation functions.

Essay questions

1 What, if any, are the benefits of redesigning jobs in accordance with psychological principles?

2 To what extent does Hackman and Oldham's job characteristics model accurately represent the processes and outcomes of job redesign?

3 Describe the effects that new technology can have upon (i) job characteristics and (ii) patterns of social interaction. What factors determine which of these effects actually occur?

4 Examine the impact of new technology on the productivity and performance of organisations.

Advanced manufacturing technology Machines involved in the manufacturing process which are controlled by microelectronic programmable systems.

Centralisation of power Movement of decision-making authority away from local units in an organisation, towards the headquarters and usually top management.

CNC machines A common example of advanced manufacturing technology, CNC machines operate on materials by precise cutting, hole-punching etc.

Core job characteristics The five aspects of jobs suggested by Hackman and Oldham as being essential in influencing satisfaction, motivation and job performance. The five are: skill variety, task identity, task significance, autonomy and feedback.

Critical psychological states The three immediate psychological effects of the core job characteristics, as proposed by Hackman and Oldham. The three are: experienced meaningfulness of the work, experienced responsibility for outcomes of the work, and knowledge of the actual results of work activities.

Empowerment A human resource management technique which (i) increases employee involvement in (and responsibility for) decision making and quality management, and (ii) encourages employees to learn a wide range of skills to ensure their capacity to make an effective contribution to organisational performance.

Functional flexibility The name often given to the second aspect of empowerment described above.

Job characteristics model The name given to Hackman and Oldham's theory (*see also* **Core job characteristics** and **Critical psychological states**).

Job redesign Collective name given to techniques designed to increase one or more of the variety, autonomy and completeness of a person's work tasks.

Motivating potential score Arithmetical combination of Hackman and Oldham's job characteristics designed to summarise the overall goodness of a job from a psychological point of view.

Organisation and end-user approach A method of introducing new technology which emphasises the importance of compatibility with individual and organisational characteristics.

Quality of working life The extent to which a person's work supports their psychological well-being and development.

Scientific management Also called Taylorism, this is an approach to management which emphasises management control, simplification and standardisation of work activities, and purely financial incentives.

Socio-technical systems Theoretical tradition which emphasises the importance of having social structures and technological systems which are compatible with each other.

SUGGESTED FURTHER READING

1 Chapters 5 and 6 of *Motivation: Strategies, Theory and Practice,* by Ivan Robertson, Mike Smith and Dominic Cooper (published in 1992 by the Institute of Personnel and Development), gives an overview of job design techniques and some practical examples.

2 The chapter by Toby Wall and Keith Davids in the 1992 *Review of Industrial and Organizational Psychology* (*see* reference list below) provides a thorough analysis of issues concerning the introduction and use of advanced manufacturing technology.

3 Although a little old now, Bernard Burnes' 1989 book (*see* reference list below) reports an informative study of how various organisations handle the introduction of new technology.

REFERENCES

Blackler, F. (1988) 'Information technologies and organizations: lessons from the 1980s and issues for the 1990s', *Journal of Occupational Psychology*, vol. 61, pp. 113–27.

Blackler, F. and Brown, C. (1986) 'Alternative models to guide the design and introduction of the new information technologies into work organizations', *Journal of Occupational Psychology*, vol. 59, pp. 287–313.

Bloomfield, B.P. and Coombs, R. (1992) 'Information technology, control and power: the central-ization and decentralization debate revisited', *Journal of Management Studies*, vol. 29, pp. 459–84.

Braverman, H. (1974) *Labor and Monopoly Capital*. New York: Monthly Review Press.

Buchanan, D.A. and Boddy, D. (1983) 'Advanced technology and the quality of working life: the effects of computerised controls on biscuit-making operators', *Journal of Occupational Psychology*, vol. 56, pp. 109–19.

Burkhardt, M.E. (1994) 'Social interaction effects following a technological change: a longitudinal investigation', *Academy of Management Journal*, vol. 37, pp. 869–98.

Burnes, B. (1989) *New Technology in Context*. Aldershot: Gower.

Campion, M.A. (1988) 'Interdisciplinary approaches to job design: a constructive replication with extensions', *Journal of Applied Psychology*, vol. 73, pp. 467–81.

Campion, M.A. and McClelland, C.L. (1993) 'Follow-up and extension of the interdisciplinary costs and benefits of enlarged jobs', *Journal of Applied Psychology*, vol. 78, pp. 339–51.

Campion, M.A. and Thayer, P.W. (1985) Development and field evaluation of an interdisciplinary measure of job design', *Journal of Applied Psychology*, vol. 70, pp. 29–43.

Carlopio, J. (1988) 'A history of social psychological reactions to new technology', *Journal of Occupational Psychology*, vol. 61, pp. 67–77.

Champoux, J.E. (1991) 'A multivariate test of the job characteristics theory of work motivation', *Journal of Organizational Behavior*, vol. 12, pp. 431–46.

Chapman, A.J., Sheehy, N.P., Heywood, S., Dooley, B. and Collins, S.C. (1995) 'The organiza-tional implications of teleworking' in Cooper, C.L. and Robertson, I.T. (eds) *International Review of Industrial and Organizational Psychology*, vol. 10. Chichester: John Wiley.

Cherns, A.B. (1976) 'The principles of sociotechnical design', *Human Relations*, vol. 29, pp. 783–92.

Cherns, A.B. (1987) 'Principles of sociotechnical design revisited', *Human Relations*, vol. 40, pp. 153–62.

Child, J. (1987) 'Organizational design for advanced manufacturing technology' in Wall, T.D., Clegg, C.W. and Kemp, N.J. (eds) *The Human Side of Advanced Manufacturing Technology*. Chichester: John Wiley.

Clegg, C. (1994) 'Psychology and information technology: the study of cognition in organiza-tions', *British Journal of Psychology*, vol. 85, pp. 449–77.

Clegg, C., Coleman, P., Hornby, P., McClaren, R., Robson, J., Carey, N. and Symon, G. (1996) 'Tools to incorporate some psychological and organizational issues during the development of computer-based systems', *Ergonomics*, vol. 39, pp. 482–511.

Conger, J.A. and Kanungo, R.N. (1988) 'The empowerment process', *Academy of Management Review*, vol. 13, pp. 471–82.

Cordery, J.L. and Wall, T.D. (1985) 'Work design and supervisory practice: a model', *Human Relations*, vol. 38, pp. 425–41.

Cordery, J., Sevastos, P., Mueller, W. and Parker, S. (1993) 'Correlates of employee attitudes toward functional flexibility', *Human Relations*, vol. 46, pp. 705–23.

Dankbaar, B. (1988) 'New production concepts, management strategies and the quality of work', *Work, Employment and Society*, vol. 2, pp. 25–50.

Davis, L.E. (1982) 'Organizational design' in Salvendy, G. (ed.) *Handbook of Industrial Engineering*. Chichester: JohnWiley.

Eason, K.D. (1982) 'The process of introducing new technology', *Behaviour and Information Technology*, vol. 1, pp. 197–213.

Fried, Y. and Ferris, G.R. (1987) 'The validity of the job characteristics model: a review and meta-analysis', *Personnel Psychology*, vol. 40, pp. 287–322.

Griffin, R.W. (1991) 'Effects of work redesign on employee perceptions, attitudes and behaviors: a long-term investigation', *Academy of Management Journal*, vol. 34, pp. 425–35.

Hackman, J.R. and Oldham, G.R. (1976) 'Motivation through the design of work: test of a theory', *Organizational Behavior and Human Performance*, vol. 16, pp. 250–79.

Hackman, J.R. and Oldham, G.R. (1980) *Work Redesign*. Reading, MA: Addison-Wesley.

Heller, F. (1989) 'On humanising technology', *Applied Psychology: An International Review*, vol. 38, pp. 15–28.

Herzberg, F. (1966) *Work and the Nature of Man*. Cleveland, OH: World Publishing.

Hogan, E.A. and Martell, D.A. (1987) 'A confirmatory structural equations analysis of the job characteristics model', *Organizational Behavior and Human Decision Processes*, vol. 39, pp. 242–63.

Huber, G.P. (1990) 'A theory of the effects of advanced information technologies on organizational design, intelligence and decision making', *Academy of Management Review*, vol. 15, pp. 47–71.

Jackson, P.R., Wall, T.D., Martin, R. and Davids, K. (1993) 'New measures of job control, cognitive demand and production responsibility', *Journal of Applied Psychology*, vol. 78, 753–62.

Keen, P. (1985) 'Information systems and organizational design' in Rhodes, E. and Wield, D. (eds) *Implementing New Technologies: Choice, decision and change in manufacturing*. Oxford: Blackwell.

Kelly, J.E. (1993) 'Does job redesign theory explain job re-design outcomes?' *Human Relations*, vol. 45, pp. 753–74.

Kolodny, H., Liu, M., Stymne, B. and Denis, H. (1996) 'New technology and the emerging organizational paradigm', *Human Relations*, vol. 49, pp. 1457–87.

Kornhauser, A. (1965) *Mental Health of the Industrial Worker*. Chichester: John Wiley.

Langley, A. and Truax, J. (1994) 'A process study of new technology adoption in smaller manufacturing firms', *Journal of Management Studies*, vol. 31, pp. 619–52.

Loher, B.T., Noe, R.A., Moeller, N.L. and Fitzgerald, M.P. (1985) 'A meta-analysis of the relation of job characteristics to job satisfaction', *Journal of Applied Psychology*, vol. 70, pp. 280–9.

Lyytinen, K. and Hirshheim, R. (1987) 'Information systems failures: a survey and classification of the empirical literature', *Oxford Surveys in Information Technology*, vol. 4, pp. 257–309.

Mantovani, G. (1994) 'Is computer-mediated communication intrinsically apt to enhance democracy in organizations?', *Human Relations*, vol. 47, 45–62.

McCann, J.E. and Buckner, M. (1994) 'Redesigning work: motivations, challenges and practices in 181 companies', *Human Resource Planning*, vol. 17, no. 4, pp. 23–41.

Oborne, D. (1985) *Computers at Work: A behavioural approach*. Chichester: John Wiley.

Patrickson, M. (1986) 'Adaptation by employees to new technology', *Journal of Occupational Psychology*, vol. 59, pp. 1–11.

Pava, C. (1983) *Managing New Office Technology*. New York: Free Press.

Roberts, K.H. and Glick, W. (1981) 'The job characteristics approach to task design: a critical review', *Journal of Applied Psychology*, vol. 66, pp. 193–217.

Sproull, L. and Kiesler, S. (1991) *Connections – New Ways of Working in the Networked Organization*. Cambridge, MA: MIT Press.

Taylor, J.C. (1979) 'Job design criteria twenty years later' in Davis, L.E. and Taylor, J.C. (eds) *Design of Jobs*. 2nd edn. Santa Monica, CA: Goodyear.

Turner, A.N. and Lawrence, P.R. (1965) *Industrial Jobs and the Worker*. Cambridge, MA: Harvard University Press.

Wall, T.D. (1982) 'Perspectives on job redesign' in Kelly, J.E. and Clegg, C.W. (eds) *Autonomy and Control in the Workplace*. London: Croom Helm.

Wall, T.D. (1987) 'New technology and job redesign' in Warr, P. (ed.) *Psychology at Work*. 3rd edn. Harmondsworth: Penguin.

Wall, T.D. and Davids, K. (1992) 'Shopfloor work organization and advanced manufacturing technology' in Cooper, C.L. and Robertson, I.T. (eds) *International Review of Industrial and Organizational Psychology*, vol. 7. Chichester: John Wiley.

Wall, T.D., Clegg, C.W. and Kemp, N.J. (eds) (1987a) *The Human Side of Advanced Manufacturing Technology*. Chichester: John Wiley.

Wall, T.D., Clegg, C.W., Davies, R.T., Kemp, N.J. and Mueller, W.S. (1987b) 'Advanced manufacturing and work simplification: an empirical study', *Journal of Occupational Behaviour*, vol. 8, pp. 233–50.

Wall, T.D., Corbett, J.M., Clegg, C.W., Jackson, P.R. and Martin, R. (1990) 'Advanced manufacturing technology and work design: towards a theoretical framework', *Journal of Organizational Behavior*, vol. 11, pp. 201–19.

Warr, P. (1987) 'Job characteristics and mental health' in Warr, P. (ed.) *Psychology at Work*. 3rd edn. Harmondsworth: Penguin.

Wilson, F.M. and Buchanan, D.A. (1988) 'The effect of new technology in the engineering industry: cases of control and constraint', *Work, Employment and Society*, vol. 2, pp. 366–80.

Zammuto, R.F. and O'Connor, E.J. (1992) 'Gaining advanced manufacturing technologies' benefits: the roles of organization design and culture', *Academy of Management Review*, vol. 17, pp. 701–28.

Understanding organisational change

Bernard Burnes

LEARNING OBJECTIVES

After studying this chapter, you should be able to:

1 identify the main approaches to organisational change;

2 describe and compare the strengths and weaknesses of the main approaches to change;

3 understand that within the different approaches there are significant variants;

4 identify the respective roles of managers, employees and outside consultants;

5 understand the difference between open-ended change projects and closed change projects;

6 appreciate how the main approaches view employee involvement and resistance;

7 explain how the different approaches view 'political' behaviour;

8 list the main reasons why change projects fail.

INTRODUCTION

This chapter provides a critical review of the main approaches to planning and implementing change which have been developed in the past 50 years. It begins by arguing that an understanding of the theory and practice of change management is crucial to organisational life in the 1990s. The chapter then goes on to review critically the two main approaches to organisational change: the *planned approach*, and the *emergent approach*. It is shown that the planned approach, which was developed by Kurt Lewin in the 1940s, views organisational change as essentially a process of moving from one fixed state to another through a series of predictable and pre-planned steps. However, it will be seen that the emergent approach, which came to the fore in the 1980s, starts from the alternative assumption that change is a continuous, open-ended and unpredictable process of aligning and re-aligning an organisation to its changing environment. Advocates of emergent change argue that it is more suitable to the turbulent environment in which modern firms now operate because, unlike the planned approach, it recognises the need for organisations to align their internal practices and behaviour with changing external conditions. Proponents of planned change, though, dispute this criticism and argue for its continuing relevance.

The review of these two approaches will reveal that, despite the large body of literature devoted to the topic of change management and the many tools and techniques available to change agents, there is considerable disagreement regarding the most appropriate approach. In an effort to bring clarity to the issue, the chapter concludes by arguing that neither the emergent nor the planned approach is suitable for all situations and circumstances. Instead, it is maintained that approaches to change tend to be situation specific and that the potential exists for organisations to exercise choice over the particular approach they adopt.

WHY IS CHANGE MANAGEMENT IMPORTANT?

Change management would not be considered particularly important if products and markets were stable and organisational change was rare: however, that is not the case, nor has it ever been so. Change is an ever-present feature of organisational life, though many leading management thinkers such as Tom Peters (1995), Rosabeth Moss Kanter (1989) and Charles Handy (1994) do argue that, in order to maintain or achieve competitiveness, the need for, and the pace and magnitude of, change have increased significantly over the past two decades. Certainly, there is more than just anecdotal evidence to support this view (*see also* Chapters 1 and 6). The Institute of Management (IM), formerly the British Institute of Management, which carried out a number of surveys of its members, supported this view. In 1991, the IM reported that 90 per cent of organisations in its survey were becoming 'slimmer and flatter' (Coulson-Thomas and Coe, 1991, p. 10). In 1992, it reported that 80 per cent of managers responding to its survey had experienced one or more corporate restructurings in their organisations in the previous five years (Wheatley, 1992). In its 1995 survey (Institute of Management, 1995), 70 per cent of respondents reported that their organisations had restructured in the previous two years. A similar picture emerged from a recent study carried out at the University of Manchester Institute of Science and Technology (UMIST). This study found that 51 per cent of respondents' organisations were experiencing major transformations (Ezzamel *et al.*, 1994).

Though change projects come in many shapes and sizes, increasingly since the early 1980s the prime objective for many organisations has been to change their culture. Indeed, a recent survey by the Industrial Society (1997) found that 94 per cent of its respondents had either recently been involved in or were currently going through a culture change programme. Therefore, we can see that even over a very short time span, most organisations and their employees have experienced or are experiencing substantial changes in what they do and how they do it. Clearly, the success or otherwise of these change initiatives can have a significant impact on an organisation's performance.

> ■ **KEY LEARNING POINT**
> *Effective organisational change is crucial to an organisation's competitiveness.*

The failure of change management programmes

Undoubtedly, the way such changes are managed, and the appropriateness of the approach adopted, have major implications for the way people experience change and their perceptions of the outcome. In both the 1995 Institute of Management study and the UMIST study, managers reported considerable levels of dissatisfaction with the outcome of change programmes. The Institute of Management (1995) study found that, as a result of recent organisational changes, managers' workloads had increased greatly and that one in five was working an extra 15 hours per week. Many also reported that increased workloads were preventing them from devoting adequate time to long-term strategic planning or to their own training and development needs. The UMIST study found that while most managers supported the case for change, many were anxious not only about the outcome of change but also about the process of change itself (Ezzamel *et al.*, 1994).

Given the vast literature on the topic, it may appear strange that many managers have doubts about both the approach to and outcome of change. Yet the reality, according to many observers, is that organisations can and do experience severe problems in managing change effectively (Howarth, 1988). It is clear that to manage change successfully, even on a small scale, can be complex and difficult. The literature abounds with examples of change projects which have gone wrong, some disastrously so (*see* Burnes and Weekes, 1989; Cummings and Huse, 1989; Kanter *et al.*, 1992; Kelly, 1982a, b). Therefore, there is substantial evidence that managers are right to be anxious about organisational change.

Organisational change comes in all shapes, sizes and forms, and for this reason it is difficult to establish an accurate picture of the degree of difficulty firms face in managing change successfully. However, there are three types of organisational change which, because of their perceived importance, have received considerable attention: the introduction of new technology in the 1980s, the adoption of total quality management (TQM) since the mid-1980s and, in recent years, the application of business process re-engineering (BPR). All three, in their time, were hailed as 'revolutionary' approaches to improving performance and competitiveness.

The impact of the (so-called) micro-electronics revolution of the 1980s, which saw the rapid expansion of computers and computer-based processes into most areas of organisational life, was the subject of a great many studies (*see* Chapter 19). These found that the failure rate of new technology change projects was anywhere between 40 per cent and 70 per cent (Bessant and Haywood, 1985; Voss, 1985; McKracken, 1986; Smith and Tranfield, 1987; Kearney, 1989; New, 1989).

The move by European countries to adopt TQM began in the mid-1980s. At its simplest, TQM is an organisation-wide effort to improve quality through changes in structure, practices, systems and, above all, attitudes (Dale and Cooper, 1992). Though seen as pre-eminently a Japanese innovation, the basic TQM techniques were developed in the USA in the 1950s (Crosby, 1979; Deming, 1982; Taguchi, 1986; Juran, 1988). Though TQM appears to be central to the success of Japanese companies, the experience of Western companies has been that it is difficult to introduce and sustain. Indeed, one of the founders of the TQM movement, Philip Crosby (1979), claimed that over 90 per cent of TQM initiatives by American organisations fail. Though a 90 per cent failure rate seems incredibly high, studies of the adoption of TQM by companies in the UK and other European countries show that they too have experienced a similarly high failure rate – perhaps as much as 80 per cent or more (Kearney, 1992; Cruise O'Brien and Voss, 1992; Economist Intelligence Unit, 1992; Whyte and Witcher, 1992; Witcher, 1993; Zairi *et al.*, 1994).

BPR has been hailed as 'the biggest business innovation of the 1990s' (Mill, 1994, p. 26). Wastell *et al.* (1994, p. 23) stated that BPR refers to 'initiatives, large and small, radical and conservative, whose common theme is the achievement of significant improvements in organizational performance by augmenting the efficiency and effectiveness of key business processes'. Though relatively new, and therefore less well documented than either new technology or TQM, Wastell *et al.* (1994, p. 37) concluded from the available evidence that 'BPR initiatives have typically achieved much less than they promised'. Other studies of BPR have come to similar conclusions (Short and Venkatraman, 1992; Coombs and Hull, 1994). Even the founding father of BPR – Michael Hammer – acknowledges that in up to 70 per cent of cases it leaves organisations worse off rather than better off (Hammer and Champy, 1993).

Therefore, even well-established change initiatives, for which a great deal of information, advice and assistance is available, are no guarantee of success. This is perhaps why managers list their ability (or inability) to manage change as the number one obstacle to the increased competitiveness of their organisations (Hanson, 1993).

> ■ **KEY LEARNING POINT**
> *Despite the plethora of advice available, the majority of change programmes fail.*

Organisations have been and still are changing radically. Some are choosing to follow the prescriptions of management gurus such as Charles Handy (1994), Rosabeth Moss Kanter (1989), and Tom Peters (1995), while others are seeking to emulate Japanese experience as popularised by writers such as Hamel and Prahalad (1989) and Whitehill (1991). However, whatever particular form change takes and whatever objectives it seeks to achieve, organisations cannot expect to achieve success unless those responsible for managing it understand the different approaches on offer and can match them to their circumstances and preferences. On this basis, understanding the theory and practice of change management is not an optional extra but an essential requisite for survival. However, as the following examination of the two main approaches to change management will show, this is by no means an easy or straightforward exercise.

THE PLANNED APPROACH TO ORGANISATIONAL CHANGE

The practice of change management is dependent on a number of factors, not least the particular school of thought involved. Not surprisingly, therefore, even among those advocating planned change, a variety of different models of change management have arisen over the years. Though these were devised to meet the needs of particular organisations, or arose from a specific school of thought, nevertheless, most of the literature on the planned approach to change has been derived from the practice of organisation development (OD). OD has been defined as 'a systemwide application of behavioral science knowledge to the planned development and reinforcement of organizational strategies, structures and processes for improving an organization's effectiveness' (Cummings and Huse, 1989, p. 1).

Within the OD field, there are a number of major theorists and practitioners who have contributed their own models and techniques to the development of change management (e.g. Blake and Mouton, 1976; French and Bell, 1984). However, most observers seem to agree that these can be related to three basic models of the change process, which in turn arise from the pioneering work of one person – Kurt Lewin. Lewin was a prolific theorist, researcher and practitioner in interpersonal, group, intergroup and community relationships. In 1945 he founded and became the first director of the hugely influential Research Center for Group Dynamics. The models of the change process which emerged from his work are:

- the action-research model
- the three-step model
- the phases of planned change model.

Action research

The term action research was coined by Kurt Lewin. Action research was designed as a collective approach to solving social and organisational problems (*see also* Chapter 3). Though American in origin, soon after its emergence it was adopted by the Tavistock Institute in Britain, and used to improve managerial competency and efficiency in the, then, newly nationalised coal industry. Since then it has acquired strong adherents on both sides of the Atlantic (French and Bell, 1984).

An action research project usually comprises three distinct groups: the organisation (in the form of one or more senior managers), the subject (people from the area where the change is to take place), and the change agent (a consultant who may or may not be a member of the organisation). These three distinct entities form the learning community in and through which the research is carried out, and by which the organisation's or group's problem is solved.

The three entities must all, both individually and collectively, agree to come together, as a group, under mutually acceptable and constructed terms of reference. This usually small face-to-face group constitutes the medium through which the problem situation may be changed, as well as providing a forum in which the interests and ethics of the various parties to this process may be investigated. It is a cyclical process, whereby the group analyses and solves the problem through a succession of iterations. The change agent (consultant), through skills of co-ordination, links the different insights and activities within the group, so as to form a coherent chain of ideas and hypotheses (Heller, 1970).

Action research is a two-pronged process. First, it emphasises that change requires action, and is directed at achieving this. Second, it recognises also that successful action is based on analysing the situation correctly, identifying all the possible alternative solutions (hypotheses) and choosing the one most appropriate to the situation at hand (Bennett, 1983). The theoretical foundations of this approach lie in gestalt-field theory, which stresses that change can only successfully be achieved by helping individuals to reflect on and gain new insights into their situation. However, it also has a strong affinity with group dynamics, given that it uses teams to solve problems and stresses the involvement of all those concerned. This is not surprising, given Lewin's role in developing both action research and group dynamics.

Nevertheless, though action research has enjoyed a large following over the years, one of the barriers to its use is the need to gain the commitment of both the organisation and the subject of the change. This becomes especially difficult when dealing with large organisations. A common strategy is to use a top-down approach, establishing senior management agreement as a first step. But this does not always work, because compliance at the top does not always guarantee co-operation at other levels in the organisation (Clark, 1972).

Even taking its drawbacks into consideration, action research is still a highly-regarded approach to managing change (Cummings and Huse, 1989). However, this did not prevent its originator, Kurt Lewin, from seeking to improve upon it.

> ■ **KEY LEARNING POINT**
> *Action research is concerned as much with individual and group learning as it is with achieving change.*

The three-step model of change

In developing the three-step model, Lewin (1958) noted that a change toward a higher level of group performance is frequently short-lived; after a 'shot in the arm', group behaviour may soon revert to its previous pattern. This indicates that it is not sufficient to define the objective of change solely as the achievement of a higher level of group performance. Permanence of the new level should also be included in the objective. A successful change project, Lewin (1958) argued, should involve three steps:

1 *unfreezing* the present level
2 *moving* to the new level
3 *refreezing* the new level.

This recognises that before new behaviour can be successfully adopted, the old has to be discarded. Only then can the new behaviour become accepted. Central to this approach is the belief that the will of the change adopter (the subject of the change) is important, both in discarding the old, 'unfreezing', and in 'moving' to the new.

Unfreezing usually involves reducing those forces maintaining the organisation's behaviour at its present level. According to Rubin (1967), unfreezing requires some form of confrontation meeting or re-education process for those involved. The essence of these activities is to enable those concerned to become convinced of the need for change. Unfreezing clearly equates with the research element of action research, just as the next step, moving, equates with the action element.

Moving, in practice, involves acting on the results of the first step. That is, having analysed the present situation, identified alternatives and selected the most appropriate, action is then necessary to move to the more desirable state of affairs. This requires developing new behaviours, values and attitudes through changes in organisational structures and processes. The key task is to ensure that this is done in such a way that those involved do not, after a short period, revert to the old ways of doing things.

CASE STUDY 20.1

Winning support for organisational change

Dolphin Electronics was introducing a new computer system. It had carried out an extensive consultation exercise with staff but, owing to previous difficulties in introducing change, it was concerned to win over key groups of staff. Dolphin targeted two groups for special attention: senior managers and production supervisors.

Senior managers were considered important because they set the climate and priorities for the company. If they were seen to understand and consistently support the new system, then others in the organisation, it was argued, would follow. Therefore, though they did not need it, all senior managers had three weeks' intensive training on the new system. As the project manager later commented, 'The result was remarkable. Managers not only talk to staff about the system but are knowledgeable and are seen to be openly committed to it. They understand its capabilities and how difficult it is to use.'

The production supervisors had six weeks' training. Once again, this was more than they actually needed to carry out their jobs, but it was clear that if they did not believe in the system and understand its benefits then its introduction would not be successful. The intention in doing this was not to create a rosy picture of the system. Instead, the idea was to give them a realistic appreciation of both its benefits (for both the company and themselves) and the difficulties in getting it up and running.

Suggested exercises

1 *How does the approach to winning support fit in with the planned approach to change?*

2 *What alternative methods of winning over staff might Dolphin have tried?*

3 *What benefits did Dolphin seek to achieve by this approach?*

4 *What other benefits might Dolphin have achieved by winning over key groups?*

Refreezing is the final step in the three-step model and represents, depending on the viewpoint, either a break with action research or its logical extension. Refreezing seeks to stabilise the organisation at a new state of equilibrium in order to ensure that the new ways of working are relatively safe from regression. It is frequently achieved through the use of supporting mechanisms that positively reinforce the new ways of working; these include organisational culture, norms, policies and practices (Cummings and Huse, 1989).

The three-step model provides a general framework for understanding the process of organisational change. However, the three steps are relatively broad and, for this reason, have been further developed in an attempt to enhance the practicable value of this approach.

Phases of planned change

In attempting to elaborate upon Lewin's three-step model, writers have expanded the number of steps or phases. Lippitt *et al.* (1958) developed a seven-phase model of planned change, while Cummings and Huse (1989), not to be outdone, produced an eight-phase model. However, as Cummings and Huse (1989, p. 51) point out, 'the concept of planned change implies that an organization exists in different states at different times and that planned movement can occur from one state to another'. Therefore, in order to understand planned change, it is not sufficient merely to understand the processes which bring about change; there must also be an appreciation of the states that an organisation must pass through in order to move from an unsatisfactory present state to a more desired future state.

Bullock and Batten (1985) developed an integrated, four-phase model of planned change based on a review and synthesis of over thirty models of planned change. Their model describes planned change in terms of two major dimensions: change phases, which are distinct states that an organisation moves through as it undertakes planned change, and change processes, which are the methods used to move an organisation from one state to another.

The four change phases, and their attendant change processes, identified by Bullock and Batten are as follows:

1 *exploration phase*: in this state an organisation has to explore and decide whether it wants to make specific changes in its operations and, if so, commit resources to planning the changes. The change processes involved in this phase are: becoming aware of the need for change; searching for outside assistance (a consultant/facilitator) to assist with planning and implementing the changes; and establishing a contract with the consultant which defines each party's responsibilities;

2 *planning phase*: once the consultant and the organisation have established a contract, then the next state, which involves understanding the organisation's problem or concern, begins. The change processes involved in this are: collecting information in order to establish a correct diagnosis of the problem; establishing change goals and designing the appropriate actions to achieve these goals; and getting key decision makers to approve and support the proposed changes;

3 *action phase*: in this state, an organisation implements the changes derived from the planning. The change processes involved are designed to move an organisation from its current state to a desired future state, and include: establishing appropriate arrangements to manage the change process and gaining support for the actions to be taken; and evaluating the implementation activities and feeding back the results so that any necessary adjustments or refinements can be made;

4 *integration phase*: this state commences once the changes have been successfully implemented. It is concerned with consolidating and stabilising the changes so that they become part of an organisation's normal, everyday operation and do not require special arrangements or encouragement to maintain them. The change processes involved are: reinforcing new behaviours through feedback and reward systems and gradually decreasing reliance on the consultant; diffusing the successful aspects of the change process throughout the organisation; and training managers and employees to monitor the changes constantly and seek to improve upon them.

According to Cummings and Huse (1989), this model has broad applicability to most change situations. It clearly incorporates key aspects of many other change models and, especially, it overcomes any confusion between the processes (methods) of change and the phases of change – the sequential states which organisations must go through to achieve successful change.

> ■ KEY LEARNING POINT
> *Both the three-step and the phases models view change as a sequential activity involving a beginning, a middle and an end.*

Planned change: summary and criticisms

As with action research and the three-step model, Bullock and Batten's model stresses that change is an iterative process involving diagnosis, action, and evaluation, and further action and evaluation. Their approach also recognises that once change has taken place it must be self-sustaining (i.e. safe from retrogression). In addition, they also stress the collaborative nature of the change effort: the organisation and the consultant jointly diagnose the organisation's problem and jointly plan and design the specific changes.

It is at this point that there appears to be a change of emphasis in Bullock and Batten's model in comparison with Lewin's action research model. Action research aims to solve organisational problems through social action (dialogue). It seeks the active participation of the change adopter (the subject) in understanding the problem, selecting a solution and implementing it. The change agent is a facilitator, not a director or a doer. More important even than the solution to the problem, the consultant's real task is to develop those involved, and to create a learning environment that allows them to gain new insights into themselves and their circumstances.

Bullock and Batten's model, and to a lesser extent the three-step model, gives the consultant a more directive and less developmental role. Their model seems to place a greater emphasis on the consultant as an equal partner rather than as a facilitator; the consultant is as free to direct and do as the others involved. Those involved are more dependent on the change agent, not just for her or his skills of analysis but also for providing solutions and helping to implement them. Therefore, the focus is on what the change agent can do for and to those involved, rather than on seeking to get the subjects to change themselves.

Action research is an offshoot of the work of the gestalt-field theorists, who believe that successful change requires a process of learning. This allows those involved to gain or change insights, outlooks, expectations and thought patterns. This approach seeks to provide the change adopters with an opportunity to 'reason out' their situation and develop their own solutions (Bigge, 1982). Bullock and Batten's approach, and to a lesser extent the three-step model as well, on the other hand, appears to owe more to the behaviourist approach. The emphasis is on the consultant as a provider of expertise that the organisation lacks. The consultant's task is not only to facilitate but also to provide solutions. The danger in this situation is that the learner (the change adopter) becomes a passive recipient of external and objective data, one who has to be directed to the 'correct' solution. Reason does not enter into this particular equation; those involved are shown the solution and motivated, through the application of positive reinforcement, to adopt it on a permanent basis (Skinner, 1974).

Nevertheless, serious though this criticism is, as Burnes and Salauroo (1995) pointed out, there are those who question not only particular aspects of the planned approach to change but also the utility and practicality of the approach as a whole. The main charges levelled against the planned approach to change are as follows.

First, it is based on the assumption that, as Cummings and Huse (1989, p. 51) pointed out, 'an organization exists in different states at different times and that planned movement can occur from one state to another'. However, an increasing number of writers argue that, in the turbulent and chaotic world in which we live, such assumptions are increasingly tenuous and that organisational change is more a continuous and open-ended process than a set of discrete and self-contained events (Nonaka, 1988; Peters, 1989; Garvin, 1993; Stacey, 1993).

Second, and on a similar note, a number of writers have criticised the planned approach for its emphasis on incremental and isolated change and for not being able to incorporate radical, transformational change (Miller and Friesen, 1984; Harris, 1985; Schein, 1985; Dunphy and Stace, 1993).

Third, the planned change approach is based on the assumption that common agreement can be reached, and that all the parties involved in a particular change project have a willingness and interest in doing so. This assumption appears to ignore organisational conflict and politics, or at least assumes that they can be easily identified and resolved. However, many studies have shown that the pursuit of organisational power and the maintenance of vested interests are a significant factor in influencing change programmes (Pfeffer, 1981; Mintzberg, 1983; Robbins, 1986; Burnes, 1996a & b). It also ignores situations where more directive approaches may be required, such as when a crisis, requiring rapid and major change, does not allow scope for widespread involvement or consultation (Dunphy and Stace, 1993).

Fourth, it assumes that one type of approach to change is suitable for all organisations, all situations and all times. Dunphy and Stace (1993, p. 905), on the other hand, argue that:

> Turbulent times demand different responses in varied circumstances. So managers and consultants need a model of change that is essentially a 'situational' or 'contingency model', one that indicates how to vary change strategies to achieve 'optimum fit' with the changing environment.

There are proponents of planned change who would argue that these criticisms are not valid, that it is a more flexible and holistic approach than its detractors would acknowledge and is capable of incorporating transformational change (French and Bell, 1984; Cummings and Huse, 1989; McLennan, 1989; Mirvis, 1990). Nevertheless, it is the case that a new approach to change has been gaining ground in recent years. Though it has been given a number of different labels, such as continuous improvement or organisational learning, it is more often referred to as the emergent approach to change. The emergent approach tends to see change as driven from the bottom up rather than from the top down; it stresses that change is an open-ended and continuous process of adaptation to changing conditions and circumstances, and it also sees the process of change as a process of learning and not just a method of changing organisational structures and practices (Wilson, 1992; Mabey and Mayon-White, 1993; Dawson, 1994).

> ■ **KEY LEARNING POINT**
> *The main criticism of the planned approach is that it is not suitable for open-ended and unpredictable situations.*

THE EMERGENT APPROACH TO ORGANISATIONAL CHANGE

As can be seen from the above, the planned change approach is relatively well developed and understood, and is supported by a coherent body of literature, methods and techniques. The emergent approach, on the other hand, is a relatively new concept which lacks an agreed set of methods and techniques. The proponents of emergent change approach it from different perspectives and tend to focus on their own particular concerns. To this extent, they are much less of a coherent group than the advocates of planned change and, rather than being united by a shared belief, they tend to be distinguished by a common disbelief in the efficacy of planned change.

Dawson (1994) and Wilson (1992) both challenged the appropriateness of planned change in a business environment that is increasingly dynamic and uncertain. They argue that those who believe that organisational change can successfully be achieved through a pre-planned and centrally directed process of 'unfreezing', 'moving' and 'refreezing' ignore the complex and dynamic nature of environmental and change processes, and do not address crucial issues such as the continuous need for employee flexibility and structural adaptation. Wilson (1992) also believes that the planned approach, by attempting to lay down timetables, objectives and methods in advance, is too heavily reliant on the role of managers, and assumes (perhaps rashly) that they can have a full understanding of the consequences of their actions and that their plans will be understood and accepted, and can be implemented.

The emergent approach, on the other hand, stresses the developing and unpredictable nature of change. It views change as a process that unfolds through the interplay of multiple variables (context, political processes and consultation) within an organisation. In contrast to the pre-ordained certainty of planned change, Dawson (1994) in particular adopted a processual approach to change. The processual approach views organisations and their members as shifting coalitions of individuals and groups with different interests, imperfect knowledge and short attention spans. Change, under these conditions, is portrayed as a pragmatic process of trial and error, aimed at achieving a compromise between the competitive needs of the organisation and the objectives of the warring factions within the organisation.

Advocates of emergent change who adopt the processual approach tend to stress that there can be no simple prescription for managing organisational transitions successfully, owing to temporal and contextual factors. Neither, as Dawson (1994, p. 181) argued, can change be characterised as 'a rational series of decision-making activities and events ... nor as a single reaction to adverse contingent circumstances'. Therefore, successful change is less dependent on detailed plans and projections than on reaching an understanding of the complexity of the issues concerned and identifying the range of available options.

> ### ■ KEY LEARNING POINT
> *The emergent approach challenges the view that organisations are rational entities, and seeks to replace it with a view of organisations as comprising moving coalitions of different interest groups.*

The rationale for the emergent approach stems from the belief that change should not be and cannot be solidified, or seen as a series of linear events within a given period of time; instead, it is viewed as a continuous process. Dawson (1994) saw change as a period of organisational transition characterised by disruption, confusion and unforeseen events that emerge over long time frames. Even when changes are operational, they will need to be constantly refined and developed in order to maintain their relevance.

From this perspective, Clarke (1994) suggested that mastering the challenge of change is not a specialist activity facilitated or driven by an expert but an increasingly important part of every manager's role. To be effective in creating sustainable change, according to McCalman and Paton (1992), managers will need an extensive and systemic understanding of their organisation's environment, in order to identify the pressures for change and to ensure that, by mobilising the necessary internal resources, their organisation responds in a timely and appropriate manner. Dawson (1994) claimed that change must be linked with the complexity of changing market realities, the transitional nature of work organisation, systems of management control and redefined organisational boundaries and relationships. He emphasises that, in today's business environment, one-dimensional change interventions are likely to generate only short-term results and heighten instability rather than reduce it.

As can be seen, though they do not openly state it, advocates of emergent change tend to adopt a contingency perspective. For them, it is the uncertainty of the environment which makes planned change inappropriate and emergent change more pertinent. A key competence for organisations is, therefore, the ability to scan the external environment in order to identify and assess the impact of trends and discontinuities (McCalman and Paton, 1992). This includes exploring the full range of external variables, including markets and customers, shareholders, legal requirements, the economy, suppliers, technology and social trends. This activity is made more difficult by the changing and arbitrary nature of organisation boundaries: customers can also be competitors; suppliers may become partners; and employees can be transformed into customers, suppliers or competitors.

Changes in the external environment require appropriate responses within organisations. Appropriate responses, according to the supporters of the emergent approach, should promote extensive and deep understanding of strategy, structure, systems, people, style and culture, and how these can function either as sources of inertia that can block change, or, alternatively, as levers to encourage an effective change process (Wilson, 1992; Pettigrew and Whipp, 1993; Dawson, 1994). A major development in this respect is the move to adopt a 'bottom-up' rather than 'top-down' approach to initiating and implementing change. The case in favour of this move is based on the view that the pace of environmental change is so rapid and complex that it is impossible for a small number of senior managers effectively to identify, plan and implement the necessary organisational responses. The responsibility for organisational change is therefore of necessity becoming more devolved. As described in Chapter 1, this is very much what the advocates of contingency theory would expect in such a situation.

> ■ KEY LEARNING POINT
>
> *'while the primary stimulus for change remains those forces in the external environment, the primary motivator for how change is accomplished resides with the people within the organization'*
> *(Benjamin and Mabey, 1993, p. 181).*

Supporters of the emergent approach identify four features of organisations which either promote or obstruct success: structures, cultures, organisational learning and managerial behaviour.

Organisational structure

This is seen as playing a crucial role in defining how people relate to each other and in influencing the momentum for change (Clarke, 1994; Dawson, 1994). Therefore, an appropriate organisation structure can be an important lever for achieving change, but its effectiveness is regarded as dependent upon the recognition of its informal as well as its formal aspects.

The case for developing more appropriate organisational structures in order to facilitate change very much follows the arguments of the contingency theorists (*see* Chapter 1). Those favouring an emergent approach to change point out that the 1990s are witnessing a move to create flatter organisational structures in order to increase responsiveness by devolving authority and responsibility. An aspect of this is the move to create customer-centred organisations with structures that reflect, and are responsive to, different markets rather than different functions. Customer responsiveness places greater emphasis on effective horizontal processes and embodies the concept that everyone is someone else's customer.

One result of attempts to respond rapidly to changing conditions by breaking down internal barriers, disseminating knowledge and developing synergy across functions is the creation of network organisations, or to use Handy's (1989) term, 'Federal' organisations. Snow *et al.* (1993) suggested that the semi-autonomous nature of each part of a network reduces the need for and erodes the power of centrally-managed bureaucracies, which in turn leads to change and adaptation being driven from the bottom up rather than from the top down. They further argue that the specialisation and flexibility required to cope with globalisation, intense competition and rapid technological change can only be achieved by loosening the central ties and controls that have characterised organisations in the past.

Organisational culture

Johnson (1993, p. 64) suggested that the strategic management of change is 'essentially a cultural and cognitive phenomenon' rather than an analytical, rational exercise. Clarke (1994) stated that the essence of sustainable change is to understand the culture of the organisation that is to be changed. If proposed changes contradict cultural biases and traditions, it is inevitable that they will be difficult to embed in the organisation.

In a similar vein, Dawson (1994) suggested that attempts to realign internal behaviours with external conditions require change strategies that are culturally sensitive. Organisations, he points out, must be aware that the process is lengthy, potentially dangerous, and demands considerable reinforcement if culture change is to be sustained against the inevitable tendency to regress to old behaviours. Clarke (1994) also stressed that change can be slow, especially where mechanisms which reinforce old or inappropriate behaviour, such as reward, recruitment and promotion structures, continue unchallenged. In addition, if these reinforcement mechanisms are complemented by managerial behaviour which promotes risk aversion and fear of failure, it is unlikely to create a climate where people are willing to propose or undertake change. Accordingly, as Clarke (1994, p. 94) suggested, 'Creating a culture for change means that change has to be part of the way we do things around here, it cannot be bolted on as an extra'.

Therefore, for many proponents of the emergent approach to change, the presence or development of an appropriate organisational culture is essential. However, not all of its proponents take this view. Beer *et al.* (1993) suggested that the most effective way to promote change is not by directly attempting to influence organisational behaviour or culture. Instead, they advocate restructuring organisations in order to place people in a new organisational context which imposes new roles, relationships and responsibilities upon them. This, they believe, forces new attitudes and behaviours upon people.

Wilson (1992, p. 91), however, took an even more sceptical approach to culture change, claiming that:

> to effect change in an organization simply by attempting to change its culture assumes an unwarranted linear connection between something called organizational culture and performance. Not only is this concept of organizational culture multi-faceted, it is also not always clear precisely how culture and change are related, if at all, and, if so, in which direction.

■ **KEY LEARNING POINT**

Adopting an emergent approach to change may require organisations to move towards radically different structures and cultures.

Organisational learning

A willingness to change often only stems from the feeling that there is no other option. Therefore, as Wilson (1992) suggests, change can be precipitated by making impending crises real to everyone in the organisation (or perhaps even engineering crises) or encouraging dissatisfaction with current systems and procedures. The latter is probably best achieved through the creation of mechanisms by managers which allow staff to become familiar with the market-place, customers, competitors, legal requirements etc., in order to recognise the pressures for change.

Clarke (1994) and Nadler (1993) suggested that individual and organisational learning stems from effective top-down communication and the promotion of self-development and confidence. In turn, this encourages the commitment to, and shared ownership of, the organisation's vision, actions and decisions that are necessary to respond to the external environment and take advantage of the opportunities it offers. Additionally, as Pugh (1993) pointed out, in order to generate the need and climate for change, people within organisations need to be involved in the diagnosis of problems and the development of solutions. Carnall (1990) took this argument further, maintaining that organisational effectiveness can only be achieved and sustained through learning from the experience of change.

Clarke (1994, p. 156) believed that involving staff in change management decisions has the effect of 'stimulating habits of criticism and open debate', which enables them to challenge existing norms and question established practices. This, in turn, creates the opportunity for innovation and radical change. Benjamin and Mabey (1993) argued that such questioning of the status quo is the essence of bottom-up change. They consider that, as employees' learning becomes more valued and visible within a company, then rather than managers putting pressure on staff to change, the reverse occurs. The new openness and knowledge of staff puts pressure on managers to address fundamental questions about the purpose and direction of the organisation which previously they might have avoided.

Managerial behaviour

The traditional view of organisations sees managers as directing and controlling staff, resources and information. However, the emergent approach to change requires a radical change in managerial behaviour. Managers are expected to operate as facilitators and coaches who, through their ability to span hierarchical, functional and organisational boundaries, can bring together and motivate teams and groups to identify the need for, and achieve, change (Mabey and Mayon-White, 1993).

To be effective in this new role, Clarke (1994) believed that managers would require knowledge of and expertise in strategy formulation, human resource management, marketing/sales and negotiation/conflict resolution. But the key to success, the decisive factor in creating a focused agenda for organisational change is, according to Clarke (1994), managers' own behaviour. If managers are to gain the commitment of others to change, they must first be prepared to challenge their own assumptions, attitudes and mindsets so that they develop an understanding of the emotional and intellectual processes involved (Buchanan and Boddy, 1992a).

Building a learning organisation

Oticon, the Danish hearing-aid manufacturer, was founded in 1904. In 1979, it was the number one hearing-aid manufacturer in the world. However, by the early 1990s, it was rapidly losing money and market share. A new chief executive was appointed to reverse the decline in the company's fortunes.

The chief executive believed that the company could no longer compete merely by supplying good technology. Instead it needed to offer its customers a high standard of service as well. It also had to accept that while it operated in a global market-place, this was composed of a number of distinct and rapidly changing local markets. Each of these demanded a different service mix and, therefore, a different approach.

In short, if Oticon was to survive, the chief executive believed it would have to move from a technological orientation to a knowledge orientation; from a technology-based manufacturing company to a knowledge-based service business. The core of this was to build a learning organisation where experts put aside their expertise and worked as a team to create satisfied customers.

Suggested exercises

1 *How does the creation of a learning organisation fit in with the emergent approach to change?*

2 *How does learning facilitate organisational change?*

3 *How might becoming a learning organisation help Oticon to deal with rapidly changing and diverse customer needs?*

4 *Is the learning organisation concept appropriate for all organisations?*

For supporters of the emergent approach, the essence of change is the move from the familiar to the unknown. In this situation, it is essential for managers to be able to tolerate risk and cope with ambiguity. Pugh (1993) took the view that, in a dynamic environment, open and active communication with those participating in the change process is the key to coping with risk and ambiguity. This very much follows Clarke's (1994, p. 172) assertion that because 'top-down, unilaterally imposed change does not work, bottom-up, early involvement and genuine consultation' are essential to achieving successful change. This in turn requires managers to facilitate open, organisation-wide communication via groups, individuals, and formal and informal channels.

An organisation's ability to gather, disseminate, analyse and discuss information is, from the perspective of the emergent approach, crucial for successful change. The reason for this, as Wilson (1992) argued, is that to effect change successfully, organisations need consciously and proactively to move forward incrementally. Large-scale change and more formal and integrated approaches to change (such as TQM) can quickly lose their sense of purpose and relevance for organisations operating in dynamic and uncertain environments. However, if organisations move towards their strategic vision on the basis of many small-scale, localised incremental changes, managers must ensure that those concerned, which could (potentially) be the entire workforce, have access to and are able to act on all the available information. Also, by encouraging a collective pooling of knowledge and information in this way, a better understanding of the pressures and possibilities for change can be achieved, which should enable managers to improve the quality of strategic decisions (Buchanan and Boddy, 1992b; Quinn, 1993).

As well as ensuring the free flow of information, managers must also recognise and be able to cope with resistance to, and political intervention in, change. They will, especially, need to acquire and develop a range of interpersonal skills that enable them to deal with individuals and groups who seek to block or manipulate change for their own benefit (Buchanan and Boddy, 1992b). In addition, supporting openness, reducing uncertainty and encouraging experimentation can be powerful mechanisms for promoting change (Mabey and Mayon-White, 1993). In this respect, Coghlan (1993) and McCalman and Paton (1992) advocated the use of organisation development (OD) tools and techniques (such as transactional analysis, teamwork, group problem solving, role playing etc.), which have long been used in planned change programmes. However, there is an enormous and potentially confusing array of these; Mayon-White (1993) and Buchanan and Boddy (1992a) argued that managers have a crucial role to play in terms of identifying and applying the appropriate ones. The main objective in deploying such tools and techniques is to encourage shared learning through teamwork and co-operation. It is this which provides the framework and support for the emergence of creative solutions and encourages a sense of involvement, commitment and ownership of the change process (Carnall, 1990; McCalman and Paton, 1992).

Nevertheless, it would be naive to assume that everyone will want to work, or be able to function effectively, in such situations. The cognitive and behaviourial changes necessary for organisational survival may be too large for many people, including, and perhaps especially, managers. An important managerial task will, therefore, be to identify sources of inertia, assess the skill mix within their organisation and, most of all, consider whether their own managerial attitudes and styles are appropriate.

> ■ KEY LEARNING POINT
> *The emergent approach requires a major change in the traditional role of managers. In future they will need to be facilitators and coaches rather than initiators and directors.*

Emergent change: summary and criticisms

The proponents of emergent change are a somewhat disparate group who tend to be united more by their scepticism regarding planned change than by a commonly-agreed alternative. Nevertheless, there does seem to be some agreement regarding the main tenets of emergent change, which are as follows:

- organisational change is a continuous process of experiment and adaptation aimed at matching an organisation's capabilities to the needs and dictates of a dynamic and uncertain environment;

- though this is best achieved through a multitude of (mainly) small-scale incremental changes, over time these can lead to a major reconfiguration and transformation of an organisation;

- the role of managers is not to plan or implement change, but to create or foster an organisational structure and climate which encourages and sustains experimentation and risk taking, and to develop a workforce that will take responsibility for identifying the need for change and implementing it;

- though managers are expected to become facilitators rather than doers, they also have the prime responsibility for developing a collective vision or common purpose which gives direction to their organisation, and within which the appropriateness of any proposed change can be judged;

- the key organisational activities which allow these elements to operate successfully are: information gathering (about the external environment and internal objectives and capabilities); communication (the transmission, analysis and discussion of information); and learning (the ability to develop new skills, identify appropriate responses and draw knowledge from their own and others' past and present actions).

Though not always stated openly, the case for an emergent approach to change is based on the assumption that all organisations operate in a turbulent, dynamic and unpredictable environment. Therefore, if the external world is changing in a rapid and uncertain fashion, organisations need to be continually scanning their environment in order to adapt and respond to changes. Because this is a continuous and open-ended process, the planned approach to change is inappropriate. To be successful, changes need to emerge locally and incrementally in order to respond to and take advantage of environmental threats and opportunities.

Presented in this fashion, there is certainly an apparent coherence and validity to the emergent approach. However, it is a fragile coherence and of challengeable validity. As far as coherence is concerned, some proponents of emergent change, especially Dawson (1994) and Pettigrew and Whipp (1993), clearly approach it from the processual perspective on organisations. However, it is not clear that Wilson (1992) and Buchanan and Boddy (1992a, b) would fully subscribe to this view. In the cases of Clarke (1994) and Carnall (1990), it is clear that they do not take a processual perspective. Partly, this is explained by the fact that some of these writers (especially Dawson, 1992; Wilson, 1992; Pettigrew and Whipp, 1993) are attempting to understand and investigate change from a critical perspective, while others (notably Carnall, 1990; Buchanan and Boddy, 1992a, b; and Clarke, 1994) are more concerned to provide recipes and checklists for successful change. Nevertheless, these differing objectives and perspectives do put a question mark against the coherence of the emergent approach.

The validity or general applicability of the emergent approach to change depends to a large extent on whether or not one subscribes to the view that all organisations operate in a dynamic and unpredictable environment to which they continually have to adapt. Burnes (1996a, b) produced substantial evidence that not all organisations face the same degree of environmental turbulence and that, in any case, it is possible to manipulate or change environmental constraints. This does not necessarily invalidate the emergent approach as a whole, but it does indicate that some organisations, by accident or action, may find the planned approach to change both appropriate and effective in their particular circumstances. Obviously, the above issues raise a major question mark regarding the emergent approach; however, even without reservations regarding its coherence and validity, there would still be serious criticisms of this approach. For example, a great deal of emphasis is given to creating appropriate organisational cultures; but many writers have questioned whether this is either easy or indeed possible (Filby and Willmott, 1988; Meek, 1988). Indeed, as mentioned earlier, even Wilson (1992) was sceptical about the case for viewing culture as a facilitator of change. Similar points can be made regarding the 'learning organisation' approach. As Whittington (1993, p. 130) commented:

> The danger of the purely 'learning' approach to change, therefore, is that ... managers [and others] may actually recognize the need for change, yet still refuse to 'learn' because they understand perfectly well the implications for their power and status. Resistance to change may not be 'stupid' ... but based on a very shrewd appreciation of the personal consequences.

A variant of this criticism relates to the impact of success on managerial learning. Miller (1993, p. 119) observed that, while managers generally start out by attempting to learn all they can about their organisation's environment, over time, as they gain experience, they 'form quite definite opinions of what works and why' and as a consequence tend to limit their search for information and knowledge. So experience, especially where it is based on success, may actually be a barrier to learning, in that it shapes the cognitive structures by which managers, and everyone else, see and interpret the world. As Nystrom and Starbuck (1984, p. 55) observed:

> What people see, predict, understand, depends on their cognitive structures ... [which] manifest themselves in perceptual frameworks, expectations, world views, plans, goals ... myths, rituals, symbols ... and jargon.

This brings us neatly to the topic of the role of managers. As the above quotations indicate, they may neither welcome nor be able to accept approaches to change which require them to challenge and amend their own beliefs, especially where such approaches run counter to their experience of 'what works and why'. Also, if, as mentioned above, the possibility exists to manipulate environmental variables and constraints to avoid having to change their behaviour, they may perceive this as a more attractive or viable option.

> ■ **KEY LEARNING POINT**
> *Though the emergent approach to change has apparent advantages over the planned approach, an examination of it reveals that there are serious question marks over its coherence, validity and applicability.*

CHOOSING AN APPROACH TO CHANGE

This chapter has examined the development and applicability of the two major approaches to change management which have emerged in the latter half of the twentieth century: the planned approach and the emergent approach. Though elaborated upon and supported by a considerable number of very useful tools and techniques, the first of these – the planned approach – has remained essentially true to Lewin's original 'unfreezing', 'moving' and 'refreezing' approach. However, in the increasingly dynamic and unpredictable business environment of the 1980s, writers began to question the appropriateness of a top-down approach which saw the process of change primarily in terms of a 'beginning, middle and end' framework. In place of the planned approach to change, the emergent approach began to gain support. With its emphasis on bottom-up and open-ended change, it appeared to offer a more appropriate method of accomplishing the stream of adaptations organisations believed they needed to make in order to bring themselves back into line with their environment. However, this chapter has shown that emergent change appears to have as many shortcomings as planned change.

CASE STUDY 20.3

Somerfield Stores and RHM

About the companies

In 1983, Somerfield (then known as Gateway) was the UK's second largest food retailer. However, owing to over-ambitious expansion plans, it finished the 1980s heavily in debt and rapidly losing market share. From the early 1990s, Somerfield began to rebuild its reputation and regain market share. The main thrust of its strategy has been to 'offer a competitive and attractive product range with an emphasis on fresh foods at excellent prices'.

RHM is one of Somerfield's main suppliers. Its products include household names such as Robertson's jams, McDougal's flour, Bisto gravy powder and the Sharwoods range of foods.

The focus of the study

As part of its strategy to rebuild its market position, Somerfield has been attempting to develop closer links with its 2000 suppliers to ensure that it can supply its customers with the best products at the most competitive prices.

Somerfield believed that it could not regain its market position merely by playing 'catch up' – it needed to leapfrog the opposition. In looking across the Atlantic, Somerfield were impressed with the vendor managed inventory (VMI) concept which had brought similar and considerable benefits to Wal-Mart.

VMI is, in essence, quite simple. Instead of a company managing its own stocks – deciding what to re-order from suppliers – it allows the suppliers to do this. It is claimed that this approach minimises the risk of 'stock outs' while ensuring that they do not carry too much stock.

Somerfield developed its own version of VMI, which it called co-managed inventory (CMI).

Putting CMI on trial

After extensive discussions with its suppliers, RHM, along with nine other companies, was chosen to take part in a CMI trial.

The purpose of the trial was to assess the benefits of CMI before any full-scale introduction could be contemplated. Therefore, in the words of one senior manager, a 'suck it and see' exercise was required to see if the promise of CMI could be fulfilled.

RHM volunteered to take part in the trial for three reasons. First, if this was the direction the industry was moving in, it wanted to be in the vanguard, not the rearguard. Second, RHM has a policy of assisting its major customers to develop their competitiveness, where possible. Third, though RHM did not see any major financial benefit to itself as such, it did see that CMI might enable it to offer Somerfield a better service in the future.

Because it was a relatively low-cost and exploratory project, RHM did not carry out a rigorous evaluation of the benefits of the project. In any case, if Somerfield eventually adopted CMI, RHM would have no alternative but to follow suit.

Up and running

The CMI trial began in 1995. The first phase involved testing the CMI software which, as might be expected, threw up a number of concerns. However, these were quickly resolved and CMI was allowed to 'go live'.

As the live phase of the trial developed, RHM came to appreciate better Somerfield's needs and it began to see areas where it could reduce stock levels and offer an improved service. RHM found that there was a lot of 'cushion' in the existing system. That is to say, rather than being in danger of stockouts, Somerfield were in the opposite position – too much stock. Partly this was because Somerfield were cautious and wanted to avoid stockouts at all costs. But it was also partly because RHM had not previously had the information to assess Somerfield's needs accurately.

Therefore, for CMI to be successful, it would require not only technical changes in ordering procedures and policies, but also a change in attitude by Somerfield's purchasing staff.

Suggested exercise

Analyse the case study to see whether it offers support for either the planned or emergent approach to change. In particular, address the following questions:

(a) To what extent was the change 'open-ended'?

(b) Was the approach adopted suitable for the situation?

(c) What reasons might a supplier have for refusing to participate in Somerfield's CMI trial?

(d) To what extent were the benefits gained due to CMI and to what extent could they be due to closer co-operation and greater information exchange?

(e) Did the unanticipated benefits which emerged justify the approach taken or did they serve to highlight shortcomings in it?

The two approaches appear to have some striking similarities, especially the stress they place on the process of change also being a learning process. They also share a common, and major, difficulty, which is that, while both claim to be universally applicable, they were developed with particular, but different, situations in mind (especially the nature of the environment in which organisations operate).

As Fig. 20.1 shows, we can locate them at either end of a business environment continuum which runs from stability and predictability to turbulence and uncertainty. This continuum of change perspective is in line with the call by Dunphy and Stace (1993, p. 905) for 'a model of change that is essentially a "situational" or "contingency model", one that indicates how to vary strategies to achieve "optimum fit" with the changing environment'.

Fig. 20.1 Change and the environment

Dunphy and Stace advocated a model of change which reflects the fact not only that organisations operate under different circumstances, but also that there is more than one approach to change.

As an example of this, Kanter *et al.* (1992) introduced two more approaches to change: 'bold strokes' and 'long marches'. Bold strokes are major and rapid change initiatives which are imposed on an organisation from the top in a directive rather than participative manner. Long marches are change initiatives which comprise a whole series of small-scale, local (incremental) changes which have little overall effect in the short term but over the long term can transform an organisation. The point to note is that while long marches can be seen as complementary to the emergent model of change, bold strokes fit neither the emergent nor the planned approach.

Therefore, while the change literature has tended to focus on the planned and emergent models, it should be recognised that these do not encompass the full spectrum of change events. This point merely reinforces Dunphy and Stace's argument that if a model of change is to be applicable to the widely-differing and dynamic circumstances under which organisations operate, it must offer an equally wide range of approaches to change. However, in wishing to base such a model on a 'contingency' approach, Dunphy and Stace ignore the criticisms of contingency models or the difficulties involved in moving from one approach to change to another.

From the point of view of applying a contingency approach to organisational change, perhaps the most pertinent criticism is that rather than managers being the virtual prisoners of organisational contingencies when making decisions regarding structure, the reverse may be the case. Managers may have a significant degree of choice and influence, not only over structure, but also over the situational variables themselves.

Whether this is called 'organisational choice' (Trist *et al.*, 1963), 'strategic choice' (Child, 1972) or 'design space' (Bessant, 1983), the meaning is the same: those senior managers responsible for such decisions can exercise a high degree of freedom in selecting and influencing the technology to be used, the environment in which they operate and even the size of the organisation. Indeed, one of the architects of the technology-structure hypothesis, Charles Perrow, later went on to argue that technology is chosen and designed to maintain and reinforce existing structures and power relations within organisations rather than the reverse (Perrow, 1983). Other writers make the case for size and environment being manipulated in similar ways (Lorsch, 1970; Abell, 1975; Leifer and Huber, 1977; Hendry, 1979; Clegg, 1984).

If it is possible to manipulate or change contingencies, then rather than adapting their approach to change to the situation in hand, the reverse may be the case – organisations can influence or manipulate contingencies to align them with their preferred way of working and their managerial style. Indeed, there is considerable evidence that those who are responsible for running organisations do manipulate contingencies in this fashion (*see* Burnes, 1996a).

A further difficulty in applying a contingency model to change is that, like other models, it ignores the difficulty that organisations may face in adopting a new approach to change. To an extent, by being so prescriptive, the change literature sidesteps these difficulties. Implicit in much of the literature is the view that 'ours is the best approach, anything else is not just sub-optimal but could be disastrous. Therefore, you *must* adopt our approach'. However, many studies appear to suggest that an organisation's preferred approach to change stems from its culture and thus cannot easily be amended or replaced (Schein, 1985; Dobson, 1988; Cummings and Huse, 1989; Burnes and James, 1995). Indeed, this may well give a clue as to why so many change projects are said to fail owing to the apparent inability of managers to follow the prescriptions for successful change laid down in the literature (Juran, 1988; Kearney, 1989; Coombs and Hull, 1994; Zairi *et al.*, 1994; Burnes, 1996b). A plausible explanation is that, where such prescriptions run counter to the organisation's culture, they will be either ignored or ineffective.

In a similar vein, the 'cultural risk' approach of Schwartz and Davis (1981) warns of the dangers of ignoring or underestimating the resistance that can arise when proposed changes clash with existing cultures. They argue that, depending on the importance of the change objectives, managers need to decide whether to adapt their organisation's culture to the desired changes or bring the changes into line with its culture. Handy (1986), in discussing different forms of organisational culture, provided evidence which supports the view that there is a strong link between culture and managerial practices. He argued that in Western organisations, 'role' and 'task' cultures are the norm. Role cultures tend to promote a top-down, bureaucratic managerial style that emphasises means over ends. Task cultures, on the other hand, tend to promote ends over means and are associated with a flexible, more decentralised style of management. It is clear that role cultures appear to align better with the planned model of change, while task cultures seem more in tune with the emergent model. Consequently, it would be difficult to see how an organisation with a role culture could easily or successfully adopt the decentralised and participative procedures of the emergent model, or for that matter, how one with a task culture could adopt a planned approach.

Therefore, while Dunphy and Stace (1993) may be right to call for a model of change which recognises the need for aligning internal and external environments, this is not necessarily best or most easily achieved by changing internal practices; sometimes it is the situational variables that may have to be changed. As an example, Burnes (1996a) argued that Nissan's attempt to promote a more stable environment in the UK motor component industry was driven by the desire to maintain its own internal managerial practices and culture. He also argued that recent changes in the British National Health Service were designed to destabilise the environment in which it operated in order to promote a change in managerial practices and culture.

Therefore, there is certainly evidence that organisations wishing to maintain or promote a particular managerial style can choose to influence situational variables to achieve this. The point is that rather than having little choice, rather than being forced to change their internal practices to fit in with external variables, organisations can exercise some choice over these issues.

> ■ KEY LEARNING POINT
>
> *Just as organisations have choice in terms of what to change, they also have choice in what approach they adopt to change.*

SUMMARY

This chapter has sought to argue that just as change comes in all shapes and sizes, so too do models or approaches to change. Therefore, rather than seeing the argument between the planned and emergent approaches to change as a clash of two fundamentally opposing systems of ideas, they can be better viewed as approaches which seek to address different situational variables (contingencies). The planned model is clearly one which is best suited to relatively stable and predictable situations where change can be driven from the top down. The emergent model, on the other hand, is one which is geared to fast-moving and unpredictable situations where it is impractical, if not impossible, to drive change from the top. It has also been argued that the appropriateness of these approaches may also have to be judged in relation to an organisation's culture.

It follows that it is misleading to speak of 'good' or 'bad' approaches to change. Instead, we need to think in terms of appropriateness of an approach with regard to the circumstances being addressed. The issue, therefore, becomes one of ensuring, as near as possible, that the approach adopted is suitable for the circumstances. Though this stress on appropriateness can encompass Dunphy and Stace's (1993) call for a contingency approach to change, it would be misleading to categorise it as such, because the issue of matching approach and circumstances does not address the possibility of influencing the circumstances to make them more amenable to the approach to change which the organisation wishes to adopt.

A contingency approach, while offering guidance, does not seek to offer choice. Instead, it merely replaces a 'one best way for *all*' with a 'one best way for *each*'. If, however, as has been argued, organisations can influence the contingencies they face, then rather than adapting their managerial style to these contingencies, they can choose to adapt the contingencies to their style.

The presence or absence of choice is no mere idle academic speculation; instead it lies at the heart of all major decisions in organisations. To ignore the presence of choice or not even to recognise its existence means taking decisions by default, and thus possibly missing major opportunities for increasing an organisation's competitiveness. In its most extreme form, it is a failure of management that can even lead to the demise of an organisation.

TEST YOUR LEARNING

Short-answer questions

1 What was Kurt Lewin's main contribution to the development of organisational change?

2 How does Bullock and Batten's phases of change model differ from Lewin's three-step model?

3 What are the main advantages of the planned approach?

4 What are the main disadvantages of the planned approach?

5 What are the key components of the emergent approach?

6 How does the emergent approach view the role of organisational culture?

7 What are the main advantages of the emergent approach?

8 What are the main disadvantages of the emergent approach?

Essay questions

1 To what extent can it be said that, in the fast-moving 1990s, the planned approach to change ceased to be relevant?

2 Discuss the proposition that the emergent approach is nothing more than an attempt to provide an intellectual justification for allowing managers an ad hoc approach to change.

3 Describe and discuss the planned and emergent approaches' view of the role of managers.

4 What are the main constraints on organisations when deciding on which approach to change to adopt?

GLOSSARY OF TERMS

Action research This is an iterative change process aimed at improving organisational performance. It involves three equal parties acting in concert: the organisation, its employees and a change agent.

Bold strokes These are major and rapid change initiatives which are imposed on an organisation from the top in a directive rather than participative manner.

Change agent An internal or external facilitator whose role is to guide an organisation through a process of change.

Contingency theory An approach to organisation design which rejects any universal best way and instead views organisation structures as being dependent (i.e. contingent) on the particular combination of situational variables each organisation faces. The main situational variables cited in the literature are environment, technology and size.

Emergent change This is a bottom-up and open-ended approach which views organisations as constantly having to adjust to changing environmental circumstances.

Long marches Change initiatives which comprise a series of small-scale, local, incremental changes which have little overall effect in the short term but over the long term can transform an organisation.

New technology A generic label used to describe any form of computer-based technology.

Organisation development (OD) The application of behavioural science knowledge to the planned creation and reinforcement of organisational strategies, structures and processes.

Organisational culture The distinctive norms, beliefs, principles and ways of behaving that combine to give each organisation its distinctive character.

Organisational learning The ability of an organisation to develop and utilise knowledge in order to create and sustain competitive advantage.

Phases of change These are distinct states through which an organisation moves as it undertakes planned change.

Planned change This is a generic term for approaches to change which have predetermined goals and a distinct starting and finishing point.

Processual approach An approach to change which sees organisations as shifting coalitions of individuals and groups with different interests and aims, imperfect knowledge and short attention spans.

Three-step model This model views change as a planned and finite process which proceeds through three stages: unfreezing, moving and refreezing.

Total quality management A strategic and organisation-wide approach to quality which is associated with Japanese manufacturing organisations.

SUGGESTED FURTHER READING

1 Bernard Burnes' book *Managing Change: A strategic approach to organisational dynamics*, 2nd edn provides a comprehensive review of the development of organisations and organisational change. It expands on this chapter and contains ten detailed case studies of major change projects in European companies.

2 *The Challenge of Organizational Change: How companies experience it and leaders guide it*, by Rosabeth Moss Kanter, Barry A. Stein and Todd D. Jick, though research-based, is less of an academic text and more of a guidebook on how to manage change. It contains many examples of change projects in American companies.

3 *A Strategy of Change: Concepts and controversies in the management of change*, by David Wilson, is a short and readable book which covers some of the key arguments concerning change management.

REFERENCES

Abell, P. (1975) 'Organisations as technically constrained bargaining and influence systems' in Abell, P (ed.) *Organisations as Bargaining and Influence Systems*. London: Heinemann.

Beer, M., Eisenstat, R.A. and Spector, B. (1993) 'Why change programmes don't produce change' in Mabey, C. and Mayon-White, B. (eds) *Managing Change*. 2nd edn. London: Open University/Paul Chapman.

Benjamin, G. and Mabey, C. (1993) 'Facilitating radical change' in Mabey, C. and Mayon-White, B. (eds) *Managing Change*. 2nd edn. London: Open University/Paul Chapman.

Bennett, R. (1983) *Management Research*, Management Development Series no. 20. Geneva: International Labour Office.

Bessant, J. (1983) 'Management and manufacturing innovation: the case of information technology' in Winch, G. (ed.) *Information Technology in Manufacturing Processes*. London: Rossendale.

Bessant, J. and Haywood, B. (1985) 'The introduction of flexible manufacturing systems as an example of computer integrated manufacture'. Brighton: Brighton Polytechnic.

Bigge, L.M. (1982) *Learning Theories for Teachers*. Aldershot: Gower.

Blake, R.R. and Mouton, J.S. (1976) *Organizational Change by Design*. Austin, Tx: Scientific Methods.

Buchanan, D. and Boddy, D. (1992a) *The Expertise of the Change Agent*. London: Prentice Hall.

Buchanan, D. and Boddy, D. (1992b) *Take the Lead: Interpersonal skills for change agents*. London: Prentice Hall.

Bullock, R.J. and Batten, D. (1985) 'It's just a phase we're going through: a review and synthesis of OD phase analysis', *Group and Organization Studies*, vol. 10, pp. 383–412.

Burnes, B. (1996a) *Managing Change: A Strategic Approach to Organisational Dynamics*. 2nd edn. London: Pitman Publishing.

Burnes, B. (1996b) 'No such thing as ... a "one best way" to manage organizational change', *Management Decision*, vol. 34, no. 10, pp. 11–18.

Burnes, B. and James, H. (1995) 'Culture, cognitive dissonance and the management of change', *International Journal of Operations and Production Management*, vol. 15, no. 8, pp. 14–33.

Burnes, B. and Salauroo, M. (1995) 'The impact of the NHS internal market on the merger of colleges of midwifery and nursing: not just a case of putting the cart before the horse', *Journal of Management in Medicine*, vol. 9, no. 2, pp. 14–29.

Burnes, B. and Weekes, B. (eds) (1989) *AMT: A strategy for success?* London: NEDO.

Carnall, C.A. (1990) *Managing Change in Organizations*. London: Prentice Hall.

Child, J. (1972) 'Organizational structure, environment and performance: the role of strategic choice', *Sociology*, vol. 6, no. 1, pp. 1–22.

Clark, P. (1972) *Action Research and Organisational Change*. London: Harper & Row.

Clarke, L. (1994) *The Essence of Change*. London: Prentice Hall.

Clegg, C. W. (1984) 'The derivation of job design', *Journal of Occupational Behaviour*, vol. 5, pp. 131–46.

Coghlan, D. (1993) 'In defence of process consultation' in Mabey, C and Mayon-White, B (eds) *Managing Change*. 2nd edn. London: Open University/Paul Chapman.

Coombs, R. and Hull, R. (1994) 'The best or the worst of both worlds: BPR, cost reduction, and the strategic management of IT', paper presented to the OASIG Seminar on Organisation Change through IT and BPR: Beyond the Hype, London, September.

Coulson-Thomas, C. and Coe, T. (1991) *The Flat Organization*. London: British Institute of Management.

Crosby, P.B. (1979) *Quality is Free*. New York: McGraw-Hill.

Cruise O'Brien, R. and Voss, C. (1992) '*In search of quality*', working paper. London: London Business School.

Cummings, T.G. and Huse, E.F. (1989) *Organization Development and Change*. St Paul, MN: West Publishing.

Dale, B. G. and Cooper, C. L. (1992) *Total Quality and Human Resources: An executive guide*. Oxford: Blackwell.

Dawson, P. (1994) *Organizational Change: A processual approach*. London: Paul Chapman.

Deming, W.E. (1982) *Quality, Productivity and Competitive Position*. Boston, MA: MIT Press.

Dobson, P. (1988) 'Changing culture', *Employment Gazette*, December, pp. 647–50.

Dunphy, D. and Stace, D. (1993) 'The strategic management of corporate change', *Human Relations*, vol. 46, no. 8, pp. 905–18.

Economist Intelligence Unit (1992) *Making Quality Work – Lessons from Europe's leading companies*. London: Economist Intelligence Unit.

Ezzamel, M., Green, C., Lilley, S. and Willmott, H. (1994) 'Change management: Appendix 1 – A review and analysis of recent changes in UK management practices'. Manchester: The Financial Services Research Centre, UMIST.

Filby, I. and Willmott, H. (1988) 'Ideologies and contradictions in a public relations department', *Organization Studies*, vol. 9, no. 3, pp. 335–51.

French, W. L. and Bell, C. H. (1984) *Organization Development*. Englewood Cliffs, NJ: Prentice Hall.

Garvin, D.A. (1993) 'Building a learning organization', *Harvard Business Review*, July/August, pp. 78–91.

Hamel, G. and Prahalad, C.K. (1989) 'Strategic intent', *Harvard Business Review*, May/June, pp. 63–76.

Hammer, M. and Champy, J. (1993) *Re-engineering the Corporation*. London: Nicolas Brealey.

Handy, C. (1986) *Understanding Organizations*. Harmondsworth: Penguin.

Handy, C. (1989) *The Age of Unreason*, London: Arrow.

Handy, C. (1994) *The Empty Raincoat*, London: Hutchinson.

Hanson, P. (1993) 'Made in Britain – The true state of manufacturing industry', paper presented at the Institution of Mechanical Engineers Conference on Performance Measurement and Benchmarking, Birmingham, June.

Harris, P. R. (1985) *Management in Transition*. San Francisco, CA: Jossey-Bass.

Heller, F. (1970) 'Group feed-back analysis as a change agent', *Human Relations*, vol. 23, no. 4, pp. 319–33.

Hendry, C. (1979) 'Contingency theory in practice, I', *Personnel Review*, vol. 8, no. 4, pp. 39–44.

Howarth, C. (1988) 'Report of the Joint Design of Technology, Organisation and People Growth Conference', Venice. Information Services News and Abstracts, 95 November/December. London: Work Research Unit.

Industrial Society (1997) *Culture Change, Managing Best Practice 35*. London: Industrial Society.

Institute of Management (1995) *Finding the Time – A survey of managers' attitudes to using and managing time*. London: Institute of Management.

Juran, J. M. (1988) *Quality Control Handbook*. New York: McGraw-Hill.

Johnson, G. (1993) 'Processes of managing strategic change' in Mabey, C. and Mayon-White, B. (eds) *Managing Change*. 2nd edn. London: Open University/Paul Chapman.

Kanter, R.M. (1989) *When Giants Learn to Dance: Mastering the challenges of strategy, management, and careers in the 1990s*. London: Unwin.

Kanter, R.M., Stein, B.A. and Jick, T.D. (1992) *The Challenge of Organizational Change*. New York: Free Press.

Kearney, A.T. (1989) *Computer Integrated Manufacturing: Competitive advantage or technological dead end?* London: Kearney.

Kearney, A.T. (1992) *Total Quality: Time to take off the rose-tinted spectacles*. Kempston: IFS.

Kelly, J.E. (1982a) 'Economic and structural analysis of job design' in Kelly, J.E. and Clegg, C.W. (eds) *Autonomy and Control at the Workplace*. London: Croom Helm.

Kelly, J.E. (1982b) *Scientific Management, Job Redesign and Work Performance*. London: Academic Press.

Leifer, R. and Huber, G.P. (1977) 'Relations amongst perceived environmental uncertainty, organisation structure and boundary-spanning behaviour', *Administrative Science Quarterly*, vol. 22, pp. 235–47.

Lewin, K. (1958) 'Group decisions and social change' in Swanson, G.E., Newcomb, T.M. and Hartley, E.L. (eds) *Readings in Social Psychology*. New York: Holt, Rhinehart and Winston.

Lippitt, R., Watson, J. and Westley, B. (1958) *The Dynamics of Planned Change*. New York: Harcourt, Brace and World.

Lorsch, J.W. (1970) 'Introduction to the structural design of organizations' in Dalton, G.W., Lawrence, P.R. and Lorsch, J.W. (eds) *Organization Structure and Design*. London: Irwin-Dorsey.

Mabey, C. and Mayon-White, B. (eds) (1993) *Managing Change*. 2nd edn. London: Open University/Paul Chapman.

McCalman, J. and Paton, R. A. (1992) *Change Management: A guide to effective implementation.* London: Paul Chapman.

McKracken, J.K. (1986) 'Exploitation of FMS technology to achieve strategic objectives', paper presented to the 5th International Conference on Flexible Manufacturing Systems, Stratford-Upon-Avon.

McLennan, R. (1989) *Managing Organizational Change.* Englewood Cliffs, NJ: Prentice Hall.

Mayon-White, B. (1993) 'Problem-solving in small groups: team members as agents of change' in Mabey, C. and Mayon-White, B. (eds) *Managing Change.* 2nd edn. London: Open University/Paul Chapman.

Meek, V.L. (1988) 'Organizational culture: origins and weaknesses', *Organization Studies*, vol. 9, no. 4, pp. 453–73.

Mill, J. (1994) 'No pain, no gain', *Computing*, 3 Feburary, pp. 26–7.

Miller, D. (1993) 'The architecture of simplicity', *Academy of Management Review*, vol. 18, no. 1, pp. 116–38.

Miller, D. and Friesen, P.H. (1984) *Organizations: A Quantum View.* Englewood Cliffs, NJ: Prentice Hall.

Mintzberg, H. (1983) *Power In and Around Organizations.* Englewood Cliffs, NJ: Prentice Hall.

Mirvis, P.H. (1990) 'Organization development: part 2 – a revolutionary perspective', *Research in Organizational Change and Development*, vol. 4, pp. 1–66.

Nadler, D.A. (1993) 'Concepts for the management of strategic change' in Mabey, C. and Mayon-White, B. (eds) *Managing Change.* 2nd edn. London: Open University/Paul Chapman.

New, C. (1989) 'The challenge of transformation' in Burnes, B. and Weekes, B. (eds): *AMT: A strategy for success?* London: NEDO.

Nonaka, I. (1988) 'Creating organizational order out of chaos: Self-renewal in Japanese firms', *Harvard Business Review*, November/December, pp. 96–104.

Nystrom, P.C. and Starbuck, W.H. (1984) 'To avoid crises, unlearn', *Organizational Dynamics*, vol. 12, no. 4, pp. 53–65.

Perrow, C. (1983) 'The organizational context of human factors engineering', *Administrative Science Quarterly*, vol. 28, pp. 521–41.

Peters, T. (1989) *Thriving on Chaos.* London: Pan.

Peters, T. (1995) *The Pursuit of WOW!* London: Macmillan.

Pettigrew, A. and Whipp, R. (1993) 'Understanding the environment' in Mabey, C. and Mayon-White, B. (eds) *Managing Change.* 2nd edn. London: Open University/Paul Chapman.

Pfeffer, J. (1981) *Power in Organizations.* Cambridge, MA: Ballinger.

Pugh, D. (1993) 'Understanding and managing organizational change' in Mabey, C. and Mayon-White, B. (eds) *Managing Change.* 2nd edn. London: Open University/Paul Chapman.

Quinn, J.B. (1993) 'Managing strategic change' in Mabey, C. and Mayon-White, B. (eds) *Managing Change.* 2nd edn. London: Open University/Paul Chapman.

Rubin, I. (1967) 'Increasing self-acceptance: a means of reducing prejudice', *Journal of Personality and Social Psychology*, vol. 5, pp. 233–8.

Robbins, S.P. (1986) *Organizational Behavior: Concepts, controversies, and applications.* Englewood Cliffs, NJ: Prentice Hall.

Schein, E. H. (1985) *Organizational Culture and Leadership: A dynamic view.* San Francisco, CA: Jossey-Bass.

Schwartz, H. and Davis, S. (1981) 'Matching corporate culture and business strategy', *Organizational Dynamics*, vol. 10, pp. 30–48.

Short, J.E. and Venkatraman, N. (1992) 'Beyond business process redesign: redefining Baxter's business network', *Sloan Management Review*. Fall, pp. 7–21.

Skinner, B.F. (1974) *About Behaviourism.* London: Cape.

Smith, S. and Tranfield, D. (1987) 'The implementation and exploitation of advanced manufacturing technology – an outline methodology', Change Management Research Unit, Research Paper no. 2, Sheffield Business School.

Snow, C., Miles, R. and Coleman, H. (1993) 'Managing 21st century network organizations' in Mabey, C. and Mayon-White, B. (eds) *Managing Change*. 2nd edn. London: Open University/Paul Chapman.

Stacey, R. (1993) *Strategic Management and Organisational Dynamics*. London: Pitman.

Taguchi, G. (1986) *Introduction to Quality Engineering*. Dearborn, MI: Asian Production Organization.

Trist, E.L., Higgin, G.W., Murray, H. and Pollock, A.B. (1963) *Organisational Choice*. London: Tavistock.

Voss, C.A. (1985) 'Success and failure in advanced manufacturing technology', Warwick University working paper.

Wastell, D.G., White, P. and Kawalek, P. (1994) 'A methodology for business process redesign: experience and issues', *Journal of Strategic Information Systems*, vol. 3, no. 1, pp. 23–40.

Wheatley, M. (1992) *The Future of Middle Management*. London: British Institute of Management.

Whitehill, A.M. (1991) *Japanese Management: Tradition and transition*. London: Routledge.

Whittington, R. (1993) *What is Strategy and Does it Matter?* London: Routledge.

Whyte, J. and Witcher, B. (1992) 'The adoption of total quality management in Northern England' Durham: Durham University Business School.

Wilson, D.C. (1992) *A Strategy of Change*. London: Routledge.

Witcher, B. (1993) 'The adoption of total quality management in Scotland'. Durham: Durham University Business School.

Zairi, M., Letza, S. and Oakland, J. (1994) 'Does TQM impact on bottom line results?', *TQM Magazine*, vol. 6, no. 1, pp. 38–43.

INDEX